America, Russia, and the Cold War
1945–2006

America, Russia, and the Cold War 1945–2006

TENTH EDITION

Walter LaFeber
Cornell University

Boston   Burr Ridge, IL   Dubuque, IA   Madison, WI   New York
San Francisco   St. Louis   Bangkok   Bogotá   Caracas   Kuala Lumpur
Lisbon   London   Madrid   Mexico City   Milan   Montreal   New Delhi
Santiago   Seoul   Singapore   Sydney   Taipei   Toronto

Mc Graw Hill Higher Education

AMERICA, RUSSIA, AND THE COLD WAR, 1945–2006
Published by McGraw-Hill, a business unit of The McGraw-Hill Companies, Inc., 1221 Avenue of the Americas, New York, NY, 10020. Copyright © 2008, 2004, 1997, 1993, 1991, 1985, 1980, 1976, 1971, 1967 by The McGraw-Hill Companies, Inc. All rights reserved. No part of this publication may be reproduced or distributed in any form or by any means, or stored in a database or retrieval system, without the prior written consent of The McGraw-Hill Companies, Inc., including, but not limited to, in any network or other electronic storage or transmission, or broadcast for distance learning.

Some ancillaries, including electronic and print components, may not be available to customers outside the United States.

This book is printed on acid-free paper.

1 2 3 4 5 6 7 8 9 0 DOC/DOC 0 9 8 7 6

ISBN: 978-0-07-353466-4
MHID: 0-07-353466-8

Vice President and Editor-in-Chief: *Emily Barrosse*
Publisher: *Lisa Moore*
Senior Sponsoring Editor *Jon-David Hague*
Editorial Coordinator: *Sora Lisa Kim*
Marketing Manager: *Jennifer Reed*
Senior Project Manager: *Rick Hecker*
Art Editor: *Robin Mouat*
Designer: *Srdjan Savanovic*
Photo Research Coordinator: *Nora Agbayani*
Media Producer: *Magdalena Corona*
Senior Production Supervisor: *Carol A. Bielski*
Composition: *Laserwords Private Limited, Chennai, India*
Printing: *R.R. Donnelley & Sons*

Library of Congress Cataloging-in-Publication Data

LaFeber, Walter.
America, Russia, and the Cold War, 1945–2006 / Walter LaFeber.—10th ed.
p. cm.
Rev. ed. of: America, Russia, and the Cold War, 1945–2002. Updated 9th ed.
Includes bibliographical references and index.
ISBN-13: 978-0-07-353466-4 (softcover : alk. paper)
ISBN-10: 0-07-353466-8 (softcover : alk. paper)
1. United States—Foreign relations—Soviet Union. 2. Soviet Union—Foreign relations–United States. 3. United States–Foreign relations–Russia (Federation) 4. Russia (Federation)—Foreign relations—United States. 5. United States—Foreign relations—1945–1989. 6. United States—Foreign relations—1989. 7. World politics—1945–1989. 8. World politics—1989. 9. Cold War. I. LaFeber, Walter. America, Russia, and the Cold War, 1945–2002. II. Title.

E183.8.S65L343 2008
327.7304709′045—dc22

2006048225

The Internet addresses listed in the text were accurate at the time of publication. The inclusion of a Web site does not indicate an endorsement by the authors or McGraw-Hill, and McGraw-Hill does not guarantee the accuracy of the information presented at these sites.

www.mhhe.com

To Sandy

About the Author

WALTER LAFEBER was born and raised in Indiana, attended
Hanover College, and then received his Master of Arts degree from
Stanford University and his Doctor of Philosophy degree from the
University of Wisconsin at Madison. His books include *The
American Age: U.S. Foreign Policy at Home and Abroad Since 1750* (2nd
ed., 1994); *Inevitable Revolutions: The United States in Central America*
(2nd ed., 1993); *The Panama Canal: The Crisis in Historical Perspective*
(2nd ed., 1989); and *The New Empire: An Interpretation of American
Expansion, 1865–1898* (1963, 1998). He also wrote *The American
Search for Opportunity*, Volume II of the *Cambridge History of
American Foreign Relations* (1994). *The Clash: U.S.-Japan Relations
Throughout History* (1997) won the Bancroft and Hawley prizes.
Michael Jordan and the New Global Capitalism was published in 1999
and *The Deadly Bet; LBJ, Vietnam and the 1968 Election* in 2005. Since
1968, Professor LaFeber has been the Marie Underhill Noll
Professor of American History at Cornell University, and in 1994,
he was named a Stephen H. Weiss Presidential Teaching Fellow. In
2002, he was named to the Andrew Tisch and James Tisch
Distinguished University Professorship.

Contents

Foreword

"The United States always wins the war and loses the peace," runs a persistent popular complaint. Neither part of the statement is accurate. The United States barely escaped the War of 1812 with its territory intact. In Korea in the 1950s the nation was forced to settle for a stalemate. A decade later in Vietnam, the United States clearly lost the war. At Paris in 1782, and again in 1898, American negotiators drove hard bargains to win notable diplomatic victories. Yet the myth persists, along with the equally erroneous American belief that we are a peaceful people. Our history, in fact, is studded with conflict and violence. From the Revolution to the Cold War, Americans have been willing to fight for their interests, their beliefs, and their ambitions. The United States has gone to war for many objectives—for independence in 1775, for honor and trade in 1812, for territory in 1846, for the Union in 1861, for humanity and empire in 1898, for neutral rights in 1917, and for national security in 1941. Since 1945, the nation has been engaged in two limited wars in Asia with disappointing outcomes, a brief conflict in the Middle East that ended in a decisive victory over Saddam Hussein, and a prolonged struggle in Iraq against an insurgency that has attracted support from extremists across the Muslim world.

This volume on the Cold War is part of a series of books designed to examine in detail critical periods relating to American involvement in foreign wars. Since the first edition appeared in 1967, Professor LaFeber has carefully revised his account to explain the course of the Cold War as it moved from periods of intense crisis and confrontation to times of relative stability. In recent editions, he has paid special attention to the dramatic events that ended the Cold War, notably the collapse of communist regimes in Eastern Europe, the tearing down of the Berlin Wall, and the demise of the Soviet Union itself in 1991. He has also surveyed the troubled state of U.S.-Russian affairs in the decade since the end of the Cold War, enabling the reader to see how the half-century of conflict between the superpowers led to today's uneasy relationship. In this edition, Professor LaFeber examines the impact of the events of 9/11 on American-Russian relations and offers a critical analysis of the way the George W. Bush administration has waged the war against terrorism.

Robert A. Divine

Preface to the Tenth Edition

Forty years is a long time for the life of either a working historian or a book on contemporary foreign policy. I am deeply indebted to those who have found this book useful (even, to judge from a number of messages, provocative), and to those who have written about the parts they learned from and the parts they believed needed improvement. When the volume initially appeared, the Vietnam War was reaching its peak and Americans were more fully involved (often on the streets) in U.S. foreign policy than at any time since 1898 or 1812. This edition is published when the tragedies of September 11, 2001, and the Bush administration's reactions to those policies, have again brought larger numbers of Americans into the discussion of, even involvement in, their nation's foreign policies than at any time since the Vietnam conflict. As hard as many of us try, we cannot escape the everyday consequences of our foreign policies. Those consequences are direct for American (and other) daily lives, take-home pay, relatives and friends serving in the military, privacy in telephone and email conversations, choices in education, career alternatives, survival. Foreign policy was unavoidable in the 1800–1850 era for nearly all Americans when major foreign powers stood just across the rivers and lakes of the United States, and it has been unavoidable after the 1940s as nuclear weapons and military—and our everyday economic—change make foreign policy an unavoidable fact of daily life.

During these recent six decades, the United States evolved into the strongest power in world history. Particularly after the end of the Cold War (or, more exactly, the end of the Soviet Union), in 1991, Americans bought the growing argument that their unmatched military power gave them the power to act unilaterally, if they believed it necessary. Such a belief actually goes back to the first two centuries after the United States became independent. Their burgeoning power after World War II only gave Americans the ability to reach farther, faster, and more furiously than before the 1940s. This book, unlike parts of some recent, so-called trans-national historical approaches, therefore examines the United States not as part of larger trans-national movements (in which American power is often, unfortunately, too easily scaled down to match its surroundings). This volume sees the United States as the major world power which often unilaterally decides much else, including on a large scale (even much larger than the 9/11 terrorist attacks), who lives and who dies. The book also assumes that American domestic needs and beliefs (and power) largely shape the foreign policies of both the United States and the countries it engages. The argument in this book is that if this U.S. power is to be responsible, Americans, not some trans-national forces outside the United States, have to take the responsibility to ensure that their nation's power is exercised both responsibly and honestly. As is pointed out in too many of the following chapters, when that power is not so exercised, people in the United States as well as in other nations are directly, and too often tragically, affected.

In this tenth edition, the final, 15th chapter, which considers the 9/11 attacks and their foreign policy aftermaths, has been almost completely rewritten and greatly lengthened. Recently published materials and documents have been included in the text and footnotes of the first fourteen chapters. New sources have led to the following additions (among others). Fresh information is provided, particularly on the North Korean side, for the Korean war. The "Project Pedro" propaganda campaign is noted in relation to U.S.-Mexican relations. Some studies on modernization theory and how it relates to the 1950s–1960s ("bombing Vietnam into the future") are included. The effects of the CIA's famous (or infamous) "Team B" are noted for the 1970s and 1980s. How Jimmy Carter's human rights commitment clashed with the Carter/Brzezinski move toward China is exemplified in a revealing study of policy toward Cambodia. Pope John Paul II's effect on

Eastern Europe and the end of the Cold War is sketched out. And important recent studies of President Bill Clinton's foreign policies have been noted.

The 1980s–1990s vividly demonstrated, in wholly different ways on the American and Russian sides, that foreign policies are no more effective than are allowed by policymakers' formulations and the officials' domestic as well as international circumstances. That axiom did not change after 9/11.

Web Site

An accompanying Web site (www.mhhe.com/lafeber) has been expanded for the tenth edition. Visit the site to find primary source documents, links to relevant Web sites, and—new to this edition—an extended and updated Bibliography.

Acknowledgments

I would like to thank the instructors who reviewed the ninth edition and offered helpful suggestions for revisions:

Clark Billings, Massachusetts College of Liberal Arts

Betty Bergland, University of Wisconsin, River Falls

David L. DiLeo, Saddleback College

Ross Gregory, Western Michigan University

A number of friends have provided conversations and materials that have helped to shape this new edition. They include Cary Fraser, Eric Alterman, Kenton Clymer, Paul Dukes, Tom Schoonover, Bob Hannigan, Jessica Wang, Bruce Jentleson, Jeff Bialos, Andrew Rotter, David Anderson, Mel Leffler, Joe Siracusa, Doug Little, Seth Fein, Amy Davis, David Langbart, Evan Stewart, Jim Siekmeier, Anne Foster, Sayuri Shimitsu, Milton Leitenberg, and at Cornell, as always, Glenn Altschuler, Joel Silbey, Michael Kammen, Mary Beth Norton, Dick Polenberg, Ted Lowi, Peter Katzenstein, Mary Katzenstein, Martin Shefter, Matt Evangelista, Fred Logevall, Sherman Cochran, Maria Cristina Garcia, and Chen Jian, as well as the invaluable Olin Library staff. Some friends have made the new edition possible for related, as well as for other special reasons: Lloyd Gardner, Tom McCormick, Frank Costigliola, Steven and Suzanne Weiss, Andrew and Ann Tisch, James and Merryl Tisch, Hunter Rawlings, David and Martha Maisel, Wayne Isom, Ed Herrold, and Hirschel Abelson, as well as the late

Marie Underhill Noll. Robert Divine, the editor of the series in which this volume has long appeared, has been a friend even longer than he has been an editor. As it has also been for at least forty years (in some cases), Sandy; Scott LaFeber and Laura Morin; Suzanne, Tom, Matt, and Trevor Kahl; and Bill and Hilde Kahl have made it all worthwhile.

Walter LaFeber, April 2006

Maps

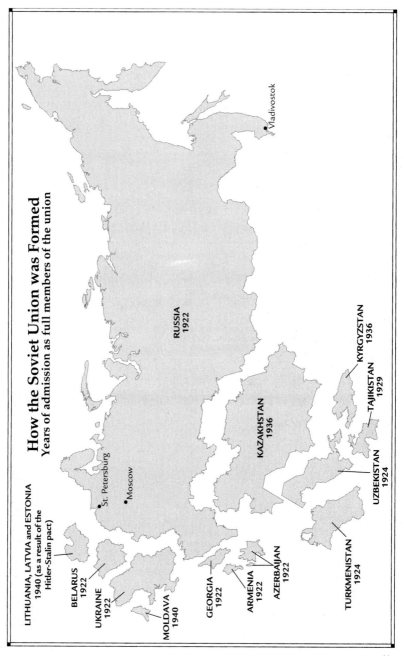

How the Soviet Union was Formed
Years of admission as full members of the union

LITHUANIA, LATVIA and ESTONIA
1940 (as a result of the
Hitler-Stalin pact)

BELARUS
1922

UKRAINE
1922

MOLDAVA
1940

GEORGIA
1922

ARMENIA
1922

AZERBAIJAN
1922

St. Petersburg

Moscow

RUSSIA
1922

KAZAKHSTAN
1936

KYRGYZSTAN
1936

TAJIKISTAN
1929

UZBEKISTAN
1924

TURKMENISTAN
1924

Vladivostok

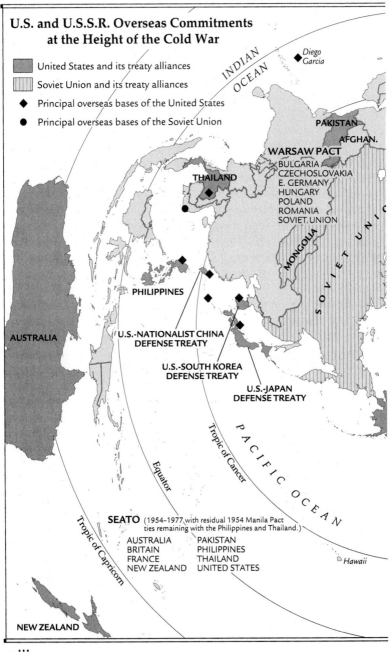

U.S. and U.S.S.R. Overseas Commitments at the Height of the Cold War

- ▨ United States and its treaty alliances
- ▥ Soviet Union and its treaty alliances
- ◆ Principal overseas bases of the United States
- ● Principal overseas bases of the Soviet Union

INDIAN OCEAN

Diego Garcia

PAKISTAN

AFGHAN.

WARSAW PACT

BULGARIA
CZECHOSLOVAKIA
E. GERMANY
HUNGARY
POLAND
ROMANIA
SOVIET UNION

THAILAND

MONGOLIA

SOVIET UNION

PHILIPPINES

AUSTRALIA

U.S.-NATIONALIST CHINA
DEFENSE TREATY

U.S.-SOUTH KOREA
DEFENSE TREATY

U.S.-JAPAN
DEFENSE TREATY

Tropic of Cancer

PACIFIC OCEAN

Equator

Tropic of Capricorn

Hawaii

SEATO (1954–1977 with residual 1954 Manila Pact
ties remaining with the Philippines and Thailand.)

AUSTRALIA	PAKISTAN
BRITAIN	PHILIPPINES
FRANCE	THAILAND
NEW ZEALAND	UNITED STATES

NEW ZEALAND

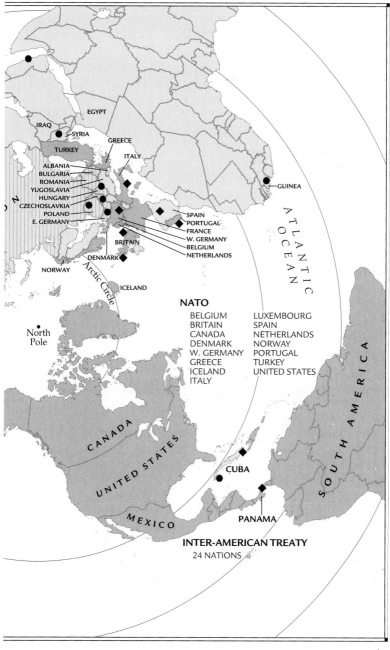

EGYPT

IRAQ
SYRIA
TURKEY
GREECE
ITALY

ALBANIA
BULGARIA
ROMANIA
YUGOSLAVIA
HUNGARY
CZECHOSLAVKIA
POLAND
E. GERMANY

SPAIN
PORTUGAL
FRANCE
W. GERMANY
BELGIUM
NETHERLANDS

BRITAIN

DENMARK

NORWAY

Arctic Circle

ICELAND

GUINEA

ATLANTIC OCEAN

North Pole

NATO

BELGIUM	LUXEMBOURG
BRITAIN	SPAIN
CANADA	NETHERLANDS
DENMARK	NORWAY
W. GERMANY	PORTUGAL
GREECE	TURKEY
ICELAND	UNITED STATES
ITALY	

CANADA

UNITED STATES

MEXICO

CUBA

PANAMA

SOUTH AMERICA

INTER-AMERICAN TREATY
24 NATIONS

The Burden of History
(to 1941)

The Cold War dominated American life after 1945. The collapse of the Soviet Union in 1991 ended one phase of the U.S.-Russian rivalry with the Americans surviving, but it gave little reason for the U.S. wave of triumphalism that followed. In terms of its history, when accurately told, the Cold War cost Americans $8 trillion in defense expenditures, took the lives of nearly 100,000 of their young men and women, ruined the careers of many others during the McCarthyite witch hunts, led the nation into the horrors of Southeast Asian and Central American conflicts, and in the 1980s helped trigger the worst economic depression in fifty years. Bloody conflicts in the developing world where Americans and Russians, or more often their surrogates, fought each other killed tens of millions of people in Korea, Vietnam, the Middle East, Central America, and Afghanistan, among other battlefields. It was not the most satisfying chapter in American diplomatic history.

These tragedies can be understood—and, it is hoped, some future disasters averted—only by understanding the causes of this struggle between the United States and Russia. The conflict did not begin in 1945 or even with the communist victory in Russia during 1917. The two powers did not initially come into conflict because one was communist and the other capitalist. Rather, they first confronted each other on the plains of north China and Manchuria in the late nineteenth century. That meeting climaxed a century in which Americans had expanded westward over half the globe and Russians had moved eastward across Asia.

1

Until that confrontation the two nations had been good friends. Whenever conflicts arose (as over settlements in California and Alaska), the Russians retreated before the demands of U.S. expansionists. Encounters outside the New World, however, could not be settled so easily. Americans swept across a continent while sending out tentacles of trade that quickly seized upon Asia as the great potential market for their magnificently productive farms and factories. By the 1890s Russia, after five centuries of expansion, controlled a grand continental empire containing (like the United States) peoples of many cultures. Americans believed that a "manifest destiny" of supernatural force directed their conquests. The Russians similarly viewed their tsar, or emperor, as an instrument of God's will.

But the two nations also differed sharply. The American empire was decentralized, or "federal," with states and outlying territory enjoying considerable freedom. The Russian empire was tightly centralized, with an army of bureaucrats working antlike for the tsar (and, later, a small Communist party elite in Moscow). Russian officials agreed that only rigidly enforced order from above could preserve the nation. Such bureaucracies are not renowned for imagination and originality. (In part because of this lack of creativity, Russia, both before and after 1917, necessarily borrowed technology and new industrial methods from the West.[1]) The oppressive bureaucracy also was brutal, especially in the post-1880 era when it condemned political dissenters to Siberian prison camps and accelerated pogroms against Russian Jews. Anti-Russian feelings spread across the United States. Congress threatened to cut trade with the tsar. Mark Twain caught the mood when he exclaimed that if the regime could be ended only with dynamite, "then thank God for dynamite."

Americans were also finding another fault with their former friends. The United States honored not bureaucracies, but businesspeople who moved across the oceans to profit in open world marketplaces. Russians, however, moved across land, not water. They developed an empire that was more political than commercial. After annexing land in Asia, they tried to control it tightly by closing the markets to foreign businesspeople with whom they could not compete. This highlighted the problem between the two

---

[1]Robert Wesson, "Soviet Russia: A Geopolitical View," *Survey*, XVII (Spring 1971): 1–13.

countries in the 1890s: the United States believed its prosperity increasingly required an "open door" to trade in China's rich province of Manchuria, but the Russians were determined to colonize and close off parts of Manchuria. Two hostile systems confronted each other, much as they would during 1945 in Eastern Europe, and for many of the same reasons.

From the 1890s until 1917 the United States tried to contain Russian expansion, usually by supporting Japan, which, for its own expansionist purposes, also wanted an open Manchuria. President Theodore Roosevelt exemplified American sentiments: the Russians "are utterly insincere and treacherous; they have no conception of the truth . . . and no regard for others." As for the tsar, he was "a preposterous little creature." More to the point, TR feared that Russia was trying to "organize northern China against us."[2]

These views did not change even at the start of World War I in 1914 when the tsar allied with two American friends, England and France, against Germany. Colonel Edward House, President Woodrow Wilson's closest adviser, starkly outlined the alternatives that were to haunt Americans throughout much of the twentieth century: "If the Allies win, it means the domination of Russia on the continent of Europe; and if Germany wins, it means the unspeakable tyranny of militarism for generations to come."[3] Either way the United States would lose.

The traditional Russian danger grew more threatening in late 1917. Vladimir Lenin's Bolshevik movement used the devastation, chaos, and poverty caused by World War I to overthrow the Russian government and establish a Soviet Union. The ever-expanding tsarist empire now possessed an ideological force, Marxism, that was supposedly driven by historical law and dedicated to world revolution. Between 1918 and 1920 Woodrow Wilson dispatched more than 10,000 American soldiers as he cooperated with Allied attempts to overthrow Lenin by force, and, simultaneously, tried to prevent an invading Japanese army from colonizing and closing off Siberia. The President finally contained the Japanese, but the Allied

---

[2]Quoted in William Henry Harbough, *Power and Responsibility: The Life and Times of Theodore Roosevelt* (New York, 1961), p. 277.
[3]Quoted in Arthur S. Link, *Wilson: The Struggle for Neutrality, 1914–1915* (Princeton, 1960), p. 48.

intervention was a disaster. In the short run many Russians fled from the foreign troops to support Lenin. In the long run Soviet leaders did not forget that the intervention seemed to confirm their belief that "capitalist encirclement" aimed at strangulating the communist regime.

At the Versailles Peace Conference in 1919, the Allies sought another approach. With the shadow of Lenin darkening every discussion, the Western powers tried to isolate the Soviets by creating such buffer states as Poland, Rumania, Czechoslovakia, and Yugoslavia in Eastern Europe. As a young, embittered American official named Walter Lippmann phrased it, the Allies created a military *cordon sanitaire*, when peace required a "sanitary Europe," that is, a prosperous, less militarized area that could build a more attractive and equitable society than Lenin could devise.[4] (In 1947, as dean of American journalists, Lippmann again condemned American postwar policy, and again was rejected by Washington officials.)

Attempting to isolate the Soviets, Woodrow Wilson refused to open diplomatic relations. Sounding like Theodore Roosevelt discussing the tsar, Wilson declared that Lenin's government "is based upon the negation of every principle of honor and good faith." But others refused to follow his lead. England began trading with Russia in 1921. A year later the two outcasts, Russia and defeated Germany, signed a treaty of cooperation. Though shocking Americans by condemning religion and private property, the Soviets were apparently here to stay.

The United States by no means ignored the Bolsheviks. An American relief mission distributed over $60-million worth of aid to starving Russians in the 1920s. When Lenin announced in 1921 that he would welcome foreign capital for reconstruction projects, Secretary of Commerce Herbert Hoover believed this meant communism was collapsing. Hoping that Americans could control as well as profit from a more capitalist Russia, Hoover encouraged businessmen to look upon Russia as an "economic vacuum" that, like all vacuums, invited invasion. They responded. Ford, General Electric, and Westinghouse were among the many major firms that invested millions of dollars. Young W. Averell Harriman began to develop a billion-dollar manganese concession in Russia during

---

[4]Walter Lippmann, *New Republic* (March 22, 1919), supplement.

1926. When his venture ran into financial trouble, the Soviets freed him from his contract. (Harriman found them less cooperative when Franklin D. Roosevelt named him U.S. ambassador to Russia during World War II.) Meanwhile, between 1925 and 1930 Soviet-American trade rose to over $100 million, well above the prewar figure, even though Washington continued to refuse to recognize officially that the Soviet Union existed.

The economic relationship was suddenly transformed after 1928, but not as Hoover had hoped. When Lenin died in 1924, Joseph Stalin used his control of the Soviet party bureaucracy to boost himself to the top. Son of a cobbler, educated at (and expelled from) an Orthodox theological seminary, and frequently arrested before 1917 for revolutionary activities, Stalin and his brutality had so alienated Lenin that the Soviet leader had nearly broken off personal relations. Lenin's death solved that potential problem; then Stalin brilliantly played faction against faction to defeat his opposition. In 1928 he enhanced his power by announcing five-year plans for rapid economic development. These schemes required a tightly run, self-sufficient society. The communist call for worldwide revolution became less important to Stalin than unchallenged personal power and a rebuilt Russia strong enough to withstand "capitalist encirclement."

American-Russian trade consequently dropped just as the United States entered the worst depression years. Many businessmen pressed the newly elected President, Franklin D. Roosevelt, to recognize Russia formally. He did so in November 1933, but only after overcoming, or ignoring, strong anti-Soviet feeling from his own State Department, as well as from the American Legion, Roman Catholic Church leaders, the Daughters of the American Revolution, and the American labor movement. Justifiably concerned that the Russians might not be warmly welcomed, Roosevelt scheduled the arrival of the Soviet diplomatic delegation at the same time his countrymen raucously celebrated the end of Prohibition.

Stalin welcomed recognition, but not for economic reasons. He wanted American help against the Japanese army that had begun rampaging through Manchuria in 1931. Roosevelt refused to respond to the Russian appeal. The State Department even assured the Japanese in 1933 that recognition of Russia should not be taken as a threat against Japan.[5] Until World War II the United States never deviated from this policy. Twice in the next five years, in 1934 and 1937, American officials rejected Soviet requests for joint policies against Japan and Nazi Germany. The administration received strong support from many American liberals, even former communists, who grew disillusioned as Stalin began bloody purges of his political enemies. After the war these liberals did not forget their earlier bitter disenchantment with communism, "the God who failed."

By 1938 Stalin's relations with the Western powers were disintegrating. The climactic blow occurred that year at the Munich conference, when the French and British appeased Hitler by giving Germany part of Czechoslovakia. At the Communist party's Eighteenth Congress in early 1939, Stalin charged that the West hoped to turn Hitler east toward war with the Soviets. This would not happen, he indicated, for although "new economic crises" in the capitalist world made inevitable another "imperialist" war, this time Russia would not pull Western "chestnuts out of the fire."[6] Making much of a terrible situation, Stalin stunned the West in late August 1939 by signing a nonaggression pact with Hitler. The two dictators agreed to divide Poland and the Balkans. A week after the treaty was negotiated, Hitler began World War II by invading Poland.

During the next eighteen months Russian-American relations hit bottom. The Soviet invasion of Finland secured a strategic buffer for Stalin but simply confirmed to Americans that Russia brutalized small neighbors. In early 1941, however, Hitler tired of negotiating with the Russians and decided to take Eastern Europe fully into his own hands. On June 22 Nazi armies swept into the Soviet Union in history's greatest military operation.

The State Department debated for twenty-four hours before issuing an announcement that condemned the Soviet view of religion, declared that "communistic dictatorship" was as intolerable as "Nazi dictatorship," said nothing good about the Russians, but concluded they must be helped since Hitler posed the larger threat.

---

[5]Stanley K. Hornbeck to Secretary of State Cordell Hull, October 28, 1933, and Hornbeck to William Phillips, October 31, 1933, 711.61/333, Archives of the Department of State, Washington, D.C. (Hereafter cited NA, followed by Record Group number.)
[6]Myron Rush, ed., *The International Situation and Soviet Foreign Policy: Key Reports by Soviet Leaders from the Revolution to the Present* (Columbus, Ohio, 1970), pp. 85–96.

Harry S Truman, Democratic senator from Missouri, bluntly expressed his and many other Americans' feelings: "If we see that Germany is winning we should help Russia and if Russia is winning we ought to help Germany and that way let them kill as many as possible, although I don't want to see Hitler victorious under any circumstances."[7]

It was not the best spirit with which to start a new partnership. But such statements only climaxed half a century of Russian-American enmity. Possessing drastically different views of how the world should be organized, unable to cooperate during the 1930s against Nazi and Japanese aggression, and nearly full-fledged enemies between 1939 and 1941, the United States and the Soviet Union finally became partners because of a shotgun marriage forced upon them by World War II.

[7]*The New York Times,* June 24, 1941, p. 7.

President Truman (back to camera) shakes hands with Stalin at the Potsdam Conference and tells the unsurprised Soviet leader about the new atomic bomb.
(U.S. Army, Courtesy of Harry S Truman Library)

CHAPTER 1

Open Doors, Iron Curtains (1941–1945)

A honeymoon never occurred. Despite exchanges of military information and nearly $11 billion of American lend-lease supplies sent to Russia, conflicts quickly erupted over war strategy and plans for the postwar peace.

As the Nazis drove deeper into Russia in 1942, Stalin desperately asked President Roosevelt and British Prime Minster Winston Churchill to draw off German armies by invading Western Europe. Soviet Foreign Minister V. M. Molotov, according to one observer, knew only four words of English: "yes," "no," and "second front." Twice Roosevelt promised an invasion. Twice he and Churchill reneged. Believing they lacked the power to attack Western Europe, they instead invaded North Africa and Italy. These campaigns stalled the opening of the second front until mid-1944. By then the Russians had themselves driven back the Nazis, although at tremendous cost.

Stalin's suspicions multiplied as he asked Roosevelt and Churchill to agree that postwar Russia should include the Baltic States and parts of Poland, Finland, and Rumania. These areas had once belonged to tsarist Russia and had been reclaimed by Stalin in 1939 with the Nazi-Soviet pact. In 1943 Roosevelt told an unhappy Stalin that millions of U.S. voters of Baltic ancestry made it impossible for him to recognize Soviet claims to Latvia, Lithuania, and Estonia—although Roosevelt added that he certainly "did not intend to go to war with the Soviet Union on this point." Roosevelt hoped to delay discussion on other territorial issues until after the war.

That was a fateful decision. By 1945 the Red Army stood astride Eastern and much of Central Europe. Roosevelt and Churchill, moreover, would then have to discuss Stalin's demands in a strikingly different world, for the Allies were destroying Germany and Japan, two nations that historically had blocked Russian expansion into Europe and Asia.

American policymakers soon discovered an even greater problem. Their own policy was contradictory. Neither Roosevelt nor his successor, Harry S Truman, ever reconciled the contradictions. That failure was a major cause of the Cold War. The contradictions contained both economic and political factors.

Washington officials believed another terrible economic depression could be averted only if global markets and raw materials were fully open to all peoples on the basis of equal opportunity, or the open door, for everyone. American domestic requirements, moreover, dictated such a policy. The world could not be allowed to return to the 1930s state of affairs, when nations tried to escape depression by creating high tariff walls and regional trading blocs that dammed up the natural flow of trade. If that recurred, Americans could survive only through massive governmental intervention into their society. If the government dominated the economy, however, it would also regulate individual choice and perhaps severely limit personal freedom.

"In the event of long-continued unemployment," Vice President Henry Wallace warned, "the only question will be as to whether the Prussian or Marxian doctrine will take us over first." Such alternatives could be avoided only if Americans realized, in the words of Assistant Secretary of State Dean Acheson, that "we cannot expect domestic prosperity under our system without a constantly expanding trade with other nations." As one official noted, "The capitalistic system is essentially an international system," and "if it cannot function internationally, it will break down completely." For these reasons the United States required an open world marketplace after the war.[1]

---

[1]Henry Wallace, Herbert Hoover, et al., *Prefaces to Peace* (New York, 1943), p. 413; Lloyd C. Gardner, *Economic Aspects of New Deal Diplomacy* (Madison, Wis., 1964), p. 344; testimony of Secretary of the Treasury Fred Vinson, *The New York Times*, March 6, 1946, p. 8.

In August 1941, at the Atlantic Conference held off Newfoundland with Churchill, Roosevelt moved to implement this policy. In Article III of the Atlantic Charter, the two leaders declared that after the war all peoples should have the right "to choose the form of government under which they will live." Article IV added the economic side to that principle: all states should enjoy "access, on equal terms, to the trade and to the raw materials of the world which are needed for their economic prosperity."[2] That "need" for Americans grew incredibly during the next four years. Their industrial output rose 90 percent. This economic power, developed while other industrial nations were decimated by war, also assured Americans they would be in the most advantageous position to win the race for "access, on equal terms" in world trade.

The Ghost of Depression Past and Depression Future thus hovered menacingly over American postwar objectives. But those objectives were political as well as economic. Closed economic blocs not only hurt trade but easily developed into political blocs. Friction between such blocs caused world wars. That was precisely what had occurred during the 1930s when the British, Germans, Japanese, and Russians had warred on one another economically, then militarily. As State Department economic adviser Will Clayton declared, "Nations which act as enemies in the marketplace cannot long be friends at the council table."[3]

In 1944 the United States tried to ensure that the postwar marketplace would be friendly. An international conference at Bretton Woods, New Hampshire, created a World Bank (the International Bank of Reconstruction and Development) and the International Monetary Fund (IMF). The World Bank would have a treasury of $7.6 billion (and authority to lend twice that amount) to guarantee private loans given for rebuilding war-torn Europe and for building up the less industrialized nations. The IMF possessed $7.3 billion to stabilize currencies so that trade could be conducted without fear of sudden currency depreciation or wild fluctuations

[2]U.S. Department of State, *Foreign Relations of the United States* [henceforth *FRUS*], *1941*, I (Washington, 1948): 366–368. This document is on the www.mhhe.com/lafeber website for this book.
[3]Quoted in Lloyd Gardner, *Architects of Illusion* (Chicago, 1970), p. 123.

in exchange rates, ailments which had nearly paralyzed the international community in the 1930s. The United States hoped these two agencies would reconstruct, then stabilize and expand world trade. Of course, there was one other implication. Voting in the organizations depended on money contributed. Since Americans would have to contribute the most, they would also control the World Bank and IMF.

American policy from the Atlantic Charter through the Bretton Woods conference seemed well thought out. Financier and self-appointed adviser to Presidents and congressmen, Bernard Baruch, caught the spirit in early 1945: if we can "stop subsidization of labor and sweated competition in the export markets," as well as prevent rebuilding of war machines, "oh boy, oh boy, what long-term prosperity we will have."[4] Like Dorothy, Americans seemed on their way to a happier land of Oz, with their immense economic power serving as ruby slippers. But, like Dorothy, they soon encountered witches—not just one, but wicked witches from both West and East.

In the West the French and British had realized since the 1920s that they could no longer compete with the efficient American industrialists in an open marketplace. During the 1930s the British had created an economic bloc in their own Empire to shut out American goods. Churchill did not believe he could surrender that protection after the war, so he watered down the Atlantic Charter's "free access" clause before agreeing to it. Yet American officials were determined to break open the British Empire. Combined, United Kingdom and American trade accounted for more than half the world's exchange of goods. If the British bloc could be split apart, the United States would be well on the way to opening the entire global marketplace.

A devastated England had no choice. Two wars had destroyed its principal industries that paid for the importation of half the nation's food and nearly all its raw materials except coal. The British asked for help. In 1945 the United States agreed to loan $3.8 billion. In return, weary London officials promised to dismantle much of their imperial trading bloc. Will Clayton, who negotiated the agreement, confided

---

[4]Baruch to E. Coblentz, March 23, 1945, Papers of Bernard Baruch, Princeton University Library, Princeton, N.J.

to Baruch, "We loaded the British loan negotiations with all the conditions that the traffic would bear."[5]

France received the same treatment. For nearly two centuries French and American interests had clashed in both the Old and New Worlds. During the war French mistrust of the United States was personified by General Charles de Gaulle, president of the French Provisional Government. De Gaulle bitterly fought American officials as he tried to maintain his country's colonies and diplomatic freedom of action. U.S. officials in turn saw de Gaulle as pro-British and a political extremist; one State Department officer even called him "this French Adolf."[6] In 1945 de Gaulle had to swallow his considerable pride to ask Washington for a billion-dollar loan. Most of the request was granted; in return France promised to curtail governmental subsidies and currency manipulation which had given advantages to its exporters in the world market.

The United States was freeing itself to deal with the witch of the East, the Soviet Union.[7] As it did, the contradictions within American policy became stunningly apparent. On the one hand, Washington demanded an open Europe. As a top official later explained, the State Department wanted all Europe "west of the Russian border . . .

---

[5]"Memorandum for Mr. Baruch," from Clayton, April 26, 1946, Baruch Papers. For the background, note especially Susan A. Brewer, *To Win the Peace; British Propaganda in the United States During World War II* (Ithaca, 1997), pp. 38–40, 163–198, 234–245; Patrick J. Hearden, *Architects of Globalism* (Fayetteville, 2002), which deals with the question of why the U.S. treated the closed, or potentially closed, Soviet and British systems different (answer: the British accepted American dollars and rules, while the Soviets did not); Warren F. Kimball, "Lend-Lease and the Open Door . . . 1937–1942," *Political Science Quarterly*, LXXXVI (June 1971): 232–259. An instructive discussion by top U.S. officials of the loan to Great Britain can be found in chapter I of this book's documents at the www.mhhe.com/lafeber website.

[6]H. F. Matthews to Ray Atherton, June 25, 1943, Papers of William Leahy, Box 4, Library of Congress, Washington, D.C.

[7]Unfortunately, the "wicked witch" analogy is not far-fetched. Louis Halle, a member of the State Department Policy Planning Staff in the late 1940s, recalled that throughout this era until "almost the end of 1962," the West lived under the terror of "the Moscovite tyranny that was spreading from the East." For those who wished to understand such fears, Halle recommended reading J. R. R. Tolkien's trilogy, *The Lord of the Rings*, which Halle believed "enshrines the mood and emotion of those long years." *The Cold War as History* (New York, 1967), p. 138.

established as a cooperative continental system economically unified in certain major particulars."[8] On the other hand, Stalin had constantly demanded that Roosevelt and Churchill recognize the Soviet right to control large parts of Eastern Europe. For Stalin this Russian "sphere" would serve as a strategic buffer against the West and could also be exploited economically for the rapid rebuilding of the Soviet economy. Making his intentions clear, Stalin refused to sign the Atlantic Charter until he added provisions that emasculated Articles III and IV.[9]

As early as 1942, therefore, Roosevelt faced the choice: he could either fight for an open postwar world (at least to the Russian borders) or agree with his ally's demands in Eastern Europe. If he chose the first alternative, Russian-American relations would probably erode until the joint effort against the Axis might collapse. At the least, Americans and Russians would enter the postwar world as enemies. (As it was, a mistrustful Stalin secretly considered a separate peace with Hitler as late as mid-1943.[10]) If Roosevelt chose the second alternative, he would undermine American hopes for the triumph of the Atlantic Charter principles, thus destroying the chances for postwar peace and American prosperity. Not that the United States required Eastern European markets. But a stable, prosperous world did require a healthy Europe, and that meant a united Europe with its eastern sectors providing food and western areas the industrial products. Each needed the other. As the State Department informed Roosevelt in early 1945, European stability "depends on the maintenance of sound economic conditions and reasonable prosperity in all parts of the Continent."[11] Besides, a dangerous precedent could be set. If Stalin got away with building his own sphere in Europe, Churchill, de Gaulle, and others might try to rebuild their blocs.

---

[8]Adolf Berle, "Diplomacy and the New Economics." In E. A. J. Johnson, ed., *Dimensions of Diplomacy* (Baltimore, 1964), pp. 93–95.

[9]Martin F. Herz, *The Beginnings of the Cold War* (Bloomington, Ind., 1966), pp. vii–viii. For Stalin's views on Soviet rights during the darkest days of the war, see the Anthony Eden account of his talks with Stalin in 1941 in the chapter I documents at the www.mhhe.com/lafeber website.

[10]Vojtech Mastny, "Stalin and the Prospects of a Separate Peace in World War II," *American Historical Review,* LXXVII (December 1972): 1365–1388.)

[11]*FRUS: The Conferences at Malta and Yalta, 1945* (Washington, 1955), pp. 235–236.

Faced with this agonizing dilemma, Roosevelt at first suggested to the Soviets that the postwar world should be stabilized by "four policemen"—the United States, Russia, Great Britain, and China. The Soviets were delighted, for they understood this plan to mean they would be the policemen patrolling Eastern Europe. By late 1943, however, State Department officials were changing Roosevelt's mind. The "four policemen" concept could not be reconciled with a unified, open world. Areas patrolled by one policeman could too easily become closed spheres controlled by one power. Roosevelt began to stall, then to modify the idea. As he delayed, the Red Army started its sweep across Eastern Europe in 1944. Stalin understood what was happening. "This war is not as in the past," he told fellow communists. "Whoever occupies a territory also imposes on it his own social system" as far "as his army can reach."[12]

Churchill also understood. In October 1944 he deserted Roosevelt's policy of delay and flew to Moscow to make a deal. The British leader had heard FDR's position: to "restrain the [Soviet] tendency toward exclusive spheres," as the President wrote him four months earlier. Knowing Stalin disagreed, and that the Red Army was in a position to deliver Eastern Europe to the Russian dictator, Churchill secretly promised Stalin in their Moscow meeting to recognize Soviet domination in Rumania and Bulgaria. In return, Stalin agreed that England could control Greece. Thus Churchill protected the Mediterranean lifeline of the British Empire while acknowledging Russia's "first say" in certain Eastern European nations. With accuracy, and sarcasm, Churchill warned Stalin that the deal had better be expressed "in diplomatic terms and not . . . use the phrase 'dividing into spheres,' because the Americans might be shocked."[13]

[12]Milovan Djilas, *Conversations with Stalin* (New York, 1961), p. 114.

[13]"Record of Meeting at the Kremlin, Moscow, October 9, 1944," PREM 3, 434/47, Public Record Office, London, England. I am indebted to Professor Lloyd Gardner of Rutgers-New Brunswick and Professor Warren Kimball of The Citadel for calling my attention to this document. Joseph M. Siracusa analyses the context of the Moscow meeting in *Into The Dark House* (Claremont, 1998), chapter 1, which has the FDR to Churchill letter, and Appendix 1 documents providing the conversations at Moscow. In much the same way, the United States excluded the Soviets from any authority in liberated Italy; see Gabriel Kolko, *The Politics of War, 1943–1945* (New York, 1968), pp. 37–39.

When he learned of the agreement, Roosevelt was shocked anyway, but worse was to come. In February 1945 the Big Three met at the Russian Black Sea resort of Yalta to shape the postwar world. An acrimonious debate erupted over the future of Poland. Throughout 1943–1944 Roosevelt had indicated he understood the need for a Polish government that would (unlike that government in the interwar years) be friendly toward Russia. But he was not prepared for Stalin's moves in early 1945. The Soviets had recognized a communist-dominated regime before the Yalta meetings began. FDR and Churchill demanded that Stalin allow pro-Western Poles in the government. The three men finally agreed that the regime must be "reorganized on a broader democratic basis." Admiral William Leahy, Roosevelt's chief military aide, accurately observed that the agreement was "so elastic that the Russians can stretch it all the way from Yalta to Washington without technically breaking it." Since the Red Army occupied Poland, however, this was the best FDR could do. He did try to make the agreement less elastic by proposing a "Declaration on Liberated Europe." This provided that each of the three powers would pledge cooperation in applying the self-determination principle to newly liberated nations. The Russians amended the declaration until it was virtually meaningless. Again, FDR had to accept the remains.[14]

Stalin left Yalta doubtless believing his allies had at least acquiesced to his domination over Eastern Europe. That must have been a relief, for throughout much of the war his policy had also been pulling in two directions. The Soviet dictator insisted on his own sphere but to this point had carefully not explained to his partners what Russian control implied. To have done so might have angered the Allies, slowed American deliveries of war matériel, and perhaps

---

[14]*FRUS: Yalta,* pp. 234–235, 668–669, 677–678, 898. The important work on these developments is Lloyd C. Gardner, *Spheres of Influence: The Great Powers Partition Europe, From Munich to Yalta* (Chicago, 1993). For Stalin's rather optimistic perspective, note Robert Service, *Stalin, A Biography* (Cambridge, Mass., 2005), pp. 465–468. On FDR's (and Truman's) dangerously misleading public statements about Yalta, note especially the excellent analysis in Eric Alterman, *When Presidents Lie* (New York, 2004), chapter 2. For key documents on the discussions at Yalta on the Polish question and the text for the "Declaration on Liberated Europe," see chapter I, at www.mhhe.com/lafeber website.

even led to a separate deal between the West and Germany. (After all, why should Stalin have expected capitalist scruples to be more elevated than his own?) With the Red Army so close to total victory, he did not want any last-minute diplomatic bungling. Yalta seemed to remove that danger.

But Stalin miscalculated. Two weeks after the conference adjourned, the Soviets turned the screws on Rumania by demanding that the king appoint a communist-controlled government. Rumanian soldiers, the Soviet leader recalled, had marched with the Nazis into Russia in 1941. Churchill, moreover, had agreed to turn his back on Rumania in return for Stalin's ignoring Greece. But the United States claimed that Stalin was breaking the Declaration of Liberated Europe. The American case was difficult to argue, and Molotov picked it apart.[15] This was not, however, a mere debate: control of Eastern Europe was at stake.

A crisis developed when Russia refused to allow any more than three pro-Western Poles into the eighteen-member Polish government. For Americans, Poland became the test case of Soviet intentions. As Secretary of State Edward Stettinius observed, Poland, not Rumania, was *"the big apple in the barrel* and we should concentrate on that."* The analogy obviously implied that one rotten apple could spoil all the others in Central and Eastern Europe. On April 1, 1945, Roosevelt gravely warned Stalin that the Soviet plan could not be accepted. On April 5 Averell Harriman, U.S. ambassador to Russia, insisted to FDR that Stalin must not be allowed to establish "totalitarianism" in Soviet-occupied territories, for "unless we are prepared to live in a Soviet-dominated world, we must use our economic power to assist countries naturally friendly to us."[16] Writing to Churchill about the crisis the next day, Roosevelt referred to yet another weapon: "Our armies will in a very few days be in a position that will permit us to become 'tougher' than has heretofore appeared advantageous to the war effort."[17]

---

[15]Daily Staff Summary, March 1, March 19, March 28, 1945, Lot File, NA, RG 59.

[16]"Record," volumes III, IV, 11–17 March 1945. Papers of Edward Stettinius, University of Virginia Library, Charlottesville. Italics in original. "Special Information for the President," from Stettinius, April 5, 1945, Lot File 53 D 444, NA, RG 59.

[17]Roosevelt to Churchill, April 6, 1945. In Francis L. Loewenheim, Harold D. Langley, and Manfred Jonas, eds., *Roosevelt and Churchill* (New York, 1975), p. 705.

Within a week Roosevelt was dead, the victim of a massive stroke. His new Vice President, Harry S Truman, inherited a decayed alliance. FDR had not discussed foreign policy (or much else) with him. Truman had privately referred to himself as a "political eunuch." But his affection for Russia had not noticeably increased since 1941. After Roosevelt appeared before Congress to put a good face on the difficulties at Yalta, journalists asked Truman what he thought of the speech. "One of the greatest ever given," he replied— and then joined them in laughter.[18]

Truman entered the White House a highly insecure man. ("I felt like the moon, the stars, and all the planets had fallen on me," he told reporters.) And he held the world's most responsible job in a world that was changing radically. Truman tried to compensate for his insecurity in several ways. First, he was extremely jealous of his presidential powers and deeply suspicious of anyone who challenged those powers. Truman made decisions rapidly not only because that was his character but also because he determined "the buck stopped" at his desk. There would be no more sloppy administration or strong, freewheeling bureaucrats as in FDR's later years.

Second, and more dangerously, Truman was determined that these decisions would not be tagged as "appeasement." He would be as tough as the toughest. After only twenty-four hours in the White House, the new President confidently informed his secretary of state, "We must stand up to the Russians," and he implied "We had been too easy with them."[19] In foreign-policy discussions during the next two weeks, Truman interrupted his advisers to assure them he would certainly be "tough."

His determination was reinforced when he listened most closely to such advisers as Harriman, Leahy, and Secretary of the Navy James Forrestal, who urged him to take a hard line. Warning of a "barbarian invasion of Europe," Harriman declared that postwar cooperation with the Soviets, especially economically, must depend on their agreement to open Poland and Eastern Europe. In a decisive meeting on April 23, 1945, Secretary of War Henry Stimson argued with Harriman. Stimson declared that peace must never be threatened by an

[18]Margaret Truman, *Harry S Truman* (New York, 1973), pp. 220–222.
[19]"Private Calendar Notes, 4/13/45," Box 224, Stettinius Papers; and note Arnold A. Offner, "'Another Such Victory,' President Truman, American Foreign Policy, and the Cold War," *Diplomatic History*, 23 (Spring 1999): 129–132.

issue such as Poland, for free elections there were impossible, Russia held total control, and Stalin was "not likely to yield . . . in substance."[20] Stimson was not an amateur; he had been a respected Wall Street lawyer and distinguished public servant for forty years, including a term as Herbert Hoover's secretary of state.

But Truman dismissed Stimson's advice, accepted Harriman's, and later that day berated Soviet Foreign Minister Molotov "in words of one syllable" for breaking the Yalta agreement on Poland. Truman demanded that the Soviets agree to a "new" (not merely "reorganized") Polish government. An astonished Molotov replied, "I have never been talked to like that in my life." "Carry out your agreements," Truman supposedly retorted, "and you won't get talked to like that."[21]

The next day Stalin rejected Truman's demand by observing that it was contrary to the Yalta agreement. The dictator noted that "Poland borders with the Soviet Union, what [sic] cannot be said of Great Britain and the United States." After all, Stalin continued, the Soviets do not "lay claim to interference" in Belgium and Greece where the Americans and British made decisions without consulting the Russians.[22] In June Truman reluctantly accepted a compromise when Stalin included several more pro-Western Poles in the government. Americans hoped that political recognition of the new regime would allow them to use their economic power to open Poland "to a policy of equal opportunity in trade, investments and access to sources of information."[23] But the Poles refused to open the door to

---

[20]The necessary context for understanding the "barbarian" reference is Frank Costigliola's pioneering, "'Like Animals or Worse' . . . ," *Diplomatic History*, 28 (November 2004), pp. 749–780; and for Harriman's emotional reaction to Soviet policies, note Costigliola's "'I Had Come as a Friend': Emotion, Culture, and Ambiguity in the Formation of the Cold War, 1943–1945," *Cold War History*, 1 (August 2000), pp. 103–128; Alterman, *When Presidents Lie*, pp. 48–59; Diary, April 23, 1945. Papers of Henry Stimson, Yale University Library, New Haven, Conn. A fine account of Truman during this decisive first month is Arnold A. Offner, *Another Such Victory* (Stanford, 2002), pp. 20–46.

[21]Harry S Truman, *Memoirs, Volume One* (Garden City, N.Y., 1955), p. 82. This precise exchange was possibly created by Truman's imagination. These words are not reported in the official records of the conversation. They doubtless suggest, nevertheless, the tone of what Truman did say.

[22]*FRUS, 1945*, V (Washington, 1967): 263–264.

[23]*FRUS: The Conference of Berlin*, I (Washington, 1960): 262–264; "Memorandum for the President," June 27, 1945, Lot File 53 D 444, NA, RG 59.

the dollar. Stimson had been correct. Truman's toughness had only stiffened Russian determination to control Poland.

An "iron fence" was falling around Eastern Europe, Churchill blurted out to Stalin in mid-1945. "All fairy-tales," the Soviet leader blandly replied. But it was partly true. The crises over Rumania and Poland raised higher the fence around those two nations. In other areas, however, the Soviet approach varied. A Russian-sponsored election in Hungary produced a noncommunist government. In Bulgaria the Soviet-conducted elections satisfied British observers, if not Americans. Stalin agreed to an independent, noncommunist regime in Finland if the Finns would follow a foreign policy friendly to Russia. An "iron fence" by no means encircled all of Eastern Europe. There was still room to bargain if each side wished to avoid a confrontation over the remaining areas.

But the bargaining room was limited. Stalin's doctrine and his determination that Russia would not again be invaded from the west greatly narrowed his diplomatic options. So too did the tremendous devastation of the war. Rapid rebuilding under communism required security, required access to resources in Eastern and Central Europe, and continued tight control over the Russian people. The experience of war was indelible. Russians viewed almost everything in their lives through their "searing experience of World War II," as one psychologist has phrased it.[24] The conflict destroyed 1700 towns and 70,000 villages and left 25 million homeless. Twenty to thirty million died; 600,000 starved to death at the single siege of Leningrad.

During those terrible years Stalin had shrewdly asked his countrymen not to sacrifice themselves for communism (in whose name, after all, millions had been executed or placed in Siberian prisons by Stalin during the 1930s), but for "Mother Russia." Little evidence exists, however, that Stalin privately changed his own peculiar brand of Marxist-Leninist doctrine. This was crucial, for all Soviet leaders cloaked their polices with this doctrine. They used it not only in determining foreign policy but also in rationalizing their

---

[24]Ralph K. White, "Images in the Context of International Conflict." In Herbert C. Kelman, ed., *International Behavior* (New York, 1965), p. 271.

own power and in silencing internal dissent. To outside observers, therefore, doctrine acted as a weather vane; once officials decided upon policy, they publicly justified it with appropriate doctrine, and the doctrinal changes indicated the policy changes.

Stalin's doctrine during the spring of 1945 differed little from the views he had uttered about Western "imperialists" in 1939. The wartime alliance apparently did not dent his outlook, or if it did the Western attempts to open Eastern Europe rekindled his earlier fears. In April 1945 Stalin told fellow communists that another war was only a matter of time. The Germans "will recover, and very quickly," he warned. "Give them twelve to fifteen years and they'll be on their feet again. And that is why the unity of the Slavs is important."[25]

During 1945 the triumphs of the Red Army and the growing tension over Eastern Europe led Stalin to tighten his control over Soviet life. Special schools opened to teach the dictator's doctrine; "Mother Russia" gave way to "Glorious Stalin." The Red Army received special attention. It had been exposed to corrupting "bourgeois" influence in Central Europe and had grown too rapidly for Stalin to impose rigid political control. He raised his close associate Lavrenti Beria, chief of the dreaded secret police, to the rank of marshal of the Red Army and promoted himself to generalissimo. Army officers, holding the only power capable of challenging Stalin, slowly disappeared from public view. By the summer of 1945 his authority was unquestioned.[26]

Some scholars have examined Stalin's acts of 1928–1945, pronounced them the work of a "paranoid," and concluded that the United States had no chance to avoid a cold war since it was dealing with a man who was mentally ill. That interpretation neatly avoids confronting the complex causes of the Cold War but is wholly insufficient to explain those causes. However Stalin acted inside Russia, where he had total control, in his foreign policy during 1941–1946 he

[25]Djilas, *Conversations with Stalin,* p. 114; John S. Curtiss and Alex Inkeles, "Marxism in the U.S.S.R.—The Recent Revival," *Political Science Quarterly,* XLI (September 1946): 349–364. A fine study of this problem is Paul Marantz, "The Soviet Union and the Western World: A Study in Doctrinal Change, 1917–1964," unpublished doctoral dissertation, Harvard University, 1971.
[26]Alexander Werth, *Russia at War* (New York, 1964), pp. 943–945; Raymond L. Garthoff, *Soviet Military Policy, A Historical Analysis* (New York, 1966), pp. 42–44.

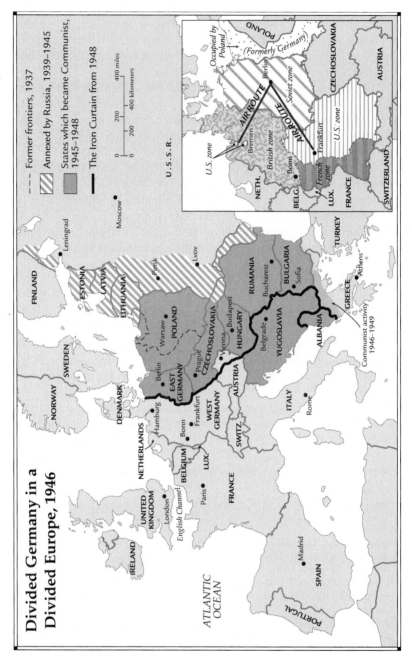

Divided Germany in a Divided Europe, 1946

Former frontiers, 1937
Annexed by Russia, 1939–1945
States which became Communist, 1945–1948
The Iron Curtain from 1948

400 miles
400 kilometers
0   200   400

Moscow

FINLAND
Leningrad
ESTONIA
LATVIA
LITHUANIA
Pinsk
Lvov
SWEDEN
NORWAY
POLAND
Warsaw
Berlin
EAST GERMANY
Prague
CZECHOSLOVAKIA
Vienna
HUNGARY
Budapest
RUMANIA
Bucharest
BULGARIA
Sofia
YUGOSLAVIA
Belgrade
ALBANIA
GREECE
Athens
TURKEY
Communist activity 1946–1949

DENMARK
Hamburg
Bonn
Frankfurt
WEST GERMANY
AUSTRIA
SWITZ.
ITALY
Rome

NETHERLANDS
BELGIUM
LUX.
FRANCE
Paris
English Channel
UNITED KINGDOM
London
IRELAND

ATLANTIC OCEAN

SPAIN
Madrid
PORTUGAL

U.S.S.R.

POLAND
(Formerly Germany)
Occupied by Poland
Berlin
Soviet zone
AIR ROUTE
AIR ROUTE
British zone
Bremen
U.S. zone
U.S. zone
Bonn
Frankfurt
U.S. zone
French zone
LUX.
NETH.
BELG.
FRANCE
SWITZERLAND
CZECHOSLOVAKIA
AUSTRIA

displayed a realism, a careful calculation of forces, and a diplomatic finesse that undercut any attempt to explain away his actions as paranoid.[27] If he and other Soviets were suspicious of the West, they were realistic, not paranoid: the West had poured thousands of troops into Russia between 1917 and 1920, refused to cooperate with the Soviets during the 1930s, tried to turn Hitler against Stalin in 1938, reneged on promises about the second front, and in 1945 tried to penetrate areas Stalin deemed crucial to Soviet security.

American diplomats who frequently saw Stalin understood this background. In January 1945 Harriman told the State Department, "The overriding consideration in Soviet foreign policy is the preoccupation with 'security,' as Moscow sees it." The problem was that Americans did not see "security" the same way. They believed their security required an open world, including an open Eastern Europe. No Western diplomat has been found who declared in 1945–1947 that Stalin showed signs of mental illness. Some actually argued that hard-line "boys" within the politburo forced him to be tougher with the West than he wished.[28] That was inaccurate. Stalin set policy and the policy was consistent. Only timing and tactics varied.

In dealing with foreign Communist parties, Stalin's priority was not world revolution but, once again, Russian security and his own personal power. In 1943 he had made a goodwill gesture by disbanding the Comintern (the organization that directed overseas Communist parties from headquarters in Moscow). It was only a gesture, however, for Stalin determined to control these parties for his own purposes. In 1944–1945 he ordered the powerful French Communist party to cooperate with the Western Allies rather than attempt to seize power. Wanting above all else Anglo-American

---

[27]Adam B. Ulam, *Stalin* (New York, 1973), pp. 685–686. The most popular expression of Stalin's supposed paranoia is in Arthur Schlesinger's essay, most easily found in Lloyd C. Gardner, Arthur Schlesinger, Jr., and Hans J. Morgenthau, *The Origins of the Cold War* (Waltham, Mass., 1970), pp. 72–73. The paranoia interpretation for 1943 to 1947 events has been undermined by Soviet documents made available after 1989; see Vladislav Zubok and Constantine Pleshakov, *Inside the Kremlin's Cold War* (Cambridge, Mass., 1996), pp. 274–277.

[28]*FRUS: Yalta,* pp. 450–451; "Mr. Macmillan to Foreign Office," 21 March 1945, FO 371 N3097/1545/38, Public Record Office, London; *FRUS: Berlin,* I: 13. For new evidence on the internal Soviet debate, 1943–1945, see Vladimir O. Pechtanov, *The Big Three After World War II.* Cold War International History Project (Washington, D.C., 1995), pp. 1–25.

acquiescence to his acts in Eastern Europe, Stalin restrained the French communists before they became dangerously overambitious.

Similarly, a leading French communist, Jacques Duclos, blasted the American Communist party in the spring of 1945 for moving too close to the New Deal, and ordered it to create a separate identity— but then advised working within the American political system. "Nothing prevents a Communist Party from adapting its electoral tactics to the requirements of a given political situation," observed Duclos. The State Department, however, informed Truman that Duclos's advice required the government "to treat the American Communist movement as a potential fifth column." Traditional American fear of communist ideology reinforced the administration's dislike of Stalin's actions in Eastern Europe. Such fear at home was hardly warranted. Fifty thousand, or half the membership in the U.S. Communist party's Political Association, left the group by 1946.[29] Ironically, Americans began their search for communists at the same time the Communist party had to begin its own search for members.

By mid-1945 Stalin's policies were brutally consistent, while Truman's were confused. The confusion became obvious when the United States, opposed to a sphere of interest in Europe, strengthened its own sphere in the Western Hemisphere. Unlike its policies elsewhere, however, the State Department did not use economic weapons. The economic relationship with Latin America and Canada could simply be assumed. During the war these two areas had fed cheap raw materials to U.S. industry. After the struggle, and despite promises to the contrary, Washington neglected its neighbors while spending goods and money to rebuild Europe.

But Latin America was not neglected politically. A young assistant secretary of state for Latin American affairs, Nelson Rockefeller, and Senator Arthur Vandenberg (Republican from Michigan) devised the political means to keep the Americas solidly within Washington's sphere. Their instrument was Article 51 of the U.N. Charter. This provision was largely formulated by Rockefeller and Vandenberg at the San Francisco conference that founded the United Nations in the spring of 1945. The article allowed for collective self-defense through

---

[29]*Daily Worker,* May 24, 1945, pp. 7–9; *FRUS: Berlin,* I: 267–282; Joseph R. Starobin, *American Communism in Crisis, 1943–1957* (Cambridge, Mass., 1972), pp. 74–120.

special regional organizations to be created outside the United Nations but within the principles of the charter. In this way, regional organizations would escape Russian vetoes in the Security Council. The United States could control its own sphere without Soviet interference.

Intimately acquainted with Latin America because of his family's investments (especially in Venezuelan oil), Rockefeller wanted Russia excluded so that North and South America could be economically integrated and developed without unwelcome advice from outsiders. He also understood that unless the United States "operated with a solid group in this hemisphere" it "could not do what we wanted to do on the world front."[30] Vandenberg had other reasons. Although he was known as a 1930s "isolationist" who became an "internationalist" by 1945, it is questionable how far he actually turned.

The portly, white-haired senator exemplified the truism that Americans tend to become political "isolationists" when they cannot dominate international affairs and "internationalists" politically when they can. (They have been economic and cultural "internationalists" since the seventeenth century.) Rarely have Americans been prepared to bargain or to compromise their freedom of action. They have joined such organizations as the United Nations when they could control them. Throughout the war Vandenberg gradually left his earlier political "isolationism" because he believed the United States would have the power to internationalize the Atlantic Charter freedoms. These principles, he proclaimed in early 1945, "sail with our fleets. They fly with our eagles. They sleep with our martyred dead." And they must be had by all, including Eastern Europeans. But the Yalta agreements shocked him. Terming the Polish settlement "awful," he doubted that the United Nations, burdened with the Soviet veto in the Security Council, could enforce the Atlantic Charter. The Western Hemisphere could nevertheless be protected. When he and Rockefeller finished with Article 51, they thought they had obtained the best of both worlds: exclusive American power in the New and the right to exert American power in the Old.

The obvious confusion in that approach was pinpointed by Secretary of War Stimson when he condemned Americans who were

---

[30]David Green, *The Containment of Latin America* (Chicago, 1971), p. 234; the background is superbly provided in Elizabeth Cobbs Hoffman, *Rich Neighbor Policy: Rockefeller and Kaiser in Brazil* (New Haven, Conn., 1992).

"anxious to hang on to exaggerated views of the Monroe Doctrine [in the Western Hemisphere] and at the same time butt into every question that comes up in Central Europe." Almost alone, Stimson argued for an alternative policy. Through bilateral U.S.-U.S.S.R. negotiations (and not negotiations within the United Nations, where the Russians would be defensive and disagreeable because the Americans controlled a majority), Stimson hoped each side could agree that the other should have its own security spheres. But as he had lost the argument over Poland, so Stimson lost this argument. Truman was prepared to bargain very little. He might not get 100 percent, the President told advisers, but he would get 85 percent. Even in Rumania, where the Russians were particularly sensitive, the State Department secretly determined in August 1945, "It is our intention to attain a position of equality with the Russians." When, however, the Americans pressed, the Soviets only tightened their control of Rumania.[31]

Not even Stimson, however, could suggest a solution for Germany, the biggest problem of all. Throughout 1943–1945 Roosevelt had wavered between virtually destroying the nation (he even once mentioned mass castration) and allowing Germany to reindustrialize under tight controls. Stimson and Secretary of State Cordell Hull fought for rebuilding Germany. They believed world recovery depended on a strong, industrialized Europe. That required at its heart, as it had for a century, a healthy Germany. Roosevelt—typically—never made a clear choice.

For his part, Stalin happily agreed when Roosevelt suggested dismemberment, but the Russian cared more about taking reparations (in the form of industrial machines and goods) out of Germany. In this way he could rebuild Russian industry while killing off any possibility that Germany could again threaten Russia in the foreseeable future. Stalin also insisted upon territorial changes. He wanted the Poles to have part of eastern Germany as compensation for the land they were being forced to give Russia in eastern Poland. At first Churchill and Roosevelt had not objected to this demand, but by 1945 they opposed the new German-Polish boundary. They rightly feared this simply masked communist control of eastern Germany.

---

[31]"Memorandum for the Secretary," August 20, 1945, Lot File, Staff Officers' Summary, NA, RG 59.

At the Potsdam conference, held outside captured Berlin in July 1945, Truman and Secretary of State James Byrnes offered Stalin a deal. The West would de facto recognize the new Polish-German boundary. The Russians could also take reparations out of their own occupation zone of eastern Germany, an area primarily agricultural. But in the three Western occupation zones (controlled by the Americans, British, and French) the Soviets could have only 25 percent of the reparations; about half of those would have to be paid for with foodstuffs from the Russian zone. With considerable grumbling, Stalin accepted the deal. The United States had finally made the choice: it would not rush to dismember Germany but would hold tightly to the nation's western industrial heartland and methodically rebuild the shattered German economy. Of course there was one other implication. An economic division of Germany could lead to a political division. The deal laid the basis for an eastern and a western Germany.[32]

Although Truman did not obtain his "85 percent" at Potsdam, en route home he received the news that a weapon of unimaginable power, the atomic bomb, had obliterated Hiroshima, Japan, on August 6. Eighty thousand had died in an instant. This was some 20,000 fewer than had been killed by a massive American fire bombing of Tokyo earlier in the year, but it was the newly opened secret of nature embodied in a single bomb that was overwhelming. Roosevelt had initiated the atomic project in 1941. He had decided at least by 1944 not to share information about the bomb with the Soviets, even though he knew Stalin had learned about the project. By the summer of 1945 this approach, and the growing Soviet-American confrontation in Eastern Europe, led Truman and Byrnes to discuss securing "further *quid pro quos*" in Rumania, Poland, and Asia from Stalin before the Russians could share the secret of atomic energy.

Truman and his advisers, however, never figured out how to use the bomb as a lever to obtain concessions they wanted from the Soviets. At Potsdam the President had used the cool approach. After hearing that the test atomic device had worked at Los Alamos, New

---

[32]See Carolyn Eisenberg, "Rethinking the Division of Germany," in Allen Hunter, ed., *Rethinking the Cold War* (Philadelphia, 1998), pp. 52–53, for a good summary of the different U.S. views. For Truman, see especially Offner, *Another Such Victory*, pp. 70–84; for Stalin's views, note Service, *Stalin*, pp. 474–476, especially on the atomic bomb issue. For documents relating to the discussion at Potsdam on the German and Polish issues, see the chapter I documents at www.mhhe.com/lafeber website.

Mexico ("Now," one conscience-stricken scientist at Los Alamos said, "we're all sons-of-bitches"), Truman nonchalantly informed Stalin that the United States possessed a new destructive weapon, but did not mention what it was. Stalin instantly understood but acted so nonchalant himself that Truman was uncertain whether the Soviet leader grasped the President's remark. Stalin, however, understood so well that he immediately instructed the chief of the supersecret Soviet atomic project to speed up the work. The chief responded that he lacked both electrical power and the equipment needed to clear forests for the laboratories. Stalin quickly ordered electricity used by civilian areas to be switched to the nuclear project, then he sent two tank divisions to clear the forests. Just hours after the atomic age began, its arms race was accelerating.[33]

Truman dropped the bomb on Hiroshima for at least three reasons. First, the weapon had been developed with the expectation that it would be used. The primary target had been the Nazis, but when Germany surrendered in May 1945, the target automatically became Japan. Given the ferocious fighting of early 1945, when in months Americans suffered more casualties in the Pacific than they had during the previous three years of warfare in that theater, Truman's more difficult decision would have been *not* to use the bomb. Second, the planned late-1945 invasion of Japan would be costly. Using the bomb would reduce, if not remove, the need for paying such costs in American blood. Third, a diplomatic object was apparent. Stalin had promised at Yalta to invade Japanese strongholds in Manchuria approximately three months after the war with Germany

---

[33]This and the following two paragraphs are drawn from Anatoly Dobrynin, *In Confidence* (New York, 1995), p. 23; Martin J. Sherwin, "The Atomic Bomb and the Origins of the Cold War . . . ," *American Historical Review,* LXXVIII (October 1973): 945–968; Barton Bernstein, "The Atomic Bombings Reconsidered," *Foreign Affairs,* 74 (January 1995), pp. 135–152; the collection of important essays in *Diplomatic History,* 19 (Spring 1995), pp. 197–365, republished as Michael J. Hogan, ed., *Hiroshima in History and Memory* (New York, 1996), especially the Walker and Bix essays; and Gar Alperovitz, *The Decision to Use the Atomic Bomb and the Architecture of an American Myth* (New York, 1995), especially pp. 303–311, 484–489. The material in these three paragraphs is also based on chapter 7 of Walter LaFeber, *The Clash: United States Relations with Japan Throughout History* (New York, 1997), where further citations are listed. For the development of the bomb, a prize-winning account is Kai Bird and Martin J. Sherwin's biography of J. Robert Oppenheimer, *American Prometheus* (New York, 2005), chapters 13–23, the last of which has the Los Alamos scientist's quote.

ended—that is, sometime in August. In early 1945 U.S. officials had been much relieved that the Soviets would help fight the Japanese. By midsummer, however, Truman and Byrnes no longer wanted Stalin's armies too close to Japan. On August 8 the Soviets declared war on the Japanese and invaded Manchuria. The next day a second atomic bomb destroyed the city of Nagasaki. If reasons existed for laying the first bomb on Hiroshima, few observers since have found reasons for dropping the second—unless the reasons were that Truman simply did nothing to stop it (he did then order no more to be dropped without his express instructions) and that the Soviet invasion, in the eyes of top U.S. officials, required a quick Japanese surrender to the Americans.

On August 10, 1945, the Emperor overruled his military and Japan began peace negotiations. After several more heavy U.S. Air Force conventional raids took thousands of Japanese lives, Tokyo and Washington worked out surrender terms during August 14–15. Those terms could probably have been settled earlier if, as Stimson urged, Truman had said that the Japanese Emperor could remain (although shorn of his divine status). Byrnes, however, warned that if Truman made such a compromise, the American people would damn the President. In the end, the President accepted the retention of the Emperor. That acceptance and the Soviet declaration of war on August 8 largely convinced the Emperor and his advisers—who greatly feared that the armies of their historic enemy, Russia, might impose a communist system on their home islands if war continued—to make peace. Soviet troops were never able to move into the main Japanese home islands. Stalin vigorously, and uselessly, protested when Truman excluded the Russians from any real power in occupied Japan.

The bomb "is the greatest thing in history," Truman boasted. Nor was he sorry he had used it. Noting the "unwarranted attack on Pearl Harbor," the President explained to a journalist, "When you deal with a beast you have to treat him as a beast." (On his deathbed in 1972, however, Truman seemed obsessed about defending his dropping of the bomb. It was a ghost that never went away.)[34] On August 19 Admiral

---

[34]Quoted in Lisle A. Rose, *Dubious Victory: The United States and the End of World War II* (Kent State, 1973), p. 363; Truman in 1972 is noted in Ralph E. Weber, *Talking with Harry* (Wilmington, Del., 2001), p. 4. For a statement of Truman's views at this time, see his October 27, 1945 speech in chapter I of the documents at www.mhhe.com/lafeber website.

Leahy announced over national radio that the United States possessed a more powerful navy than any other two fleets in existence, the best-equipped ground force in the world, the "largest and most efficient air force," and "with our British allies, the secret of the world's most fearsome weapon." Clearly, Americans held most of the high cards as World War II ended. That same month Secretary of State Byrnes publicly announced the stakes for which the game would be played.

"Our international policies and our domestic policies are inseparable," he began. "Our foreign relations inevitably affect employment in the United States. Prosperity and depression in the United States just as inevitably affect our relations with the other nations of the world." Byrnes expressed his "clear conviction that a durable peace cannot be built on an economic foundation of exclusive blocs . . . and economic warfare." Specifically he warned: "In many countries . . . our political and economic creed is in conflict with ideologies which reject both of these principles." Byrnes concluded: "To the extent that we are able to manage our domestic affairs successfully, we shall win converts to our creed in every land."[35] John Winthrop had not expressed it more clearly 300 years earlier at Massachusetts Bay. Only now the City Upon a Hill, as Winthrop called it, was industrialized, internationalized—and held the atomic bomb.

But the Soviets refused to budge. Byrnes and Molotov agreed on little at a Foreign Ministers conference in the autumn of 1945. Inside Russia the threat of "capitalist encirclement" was trumpeted. Ominous rumors spread that Stalin would respond by further regimenting the Soviets with more five-year plans. Stimson, about to retire from the War Department, made one final attempt to stop an East-West confrontation. In a September 11 memorandum to Truman, Stimson prophesied "that it would not be possible to use our possession of the atomic bomb as a direct lever to produce the change" desired inside Eastern Europe. If Soviet-American negotiations continue with "this weapon rather ostentatiously on our hip, their suspicions and their distrust of our purposes and motives will increase." He again urged direct, bilateral talks with Stalin to formulate control of the bomb and to write a general peace settlement.[36]

---

[35]Raymond Dennett and Robert K. Turner, eds., *Documents on American Foreign Relations*, VIII (1945–1946) (Princeton, 1948): 601–602.
[36]See Henry Stimson and McGeorge Bundy, *On Active Service in Peace and War* (New York, 1948), pp. 638–650.

Stimson's advice was especially notable because several months before he himself had hoped to use the bomb to pry the Soviets out of Eastern Europe. Now he had changed his mind.

Truman again turned Stimson's advice aside. A month later the President delivered a speech larded with references to America's monopoly of atomic power, then attacked Russia's grip on Eastern Europe. Molotov quickly replied that peace could not be reconciled with an armaments race advocated by "zealous partisans of the imperialist policy." In this connection, he added, "We should mention the discovery of . . . the atomic bomb."[37]

With every utterance and every act, the wartime alliance further disintegrated. Stalin understood and regimented the Russian people for the struggle. Americans did not yet understand. Public and congressional opinion followed, not shaped, presidential and State Department policy. Harriman and other officials had defined the issues and called for a tough policy before Congress or its constituents knew about an "iron fence." In this, as in most foreign-policy issues, the executive branch could create a public opinion for policies it believed were in the national interest.[38] American interest was not threatened by a possible Soviet invasion of Western Europe. As the State Department informed Truman in June 1945, the Russians "are not too greatly concerned about developments in Western Europe so long as the Western European countries do not show signs of ganging up on them."[39]

A U.S. intelligence report spelled out Stalin's military problems in a stunning analysis of November 1945. The report listed Soviet military weaknesses and "the time required to remedy" them so that the U.S.S.R. would be "willing to risk a major armed conflict":[40]

1. War losses in manpower and industry (15 years)
2. Lack of technicians (5–10 years)
3. Lack of Strategic Air Force (5–10 years)

---

[37]*Department of State Bulletin*, XIII (October 28, 1945): 653–656; V. Molotov, *U.S.S.R. Foreign Policy* (Shanghai, 1946), pp. 7–8. Stimson's letter to Truman is in chapter I documents at www.mhhe.com/lafeber website.

[38]For a good analysis of this general problem, see Bernard Cohen, *The Public's Impact on Foreign Policy* (New York, 1943), especially pp. 155–156 on Acheson.

[39]*FRUS: Berlin*, I: 264.

[40]A superb analysis is in Matthew A. Evangelista, "Stalin's Postwar Army Reappraised," *International Security*, VII (Winter 1982–1983): 121–122.

4. Lack of a modern navy (15–20 years for a war involving major naval operations)
5. Poor condition of railway and military transportation systems and equipment (10 years)
6. Vulnerability of Soviet oil, rail, and vital industrial centers to long-range bombers
7. Lack of atomic bomb (5–10 years, possibly less)
8. Resistance in occupied countries (5 years or less)
9. Quantitative military weakness in the Far East—especially naval (15–20 years)

The report concluded that Russia would be unlikely to chance a major war for at least fifteen years. Since half the transport of the standing Soviet army was horse-drawn (and would remain so until 1950), fifteen years seemed a safe estimate.

Thus at the outset of the Cold War, Truman's problem was certainly not the threat of Soviet invasion of Asia or Europe. Nor was it American public opinion. The problem lay in Eastern Europe, where Stalin militarily roped off the region—and thus directly challenged the Atlantic Charter principles and the growing belief in Washington that the American system could only work globally. The division of Germany was set. Poland and Eastern Europe sank behind an "iron fence." The question now became this: how would the world's most powerful nation respond to these frustrations of its dreams for the postwar world? And there was a related question: when they responded, how would Americans use their tremendous power—not least their new atomic bomb? Some recalled the words of the famous nineteenth-century science-fiction writer Jules Verne: "The end of the earth will be when some enormous boiler . . . shall explode and blow up our globe. And [the Americans] are great boilermakers."[41]

---

[41]Paul Boyer, *By the Bomb's Early Light* (New York, 1985), p. 248.

President Truman (left) was not always an agreeable host when Winston Churchill (center) gave his famous Iron Curtain speech in 1946.
(Terry Savage, Courtesy of Harry S Truman Library)

CHAPTER 2

Only Two Declarations of Cold War (1946)

In late 1945 General George Patton, an heroic figure to some Americans in the 1940s and for decades thereafter, addressed eight-year-olds in a Sunday school class. "You are the soldiers and nurses of the next war. There will be another war," Patton assured the children. "There has always been."[1]

During 1946 war became more imminent than even Patton had expected. In Manchuria, Iran, Turkey, and Europe, the American and Russian military forces confronted each other. Several times they approached flash point. The crisis did not develop quite so far in China, but that situation was nevertheless critical, for the United States was losing a position in the western Pacific won during the war with American blood.

Harry Truman determined to maintain that position. "The future foreign interests of the United States will be in the Western Hemisphere and in the Pacific," he told an adviser in September 1945. The President believed Asian interests depended upon strengthening the Nationalist Chinese regime of Chiang Kai-shek. Chiang was to replace Japan as the stabilizing force in the area. And then there would also be economic benefits. By working through Chiang, Washington officials believed they could develop not only the great China market but other Asian countries as well. For more than a century Yankee tradesmen had pursued the mirage of that market. It now finally seemed real. A billion Asian customers would be of considerable help in avoiding

---

[1]Quoted in L. Wittner, *Rebels Against War . . . 1941–1960* (New York, 1969), p. 98.

another economic depression. John Carter Vincent, the State Department's expert on China, encouraged restoration of postwar trade "with all the speed we can generate. We are endeavoring to get businessmen back into China for their sake and for China's sake."[2] Whether a China could be created that would be both strong and friendly to Western interests was a question the West had avoided facing for a century.

This ambitious policy banged immediately into a major obstacle. Chiang's control was being chipped away by communist forces led by Mao Ze-dong. Although outnumbered five to one in 1945, Mao's army had increased dramatically since 1935 when Chiang had isolated it in northern China. At the end of World War II, the communists controlled one-fifth of China and more than 105 million people. Chiang's regime, meanwhile, was shot through with corruption, squandered more than a billion dollars of American aid, and drove many peasants (who comprised four-fifths of the population) into Mao's hands. Of special importance, the Nationalists could not control a roaring inflation that rocketed prices up some 2000 percent between 1937 and 1945; the middle classes were nearly wiped out.

Intent on preventing a Communist China, Roosevelt, then Truman, developed a policy that first aimed at separating Mao from the Soviets. In 1945 FDR obtained Stalin's promise to deal with Chiang, not Mao. In return for this pledge and his promise to enter the war against Japan, Stalin received substantial territorial concessions in Asia: the lease of Port Arthur as a Soviet naval base, internationalization of the port of Dairen, joint Sino-Soviet operation of the Chinese Eastern and South Manchurian railroads, possession of southern Sakhalin and the Kurile Islands (then held by Japan), and a plebiscite to be held in Outer Mongolia (which in October 1945 voted under Soviet supervision to become independent of China and move closer to Russia by the amazing score of 483,290 to 0). Chiang and Stalin agreed to most of these terms in a Treaty of Friendship and Alliance. The State Department and such periodicals as Henry Luce's *Time-Life* publications, which kept close watch over American interests in Asia, cheered the treaty.

Only Mao was bitter. He later recalled that "Stalin tried to prevent the Chinese Revolution by saying . . . we must collaborate with

[2]Seymour to Foreign Office, 24 November 1945, FO 371 F11517/36/10, Public Record Office, London.

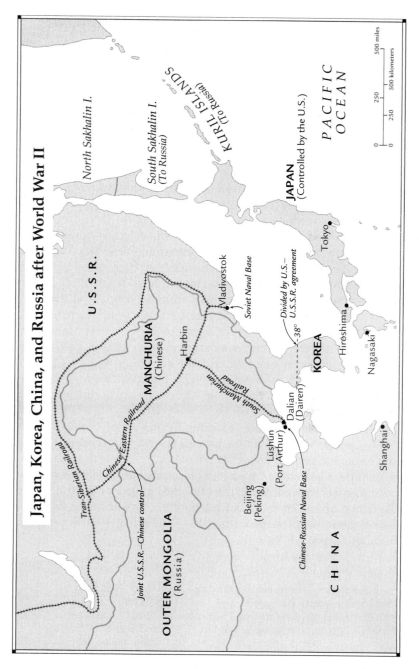

Japan, Korea, China, and Russia after World War II

North Sakhalin I.

South Sakhalin I.
(To Russia)

KURIL ISLANDS
(To Russia)

U.S.S.R.

JAPAN
(Controlled by the U.S.)

PACIFIC
OCEAN

500 miles

500 kilometers

250

250

Tokyo

Vladivostok

Soviet Naval Base

MANCHURIA
(Chinese)

Harbin

Divided by U.S.–
U.S.S.R. agreement

38°

KOREA

Hiroshima

Nagasaki

Chinese Eastern Railroad

South Manchurian
Railroad

Trans-Siberian Railroad

Joint U.S.S.R.–Chinese control

Dalian
(Dairen)

Lüshun
(Port Arthur)

Beijing
(Peking)

Chinese-Russian Naval Base

Shanghai

OUTER MONGOLIA
(Russia)

CHINA

37

Chiang." Soviet policy was clear. Stalin preferred a chaotic, divided China that would not threaten Russia, rather than a united China under either Chiang or Mao. As head of such a giant nation, Mao could particularly challenge Stalin within the communist world.[3]

With Mao's regime apparently isolated, the State Department moved to the next goal: ending the civil war by forcing Mao and Chiang into a coalition that Chiang could control. But Chiang refused to be locked into the same room with the communists. He had more direct methods. When asked about the danger of Russian-Chinese communist cooperation, Chiang replied "there is nothing to worry about" because he "was going to liquidate Communists."[4] Knowing that approach would not work, Truman pressured Chiang to accept the coalition idea.

Chiang-Mao talks broke down over whose army would control Manchuria, a key industrial area of northern China occupied by Japan since 1931. In the autumn of 1945 the problem became more complicated and ominous. Russian armies moved into Manchuria to disarm the Japanese, then remained to carry out what officials on the scene termed "scientific looting" of industrial machinery for the rebuilding of Russian industry.[5] Mao and Chiang raced to control Manchuria. Mao won, despite Truman's attempt to help Chiang by keeping Japanese soldiers in place against the communists until Chiang's troops could move into position. The President even dispatched 50,000 American soldiers to help Chiang push northward. Soon 100,000 Americans were in China.

With Chiang's position eroding, Truman sent General of the Army George Marshall on his famous mission to reconcile Chiang and Mao. The general hoped, in his words, to avert "the tragic consequences of a divided China and of a probable Russian reassumption of power in Manchuria, the combined effect of this resulting in the defeat or loss of the major purpose of our war in the Pacific."[6] Few Americans dissented from Marshall's fear of the potential Russian danger.

---

[3]Seymour Topping, *Journey Between Two Chinas* (New York, 1972), p. 54.
[4]Daily Staff Summary, February 26, 1945, Lot File, NA, RG 59.
[5]"Memorandum for the President," September 17, 1945, OSS Memoranda for the President, Donovan Chronological File, Box 15, Truman Library.
[6]Quoted in Tang Tsou, *America's Failure in China, 1941–1950* (Chicago, 1963), pp. 355–356.

By late February 1946 Marshall had worked out an agreement, including a cease-fire. This was the closest the United States or the Chinese themselves would come to a peaceful settlement. By mid-April the arrangement had collapsed. Marshall later placed much blame on Chiang for this disaster, because the Chinese leader insisted on taking Manchuria by force. The American, however, also noted that toward the end of the negotiations the communists were unwilling "to make a fair compromise," particularly on the disposition of their army.[7]

Believing he could defeat the communists militarily and that the United States had no alternative but to provide him with all the arms he required, Chiang refused Marshall's suggestions for further compromise. The Nationalists' leader sadly miscalculated. As the State Department had feared, Mao's armies obtained a treasure when, in March and April 1946, Soviet occupation troops in Manchuria suddenly withdrew, leaving behind vast stores of Japanese arms and equipment for Mao's forces. Chiang launched a major military offensive into Manchuria. At first he was successful, then his army overstretched its supply lines. By late 1946 Mao was successfully counterattacking.

As the military tide began to turn, even worse lay in wait for Americans. Washington officials warned the "widespread resentment" by the Chinese people "which cannot be openly expressed is being turned almost entirely against the U.S." Even the American troops were being pressured to leave. It was a terrible dilemma. If the United States remained, it would be "an immediately available target . . . for . . . Chinese xenophobia." On the other hand, Chiang had to have American aid. "If we break" with him, a top White House adviser observed, "the result will be that we will have no friends in either of the Chinese factions and no friends in China."[8]

Marshall cut through to the core of the problem. If Americans tried to save Chiang they would "virtually [have] to take over the Chinese government. . . . It would involve the [United States] in a continuing commitment from which it would practically be impossible to withdraw" and could make China "an arena of international

---

[7]For Marshall's later assessment and hope for a liberal middle way for China, see Department of State, *U.S. Relations with China* (Washington, 1949), pp. 686–689.
[8]Daily Staff Summary, January 8, 1947, Lot File, NA, RG 59.

conflict."[9] Neither Truman nor Marshall would get sucked into that kind of war. The President tried to cover his retreat after late 1946 with a small aid program for Chiang, but Truman was pulling out of China. He and Marshall could only hope that the revolution would not be completed "for a long time."

Stalin shared that hope. Indeed, Truman could downgrade China precisely because the Russians had withdrawn from Manchuria and now seemed to be behaving throughout Asia. On the other hand, viewing international events in the context of the American-Soviet confrontation forced Washington officials to give top priority to European and Middle Eastern affairs. As China dropped down the American priority list in 1946, these two elements—Washington's determination to counter all Soviet threats, and total commitment to keeping Western Europe within the American camp—fused and exploded into a dramatic crisis in the Middle East.

For nearly a century the Middle East had formed the lifeline of the British and French empires. More recently it provided the Western world with oil. American companies had moved into a dominating position in the petroleum industry. To protect this vital area, the British, Russians, and Americans had agreed in 1942 to occupy Iran jointly. They further agreed to withdraw six months after the conflict ended. Several times during the war Churchill and Roosevelt assured Stalin that Russia, which bordered Iran, would have its interests protected in the postwar settlement. By 1944, however, the State Department was developing a tougher policy to fight Soviet claims.

By early 1946 most of the British and American forces had withdrawn, but the Russians stalled. Stalin demanded oil concessions approximating those obtained by the British. The Soviets then supported a revolt of the Azerbaijanian population in northern Iran. The State Department panicked. The Russians seemed on the move everywhere, a top official warned, not only in the east and west but through this "third barrier" in the south. They threatened to "sweep unimpeded across Turkey . . . into the Mediterranean and across Iran . . . into the Indian Ocean."[10]

[9]Daily Staff Summary, January 8, 1947, Lot File, NA, RG 59; Leahy Diaries, Box 5, August 12, 1946, Leahy Papers; Akira Iriye, *The Cold War in Asia* (Englewood Cliffs, N.J., 1974), p. 166.

[10]The best analysis is Mark Lytle, *The Origins of the Iranian-American Alliance, 1941–1953* (New York, 1987), especially chapters III–VI. *FRUS, 1946, Near East*, pp. 1–5.

Washington officials decided on a two-pronged policy. First they took the Iranian case to the United Nations. The opening session of the new Security Council was thus poisoned by a bitter exchange between the Soviets and Americans. Second, when Russian tanks rumbled toward the Iranian border in early March, Secretary of State James F. Byrnes smacked one fist into his other hand and declared, "Now we'll give it to them with both barrels." Byrnes sent a message to the Soviets that they must withdraw from the country. In late March Iran and Russia announced that the Red Army would leave and a joint Iranian-Soviet oil company would be formed subject to ratification of the Iranian Parliament (the Majlis). The Iranian army then squashed the Azerbaijan revolt. Several months later the Majlis rejected the oil company. Russia had suffered a humiliating diplomatic defeat. Soviet records released in the 1990s revealed that Stalin did not leave Iran because of Byrnes's threats, but because the Soviets believed they had made an acceptable deal with the Iranians. At no point in 1945–1946 did Stalin plan to divide Iran. But the Iranians, with U.S. encouragement, double-crossed him, while his actions had mobilized an Anglo-American anti-Soviet movement. He thus lost twice.[11]

Another setback quickly followed in Turkey. This crisis had grown from historic Russian-Turkish antipathy, Soviet determination to gain joint control of the strategic Dardanelles Straits (the key link between the Mediterranean and Soviet ports on the Black Sea), and Stalin's inherited Georgian trait of hating everything Turkish except tobacco. In early 1945 he revived an ancient Russian demand for partnership with the Turks to control the straits. Again, during the war FDR and Churchill had assured Stalin that Russia was "justified" in having access to the Mediterranean, particularly since Turkey had collaborated with Hitler.[12] And again, as in Iran, by 1945 the British and Americans had changed their minds. They were determined to keep the Soviets away from the Mediterranean.

Quiet diplomatic probing by both sides followed until August 1946, when Stalin sent a note to Turkey which Under Secretary of

---

[11]Natalia I. Yegarova, *The "Iran Crisis" of 1945–1946: A View from the Russian Archives,* Cold War International History Project (Washington, D.C., 1996), pp. 12–19.

[12]Adam Ulam, *Expansion and Coexistence* (New York, 1968), pp. 430–431; "Record of Meeting at the Kremlin," 9 October 1944, PREM 3, 434/7, Public Record Office, London.

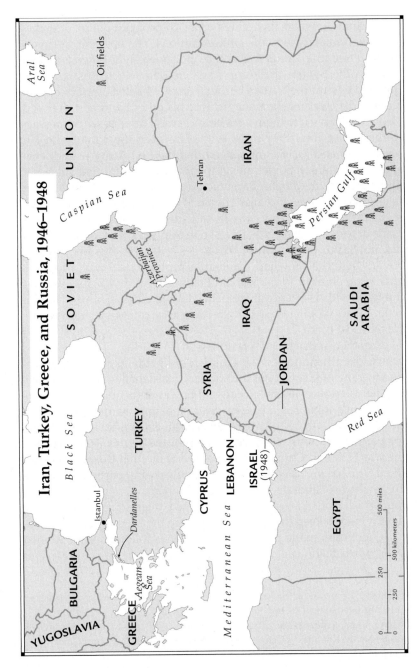

Iran, Turkey, Greece, and Russia, 1946–1948

Oil fields

Aral Sea

SOVIET UNION

Caspian Sea

Tehran

IRAN

Persian Gulf

SAUDI ARABIA

Azerbaijan Province

IRAQ

JORDAN

SYRIA

Black Sea

Istanbul

Dardanelles

TURKEY

CYPRUS

LEBANON

ISRAEL (1948)

Mediterranean Sea

Red Sea

EGYPT

BULGARIA

YUGOSLAVIA

GREECE

Aegean Sea

0   250   500 miles

0   250   500 kilometers

State Dean Acheson interpreted as a Soviet attempt to dominate Turkey, threaten Greece, and intimidate the remainder of the Middle East. Acheson advised a showdown with the Russians before the fall of Turkey led to the collapse of "the whole Near and Middle East," then even "India and China." Here, as in the Iranian crisis, American officials justified their policy on the basis of what would later be termed the "domino theory." This theory rested on the assumption that Stalin, like Hitler, was intent on—and capable of—unlimited conquest. Soviet policy in 1946 and Hitler's ambitions of 1938 were not comparable. But few officials (or historians) wished to point that out at the start of the Cold War.

Harry Truman saw nothing wrong with Acheson's view. "We might as well find out whether the Russians were bent on world conquest now as in five or ten years," the President asserted.[13] So he informed the Soviets that Turkey would continue to be "primarily responsible" for the straits. The State Department then reinforced an American naval unit (including marines) which had been sailing in the Mediterranean since early spring. The *Franklin D. Roosevelt*, the most powerful American aircraft carrier, moved into the area. By the autumn of 1946 Soviet pressure on Turkey had eased. A tough Washington response had kept the dominoes upright.

Stalin probably believed that, because of its wartime sacrifices and geographic location, Russia had as much right to Iranian oil and control of the Dardanelles as any other power. Thwarted in these areas, in February 1946, Stalin brought charges in the Security Council against the British repression of the Greek rebellion and British and Dutch attempts to suppress revolution in Indonesia. The bitterest outburst occurred three months later at the Paris Foreign Ministers conference. Molotov gave the Soviet view of what was occurring:

> Nineteenth century imperialism may be dead in England, but there are new twentieth century tendencies. When Mr. Churchill calls for a new war and makes militant speeches on two continents, he represents the worst of 20th century imperialism. . . . Britain has troops in Greece, Palestine, Iraq, Indo-China and elsewhere. Russia has no troops outside of security zones and their lines of communication. This is different. We have troops only where provided by

---

[13]James Forrestal, *The Forrestal Diaries*, Walter Millis, ed. (New York, 1951), p. 192; Thomas Paterson, *Soviet-American Confrontation* (Baltimore, 1973), pp. 192–193.

treaties. Thus we are in Poland, for example, as our Allies are in Belgium, France and Holland. I also recall that Egypt is a member of UNO [the United Nations]. She demands that British troops be withdrawn. Britain declines. . . . What shall we say of UNO when one member imposes its authority upon another? How long can such things go on?[14]

During early 1946 Stalin and Churchill issued their declarations of Cold War. In an election speech of February 9, the Soviet dictator announced that Marxist-Leninist dogma remained valid, for "the unevenness of development of the capitalist countries" could lead to "violent disturbance" and the consequent splitting of the "capitalist world into two hostile camps and war between them." War was inevitable as long as capitalism existed. The Soviet people must prepare themselves for a replay of the 1930s by developing basic industry instead of consumer goods and, in all, making enormous sacrifices demanded in "three more Five-Year Plans, I should think, if not more."[15] There would be no peace, internally or externally. These words profoundly affected Washington. Supreme Court Justice William Douglas, one of the reigning American liberals, concluded that Stalin's speech meant "The Declaration of World War III." *The New York Times* front-page story of the speech began by declaring that Stalin believed "the stage is set" for war.[16]

Winston Churchill delivered his views at Westminister College in Fulton, Missouri, on March 5. The former prime minister exalted American power with the plea that his listeners recognize that "God has willed" the United States, not "some Communist or neo-Fascist state" to have atomic bombs. To utilize the "breathing space" provided by these weapons, Churchill asked for "a fraternal association of the English-speaking peoples" operating under the principles of the United Nations—but not inside that organization—to reorder the world. This unilateral policy must be undertaken because "from Stettin in the Baltic to Trieste in the Adriatic, an iron curtain has descended across the Continent" allowing "police government" to rule Eastern Europe. The Soviets, he emphasized, did not want war:

[14]Arthur H. Vandenberg, Jr., ed., *The Private Papers of Senator Vandenberg* (Boston, 1952), pp. 277–278.
[15]J. V. Stalin, *Speech Delivered by J. V. Stalin at a Meeting of Voters of the Stalin Electoral Area of Moscow, February 9, 1946* (Washington, Embassy of the U.S.S.R., March 1946).
[16]*Forrestal Diaries*, pp. 134–135; *The New York Times*, February 10, 1946, p. 1.

"What they desire is the fruits of war and the indefinite expansion of their power and doctrines."[17]

The "iron curtain" phrase made the Westminister College speech famous. But, as Churchill himself observed, the "crux" of the message lay in the proposal that the Anglo-Americans, outside the United Nations and with the support of atomic weaponry (the title of the address was "The Sinews of Peace"), create "a unity in Europe from which no nation should be permanently outcast." The Soviets perceived this as a direct challenge to their power in Eastern Europe. Within a week Stalin attacked Churchill and his "friends" in America, who, he claimed, resembled Hitler by holding a "racial theory" that those who spoke the English language "should rule over the remaining nations of the world." This, Stalin warned, is "a set-up for war, a call to war with the Soviet Union."[18]

Within a short period after the Churchill speech, Stalin launched a series of policies which, in retrospect, marks the spring and summer of 1946 as a milestone in the Cold War. During these weeks the Soviets, after having worked for a loan during the previous fifteen months, finally concluded that Washington had no interest in loaning them $1 billion, or any other amount. They refused to become a member of the World Bank and the International Monetary Fund. These rejections ended the American hope to use the lure of the dollar to make the Soviets retreat in Eastern Europe and join the capitalist-controlled bank and IMF.

Actually there had never been reason to hope. Control of their border areas was worth more to the Russians than $1 billion, or even $10 billion. Moreover, as early as September 1944 an American intelligence report had indirectly warned against trying to use financial pressure. It observed that with internal sacrifices Russia "could carry through this reconstruction with its domestic resources, without foreign loans or reparations." The State Department agreed with this conclusion in April 1946 when Byrnes told the Cabinet that "the only place where money has not influenced national interest is Russia." (The secretary of state notably added that "we are in this thing all

[17]Text in *The New York Times,* March 6, 1946, p. 4 and in the chapter II documents at www.mhhe.com/lafeber website.
[18]Interview in *Pravda,* reprinted in *The New York Times,* March 14, 1946.

over the world to an extent that few people realize.")[19] Thus the attempt to buy off the Soviets had worked no better than Washington's vague hope that the atomic bomb might somehow make them more "manageable."

At home Stalin announced a new five-year plan, then initiated an intense ideological effort to eliminate Western influences, purify and propagate Stalinist dogma, and deify the dictator himself. The name of Andrei Zhdanov soon became synonymous with this campaign. One close observer described this supposed "intellectual" of the politburo as "short, with a brownish clipped mustache, high forehead, pointed nose, and sickly red face," who had "some knowledge of everything," but did not know a single field thoroughly, "a typical intellectual who became acquainted with and picked up knowledge of other fields through Marxist literature." Zhdanov prophesied that Marxism-Leninism had a messianic destiny, "the right to teach others a new general human morality."[20]

The Stalinist and Churchillian declarations of Cold War appeared by the summer of 1946 to have a dramatic effect on the two touchstones of world politics, Germany and the control of atomic weapons. In Germany reparations were the central issue. Secretary of State Byrnes attempted to meet Russian fears of a remilitarized Germany by proposing that the Big Four powers sign a treaty unifying the country and guaranteeing its demilitarization. Molotov rejected this because of a key Russian policy change on reparations. Sometime during the spring the Soviets stopped removing machinery from eastern Germany and determined instead to produce goods in their zone, where labor and resources were more readily available, then ship the products to Russia. While Molotov was rejecting Byrnes's overture, General Lucius Clay informed Russian commanders in Germany in May that no more reparations would be removed from the Western zones. These areas, Clay feared, were becoming bankrupt. Unless

---

[19]"Memorandum for Baruch from Sam Lubell," March 1945, Papers of Bernard Baruch, Princeton University Library, Princeton, N.J.; "Cabinet Meeting, April 19, 1946." Notes on Cabinet Meetings, 1945–1946, White House File, Truman Library.

[20]Milovan Djilas, *Conversations with Stalin* (New York, 1961), pp. 149–150; Frederick C. Barghoorn, "Great Russian Messianism in Postwar Soviet Ideology." In Ernest J. Simmons, ed., *Continuity and Change in Russian and Soviet Thought* (Cambridge, Mass., 1955), pp. 545–546.

reparations were stopped and the zones rebuilt, he was convinced, the population had little chance for survival. Molotov's and Clay's moves were decisive moments in the Cold War, for they terminated any real hope of useful negotiations to reunite Germany. Each power had now set out to develop its own zone.

Byrnes analyzed this growing rigidity in a highly publicized speech at Stuttgart, Germany, on September 6. The secretary of state announced that Germany must develop exports in order to be "self-sustaining," and refused to recognize the Oder-Neisse boundary for eastern Germany. He asserted that Germans should be given primary responsibility for running their own affairs (this was particularly frightening to both the Russians and the French), and emphasized that the American presence in Central Europe would not be withdrawn. This was the first time a high American official had said such things publicly. The speech, however, was historic, not prophetic; it only summarized events of the previous eighteen months. [Byrnes's speech may be read in the chapter II documents at website www.mhhe.com/lafeber.]

A second clash in the summer of 1946 intensified the Cold War. Since Hiroshima the horror of atomic energy had overhung every diplomatic exchange. In March 1946 the United States released a plan for the control of the atom, the so-called Acheson-Lilienthal proposal. This report suggested a series of stages through which the world could pass to international control of atomic weapons. Throughout the transition period the United States, possessing the only atomic bombs, would remain in a favored position while other nations agreed to be inspected by international agencies. A month later Truman named Wall Street financier Bernard Baruch as the first American delegate to a new UN Atomic Energy Commission. American policy soon began to change. Deeply suspicious by nature, Baruch distrusted the Acheson-Lilienthal report, partly because he had not sat on the committee and partly because it said nothing about the Russian veto in the Security Council.

Baruch determined to eliminate any Soviet power to veto inspections or sanctions. The Acheson-Lilienthal report, on the other hand, planned to obtain Russian agreement to general principles and then discuss the veto problem. Baruch became increasingly bitter about Under Secretary of State Acheson (whom he mistakenly accused of recording their telephone conversations) and those "One Worlders" like columnist Walter Lippmann "whom I can't understand any more." All the "One Worlders" criticized Baruch's belief that he could force the Soviets to surrender their veto power.[21] But he finally triumphed by convincing Truman that it was better to be tough with Russia sooner rather than later. After recalling the dismantling of the American Navy in the 1920s, the President agreed: "We should not under any circumstances throw away our gun until we are sure the rest of the world can't arm against us."[22] Military and political advisers bolstered this view by avowing that Russia could not build atomic bombs for at least five to fifteen years. Only a few scientists warned that the period might be considerably shorter.

In a dramatic speech at the United Nations in June 1946, Baruch presented his plan: atomic energy would be controlled through international management of the necessary raw materials and inspection by international agencies. No vetoes of these controls and inspections would be allowed, and majority vote would rule. In the realm of peaceful uses of atomic energy, an Atomic Development Authority, again free of the veto, would establish atomic plants not according to need (as in underdeveloped areas or in large stretches of Russia) but according to strategic and geographic criteria. By controlling a majority within the authority, the United States could thus control the development of the industrial uses of nuclear energy *within* the Soviet Union. [Baruch's speech may be read in the chapter II documents at website www.mhhe.com/lafeber.]

This was, not surprisingly, totally unacceptable to the Russians. They countered by demanding destruction of all atomic bombs, the cessation of their production, agreement of all powers not to use these weapons, and then a discussion of controls. Baruch retorted that they must accept the entire American plan or there would be no plan. So there was no plan. Instead, Congress established a U.S. Atomic Energy Commission under the Atomic Energy Act of 1946. Under strong military pressure, the act prohibited an exchange of information on the use of atomic energy with any nation until Congress should decide by joint resolution that "effective" international controls were in force. That, obviously, would be a long time off.

[21]Acheson file, Atomic Energy, Baruch Papers, especially telephone conversation between Baruch and Acheson, November 26, 1946.
[22]"BMB [Bernard M. Baruch] Memorandum of Meeting on June 7, 1946, with the President and J. F. Byrnes," Truman File, Atomic Energy, Baruch Papers.

So, a year after Japan's surrender, the Pandora's box of atomic power remained open, Byrnes's speech illustrated the deadlock over Germany, and Russian-American loan discussions had collapsed. Stalin and Churchill had issued world-shaking statements. But—significantly—Harry Truman had not. He and other Americans even reacted coldly to Churchill's suggestion of an Anglo-American partnership that would tie the United States to a declining, nearly bankrupt England. The President publicly offered no alternative to Churchill's. Throughout 1946, even during the Iranian and Turkish crises, Truman never publicly condemned Soviet policy.

No one doubted that the Western world would be shaped by Truman's decisions. On the train ride to Fulton, Missouri, Churchill delighted his hosts when he recited by memory long portions of John Greenleaf Whittier's poetry. Truman meanwhile walked up to the engine. While the Britisher quoted American authors, the President drove the train. It was all appropriate. Throughout 1945–1946 Truman had confronted the Russians, but he had not formulated a coherent policy or a consensus at home to support such a comprehensive policy. The question was in which direction, and how rapidly, Truman would drive the train of the Western nations.

By autumn the President's task was, oddly, made more difficult as the Soviets became quiet. Truman's problem was no longer centered on the threat of immediate Russian expansion, as in Iran or Turkey. It rapidly became the infinitely more complex chore of rebuilding war-devastated Western Europe as it entered perhaps the harshest winter in living memory. Great Britain was so deeply discouraged that a radical swing to the left seemed politically possible. Parts of Central Europe faced starvation. France was chaotic. Truman had so feared a French Communist party seizure of power from within that in May he secretly ordered the U.S. Army in Germany to prepare for a march into France.[23] The West was threatened not by the Red Army, but by internal collapse. Truman's closest advisers urged him to use massive economic and military aid "to build up a world of our own" before the Soviets won by default.[24]

---

[23]*FRUS, 1946, Europe*, V: 435–438.
[24]The best brief discussion of this approach is Richard M. Freeland, *The Truman Doctrine and McCarthyism* (New York, 1972), pp. 56–57.

But for the President this advice seemed only a pipe dream. Congress and the American people would respond to a Soviet attack. Spending billions of the taxpayers' dollars in Europe, however, was different. Americans recalled with bitterness how ungrateful Europeans appeared for help given during World War I. Nor would it be popular to enrich England and France, whose trade practices and imperial policies had long angered the United States. Moreover, Americans had sacrificed during the war. Now they wanted to spend on themselves. This was not easy, for a rush of inflation, labor strikes, and meat shortages in late 1946 wounded both the economy and Truman's popularity. Many Americans believed that if the President wanted to help someone he should help them by cutting taxes. Truman's difficulties came into the open during the autumn of 1946, when he was attacked by liberals for being too militaristic and by conservatives for his economic policies.

The liberal attack was led by Henry Agard Wallace, a great secretary of agriculture during the early New Deal, Vice President from 1941–1945, maneuvered out of the vice-presidential nomination in 1944 so that Harry Truman could be FDR's running mate, and finally secretary of commerce in 1945. Here he devoted himself to the cause of what he liked to call the "Common Man," by extending increased loans to small businessmen and, above all, enlarging the economic pie by increasing foreign trade. Wallace soon discovered that Truman threatened to clog the trade channels to Russia, Eastern Europe, perhaps even China, with his militant attitude toward the Soviets.

At a political rally in New York on September 12, 1946, Wallace delivered a speech, cleared personally, and too rapidly, by Truman. The address focused on the necessity of a political understanding with Russia. This, Wallace declared, would require guaranteeing Soviet security in Eastern Europe. He hoped the capitalist and communist systems could compete "on a friendly basis" and "gradually become more alike." Wallace, however, added one proviso for his happy ending: in this competition "we must insist on an open door for trade throughout the world. . . . We cannot permit the door to be closed against our trade in Eastern Europe any more than we can in China."[25] At that moment Byrnes and Vandenberg were in Paris, painfully and unsuccessfully trying to negotiate peace treaties with

---

[25]Henry Wallace, "The Way to Peace," *Vital Speeches,* October 1, 1946, pp. 738–741.

Molotov. They immediately demanded Wallace's resignation. On September 20, Truman complied.[26]

The vigor of their reaction to Wallace's speech measured the distance American policy had moved since the close of World War II. Wallace was essentially pleading for a renewal of the administration's invitation of 1945 to the war-decimated Soviet economy to join a friendly game of economic competition with the American industrial mammoth and to play the game according to American rules. By mid-1946 Truman and Byrnes had moved far beyond this. They now assumed that Stalin would not accept such rules but would cooperate only when directly faced with the threat of superior force. Given this background and the ringing declaration of a worldwide open door, little wonder that the Communist party newspaper *Daily Worker* in New York at first attacked Wallace's speech as a cover for "American imperialism." Only after Byrnes and Truman blasted Wallace did the *Worker* discover virtue in his ideas.

Wallace nevertheless voiced the concerns of many New Dealers. In late September a group of labor leaders met with Harold Ickes and Henry Morgenthau, Jr., two stalwarts of the Roosevelt years, to proclaim support of Wallace's views and to issue a plea to end tests of atomic bombs. Truman was meanwhile convinced that Wallace was a "pacifist," more dangerous than the pro-Nazi groups in the country during World War II, and part of "a sabotage front for Uncle Joe Stalin."[27]

This splitting of the New Deal coalition badly wounded Truman's political fortunes, but worse lay ahead. The President had become so unpopular that only 32 percent of those polled thought he provided adequate leadership. His fellow Democrats did not even ask him for support in the 1946 congressional campaign. They preferred to broadcast recordings of Roosevelt's speeches. The election was a disaster for the administration. Republicans gained solid control of both Senate and House for the first time since 1928. The Republican "Class of 1946," moreover, included such red-blooded conservatives as Joseph McCarthy of Wisconsin, John Bricker of

[26]See John C. Culver and John Hyde, *American Dreamer: The Life and Times of Henry A. Wallace* (New York, 2000), chapters 5–14, 20–21 for background, and pp. 411–431 on the resignation. Wallace's speech may be read in the chapter II documents of this book's www.mhhe.com/lafeber website.

[27] Margaret Truman, *Harry S Truman* (New York, 1973), pp. 346–347.

Ohio, and William Knowland of California. The new legislators had stressed their anticommunism during the campaign but had also called for deep tax cuts. There seemed little chance they would support any large-scale economic and military program to help Europe, particularly if Stalin remained quiet.[28] Several leading Americans, including Senator J. William Fulbright (Democrat of Arkansas) and columnist Walter Lippmann, suggested that Truman could best serve his country by resigning.

During the last days of 1946, the counterattack began. A group of liberals prepared to meet in Washington to form the Americans for Democratic Action. This organization, in contrast to Wallace's, pledged to continue working within the Democratic party and to fight communism both at home and abroad. Chairing the founding session was Reinhold Niebuhr, theologian, philosopher, historian, and perhaps the most important contemporary influence on American thought. Not since Jonathan Edwards's day of the 1740s had an American theologian so affected his society. Like Edwards, Niebuhr emphasized the importance of sin and sinful power in that society. He disavowed the "sentimental optimism" that had shaped American thought during the 1900–1930 era and which again was appearing in the post-1945 world under the guise of "positive thinking."

In a remarkable series of books and lectures, Niebuhr developed his central theme that, because of avarice, finiteness, and inability to realize the limits of their own power, humans were overwhelmed with anxieties and unable to use freedom constructively. This anxiety led to a will-to-power and this, in turn, to conflict. Given such "egoistic corruption in all human virtue,"[29] Niebuhr warned that reason, and particularly faith in science, could not be wholly trusted, for both reason and science often refused to use the religious and historical insights required to solve secular problems.

As the Cold War heightened, Niebuhr stood ready with an explanation and a solution. Communism, he proclaimed, was at once the worst and most aggressive of societies because its faithful believed they could find a perfect union among the sinful simply by changing economic relationships. Private property, he warned, "is

---

[28] Susan M. Hartmann, *Truman and the 80th Congress* (New York, 1971) p. 49.
[29] Reinhold Niebuhr, "The Foreign Policy of American Conservatism and Liberalism." In *Christian Realism and Political Problems* (New York, 1953), p. 66.

not the cause but the instrument of human egotism."[30] Niebuhr charged that communists overlooked what was more important and ineradicable, each individual's will-to-power. Worse, communism historically had sought to achieve the better society by centralizing power in one or several leaders rather than working out a balance of power within that society. By employing science and so-called scientific rationales, moreover, communism had proved once again to Niebuhr that science is highly serviceable to, and easily maneuvered by, a totalitarian society.

Since "all life is an expression of power," he believed that the West could preserve its freedoms only by creating the best possible balance-of-power situations. He thought New Deal capitalism offered the most promise inside the United States because Roosevelt had created government agencies to check irresponsible private corporations. Abroad, no trust could be placed in world government. He supported instead the Baruch Plan for atomic energy and wrote article after article in 1946 and 1947 pleading for a revitalized Europe to offset the communist threat.[31]

After a visit to Europe in 1946, Niebuhr fixed upon the German problem. Here again he became an important symbol, and a strong influence, in American foreign policy. Niebuhr was one of the earliest to spell out in detail the spiritual, political, and economic unity of the Atlantic community and the pivotal role that Germany must play if Europe was to be saved from communism. "Russian truculence cannot be mitigated by further concessions," he wrote in October 1946. "Russia hopes to conquer the whole of Europe strategically or ideologically." Then came a thrust at Wallace: "It has been the unfortunate weakness of both liberalism and liberal Christianity that they have easily degenerated into sentimentality by refusing to contemplate the tragic aspects of human existence honestly."[32] In applauding the rapid development of the German steel industry in 1947, Niebuhr accepted the "explicit division between East and West which has taken place. . . . Only God can bring order out of this kind of mixture of good and evil. We must, meanwhile, keep our powder dry."[33]

---

[30] *The Nation,* March 6, 1948, p. 268.
[31] *Christianity and Crisis,* July 8, 1946, p. 2.
[32] *Life,* October 21, 1946, pp. 65–72.
[33] *Christianity and Crisis,* August 4, 1947, p. 2.

Niebuhr's work thus provided points of departure for criticizing Wallace, condemning communism, formulating a Europe-first policy, and rebuilding Germany. Most important, he provided a historical basis and rationale for the tone, the outlook, and the unsaid, and often unconscious, assumptions of these years.

But transforming Niebuhr's views into policy would require time. Given the slide of Western Europe and the Republican hold on Congress, Harry Truman did not appear to have enough time or support. Knowledgeable Americans who were usually calm began to sound shrill and desperate. For example, exactly one year after Henry Stimson had advised reasoning with the Soviets, Secretary of the Navy James Forrestal counseled with the retired statesman. "He said," Forrestal recorded in his diary that night, "the way things had now developed he thought we should not delay in going forward with the manufacture of all the atomic missiles we could make."[34] Others agreed with Stimson's suggestion, but it would not prevent the economic collapse of Europe no matter how many missiles were built.

Truman, unlike Churchill and Stalin, had not yet publicly joined the Cold War. The direction and speed of the Western train remained to be determined. Meanwhile the President's winter promised to be nearly as bleak as Europe's.

---

[34] *Forrestal Diaries,* p. 200.

The President worded his Truman Doctrine so the American people had little choice but to swallow the bitter medicine of fighting a Cold War—in 1947 and for 40 years thereafter.
(Fred O. Seibel Cartoonist's Research Collection, MSS 2531, Special Collections, University of Virginia Library)

CHAPTER 3

Two Halves of the Same Walnut (1947–1948)

On March 12, 1947, President Truman finally issued his own declaration of Cold War, and did so with an act that became historic. Dramatically presenting the Truman Doctrine to Congress, he asked Americans to join in a global commitment against communism. The nation responded. A quarter of a century later, Senator J. William Fulbright declared, "More by far than any other factor the anti-communism of the Truman Doctrine has been the guiding spirit of American foreign policy since World War II."[1]

An odd circumstance, however, must be explained if the Truman Doctrine is to be understood. The Soviet Union had been less aggressive in the months before the President's pronouncement than at any time in the postwar period. State Department officials privately believed that "the USSR is undergoing serious economic difficulties" which have led to "the less aggressive international attitude taken by Soviet authorities in recent weeks." This policy was only "a temporary retreat." Nonetheless, the problems seemed so great that the Russians gave military discharges to "hundreds of thousands of young men [who] will now become available for labor force in industry, agriculture and construction."[2] Stalin reduced his 12 million military men of 1945 to between 3 and 4 million in 1947. (American forces

---

[1]J. William Fulbright, *The Crippled Giant* (New York, 1972), pp. 6–24 for quote and context.

[2]Daily Staff Summary, January 3, January 15, February 24, February 10, 1947, Lot File, NA, RG 59.

dropped from 10 million to 1.4 million, but Americans enjoyed a monopoly of atomic weapons.) Russian military levels would go no lower, for the Red Army was Stalin's counter to Truman's atomic bomb. Poised in Eastern Europe, the troops threatened to take the continent hostage in case of atomic attack on Russia. Stalin had no navy capable of long-range offensive strikes. His fleet depended on 300 submarines geared for defensive purposes.[3]

Truman's immediate problem was not the threat of a Russian invasion. As Dean Acheson privately remarked, the Russians would not make war with the United States "unless they are absolutely out of their minds." The greater danger was that Stalin might be proved correct when he indicated that the communists could bide their time since a "general crisis" was becoming so "acute" in the West that it would sweep away "atom-dollar" diplomacy. Communist party power rose steeply in Europe, particularly in France where the first cabinet of the new Fourth Republic contained four communists, including the minister of defense. Chaotic conditions in former colonial areas also opened exceptional opportunities to revolutionaries. The two gems of the British Crown, India and Egypt, shattered the empire with drives for independence. They were soon joined by Pakistan, Burma, Ceylon, and Nepal. France began a long, futile, eight-year war to regain Indochina. The Dutch faced full-scale revolution in Indonesia. The Middle East was in turmoil over the determination of a half-dozen countries to be totally independent, as well as over the influx of 100,000 Jews who hoped to establish a homeland in Palestine.

In late 1946 and early 1947, American officials gave increasing attention to these newly emerging areas. Europe could not be fully stabilized until England, France, and the Netherlands settled their colonial problems. Adolf Berle, economist, adviser to Roosevelt and Truman, and State Department official, declared in late 1946 that the Soviets and the United States had begun a battle for the allegiance of the less industrialized nations. "Within four years the world [will] be faced with an apparent surplus in production beyond any previously known," Berle explained. If American surpluses were used to "take the lead in material reconstruction" of the newly emerging

---

[3]Thomas Wolfe, *Soviet Power and Europe, 1945–1970* (Baltimore, 1970), pp. 10–11, 33, 45–46.

countries, the United States could level off those "cycles of 'boom and bust' which disfigured our prewar economy."[4]

"Boom and bust" already threatened. The American economy sagged, and unemployment rose in early 1946 before some expansion began. State Department experts worried that the improvement was temporary, for it rested on a $15-billion American export trade, nearly four times the level of the 1930s. Most of these exports were rebuilding Western Europe, but the Europeans were rapidly running out of dollars to pay for the goods. When its remaining dollars and gold were spent, Europe would stagnate, then perhaps grasp at socialism to save itself. Americans would face the loss of their most vital market and probably the return of the 1930s state of affairs with all the terrible political consequences. Truman understood this by early 1947, but a tax-cutting Republican Congress and his own low popularity seemed to block any action.

The turn came on February 21, 1947, when a British embassy official drove to the State Department building. He informed Acheson that because of its own economic crisis (more than half its industry was quiet), England could not provide the $250 million of military and economic support needed by Greece and Turkey. As Secretary of State George Marshall later observed, "It was tantamount to British abdication from the Middle East with obvious implications as to their successor."[5]

American officials were not taken by surprise. From 1944 until early 1947 they had closely watched the British attempt to regain control of Greece become bogged down in a Greek civil war. On one side was a conservative-monarchical group supported by London. On the other was the National Liberation Front (NLF), with communist leadership, which had gained popularity and power by leading resistance efforts against the Nazis. By 1947 the NLF received support from Yugoslav communist leader Josip Broz (Marshal Tito). The Yugoslav was not motivated by affection for his fellow communists in Greece. Rather, he hoped to annex parts of Greece to a large Yugoslav federation. Stalin was not directly involved and indeed developed a strong dislike for Tito's overly large ambitions.

---

[4]R. Dennett, ed., *Documents on American Foreign Relations*, VIII (Princeton, 1951): 607–608.

[5]James Forrestal, *The Forrestal Diaries*, Walter Millis, ed. (New York, 1951), p. 245.

But as NLF strength grew, the United States did become involved. Throughout 1946 it sent special missions, poured in $260 million of aid, and sided with the British. Drawing on this experience, the State Department was able to work out a detailed proposal for assistance within a week after Acheson received the British message. After only nineteen days Truman could appear before Congress with a complete program. Clearly, the President's request on March 12 for $400 million in Greek and Turkish aid (the Truman Doctrine speech) was not a sudden, drastic departure in American foreign policy.

The reasoning in Truman's speech, however, was radically new. That reasoning was worked out by American officials who had long been waiting for this opportunity. As they developed the speech, "they found release from the professional frustrations of years," as one later declared. "It seemed to those present that a new chapter in world history had opened and they were the most privileged of men."[6] Those words help explain why the officials made certain choices. For example, they could have determined simply that Greece was in a civil war and therefore the United States had no business intervening. Or they could have quietly asked Congress to continue aid to Greece and Turkey while transferring to those nations weapons left from the war. The administration, however, rejected those alternatives. Truman chose instead to appear dramatically before Congress to request support for a global battle against communism. A White House adviser remarked that the message would be "the opening gun in a campaign to bring people up to [the] realization that the war isn't over by any means."

As State Department officials prepared drafts of the speech, Truman, Secretary of State Marshall, and Acheson met with congressional leaders. It was not a warm audience. The Republicans were busily cutting taxes 20 percent and chopping $6 billion from Truman's already-tight budget. The legislators remained unmoved until Acheson swung into the argument that the threat was not a Greek civil war but Russian communism; its aim was the control of the Middle East, South Asia, and Africa; and this control was part of a communist plan to encircle and capture the ultimate objective, Germany, and indeed all of Europe. It was a struggle between liberty and dictatorship. By defending Greece and Turkey, therefore, Americans were defending their own freedoms. "The Soviet Union

---

[6]Joseph M. Jones, *The Fifteen Weeks* (New York, 1955), pp. 146–147.

was playing one of the greatest gambles in history at minimal cost," Acheson concluded, "We and we alone are in a position to break up the play."[7]

The congressmen were stunned. Silence followed until Arthur Vandenberg (now the chair of the Senate Foreign Relations Committee) told Truman that the message must include Acheson's explanation. As the senator advised, the President "scared hell" out of the American people. Insofar as public opinion was concerned, this tactic worked well for Truman (at least until three years later when Senator Joseph McCarthy and others turned the argument around and accused the administration of handling such a horrible danger too gently). The President also won over Congress with assurances that the United States would not only control every penny of America's aid to Greece but run the Greek economy by controlling foreign exchange, budget, taxes, currency, and credit.

Inside the State Department, however, Acheson ran into opposition. George Kennan, the top expert on Soviet affairs, objected bitterly to sending military assistance to nations such as Turkey that had no internal communist problems and bordered the Soviet Union. Unlike economic help, military aid could be provocative. Acheson rejected the argument. The opportunity to build Turkey's military strength was too good to miss. Thus in the words of one official, "Turkey was slipped into the oven with Greece because that seemed the surest way to cook a tough bird." Kennan also protested against the harsh ideological tone and open-ended American commitment in the speech drafts. He was joined by Secretary of State Marshall and Charles Bohlen, another expert on Russia, who told Acheson that "there was a little too much flamboyant anticommunism in the speech." Acheson stood his ground. Marshall was informed that Truman believed the Senate would not approve the doctrine "without the emphasis on the Communist danger."[8]

Acheson, however, carefully kept the central economic factors out of the speech. He and Truman wanted a simple ideological call to action that all could understand, not a message that might trigger

---

[7]Dean Acheson, *Present at the Creation* (New York, 1969), pp. 292–293. For a superb biography of Acheson that analyzes his background and worldview, see Robert Beisner, *Dean Acheson: A Life in the Cold War* (New York, 2006).
[8]George Kennan, *Memoirs, 1925–1950* (Boston, 1967), pp. 315–322; Charles E. Bohlen, *Witness to History, 1929–1969* (New York, 1973), p. 261.

arguments over American oil holdings in the Middle East. The economic interests were nevertheless crucial. As State Department official Joseph Jones noted, if Greece and similar key areas "spiral
downwards into economic anarchy, then at best they will drop out
of the United States orbit and try an independent nationalistic policy; at worst they will swing into the Russian orbit," and the result
would be a depression worse than that of the 1930s.[9]

Jones's insight was incorporated into a major speech made by
Truman at Baylor University on March 6. The address provided the
economic dimension to the Truman Doctrine pronounced six days
later. The President frankly declared that if the expansion of state-
controlled economies (such as the communists') was not stopped,
and an open world marketplace restored for private business, a
depression would occur and the government would have to intervene massively in the society. Americans could then bid farewell to
both their traditional economic and personal freedoms. "Freedom
of worship—freedom of speech—freedom of enterprise," Truman
observed. "It must be true that the first two of these freedoms are
related to the third." For "Peace, freedom and world trade are indivisible." He concluded, "We must not go through the thirties
again."[10] The President had given the economic reasons for pro-
nouncing the Truman Doctrine. The Baylor speech (written by
Acheson and Will Clayton) explained why Americans, if they
hoped to preserve their personal freedom, had to rebuild the areas
west of the Iron Curtain before these lands collapsed into anarchy,
radical governments, or even communism.

The Truman Doctrine speech itself, given before Congress on
March 12, 1947, laid out the ideological and political reasons for the
commitment. The President requested $400 million for military and
economic aid, but he also asked for something else. Truman warned
Congress that the world must now "choose between alternative
ways of life." He urged Americans to commit themselves to helping
"free peoples" and to opposing "totalitarian regimes." This request,
plus Truman's failure to place any geographic limits on where

---

[9]Barton J. Bernstein, ed., *Politics and Policies of the Truman Administration* (Chicago,
1970), p. 57.
[10]*Public Papers of the Presidents . . . Truman . . . 1947* (Washington, 1963), pp. 167–172.
This speech can be read in chapter III documents at the www.mhhe.com/lafeber website.

Americans must commit themselves (Africa as well as Germany? Southeast Asia as well as Western Europe?), raised criticism. [The Truman Doctrine speech can be read in chapter III documents at website www.mhhe.com/lafeber.]

Robert Taft of Ohio, the Senate's Republican leader, accused Truman of dividing the world into communist and anticommunist zones, then said flatly, "I do not want war with Russia." On the left, Henry Wallace, traveling in Europe, accused Truman of "reckless adventure" that would cost the world "a century of fear." Senator Vandenberg rushed to the President's defense by calling Wallace an "itinerant saboteur." But such fear was not only on Taft's and Wallace's minds. Shortly before the speech, Acheson told J. Robert Oppenheimer, who had supervised the building of the first atomic bombs and remained a leading scientist in the atomic weapons field, "We are entering an adversary relationship with the Soviet," and "we should bear that in mind" while making atomic plans.[11]

Congress wriggled uncomfortably. As Senator Vandenberg began closed-door hearings on what he called "the most fundamental thing that has been presented to Congress in my time," Acheson hedged on whether the Truman Doctrine had any limitations. "If there are situations where we can do something effective, then I think we must certainly do it." But he was clear on one issue: "I think it is a mistake to believe that you can, at any time, sit down with the Russians and solve questions." Only when the West built unbeatable bastions of strength would Stalin listen to American terms. Acheson assumed Russia was primarily responsible for the Greek revolution. After all, said Lincoln MacVeagh, U.S. ambassador to Greece, "Any empire that bases itself on revolution always has expansionist tendencies." (The ambassador was alluding to the revolution of 1917, not 1776.) This view of Soviet involvement was wrong. The Greek problem was caused by internal forces and fueled by Tito for his own purposes. But this point made little difference. The administration asked for a commitment against communism anywhere, not just against the Soviets.

---

[11]Jones, *Fifteen Weeks*, pp. 175–178; Lloyd Gardner, *Architects of Illusion* (Chicago, 1970), p. 201.

That caused a special problem in Greece, for as MacVeagh secretly admitted, "the best men" in Greece "are the heads of the Communist movement. . . . That is the sad part of it." But Americans had to keep on "trying to make bricks without straw . . . or you are going to lose the country." The Greek government became so brutal that the State Department privately warned that it must stop torturing its political prisoners or "the President's program" would be damaged. When criticized for helping the Greek and Turkish right-wing parties, however, Truman could simply ask Americans whether they preferred "totalitarianism" or "imperfect democracies." This settled that question.[12]

The President and Acheson mousetrapped those in Congress who wanted to be both anticommunist and penny-pinchers. As a leading Democrat chuckled privately, of course the Republicans "didn't want to be smoked out. . . . They don't like Communism but still they don't want to do anything to stop it. But they are all put on the spot now and they all have to come clean." The President, moreover, had moved so quickly that Congress had no choice but to give him increased powers. "Here we sit," mourned Vandenberg, "not as free agents," but dealing with something "almost like a Presidential request for a declaration of war." "There is precious little we can do," the senator concluded, "except say 'yes.'"[13] Vandenberg was correct. Congress's acceptance of Truman's definition of the crisis marked the point in the Cold War when power in foreign-policy formulation began shifting rapidly from Capitol Hill to the White House. The power remained with the presidency after the Cold War as well, thanks in part to Truman's 1947 example of how to obtain agreement in a divided, pluralistic democracy.

Nine days after his speech Truman helped ensure his victory by announcing a loyalty program to ferret out security risks in government. The first such peacetime program in American history, it was so vaguely defined that political ideas and long-past associations were suddenly made suspect. Most ominously, the accused would

[12]Material in the preceding two paragraphs is from U.S. Senate, Committee on Foreign Relations, 80th Cong., 1st Sess., *Legislative Origins of the Truman Doctrine; Hearings . . .* (Washington, 1973), pp. 5, 17, 95, 46, 45; *FRUS, 1947*, V: 142–143.

[13]Phone conversation between Carl Vinson and Forrestal, Speech to Congress on Greece file, March 13, 1947, Box 28, Papers of Clark Clifford, Truman Library; Senate, *Legislative Origins*, p. 128.

not have the right to confront the accuser.[14] Truman thus strikingly dramatized the communist issue and exerted new pressure on Congress to support his doctrine. By mid-May Congress had passed his request by large margins.

▬ The Truman Doctrine was a milestone in American history for at least four reasons. First, it marked the point at which Truman used the American fear of communism both at home and abroad to convince Americans they must embark upon a Cold War foreign policy. This consensus would not break apart for a quarter of a century. Second, as Vandenberg knew, Congress was giving the President great powers to wage this Cold War as he saw fit. Truman's personal popularity began spiraling upward after his speech. Third, for the first time in the postwar era, Americans massively intervened in another nation's civil war. Intervention was justified on the basis of anticommunism. In the future, Americans would intervene in similar wars for supposedly the same reason and, as in Vietnam, with less happy results. Even Greek affairs went badly at first, so badly that in late 1947 Washington officials discussed sending as many as two divisions of Americans to save the situation. That luckily proved unnecessary. When Yugoslavia left the communist bloc in early 1948, Tito turned inward and stopped aiding the rebels. Deprived of aid, the Greek left wing quickly lost ground. But it had been close, and Americans were nearly involved massively in a civil war two decades before their Vietnam involvement. As it was, the success in Greece seemed to prove that Americans could, if they wished, control such conflicts by defining the problem as "communist" and helping conservatives remain in power.[15]

Finally, and perhaps most important, Truman used the doctrine to justify a gigantic aid program to prevent a collapse of the European and American economies. Later such programs were expanded globally. The President's arguments about the need to fight communism

---

[14]Richard Freeland, *The Truman Doctrine and the Origins of McCarthyism* (New York, 1972), pp. 208–211.

[15]*FRUS, 1947*, V: 466–469; Thomas Paterson, *Soviet-American Confrontation* (Baltimore, 1973), p. 205. A good analysis showing how Truman could use the doctrine with—or against—European allies is Mark A. Lawrence, *Assuming the Burden* (Berkeley, 2005), pp. 184–185. An interesting State Department view on how American opinion was changed is in H. Schuyler Foster, "American Public Opinion and U.S. Foreign Policy," *Department of State Bulletin*, XLI (November 30, 1959).

now became confusing, for the Western economies would have been in grave difficulties whether or not communism existed. The complicated problems of postwar reconstruction and U.S. dependence on world trade were not well understood by Americans, but they easily comprehended anticommunism.

So Americans embarked upon the Cold War for the good reasons given in the Truman Doctrine, which they understood, and for real reasons, which they did not understand. Thus, as Truman and Acheson intended, the doctrine became an ideological shield behind which the United States marched to rebuild the Western political-economic system and counter the radical left. From 1947 on, therefore, any threats to that Western system could be easily explained as communist-inspired, not as problems that arose from difficulties with the system itself. That was a lasting and tragic result of the Truman Doctrine.

The President's program evolved naturally into the Marshall Plan. Although the speech did not limit American effort, Secretary of State Marshall did by concentrating the administration's attention on Europe. Returning badly shaken from a Foreign Ministers conference in Moscow, the secretary of state insisted in a nationwide broadcast that Western Europe required immediate help. "The patient is sinking," he declared, "while the doctors deliberate." Personal conversations with Stalin had convinced Marshall that the Russians believed Europe would collapse. Assuming that the United States must lead in restoring Europe, Marshall appointed a policy-planning staff under the direction of George Kennan to draw up guidelines.

Kennan later explained the basic assumption that underlay the Marshall Plan and, indeed, the entire range of America's postwar policies between 1947 and the mid-1950s. Excluding the United States, Kennan observed,

> . . . there are only four aggregations which are major ones from the standpoint of strategic realities [that is, military and industrial potential] in the world. Two of those lie off the shores of the Eurasian land mass. Those are Japan and England, and two of them lie on the Eurasian land mass. One is the Soviet Union and the other is that of central Europe. . . .
>
> Viewed in absolute terms, I think the greatest danger that could confront the United States security would be a combination

and working together for purposes hostile to us of the central European and the Russian military-industrial potentials. They would really create an entity . . . which could overshadow in a strategic sense even our own power. It is not anything, I think, which would be as easy of achievement as people often portray it as being here. I am not sure the Russians have the genius for holding all that together. . . . Still, they have the tendency of political thought, of Communist political expansion.[16]

Building on this premise, round-the-clock conferences in May 1947 began to fashion the main features of the Marshall Plan. The all-important question became how to handle the Russians. Ostensibly, Marshall accepted Kennan's advice to "play it straight" by inviting the Soviet bloc. In reality the State Department made Russian participation improbable by demanding that economic records of each nation be open for scrutiny. For good measure Kennan also suggested that the Soviets' devastated economy, weakened by war and at that moment suffering from drought and famine, participate in the plan by shipping Soviet goods to Europe. Apparently no one in the State Department wanted the Soviets included. Russian participation would vastly multiply the costs of the program and eliminate any hope of its acceptance by a purse-watching Republican Congress, now increasingly convinced by Truman that communists had to be fought, not fed.

Acheson's speech at Cleveland, Mississippi, in early May and Marshall's address at Harvard University on June 5 revealed the motives and substance of the plan. In preparing for the earlier speech, Acheson's advisers concluded that American exports were rapidly approaching the $16-billion mark. Imports, however, amounted to only half that amount, and Europe did not have sufficient dollars to pay the difference. Either the United States would have to give credits to Europeans or they would be unable to buy American goods. The President's Council of Economic Advisers predicted a slight business recession, and if, in addition, exports dropped

---

[16]U.S. Senate, Subcommittee to Investigate the Administration of the International Security Act . . . of the Committee on the Judiciary, 82nd Cong., 1st Sess., *The Institute of Pacific Relations* (Washington, 1951), pp. 1557–1558. (Hereafter cited as *I.P.R. Hearings.*) An important exchange on the Marshall Plan and U.S. and Soviet motives is "Special Forum: The Marshall Plan and the Origins of the Cold War Reassessed," *Journal of Cold War Studies*, 7 (Winter 2005).

in any substantial amount, "the effect in the United States," as one official wrote,"might be most serious."[17] Acheson underlined these facts in his Mississippi speech.

At Harvard, Marshall urged Europeans to create a long-term program that would "provide a cure rather than a mere palliative." On June 13 British Foreign Minister Ernest Bevin accepted Marshall's suggestion that Europeans take the initiative. Bevin traveled to Paris to talk with French Foreign Minister Georges Bidault. The question of Russian participation became uppermost in their discussions. *Pravda* had labeled Marshall's speech as a Truman Doctrine with dollars, a useless attempt to save the American economy by dominating European markets. Bidault ignored this; pressured by the powerful French Communist party and fearful that Russia's absence might compel France to join the Anglo-Saxons in a divided Europe dominated by a resurrected Germany,[18] he decided to invite Molotov. The Russian line immediately moderated. (Marshall's historic speech may be read in chapter III documents at the www.mhhe.com/lafeber website.)

On June 26, 1947, Molotov arrived in Paris with eighty-nine economic experts and clerks, then spent much of the next three days conferring over the telephone with Moscow officials. The Russians were giving the plan serious consideration. They had even ordered their East European satellites to be prepared to join the plan. Molotov finally proposed that each nation individually establish its own recovery program. The French and British proposed instead that Europe as a whole create the proposal for American consideration. They also watered down his demands that new controls be clamped on Germany. Molotov angrily quit the conference. He warned that the plan would undermine national sovereignty, revive Germany, allow Americans to control Europe, and, most ominously, divide "Europe into two groups of states . . . creating new difficulties in the relations between them."[19] Within a week after his return to Moscow, the Soviets set their own "Molotov Plan" in motion. The Poles and

---

[17]Jones, *Fifteen Weeks*, p. 207. Acheson's speech may be read in the chapter III documents at the www.mhhe.com/lafeber website.

[18]For example, *The New York Times*, June 19, 1947, p. 1.

[19]Text in *The New York Times*, July 3, 1947, p. 3; Scott D. Parrish and Mikhail M. Narinsky, *New Evidence on the Soviet Rejection of the Marshall Plan, 1947: Two Reports*. Cold War International History Project (Washington, D.C., 1994), pp. 4–29.

the Czechs, who had expressed interest in Marshall's proposal, now informed the Paris conference that they could not attend because it "might be construed as an action against the Soviet Union." (The background of the Soviet objections may be read in Molotov's 1946 speech in chapter III documents at www.mhhe.com/lafeber website.)

As the remaining sixteen European nations hammered out a program for Marshall to consider, the United States moved on a closely related front: it determined to revive Germany quickly. In late 1946 the Americans and British had overridden French opposition to merge economically the U.S. and British zones in Germany. Administrative duties were given to Germans. By mid-July 1947 Washington officials so rapidly rebuilt German industry that Bidault finally pleaded with Marshall to slow down or else the French government would never survive to carry through the economic recovery program.

The European request for a four-year program of $17 billion of American aid now had to run the gauntlet of a Republican Congress, which was dividing its attention between slashing the budget and attacking Truman, both in anticipation of the presidential election only a year away. In committee hearings in late 1947 and early 1948, the executive presented its case. Only large amounts of government money which could restore basic facilities, provide convertibility of local currency into dollars, and end the dollar shortage would stimulate private investors to rebuild Europe, administration witnesses argued.

George Kennan summarized the central problem in a note to Acheson. "Communist activities" were not "the root of the difficulties of Western Europe" but rather "the disruptive effects of the war on the economic, political, and social structure of Europe." So in the final plan Italy, with Europe's largest Communist party, received less aid than other, more economically important nations. In this sense the plan revolved around a rebuilt and autonomous Germany. As Secretary of State Marshall told Congress, "The restoration of Europe involves the restoration of Germany. Without a revival of German production there can be no revival of Europe's economy. But we must be very careful to see that a revived Germany cannot again threaten the European community." The Marshall Plan offered a way to circumvent Allied restrictions on German development, for it tied the Germans to a general European program and then offered vast sums to such nations as France which otherwise would be most reluctant to support reconstructing Germany.[20]

The Marshall Plan served as an all-purpose weapon for Truman's foreign policy. It charmed those who feared a slump in American exports and who believed, communist threat or no communist threat, that American and world prosperity rested on a vigorous export trade. A spokesman for the National Association of Manufacturers, for example, appeared considerably more moderate toward communism than some government officials when he argued that Europe suffered not from "this so-called communistic surge," but from a "production problem" which only the Marshall Plan could solve.[21] Appropriately, Truman named as administrator of the plan Paul Hoffman, a proven entrepreneur who, as Acheson once observed, preached a "doctrine of salvation by exports with all the passion of an economic Savonarola."[22] The plan also attracted a group, including Reinhold Niebuhr, which placed more emphasis upon the containment of communism. The plan offered all things to all people who were not Soviet.

The Marshall Plan now appears to have signaled not the beginning but the end of an era. It marked the last phase in the administration's use of economic tactics as the primary means of tying together the Western world. The plan's approach, that more peaceful and positive approach which Niebuhr applauded, soon evolved into military alliances. Truman proved to be correct in saying that the Truman Doctrine and the Marshall Plan "are two halves of the same walnut." Americans willingly acquiesced as the military aspects of the doctrine developed into quite the larger part.

Why such programs could so easily be transformed into military commitments was explained by George Kennan in a well-timed article appearing in July 1947 under the mysterious pseudonym Mr. "X." Washington's most respected expert on Soviet affairs, Kennan (who once called Niebuhr "the father of us all") had warned throughout the

---

[20]*FRUS, 1947*, III: 225–229; U.S. House of Representatives, Foreign Affairs Committee, 80th Cong., 1st and 2nd Sess., *United States Foreign Policy for a Post-War Recovery Program . . .* I (Washington, 1948): 354–359.

[21]U.S. House of Representatives, *U.S. Foreign Policy for a Post-War Recovery Program*, I: 680–681.

[22]Dean Acheson, *Sketches from Life of Men I Have Known* (New York, 1959), p. 19.

early 1940s against any hope of close postwar cooperation with Stalin. In early 1946 he sent a long dispatch to Washington from Moscow suggesting that at the "bottom of the Kremlin's neurotic view of world affairs is the traditional and instinctive Russian sense of insecurity." In post-1917 Russia this "insecurity" became highly explosive when mixed with communist ideology and "Oriental secretiveness and conspiracy."[23] This dispatch brought Kennan to the attention of Secretary of the Navy James Forrestal, who helped bring the diplomat back to Washington and then strongly influenced Kennan's decision to publish the "X" article.

The article gave the administration's view of what made the Russians act like communists. The analysis began, however, not by emphasizing "the traditional Russian sense of insecurity" but by assuming that Stalin's policy was shaped by a combination of Marxist-Leninist ideology, which advocated revolution to defeat the capitalist forces in the outside world, and the dictator's determination to use "capitalist encirclement" as a rationale to regiment the Soviet masses so that he could consolidate his own political power. Kennan belittled such supposed "encirclement," although he recognized Nazi-Japanese hatred of the Soviets during the 1930s. (He omitted mentioning specifically the American and Japanese military intervention in Russia between 1918 and 1920 and the U.S. attempt to isolate the Soviets politically through the 1920s.) Mr. "X" believed that Stalin would not moderate communist determination to overthrow the Western governments. Any softening of the Russian line would be a diversionary tactic designed to lull the West. For in the final analysis Soviet diplomacy "moves along the prescribed path, like a persistent toy automobile wound up and headed in a given direction, stopping only when it meets some unanswerable force." Endemic Soviet aggression could thus be "contained by the adroit and vigilant application of counterforce at a series of constantly shifting geographical and political points." The United States would have to undertake this containment alone and unilaterally, but if it could do so without weakening its prosperity and political stability, the Soviet party

[23]Barton J. Bernstein and Allen J. Matusow, *The Truman Administration: A Documentary History* (New York, 1966), pp. 198–212; *Forrestal Diaries*, pp. 135–140. Kennan's view of Niebuhr was confirmed in Kennan's remark to the author at Cornell University in 1966.

structure would undergo a period of immense strain climaxing in "either the breakup or the gradual mellowing of Soviet power."[24]

The publication of this article triggered one of the more interesting debates of the Cold War. Walter Lippmann was the dean of American journalists and one of those who did not accept the "two halves of the same walnut" argument. He condemned the military aspects of the Truman Doctrine while applauding the Marshall Plan because he disagreed with Kennan's assessment of Soviet motivation. And that, of course, was a crucial point in any argument over American policy. In a series of newspaper articles later collected in a book entitled *The Cold War*,[25] Lippmann argued that Soviet policy was molded more by traditional Russian expansion than by communist ideology: "Stalin is not only the heir of Marx and of Lenin but of Peter the Great, and the Czars of all the Russias." Because of the victorious sweep of the Red Army into Central Europe in 1945, Stalin could accomplish what the czars for centuries had only hoped to obtain. This approach enabled Lippmann to view the Soviet advance as a traditional quest for national security and, in turn, allowed him to argue that Russia would be amenable to an offer of withdrawal of both Russian and American power from Central Europe. The fuses would thus be pulled from that explosive area.

Lippmann outlined the grave consequences of the alternative, the Mr. "X"–Truman Doctrine policy: "unending intervention in all the countries that are supposed to 'contain' the Soviet Union"; futile and costly efforts to make "Jeffersonian democrats" out of Eastern European peasants and Middle Eastern and Asian warlords; either the destruction of the United Nations or its transformation into a useless anti-Soviet coalition; and such a tremendous strain on the American people that their economy would have to be increasingly regimented and their soldiers sent to fight on the perimeter of the Soviet bloc. The columnist warned that if Mr. "X" succeeded in applying counterforce to the "constantly shifting geographical and political points," the Soviets would therefore be allowed to take the

---

[24]"The Sources of Soviet Conduct," *Foreign Affairs*, XXV (July 1947): 566–582; it also can be read in the chapter III documents at the www.mhhe.com/lafeber website. Kennan much later believed that the essay had been misinterpreted; see George Kennan, *Memoirs, 1925–1950* (Boston, 1967), pp. 364–367. But also see Gardner, *Architects of Illusion*, pp. 270–300.

[25]Walter Lippmann, *The Cold War: A Study in U.S. Foreign Policy* (New York, 1947).

initiative in the Cold War by choosing the grounds and weapons for combat. Finally, Lippmann, like the administration, emphasized Germany's importance. But he differed by observing that Russia, which controlled eastern Germany, could, at its leisure, outmaneuver the West and repeat the 1939 Nazi-Soviet pact by offering the ultimate reward of reunification in return for German cooperation.

Lippmann was profound, but he had no chance of being persuasive. By the end of August 1947, the State Department rejected Lippmann's proposals for disengagement in Germany. American officials instead assumed that the "one world" of the United Nations was "no longer valid and that we are in political fact facing a division into two worlds."[26] The "X" article also indicated that the administration was operating on another assumption: economic development could not occur until "security" was established. This increasing concern with things military became evident in late 1947 when Kennan suggested that the United States change its long-standing hostility to Franco's dictatorship in Spain in order to cast proper military security over the Mediterranean area. Only a year earlier the United States had joined with Britain and France in asking the Spanish people to overthrow Franco by political means because his government was pro-Nazi and authoritarian. Kennan's suggestion marked the turn in Spanish-American relations, which ended in close military cooperation after 1950.[27]

The quest for military security also transformed U.S. policy in Asia. With Chiang Kai-shek's decline the State Department searched for a new partner who could help stabilize the Far East. The obvious candidate was Japan, which from the 1890s until 1931 had worked closely with Washington. It was also the potential industrial power-house of the area, the Germany of the Orient. Since 1945 the United States had single-handedly controlled Japan. The Soviets had been carefully excluded. Even Australia was allowed to send occupation forces only after promising not to interfere with the authority of General Douglas MacArthur, head of the American government in Japan. MacArthur instituted a new constitution (in which Japan renounced war for all time), then conducted elections, which allowed him to

[26]*Forrestal Diaries*, p. 307.
[27]*Forrestal Diaries*, p. 328.

claim that the Japanese had overwhelmingly repudiated communism. To the general, as to Washington officials, this was fundamental. In 1946 MacArthur privately compared America in its fight against communism to the agony of Christ at Gethsemane, for "Christ, even though crucified, nevertheless prevailed."[28]

He added that Japan was becoming "the western [sic] outpost of our defenses." In 1947–1948 Japan received the "two halves of the same walnut" treatment. The State Department reversed its post-1945 policy and decided to rebuild Japanese industry and develop a sound export economy. At the same time, American bases on the islands were to be expanded and maintained until, in one official's words, "the at present disarmed soldiers of Japan are provided with arms and training to qualify them to preserve the peace."[29] As in Europe, economic development and security moved hand in hand as Americans made Japan, the hated recent enemy, their most important economic and military ally in Asia.

The new security policy underwent a trial run in that longtime laboratory of U.S. policies, Latin America. After several postponements, the American nations convened at Rio de Janeiro in late summer of 1947. The U.S. delegation candidly laid out the rules for the conference. There would be no discussion of economic aid, Secretary Marshall explained, because European recovery took precedence over Latin American development. The conference must instead initiate steps toward a collective security arrangement. In doing so, the United States expected each nation to take some action against future aggressors, whether that action be military or otherwise. No nation, the American delegation argued, could remain truly neutral.

On September 2, 1947, the delegates signed the Rio Treaty providing for collective self-defense for the hemisphere, the first such treaty formulated under Articles 51 and 52 of the UN Charter. The treaty provided that an attack against one American nation would be considered as an attack upon all, and that when two-thirds of the hemispheric nations agreed to resist such an attack, all states must cooperate by contributing either troops or supplies.[30] Nine months earlier Vandenberg had lamented that a "Communistic upsurge" in

---

[28]*Forrestal Diaries*, pp. 177–178.
[29]Leahy Diaries, Box 6, September 22, 1948, Leahy Papers.
[30]Raymond Dennett and Robert K. Turner, eds., *Documents on American Foreign Relations*, IX (1947) (Princeton, N.J., 1948): 531–543.

Latin America was dividing the hemisphere, although he provided no evidence of the "upsurge."[31] After the signing of the Rio Treaty, Vandenberg rested more easily: "This is sunlight in a dark world," he informed his Senate colleagues.

The following March, the Ninth Inter-American Conference convened at Bogotá, Colombia, to provide yet more sunlight for depressed Washington officials. Again, the United States refused to make any economic commitments. At the most, Marshall hoped that he could use the occasion to create the proper atmosphere so that Latin American laws, particularly those relating to oil resources, might be made more attractive to U.S. investors. Out of this approach came the Charter of the Organization of American States, which established administrative machinery for hemispheric consultation and an Advisory Defense Committee for military strategy.

This much the United States welcomed. The Latin Americans, however, stubbornly insisted on adding a statement of the principles and standards that would govern hemispheric relations. Despite U.S. objections, the motion passed. Articles 15 and 16 were incorporated in the charter. The first stated: "No State or group of States has the right to intervene, directly or indirectly, for any reason whatever, in the internal or external affairs of any other State." Article 16 was more specific: "No State may use or encourage the use of coercive measures of an economic or political character in order to force the sovereign will of another State and obtain from it advantages of any kind."[32] The U.S. Senate ratified the charter, but this was the last major inter-American conference held during Truman's presidency. The administration had obtained the desired military arrangements and, perhaps, too many political obligations.

Of special importance to Truman's "security" effort, the President transformed what he termed "the antiquated defense setup of the United States" by passing the National Security Act through Congress in July 1947. This bill provided for a single Department of Defense to replace the three independently run military services, the statutory establishment of the Joint Chiefs of Staff, a National Security Council to advise the President, and a Central Intelligence Agency to correlate and

---

[31]Arthur H. Vandenberg, Jr., ed., *The Private Papers of Senator Vandenberg* (Boston, 1952), p. 335.

[32]Raymond Dennett and Robert K. Turner, eds., *Documents on American Foreign Relations*, X (1948) (Princeton, N.J., 1950): 484–502.

evaluate intelligence activities. James Forrestal, the stepfather of Mr. "X" and the leading advocate among presidential advisers of a tough military approach to Cold War problems, became the first secretary of defense. Forrestal remained until he resigned in early spring 1949. Two months later on the night of May 22, Forrestal, suffering from mental and physical illness, jumped or accidentally fell to his death from the twelfth floor of the Bethesda Naval Hospital in Maryland.

The military and personal costs of the Truman Doctrine–Mr. "X" policy were higher than expected. And the cost became more apparent as Truman and J. Edgar Hoover (director of the Federal Bureau of Investigation) carried out the President's Security Loyalty program. Their search for subversives accelerated after Canadians uncovered a Soviet spy ring.

The House Un-American Activities Committee began to intimate that Truman was certainly correct in his assessment of communism's evil nature but lax in destroying it. In March 1948 the committee demanded the loyalty records gathered by the FBI. Truman handled the situation badly. Unable to exploit the committee's distorted view of the internal communist threat, he accused it of trying to cover up the bad record of the Republican Congress. He refused to surrender the records, ostensibly because they were in the exclusive domain of the executive, more probably because of his fear that if the Republicans saw the FBI reports, which accused some federal employees of disloyalty on the basis of hearsay, unproven allegations, and personal vendettas, November might be an unfortunate month for Truman's political aspirations.[33] Unable to discredit the loyalty program he had set in motion, trapped by his own indiscriminating anticommunist rhetoric designed to "scare hell" out of the country, Truman stood paralyzed as the ground was carefully plowed around him for the weeds of McCarthyism.

Since the Iranian and Turkish crises of 1946, the Soviets had not been active in world affairs. But Molotov's departure from the Marshall Plan conference in Paris during July 1947 marked the turn. Russian attention was riveted on Germany. Documents opened in the 1990s confirmed that the politburo interpreted the Marshall Plan to mean that Americans intended "to restore the economy of Germany and Japan on

---

[33] A useful analysis is Athan Theoharis, *Seeds of Repression: Harry S. Truman and the Origins of McCarthyism* (New York, 1971).

the old basis [of pre-1941] provided it is subordinated to interests of American capital." Rebuilding Europe through the plan and tying it closer to American economic power threatened Stalin's hope of influencing Western European policies. Stalin believed—correctly—that the Marshall Plan also aimed to break up Soviet control of Eastern Europe by tying that region into a general multilateral capitalist reconstruction of all Europe. The Soviet dictator sharply reacted. The Cold War itself drastically changed.[34]

Molotov quickly initiated a series of moves to tighten Soviet control of the bloc. A program of bilateral trade agreements, the so-called Molotov Plan, began to link the bloc countries and Russia in July 1947. The final step came in January 1949, when the Council for Mutual Economic Assistance (COMECON) provided the Soviet answer to the Marshall Plan by creating a centralized agency for stimulating and controlling bloc development. As a result of these moves, Soviet trade with the East European bloc, which had declined in 1947 to $380 million, doubled in 1948, quadrupled by 1950, and exceeded $2.5 billion in 1952. Seventy percent of East European trade was carried on with either the Soviet Union or elsewhere within the bloc.[35]

Four days after his return from Paris, Molotov announced the establishment of the Communist Information Bureau (Cominform). Including communists from Russia, Yugoslavia, France, Italy, Poland, Bulgaria, Czechoslovakia, Hungary, and Rumania, the Cominform provided another instrument for increasing Stalin's control. This was his answer to the Czech and Polish interest in joining the Marshall Plan. In late August, a month before the first Cominform meeting, Soviet actions in Hungary indicated the line that would be followed. After a purge of left-wing anticommunist political leaders, the Soviets directly intervened by rigging elections. All anticommunist opposition disappeared.[36]

---

[34]The quote is in a telegram from the Moscow Embassy to Secretary of State Marshall, May 26, 1947, Papers of Joseph Jones, Truman Library; newly available documents are analyzed in Parrish and Narinsky, *New Evidence on the Soviet Rejection of the Marshall Plan*, pp. 1–51. For a Soviet view at this time, see Andrei Vyshinsky's September 1947 statement in chapter III documents of the www.mhhe.com/lafeber website.

[35]Stanley J. Zyzniewski, "Soviet Foreign Economic Policy," *Political Science Quarterly*, LXXIII (June 1958): 216–219.

[36]An especially revealing document on this turn is Andrei Zhdanov, "The International Situation," reprinted in *The Strategy and Tactics of World Communism*, Supplement I (Washington, 1948): 212–230.

American officials fully understood why the Soviets were trying these new policies. As Secretary of State Marshall told Truman's cabinet in November 1947, "The advance of Communism has been stemmed and the Russians have been compelled to make a reevaluation of their position."[37] America was winning its eight-month Cold War. But the Soviets' difficulties provided an excuse for Congress, which was not anxious to send billions of dollars of Marshall Plan aid to Europe if the Russians posed little threat. Congress dawdled as the plan came under increased criticism. In speeches around the country Marshall tried to sell the program for its long-term economic and political benefits. His arguments fell on deaf ears. The American economy seemed to be doing well. Just weeks before the 1948 presidential campaign was to begin, Truman faced a major political and diplomatic defeat.

And then came the fall of Czechoslovakia. The Czechs had uneasily coexisted with Russia by trying not to offend the Soviets while keeping doors open to the West. This policy had started in late 1943, when Czech leaders signed a treaty with Stalin that, in the view of most observers, obligated Czechoslovakia to become a part of the Russian bloc. President Edvard Beneš and Foreign Minister Jan Masaryk, one of the foremost diplomatic figures in Europe, had nevertheless successfully resisted complete communist control. Nor had Stalin moved to consolidate his power in 1946 after the Czech Communist party emerged from the parliamentary elections with 38 percent of the vote, the largest total of any party. By late 1947 the lure of Western aid and internal political changes began to pull the Czech government away from the Soviets. At this point Stalin, who like Truman recalled the pivotal role of Czechoslovakia in 1938 (see p. 6), decided to put the 1943 treaty into effect. Klement Gottwald, the Czech Communist party leader, demanded the elimination of independent parties. In mid-February 1948 Soviet armies camped on the border as Gottwald ordered the formation of a wholly new government. A Soviet mission of top officials flew to Prague to demand Beneš's surrender. The communists assumed full control on February 25. Two weeks later Masaryk either committed suicide, or, as Truman believed, was the victim of "foul play."

---

[37]*Forrestal Diaries*, pp. 340–341.

Truman correctly observed that the coup "sent a shock throughout the civilized world." He privately believed, "We are faced with exactly the same situation with which Britain and France were faced in 1938–9 with Hitler."[38] In late 1947 Hungary had been the victim of a similar if less dramatic squeeze. Within two months new opportunities would beckon to the Cominform when the Italian election was held. On March 5, 1948, a cable arrived from General Clay in Germany. Although "I have felt and held that war was unlikely for at least ten years," Clay began, "within the last few weeks, I have felt a subtle change in Soviet attitude which . . . gives me a feeling that it may come with dramatic suddenness." For ten days government intelligence worked furiously investigating Clay's warnings and on March 16 gave Truman the grim assurance that war was not probable within sixty days.[39] Two days before, on March 14, the frightened U.S. Senate had endorsed the Marshall Plan by a vote of 69 to 17. As it went to the House for consideration, Truman, fearing the "grave events in Europe [which] were moving so swiftly," decided to appear before Congress.

In a speech remarkable for its repeated emphasis on the "increasing threat" to the very "survival of freedom," the President proclaimed the Marshall Plan "not enough." Europe must have "some measure of protection against internal and external aggression." He asked for Universal Training, the resumption of Selective Service (which he had allowed to lapse a year earlier), and speedy passage of the Marshall Plan.[40] Within twelve days the House approved authorization of the plan's money.

With perfect timing and somber rhetoric, Truman's March 17, 1948, speech not only galvanized passage of the plan but also accelerated a change in American foreign policy that had been heralded the previous summer. Congress stamped its approval on this new military emphasis by passing a Selective Service bill. Although Universal Military Training, one of Forrestal's pet projects, found little favor, a supposedly penny-proud Congress replaced it with funds to begin a seventy-group air force, 25 percent larger than even Forrestal had requested.

[38]Margaret Truman, *Harry S Truman* (New York, 1973), p. 392; for the Czech-U.S.S.R. background, see Vojtech Mastny, *Russia's Road to the Cold War* (New York, 1979), pp. 133–142, 281–282.
[39]*Forrestal Diaries*, pp. 387, 395.
[40]*Documents on American Foreign Relations*, X (1948): 5–9.

Perhaps the most crucial effect of the new policy, however, appeared in the administration's determination to create great systems that would not only encourage military development but also compel the Western world to accept political realignments. The first of these efforts had been the Rio Pact and the new policies toward Japan. The next, somewhat different, and vastly more important effort would be the North Atlantic Treaty Organization (NATO).

Some forty-five years later documents came to light revealing that much of the March 1948 crisis had been invented. The fall of Czechoslovakia was certainly real, although its causes and implications were more complex and ambiguous than Truman announced in 1948. A top secret intelligence analysis told Truman in late March 1948 that the Soviets would "not resort to direct military action during 1948" unless the United States seemed ready to attack Russia— which was most unlikely. Less complex and ambiguous were the other causes of the war scare. It is now clear that U.S. officials, especially Forrestal and his Pentagon advisers, concocted the scare (including General Clay's remarkable telegram) to terrify Congress into passing bills for a major military buildup (especially in the air force, where U.S. aircraft manufacturers lobbied for more money) and Universal Military Training. The scare was also designed to push neutral-minded Europeans into seeking the protection of a U.S.-dominated military alliance. Except for the Universal Training, the scare tactics worked to a remarkable degree. Domestic needs, at least as some officials and interests defined those needs, again determined foreign policy.[41]

---

[41]Gerald K. Haines and Robert E. Leggett, eds., *CIA's Analysis of the Soviet Union, 1947–1991* (Washington, D.C., 2001), p. 21; the author is indebted to David Laughart for a copy of this document. Frank Kofsky, *Harry S. Truman and the War Scare of 1948* (New York, 1995), especially "Foreword" to 1995 edition.

Reinhold Niebuhr, an intellectual godfather of U.S. Cold War policies, was a prophet with honor in his own country.
(© Time Life Pictures/Getty Images)

CHAPTER 4

The "Different World" of NSC-68 (1948–1950)

During the spring of 1948 a united administration, enjoying strong support on foreign policy from a Republican Congress, set off with exemplary single-mindedness to destroy the communist threat that loomed over Europe. Within two years this threat had been scotched. But the U.S. officials who created the policy had split, the Congress that ratified the policy had turned against the executive, the administration had fought off charges that it had been infiltrated by communists, and the United States found itself fighting a bloody war not in Europe but in Asia. These embarrassments did not suddenly emerge in 1950 but developed gradually from the policies of 1948–1949.

During March 1948, as Congress approved the Marshall Plan, the British, the French, and the Benelux signed the Brussels Treaty. In this defense arrangement each signatory promised to aid the other parties in the event of attack with all military and other aid "in their power." Truman applauded the treaty, and soon Senator Vandenberg and Robert Lovett, Acheson's successor as under secretary of state, were spending long evenings in Vandenberg's Wardman Park Hotel suite drawing up a congressional resolution to pave the way for American entry into the new European association. Presented to the Senate on May 19, the Vandenberg Resolution genuflected briefly before the UN Charter, then passed on to the more vital business of requesting a regional arrangement, under Vandenberg's pet UN Charter Article 51, in which the United States would participate militarily. This breezed through the Senate on June 11 by a 64 to 4 vote, and Lovett began a three-month-long series of conferences with European leaders to draft a final treaty. These discussions had barely begun when they were shaken by two events. In Europe the Berlin blockade severely tested Western unity. In the United States a foreign-policy debate erupted during the presidential campaign.

The Berlin blockade had its beginnings in those moments of 1945 and 1946 when the breakdown of the Four Power Allied Control Council made impossible the reunification of Germany. The Soviets continued to hope they could create a unified but demilitarized Germany under their own aegis, or, as Molotov told Byrnes in 1946, a united Germany which could be neutralized after Russia received adequate industrial reparations. As Americans stressed, however, the prosperity of Western Europe depended on German industrial recovery. If it could not reunify Germany, the West could at least develop the western, industrial portions controlled by France, Great Britain, and the United States and integrate the areas into a new European community. These three powers plus the Benelux reached agreement on this approach during intermittent meetings in London from February into June. The Ruhr's great resources were to be brought under joint control of the Western powers.[1] By late June the conference began a currency reform to stop the inflation and widespread black market activities caused in Germany and West Berlin by the weak reichsmark.

For the Soviets the crisis was at hand. The Western moves were obviously designed to accept and exploit the status quo in Germany. The Soviets, however, based their European policy on a weakened, non-Western Central Europe, and with the passage of the Marshall Plan and the rebuilding of West Germany they now faced the imminent defeat of that policy. Worse, Stalin confronted the prospect of a revitalized West Berlin deep inside the Soviet zone. Then, suddenly, the dictator's authority was challenged from within the bloc itself.

Tito was quite unlike Stalin's other followers in Eastern Europe. As a guerrilla leader he had successfully resisted the Nazis, and in doing so had created a mass basis of support in Yugoslavia at a time when Stalin and other communist leaders increasingly rested their power on elite groups. His country, unlike Czechoslovakia, did not border on the Soviet Union and enjoyed access to the Mediterranean

---

[1] U.S. Senate, Committee on Foreign Relations, 87th Cong., 1st Sess., *Documents on Germany, 1944–1961* (Washington, 1961), pp. 87–88.

area. Tito's belief in communism had never been in question. He was the only bloc leader who fully supported Stalin's and Zhdanov's creation of the Cominform. Tito's nationalism, however, had never been questioned either. When Stalin began to demand full Yugoslav adherence to the new economic and mutual assistance pacts, Tito balked. Enraged, Stalin claimed, "I will shake my little finger—and there will be no more Tito."[2]

The Yugoslav's secret police, however, proved superior to Stalin's. After the Soviet dictator tried in vain to overthrow Tito with an internal coup, Stalin called a special Cominform meeting in June 1948 to expel Yugoslavia from the bloc for "taking the route of nationalism." Tito not only successfully challenged Stalin's power but also disproved Stalin's key assumption that the world was divided into "two camps," with any so-called third force only a cover for capitalism. Having shaken both Stalin's power and theory, Tito's example threatened Soviet control throughout Eastern Europe. At that moment in mid-June when Stalin was preparing to bring Tito's many supposed sins into the open, the Allies challenged Soviet policies in Germany. Stalin's first reaction was the ordering of bloody purges in Eastern Europe to exterminate nascent Titos. During the next two years probably one of every four communist members in the bloc fell from grace.

He next attempted to sever the West from the 2.4 million West Berliners. On June 24 the Soviets stopped all surface traffic between Berlin and the Western zones. The Western powers had never negotiated a pact guaranteeing these rights. The Soviets now rejected arguments that occupation rights in Berlin and the use of the routes during the previous three years had given the West legal claim to unrestricted use of the highways and railroads. On June 28 came the American response. Without consulting anyone but a few cabinet members, Truman decided, as Forrestal recalled the President's words, "We [are] going to stay, period." Secretary of State Marshall later placed this decision within a context that bore an eerie resemblance to Stalin's policy framework: "We had the alternative of following a firm policy in Berlin or accepting the consequences of

---

[2]Nikita S. Khrushchev, *The Crimes of the Stalin Era. Special Report to the 20th Congress of the Communist Party of the Soviet Union,* annotated by Boris I. Nicolaevsky (New York, 1956), p. 48. This copy from *The New Leader* is well annotated.

failure of the rest of our European policy."[3] The domino theory could work, apparently, on both sides of the Iron Curtain, and Germany had become the first domino.

The United States began a massive airlift, ultimately lasting 324 days, which soon delivered 13,000 tons of supplies daily to West Berlin. Stalin was playing for high stakes, but so was Truman. In July he transferred to England two groups of B-29 bombers, the planes designated to carry atomic bombs. Truman's action indicated how the monopoly of these bombs allowed the administration to balance the budget and cut back conventional army forces, yet not diminish its capacity or willingness to brandish military force. The President assured Forrestal and Marshall that, although he prayed the bomb would not have to be used, "if it became necessary, no one need have a misgiving but what he would do so." The evening after Truman made this remark, a meeting of leading newspaper publishers agreed that if war occurred over Berlin, the American people would expect the bomb to be dropped. Taking these words at face value, the Pentagon requested that control of the bomb be transferred from the President to the military so that preparations could be made for its use. Here Truman drew the line: he did not intend "to have some dashing lieutenant colonel decide when would be the proper time to drop one." This decision became more significant when Lovett brought word back to Washington that General Clay, the American commander in Berlin, "was now drawn as tight as a steel spring."[4]

In mid-May 1948 Truman gave further evidence of his presidential power, although this occurred less in the context of possible atomic war against the Soviets than inevitable political war against Republicans. Shortly after 6:00 P.M. on May 14, the President recognized the state of Israel just minutes after the Israelis had proclaimed the existence of their new nation. Truman did this after rejecting the advice of both his military and diplomatic advisers. For months Forrestal had warned that the recognizing of the Israelis, who were fighting a bloody war against the Arabs for possession of Palestine, would lead to the loss of vital Middle Eastern oil resources in the Arab states.

---

[3]James Forrestal, *The Forrestal Diaries*, Walter Millis, ed. (New York, 1951), pp. 454–455.
[4]*Forrestal Diaries*, pp. 487–489, 460–461, 480–481.

Truman, however, had supported large-scale Jewish immigration into Palestine. Moreover, even State Department experts agreed with many Americans' unfortunate stereotypes of Arabs as cartoon-like and irrational. "As for the emotions of the Arabs," one U.S. official privately wrote, "I do not care a dried camel's hump," just as long as they don't attack "our oil investments." In 1947 Truman hoped Palestine could be partitioned so that a separate Jewish state could be created. Not illogically, therefore, he agreed with his political rather than his diplomatic advisers. The Jewish vote could be decisive in such key states as Ohio, New York, and California. Although the President sincerely sympathized with the Israeli effort in Palestine, British Prime Minister Clement Attlee was also correct when he observed that Truman overrode his diplomatic advisers because "there's no Arab vote in America but there's a very heavy Jewish vote and the Americans are always having elections."[5]

In the decisions on Berlin and Israel, Truman enjoyed such strong congressional support (although Congress had not been formally consulted in either instance) that foreign policy never became a major issue between Truman and the Republican nominee, Thomas E. Dewey of New York, during the 1948 presidential campaign. Reinhold Niebuhr summarized the basic viewpoint of most Republicans and Democrats when he wrote in *Life* magazine in September 1948, "For peace we must risk war." The Soviets were weaker and would not fight, Niebuhr declared. "We cannot afford any more compromises. We will have to stand at every point in our far-flung lines."[6] These views underlay the foreign-policy planks of both parties, although the platforms did not agree in every particular. In contrast to the Democrats, the Republicans emphasized the need to save China, lauded bipartisanship, placed heavier emphasis on building the military, and accused the President of not comprehending the real nature of the Russian peril. The Democrats answered the last charge by inserting a

---

[5]The best historical overview is Douglas Little, *American Orientalism; The United States and the Middle East since 1945* (Chapel Hill, 2002), especially. pp. 25–27 for the U.S. official's quote & context; Clement Attlee, *Twilight of Empire* (New York, 1961), p. 181. A succinct, useful, and well-done overview is Michelle Mart, "Constructing a Universal Ideal: Anti-Semitism, American Jews, and the Founding of Israel," *Modern Judaism,* 20 (2000), especially pp. 196–199 on Truman.

[6]Reinhold Niebuhr, "For Peace We Must Risk War," *Life,* XXV (September 20, 1948): 38–39.

plank (which had no counterpart in the Republican platform) condemning communism "overseas and at home," and pledging strong
enforcement of antisubversive laws.

The Cold War entered the campaign, but the clash occurred
between the Democrats and Henry Wallace's Progressive party. As
the Progressives cried that the "old parties" did not want a settlement with Russia, Wallace, along with many of his noncommunist
supporters, became fair game to those Americans committed to
fighting the Cold War with no holds barred. Apparently because of
his political views, one Wallace supporter was stabbed to death in
Charleston, South Carolina. At Evansville College, Bradley University, Northwestern, the University of Georgia, the University of
Miami, and the University of New Hampshire, Progressive party
adherents were either fired or made to suffer in other ways for their
political convictions. The Americans for Democratic Action, afraid
that Wallace might split the liberal vote and hand the victory to
Dewey, tried to use guilt-by-association tactics by printing in major
urban newspapers the names of the Progressive party's principal
contributors and then listing the organizations on the attorney general's list of subversive groups to which these contributors belonged—or
had belonged long before.[7]

The growing tension over Berlin and Truman's shift to the left on
domestic issues killed any hopes the Progressives nursed of determining the election. Clark Clifford, Truman's closest political adviser, was
prophetic, for a year before he had told the President: "There is considerable political advantage to the Administration in its battle with the
Kremlin. . . . The worse matters get, up to a fairly certain point—real danger of imminent war—the more there is a sense of crisis. In times of crisis the American citizen tends to back up his President."[8] Wallace
received only 1,157,326 votes; half came from New York. Overcoming
handicaps imposed by defections to the Wallacite left and the Dixiecrat
right, and by public opinion polls which showed him trailing Dewey,
Truman lustily enjoyed scoring the greatest upset in twentieth-century
American politics. The Progressive party rapidly declined, with Wallace
finally quitting in 1950 when he supported Truman's actions in Korea.
In Europe negotiations resumed on the NATO treaty.

---

[7]Karl M. Schmidt, *Henry A. Wallace: Quixotic Crusade, 1948* (Syracuse, 1960), pp. 86–88,
159, 252; John C. Culver and John Hyde, *American Dreamer: The Life and Times of Henry
A. Wallace* (New York, 2000), pp. 456–478, 496–502.
[8]Allan Yarnell, *Democrats and Progressives* (Berkeley, 1974), chapter III, especially p. 37.

These negotiations for a military alliance moved to the front of American diplomatic activity. In his Inaugural Address of January 20, 1949, Truman made a slight effort to restore some balance when, in outlining the four major points of his foreign policy, he suggested as the so-called Point Four "a bold new program" to spread scientific and industrial knowledge to the newly emerging areas. It was to be a kind of private-enterprise Marshall Plan to help the impoverished, and increasingly important, Third World. The President and Congress moved slowly in implementing this glamorous concept. The business community, on which Truman depended for the passage and implementation of any large aid program, attacked the probability of more governmental interference in the less industrialized countries. That community asked instead that Truman negotiate with these nations treaties assuring fair and equitable treatment of private investment and personnel. For a year and a half, Truman could obtain no Point Four legislation. In the summer of 1950 Congress finally passed a token appropriation of $27 million to begin a technical aid program in conjunction with the United Nations. Even the method was attacked by Senator Tom Connally, Democratic chairman of the Foreign Relations Committee: "I don't see why in the world we need to turn this over and let . . . the United Nations run it and . . . mess it all up."[9] Senator Connally's feeling ran somewhat contrary to Point One of Truman's Inaugural Address—full support of the United Nations.

The other two points of the address—the encouragement of European recovery and the pledging of aid to help nations defend themselves—were more popular. Here Truman dealt with the familiar cultures and policies of Europe. He also worked with a new secretary of state who knew Europe intimately. The most important American foreign policymaker in the post–World War II era, Dean Acheson founded his policy on those Atlantic ties which statesmen in Europe traditionally considered the last hope of Western civilization. As a young, brilliant lawyer whom Roosevelt had plucked in 1933 out of Washington's most august law firm, Acheson had resigned from the early New Deal because he considered Roosevelt's experimental monetary policies rather weird. The approach of war, however, drew Acheson back into government, and between 1941 and 1947 he devoted himself to the European polices which climaxed with the Marshall Plan.

[9]Quoted in Richard P. Stebbins, *United States in World Affairs, 1950* (New York, 1951), p. 98.

As a good conservative, Acheson gave his allegiance to the Western partnership, in which he correctly viewed the United States to be senior partner. His fear of the Soviet menace satisfied even Vandenberg: Acheson "is so totally anti-Soviet and is going to be so *completely* tough," the Michigan senator wrote from a Foreign Minister's conference in May 1949, "that I really doubt whether there is any *chance at all*" for an agreement.[10]

Nor did Acheson allow the wishes of the multitude to disturb his outlook. The growing popularity of public opinion polls, he remarked in 1946, signifies that "we have become of a somewhat hypochondriac type, and ascertain our state of health by this mass temperature taking. Fortunately this was not one of the hardships of Valley Forge." As for the United Nations, "in the Arab proverb, the ass that went to Mecca remained an ass, and a policy has little added to it by its place of utterance." Congress did not escape his wrath. Its function in foreign policy, he later observed, "is the function of people who don't know and don't care and are obstructive, and they are just generally raising hell around." As for individuals, "the question of sincerity of a United States Senator is beyond me. . . . He is an honest man, he is an intense fellow, he gets all worked up, the blood rushes to his head, he takes on kind of a wild, stary look at you, and I just do not think his mind works in a normal way when he gets excited."[11]

Acheson preferred to place his confidence in power manipulated by an elite. He sounded much like Niebuhr. After World War II, Acheson declared, Americans "learned how wrong the prophets of the Enlightenment had been about what moved peoples. These prophets overestimated the influence of wisdom, virtue, and understanding of experience, and underestimated prejudice, passion and dogma." And there was power: "Power politics had no place in our Celestial City; but a substantial place in the twentieth century." So there they were, sin and power. His war against communism, his trust in power (especially military power) to contain sin, and the

---

[10]The best and most detailed biography is Robert Beisner, *Dean Acheson: A Life in the Cold War* (New York, 2006); Arthur H. Vandenberg, Jr., ed., *The Private Papers of Senator Vandenberg* (Boston, 1952), p. 485. For Acheson's pro-British imperial views, note John T. McNay, *Acheson and Empire* (Columbia, Mo., 2001).

[11]Princeton Seminar, October 10–11, July 22–23, 1953, Acheson Papers, Truman Library.

veneration he had for traditional Europe admirably suited Acheson for the new era to be opened by the NATO pact.[12]

The world in which NATO was to be born was undergoing rapid change. Nowhere was this more evident than in the Soviet Union. The successful Allied response to the Berlin blockade and Tito's defiance of the Cominform forced Stalin to question Zhdanov's fanaticism. By the end of July 1948, Zhdanov was dead, perhaps poisoned, more likely the victim of a heart attack after violent arguments with Stalin. Zhdanov's supporters disappeared in a mass purge, and Georgy Malenkov and Nikita Khrushchev, both of whom wanted Stalin to devote more attention to internal economic problems, moved up the rungs of power.

During April 1949 the Soviets began lifting the Berlin blockade. In Western Europe, which NATO was to undergird, Italian and French communists lost considerable ground. Despite a recession caused by an American economic downturn, overall production in Western Europe exceeded the 1938 level by 15 percent. As Truman's chief diplomatic troubleshooter W. Averell Harriman testified, fear in Europe "no longer exists as it existed 18 months ago."[13]

In this changing, quieter international environment, the Senate opened hearings on the NATO pact. Twelve nations had signed it: the United States, Canada, Denmark, France, Iceland, Italy, Portugal, Norway, Great Britain, and the Benelux. They pledged to use force only in self-defense and to develop "free institutions," particularly through the encouragement of "economic collaboration between any or all" of the parties. Article 5 was central:

> The Parties agree that an armed attack against one or more of them in Europe or North America shall be considered an attack against them all; and consequently they agree that, if such an armed attack occurs, each of them . . . will assist the Party or Parties so attacked by taking forthwith, individually and in concert with the other Parties, such action as it deems necessary, including the use of armed force.

---

[12]Dean Acheson, *Pattern of Responsibility; Edited by McGeorge Bundy from the Record of Secretary of State Dean Acheson* (Boston, 1952), pp. 17, 21; Dean Acheson, "The Truman Years," *Foreign Service Journal*, XLII (August 1965): 23.

[13]U.S. Senate, Committee on Foreign Relations, 81st Cong., 1st Sess., *Hearings . . . on . . . The North Atlantic Treaty* (Washington, 1949), p. 203.

Article 11 modified this commitment by adding that the pact's provisions shall be carried out in accordance with each nation's "constitutional processes." Vandenberg and Connally had inserted this clause
in an attempt to curb executive powers.

At first the hearings went well. Acheson calmed some fears by
emphasizing that no one "at the present time" contemplated following
NATO with "a Mediterranean pact, and then a Pacific pact, and so
forth." Everyone present agreed that European defense could not be
entrusted to the United Nations. A consensus formed on the proposi-
tion that NATO "is to create not merely a balance of power, but a preponderance of power." This fitted into Truman's and Acheson's
policies of dealing with the Russians from "positions of strength." The
West, however, already enjoyed such a "preponderance" because of its
possession of the atomic bomb. NATO promised to add little more.
This led to questions which soon revealed that even administration
spokesmen had difficulty discovering the pact's military importance.

At the time, the West's dozen underequipped divisions faced
twenty-five fully armed Russian divisions in Central Europe. When
asked whether the administration planned to send "substantial"
numbers of U.S. troops to shore up the European defenses, Acheson
and General Omar Bradley, Chairman of the Joint Chiefs of Staff,
assured the Senate, in Acheson's words, "The answer to that question, Senator, is a clear and absolute 'no.'" Continuing their search
for the manpower that would fill NATO, Acheson was asked
whether he contemplated putting Germans back into uniform. "We
are very clear," he replied, "that the disarmament and demilitarization of Germany must be complete and absolute."[14]

The questioning necessarily took another line. Perhaps NATO was
then aimed at preventing internal subversion in Western Europe?
Acheson called the possibility of successful subversion "remote" and
thought the American reaction to a coup would be the less-than-drastic
response of allowing the victim to leave the NATO alliance. Clearly the
treaty's military significance seemed not to be overwhelming.[15]

The key to the American view of the treaty emerged when
Harriman remarked that if NATO were not carried through "there
would be a reorientation" in Europe climaxing in "a restrengthening

---

[14]Committee on Foreign Relations, *Hearings on* [NATO], pp. 54, 57, 47, 183, 144.
[15]Committee on Foreign Relations, *Hearings on* [NATO], pp. 25, 310, 317.

of those that believe in appeasement and neutrality." In a similar vein, Acheson commented a year later, "Unity in Europe requires the continuing association and support of the United States. Without it free Europe would split apart." Now that the Marshall Plan was apparently reviving Europe economically, the United States, in the full splendor of its postwar power, was attempting to strengthen its political ties with, and influence over, Europe through the creation of common military institutions. Senator Connally succinctly phrased this in the Senate debate: "The Atlantic Pact is but the logical extension of the principle of the Monroe Doctrine."[16]

The Senate ratified the treaty 82 to 13. On the day he added his signature in mid-July 1949, Truman sent Congress a one-year Mutual Defense Assistance (MDA) bill providing for $1.5 billion for European military aid. This was the immediate financial price for the NATO commitment. A memorandum circulating through the executive outlined the purpose of MDA: "to build up our own military industry," to "create a common defense frontier in Western Europe" by having the Allies pool "their industrial and manpower resources," and particularly, to subordinate "nationalistic tendencies."[17] In the House, however, the bill encountered tough opposition from budget-cutting congressmen. On September 22 President Truman announced that Russia had exploded an atomic bomb. Within six days the NATO appropriations raced through the House and went to the President for approval.

Although publicly playing down the significance of the Russian bomb, the administration painfully realized that, in Vandenberg's words, "This is now a different world." Few American officials had expected the Soviet test this early. Because it was simultaneous with the fall of China, the American diplomatic attitude further stiffened. As Leo Szilard, one of the foremost scientists in the development of

[16]Committee on Foreign Relations, *Hearings on* [NATO], p. 231; Acheson, *Pattern of Responsibility*, p. 55; Tom Connally, *My Name Is Tom Connally* (New York, 1954), p. 231. This political (rather than military) importance of NATO is also emphasized in U.S. Senate, Committee on Foreign Relations, 81st Cong., 1st and 2nd Sess., *Review of the World Situation, 1949–1950* [Executive hearings of 1949–1950 made public in 1974] (Washington, 1974), pp. 6, 12–13. The NATO treaty and a Senate "interpretation" of it can be read in chapter IV documents at the www.mhhe.com/lafeber website of this book.

[17]"Effect of the MAP on U.S. Security," draft from Foreign Assistance Coordinating Committee, June 22, 1949, Papers of David D. Lloyd, Truman Library.

the American bomb, explained, "The Russians can affect the political attitude of Western Europeans just by threatening to bomb them."[18] Despite the Marshall Plan and NATO, for American policymakers the struggle for Europe had reopened.

Truman took a first step in the new battle by ordering that development of the hydrogen bomb be accelerated. The second step occurred when American military authorities determined to build a large conventional European army which would include German military units. In August the first elections in West Germany for a national parliament had given Konrad Adenauer's Christian Democratic Union a plurality of 31 percent of the votes. A vigorous seventy-three years of age, Adenauer had spent his early political life in Cologne city government and then, from 1933 to 1945, in Nazi prisons. His rise to power in 1949 resulted more from ruthless political infighting than from charisma. He personally enjoyed little national support, but he had a clear vision: a restored, independent Germany could develop only through close cooperation with the United States. Adenauer dedicated the last two decades of his long life to realizing this vision.

American officials appreciated Adenauer's obvious statesmanship but disagreed over tactics. A U.S. Army planning unit outlined a program for German rearmament and launched a campaign to procure NATO's acceptance. The State Department, however, argued that building a German army could create political reaction at home, unpleasant responses from Poland and Russia, and strong hostility in France.[19] The French probably knew little about this Washington infighting, but they fully comprehended the threat that overpowering American influence in NATO, and a possibly rearmed Germany, posed to their own independence. As it had in the past and would in the future, France retaliated by trying to increase its power on the continent at the expense of the Americans.

French Foreign Minister Robert Schuman proposed in early 1950 that "Little Europe" (France, Germany, Italy, and the Benelux) combine

---

[18]Leo Szilard, "A Personal History of the Bomb." In "The Atlantic Community Faces the Bomb," *University of Chicago Roundtable,* September 25, 1949, p. 4.
[19]Laurence W. Martin, "The American Decision to Rearm Germany." In Harold Stein, ed., *American Civil-Military Decisions: A Book of Case Studies* (Birmingham, Ala., 1963), pp. 646–651.

their heavy iron, coal, and steel industry. Like the American military's plans for German rearmament, the "Schuman Plan" would have political repercussions. Germany's basic industry would be integrated into Western Europe; the Ruhr would essentially be internationalized, thus (the French hoped) destroying Germany's military capacity while giving France entry to the area's rich coal deposits. The combining of basic industries would shortly force transport and agriculture to follow in a movement of spectacular European integration. Last, but not least, exclusion of England and the United States from the plan would increase France's ability to influence all of Western Europe.

The French hoped to tie down Germany and shape Western Europe through economic means. Americans planned to influence Germany and Western Europe through the military structure of NATO. These two approaches, in full view by early 1950, posed the alternatives for European development through the early twenty-first century. They also made understandable the growing competition and bitterness between the United States and France. In 1949–1950 George Kennan offered a third alternative. He concluded that Russia could be contained, yet Cold War tensions eased, through some kind of neutralization plan for Central Europe. Kennan considered NATO an obstacle to such neutralization, since the new alliance permanently divided and threatened to rearm Germany.[20]

When Kennan made such arguments within the State Department, he encountered vigorous opposition from Acheson.[21] The secretary of state preferred the old to the new Mr. "X." But the Russian atomic bomb explosion deepened Kennan's convictions. In early 1950 he announced he was leaving the State Department for a year of study at Princeton. So ended another "disengagement" debate within the State Department.

Kennan's departure did not free Acheson from criticism. As a Europe-first advocate, and as secretary of state during the months when Chiang Kai-shek finally lost China, Acheson became the target for a growing body of Chiang's supporters known as the China Lobby. The lobby had begun in the Chinese embassy during World War II. It coordinated pro-Chiang propaganda in the United States

---

[20]George Kennan, *Memoirs, 1925–1950* (Boston, 1967), pp. 446–449.
[21]*U.S. News and World Report,* XLIV (January 17, 1958): 63.

and helped pay its expenses by illegally smuggling narcotics into the country. Until 1948 the China Lobby was not significant but then became transformed into a highly effective pressure group. First, it gained the adherence of wealthy, conservative Americans who believed Truman was selling out China and the free enterprise system to communists. Second, many Americans could not understand why the greatest power in the world stood helplessly by while Mao Ze-dong's communist forces conquered China. Such frustration and their incredible ignorance of China (and of the limits of American power) led to the easy conclusion that communist sympathizers hidden in the bowels of the State Department must be doing the dirty work. The wealth, the political attractiveness of these reasons for China's fall, and, in some cases, their own personal experience in Asia attracted political support from key congressmen. These included William Knowland (later Senate majority leader for the Republicans) and Senator Kenneth Wherry (who had uttered, "With God's help we will lift Shanghai up and up, ever up, until it is just like Kansas City.")[22]

When the China enthusiasts argued that more American aid could save Chiang, Acheson correctly responded that lack of supplies was not causing the Nationalists' headlong retreat. The chief of the American advisory group in China reported in late 1948 that these "military debacles in my opinion can all be attributed to the world's worst leadership and many other morale destroying factors that led to a complete loss of will to fight."[23] By February 1949 the Nationalists had lost nearly half their troops, mostly by defection. Eighty percent of the American equipment given Chiang had fallen into communist hands. In April, as Mao's troops successfully crossed the Yangtze and began to sweep across southern China, Truman finally moved to terminate aid. This aroused the full fury of the China bloc, but the critics could only attack the administration, for they had no useful alternatives to offer. As Knowland candidly admitted, no responsible opponent of the Truman policy had ever proposed sending an American army to fight in China.

---

[22]Quoted in Eric Goldman, *The Crucial Decade and After, 1945–1961* (New York, 1960), p. 116; Ross Koen, *The China Lobby* (New York, 1960).
[23]Tang Tsou, *America's Failure in China* (Chicago, 1963), pp. 482–483.

In August 1949 Acheson tried for the knockout blow by releasing the so-called White Paper, a 1054-page compilation of documents to support the administration's thesis that, as Acheson wrote in a long introduction, "The unfortunate but inescapable fact is that the ominous result of the civil war in China was beyond the control of the government of the United States. . . . It was the product of internal Chinese forces, forces which this country tried to influence but could not." The only alternative policy would have been a "full-scale intervention" of American troops, which "would have been resented by the mass of the Chinese people, would have diametrically reversed our historic policy, and would have been condemned by the American people." He looked forward to the time when the Chinese would throw off the "foreign yoke" of communism. The China Lobby retaliated by terming the White Paper a "whitewash of a wishful, do-nothing policy which has succeeded only in placing Asia in danger of Soviet conquest."[24]

Despite the China Lobby, Truman and Acheson almost took a historic step during midsummer 1949: they nearly gave their approval when the American ambassador to China, J. Leighton Stuart, asked if he could talk with Mao. The initiative had come from the communists, some of whom clearly hoped to have some kind of diplomatic relationship with the United States. State Department officials urged that Stuart be sent to the new government. After hurried meetings at the White House, however, Acheson told Stuart that a decision "at the highest level" forbade him from talking with Mao. They believed—correctly, as it turned out—that Mao had determined to move his revolution closer to Stalin, not the United States, and that Truman would pay a bitter political price at home if he reached out to Mao. Acheson made the decision final by announcing on October 12 that the new Chinese regime could not be recognized by the United States. Americans were particularly angered when Mao's government seized American consular property and later jailed American Consul Angus Ward.

Chiang Kai-shek fled to Formosa (now Taiwan) to establish a rival Chinese government. This presented another set of problems to

---

[24]Dean Acheson, "Letter of Transmittal, July 30." In *United States Relations with China . . . 1944–1949* (Washington, 1949), pp. xiv–xvii. Quoted in H. B. Westerfield, *Foreign Policies and Party Politics: Pearl Harbor to Korea* (New Haven, 1955), p. 356.

Washington. In late December the Joint Chiefs and Acheson agreed that since Mao would probably conquer Formosa sometime in 1950, the United States should not give military aid to the Nationalists.[25] Chiang's supporters again organized for battle in Congress and forced the administration to compromise when they threatened to cut off aid to Korea if some assistance was not immediately sent to Formosa. The battle was bitter, and Vandenberg, seriously ill in Michigan, could not heal the wounds suffered by bipartisanship. This fight, waged just five months before the outbreak of the Korean War, left bipartisanship a shattered ideal and no longer a practice.

Truman and Acheson determined to move slowly in the revolutionary Asian situation. American experts were not certain whether a common allegiance to Marxism-Leninism would suffice to link China and Russia in a friendly partnership. Stalin remembered the debacle of his China policies during the 1920s. The Chinese communists bitterly recalled how Stalin had cooperated with Roosevelt in recognizing Chiang's government and had kept a Soviet ambassador with the Nationalists in 1949 after most Western governments had deserted Chiang. Soviet and Chinese documents made public in the 1990s revealed that a suspicious and fearful Stalin had urged Mao not to launch the revolution in 1945, and—stunningly—apparently tried to keep China divided between Mao and Chiang as late as 1949. Fearful of growing crises with the United States in Europe, Stalin wanted no confrontation in Asia.[26]

But one of the most important confrontations in all the Cold War did loom in Asia. A top-secret U.S. intelligence report to Truman in April 1949 proved to be prophetic: there was no "factual evidence of Soviet preparation for direct military aggression during 1949," but since "international tension has increased," there could be war "through miscalculation on either side."[27]

[25]U.S. Senate, Committee on Armed Services and Committee on Foreign Relations, 82nd Cong., 1st Sess., *Hearings to Conduct an Inquiry into the Military Situation in the Far East* . . . (Washington, 1951), pp. 1770–1771; cited hereafter as *Military Situation in the Far East. . . .*

[26]Noted in Donald S. Zagoria, *The Sino-Soviet Conflict, 1956–1961* (Princeton, 1962), pp. 14–15. This paragraph is also based on Brian Murray, *Stalin, the Cold War, and the Division of China. . . .* Cold War International History Project (Washington, D.C., 1995), pp. 1–17.

[27]Gerald K. Haines and Robert E. Heggett, eds., *CIA's Analysis of the Soviet Union, 1947–1991* (Washington, D.C., 2001), p. 29.

The beginnings of miscalculation in the East became apparent in discussions between Chinese and Russian leaders which began in December 1949. More than two months of hard bargaining ensued. Stalin gave restricted credit arrangements to China for the purchase of Soviet exports to the value of a paltry $300 million spread over five years. The Soviets later cut the value of the loan about one-fifth by devaluing the ruble. China did succeed in making the treaty one of "mutual assistance": Russia would consult with China in the event that Japan "or any other state that should unite" with Japan threatened aggression against China. Perhaps of most importance to Mao, the Soviets promised to surrender to him their special rights in Manchurian ports and the Manchurian railway system. While these points were argued, Stalin moved unsuccessfully back of the scene to loosen the allegiances of Manchuria and Inner Mongolia to Mao. The "fraternal alliance" was enduring an uncommon amount of horse trading and attempted backstabbing.

On January 12, 1950, as the Mao-Stalin talks edged along, Acheson publicly and, as it turned out, dangerously miscalculated when he spoke before the National Press Club in Washington.[28] He viewed the Soviet attempt to control Outer and Inner Mongolia, Manchuria, and Sinkiang as "the single most significant, most important fact" in Asia. Such attempts would prove to Mao that the Soviets wished not to help but to dominate. Acheson stressed that nationalism, not communism, had become the dominant fact in postwar Asia and that consequently the United States, not Russia, would prove to be the best friend of those Chinese who want "their own national independence." In this context Acheson issued his famous declaration that the Pacific "defensive perimeter" of the United States ran from the Aleutians to Japan, the Ryukyus, and down to the Philippines. (This was not a newly announced policy. In March 1949 General MacArthur defined the perimeter as encompassing exactly the same area.[29]) Acheson doubted that the Far East was threatened as much by military aggression as by "subversion and penetration." The secretary of state, however, carefully made two exceptions to these general policies: first, in both Japan

[28]An excellent, succinct context is Arnold A. Offner, *Another Such Victory; President Truman and the Cold War, 1945–1953* (Stanford, 2002), pp. 348–358, 378–379.
[29]*The New York Times,* March 2, 1949, p. 22.

and Korea, the United States had special economic responsibilities; second, if attack occurred west of the defense perimeter (for example, in Korea), the "entire civilized world under the Charter of the United Nations" would aid "people who are determined to protect their independence."[30]

Acheson had issued a fascinating document, acute in its view of Asian nationalism, accurate in this pinpointing of a Sino-Soviet split, precise in its sorting out of Japan and Korea as of paramount importance to American policy, but dead wrong in its assumption that military aggression in the area was not imminent. He had left many options open for policy maneuvers. Within a month these options were severely cut. On January 13 Yokov Malik, the Soviet delegate to the Security Council, walked out of the United Nations after his proposal to unseat Chiang's regime in favor of Mao's lost 6 to 3. The next day the Chinese communists raided American consulate grounds in Peking. The U.S. view toughened. A month later the Sino-Soviet treaty became public. Acheson interpreted the agreement as Mao's selling out the Chinese people to Stalin.[31]

The Sino-Soviet pact, the explosion of the Russian bomb, the divisive arguments over NATO, and the whimpering end of bipartisanship added up to an unpleasant winter for the Truman administration. Peace would not be found soon. Indeed, it was not to be found at all. Americans, who, like other peoples, prefer their wars short and triumphant, wondered why.

One answer had already been suggested on July 30, 1948, as the nation felt the reverberations of the Czech coup and the Berlin blockade. Elizabeth Bentley and Whittaker Chambers, a self-confessed former Communist party member, claimed before the House Un-American Activities Committee that communists had infiltrated the State Department a decade before. Chambers specifically accused Alger Hiss of being a party agent. Hiss had worked in several executive departments after 1933, including the State Department, where in 1944 he helped lay the groundwork for the United Nations. His friends included Dean Acheson and John Foster Dulles. Hiss replied to Chambers with a $75,000 libel suit. Chambers then took federal agents to his

---

[30]Dean Acheson, "Crisis in Asia," *Department of State Bulletin,* XXII (January 23, 1950): 111–117.
[31]Dean Acheson, "United States Policy Toward Asia," *Department of State Bulletin,* XXII (March 27, 1950): 4–8.

Maryland farm and picked from a hollowed-out pumpkin microfilms of State Department documents which Chambers claimed Hiss had passed to him in 1938. The typing irregularities on the microfilms, so the FBI claimed, seemed to match those of one of Hiss's old typewriters. Acheson supported the former Harvard Law School graduate in the strongest terms. But a newly arrived congressman from California, Richard Nixon, determined to pursue the case until Chambers was vindicated. After one hung jury Hiss was finally convicted of perjury on January 21, 1950. Many Americans now believed they understood why the Cold War was not ending quickly and happily.[32]

The American mood by 1949 was not founded on reform but conservativism and consensus. Perhaps nowhere was this more noticeable and explicit than in the writing of American history. In 1948 Charles Beard, the greatest of those historians who between 1910 and 1940 had emphasized and applauded reform, and class and political divisions, in American history, published *President Roosevelt and the Coming of the War*. Charging that FDR had knowingly broken the constitutional boundaries imposed on the executive branch so that he could take the nation into war, Beard warned that this tragedy could be repeated by a future President in any new campaign undertaken by Americans to bring peace to "the whole world." Such a campaign would undermine the Constitution, Beard argued, for the President would possess "limitless authority publicly to misrepresent and secretly to control foreign policy, foreign affairs, and the war power." As he had throughout his life, Beard used James Madison and *The Federalist* as his primary references.

Such dissent from waging the Cold War was not the fashion in 1948 and 1949, and most American historians wanted to be fashionable. Samuel Eliot Morison, Boston Brahmin, rear admiral (appointed by Roosevelt), and president of the American Historical Association, attacked Beard's legacy in an article subtitled, "History Through a Beard." The year after Morison's article appeared, Arthur Schlesinger, Jr., whose intellectual debt to Niebuhr was great, published a primer for the new liberals, which viewed their role not to the left, where Beard had wanted it, but in *The Vital Center*. Schlesinger

---

[32]John Earl Haynes and Harvey Klehr, *Venona: Decoding Soviet Espionage in America* (New Haven, Conn., 1999), pp. 62–72, 97–98, 122–127, 155–173 uses newly released Soviet records to trace Bentley's, Chambers's, and Hiss's relationships with Soviet spying.

attacked American businessmen ("capitalists") who, since they were "incapable of physical combat," developed "a legal system which penalized the use of force and an ethic which glorifies pacifism." War had been useful, particularly when it closed domestic "rifts" between Americans, as in 1917 and 1941.[33] Like the historians, President Truman took pride in his ability to search the past for present policies, but he looked elsewhere as well. "We are on the right track, and we will win," he announced in early 1950, "because God is with us in that enterprise."

The Antichrist nevertheless seemed to be everywhere, even in an age that demanded consensus. On January 14 the Chinese communists attacked the American consulate offices, a week later Hiss was convicted, and on January 31 the White House announced orders to make a hydrogen bomb. "Annihiliation of any life on earth has been brought within the range of technical possibilities," Albert Einstein reported over national television. On February 3 London announced that a British spy ring headed by German-born, British-naturalized Klaus Fuchs had been discovered relaying atomic secrets to Soviet agents. (Russian scientists claimed in the 1990s that Fuchs's information enabled them to explode a bomb two years earlier than they had planned. After serving a prison term, Fuchs died in East Germany in 1988.) At Wheeling, West Virginia, the junior senator from Wisconsin, Joseph McCarthy (Republican), announced on February 9 that he held in his hand proof that the Department of State was riddled with communists. The paper he waved could prove nothing even faintly related to his charges, but no matter. The timing was perfect.

The senator had not previously been known for such ideological zeal, but for an uncommon amount of political savvy. In 1946 he overcame a reputation as one of the worst circuit court judges in Wisconsin history to win the Senate seat from the popular Robert M. LaFollette, Jr. McCarthy accomplished this in part by running on the slogan, "Congress needs a tail-gunner," which he had never been, and by apparently destroying the legal records that reflected unfavorably on his judiciary abilities. In early 1950, with another election fight in Wisconsin only two years away, he searched for an issue. During a conversation with advisers McCarthy first dismissed the

---

[33]Samuel Eliot Morison, "Did Roosevelt Start the War: History Through a Beard," *Atlantic Monthly*, CXLII (August 1948): 91–97; Arthur Schlesinger, Jr., *The Vital Center* (Boston, 1949, 1962), especially pp. 13–14, 173.

St. Lawrence Seaway project as a possibility; then, with the Hiss case in the headlines, he eagerly seized on the communist issue. After the Wheeling speech he became the center of some of the wildest scenes in Senate history. As his fellow legislators tried to pinpoint what he had charged, McCarthy's figures whirled from the 205 communists, at Wheeling, to 57 the following night, 81 on February 20, and when brought before a special Senate committee headed by the highly respected Millard Tydings, Democrat of Maryland, his figures changed again to 10, then to 116, and finally to 1. The one was Owen Lattimore, a specialist on Far Eastern studies at Johns Hopkins University. On Lattimore's conviction, McCarthy said, he would "stand or fall." When pressed for evidence the senator responded in part by reverting to Truman's refusal to allow Congress to examine the loyalty files. The President, McCarthy claimed, was keeping the evidence locked up. The Tydings committee dismissed McCarthy as a fraud and exonerated Lattimore, but the Wisconsin senator had only begun.[34]

Mao, the China Lobby, McCarthy, Stalin, and Truman had learned that forming consensus on the Cold War was not free of complications. A grim President, pressed by domestic critics and the new Soviet bomb, demanded a wide-ranging reevaluation of American Cold War policies. In early 1950 the National Security Council began work on a highly secret document (declassified only a quarter of a century later, and then through an accident) that would soon be known as NSC-68. Truman examined the study in April, and it was ready for implementation when Korea burst into war.

NSC-68 proved to be the American blueprint for waging the Cold War. It began with two assumptions that governed the rest of the document. First, the global balance of power had been "fundamentally altered" since the nineteenth century so that the Americans and Russians now dominated the world: "What is new, what makes the continuing crisis, is the polarization of power which inescapably confronts the slave society with the free." It was us against them. Second, "the Soviet Union, unlike previous aspirants to hegemony, is animated by a new fanatic faith, antithetical to our own, and seeks to impose its absolute authority," initially in "the Soviet Union and

---

[34]Richard N. Rovere, *Senator Joe McCarthy* (New York, 1959), pp. 6, 54, 39–100, 120–122, 130, 140–160; for Fuchs's importance, see *The New York Times,* January 14, 1993, p. A12; and Haynes and Klehn, *Venona,* especially pp. 304–307.

second in the area now under [its] control." Then the crucial sentence: "In the minds of the Soviet leaders, however, achievement of this design requires the dynamic extension of their authority and the ultimate elimination of any effective opposition to their authority. . . . To that end Soviet efforts are now directed toward the domination of the Eurasian land mass."[35]

The two top State Department experts on Russia, George Kennan and Charles Bohlen, fought against using these phrases. They believed that Stalin had no grand design for world conquest, that his attention was focused almost entirely within the Soviet bloc, and that as a conservative he actually feared overextending Russian power. Kennan went further by arguing that NSC-68 should not be drawn up at all, for it could make American policies too rigid, simple, and militaristic. Acheson overruled Kennan and Bohlen.[36] The secretary of state determined to launch a global offensive to reclaim the initiative in the Cold War and to shut up critics at home.

Given Acheson's outlook, the document moved to the inevitable conclusion: the United States "must lead in building a successfully functioning political and economic system in the free world," for "the absence of order among nations is becoming less and less tolerable." To impose "order" around the globe was a rather large task, but the United States was up to it. The key would be having military power that could deter "an attack upon us" while Americans went about arranging the world so that "our free society can flourish." But the administration's confidence in the use of military power went beyond mere deterrence: limited wars could be fought "to compel the acceptance of terms consistent with our objectives." To wage this kind of war, the country had to mobilize its own and its allies' economies for a vast military effort. This military rebuilding was immediately required,

---

[35]"NSC-68. A Report to the National Security Council by the Executive Secretary on United States Objectives and Programs for National Security, April 14, 1950, Washington," pp. 4, 8, 6, 34. (Hereafter cited as "NSC-68.") The NSC-68 document and some of the internal criticism of it may be found at chapter IV documents of the www.mhhe.com/lafeber website.

[36]Joseph M. Siracusa, *Into the Dark House* (Claremont, 1998), especially pp. 74–83 on Kennan and a slightly different view of NSC-68; Paul Y. Hammond, "NSC-68: Prologue to Rearmament." In Warner P. Schilling et al., eds., *Strategy, Politics and Defense Budgets* (New York, 1962), pp. 308–311.

particularly since the Western economies were going to decline "within a period of a few years at most . . . unless more positive governmental programs are developed." The crisis was at hand.

In conclusion, therefore, NSC-68 recommended (1) against negotiations with Russia since conditions were not yet sufficient to force the Kremlin to "change its policies drastically"; (2) development of hydrogen bombs to offset possible Soviet possession of an effective atomic arsenal by 1954; (3) rapid building of conventional military forces to preserve American interests without having to wage atomic war; (4) a large increase in taxes to pay for this new, highly expensive military establishment; (5) mobilization of American society, including a government-created "consensus" on the necessity of "sacrifice" and "unity" by Americans; (6) a strong alliance system directed by the United States; and—as the topper—(7) undermining the "Soviet totalitariat" from within by making "the Russian people our allies in this enterprise." How this was to be done was necessarily vague. No matter. Truman and Acheson were no longer satisfied with containment. They wanted Soviet withdrawal and an absolute victory.[37]

But, as in early 1947 before Truman "scared hell" out of them, the American people were by no means prepared to pay such costs for victory. Republicans and many Democrats demanded lower taxes. Even Secretary of Defense Louis Johnson fought against NSC-68 by arguing that Acheson's policies could bankrupt the country. The secretary of state finally brought the military around to accept the civilian call for larger defense budgets. The Soviet Union meanwhile appeared quiet and contained. The political circumstances threatened to destroy Acheson's hopes that NSC-68 could be used to build global "positions of strength." Only he, the President, and a few others seemed to have a clear idea of what had to be done. NSC-68 was a policy in search of an opportunity. That opportunity arrived on June 25, 1950, when, as Acheson and his aides later agreed, "Korea came along and saved us."[38]

---

[37]"NSC-68," pp. 9, 12, 25–26, 28, 31, 45, 57, 23, 65, 24, 10. See also the various perspectives on this document in Ernest R. May, ed., *American Cold War Strategy: Interpreting NSC-68* (Boston, 1993). Part of the effort to win over the Russian people was to use U.S. religious values. Even Kennan tended to agree with this approach. David Foglesong, "Roots of 'Liberation'. . . . *International History Review*, 21 (March 1999), pp. 68–70.

[38]Princeton Seminar, July 8–9, 1953, Acheson Papers, Truman Library.

A worried British Prime Minister Clement Attlee (seated right) expresses his concern over U.S. policies in Korea to President Truman (seated left), Secretary of State Acheson, and Secretary of Defense Marshall (standing left and right respectively), in December, 1950.
(Abbie Rowe, National Park Service, Courtesy of Harry S. Truman Library)

CHAPTER 5

Korea: The War for Both Asia and Europe (1950–1951)

In June 1950 Korea was a Cold War–wracked country which lacked nearly everything except authoritarian rulers, illiteracy, cholera epidemics, and poverty. For nearly a century it had been a pawn in Far Eastern power plays. In 1905 Japan, after using force to stop a Russian thrust, had established a protectorate over Korea and in 1910 annexed that country. In 1945 Japanese armies, according to Soviet-American agreement, were disarmed north of the 38th parallel by Russia and south of the line by the United States. Lengthy conferences failed to unify the nation, for neither the Soviets nor the Americans wanted to chance the possibility that a unified Korea would move into the opposing camp.

Both superpowers, however, found themselves trapped in a bloody civil conflict, Korean killing Korean, which astonishingly claimed 100,000 lives after 1946 and *before* the formal beginning in June 1950 of what Americans call the "Korean War." New scholarship reveals that the main struggle was not the United States versus the Soviet Union but left-wing Koreans (including both communists and noncommunists) against right-wing Koreans.[1] The United States

---

[1] A superb overview of the recent literature is Allan R. Millett, "The Korean War: A 50-Year Critical Historiography," *The Journal of Strategic Studies*, 24 (March 2001): 188–224. Excellent accounts are Bruce Cumings's prize-winning *The Origins of the Korean War. Volume I* (Princeton, 1981); and the essays by Cumings, Mark Paul, Stephen Pelz, John Merrill, and James I. Matray in *Child of Conflict: The Korean-American Relationship, 1943–1953,* Bruce Cumings, ed. (Seattle, 1983).

worked desperately to keep the rightist groups in power. These groups were led by the venerable Syngman Rhee, who had spent long years of exile in the United States. Meanwhile middle-of-the-road factions moved increasingly to the left, for the leftists espoused an ardent nationalism aimed at uniting the divided nation, while Rhee appeared to be dependent on the United States for survival and was willing to accept elections only in South Korea. Vicious guerrilla war erupted between left and right in 1946. As it continued over the next two years, several crack South Korean military units defected to leftist forces.

Harry Truman never wavered in his determination to keep South Korea in the West's camp, but the growing bloodshed and Rhee's authoritarian methods (including press censorship and mass arrests of political opponents) embarrassed Truman. In 1948 he moved to pull out the remaining U.S. troops and turn the headache of pacifying the area over to the United Nations. Soviet troops also retreated from the North, but they left behind the communist regime of Kim Il Sung and Red Army advisers to whip the North's army into shape. By 1949, with North and South Korea independent nations, the fighting escalated into conventional battles. Many of these were launched by Rhee to show that he was serious about reuniting the country by force. In early 1950 the fighting died down, but the pause lasted only until Kim believed he had amassed the forces to overthrow Rhee and unite Korea under his own control.

When, therefore, Harry Truman decided in late June 1950 to commit U.S. men and machines to war, he was involving Americans not in a conflict against Stalin but in a Korean civil war that had long been waged between Rhee and Kim. Three causes triggered the invasion from the North on June 24, 1950. The first was Kim's belief that Rhee was highly vulnerable. The State Department had even issued public protests against Rhee's crackdown on his own people. In a May 1950 election the South Korean leader lost control of his legislature, despite arrests of leading political opponents before the balloting.

Second, since 1946 Kim had been closely tied to Mao's Chinese communists, indeed too closely for a Korean who was a nationalist as well as a communist. He had gained a measure of independence by moving closer to the Soviet military in 1949. In early 1950 Kim traveled to Moscow several times to ask Stalin for help in conquering the South. After initially refusing, the Russian dictator finally gave the green light and promises of supplies, but he made clear that neither Soviet forces nor prestige would be involved. If Kim's grand plans collapsed, the cautious Stalin was going to be standing clear of the debris. If Kim succeeded, however, he would break free of Mao and unite Korea. It was worth the risk, Stalin could conclude.

Third, Kim's plan fit with a general strategy which Stalin was designing to counter two threats. In mid-May Truman announced that discussions on a Japanese peace treaty would receive high priority. The negotiations would particularly consider Japanese independence and the establishment of American military bases on Japan's soil under long-term agreements. The talks, American officials said, were not to be burdened with Russian representation. For Stalin this announcement opened the unhappy prospect of unity between the two greatest industrial nations in the Pacific, perhaps even the extension of a NATO-like organization to the Asian periphery of the Soviet Union. The Sino-Soviet pact in February had singled out Japan as a potential threat to Asian communism, and this had been followed by the Soviet press accusing Truman of attempting to "draw the Asiatic and Pacific countries into aggressive military blocs, to entangle those countries in the chains of some 'little' Marshall Plan for Asia."[2] If North Korea could unify all of Korea, peacefully or otherwise, the threat of a militarized, Western-oriented Japan would be blunted, perhaps neutralized.

Another threat might well have caused Stalin even more concern. Mao's success had not created but probably encouraged revolutions throughout Asia, particularly in Indochina, the Philippines, and Indonesia. The possibility that some of these revolutions might triumph, perhaps following the pattern set by Mao, could weaken Stalin's two-camp premise and loosen his direction over the world communist bloc. Stalin's view of world matters had become so rigid that he could not accept the nationalist content of these revolts. A short and successful war by a Russian-controlled North Korea could both intimidate Japan and check the expansive aims and reputation of Mao. Thus, as a later study based on formerly secret Russian documents concludes, "It was Soviet weakness that drove Stalin to support the attack on South Korea, not the unrestrained [Russian] expansionism imagined by the authors of NSC-68."[3]

---

[2]*Current Digest of the Soviet Press*, II (April 22, 1950): 19; Nikita Khrushchev, *Khrushchev Remembers*, Strobe Talbott, trans. and ed. (Boston, 1970), pp. 367–370.

[3]Kathryn Weathersby, *Soviet Aims in Korea and the Origins of the Korean War*. Working Paper No. 8, Cold War International History Project (Washington, D.C., 1993), p. 32.

Attending to family business in Independence, Missouri, when the attack occurred, Truman immediately returned to Washington. He and Acheson assumed the invasion was Russian-directed, perhaps the beginning of an extensive Sino-Soviet thrust. Their initial reaction, however, was carefully measured. They ordered General MacArthur in Tokyo to dispatch supplies to the South Korean troops. Then, moving to contain the action, Truman ordered the American Seventh Fleet to sail between China and Formosa, and sent additional assistance to counterrevolutionary forces in the Philippines and Indochina. In a hurriedly called session of the UN Security Council, an American resolution branding the North Koreans as aggressors, demanding a cessation of hostilities, and requesting a withdrawal behind the 38th parallel, passed 9 to 0, with Yugoslavia abstaining. The Soviet Union was not represented, for Yakov Malik continued his boycott to protest the exclusion of Red China.

Two days later, as the military situation worsened, Truman ordered American air and naval units into action. That same day, June 27, 1950, the United Nations passed a resolution recommending that its members aid South Korea in restoring peace. This passed 7 to 1, with Yugoslavia opposing and Egypt and India abstaining. Malik still had not appeared; the rapidity and extent of Truman's reaction had taken the Soviets by surprise. (Truman's June 27th policy statement can be read at this book's www.mhhe.com/lafeber website, at chapter V documents.)

The day after American units had been committed, the President conferred with congressional leaders for the first time to inform them of this action. The only strong objection was voiced by Senator Taft, who approved of Truman's action but disliked sending Americans to war without consulting Congress. Neither then nor later did the President discuss Taft's objection with the full Congress. On June 30 Truman made the final commitment. The South Korean army of 65,000 men had suffered heavy losses in the first week of fighting. The President decided that only American ground units could stop the southward flood. In sending these troops Truman emphasized that the United States aimed only "to restore peace there and . . . restore the border." Supporting air attacks were similarly to be limited to the area around the 38th parallel.

Throughout the first week of the war, the President carefully refrained from publicly linking the Russians to the attack. He hoped

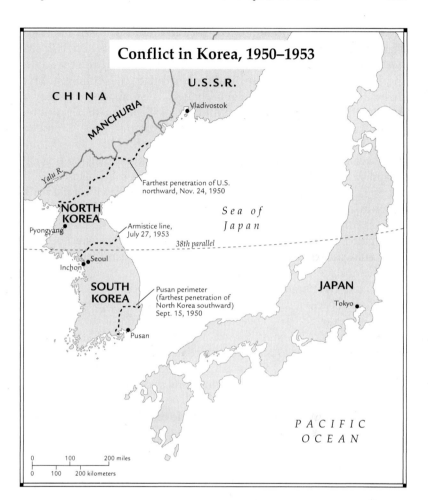

Conflict in Korea, 1950–1953

CHINA

MANCHURIA

U.S.S.R.

Vladivostok

Yalu R.

Farthest penetration of U.S. northward, Nov. 24, 1950

NORTH KOREA

Pyongyang

Armistice line, July 27, 1953

S e a   o f   J a p a n

38th parallel

Seoul

Inchon

SOUTH KOREA

Pusan perimeter (farthest penetration of North Korea southward) Sept. 15, 1950

JAPAN

Tokyo

Pusan

P A C I F I C   O C E A N

0   100   200 miles

0   100   200 kilometers

thereby to enable them to stop the aggression without loss of public face. Truman also used his questionable grasp of history to warn that Korea might be only a diversion. "We must be careful not to cause a general war," he told a top adviser on June 30. "Russia is figuring on an attack in the Black Sea and toward the Persian Gulf. Both are prizes Moscow has wanted since Ivan the Terrible [the sixteenth-century Russian tsar] who is now their hero along with Stalin and Lenin." On June 27 Truman dispatched a note to Moscow assuring Stalin that

American objectives were limited; the President expressed the hope that the Soviets would help in quickly restoring the *status quo ante bellum*. The Soviets initially responded to Truman's overtures by accusing South Korean forces of invading North Korea. Within ten days this view underwent considerable change. The war was a "civil war among the Koreans," Deputy Minister of Foreign Affairs Andrei Gromyko claimed on July 4. Under these circumstances, Gromyko concluded, the Soviet Union could take no action.[4]

Privately in June and publicly during the late summer, the Truman administration became less restrained in defining the Soviet role. "In Korea the Russians presented a check which was drawn on the bank account of collective security," Acheson claimed. "The Russians thought the check would bounce. . . . But to their great surprise, the teller paid it."[5] The terms "collective security" and "UN action" became the catchwords which supposedly explained and justified Truman's decision in late June. Both terms were misleading. The United States had no collective security pact in the Pacific in 1950. As Acheson used the term "collective security," it meant the United States would both define the extent of the "collective" and unilaterally, if necessary, furnish the "security." Nor is there any indication that the President consulted his European or Asian allies before committing American air and naval units on June 27.[6] This was not the first nor would it be the last time the United States would take unilateral action in an explosive situation without consulting its Western European partners.

As for the sudden American concern to bolster the United Nations, this concern had not been apparent when the United States acted unilaterally or with some Western powers to establish the Truman Doctrine, the Rio Pact, the Marshall Plan, and NATO. American actions in Korea were consistent with this history, for the United States used the resolution of June 27 to establish a military command in Korea that took orders not from the United Nations but from Washington. "The entire control of my command and everything I did came from our own Chiefs of Staff," MacArthur later recalled. "Even the reports which were normally made by me to the United Nations were subject to censorship

---

[4]"June 30, 1950—Friday," Subject File, Box 71, Papers of George Elsey, Truman Library; Harry S. Truman, *Memoirs*, II (Garden City, N.Y.; 1955–1956): 341, 346; Max Beloff, *Soviet Policy in the Far East, 1944–1951* (London, 1953), p. 186.
[5]Dean Acheson, *Pattern of Responsibility*, McGeorge Bundy, ed. (Boston, 1952), p. 254.
[6]For example, Truman, *Memoirs*, II: 330–340.

by our State and Defense Departments. I had no direct connection with the United Nations whatsoever."[7] Sixteen nations finally contributed to "UN" forces, but the United States provided 50 percent of the ground forces (with South Korea providing most of the remainder), 86 percent of the naval power, and 93 percent of the air power. In October, during the Truman-MacArthur conference at Wake Island, a dozen American officials prepared plans for the reconstruction of *all* Korea without consulting anyone, not even the United Nations or Syngman Rhee. The United States suffered 142,000 casualties in Korea, not for the sake of "collective security" or the United Nations, but because the executive branch of the government decided that the invasion signaled a direct threat to American interests in both Asia and Europe.

Indeed, although the fighting was limited to Korea, Truman and Acheson used the war as the opportunity to develop new American policies around the globe. Because of these American initiatives, the six months between June and December 1950 rank among the most important of the Cold War era.

Truman and Acheson moved to the offensive globally for two particular reasons: the Korean War gave them an opportunity to shut up their critics at home and to take advantage of new openings abroad. Within the United States Acheson was in trouble because he had happened to be in office when China fell to Mao. He compounded this problem by courageously reaffirming his faith in Alger Hiss while Hiss was convicted for perjury. Of perhaps equal importance, Acheson's impeccable mustache and attire, his sarcastic and brilliant arguments, and his Ivy League background did not endear him to people who disliked so-called eggheads who made the world seem more complicated than did down-home folks like Joseph McCarthy. In his memoirs Acheson termed the onslaught "The Attack of the Primitives," and he viewed some critics as "animals."[8] But his January 1950 remarks implying that Korea was outside the primary area of American military responsibility left him open for those who had been waiting for just such a mistake. Never

---

[7]U.S. Senate, Committee on Foreign Relations and Committee on Armed Services, *Hearings: Military Situation in the Far East* (Washington, 1951), p. 10.

[8]Dean Acheson, *Present at the Creation* (New York, 1969), chapter 39.

again would he make that error. Instead of defining defense perimeters, he would take the offensive and undercut the "primitives."

The offensive would also allow the administration to put plans into motion that had been on drawing boards up to a year or more. These included the NSC-68 blueprint and the revitalization of American military alliances around the world. So began the spectacular summer of 1950 in which Truman and Acheson transformed the United Nations, committed the United States to Formosa and Indochina, began rearming Germany, nearly tripled American defense spending, and—in the climactic act—invaded North Korea to show opponents at home and abroad that the United States was no longer content with mere "containment" but now aimed for liberation.

The secretary of state first went to the United Nations, which had given its support to the American commitment in Korea. It had done so, however, only because the absence of the Soviet delegation had prevented a Russian veto of the UN resolution. The United States could not trust such luck in the next crisis. During the autumn Acheson pushed through the General Assembly a "United for Peace" proposal giving the assembly the right to make recommendations to members for collective security measures, including the use of force, if the use of the veto stopped the Security Council from acting. This resolution transfigured the United Nations. It now rested much less on agreements among the great powers, without which neither the United Nations nor the world peace could be viable. Instead power was thrown into the General Assembly, where Costa Rica had voting power equal to that of the United States or the Soviet Union. Weakening the Russian veto, the United States also weakened its own. Assuming, however, that it could control the General Assembly, the administration had taken a calculated risk. It had, to paraphrase Acheson, issued a blank check on the future. After a decade of increased neutralist feelings among the multiplying nations in Africa and Asia, that check would appear increasingly rubberized by the 1970s.

A second part of the diplomatic offensive involved Formosa. During early 1950 Truman and his military advisers expected Communist China to conquer the island. When North Korea attacked, however, the President placed the American Seventh Fleet between the mainland and Formosa to stop any possible conflict in the area. The next step occurred in August when MacArthur's recommendations that American advisers and assistance be sent to Chiang were accepted by Truman. The early 1950 policy had been reversed. The United States had bedded down with Chiang Kai-shek and had placed itself on his side in the intra-Chinese dispute over Formosa. Mao Ze-dong was shocked at the sudden U.S. move into China's civil war. Truman's protection of Formosa was one reason why Mao was ready to fight the Americans in Korea months later.[9]

A similar turn occurred in American policy toward Indochina. The French had been the dominant colonial power in Southeast Asia since the late nineteenth century. The area's riches made it a formidable prize: Burma, Thailand, and Indochina provided rice for much of Asia. Southeast Asia produced nearly 90 percent of the world's natural rubber, 60 percent of the world's tin, and the bulk of Asia's oil. During World War II Franklin D. Roosevelt became convinced the French could not control this strategic area (particularly after the Japanese had humiliated the white colonial rulers in warfare during 1940–1941). He tried to ease the French out so that Indochina could become a UN trusteeship, with actual control in Chinese and American hands. In the weeks before his death, however, Roosevelt changed his mind. Chiang could no longer be trusted, and the United States had major problems elsewhere. FDR's alternatives were clear: either allow the French to reenter, or part of the area would be controlled by the revolutionary nationalism of the Vietnamese communist leader Ho Chi Minh. Ho's forces made overtures to the United States throughout 1945, but neither Roosevelt nor Truman was in any mood to allow Ho to control such a vital area. First FDR and then Truman allowed the French to reclaim their colonies. By late 1946 France and Ho's forces were locked in war, a war that would not end for Vietnam until nearly thirty years later.

The Soviets also refused to recognize Ho's Republic of Vietnam. By 1948 Ho was turning to Communist China for aid. He had not easily reached this decision, for the Indochinese had feared and fought against their giant neighbor for 1000 years. (In 1946, when he tried to negotiate with the French, Ho quieted his Vietnamese critics by declaring, "It is better to sniff the French dung for a while than eat China's all our lives."[10]) In January 1950 China recognized Ho's government. The Soviets followed within two weeks. After an intensive policy review, the United States fully committed itself to the French

---

[9]This is an important theme in Thomas J. Christensen, "A 'Lost Chance' for What?" *Journal of American–East Asian Relations,* IV (Fall 1995): 250–276.
[10]Jean Lacouture, *Ho Chi Minh* (New York, 1968), p. 119.

cause in early February, four and one-half months before the Korean War began. Financial aid began to flow from Washington to the French in May. But not until after the Korean War began did American personnel become involved. On July 27, in the same announcement giving American support to South Korea, Truman revealed that he was dispatching a military mission to Vietnam.

The commitment had been made, as a State Department pamphlet noted in 1951, because the United States had such vital interests as the "much-needed rice, rubber, and tin" in Southeast Asia. The pamphlet added, "perhaps even more important would be the psychological effect of the fall of Indochina. It would be taken by many as a sign that the force of communism is irresistible and would lead to an attitude of defeatism." Without American aid, "it is doubtful whether [the French] could hold their ground against the Communists." A top State Department official, John Foster Dulles, was more specific at a private dinner of Asian experts in October 1950. Japan, Dulles warned, could move in only one of two directions if it hoped to become prosperous and stable: either toward its traditional markets in China, now communist, and thus deal with Mao's government, or else find markets in Southeast Asia.[11] Because Japan was the key to the entire American position in the Pacific, Southeast Asia had to remain open for Japanese exploitation.

At the same time new American commitments were forged in Asia, Acheson concentrated on Europe, the area he and Truman considered of most importance. The secretary of state moved quickly to tighten the American military alliance with Western Europe, but he did not do so solely for military objectives. Acheson never believed that the military, political, or economic aspects of a problem could, in his words, "be separated in the intellectual equivalent of a cream separator."[12] Acheson knew that intelligence reports interpreted the Korean invasion as a "local affair" which did not apparently foreshadow a communist attack in Europe.[13] He nevertheless believed that future European political problems, particularly those which

---

[11]U.S. Department of State, *Indochina: The War in Southeast Asia* (Washington, 1951), pp. 1–7; Dean Rusk, *The Underlying Principles of Far Eastern Policy* (Washington, 1951), p. 8222; Council of Foreign Relations Study Group Reports, October 23, 1950, Conference Dossiers, Draft of Japanese Peace Treaty, Dulles Papers, Princeton. In a fine analysis of U.S.-French-Indochina relations, 1944–1950, Mark A. Lawrence calls Truman's policy a "tragedy." (*Assuming the Burden* [Berkeley, 2005], p. 286.)

[12]Dean Acheson, *Sketches from Life of Men I Have Known* (New York, 1961), p. 103.

[13]Richard J. Barnet and Marcus Raskin, *After 20 Years* (New York, 1965), p. 29.

threatened American interests, could be solved through the use of military alliances. It was in this context, not in that of an imminent Russian invasion which few expected, that Acheson proposed to horrified British and French officials that Germany be rearmed.

The Joint Chiefs had approved a German rearmament plan as early as April 1950. During long and bitter discussions the State and Defense Departments worked out a package deal in September. Germany would be rearmed and Western European qualms quieted with three devices: more American money to aid Europe with its financial problems, four to six divisions of American troops to assure Europe of American aid in case of future Russian—or German—aggression, and an integrated military command headed by an American general. Agreement was reached just before British Foreign Minister Bevin and French Foreign Minister Robert Schuman sailed from Europe to meet Acheson at the Waldorf-Astoria Hotel in New York City for the September NATO Council meetings.[14]

On September 12 Acheson dropped, as one official called it, "the bomb at the Waldorf." To the unbelieving British and French, he proposed the creation of ten German divisions. Bevin finally went along, believing that the French would never accept the plan anyway.

In December the NATO foreign ministers discussed a compromise: German troops at the regimental level would be incorporated into the NATO establishment but would not constitute more than 20 percent of its strength. Despite strong last-minute Soviet protests, which some officials believed threatened war if Germany were rearmed, the foreign ministers finally accepted in principle German participation, but they could not agree on details. The ministers did approve an integrated force under a supreme commander. President Truman appointed General Dwight D. Eisenhower to this post on December 19.

Truman and Acheson next sent four divisions of American soldiers to Europe in September. This immersed the administration in deep political trouble. During congressional hearings in April 1949, Acheson had assured touchy senators that he expected no large numbers of American troops would be sent to the NATO command. In early 1950, however, NSC-68 secretly proposed rapid and costly rebuilding of Western defenses. The Korean conflict provided the

---

[14]Laurence W. Martin, "The American Decision to Rearm Germany." In Harold Stein, ed., *American Civil-Military Decisions: A Book of Case Studies* (Birmingham, Ala., 1963), pp. 653–659.

opportunity to move ahead. On January 5, 1951, Taft accused Acheson of misleading the American people with his April 1949 statement. Truman hurriedly told the rebellious congressmen that the serious European situation demanded four divisions but no more. After hearings in which Acheson described the troops as serving political as well as military objectives, the Senate on April 4, 1951, approved by a 69 to 21 vote a resolution that endorsed the administration's proposals for NATO, including the integrated command; urged the military utilization of Germany, Italy, and Spain in order to protect Europe; and approved the sending of the four divisions but asked the President to send no more without consulting Congress. Truman and Acheson had successfully used the Korean War to create a new framework for global affairs.

This debate over the commitment to NATO did not occur in an atmosphere of congenial executive-legislative relations. The junior senator from Wisconsin had just launched a new onslaught against "communists," especially those in the State Department. As Cold War passions rose, rational public debate correspondingly sank, and as the Korean War intensified, McCarthyism received a second life. "Today American boys lie dead in the mud of Korean valleys. Some have their hands tied behind their back, their faces shot away by Communist machine guns," the senator wrote the President in mid-July 1950. These horrors occurred, McCarthy charged, because the congressional program for Korea "was sabotaged."[15] He was not clear on the substance of that program, but during the following months he did not hesitate in condemning the man he believed to be the chief saboteur. George Catlett Marshall, former army chief of staff, architect of military victory over Germany and Japan, secretary of state, now secretary of defense, was, McCarthy claimed, part of a "conspiracy so immense and an infamy so black as to dwarf any previous such venture in the history of man." Because Henry Stimson, a man with impeccable credentials as an anticommunist and a conservative, had ranked Marshall only with George Washington, McCarthy felt compelled to have his aides document his accusations with a book on

---

[15]Joseph R. McCarthy to President Truman, July 12, 1950, Office File 20, Truman Papers, Truman Library.

Marshall. The senator himself probably never read the book through; if he did, he found no evidence to substantiate his charges.

Truman also considered Marshall one of the greatest Americans who ever lived, and the President began replying to McCarthy's charges by calling the senator, among other things, the Kremlin's greatest asset. In the ensuing war of slanderous personal abuse, Truman did not stand a chance. McCarthy's use of the "multiple lie" (an accusation so long and containing so many untruths that no one could ever pin down all the lies at one time), and his repeated emphasis on so-called facts and documents in an American society which easily accepts the superficial appearance of truth for the truth itself, made McCarthy invulnerable to Truman's retaliation.[16] Nor had Truman helped his cause by advancing his own conspiratorial view of Soviet activity and creating a noxious loyalty program. In 1949 and 1950 Attorney General J. Howard McGrath crossed the country protesting against professors of dubious political beliefs who infected student minds, and warned that the "many Communists in America" were "everywhere—in factories, offices, butcher stores, on street corners." With such tactics, the President and the attorney general played into the hands of the spreading McCarthyism.

Soon few were free of suspicion. A McCarthyite line properly applied could end any controversy. "It seems that the only argument some persons can present is to holler about Alger Hiss and then refer to Yalta," Senator Tom Connally complained. "Every time something comes up, they get out a Communist and chase him around."[17] In too many cases this sufficed.

Congress demonstrated its patriotism in September by passing the McCarran Internal Security bill. A measure so confused that its supporters could not explain parts of it, the act required communist organizations and their members to register with the attorney general. It did not call such membership a crime, but this was covered by the Smith Act of 1940, which prohibited membership in any group advocating violent overthrow of the government. If the Supreme Court declared the Communist party to be such a group, those registering under the McCarran Act would automatically incriminate themselves. With such conditions, skeptics doubted that registrars would be overwhelmed by

[16]Richard Rovere, *Senator Joe McCarthy* (New York, 1959), pp. 110, 167–170. The book on Marshall is *America's Retreat From Victory: The Story of George Catlett Marshall* [n.p.], 1952.
[17]Tom Connally, *My Name Is Tom Connally* (New York, 1954), pp. 351–352.

people insisting on labeling themselves criminals. Truman gave the bill a ringing veto on September 20, arguing that the act could not work properly and so would result in an even more repressive act in the future. The House took one hour to pass the act over the President's veto. The Senate did so after a handful of liberals led by Hubert Humphrey and Paul Douglas tried to hold back the inevitable with a twenty-two-hour filibuster.

The political facts were plain for all to see, and any doubters were soon convinced by the results of the November congressional election. The Republicans picked up twenty-eight seats in the House. In the Senate they won five more seats, and in three of those contests (John Marshall Butler's victory over McCarthy nemesis Millard Tydings in Maryland, Everett Dirksen's defeat of Senate Majority Leader Scott Lucas in Illinois, and Richard Nixon's triumph over Helen Gahagan Douglas in California), McCarthy happily accepted credit for helping the winners.

The election occurred when American forces were advancing to greater victories in Korea. What uplifting effects some battle losses would have on Republican power and McCarthyism, Democrats did not wish to contemplate. Truman and Acheson, however, believed they had removed that danger—indeed, had cut the ground out from under the "primitives"—by deciding to cross the 38th parallel and liberate North Korea. This decision can be fully understood only when placed with the administration's initiatives in Korea, the United Nations, Formosa, Indochina, and Germany. Together these commitments provided Acheson with new and exceptionally strong "situations of strength" from which he could deal with communists and domestic critics.

The origins of the decision to cross the 38th apparently date from mid-July. MacArthur had finally halted the North Korean advance. Rumors circulated in the State Department that plans were being made to advance beyond the 38th. George Kennan considered such a move highly dangerous. He did not want MacArthur to go to "the gates of Vladivostok [the giant Soviet naval base bordering North Korea]. The Russians would never under any circumstances agree to this." Kennan had intense arguments with Dulles and Assistant Secretary of State for the Far East Dean Rusk, both of whom apparently supported Acheson's hope that the United States could forcefully unite the Koreas.

The decision was finally based upon an evaluation of possible Soviet reaction. By August Stalin had defined Russia out of Korea's "civil war." Moreover, Secretary of Defense Louis Johnson privately told the Senate Foreign Relations Committee that the Soviets would not attack in either Asia or Europe "because Russia was probably aware of the fact that at the present time we had a greater supply of atomic bombs than she had."[18] China was of less concern, partly because Acheson believed Stalin controlled Chinese movements, and also because Mao's army, after the long civil war, did not seem capable of effectively fighting the United States.

On September 1 the directive allowing MacArthur to drive beyond the 38th was completed by the National Security Council. Truman signed it on September 11. Four days later MacArthur made a brilliant landing at Inchon, back of North Korean lines, cut off large numbers of enemy troops, and began a rapid northward drive. With the general's triumph, Truman instructed him on September 27 to move through North Korea if he did not encounter Chinese or Russian resistance and if he were certain of success in the field. Given MacArthur's self-confidence, if not arrogance, that was an invitation for him to drive to the Yalu River bordering China itself. On October 7 the United Nations followed obediently by endorsing Truman's order with a lopsided vote.

All eyes now turned to China. In late August American officials had asked for the open door "within all parts of Korea." At that point Foreign Minister Jou En-lai reminded the world that "Korea is China's neighbor" and asked for negotiations so that the affair could be settled "peacefully." In late September China warned India, which had become China's main link with the Western world, that it would not "sit back with folded hands and let the Americans come to the border." Jou formally told India in a dramatic midnight meeting that China would attack if UN troops moved into North Korea. The United States discounted the threat. MacArthur, never one to pass up the opportunity for the grand if empty gesture, responded

---

[18]Kennan's views are in George Kennan, *Memoirs, 1925–1950* (Boston, 1967), p. 488; Johnson's, in "Memorandum of Executive Meeting of the Foreign Relations Committee," August 23, 1950, Foreign Relations, 1950, Secretary Louis Johnson, Box 101, Papers of H. Alexander Smith, Princeton. The decision to cross the 38th is discussed at length, and with more extensive bibliographical references, in William Stueck, "The March to the Yalu," in Bruce Cumings, ed., *Child of Conflict* (Seattle, 1983), pp. 195–238.

by demanding North Korea's total surrender. The Americans were ignorant of two vital facts: the Chinese were willing to die to keep a U.S. force away from their borders, and they were being egged on to fight by Stalin. A major restraint on China was Kim Il Sung's hatred of the thought of Chinese intervention. China had intervened in Korea, quite uninvited, for centuries. Kim, moreover, had thought his troops could win on their own. But Inchon and the U.S. drive above the 38th forced him to accept Chinese help.[19]

Soviet and Chinese documents opened in the 1990s revealed that Stalin told Chinese leader Mao Ze-dong on October 5–7, 1950, that if China sent in "at least five or six divisions," the United States could be beaten. But if Mao waited, Stalin warned, the Americans and their rebuilt Japanese allies would become all-powerful in Asia. The Soviet dictator had many motives for giving this advice, including the hope that China would drive back the Americans without the need to shed any Russian blood. Of special importance, Stalin wanted China and the United States to sink into a full conventional war with each other—a conflict that would make the already war-ravaged Chinese more dependent on the Soviets, while weakening and distracting the Americans. Stalin assured China that the Soviet Union "stands [behind] its ally."

He apparently meant far behind. For when China moved toward war in mid-October, Stalin suddenly refused to honor his promise to provide at least air support for Mao's exposed troops. The Soviet dictator did send China large amounts of arms and planes, but he wanted no part of any direct Russian confrontation with the Americans. Knowing Stalin's deviousness, Mao first hesitated; he had no desire for war with the United States either. But under Soviet pressure and the relentless U.S. advance toward China, Mao decided to throw the dice. His decision was also shaped by Truman's earlier move in June to use the U.S. Navy to protect Chiang's exiled regime

[19]Shen Zhihua, "Sino-North Korean Conflict and Its Resolution during the Korean War," *Cold War International History Project Bulletin*, 14/15 (Winter 2003–Spring 2004), pp. 11–14. The account in this and the following paragraph follows in most respects that of Allen Whiting, *China Crosses the Yalu* (New York, 1960); *Washington Post*, December 20, 1995, p. A27; Chen Jian, *The Sino-Soviet Alliance and China's Entry into the Korean War*. Cold War International History Project (Washington, D.C., 1991). For Stalin's brinksmanship with, and pressures on, Mao to intervene, see Robert Service, *Stalin, A Biography* (Cambridge, Mass., 2005), pp. 554–557.

on Taiwan, a move a surprised Mao had seen as direct American intervention in China's civil war. Mao nevertheless apparently paced the floor some sixty hours before he decided to fight the world's strongest power. On October 16, 1950, the first Chinese "volunteers" moved across the Yalu into North Korea. (China's public reasons why it went to war against the United States can be found in the chapter V documents at the www.mhhe.com/lafeber website.)

Americans and Chinese were now headed for a conflict that was to poison and misshape their relationship, and indeed the entire global arena, for nearly the next quarter century. But neither would retreat. On September 10, 1950, Acheson commented on national television, "I should think it would be sheer madness for the Chinese to intervene." On October 9 the danger reached a new high when two American F-80 jets strafed a Soviet airfield only a few miles from Vladivostok. After the Soviets protested, the United States apologized. Vexed that the crisis arose, and angered that he had to back down before the Soviets just a month before national elections, Truman canceled a trip to Independence and flew to Wake Island to check on MacArthur. In the heavily censored text of the meeting, the general assured the President, "We are no longer fearful of [Chinese] intervention. We no longer stand hat in hand." China might move 60,000 men across the Yalu, but if these troops tried to move farther south without air cover (and the Chinese had no air force), "there would be the greatest slaughter."[20]

On October 26 the first Chinese prisoner was captured, "so that you began to know, at that point," Acheson later commented, "that something was happening." MacArthur nevertheless continued his drive toward the Yalu. On November 21 advanced elements of American troops peered at Chinese sentries stationed across the river. Three days later MacArthur grandly announced the launching of the end-the-war offensive. On November 26 the Chinese moved across the Yalu in mass, trapping and destroying large numbers of UN troops, including 20,000 Americans and Koreans at the frozen horrors of the Chosin Reservoir. Three weeks later the retreating UN forces again

---

[20]Arnold A. Offner, " 'Another Such Victory': President Truman, American Foreign Policy, and the Cold War," *Diplomatic History*, 23 (Spring 1999): 149–152; U.S. Senate, Committee on Armed Services and Committee on Foreign Relations, *Substance of Statements Made at Wake Island Conference on October 15, 1950*, compiled by General of the Army Omar N. Bradley (Washington, 1951), p. 5.

fought below the 38th, and now it was Jou En-lai who proclaimed his nation's intention of reunifying Korea. "They really fooled us when it comes right down to it, didn't they?" a senator once asked Acheson. "Yes, sir," the secretary of state replied.[21]

On November 15 Acheson, usually so debonair in his public appearances, became nearly incoherent in explaining why the Chinese should not fear American forces on the Yalu. "Everything in the world" was being done to reassure the Chinese that their interests were not jeopardized, he declared, "and I should suppose that there is no country in the world which has been more outstanding in developing the theory of brotherly development of border waters than the United States."[22] Such an American "brotherly development" of the Yalu, of course, was precisely what the Chinese were determined to prevent. From a position on the Yalu, the United States could exert pressure on both Mao's internal and external policies. China's intense hatred for the West, reaching a peak after a century of Western exploitation of the country, and Mao's determination to restore Chinese power in Asia made impossible the acceptance of such an American presence.

The decision to cross the 38th proved exceptionally costly to the United States. Four-fifths of all American casualties in the war occurred after UN forces crossed the parallel. The war froze the United States into a Cold War posture for the next two decades, paralyzing particularly American-Chinese relations. As one observer noted, "700 million potential customers had turned into the apparition of 700 million dangerous adversaries."[23] The United States began to look upon ferocious Chinese armies as a new and more dangerous form of the "Yellow Peril" that had long haunted Americans. The "Peril" became more dangerous in the 1950s and 1960s precisely because so few Americans knew anything about it.

Washington officials were frightened. But the aggression must be crushed, the President declared, or "we can expect it to spread

---

[21]*Military Situation in the Far East,* pp. 1832–1835. Much in this section depends on two superb accounts: Thomas J. Christensen: "A 'Lost Chance' for What?" *Journal of American–East Asian Relations,* IV (Fall 1995): 249–278; and the best analysis of China's policies, Chen Jian, *Mao's China and the Cold War* (Chapel Hill, 2001), pp. 64–71, especially on the Mao-Stalin relationship.

[22]*Department of State Bulletin,* XXIII (November 27, 1950): 855.

[23]A. T. Steele, *The American People and China* (New York, 1966), p. 60.

throughout Asia and Europe to this hemisphere." Truman's views on the need to continue the war were shaped by yet another belief—a belief voiced especially by Acheson and his advisers who had written NSC-68. Acheson and now even the President had come to realize that the war with China allowed the passage of huge defense budgets through Congress. It was the opportunity to put the United States, finally, on full military footing to fight the larger Cold War. Truman, as one record revealed, told a secret meeting of the NSC in late November 1950, "If the Chinese threat evaporates, the President doubts that you could go ahead with a $45 billion program." (The prewar military "program" had been under $14 billion.) Thus domestic politics provided a key, if not *the* key, to understanding Truman's historic decisions to move above the 38th and then fight a war with China. For those decisions were shaped by the President's determination (1) to quiet Republican critics who wanted "Asia first," (2) to silence Senator Joseph McCarthy's screeching attacks, (3) to push through the massive defense budgets envisioned by NSC-68—budgets that ushered in the high military spending of at least the next fifty-five years, and (4) to unite Korea with force by liberating the communist North.[24]

Truman's public response, however, seemed more cautious at first. He countermanded MacArthur's order to bomb Chinese troops and supplies in Manchuria. Then, in a news conference of November 30, Truman showed signs of losing this restraint. He intimated that the United States would use all its power to contain the Chinese. He explicitly did not exclude using atomic bombs. This remark brought British Prime Minster Attlee flying to the United States on December 4.

Attlee was not without responsibility for the crisis; his government had participated in the decision to send UN troops to the Yalu. He now worried that in the newly expanded war Truman would not be able to control the military and particularly wondered at the spectacle of Truman's flying 5000 miles to Wake Island to meet MacArthur, who had flown 1900. ("I thought it a curious relationship between a Government and a general," Attlee commented later.) The

---

[24]U.S. Government, *Public Papers of the Presidents of the United States . . . Truman . . . 1950* (Washington, 1965), pp. 724–727; the interpretation linking the war to the new defense budgets is based on Christensen, "A 'Lost Chance' for What?" pp. 268–278, and the work of the late Professor Frank Kofsky.

prime minister received Truman's assurances that the United States was not planning to use the bomb. The two men then undertook a full, candid, and most revealing evaluation of the Asian tinderbox.

Both agreed that a general war must be averted and that the UN forces should not evacuate Korea unless forced out militarily. Then basic differences emerged. Attlee argued that China's admission to the United Nations could bring it into regular consultations leading to a cease-fire. Acheson doubted that in their present advantageous military position the Chinese would want a cease-fire; if they did and negotiations resulted, Mao would next demand a UN seat and concessions on Formosa. The United States had refused to discuss these two items before the intervention, and Acheson now was in no mood to reward aggressors. Attlee countered that a cease-fire would make explicit the divisions between China and Russia: "I want them [the Chinese] to become a counterpoise to Russia in the Far East," Attlee argued. If "we just treat the Chinese as Soviet satellites, we are playing the Russian game."

But Truman now hardened his earlier view of the Chinese. They were "Russian satellites," and if they succeeded in Korea "it would be Indo-China, then Hong Kong, then Malaya." Acheson interposed that he did not think it mattered whether China was a satellite or not, for it would act like Russia anyway. He believed the invasion into Korea "had design," and, like Truman, he adopted the domino theory to warn that any compromise with the Chinese would have a "serious" effect on the Japanese and Philippine Islands. Acheson recalled a "saying among State Department officials that with communistic regimes you could not bank good will; they balanced their books every night."

Although the military situation steadily eroded, not even the other nations in the Western Hemisphere offered much assistance. The Latin Americans dutifully voted with the United States on resolutions in the United Nations and the Organization of American States, but in the early spring of 1951, when Truman personally appealed to Latin American foreign ministers to "establish the principle of sharing our burdens fairly," only Colombia responded with troops. Several other nations sent matériel, but Latin America as a whole failed to see the relevance of Korea to its own economic deprivation and political instability.

The United States would have to depend primarily upon its own resources in defending what Niebuhr had called "our farflung lines." In December and January the President requested emergency powers to expedite war mobilization. Closely following the guidelines suggested in NSC-68, he submitted a $50-billion defense budget; this contrasted with the $13.5-billion budget of six months before. The administration doubled the number of air groups to ninety-five and obtained new bases in Morocco, Libya, and Saudi Arabia. Army personnel increased 50 percent to 3.5 million men.

In Asia the administration focused on tightening American military ties with Japan through a new peace treaty. John Foster Dulles assumed control of the negotiations and almost single-handedly drove the treaty through to a successful conclusion in September 1951. It was a bravura performance. The pact restored Japanese sovereignty over the home islands but not over the Ryukyus (which included the large American base at Okinawa). In an accompanying security agreement Japan allowed the stationing of American troops and planes on its soil but not those of any third power. Dulles simply excluded Russia from the early, decisive negotiations. When the Soviets were allowed to participate, Dulles interpreted their proposal as an attempt to dominate the area around Japan. As one participant recalled, Dulles demonstrated the effect of the Soviet plan on a map, "took this map dramatically and held it up like this . . . and then threw it on the floor with the utmost contempt. And that made a tremendous impression."[25]

Dulles also ran roughshod over American allies and neutrals in Asia who demanded reparations from Japan for its occupation during World War II. He warned that the United States would brook no "Carthaginian peace" which would "lead to bitter animosity and in the end drive Japan into the orbit of Russia." Some American allies wanted reparations to weaken Japanese potential for producing weapons. Dulles solved this problem by negotiating a series of mutual defense treaties to ensure the Philippines, Australia, and New Zealand against both reemerging Asian giants, Japan and China. Thirty months before, Acheson had assured the Senate that other than NATO the administration contemplated no further regional pacts. On September 1, 1951, the United States nevertheless signed with Australia and New Zealand the so-called ANZUS Treaty, pledging the security of those two nations.

---

[25]Interview with C. Stanton Babcock, in Dulles Oral History Project, Dulles Papers, Princeton.

Because Australia and New Zealand belonged to the British Commonwealth, Great Britain was conspicuous by its absence from ANZUS. As early as March 1914 Winston Churchill, then First Lord of the Admiralty, predicted that with British resources increasingly devoted to Europe, the "white men" in the Pacific would soon have to seek American protection. Thirty-seven years later the British were not so understanding. When Great Britain protested that the United States had not adequately consulted it on the Japanese or ANZUS pacts, Dulles granted the point, but countered that if Britain came in, the French and Dutch would also and thereby transform ANZUS in the eyes of suspicious Asians into a colonial alliance. This argument effectively reduced British influence in the Pacific. "All roads in the Commonwealth lead to Washington," a Canadian official observed.[26] The United States was almost single-handedly preparing Asia for the containment of China.

These negotiations determined the geographic extent of the American commitment in the Pacific. During the spring of 1951, with drama and flourishes seldom seen in American history, the military extent of that commitment was decided. In late January UN forces opened a successful drive back to the 38th parallel. As the battle stalemated along the former boundary line, State Department and Pentagon officials cautiously explored the possibility of negotiations with the Chinese on March 20. Three days later General MacArthur issued a personal statement urging that the Red military commanders "confer in the field" with him on surrender; if he could attack China's "coastal areas and interior bases," the general insisted, that nation would be "doomed" to military collapse. MacArthur had again undercut his superiors in Washington.

As early as July 1950 he had shown reluctance to accept Truman's decision that Chiang Kai-shek should be contained on Formosa rather than unleashed on the mainland or allowed to ship troops to Korea. A month later MacArthur sent a message to the annual U.S. convention of the Veterans of Foreign Wars, which the President viewed as an

[26]Interview with General Matthew Ridgway, in Dulles Oral History Project, Dulles Papers, Princeton; Churchill and the Canadian official are quoted in Geoffrey Barraclough, *An Introduction to Contemporary History* (New York, 1964), p. 67. For the U.S.-Australian disagreement over ANZUS, and Australia's road into the Cold War, note Joseph M. Siracusa, *Into the Dark House* (Claremont, 1998), chapter 5.

attack upon his policy toward Chiang. Truman angrily demanded that this message be recalled, and MacArthur complied although it had already been published. The Wake Island conference muted these differences, but the published minutes are embarrassing in their revelation of MacArthur's incredible condescension and Truman's tittering insecurity. Once the President was back in Washington, this insecurity disappeared. After MacArthur again recommended a naval blockade of China, air attacks to level Chinese military and industrial installations, and the use of 30,000 Formosan troops in Korea, Truman patiently explained on January 13 "the political factors" involved in the "world-wide threat" of the Soviet Union which made containment of the Korean War necessary.[27] When MacArthur issued his ultimatum of March 23, Truman's patience, never inexhaustible, evaporated.

Only the method and timing of relieving the general remained to be decided. On April 5, 1951, Joe Martin, the leading Republican in the House, read a letter from MacArthur which charged that "here we fight Europe's war with arms while the diplomats there still fight it with words." "We must win," the letter emphasized. "There is no substitute for victory." The Joint Chiefs of Staff agreed with Truman that MacArthur would have to be relieved immediately. Reports from the field indicated that the general was losing the confidence of his men and had already lost confidence in himself.[28] On April 11 the President recalled MacArthur.

Truman knew the political dynamite in the decision. Less than two weeks earlier he had agreed with top advisers that an all-out speaking campaign would have to be undertaken by cabinet-level officers because the administration's "'story' was not reaching the American public."[29] The American people preferred quick victory to containment. This preference was dramatically demonstrated when the general returned home to the greatest popular reception in American history. Senator McCarthy expressed the feelings toward Truman of not a few Americans when, with characteristic restraint,

[27]*Military Situation in the Far East*, pp. 503–504.

[28]Cabell Philipps, *The Truman Presidency* (New York, 1966), pp. 337–347.

[29]"Memorandum for the President," from Joseph Short, Secretary to the President, April 2, 1951, Office File 386, Truman Papers, Truman Library. A superb analysis stressing the domestic politics–foreign policy relationship is Roger Dingman, "Politics in Peril: The Truman-MacArthur Controversy," a paper given at the Georgetown University conference, *The Korean War: An Assessment of the Historical Record*, July 24–25, 1995.

he told a press conference, "The son of a bitch ought to be impeached." Congress warmly received MacArthur's speech before a joint session, then in April and May settled down to investigate the case of the President versus the general.

In a battle of MacArthur versus Truman, the long-range issues tended to be overshadowed by the personalities involved. In MacArthur's case this was not an advantage. Having last set foot in the United States fourteen years before, the general seemed unable or unwilling to grasp the political and social as well as the diplomatic views of his country. Although he had repeatedly advocated policies that contained the most somber worldwide ramifications, he now admitted having only a "superficial knowledge" of NATO and European affairs.

His basic message was curiously close to Truman's and Niebuhr's in 1948: because communism posed a threat to all civilization, "you have got to hold every place." Like Acheson, he insisted on not putting military power and politics into the intellectual equivalent of a cream separator. In time of war, however, MacArthur demanded the reversal of Acheson's priority: once involved in war, the general argued, the military commander must be supreme over all military and political affairs in his theater, "or otherwise you will have the system that the Soviets once employed of the political commissar, who would run the military as well as the politics of the country." Such a remark cut across the grain of traditional American policies of subordinating military to civilian officials even if the nation was involved in total war. When the embattled general heard the suggestion of Assistant Secretary of State Dean Rusk that war in Korea must not become a "general conflagration," MacArthur branded it "the concept of appeasement, the concept that when you use force you can limit the force." Americans who had a dim view of nuclear war did not care for such words.

The general expressed contempt for the Chinese communists. "Never, in our day, will atomic weapons be turned out of China. They cannot turn out the ordinary weapons." Nor was there a threat of Soviet intervention. Time, however, was short. If, as MacArthur once remarked, Europe was a "dying system," and the Pacific would "determine the course of history in the next ten thousand years," victory must be won immediately. The "dreadful slaughter" had to end, MacArthur pleaded; American blood as well as dust is settling in Korea, and the "blood, to some extent" rests "on me." But now, he concluded emotionally, "There is no policy—there is nothing, I tell you, no plan, or anything."[30]

The administration had a plan, and Acheson outlined it in his testimony after MacArthur finished. Korea must be viewed as part of a "collective security system," Acheson argued. When so viewed, two things readily became apparent. First, all-out war in Korea would suck in Russian force to aid Stalin's "largest and most important" satellite. If Russia did intervene, there could be "explosive possibilities not only for the Far East, but for the rest of the world as well." Unlike MacArthur, Acheson insisted on keeping the European picture uppermost in dealing with Korea. Second, if Europe and the prevention of Russian entry in force were the main objectives, American forces were not engaged in a "dreadful slaughter" or, as Acheson remarked, "a pointless and inconclusive struggle," but had "scored a powerful victory" by dealing "Communist imperialist aims in Asia a severe setback" in preventing the armed conquest of all Korea.[31]

U.S. policies in the Pacific between 1949 and 1952 were not mousy. Indeed, as Dean Rusk recalled years later, "Our general attitude was . . . that it was important for the United States to have control of every wave in the Pacific Ocean."[32] The only argument was over the best strategy to control those waves, as well as the waves in the Atlantic. MacArthur lost the argument. He lost it so decisively, moreover, that, while negotiations to conclude a stalemated war fitfully began in Korea during the summer of 1951, Acheson accelerated the military buildup of Europe.

[30] *Military Situation in the Far East,* pp. 39, 45, 54, 66–68, 78, 81, 83, 86–87.
[31] *Military Situation in the Far East,* pp. 924–926.
[32] Ronald L. McGlothlen, *Controlling the Waves* (New York, 1993), p. 21.

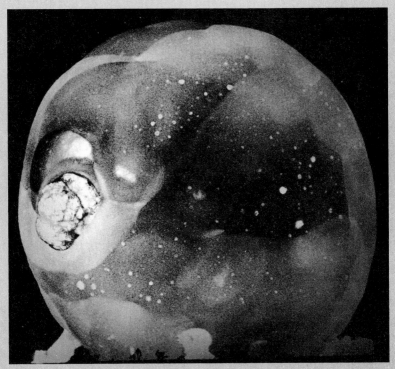

A new world. The fireball of the first Hydrogen (or "Super,") Bomb test 1952.
(© Harold & Esther Edgerton Foundation, 2008, courtesy of Palm Press, Inc.)

CHAPTER 6

New Issues, New Faces (1951–1953)

By the time a de facto armistice was agreed upon in July 1953, the Korean War had made as much impact upon American aid to Europe as to Asia. The agreement in principle on German rearmament and the sending of additional American troops to Europe (where they would stay for the next half-century and more) were major steps in this direction. American strategy in NATO during 1951 and 1952 rested first upon the "trip-wire" theory that any Soviet attack upon a NATO command containing American troops would automatically trip a nuclear attack from the United States. One European official stated this theory in elementary terms; when asked how many American soldiers must be stationed in Europe to protect the West, he replied one would be enough if that one was shot during the first wave of an attack. To further its nuclear capability, the United States conducted its first successful thermonuclear test at Eniwetok Island in the Pacific during March 1951. In mid-June 1952 the keel went down for the *USS Nautilus*, the first submarine to be powered by atomic energy. Truman proposed a $60-billion defense budget for 1952, 20 percent above that of 1951. If the wire was tripped, the United States was preparing to respond massively.

NATO strategy also rested upon the hope that the war could be contained east of the Elbe River. For this, a large conventional force would be needed; Eisenhower wanted thirty-five to forty ready divisions and ninety-six more that could be brought up within a month. The present 300 aircraft would have to multiply ten times. These grandiose plans, Truman observed, "tripped over one hard, tough fact. This fact was the poverty of western Europe."[1] Three years after the launching of the Marshall Plan, the recipient nations were sinking back into an economic morass. Only Germany gained ground; it used the new focus on military power to rearm and end the Allied occupation of its territory.[2]

In 1951 Congress passed the Mutual Security Act (MSA), which coalesced the economic, military, and technical assistance programs. This allowed an injection of a stronger military emphasis than ever before. As Acheson remarked, the "whole impact" of MSA would be "to carry out the rearmament program," for, he somehow concluded, the Marshall Plan's "original task has been accomplished."[3]

NATO strategy, as well as Cold War politics, rested also on another approach: that the basis of the alliance be expanded as far as possible. In May 1951 the United States proposed adding Greece and Turkey to the military pact to prevent those two nations from entertaining ideas of becoming politically neutral. Yugoslavia, although not wishing to enter NATO, began requesting military assistance in addition to the economic aid that Tito had already obtained from the West. In September 1951 the Western Foreign Ministers agreed to release Italy from restrictions imposed in 1945 upon its military. Most notable was the rapidly evolving American attitude toward Franco's dictatorship in Spain.

Kennan had observed in 1947 that the Truman Doctrine implied a new view of Franco. By 1949 a congressional–Defense Department axis had formed to force the issue. Conservative senators Pat McCarran, Owen Brewster, and Robert Taft urged the administration, in Taft's words, to "shake loose from its communist-front philosophy" by working with Franco. One congressman, among the many who junketed to Madrid in 1949 and 1950, publicly called the Spanish dictator a "very, very lovely and loveable character." In March 1950 McCarran succeeded in securing a $62.5-million loan for Franco. For ideological reasons, Truman despised this and every other pro-Spanish move, but after June 1950 the logic of his own military policy forced him to recognize the Franco government late that year. The following summer the

---

[1]Harry S. Truman, *Memoirs*, II (Garden City, N.Y., 1955–1956): 258.
[2]Charles Wolf, Jr., *Foreign Aid: Theory and Practice in Southern Asia* (Princeton, 1960), pp. 115–116.
[3]Wolf, *Foreign Aid*, pp. 114–116.

administration began negotiations to obtain Spanish military bases. Franco drove a hard bargain. The United States granted economic assistance and a quarter-billion dollars of military aid in return for the right to construct and use military bases which would remain under Spanish sovereignty.[4]

The Spanish base treaty augmented American military power in Europe but contributed less to Acheson's political objectives; most of Western Europe too vividly remembered Franco's cooperation with Hitler. The political aims rested instead on the success of the Pleven Plan and German rearmament. To the accompaniment of shrill Soviet protests, the Western Foreign Ministers worked on these issues throughout 1951, then gathered at Lisbon in February 1952 to hammer out final ground rules for the new Western alliance. Agreement did not come easily. A new U.S.-West German alliance began to appear. "More often than not, I found myself agreeing with . . . Adenauer," Acheson recalled, "and Eden [agreed] with Schuman."[5]

The French and British divided, however, on the critical issue. The Pleven Plan had been transformed in earlier negotiations into a European Defense Community (EDC) comprising France, Germany, and the Benelux. The EDC would operate under separate European control but be linked with NATO so that Germany could directly participate in NATO defenses. Schuman and the Netherlands officials now insisted that Great Britain formally join the EDC. They did not want to be in the EDC virtually alone with German power. They also refused to consider the American and British presence in NATO sufficient to prevent the possibility of German domination of the new grouping. After all, Americans were known for suddenly picking up and leaving Europe, as they had in 1919–1920. The newly elected British government of Winston Churchill refused to commit itself so solidly to European affairs. Too many Anglo-American ties would be severed. Any British integration into European affairs would have to come "in doses rather than at a gulp," Eden later remarked.[6] Acheson could not quiet French fear. Several months after the Lisbon conference, President Vincent Auriol of France told the secretary of state "with considerable passion," as Acheson later

---

[4]Theodore J. Lowi, "Bases in Spain." In Harold Stein, ed., *American Civil-Military Decisions: A Book of Case Studies* (Birmingham, Ala., 1963), pp. 667–697.
[5]Dean Acheson, *Sketches from Life of Men I Have Known* (New York, 1961), p. 47.
[6]Anthony Eden, *Full Circle: The Memoirs of Anthony Eden* (New York, 1960), p. 34.

recalled, "that our policy toward Germany was a great mistake. He knew Germany; he reviewed German history since Bismarck. We were wrong in thinking that the greater danger came from Russia. It came from Germany."[7]

Acheson finally obtained Schuman's consent to allow 500,000 Germans in twelve divisions to enter the EDC, but the French exacted a price. Adenauer agreed to allow Western forces to remain in Germany for internal security as well as military purposes, swore to deal with Russia only through the Allies, and allowed the West to continue governing Berlin. Acheson opened wide the American and German pocketbooks by promising to help France meet its defense expenditures in Vietnam and Europe. For this, Acheson even won an agreement to double NATO manpower to fifty divisions (including twelve French) by the end of 1952.

There would never be fifty NATO divisions; there would never be an EDC. In the long run the Lisbon conference produced much ill will. Acheson's troubles began immediately after the conference adjourned. On March 10 the Soviets proposed to the three Western powers that discussions be held on a peace treaty which would declare Germany united and independent. Russia further suggested allowing Germany to have a national army with ties to neither the East nor the West, withdrawing all foreign troops, and admitting Germany to the United Nations. This breathtaking proposal came out of cold Russian fear of a rearmed, Western-oriented Germany. Acheson refused to follow up on the proposal. The West had to be kept together. This meant Germany had to be rearmed under Western guidance. The "peace offensive" out of Moscow was a "'golden apple' tactic," Acheson announced in April. The Soviets resembled the Goddess of Discord who, angered that she had not been invited to a wedding party, threw a golden apple over the fence "hoping to cause a ruckus among the guests and break up the party." The wall would be built higher to make such apple throwing more difficult, and so on May 26 and 27 Acheson, Eden, and Schuman signed the agreement ending the occupation of Germany. They then initialed the EDC treaty. Now the EDC had only to pass the various parliaments before coming into effect. In the 1990s, newly released Soviet records indicated that Acheson was correct. Stalin wanted no deal because he knew the West would demand a united, democratic

[7]Acheson, *Sketches from Life,* p. 53.

Germany, and then he would lose East Germany. But he was frightened of a rearmed West Germany and hoped to stall that nightmare.[8]

Even as Acheson threaded his way through the EDC negotiations of 1951 and 1952, Americans vigorously debated new policies which, by the middle-1950s, would set their foreign policies on new paths. In short, the debates of 1951–1952 thrashed out the premises which governed American foreign policy for at least the next decade and a half. At the simplest level, the arguments pivoted on the question of whether Asia should enjoy equal priority with Europe in American policy. Overall the debate was far more complex. It became a prime example of how oversimplified (often unquestioned) premises of one historical era could, almost inevitably, develop into apparently unrelated but far-reaching policies affecting life and death in a later era. The arguments can now be found in Senator Robert Taft's *A Foreign Policy for Americans,* Hans Morgenthau's *In Defense of the National Interest,* Reinhold Niebuhr's *The Irony of American History,* and, finally, the 1952 election campaign.[9]

Taft's and Morgenthau's books chalked in the boundaries of the debate. Like the majority of Americans, both men agreed on the need to contain Russia. Morgenthau was a distinguished professor of international relations at the University of Chicago, and Taft was running for the 1952 Republican presidential nomination, but despite their different vantage points, the two men surprisingly agreed on a number of issues. Both considered the United Nations, particularly after the passage of the U.S.-sponsored "United for Peace" resolution, to be a useless fifth wheel in world diplomacy. More fundamentally, both feared that Truman and Acheson too easily trotted out American military power. Morgenthau attacked Acheson for harping about "positions of strength" when "the supreme test of statesmanship," to Morgenthau's mind, was not building power blocs but discovering

---

[8]Dean Acheson, "Progress Toward International Peace and Unity," *Department of State Bulletin,* XXVI (April 28, 1952): 648; Ruud Van Dijk, *The 1952 Stalin Note Debate* . . . Cold War International History Project Working Paper #14 (Washington, D.C., 1996), pp. 16, 35.

[9]Robert A. Taft, *A Foreign Policy for Americans* (New York, 1951); Hans J. Morgenthau, *In Defense of the National Interest* (New York, 1951); Reinhold Niebuhr, *The Irony of American History* (New York, 1952).

areas in which tensions could be reduced through negotiations. Morgenthau did not believe Acheson could stand up to that test.

On four basic points, however, the senator and the professor profoundly differed. Taft tended to see the Cold War as a crusade against the Antichrist, and he bolstered this view by emphasizing the purity of American intentions. Morgenthau realized the unique virtues of American democracy, but he held no brief for the spotlessness of American morality or ideology. After all, he was not running for office. Nor in this particular did he share Taft's view of history, for Morgenthau believed that the new technological and political problems which appeared in 1945 marked "the definite and radical end of the . . . conditions under which the Western world lived for centuries." The professor drily observed that Russia's use of the "religious order" of communism to remake the world in its image was not unlike those Americans who "heed the noble words of Jefferson, Wilson, and Franklin D. Roosevelt, and . . . set out on a crusade to make the world safe for true democracy."

Taft would not entirely discard military power. He advocated the development of air and naval units but not the infantry. He believed that this policy would save manpower, cut military expenditures, and, in all, be politically attractive. Taft could also in this way slash the executive power to involve the United States in European problems through the commitment of American troops. Morgenthau would have none of this. He deplored the common tendency of both Taft and the Truman Doctrine to lay out "a world-embracing moral principle" that committed American power, of whatever nature, to such broad, undefined, and dangerous limits. The United States must realize, Morgenthau admonished, that military threats to its interests in Europe called for different solutions than did dangers posed by "genuine revolutions" in Asia. American policymakers must follow not the dictates of "moral principle" but the classic formula of spheres of interest. The United States could no longer wish for a wholly open world.

The professor considered the spheres-of-interest approach feasible because the Soviet threat, he believed (much as had journalist Walter Lippmann in 1947 [see p. 71]), was fueled not by communist ideology but by traditional Russian national power. Unlike the religious passion of communism, Russian national power would have to compromise because it was subject to the same restraints and limitations as American power. Taft, on the other hand, viewed communist ideology as the principal threat. He cared little whether it was attached to Soviet national power, except that by being so attached, its power became immeasurably increased. The senator, therefore, refused to settle for the spheres-of-interest approach, for this would not neutralize communist ideology; instead, he advocated fighting communism everywhere, including inside the bureaucracy of the State Department.

These differences on the roles of morality, the place of power, and the nature of the Soviet threat inevitably led Taft and Morgenthau to opposite conclusions on the climactic question of Asia. The Ohio senator deplored past American policy which, as he saw it, treated Western Europe like one big happy family while allowing Asia to go communist almost by default. Running close to the MacArthur line, Taft sought "only . . . the same policy in the Far East as in Europe." That is, he wanted the use of air and naval power as a deterrent in both Europe and Asia. In case of a conflict, his policy lessened the chances for limiting the war short of nuclear exchange. He left unanswered the question of how this naval and air power could deflect the considerably more subtle threat of communist ideology.

Morgenthau necessarily reversed Taft's priorities. Europe, particularly Germany, he argued, comprised such a technological, industrial, and cultural powerhouse that "he who controls all of Europe is well on his way toward controlling the whole world." Europe could not be left to chance, possibly to communism. A further point necessarily shaped American policy: the United States could understand and cooperate with Europe because of common backgrounds and values. Asia, however, was wholly different. Unlike the "phony" revolutions in Eastern Europe, those in Asia were "genuine." This meant that Russian imperialism and "genuine" revolution were by no means the same thing. To confuse the two could lead to an American involvement in Asia which would be calamitous. Asian revolutions, Morgenthau observed, were generated not by communism but, ironically, by the political, technological, and moral revolutions which the West transferred to the Orient. Once Asia mastered this technology, a "shift in the distribution of power" would result which, "in its importance for the history of the world, transcends all other factors. It might well mean the end of the bipolarity centered in Washington and Moscow." Given their different race and culture, Americans could not hope to control this momentous change, but only adjust to it.

In 1951 and 1952 Niebuhr neatly combined Taft's emphasis on ideology with Morgenthau's conclusions. Partly because of such feats, one observer called Niebuhr's views "part of the canon of a new generation of American liberals and the spiritual guide of those who are now revisiting conservatism."[10] More significant than his appeal to various shades of the political spectrum was Niebuhr's change of tone. Something had happened to the earlier advocate of a quickly revitalized Germany. Now he acknowledged that the rearming of Germany "was too precipitate and too indifferent" to European feelings. His loud cry of 1948 to guard the far-flung battle lines became a quiet listing of the reasons why American policymakers must not become overly committed to battle lines in the newly emerging world, especially Asia. Niebuhr now lectured the wielders of the titanic American power that they too were subject to the sins of all humankind.

The Irony of American History argued that because of pride, presumed innocence, and lack of restraint, American power was walking the rim of the abyss. American idealism, which had been instrumental in developing immense national power, now ironically blinded the United States to the dangers of overusing that power. "American power in the service of American idealism," Niebuhr approvingly quoted a European official as saying, "could create a situation in which we would be too impotent to correct you when you are wrong and you would be too idealistic to correct yourself."

To Niebuhr, communism remained as evil as it had been in 1947 and 1948, but the United States had become the victim of many of the same inconsistencies and delusions about human nature and the so-called virtues of science that had corrupted communism. In the past, Americans had been protected from themselves by the Constitution, whose authors knew more about human nature and the limitations of science than their twentieth-century descendants. Niebuhr cited John Adams: "Power always thinks it has a great soul and vast views beyond the comprehension of the weak; and that it is doing God's service when it is violating all His Laws." Niebuhr extended Adams's observation by adding that Americans believed they could solve problems simply "by the expansion of our economy." The frontier, Niebuhr intimated, had closed; expanding production "has

---

[10]Morton White in *New Republic,* May 5, 1952, pp. 18–19.

created moral illusions about the ease with which the adjustment of interest to interest can be made in human society."

In the penultimate section of *Irony*, Niebuhr applied his views to the Asian situation. The United States, he echoed Morgenthau, had little in common with the Orient. Any attempt to use the present American Cold War weaponry to save Asia from communism would be, as he had mentioned earlier in the book, like the "spears of the knights when gunpowder challenged their reign." In phrases tinged with condescension, Niebuhr warned that Asia wanted Western technology but refused to accept the West's view of human nature, society, or history. He advised working with Japan and the Philippines to contain Asian communism by means of a militarized Pacific "island littoral." So contained, communism would repeat the history of Islam during the Middle Ages and be destroyed "not so much by its foes as by its own inner corruptions." But if it hoped to witness that collapse, the United States would have to remedy its own "inner corruptions" first.

Niebuhr's fear of extending the Cold War to the mainland of Asia partly explained the changed tone in his writings. Above all, Niebuhr distrusted the new Republican administration of Dwight D. Eisenhower. Niebuhr feared Eisenhower's Asian policies, for "American conservatives" wrongly viewed communist gains in that area as resulting simply from State Department spies

> and as capable of rectification by rigorous military action on our part. This "illusion of American omnipotence," . . . is a natural mistake of a commercial community which knows that American hegemony is based upon our technical-economic power but does not understand the vast complexities of ethnic loyalties, of social forces in a decaying agrarian world, of the resentments which a mere display of military power creates among those who are not committed to us.[11]

Niebuhr's abhorrence of "the budding American imperium" did not noticeably brake the Eisenhower steamroller in 1952. The general won on a platform that committed the party to save Asia and with a campaign in which he refused to repudiate McCarthyism. Adlai Stevenson ran a more literate and less successful campaign for the

---

[11]Reinhold Niebuhr, "The Foreign Policy of American Conservatism and Liberalism." In *Christian Realism and Political Problems* (New York, 1953), pp. 58, 64.

Democrats but the Illinois governor significantly patterned his appeal after Eisenhower's in two respects: Stevenson refused to embrace the record of the Truman administration with any enthusiasm (at one point asking privately that Acheson publicly announce his intention to resign after the election), and he once went further than Eisenhower in a specific commitment to save Asia.

On October 24 the Democratic nominee warned that to withdraw American troops from Korea and allow "Asians to fight Asians," as the general wanted, "we would risk a Munich in the Far East, with the probability of a third world war not far behind." On September 4 the Republican candidate had believed the United States must protect "the far corners of the earth" which provided the nation with "materials essential to our industry and our defense." Yet on October 24, when Eisenhower dramatically pledged, "I shall go to Korea," he advocated as a military backstop only the building up of the South Korean forces and shaping "our psychological warfare program into a weapon capable of cracking the Communist front." This was a less militant course than Stevenson was advocating in a speech that same day.[12]

Beneath the Eisenhower moderation, however, was the less restrained Republican platform. It contrasted "Russia's 'Asia-first' policy" with "the 'Asia-last' policy" of the Truman administration. "Containment is defensive," one plank read, "negative, futile and immoral [in abandoning] countless human beings to a despotism and Godless terrorism." John Foster Dulles, who was largely responsible for these sections of the platform, later announced in a campaign speech at Buffalo, New York, that the new Republican administration would, if elected, use "all means to secure the liberation of Eastern Europe." When Eisenhower heard this, he immediately phoned Dulles to inform him that the phrase should have read "all peaceful means." "Yes," Dulles promptly replied, "it's just a complete oversight."[13] It was a strange oversight for a renowned international lawyer who had spent forty years honing words to great precision.

Behind Eisenhower also loomed the figure of Joseph McCarthy. We will "eliminate" from the federal government, the platform pledged, those "who share responsibility for the needless predicaments and perils

---

[12]*The New York Times,* October 25, 1952, pp. 1, 8.
[13]Interview with Dwight Eisenhower, Dulles Oral History Project, Papers of John Foster Dulles, Princeton.

in which we find ourselves." This was a rather loose definition of wrong-doing, but the Republicans were not to be denied the profit of hammering the point at the voters. "There are no Communists in the Republican Party," began one long party plank.[14]

Eisenhower's speeches were not that blunt. He also refused to invite General Douglas MacArthur to participate in the campaign, although this would have appeased a large number of conservative Republicans. Eisenhower, however, never publicly repudiated McCarthy's activities. That would not have been sound politics. Sitting on the same stage with McCarthy in Milwaukee, Eisenhower held in his hands a speech paying loving tribute to General George Marshall, who had been a sponsor of Eisenhower's rise in the military but had been termed a traitor by McCarthy. At the last minute Eisenhower bowed to McCarthy's brand of Americanism and deleted the tribute. Truman quickly accused Eisenhower of surrendering to a "moral scoundrel" and "moral pygmies." The two men became bitter enemies.[15]

Stevenson and many other Democrats seemed particularly open to the charge that, as one McCarthyite journal phrased it, "Chinese coolies and Harvard professors are the people . . . most susceptible to Red propaganda." At Wheeling, West Virginia, in 1950, McCarthy had declared that it was "not the less fortunate" Americans who "have been selling this nation out, but rather those who have had all the benefits." Those "bright young men" in the State Department who were "born with silver spoons in their mouths are the ones who have been worse." Such attacks on the "Eastern intellectual establishment" paid dividends. Many of the "less fortunate" supported McCarthy and the Republicans, and thus one more group left the New Deal coalition. Polls revealed that the most earnest supporters of the Wisconsin senator were the small businessmen, who felt squeezed between the big unions and big corporations, and manual laborers. Other support came from the new wealth groups (such as oil wildcatters and real estate manipulators), ethnic groups such as Irish and Germans determined to prove their "Americanism," and, paradoxically, some Eastern intellectuals who had prayed to the communist "God who failed"

---

[14]Clarence W. Baier and Richard P. Stebbins, (eds.,) *Documents of American Foreign Relations, 1952* (New York, 1953), pp. 80–85.

[15]Ralph E. Weber, *Talking with Harry* (Wilmington, Del., 2001), p. 133.

in the 1930s and now attempted to gain redemption by embracing McCarthy.[16] These groups endorsed the senator's definition of McCarthyism as "Americanism with its sleeves rolled." No Republican politician tried to buck that slogan in 1952.

Having won on issues Republican Senator Karl Mundt neatly formulated as K_1C_2—Korea, Communism, and Corruption—the Eisenhower administration's foreign policy could not be impervious to McCarthy or the Cold War mentality which had spawned McCarthyism. In early 1953 the new chief counsel for McCarthy's committee, Roy M. Cohn, and a friend, David Schine, junketed throughout Europe upbraiding American diplomats supposedly soft on communism, attacking U.S. Information Service libraries for exhibiting the work of such "radicals" as Mark Twain and Theodore Dreiser, and provoking the wrath of the European press. Secretary of State Dulles did nothing to stop Cohn and Schine.

Within four months after taking office, the administration bragged that it had fired 1456 federal employees under its "security program." The program had not, however, uncovered one proven communist. So challenged, the Democrats replied that they had effectively fired even more "risks" under Truman's loyalty program.[17] In the midst of this frenzy, one distinguished American Foreign Service officer who had never been tainted by any McCarthyite accusation commented, "If I had a son, I would do everything in my power to suppress any desire he might have to enter the Foreign Service of the United States."[18] The McLeod-McCarthy group countered with the slogan, "An ounce of loyalty is worth a pound of brains." The price, however, would soon be paid for such slogans. As the McCarthyites threw many of the ablest people out of the State Department (and Dulles and Eisenhower uttered too little protest), experts, particularly in the areas of China and South Asia, left government. A decade later they would not be on hand to inform Presidents about the realities of China and Vietnam. The 1960s' generation paid in blood and treasure for the ignorance of the early 1950s.

---

[16]Seymour Lipset, *Political Man: The Social Bases of Politics* (New York, 1960), pp. 171–172; Daniel Bell, *The End of Ideology: On the Exhaustion of Political Ideas in the Fifties* (Glencoe, Ill., 1960), pp. 110–112; Richard Rovere, *Senator Joe McCarthy* (Cleveland, 1959), p. 13.

[17]Rovere, *McCarthy*, pp. 17–18, 32–33.

[18]Emmet John Hughes, *The Ordeal of Power: A Political Memoir of the Eisenhower Years* (New York, 1963), p. 91.

Dulles contented himself with his favorite biblical quotation: "All things work together for good to them that love God, to them who are called according to His purpose."[19] Like Truman, the new secretary of state was confident about whom the Creator was calling. Dulles nevertheless left little to chance. He built his power base within the administration with care. No cabinet officer in American history had a closer working relationship with a President than did Dulles. When competing power centers began to appear in the White House in the person of Harold Stassen or Nelson Rockefeller, the secretary of state moved ruthlessly. "He cut off Nelson at the ankles," was the way one official described the encounter. "We will make the most successful team in history," Dulles supposedly told Eisenhower.[20]

Few could challenge Dulles's grasp of world events. He had learned much about Europe as a young law student in Paris. As a senior partner in the powerful law firm of Sullivan and Cromwell of New York City, he operated regularly during the 1920s and 1930s out of the firm's Paris and Berlin offices. He had undertaken his first important diplomatic mission in 1919–1921 with his uncle, Robert Lansing, who was Woodrow Wilson's secretary of state. In cabinet meetings few took issue with him. "After all," one Eisenhower assistant remarked, "how are you going to argue with a man who has lived with a problem—for instance, in respect to Iran—for longer than most of us knew there was such a country?"[21]

But one person did have greater knowledge about, and experience with, world issues and leaders than Dulles—Eisenhower. The general from Abilene, Kansas, not only had commanded the greatest invasion force in history during World War II but had almost daily dealt successfully with some of the most complex giants of the twentieth century, including Roosevelt, Churchill, and French leader Charles de Gaulle. After he became President, Eisenhower seemed to do little but flash his famous grin and play many rounds of golf. The joke circulated that an Eisenhower doll was one that could be wound up and then do nothing for eight years. Fresh research and the opening of new documents from

[19]Dulles to John Nagel, January 21, 1952, Correspondence, Papers of John Foster Dulles, Princeton.

[20]Sherman Adams, *First-Hand Report* (New York, 1961), p. 89; succinct, useful background on this relationship is in Richard Immerman, *John Foster Dulles* (Wilmington, Del., 1999), pp. 39–53.

[21]Interview with Sherman Adams, Dulles Oral History Project, Princeton.

the 1950s, however, now reveal that Eisenhower's calm exterior hid a strong hand, which he wielded to control policy behind the scenes.[22] Nor was the exterior always calm. Privately he could explode and become what one friend called "a human Bessemer furnace." His Vice President, Richard Nixon, later observed that the avuncular Ike was "a far more complex and devious man than most people realized." Eisenhower had early learned how to control those around him. "He's a great poker player," a chief military aide remarked, "and [an] extremely good bridge player. . . . He's a tremendous man for analyzing the other fellow's mind, what options are open to the other fellow, and what line he [Eisenhower] can best take to capitalize or exploit the possibilities." Truman, with his penchant for desk pounding, liked the phrase, "The buck stops here." On his desk Eisenhower had a plaque with a Latin phrase that translated, "Gently in manner, strong in deed." Part of the manner was delegating authority and allowing his subordinates, such as Dulles, to act as lightning rods for both public praise and criticism. Eisenhower once told his press secretary to take a certain action. The secretary objected that if he did that he "would get hell." Eisenhower patted him on the back and said, "My boy, better you than me."

A major reason why he had run for the presidency was his fear that the Republican party might fall into the hands of the Asia-first, "isolationist" faction that rallied around Senator Robert Taft. Eisenhower agreed with Taft on the need for smaller military budgets and on drastically slicing government spending, but he determined to make the party accept its global, not merely Asian, responsibilities. He once told a friend that Senator William Knowland (Republican of California), a leader of the pro–Chiang Kai-shek group, had "no foreign policy except to develop high blood pressure whenever he mentions the words 'Red China.' "

With such views, Eisenhower became the transition figure that transformed the Republican party of Taft into the party of Ronald Reagan. While agreeing with Taft on spending cuts, Eisenhower anticipated Reagan (and before him, Senator Barry Goldwater's conservative campaign of 1964) by creating a strong presidency that was especially active in foreign policy; by showing a determination to exercise U.S. power globally; and by holding fast to the belief that

[22]Much of the following is based on the pioneering work of Fred I. Greenstein, *The Hidden-Hand Presidency: Eisenhower as Leader* (New York, 1982), especially pp. 9, 26, 57, 69, 91–92; Richard Immerman, "Eisenhower and Dulles: Who Made the Decisions?" *Political Psychology,* I (Autumn 1979): 3–19.

the overriding threat to world stability was communism, not starvation, inequality, or other wants that led the have-nots to rebel against the haves. Eisenhower understood the demands of the have-nots and could eloquently articulate the policy problems they presented. But he believed they could be handled in the long run by private investment, while communism posed an immediate threat and had to be destroyed by various forms of military power. Eisenhower changed the more limited commitments of Taft Republicanism into the virtually unlimited commitments of Reagan Republicanism. And he did this by shaping a consensus at home that has been unsurpassed by any other President after 1945. In a 1955 Gallup Poll nearly two-thirds of those calling themselves liberals saw Eisenhower as liberal, and almost the same percentage considering themselves conservatives saw him as conservative.

Similar dramatic changes occurred in the Soviet Union. In August 1952 Stalin surprised the world by calling the Nineteenth Party Congress to convene on October 5. Thirteen years had passed since the eighteenth session of 1939. The Soviet dictator obviously had a task for the obedient members to perform.

Western officials doubted that Stalin aimed to ease tensions. Throughout 1951 and 1952 he had taken a tougher foreign-policy line than before and nearly doubled the Red Army to 4.9 million men while increasing defense expenditures by 50 percent. Stalin then assaulted those who challenged his foreign polices. The West, he predicted, would soon be overwhelmed by economic catastrophe. Communist successes since 1945 had contracted the capitalists' market. This contraction had so aggravated the Western economic system that the capitalists would soon begin a death struggle among themselves. This development, Stalin concluded in a brief speech at the congress, indicated two courses for communists: the tightening of party control to prepare fully for the protection of the bloc against capitalist warfare, and cooperative efforts with nationalists everywhere, but especially those in Germany, Japan, and France, in order to accelerate the revolt against American control.[23]

---

[23]J. V. Stalin, "Economic Problems of Socialism in the U.S.S.R." in *Current Soviet Policies: The Documentary Record of the 19th Communist Party Congress and the Reorganization After Stalin's Death*, edited and with an introduction by Leo Gruliow (New York, 1953), pp. 1–10, 235–236. This is an exceptionally useful compendium of primary documents which emerged from those events between October 1952 and April 1953.

A theme of the congress was a renewed emphasis on the inevitability of war. Another outcome of the congress was the most significant. In an apparent attempt to cement his control over both the Malenkov and Khrushchev factions, Stalin announced at the congress the creation of a new politburo, to be named the Party Presidium, consisting of twenty-five instead of eleven members. The new additions would be fervent young Stalinists. This stroke cut the power of both Malenkov and Khrushchev while giving Stalin even greater authority.[24]

On January 13, 1953, concrete evidence dramatically appeared to support Stalin's belief that he was threatened with "capitalist encirclement." A group of Kremlin doctors was suddenly arrested by Soviet security police for the killing of Andrei Zhdanov in 1948 and accused of being in the hire of American and British espionage agents. Some observers believed that the episode indicated Stalin's firm belief that an East-West détente of any kind, including possible armistice in Korea, was impossible. Inside the ruling circles of the Kremlin, the "Doctors Plot" had another meaning. As the plot unfolded, Stalin evidently made indirect threats to the lives of Central Committee members, including some as close to him as Molotov and Anastas Mikoyan. These threats, apparently, were the breaking point. On February 17 the chief of security in the Kremlin who had protected Stalin for thirty years suddenly was announced by the Soviet press to be dead. Within three weeks Stalin fell victim to what was officially termed "hemorrhage of the brain."

The truth, as usual, was more complex and interesting. Stalin's policies were failing abroad (especially in the key area of West German rearmament) and becoming yet more terrifying at home. He had seemed determined to eliminate even those closest to him in the Kremlin. Harrison E. Salisbury, correspondent of *The New York Times* in Moscow during those extraordinary days of 1953, later concluded that the cause of Stalin's death was suspect. On the night of Saturday, February 28, Georgi Malenkov, Lavrenti Beria, Nikolay Bulganin, and Nikita Khrushchev—the four leading contenders for Stalin's throne—had an all-night drinking bout with the dictator at his villa outside Moscow. The next day Stalin was found asleep on the floor. He reportedly had suffered a stroke. The four contenders were summoned

---

[24]*Current Soviet Policies*, p. 105; Robert C. Tucker, *The Soviet Political Mind* (New York, 1963), pp. 30–31.

for advice. But they did nothing for twenty-four hours. Salisbury surmised that the four men decided that "if they let him go a few more hours they might be rid of him for all time." A visitor to Stalin's home on the day of his death, March 5, believed that he "was speeded to his grave."[25]

Malenkov quickly took over Stalin's top jobs. He immediately cut back politburo membership to throw out the ardent young Stalinists whom the old dictator had just appointed. Malenkov also announced that new policies would arise from a "collective" rather than from the whims of one man. He issued amnesties for many political prisoners, including those locked up by Stalin for the alleged "Doctors Plot." The doctors' confessions, the Soviet press suddenly discovered, had been obtained "through the use of impermissible means of investigation which are strictly forbidden under Soviet law."[26]

This final twist to the "Doctors Plot" indicated changes in Soviet foreign policies. Malenkov confirmed the changes in a speech before the Supreme Soviet: "At the present time there is no disputed or unresolved question that cannot be settled peacefully by mutual agreement of the interested countries," he announced. "This applies to our relations with all states, including the United States of America."[27] Soon the new Russian leaders allowed Soviet citizens married to foreigners to leave the country; reestablished diplomatic relations with Greece, Israel, and later Yugoslavia; renounced Soviet claims to Turkish territory; and, most important, agreed to an end to the Korean War.

Eisenhower and Dulles suddenly found themselves dealing with a new set of Soviet policies. A fresh set of issues, a different kind of Soviet challenge had dramatically appeared. The question became whether the new American leaders could become flexible enough to deal with the new faces in Moscow, particularly in the aftermath of the terrible war in Korea and amidst the plague of McCarthyism.

---

[25]Harrison E. Salisbury, "The Days of Stalin's Death," *The New York Times Magazine*, April 17, 1983, pp. 38–48; Vladislav Zubok and Constantine Pleshakov, *Inside the Kremlin's Cold War* (Cambridge, Mass., 1996), pp. 144–146. A good overview of the death and its immediate effects is Robert Service, *Stalin, A Biography* (Cambridge, Mass., 2005), pp. 578–590.
[26]*Current Soviet Policies*, pp. 249–251.
[27]*Current Soviet Policies*, pp. 256–260.

A beginning of a not-so-beautiful friendship. South Vietnam leader Ngo
Dinh Diem (at left) is welcomed in Washington by President Eisenhower
and behind him, Secretary of State Dulles.
(National Archives and Records Administration)

CHAPTER 7

A Different Cold War (1953–1955)

Former Secretary of the Treasury George Humphrey recalled his impressions of Washington when the Eisenhower administration moved into power. "We were under war controls," Humphrey remembered, "and we were in war."[1] Entering office as the struggle continued in Korea, the President pledged that he would more efficiently and successfully wage the Cold War against Stalinist Russia. "Let's face it," one Republican adviser had remarked in early 1952. "The only excuse for Ike's candidacy is that he's the man best qualified to deal with Stalin."[2]

In early March 1953 Stalin died. The Cold War that began to confront Eisenhower and Dulles during their first months in power assumed new and puzzling traits. Georgi Malenkov took over Stalin's place in the Soviet government, but he did not accept the departed leader's foreign policies. Malenkov instead began urging friendly negotiation in Europe and peace in Korea. Rapid changes in other parts of the world also began to confuse Americans. The Republicans had won with a platform promising more military firepower and a firming up of the containment policy, but new international crises increasingly revolved around rampaging nationalisms in the Middle East, Latin America, and Southeast Asia rather than around military problems in Europe or Korea. As Morgenthau and

---

[1]Interview with George Humphrey and Herbert Hoover, Jr., Dulles Oral History Project, Princeton.
[2]Norman A. Graebner, *The New Isolationism* (New York, 1956), p. 98.

Niebuhr had foreseen, the Eisenhower administration was soon engaged in a different kind of Cold War.

Immediately after Stalin's death American intelligence informed the President that the new Soviet premier would have to consolidate his internal control and consequently would not undertake new departures in foreign affairs.[3] Many Americans believed that Stalin's death would create a chaos which might permanently damage Soviet power, or at least force a long, painful, and unproductive transition period upon new leadership. This did not happen. The possibility of one-man rule by Malenkov apparently disappeared after a severe internal party struggle. He maintained his premiership but surrendered the key post of first party secretary to Nikita Khrushchev.

A precarious collective leadership emerged as Malenkov, with his power based on the technicians and government bureaucracy, and Khrushchev, with his strong support from the party, began a struggle for supreme power. The first important casualty in the battle was Lavrenti Beria. When Beria moved too fast and overtly in making the secret police his own political tool, the new rulers arrested and executed him in July. In stark contrast to Stalin's methods, however, Beria was probably the only victim of execution within the high party hierarchy. While conveniently blaming Beria for many of the excesses of previous years, Malenkov cautiously moved to liberalize the functioning of the party and demanded a reduction of investment in heavy industry so that Russians could enjoy more consumer goods.

This policy of relaxation soon stretched to foreign affairs. If the Western alliance was unable to agree upon such ventures as the European Defense Community in the present "tense international situation," Malenkov observed to the Supreme Soviet on August 8, 1953, "a lessening of this tension might lead to [the] disintegration" of that alliance. The premier, however, hedged his bet. In the same speech he announced that the Soviets had successfully tested a thermonuclear, or hydrogen, bomb. With the American thermonuclear monopoly broken, the Soviets stood ready to negotiate on European problems. To strengthen their position further, they dropped their emphasis on revolution by an international proletariat and attempted

---

[3]Dwight D. Eisenhower, *The White House Years: Mandate for Change, 1953–1956* (Garden City, N.Y., 1963), pp. 148–149.

to influence Western policies by playing upon the peace hopes of the European middle classes.[4]

The American response to these Soviet changes was slow and unsure. The Washington bureaucracy was fearful and confused, partly because of its terror of the ubiquitous McCarthyism. Underneath this confusion lay a deeper problem. Soviet communism, Dulles told the Senate Foreign Relations Committee in January, "believes that human beings are nothing more than somewhat superior animals . . . and that the best kind of a world is that world which is organized as a well-managed farm is organized, where certain animals are taken out to pasture, and they are fed and brought back and milked, and they are given a barn as shelter over their heads." Apparently the secretary of state had read George Orwell's *Animal Farm* literally. "I do not see how, as long as Soviet communism holds those views," Dulles concluded ", . . . there can be any permanent reconciliation. . . . This is an irreconcilable conflict."[5] By defining the conflict as so intensely ideological, Dulles severely limited the possibility of easing tensions through a flexible diplomacy.

On April 16, 1953, Eisenhower made the first formal response to Malenkov's new tactics. It was breathtaking. If the Soviets sincerely desired détente, the President remarked, there must be "free elections in a united Korea"; the end of communist revolts in Malaya and Indochina; "United Nations control and inspection" of disarmament; "a free and united Germany, with a government based upon free and secret elections"; the "free choice" of governments in Eastern Europe; and a treaty restoring Austria's independence.[6] The day following this address Dulles appeared before the Senate Foreign Relations Committee; his testimony was headlined by *The New York Times* as "Dulles Bids Soviet Cooperate or Face Vast West Arming."

Within a month, however, the American approach was questioned by the most eminent statesman within that alliance. Without

---

[4]*Current Digest of the Soviet Press,* V (September 5, 1953): 3–12, 26; an important case study is Kimmo Rentola, "From Half-Adversary to Half-Ally; Finland in Soviet Policy, 1953–1958," a paper at the International Conference on the Cold War, Helsinki, 1999, in possession of the author.
[5]U.S. Senate, Committee on Foreign Relations, 83rd Cong., 1st Sess., *Nomination of John Foster Dulles . . . , January 15, 1953* (Washington, 1953), pp. 10–11.
[6]Department of State, *American Foreign Policy, 1950–1955, Basic Documents,* 2 vols. (Washington, 1957): I, 65–71.

previously informing either Eisenhower or his own Foreign Office, Winston Churchill announced on May 11 that the time had arrived for world leaders to confer "on the highest level" to see which problems might be solved. The prime minister indirectly attacked Eisenhower's demand that a multitude of questions would have to be settled at once. This was obviously impossible and, moreover, might unfortunately "impede any spontaneous and healthy evolution which may be taking place inside Russia." Churchill instead recommended a piecemeal approach by tackling solvable problems but assuming all the while that Russian security must be assured.[7]

Senate Majority Leader William Knowland responded by accusing Churchill of "urging a Far Eastern Munich." The official Washington response was characterized as "cool." Eisenhower explained why to a news conference. "The world happened to be round and it had no end and he [Eisenhower] didn't see how you could discuss the problem, the great basic problems of today, which were so largely philosophical in character, without thinking in global terms," or so reported the official text of the conference.[8] The President was arguing that, because the Soviet menace was basically ideological, or "philosophical," it was also indivisible and thus posed a threat everywhere in the world. Churchill disagreed.

In May 1952 and again in January 1953, Dulles had condemned "containment" as a "policy which is bound to fail because a purely defensive policy never wins against an aggressive policy." He advocated instead "liberation of these captive peoples" in Eastern Europe through such "processes short of war" as "political warfare, psychological warfare and propaganda." In late May 1953 Dulles suddenly faced his moment of truth. The Soviets loosened political controls in East Germany but also demanded more production from workers for the same wages. Laborers protested with a march down East Berlin's Stalinallee on June 16. The next day began with a general strike and demonstrations which climaxed with the tearing down of communist flags and demands for free elections. The American radio in West Berlin broadcast encouragement to the workers and lauded the spreading of the strikes throughout East Germany. Then suddenly Soviet tanks appeared in Berlin, Dresden, Leipzig, Magdeburg, and

[7]*The New York Times,* May 12, 1953, pp. 8–9.
[8]*The New York Times,* May 15, 1953, p. 6; Vojtech Mastny, *The Cold War and Soviet Insecurity* (New York, 1996) well describes Soviet intentions and U.S. reluctance on pp. 174–178.

Jena. As the armor smashed the demonstrations, Dulles made no move other than sending food ("Eisenhower packages") to try to win East Germans and undermine communist control. "Liberation" had failed its first test and had done so in Germany, the European prize of the East-West struggle.[9]

Facing the problem of captive peoples in North Korea shortly after, the administration came up with a more satisfactory, if not exactly happy, solution by recognizing the limits of its military and political power. Eisenhower's trip to Korea in December 1952 buttressed his belief that the United States should not be entrapped in a conventional war on the Asian mainland. For his own reasons, Secretary of the Treasury Humphrey supported this view. One-third of the budget had to be cut to eliminate deficit spending, Humphrey told the President, and that means "you have to get Korea out of the way."

To get Korea "out of the way," the administration first employed what would later be called "brinksmanship." Returning from Korea on December 14, Eisenhower warned that, unless the war ended quickly, the United States might retaliate "under circumstances of our choosing." Six weeks later in his first State of the Union message, the President announced that the American Seventh Fleet would "no longer be employed to shield Communist China." He hurriedly added that this meant no intended aggression "on our part," but this so-called unleashing of Chiang Kai-shek so frightened England and France that Dulles flew to Europe to reassure the Allies.

As tension mounted, Stalin conveniently died. The new Soviet leaders hinted their willingness to sponsor negotiations. On the crucial question of prisoner exchange (the UN forces reported that many North Korean and Chinese prisoners did not want to return home and should not be compelled to do so), the Chinese suggested on March 30 that prisoner repatriation be placed in the hands of international authorities. On April 23 armistice talks recommenced, but Dulles soon concluded that the Chinese were raising unnecessary barriers to a peace. On May 22 he hinted to Peking through Indian diplomats that if peace were not forthcoming the United States would bring in atomic weapons. The next day the State Department issued more moderate instructions on the prisoner-exchange problem.

[9]Christian F. Ostermann, *The United States and the East German Uprising of 1953* . . . , Cold War International History Project (Washington, D.C., 1994), pp. 2–3, 27, 43.

Within eleven days the communists accepted the plan with minor changes. They held to the agreement even after President Syngman Rhee of South Korea tried to sabotage the negotiations by releasing 27,000 Chinese and North Korean prisoners on June 18. The seventy-eight-year-old Rhee was outraged that the American acceptance of a division roughly along the 38th parallel would prevent him from ever ruling a unified Korea. The final armistice was signed on July 27. Talks in 1953 and 1954 on reunification failed, and the United States proceeded to pour $6 billion of aid into South Korea over the next decade. Industrial production tripled, exports increased eight times to nearly $250 million, and the economy became increasingly self-sufficient. Rhee was not as fortunate politically. He fell from power after students rioted against his autocratic regime in April 1960 and was replaced by a military-controlled government. The North Korean government also endured political upheavals, although on lower levels, and rebuilt its air force with hundreds of modern Soviet fighter planes. The United States installed tactical guided missiles with atomic warheads pointing northward. Outside Panmunjom, where negotiators would meet for forty years to insult one another, grandstands and loudspeakers accommodated tourists who liked to witness the spectacle of international diplomacy and peer out over the desolate, bare hills where thousands of men died in a "limited" war.

Now free to concentrate on Europe, Dulles made Germany the pivot. As a lawyer in Germany between the wars, he had come to admire the German people; he prized Germany's location, industrial power, and military potential as a bulwark against Soviet expansion; and, by means of a steadily developing friendship, he enjoyed a similarity of views with Konrad Adenauer that he had with no other world leader.

In 1953 Dulles made these views clear to everyone. He continued the pro-German strategies inherited from Acheson, including West Germany's rearmament, in the belief that any immediate détente was impossible, for, as he had told a distinguished assemblage of European statesmen, "The Soviet leaders are to a very large extent the prisoners of their own doctrine which is intensively held by their followers, who are fanatics."[10]

---

[10]"Statement of Secretary Dulles at April 23 Session of North Atlantic Council Ministers' Meeting," Conference Dossiers, Dulles Papers, Princeton.

Accepting the status quo in Europe, or at least the status quo once the French formally endorsed the EDC, Dulles turned to ponder the explosive problems of the newly emerging areas. These now required more and more attention.

From the Declaration of Independence until the Civil War, Americans generally sympathized with revolutions abroad. In several respects, however, they handed out their sympathy with care. They disliked revolutions that went beyond the political, social, and economic boundaries of their own. Americans also believed their own revolution superior to revolutions on the "right" (as John Quincy Adams viewed the Latin American upheavals in the 1820s) or on the "left." They best liked revolts on the North American continent, such as those in Florida, Texas, California, and Canada, which opened possible areas for annexation to the expanding Union.

In the middle of the nineteenth century, two events began to reshape American views toward revolutions: the continental conquest was completed, and Americans began emphasizing the commercial aspects of their foreign policy instead of landed expansion. These overseas commercial interests became especially important, for stability, peace, and confidence in the sanctity of contract—that is, decidedly nonrevolutionary virtues—were essential to any great trading venture. By 1900 the United States had burgeoned into a power which combined the interesting characteristics of being conservative ideologically and expansive economically. Such a combination would not be encouraging to revolution. Interventions against rebellions in Cuba and the Philippines were followed by Theodore Roosevelt's pronouncement that the United States would act as a policeman to prevent upheavals in the Caribbean area. A decade later Woodrow Wilson rationalized the use of economic and military force against the Mexican revolution with an ideological justification that employed the traditional American liberal rhetoric. The threat of revolution reached a crisis when, in 1917, Lenin joined the use of force to a communist doctrine worldwide in its ambitions and deeply repugnant to most Americans.

The Eisenhower administration inherited this significant historical legacy. It became an heir to this tradition of opposing revolutions, moreover, at the point when European colonial rule and conservative monarchies crumbled before nationalist uprisings in the Middle East, Africa, Asia, and Latin America. The new spirit was captured by the highly corrupt King Farouk of Egypt. As nationalist army officers threw him out of Egypt, Farouk predicted that in a decade there would only "be five kings left: Hearts, Clubs, Diamonds, Spades, and England." He was not far wrong.

Eisenhower and Dulles understood and sympathized with much of the new nationalism. Their own people, after all, had won the first modern anticolonial struggle in 1776. Both men realized, moreover, that the worn-out British and French empires were breathing their last. They wanted the colonials quickly out of the way. When colonials remained, revolutionaries tended to move leftward in order to continue the struggle. Eisenhower preferred to attack that problem at the root by pushing out the Europeans. But Americans seldom seemed able to move fast enough. Revolutionaries in Iran, Indochina, and Guatemala gained ground. The President determined to stop them with force if necessary.

The problem thus became what kind of force Americans should use to control revolutions abroad. Eisenhower and Dulles, and indeed all later Americans, found themselves in a terrible bind. They did not want to fight conventional ground wars in Asia and Africa. Korea had vividly proved the dangers of such involvements. Using covert weapons employed by the Central Intelligence Agency could work in certain instances (and Eisenhower proved to be exceedingly skillful in employing the CIA), but in other cases the revolutionaries had gathered too much strength to be beaten by James Bond–like operations.

Eisenhower devised a package of tactics for dealing with unwanted revolutionaries. First, he turned loose the CIA in such places as Iran and Guatemala, which were not yet out of control. Second, he sent U.S. military advisers to train native troops, as in Vietnam, where Eisenhower began the so-called Vietnamization of the war. Third, Eisenhower and Dulles engineered a series of military alliances to tie friends together in a common fight against the Soviets outside, and left-wing revolutionaries inside, various regions. The Baghdad Pact in the Middle East and the Southeast Asia Treaty Organization (SEATO) became two of the more famous examples of "pactomania," as Dulles's critics labeled the policy. Fourth, Eisenhower based his over-all military policy on the use of huge hydrogen bombs as well as small tactical atomic weapons that planners believed could be deployed with almost surgical precision on battlefields. He especially threatened to use these weapons if Soviet or Chinese forces launched a direct invasion or became heavily involved with the revolutionaries (as, indeed, he had already threatened in Korea in mid-1953).

The President's growing reliance on nuclear bombs also came out of his determination to cut back government spending. No President in the post-1945 years has been as fanatic in this regard as this famous military commander who dedicated himself to slashing military budgets. He preached repeatedly that the key to American power was its economic system and marvelous productivity, not its weapons. Military spending on the level of Truman's $50 billion annually, he feared, would set off a terrible inflation and ruin the economy. "We must not go broke," he reiterated. To Eisenhower, "broke" meant either a deficit in the federal budget, or an economy growing dependent on a "military-industrial complex," as he later termed it. "To Eisenhower," a close observer later remarked, "the United States economy was like the source of a mother's milk—tender and soft and not to be abused."[11]

At the same time, however, the President set out to stop left-wing revolutions and continue Truman's "containment" policy. These conclusions had been hammered out in a series of discussions during 1953 in "Operation Solarium" (named after the White House sun room in which they were held). If Eisenhower hoped to carry out Truman's policies without Truman's budget, his only solution was to rely on the CIA and nuclear weapons that were cheaper than maintaining soldiers in a conventional force. In two years Eisenhower reduced Truman's military budget by nearly one-third to about $34 billion. His reliance on nuclear armaments to accomplish this reduction soon became evident as he allowed the development of the B41 bomb of over 20 megatons, or the equivalent of 400 Hiroshima-type bombs. (The B41 proved less usable than originally anticipated after tests revealed that if it were dropped close to Soviet coastlines, the radiation would pose greater dangers to U.S. forces and ships at sea than it would to large parts of Russia itself.)

The size of the nation's nuclear stockpile doubled between 1953 and 1955, while new, huge B-52 bombers rolled off assembly lines to

---

[11]Douglas Kinnard, *The Secretary of Defense* (Lexington, Ky., 1980), pp. 44–45. The paradox of Eisenhower's policy—condemning too much military spending while undertaking a major buildup in new weapons—is analyzed in Richard V. Damms, "James Killian . . . and the Emergence of President Eisenhower's 'Scientific-Technological Elite,'" *Diplomatic History*, 24 (Winter 2000): 57–78.

deliver the weapons. Eisenhower became the first President to consider atomic and nuclear bombs "conventional" weapons—to "be used exactly as you would use a bullet or anything else," as he remarked publicly in 1955. Eisenhower refused repeatedly to accept a nuclear test ban that would have stopped the deadly radioactive fallout from weapons tests that began to infect the world's food supplies. His refusal was based in part on the Soviets' refusal to agree to what he considered adequate inspections, in part on the belief that the development of his main weapons systems depended on such tests. Thus, Eisenhower was prepared to consider starting a nuclear war if necessary—not only if the Soviets invaded Europe but also if Cold War costs became so high that they were forcing "us to war—or into some form of dictatorial government."[12]

His strategy became known as "the new look," or "more bang for a buck." Dulles used the phrase "massive retaliation," by which he meant being "willing and able to respond vigorously at places and with means of [our] own choosing."[13] Eisenhower had some sense of when he might launch "massive retaliation," as noted above. But he also had an idea of the destruction that could result. In certain situations, no matter how tempting, war had to be avoided. For example, he made a remarkable response to Syngman Rhee in mid-1954 when the South Korean leader tried to shame him into supporting a war to unify Korea. Eisenhower interrupted to say that he "regretted very much" the division of Korea, Germany, Austria, and Vietnam, "but . . . no one in this world will get America to go to war over these problems. . . . We cannot undertake any engagement that involves [the] deliberate intention of going to war with Iron Curtain countries."[14]

---

[12]"Memorandum for the Secretary of State," September 8, 1953, Dulles Papers, Princeton. The discussion in this paragraph is also from Lawrence Freedman, *The Evolution of Nuclear Strategy* (New York, 1983), pp. 77–78, 81–83; David Alan Rosenberg, "'A Smoking Radiating Ruin at the End of Two Hours,'" *International Security,* VI (Winter 1981–1982): 3–38; Robert A. Divine, *Blowing on the Wind: The Nuclear Test Ban Debate, 1954–1960* (New York, 1978), especially chapters 2, 3, 7; Samuel F. Wells, Jr., "The Origins of Massive Retaliation," *Political Science Quarterly,* XCVI (Spring 1981): 31–52; and *Washington Post,* December 27, 1983, p. A9.

[13]A standard version of Dulles's theory is his "Policy for Security and Peace," *Foreign Affairs,* XXXII (April 1954): especially 357–358.

[14]"Korean-American Talks, July 27, 1954," Dwight D. Eisenhower Diary Series, Box 4, Dwight D. Eisenhower Library, Abilene, Kan.

Eisenhower thereby defined the two extremes in which he would or would not go to war. But the extremes turned out not to be the problems. His dilemma involved the "gray areas"—as a young college professor, Henry Kissinger, called them in 1955—the newly emerging areas where kings and colonials were giving way to nationalist revolutionary movements. In these areas Eisenhower faced the great challenge that has confronted all his successors: finding a way of successfully using U.S. power and—most important—understanding these movements. His first challenges arose in Iran, Guatemala, and Vietnam.

In 1951 an Iranian nationalist movement headed by Mohammed Mossadegh had undercut the power of the shah and proceeded to nationalize the Anglo-Iranian Oil Company. The British government had received more taxes from the company than the Iranian government had received for its own natural resource. The company consequently provided a convenient target in an impoverished land where 500 of every 1000 newborns died. The British demanded payment for the confiscated holdings, a demand that the Iranians could not meet without binding themselves to foreign lenders. With oil exports at a standstill the Iran economy began to sink, since income from oil provided 30 percent of its total income and 60 percent of its foreign exchange. When Eisenhower entered office, the United States, despite extensive efforts by Acheson, had not been successful in acting as a mediator.

After a three-week trip through the Middle East in May 1953, Dulles reached some disturbing conclusions. Western power had "deteriorated" in the area, he believed, and unless drastic action was taken, the Arab nations would become "outright" neutrals in "the East-West struggle." Israel and intra-Arab squabbles accounted for some of the problems, but Dulles also wondered about the British. "They interpret our policy as one which in fact hastens their loss of prestige in the area. To some extent," the secretary admitted, ". . . this may be true," but Great Britain's loss of power was also due to "altered world power relationships." Dulles decided that he would have to convince the Middle East that the United States had little to do with British and French colonialism.[15]

---

[15]"Conclusions on Trip," May 9 to May 29, 1953, Conference Dossiers, Dulles Papers, Princeton. An important analysis that argues for more continuity of U.S. policies is Steve Marsh, "Continuity and Change: Reinterpreting the Policies of the Truman and Eisenhower Administrations Toward Iran, 1950–1954," *Journal of Cold War Studies*, 7 (Summer 2005), pp. 79–123.

The opportunity came within the next two months when the State Department concluded that Mossadegh was moving into the Soviet orbit. Rumors of a Soviet loan to Iran began to circulate, and in August Mossadegh received 99.4 percent of the votes in a plebiscite, a percentage which Eisenhower later used as proof of increased communist influence.[16] Having earlier refused to help Mossadegh rebuild the Iranian economy, the United States now cut off all aid.

In August the shah staged a successful coup to regain power. As revealed by CIA documents, finally made public in 2000 (after the Agency lied that they did not exist), the United States provided guns, trucks, armored cars, and radio communications for the shah's forces. The CIA effort, led by Kermit Roosevelt (Theodore Roosevelt's grandson), helped trigger the uprisings, but the Iranians did most of the work themselves. The grateful shah toasted Roosevelt: "I owe my throne to God, my people, my army—and to you."[17] The new government quickly undertook discussions with representatives of the oil company, but the representatives were not those of the year before. Since the turn of the century, the United States had been trying to get into the Iranian oil fields only to be constantly repulsed by the British.

Now the breakthrough occurred by the grace of the shah and under the guidance of State Department official Herbert Hoover, Jr., who had gained wide experience in the complexities of the international oil problem as a private businessman. A new international consortium was established giving the British 40 percent, five American firms (Gulf, Socony-Vacuum, Standard Oil of California, Standard Oil of New Jersey, and Texaco) 40 percent, and Dutch Shell and French Petroleum the remaining 20 percent of Iranian oil production. Profits would be divided equally between the consortium and Iran. Iranian oil once more freely flowed into international markets, the shah's government was securely within the Western camp, and the British monopoly on the oil fields had been broken. For Dulles and Eisenhower it was one revolution with a happy ending. More accurately it was not a revolution at all. And the United States paid for its actions in 1978 when

[16]Eisenhower, *The White House Years*, pp. 160–166.

[17]*New York Times*, April 16, 2000, pp. 1, 14; Robert Engler, *The Politics of Oil* (New York, 1961), p. 206; Kermit Roosevelt, *Countercoup: The Struggle for the Control of Iran* (New York, 1979); Mary Ann Heiss, *Empire and Nationhood* (New York, 1997), is especially important on the role of the oil companies. The context, including references to American television takeoffs of such *coups*, and the shah's toast, is in Douglas Little, "Mission Impossible . . . ," *Diplomatic History*, 28 (November 2004), especially p. 666.

Iranians overthrew the shah (see Ch. 12) and became bitterly anti-American. In 2000, Secretary of State Madeleine Albright essentially apologized for the 1953 CIA role: " . . . it is easy to see now why so many Iranians continue to resent this intervention by America in their internal affairs."[18]

American diplomats had hoped that similar problems would be avoided in Latin America by the formation of the Rio Pact and the Organization of American States (OAS) (see Ch. 3). Dulles found to his frustration that Latin American governments too often moved outside the U.S. interpretation of these agreements. He had phrased the problem dramatically in February 1953. Latin American conditions, he stressed, "are somewhat comparable to conditions as they were in China in the mid-thirties when the Communist movement was getting started. . . . Well, if we don't look out, we will wake up some morning and read in the newspapers that there happened in South America the same kind of thing that happened in China in 1949."[19] Despite this awareness Dulles never attempted to work out a comprehensive policy for encouraging Latin America to follow a path different from that which China trod in the 1930s. He instead approached the problem piecemeal. The first test for this approach came in Guatemala during the spring of 1954.

That country's population mainly comprises diverse groups of Indians who are poor, illiterate, and isolated. In an area roughly the size of Tennessee, only 10 percent of the land is tillable, yet 74 percent of the population is agrarian. Two percent of the landowners own 60 percent of the usable land. Until 1944 a succession of strongmen prevented any radical change in this society, but in that year student riots and unrest among professional classes brought in a new government, led by Juan José Arévalo, which supported land and labor reform. In 1951 Colonel Jacobo Arbenz Guzmán replaced Arévalo through proper constitutional procedures. Guatemalan politics polarized; the communists, who supported Arbenz, insisted, against strong conservative opposition, that further reforms were required. Arbenz's main objective became the United Fruit Company. For more than a half century that U.S. company had employed as many as 40,000 Guatemalans; monopolized shipping, communications, and railroads; and helped shape the country's politics.

---

[18]*New York Times*, April 16, 2000, p. 14; Engler, *Politics of Oil*, p. 207.
[19]U.S. Senate, *Nomination of Dulles*, p. 31.

In 1953 Arbenz confiscated 178,000 acres of company property. The State Department demanded proper payment, a demand Arbenz could not meet partly on nationalist grounds but also because it would require his country to tie itself economically to obligations which would prevent the financing of desperately needed internal reforms. When Arbenz refused to take the dispute to the Court of Arbitration at The Hague, Dulles moved to isolate Guatemala at the Tenth Inter-American Conference meeting at Caracas, Venezuela, in March 1954. He pushed through by a 17 to 1 vote a declaration that because "international communism . . . is incompatible with the concept of American freedom," the American states would "adopt within their respective territories the measures necessary to eradicate and prevent subversive activities."[20] Guatemala voted against, Mexico and Argentina refused to vote, and Costa Rica did not attend the meeting. Dulles interpreted the resolution as an application of the historic Monroe Doctrine. As Monroe's original message had been aimed at the political system of Europe's Holy Alliance, now the doctrine sent a similar warning to international communism, a political threat "more dangerous than the open physical aggression."[21]

On May 15, 1954, Guatemala unloaded 1900 tons of arms from Czechoslovakia. The United States responded by airlifting arms to Nicaragua and Honduras, where the CIA trained Guatemalan exiles for an invasion of their homeland. The Eisenhower administration also secretly planned to erect a blockade around Guatemala and stop any "suspicious foreign-flag vessels" possibly carrying arms.[22] That decision could have led to a direct confrontation with Soviet ships. On June 18 Colonel Carlos Castillo Armas and his American-trained force of 150 men moved across the Honduran border into Guatemala. Armas did not distinguish himself in battle, but at the decisive moment several small planes, piloted by CIA operatives,

---

[20]Department of State, *American Foreign Policy, 1950–1955, Basic Documents*, I: 1300–1302; crucial background is Paul Jo Dosal, *Doing Business with the Dictators: A Political History of United Fruit in Guatemala, 1899–1944* (Wilmington, Del., 1993).

[21]U.S. Senate, Committee on Foreign Relations, 83rd Cong., 2nd Sess., *Statements of Secretary John Foster Dulles and Admiral Arthur Radford . . . , March 9 and April 14, 1954* (Washington, 1954), p. 18.

[22]"Memo for President for Leaders' Meeting, May 24/53," May 22, 1954, Meetings with the President, 1954 (3), White House Memoranda Series, Dulles papers, Eisenhower Library, Abilene, Kan. Dulles's public reasons for the overthrow of Arbenz can be read in the chapter VII documents at www.mhhe.com/lafeber website.

bombed Guatemala City and key towns. U.S. aid was crucial, but, equally significant, Arbenz lost support from his army and the supposedly communist-controlled labor unions. By late June 1954 Castillo Armas ruled Guatemala.

Eisenhower's overthrow of Arbenz marks a turning point in U.S. foreign policy for at least four reasons. First, Americans misunderstood the Guatemalan situation. Arbenz had been constitutionally elected and headed a reform—not communist—movement. A handful of communists sat in the national legislature and influenced the labor movement, but no one ever argued that they shaped the country's most important institutions: the presidency, the army, and the Roman Catholic Church. Americans, in other words, too easily confused nationalism with communism. Second, despite the confusion, the administration pulled off such a successful and covert operation that Dulles could deny that his brother Allen (director of the CIA) was involved with Arbenz's removal. The administration announced that the Guatemalan people themselves had deposed their president. Americans too quickly and mistakenly concluded that such an operation could easily be repeated elsewhere. Third, Arbenz finally fell when his military deserted. Future Latin American revolutionaries drew the appropriate lesson. Fidel Castro of Cuba and, in the 1980s, the Sandinista government of Nicaragua would make the army and the government parts of a single unit. Overthrowing such regimes would require a war, not simply a covert CIA operation.

Finally, the United States won the battle but lost the longer war. In Guatemala (and later elsewhere) Americans failed to replace the deposed regime with an effective liberal reformer. Castillo Armas carried out large-scale executions that killed more Guatemalans after the invasion than had died during the conflict. Reactionary and ineffective, he was assassinated by members of his own regime three years later. The United States poured more aid into Guatemala between 1954 and 1965 than into any other Latin American nation, but the only results by the mid-1960s were a brutal military government and the growth of a revolutionary guerrilla movement more radical than any group in the country before 1954. (A contemporary critique of the Guatemala operation can be found in the chapter VII documents at the www.mhhe.com/lafeber website.)

During the same hours that the Dulles brothers acted in Guatemala, Eisenhower made an equally fateful decision in another rapidly emerging area: the crisis in Southeast Asia. The United States was deeply involved in the conflict between the French colonial forces and the army of the nationalist communist leader, Ho Chi Minh. Between 1950 and 1954 Washington sent $1.2 billion for the French effort, and by 1954 it had paid for over 70 percent of the French military budget. Several hundred American military technicians were also helping. In early 1954 Eisenhower viewed the implications of such aid with some concern. "I cannot conceive of a greater tragedy for America," he told a press conference in February, "than to get heavily involved now in an all-out war in any of those regions, particularly with large units."[23] Then came Dien Bien Phu.

Ground down by the guerrilla tactics of Ho and the political instability in Paris, the dispirited French army decided to make its major stand at Dien Bien Phu. It was an odd choice. The town was located away from the coast, close to the Laotian and Chinese borders, and lay at the bottom of a valley easily commanded by the Viet Minh forces controlling the mountaintops. Wheeling up large artillery pieces, a feat the French refused to believe Ho's forces could accomplish, the Viet Minh lobbed a murderous bombardment upon the French garrison. On March 20 General Paul Fly, the French chief of staff, flew to Washington to request U.S. intervention. This set off a tumultuous six-week debate within Washington and among the Western Allies. Dulles and the chairman of the Joint Chiefs, Admiral Arthur W. Radford, urged an American air strike to save the French. Air Force Chief of Staff Nathan Twining agreed and later outlined his thoughts on how the crisis might have been handled:

> I still think it would have been a good idea [to have taken] three small tactical A-bombs—it's a fairly isolated area, Dien Bien Phu—no great town around there, only Communists and their supplies. You could take all day to drop a bomb, make sure you put it in the right place. No opposition. And clean those Commies out of there and the band could play the Marseillaise and the French would come marching out of Dien Bien Phu in fine shape. And those Commies would say, "Well, those guys might do this again to us. We'd better be careful." And we might not have had this problem we're facing in Vietnam now had we dropped those small "A" weapons.[24]

---

[23]*Public Papers of the Presidents . . . , Eisenhower, 1954* (Washington, 1960), pp. 247–253.
[24]Interview with General Nathan Twining, Dulles Oral History Project, Princeton.

Dulles and Eisenhower disagreed with Twining on the use of atomic bombs, but the President began to waver on the question of American intervention in any form. On April 3, 1954, Dulles intimated to congressional leaders that the administration would appreciate a resolution allowing the commitment of U.S. forces. The congressmen and senators refused after questioning revealed that the Joint Chiefs were split on the problem (Army Chief Matthew Ridgway especially opposed any massive intervention) and that the Western Allies had not been consulted. The next day Eisenhower wrote Churchill that the threat in Vietnam compared with the dangers of "Hirohito, Mussolini, and Hitler" and asked that the United States and Great Britain form a coalition to prevent a catastrophe.[25]

Three days later the President outlined what was at stake by presenting his "domino theory" to a news conference. The struggle was crucial, Eisenhower observed, because the area contained tin, tungsten, and rubber; if, moreover, France lost, "many human beings [would] pass under a dictatorship. . . . Finally you have . . . what you would call the 'falling domino' principle. You have a row of dominoes set up, you knock over the first one, and what will happen to the last one is the certainty that it will go over very quickly. So you could have a beginning of a disintegration that would have the most profound influences." He especially worried about the economic and political effects upon Japan, the key to the containment of Russia and China in the Far East.[26]

The administration next intensified the pressure on the British. At the height of the crisis, April 20–24, 1954, Dulles flew to London to ask for the go-ahead from Churchill so that the President could send Congress the intervention resolution. The prime minister never flashed the green light. He refused to commit his government to the lost French effort, particularly during the forty-eight hours before the interested powers were to meet in Geneva on April 26 to negotiate the Indochinese problem. Without British cooperation Senate and House leaders refused to support the intervention resolution. Within

---

[25]Eisenhower, *The White House Years*, pp. 346–347.

[26]*Public Papers of the Presidents . . . , Eisenhower, 1954*, pp. 382–383. The full response can be read in chapter VII documents at the book's www.mhhe.com/lafeber website. For the importance of a newly industrializing Japan in Eisenhower's "Theory," note Sayuri Shimizu, *Creating People of Plenty* (Kent, Ohio, 2001), pp. 20–28, and Japan's notable reaction on pp. 174–179.

the White House General Ridgway was persuading Eisenhower not to follow any line that might lead to the landing of American conventional forces. Logistics, politics, and the memories of Korea, Ridgway argued, worked against such a commitment. On May 7 the decimated French garrison surrendered.

Despite the debacle at Dien Bien Phu, the diplomats made little progress in their negotiations at Geneva. Then in mid-June the government fell in Paris and was replaced by a Gaullist-radical coalition led by Pierre Mendés-France. The new premier promised either peace in Indochina or his resignation by July 20. In the two pacts concluded on July 20–21, 1954, the Geneva Accords (or Final Declaration) and the Geneva Armistice Agreement, the parties agreed: first, that a truce would occur between Ho's forces and the French (not, it is important to note, any southern Vietnamese government); second, on a temporary partition at the 17th parallel with French troops withdrawing from north of that line; third, that North and South Vietnam would neither join military alliances nor allow foreign military bases on their territories; fourth, that national elections, supervised by a joint commission of India, Canada, and Poland, would be held within two years to unify the country, and—the parties understood—France would remain in the south to carry out those elections; fifth; that regrouping of pro-communist Pathet Lao forces would be allowed in Laos, and in that country and Cambodia general elections would be held.

Ho's armies controlled two-thirds of Vietnam, but by accepting these agreements he pulled his troops into the northern half of the nation. He gave up half his country because his closest allies, China and the Soviets, demanded it. They wanted no further excuse for U.S. military involvement, no wider war. Ho never forgot this—it haunted Vietnam's relations with his two allies "like memories of a past infidelity casting shadows over a marriage," as one historian phrased it. When the worried Chinese and Russians would ask Ho to talk with the Americans in the 1960s, he ignored their advice.[27] Ho also compromised because he apparently preferred to deal with Mendés-France rather than with another premier who might come in after the July 20 deadline, and because Ho further believed that

---

[27]Odd Arne Westad, et al., "*77 Conversations Between Chinese and Foreign Leaders . . .*," Cold War International History Project (Washington, D.C., 1996), p. 16.

the French would hold to their promise of conducting elections in 1956. In such an election the North Vietnamese leader would certainly win, for he was the best-known and most powerful nationalist in all Vietnam. (Eisenhower later estimated that Ho would have received possibly 80 percent of the vote if the elections had been held at that time.) In his careful analysis of the situation, Ho had overlooked just one possibility: the United States might replace the French in South Vietnam. If this occurred, the Geneva agreements could become more like wastepaper than solemn treaties.

The American delegation had not been a party to the negotiations on the armistice and refused to agree formally to the accords. Affixing an American signature to an agreement with communists that turned over half of Vietnam to Ho would not have enhanced Dulles's popularity at home. The United States announced only that it would support "free elections supervised by the United Nations" and look on with "grave concern and as seriously threatening international peace and security" any renewal of "aggression in violation of the aforesaid agreements." (The Geneva agreement and the U.S. dissent can be read in the chapter VII documents at the www.mhhe.com/lafeber website.)

Within a year the United States replaced France as the Western power in South Vietnam. The process began at least as early as September–October 1954, when Dulles announced that henceforth American aid would go directly to the South Vietnamese and not through the French. As the secretary explained, this change would destroy the French "protected preferential market" and allow close friends like the Japanese to sell goods directly to the Vietnamese. Dulles denied any "desire" to "displace" French influence, but "a certain displacement is, I think, inevitable."[28]

Military advisers under General J. Lawton Collins began training a South Vietnamese Army; they hoped it could defend its homeland without the aid of American troops. The effect of Korea upon American thinking was immense. Collins had been chief of staff during the Korean War and was a charter member of the "Never-Again Club," a group of American Army officers, including Matthew Ridgway, who

[28]Press Conference in Manila, March 2, 1955, Conference Dossiers, Dulles Papers, Princeton.

swore they would never again commit American troops to Asia without having an ironclad promise from Washington that the troops would be supported by the bombing of such enemy cities and supply lines as sanctuaries in Manchuria and China. The Vietnamese Army now learned from its American advisers how to move in large units with heavy weapons from fortified points. The Vietnamese were being prepared to fight the Korean War all over again.[29]

This American aid carried political implications. For example, the revitalized Vietnamese Army soon was plotting against the government. That government had been placed in the hands of Ngo Dinh Diem over strenuous French objections. The United States had brought in Diem, a Roman Catholic, from his self-imposed exile at Maryknoll Seminary in Ossining, New York. (Most Vietnamese were Hindus. Roman Catholics made up only ten percent of the population.) Eisenhower pledged in a letter of October 1954 that the United States would support the Vietnamese government in the south with economic aid in order to enable Diem to resist subversion or aggression. The President made no offer of open-ended military aid, further hedging his pledge by asking Diem for economic and social reforms so that the aid could be beneficially used.

By July 1955 most of the French had left Vietnam. Diem announced that the elections agreed to in the Geneva Accords would not be held. Dulles fully supported the announcement with the argument that Diem's government had not signed the accords which promised the elections. More to the point, Dulles and Diem knew that the latter would have grave difficulties defeating Ho in a fair election, and American officials did not believe that the northern government had any intention of running a fair election. The secretary of state had set the stage for this announcement in May 1955, when he gave reporters a lesson in comparative history. The United States, he warned, would recognize an anti-Diem government in the south only if "it seems to be expressive of the real will of the people and if it is truly representative." The American Revolution, Dulles observed, deferred to what "is called a decent respect for the opinions of mankind," and, he continued, all "changes" should be undertaken soberly and "with a decent respect for the opinions of mankind."[30]

---

[29]Joseph Kraft, *Profiles in Power* (New York, 1966), pp. 139–143.
[30]Off the Record News Conference, May 7, 1955, in Paris, Conference Dossiers, Dulles Papers, Princeton.

Despite such remarks Dulles no doubt realized that Asian revolutions bore a closer relationship to the ideas of Mao Ze-dong than to those of Thomas Jefferson. At least he acted upon such an assumption shortly after the Geneva Conference, when he led the drive to establish the Southeast Asia Treaty Organization. Such a military pact had long been discussed. Dulles brought the idea into reality in a treaty signed at Manila on September 8, 1954, by the United States, France, Great Britain, Australia, New Zealand, Thailand, Pakistan, and the Philippines. These nations agreed that any armed attack upon them "or against any State or territory which the Parties by unanimous agreement may hereafter designate" (which would include, through a separate protocol, Cambodia, Laos, and Vietnam) would endanger the "peace and safety" of each of the signatories.[31]

This agreement hid crucial differences among the signatories. Dulles realized that the treaty would have to run the gamut of the U.S. Senate, so he carefully provided for sending American forces only when "communist aggression" was evident, and only then after due "constitutional processes," which supposedly meant that Congress would have to approve. Pakistan, however, did not like the "communist aggression" clause because it wanted help against possible trouble with India. (India refused to join because Prime Minister Pandit Nehru feared association with the Western colonial powers.) After an intense debate the defensive zone of SEATO was not extended to either Taiwan or Hong Kong but did include Cambodia, Laos, and South Vietnam. This left the treaty open to the charge that it was violating the Geneva Accords by implicitly bringing the former French colonies into an alliance system. Despite such potentially explosive issues the treaty sailed through the Senate by a vote of 82 to 1.

The Senate ratification is of major significance in American diplomatic history. As Republican Senator Alexander Wiley of Wisconsin observed, SEATO differed from NATO because the United States was now committed not only "to resist armed attack, but also to prevent and counter subversive activities directed from without."[32] Dulles acknowledged this and had earlier warned the cabinet of the inherent

---

[31]U.S. Senate, Committee on Foreign Relations, 83rd Cong., 2nd Sess., *Hearing . . . on the Southeast Asia Collective Defense Treaty . . .* (Washington, 1954), Part 1, pp. 4–5, 28. The SEATO treaty and Dulles's arguments for it before the U.S. Senate can be found in the chapter VII documents at the www.mhhe.com/lafeber website.

[32]U.S. Senate, *Hearing . . . on the Southeast Asia Collective Defense Treaty*, Part 1, p. 10.

dangers in such an agreement: "If we take a position against a Communist faction within a foreign country, we have to act alone," he lamented. "We are confronted by an unfortunate fact—most of the countries of the world do not share our view that Communist control of any government anywhere is in itself a danger and a threat."[33] Dulles was nevertheless willing to commit the United States to such a view. He thus also noted another crucial difference between NATO and SEATO. In NATO the United States acted multilaterally with its European allies, but in SEATO Americans would end up acting virtually alone because most Asian nations had little interest in helping them.

This carried another historic implication. Since the 1840s the United States had demanded an "open-door" policy to allow American goods and ideas into Asia. But now the traditional "open-door" policy would no longer be followed. Instead of a policy of "fair field and no favor" to anyone, as Secretary of State John Hay had asked for at the turn of the century, Dulles announced that the Monroe Doctrine was instead being extended to Asia. As the doctrine had warned the Holy Alliance to keep "hands-off" Latin America in the nineteenth century, now the United States, in Dulles's words, "declared that an intrusion [in the Far East] would be dangerous to our peace and security."[34] Whether the United States could unilaterally enforce that doctrine in Asia remained to be seen.

A first challenge was successfully blunted in 1954 and 1955 when the Chinese communists threatened the offshore islands of Quemoy, Matsu, and the Tachens, which lay between the mainland and Taiwan. As the communists shelled the islands and then announced the imminent "liberation" of Taiwan, Eisenhower warned that such liberation forces would have to run over the American Seventh Fleet stationed in the Formosa Straits. Dulles flew to Taiwan in December and signed a mutual defense pact with Chiang Kai-shek that pledged the United States to defend Chiang in return for his promise not to try to invade the mainland without American approval. Nothing was said in the pact about the offshore islands. On January 18, 1955, the communists took the small northernmost island of the Tachen group. Eisenhower declared that, because this island had no relationship to the defense of Taiwan, the attack required

---

[33]Sherman Adams, *First-Hand Report* (New York, 1961), p. 124.
[34]U.S. Senate, *Hearing . . . on the Southeast Asia Collective Defense Treaty*, Part 1, p. 21.

no counteraction. Within five days, however, he asked Congress for authority to "assure the security of Formosa and the Pescadores [Matsu and the rest of the Tachen group]" and, if necessary, "closely related localities." Congress whipped through the resolution by a vote of 409 to 3 in the House and 85 to 3 in the Senate.

Some questioned the means involved. Perhaps the resolution was a dangerous precedent for less responsible Presidents who would demand open-ended authorizations from Congress to use force against communism. Herman Phleger, the legal adviser of the Department of State who helped Dulles draft the resolution, called it a "monumental" step, for "never before in our history had anything been done like that." The method, Phleger later observed, solved for future Presidents the problem that had brought down severe criticism upon Truman when he did not obtain congressional assent for the Korean intervention.[35] The 1955 resolution turned out to be a major step in creating an imperial presidency.

Bitter arguments soured the Western alliance between 1953 and 1956. Many of the disputed points became clear when Dulles struggled to obtain French ratification of the EDC. The secretary of state had tried to force the hand of the French government in mid-December 1953, when he warned that France must ratify or face an "agonizing reappraisal" by Washington of American commitments to Europe. This implied a retreat to a "Fortress America" concept, which would leave Great Britain and France alone to face once again a revitalized Germany. Dulles was playing a risky game, but he was deadly serious. Realizing that any French government which forced the passage of the EDC could well be committing political suicide, Dulles was willing to have one French coalition do exactly this, for without the EDC Adenauer might well lose interest in his links with the West. The French also seemed expendable because Dulles wondered if they could ever again become a great power.[36]

The French had become the pawns in a climactic power struggle. They tried to stall the fateful vote by following a policy best described as *de conserver la cadavre dans le placard* ("keeping the corpse in the closet"). Three governments refused to bring the agreements to

[35]Interview with Herman Phleger, Dulles Oral History Project, Princeton.
[36]Anthony Eden, *Full Circle: The Memoirs of Anthony Eden* (Boston, 1960), pp. 64, 108.

a vote. With the delay, French hostility grew. France, opponents of
EDC argued, had an army that could lose its nationality in such a
community; but West Germany had nothing to lose for it had no
army. Anyway, why create a German army? France would also have
to divide its armies between Europe and overseas possessions; any
German military force could concentrate on Europe. And why do
such things when Malenkov was attempting to ease tensions?

In a dramatic last-minute meeting in August 1954, Mendés-France
told Western diplomats he would finally take the corpse from the
closet, but only after conditions were attached to the EDC. But not
even these modifications were enough. After a bitter debate on August
30 in which Mendés-France significantly refused to stake his government's life upon the outcome, the Assembly defeated the EDC 314 to
264 with 43 abstentions.

France had miscalculated. Not fully realizing how they were being
acted upon rather than acting in the unfolding diplomacy, the French
believed the defeat of the EDC had scotched, perhaps killed, German
rearmament. Instead they had simply exchanged the EDC, which provided for controls upon that rearmament, for perhaps NATO, which
had no such controls and would allow the development of a national
German army. For Dulles insisted that West Germany must be
rearmed. U.S. policy rested upon that imperative. As Dulles defined
the aftermath of the French vote as "a crisis of almost terrifying pro-
portions," Anthony Eden worked out a solution.

While lounging in his Sunday bath, Eden hit upon an idea. He
advocated enlarging the Western European Union (WEU) of 1948
(which originally had been an anti-German tool) by including West
Germany. The WEU would not allow complete supranational control, but it would give France what it had begged for during the EDC
struggle, the commitment of four British divisions to mainland
Europe. The French were doubly assured when Dulles pledged that
American troops would remain in Europe if France accepted the
WEU idea. Adenauer cooperated by promising that Germany would
not manufacture long-range missiles, or atomic, bacteriological, or
chemical weapons, without the approval of the NATO commander
and a two-thirds majority of the WEU Council. The other signatories
pledged that West Germany would not "have recourse to force to
achieve the reunification of Germany or the modification of the present boundaries" of Germany. These promises were written into the

Paris Agreements of October 1954.[37] On Christmas Eve Mendés-France drove the pact through the French Assembly but only after overcoming strong opposition. West German armies entered NATO in 1955.

In Indochina and Europe, Paris officials had learned lessons in Cold War power politics which would reorient their foreign polices and make them less amenable to American pressure. By no means coincidentally, Mendés-France secretly initiated the independent development of a French atomic and nuclear power project in the midst of these crises. Dulles, on the other hand, believed that the Paris Agreements created a situation which was in the best interests of both Europe and the United States. With that status quo apparently ensured, the Eisenhower administration returned its attention to the new Cold War erupting among the newly emerging nations.

[37]Department of State, *American Foreign Policy, 1950–1955, Basic Documents,* I: 1476–1496.

Jazz great Louis Armstrong spread some of the best of American culture abroad to the delight of Vice President Richard Nixon. But Armstrong condemned Eisenhower-Nixon civil-rights policies at home.
(© Bettman/Corbis)

CHAPTER 8

East and West of Suez (1954–1957)

The mass of the newly emerging peoples had little interest in the ideological struggle between the Soviet Union and the United States. They wanted only political independence and release from grinding poverty. To obtain these, they were willing to borrow from both systems, and if Soviets and Americans would compete for their allegiance and resources, so much the better. That was indeed a compelling argument not to become too firmly aligned with either side but to remain in a "Third World." Neither Russians nor Americans, however, appreciated such views. When in April 1953 Dulles accused the Russians of looking "upon anybody who is not for them as against them," he was unfortunately also characterizing American attitudes. The secretary of state knew that, as he once phrased it, "to oppose nationalism is counter-productive," but as late as June 1956 his views of communism and an apparent confusion over the meaning of nationalism enabled Dulles to say that neutrality had "increasingly become an obsolete conception and, except under very exceptional circumstances, it is an immoral and short-sighted conception."

By the mid-1950s each superpower believed that the future vitality of its ideological, economic, and strategic systems depended upon "winning" the Third World. Each would have believed this even if the other superpower had not existed. The United States and Russia were expansive forces and had been so in many areas (as, for example, in Asia) since at least the nineteenth century. The Cold War sharpened these drives by allowing each side to intensify its dynamic, historic expansion. As the nature of the Cold War changed between

1953 and 1956, pulling the attention of the United States and Russia away from Europe and toward longtime interests in the less developed world, this different Cold War required important adjustments in the Soviet and American societies.

In the Soviet Union a bitter internal party struggle obscured the meaning and extent of the Russian adjustment. On New Year's Day 1955 Malenkov announced that the Russian possession of hydrogen bombs made peaceful coexistence "necessary and possible." Khrushchev immediately accused the premier of attempting to intimidate the proletariat revolution with atomic weapons.[1] This line of attack won the support of such military leaders as Defense Minister Nikolay Bulganin and World War II hero Georgi Zhukov, and brought old-time Stalinists like Molotov to Khrushchev's side. On February 8 Khrushchev demanded and obtained Malenkov's resignation. Bulganin became premier, but Khrushchev held the real power as first party secretary. With the simultaneous fall from power of some of Malenkov's more liberal associates in Russia and throughout the bloc (such as Imre Nagy as prime minister in Hungary), Russia appeared to be sinking back into Stalinist political, economic, and foreign policies.

Such appearances deceived. By the middle of 1955 Khrushchev turned against Stalinist policies and worked out a rapprochement with Yugoslavia and a peace treaty for Austria. Having used the questions of economic investments and foreign policy to oust Malenkov, Khrushchev now shrewdly adopted the former premier's policies. (The victor never thought much of his vanquished colleagues. Americans, Khrushchev once remarked, "are from a highly educated nation and they look upon us as being equally highly educated. They don't know that we [in Russia] are dominated by an unimaginative and unattractive bunch of scoundrels.")[2]

Khrushchev structured his new approach carefully. He safeguarded Soviet security both ideologically and militarily by developing the Warsaw Pact—a bloc military alliance, patterned after NATO, which could allow Soviet military control of Eastern Europe after the political controls were relaxed. On Aviation Day 1955 the Soviets flexed awesome military muscles by flying unit after unit of

---

[1]Myron Rush, *Political Succession in the U.S.S.R.* (New York, 1965), pp. 48, 60; Arnold L. Horelick and Myron Rush, *Strategic Power and Soviet Foreign Policy* (Chicago, 1966), pp. 17–30.

[2]Quoted in Dino A. Brugioni, *Eyeball to Eyeball* (New York, 1990), p. 250.

new jet planes over Moscow. (Only later did American intelligence learn that Khrushchev simply had a relatively few planes fly around in circles.) He also tried to deal with the challenges posed to Soviet authority by independently minded Yugoslavia and China. Khrushchev first announced that Russia was further along the road to communism than any other nation. This supposedly assured the Soviets of acting as the chief ideologist within the communist world. In 1954 he had magnanimously traveled to China and had personally returned to Mao the former Chinese possessions of Port Arthur and the Chinese Eastern Railway, long controlled by Russia. A similar line was followed in Yugoslavia, despite Molotov's warning that easing relations with Tito would weaken Soviet control over the satellites. Khrushchev nevertheless went to Belgrade, blamed past Soviet-Yugoslav troubles on Stalin, and negotiated improved diplomatic and economic ties.

With the communist world supposedly reconsolidated, Khrushchev launched an aid program for the newly emerging nations which, as he candidly told a group of junketing American congressmen in 1955, he valued "least for economic reasons and most for political purposes." By the end of 1956 fourteen economic and military assistance agreements had been signed with nations in Asia and the Middle East. Khrushchev was highly selective in compiling the list. North Vietnam and Indonesia were favored in Southeast Asia. In the Middle East, Iran, Afghanistan, Turkey, and Egypt were targets of the Soviet economic offensive.

The Chinese provided the proper ideological accompaniment for this drive by attending the Bandung conference of nonaligned states in April 1955 and reaffirming the Five Principles of Peaceful Coexistence, which had been agreed upon between India and China the year before. These promised mutual respect for sovereignty and territorial integrity, noninterference in one another's domestic affairs, and peaceful coexistence. Soviet ideologists supported the Chinese proclamation by emphasizing that Stalin's old two-camp approach had been replaced with a confidence that communists and nationalists could work against Western imperialism and enter the promised land of socialism hand in hand. Never had the reputation of Communist China and Russia been higher among the newly emerging nations. Like the Eisenhower administration, Khrushchev was also thinking in global terms.

Dulles fully appreciated what communism was accomplishing. The secretary of state analyzed in detail the new world situation for the NATO Foreign Ministers during the May meetings of 1955 and 1956. Communism was on the move in Asia, Dulles warned. The Chinese brand posed a greater threat than the Russian, since it controlled a greater population mass and possessed a cultural prestige in Asia not enjoyed by Russia in either Europe or Asia. The secretary noted the major Chinese colonies which existed in many free Asian nations. He feared that Mao could follow a rule of divide and conquer because the noncommunist countries were scattered geographically and divided politically, culturally, and economically. The West, Dulles declared, must never surrender those nations: "The stakes are too high." There were 1.6 billion people in the underdeveloped areas now exposed to communist economic tactics. If those tactics prevailed, "the world ratio as between communist dominated peoples and free peoples would change from a ratio of two-to-one in favor of freedom to a ratio of one-to-three against freedom." "That," Dulles emphasized, "would be an almost intolerable ratio given the industrialized nature of the Atlantic Community and its dependence upon broad markets and access to raw materials."[3]

The central question then arose: What kind of military strategy was needed to fight this new Cold War? During the mid-1954 Dien Bien Phu crisis in Vietnam, one slight swing in American strategic thinking had begun to appear. Because NATO did not have manpower to match the communists, Dulles argued that the West should "use atomic weapons as conventional weapons against the military assets of the enemy whenever and wherever it would be of advantage to do so, taking account of all relevant factors."[4] When this tactic was employed in NATO war games in Europe, however, the results demonstrated that the type of limited war Dulles urged would incinerate most of Central Europe.

The only alternative seemed to be the development of American forces to fight wars that would stop short of nuclear exchanges. Scholars such as Bernard Brodie and Henry Kissinger began to advance this argument in late 1954. Within a year Army Chief of Staff General

---

[3]"Far East Presentation," May 10, 1955, and "NATO Meeting, Etc.," Paris, May 1–7, 1956, Conference Dossiers, Dulles Papers, Princeton.
[4]"Proposed 'Talking Paper,'" April 23, 1954, Conference Dossiers, Dulles Papers, Princeton.

Maxwell D. Taylor split the Joint Chiefs by unsuccessfully demanding, against Admiral Arthur Radford's opposition, that the military response become more flexible. Radford won the argument, but the new trend, which would become fully apparent in 1961, had set in and had done so as experts realized that massive retaliation was too inflexible for the demands of the changing Cold War. Whether, on the other hand, limited conventional war could adequately protect American interests in the less developed areas remained to be seen.

Similar problems bedeviled the administration in the economic realm. Here Dulles recognized the importance of aid for the newly emerging nations, but he overestimated its power. In dealing with proud, newly independent India he privately said that if he offered economic aid, Indian officials "will come crawling on their hands and knees." U.S.-India relations worsened until they became near adversaries after the 1960s. Washington officials overestimated their economic influence (much as Truman had with the Soviets in 1945). Eisenhower placed strong faith in productivity, "because it relieves pressures in the world that are favorable to Communism." He defined China as one huge claw reaching out for anyone who had five cents. Dulles's comment was dry and to the point: "In India today, the great peril of Communism comes from intellectual centers."[5] In his concern with productivity Eisenhower had overlooked the demand of newly emerging peoples for a rapidly developing productivity regardless of the social and political costs.

Innovation was also wanting in the field of foreign aid. In the newly emerging areas development had to occur literally from the ground up. This required internal stability and huge amounts of outside capital and technical aid. The Marshall Plan had worked as well as it did because the Europeans had the technical know-how and capital resources to turn every dollar of American aid into six dollars of capital formation. This would obviously not be the case in Asia, Africa, or Latin America. Secretary of the Treasury George Humphrey warmly endorsed placing the burden on private capital, while allowing the World Bank (which depended upon the private money market) to make necessary long-term capital loans.

---

[5]Robert J. Donovan, *Eisenhower: The Inside Story* (New York, 1956), pp. 3, 9; the Dulles quote on India is in Andrew Rotter's pioneering account on U.S.-India, *Comrades at Odds* (Ithaca, N.Y., 2000), p. 267.

Humphrey essentially won the argument.[6] Primary reliance was placed upon private capital. But private capital was uninterested in most newly emerging nations, for it favored more stable areas; between 1953 and 1956, for example, U.S. investments in Latin America increased $1.4 billion, or 19.2 percent, while in Western Europe and Canada they climbed $3.4 billion, or over 30 percent.[7]

Over all these debates hung the pall of McCarthyism. Wisconsin's junior senator, according to a public opinion poll, was regarded favorably by over half those surveyed in early 1954. His popularity had jumped sixteen points in six months, the same months he was encouraging the burning of supposedly "left-wing" books and accusing the President of the United States of allowing the American allies to carry on a "blood trade" with China. One ramification of this feeling occurred early in 1954 when Senator John Bricker of Ohio proposed an amendment to the Constitution which aimed to eliminate the possibility of any more one-man "sellouts" similar, as some claimed, to that which Roosevelt accomplished at Yalta through executive agreements made between himself and Stalin or Churchill. The Bricker amendment, like McCarthyism, was both anti-Democrat and antipresidential. "Since 1948," Bricker had charged in 1951, "the outstanding characteristic of the Truman administration has been its persistent effort to usurp legislative functions." The Republican senator warned that "the constitutional power of Congress to determine American foreign policy is at stake."

Discussed since 1951, Bricker's proposal was softened until in 1954 the Senate voted on a version whose key section provided that an international agreement other than a treaty (for example, an executive agreement) could become internal law "only by an act of Congress." Eisenhower fought the measure, warning that foreign leaders would view such restraints upon presidential power as redolent of 1930's isolationism. The proposal nevertheless was supported by a majority, 60 to 31, although falling just one vote shy of the two-thirds needed for a constitutional amendment. The most fascinating result was that the debate produced the exact opposite of Bricker's intentions. In 1955 and

---

[6]"Memorandum Re NAC Meeting," September 30, 1953, in file on NATO Meeting, December 8–15, 1956, Conference Dossiers, Dulles Papers, Princeton.
[7]U.S. Bureau of the Census, *Historical Statistics of the U.S., Colonial Times to 1957* (Washington, 1960), p. 566.

1958 during international crises, Eisenhower carefully asked Congress to authorize his actions (as Bricker wanted), but he did it so ingeniously that Congress gave the President a virtual blank check. Lyndon Johnson later used Eisenhower's tactics in obtaining congressional support for his intervention in Vietnam.[8]

In 1953–1954 McCarthyism did not stop at the boundaries of politics. Although American scientists were increasingly needed for judgments and weapons in fighting the Cold War, the scientific community was not immune to attack. The anti-intellectualism which imbued McCarthyism, and the lack of ardor for the Cold War shown by some scientists, climaxed in the case of J. Robert Oppenheimer in 1954. Oppenheimer was perhaps the most distinguished physicist in the United States. He had directed the laboratory at Los Alamos, which produced the first atomic bomb in 1945. His downfall began when he questioned the building of the hydrogen bomb in 1949–1950. He was not alone. Many scientists, their political awareness made acute by their participation in the A-bomb project, had moved into Washington after 1946 to lobby long and earnestly for the imposition of strong controls upon the development and use of atomic energy. Probably a majority of American physicists opposed the decision to make the hydrogen bomb because they believed it strategically unsound and politically dangerous.[9]

Oppenheimer shared such sentiments, but unlike most of the other scientists, long ago—before and during World War II—he had had personal relations with Communist party members in the United States and later had made personal enemies on the Atomic Energy Commission. A four-foot-six-inch-high FBI folder on Oppenheimer detailed his past but concluded that no evidence indicated that he had worked against the national interest. Eisenhower (who once defined an intellectual as "a man who takes more words than is necessary to say more than he knows") refused to take a public position. A special three-man board unanimously declared Oppenheimer to be "a loyal citizen" but nevertheless voted 2 to 1 against giving him continued

[8]A standard account is Duane Tananbaum, *The Bricker Amendment Controversy: A Test of Eisenhower's Political Leadership* (New York, 1988).

[9]The background for and details of this story are now in Jessica Wang's important *American Science in an Age of Anxiety* (Chapel Hill, N.C., 1999); and the now standard biography of Oppenheimer by Kai Bird and Martin J. Sherwin, *American Prometheus* (New York, 2005), especially chapters 26, 30–37.

access to classified information. This effectively removed Oppenheimer's voice from top governmental councils. The Atomic Energy Commission upheld this judgment 4 to 1 not on the basis of disloyalty but because of "fundamental defects in his 'character.'" No one ever proved that Oppenheimer was disloyal; the one AEC member who thought so in 1954, Thomas E. Murray, several years later admitted that his vote had been cast "within the exigencies of the moment." This was a euphemism for ignorant, anti-intellectual McCarthyism.

With the cabinet, the military, Congress, and intellectuals increasingly immobile, Dulles found himself torn between these political restraints on the one hand and, on the other, his recognition of the critical changes in international affairs. He had, for example, stalled off a summit meeting by arguing that the Soviets would have to show their sincerity in wanting negotiations by signing an Austrian peace treaty. As a part of their reorientation of policy, the Russians suddenly signed the treaty in mid-May 1955. As Eisenhower later related, "Well, suddenly the thing was signed one day and [Dulles] came in and he grinned rather ruefully and he said, 'Well, I think we've had it.'" Dulles's interpretation of the breakthrough on the treaty revealed the American dilemma. He initially claimed that "liberation" had borne rich fruit: "an area of Europe is, in a very literal sense, liberated." At the same time, however, Dulles felt compelled to warn Americans that "the new set of dangers comes from the fact that the wolf has put on a new set of sheep's clothing, and while it is better to have a sheep's clothing on than a bear's clothing on, because sheep don't have claws, I think the policy remains the same."[10]

Dulles adopted that latter approach in preparing for the 1955 summit. He was concerned that the Soviets would use the conference to gain "moral and social equality" with the United States in order to encourage neutralism. The secretary consequently warned Eisenhower to maintain "an austere countenance on occasions where photographing together [with Russians] is inevitable" and to push hard publicly for "satellite liberation." The secretary then set up American demands that would be quite difficult to realize. His

[10]Interview with Dwight D. Eisenhower, Dulles Oral History Project, Dulles Papers, Princeton. "Press and Radio News Conference . . . , May 15, 1955," Conference Dossiers, Dulles Papers, Princeton.

first goal was the unification of Germany "under conditions which will neither 'neutralize' nor 'demilitarize' united Germany, nor subtract it from NATO."[11] To this the Russians would not agree. Dulles effectively sealed this policy when West Germany formally regained its sovereignty, commenced rearming, and entered NATO in May, just weeks before the summit conference was to begin. On the eve of the meeting, Republican leader Senator William Knowland proposed the "Captive Nations" resolution; this expressed the Senate's hope that Soviet satellites "subjected to the captivity of alien despotisms shall again enjoy the right of self-determination."

Given this background, the summit was lucky to produce even a "spirit of Geneva." Eisenhower, Eden (who had succeeded Churchill as prime minister), Bulganin (who fronted for Khrushchev), and Edgar Faure of France opened the meetings on July 18 and immediately ran into a deadlock over Germany. A dead end was reached when Khrushchev overruled a wavering Bulganin by announcing that the Soviets would allow no elections in East Germany until West Germany was disarmed. The United States had thus successfully armed and tied West Germany to the Western alliance, at the same time pushing onto the Soviets the blame for blocking reunification through free elections.

The only major American initiative at Geneva was Eisenhower's "open skies" plan. He proposed the exchange of plans of each nation's military facilities and urged allowing planes to photograph each nation's territory to ensure against surprise attacks. This plan emanated from a panel, headed by Nelson Rockefeller, which was concerned with quieting European fears over the stationing of American nuclear bombs in Europe.[12] The "open skies" proposal would quiet such fears while allowing the bombs to remain. Khrushchev predictably rejected the plan on the grounds that it would infringe on Soviet territorial sovereignty. (This proposal was Eisenhower's second move in the controlled-armaments field. In December 1953 he had proposed before the United Nations a plan to establish an international agency that would control the use of atomic materials for peaceful purposes. Although meeting initial resistance from the Russians and from the American

---

[11]"Estimate of Prospect of Soviet Union Achieving Its Goals," July 1, 1955, Conference Dossiers, Dulles Papers, Princeton.
[12]Donovan, *Inside Story,* pp. 345–346.

Congress, the speech bore fruit three years later with the creation of the International Atomic Energy Agency.)

The Soviets made the best of a bad situation. They worked out formal diplomatic relations with the Adenauer government in mid-September 1955 and a week later gave East Germany full powers in foreign affairs; the latter move would force Adenauer theoretically to deal with affairs in East Germany directly through the East German communist regime instead of through the Russians. That was most repugnant to the West Germans and consequently reinsured the division of Germany. The split was widened in January 1956, when the East German People's Army entered the Warsaw Pact. Dulles's earlier hopes for reunification of Germany on Western terms now disappeared.

Dulles and Eisenhower also failed to imagine the extent to which Khrushchev would reorient the Kremlin. At the Twentieth Party Congress in February 1956, Khrushchev surprised his listeners, shocked the satellites, and astonished the West by detailing Stalin's crimes against the Communist party and (the same thing) Russian national interest.[13] But he exorcised the dictator's ghost with a scalpel, not a meat ax. Nothing was said about the particular purges in which Khrushchev himself had controlled the cattle cars full of human beings slowly moving out of the Ukraine toward Siberian concentration camps during the late 1930s. Instead, he discussed the bloodlettings in which his present enemies on the Presidium had been more closely involved. Khrushchev further emphasized that Stalin and the "cult of the individual" had been at fault, not the communist systems. He also carefully defended the party and the army against the Stalinist crimes, but not the masses or the intellectuals whom he himself would soon restrict and attack. Domestically Khrushchev was trying to increase his personal power, loosen Stalinist restrictions so that the Soviet economy could boom, and yet keep the society under absolute control without resorting to terrorist methods.

Foreign policy could not be walled off from this internal reorientation. The East European satellites were stunned. Khrushchev destroyed their supposedly unquestioning belief in Stalin and all acts of the Soviet Union. Khrushchev substituted the idea that several roads led to communism while emphasizing, nevertheless, that communism was the destiny toward which all were heading. The

[13]Nikita S. Khrushchev, *The Crimes of the Stalin Era* . . . annotated by Boris I. Nicolaevsky (New York, 1956, 1962).

point was made most clearly in the apology for Stalin's brutal tactics toward Tito. Khrushchev recalled Stalin saying that he would shake his little finger and Tito would fall; "we have," Khrushchev concluded, "dearly paid for this shaking of the little finger."

In this and other speeches at the congress, the Soviet leadership announced that the two-camp approach, the belief that war was inevitable, and the fear of "capitalist encirclement" were all now unsound doctrines. This turn in Russian thinking somewhat resembled the change in American thinking when the United States began to view the surrounding oceans not as barriers ensuring isolation, but as highways for internationalism. Within a general policy of détente with the Western world, the Soviets would tear down Stalinist-imposed barriers and move down adjoining highways into the third, uncommitted world. In keeping with this more open policy, Mikoyan, head of the Presidium, announced the dissolution of the Cominform on April 17, 1956.

After the Geneva conference of 1955, Dulles wondered whether the Soviet "maneuver" of easing tension "may in fact assume the force of an irreversible trend." Such seemed to be the case within weeks after Khrushchev's speech. In March 1956 riots erupted in Soviet Georgia, the home of the now degraded Stalin. In June mobs rioted against Communist party leaders in Poland and Hungary. Khrushchev also came under attack from the other side when such old-line Stalinists as Lazar M. Kaganovich and Molotov demanded that he forcefully quiet the East Europeans before things got completely out of hand.

In a sense, the moment of "liberation" seemed to be approaching. At the crucial point where the prophecy needed a nudge, however, the prophet was looking the other way. Throughout the summer and autumn Dulles was caught in the maelstrom of Middle Eastern politics. A year and a half before, Israel had dramatically revealed the weakness of the Egyptian Army with a quick, overpowering raid into the disputed Gaza Strip. Egyptian leader Gamal Abdel Nasser soon opened negotiations with Western and communist powers for more modern military weapons. Declaring that American prices were not competitive, he discovered the communists anxious to do anything that would weaken the Baghdad Pact. In late September 1955 Nasser signed an agreement to buy arms from the Czechs.

Dulles suddenly became interested in helping Egypt finance the planned Aswân Dam, a huge project which Nasser hoped would harness the vast power of the lower Nile River and serve as a symbol of how his regime was triumphantly taking Egypt into the twentieth century. In December 1955 the United States and Great Britain offered to help Nasser. As the United States realized, Egypt would have difficulty in paying for both the arms deal and the dam. To double-check this point, World Bank President Eugene Black traveled to Cairo to work out a deal whereby the World Bank, Great Britain, and the United States would supply the immediate funding for the $1.3-billion project. In February 1956 Black and Nasser reached agreement. The Egyptian leader then wrote to Washington regarding discussions on the proposal. Five months later he was still waiting for a reply.

Dulles had become trapped in Washington. Testifying before the Senate Foreign Relations Committee in February 1956, the secretary argued that, although Egypt and Syria might receive communist arms, he should not have to bow before domestic political pressure and send arms to Israel. This could only lead to an all-out arms race in which Arabs would triumph because "thirty-odd million Arabs [have] far greater . . . absorptive capacity" than 1.7 million Israelis. Dulles was forced to admit, however, that the United States was sending tanks to another of Israel's enemies, Saudi Arabia, under terms of a mid-1951 agreement in which the Saudis had allowed the United States to occupy Dhahran Airfield. Asked whether the arms buildup might cause Israel to launch a preventive war, Dulles admitted "there is some danger."[14] Having to take a stand on such questions in an election year was bad enough, but Dulles soon found his position worsening.

In April Egypt, Saudi Arabia, Syria, and Yemen formed a joint military alliance obviously aimed at Israel. These nations, along with Iraq, Lebanon, and Jordan, had refused to recognize the Israeli government. The Czech arms deal with Egypt now assumed a more ominous aspect. In May Nasser withdrew recognition from Chiang Kai-shek and recognized Communist China. This quickly mobilized the many American champions of Chiang to inform Dulles that they staunchly opposed any kind of deal with Nasser. On Capitol Hill this China Lobby found an easy alliance with southern congressmen, who demanded to know why the United States was offering to build a dam that would allow huge crops of Egyptian cotton to compete with American cotton.

---

[14]U.S. Senate, Committee on Foreign Relations, 84th Cong., 2nd Sess., *Hearing . . . on the Situation in the Middle East, February 24, 1956* (Washington, 1956), pp. 43–46, 68.

Dulles concluded that if he suddenly withdrew the offer, Nasser would suffer a disastrous political blow. The secretary also assumed that Khrushchev would not, in fact could not, replace American aid, an assumption with which Eugene Black concurred because of his belief that Nasser could not afford to become further involved with the communist bloc. Black nevertheless warned Dulles to go through with the deal or "hell might break loose."[15] Both of Dulles's assumptions were tragically wrong. He compounded the mistake by announcing the American decision in a cold, direct announcement on July 19, 1956, at the moment the Egyptian foreign minister was arriving to discuss the project and as Nasser himself sat in a widely publicized meeting with Tito and Nehru.

One week later Nasser struck back. He seized the Suez Canal by nationalizing the British-controlled Universal-Suez Canal Company. With a single stroke he recovered his lost prestige and gained the $25-million annual profit of the company for use in building the dam. The Egyptian leader also had his thumb on the jugular of the European economy; 67 million tons of oil had moved to Europe through Suez in 1955. As long as he compensated the shareholders of the company, Nasser was legally justified in seizing the canal. He promised, moreover, to keep the waterway open to all former users of the canal. This was not enough for Great Britain and France. Acutely aware of Western shipping interests and the possible disintegration of the Baghdad Pact, perhaps even of NATO, Dulles tried to ameliorate the crisis by establishing a users' association to manage the canal. This proved unacceptable; the British and French had no inclination to put their vital petroleum imports in the hands of Nasser, and the Egyptians refused to share control of the canal. As early as the end of July, British official Harold Macmillan revealed to Dulles Britain's plans for military action if the problem was not quickly settled.[16] Dulles, however, refused to put excessive pressure on Nasser, did not take the British and French threats seriously, and of course was reluctant to be too closely associated with the former colonial powers.

---

[15]Interview with Eugene Black, Dulles Oral History Project, Dulles Papers, Princeton.
[16]Interview with Robert Murphy, Dulles Oral History Project, Dulles Papers, Princeton; excellent background, especially on Eden's mistaken belief that the United States would stay with him through thick and thin, is in Richard H. Immerman, *John Foster Dulles* (Wilmington, Del., 1999), pp. 150–157.

These policy differences were compounded by the growing personal animosity between Eden and Dulles. Before the 1952 election Eden had dropped an unsubtle hint to Eisenhower that he preferred a secretary of state other than Dulles. The Eden-Dulles relationship never improved much beyond this point. Yet Anglo-American relations depended upon these two men in the autumn of 1956, for their ambassadors in Washington and London were relatively uninformed; the British ambassador actually left the United States on October 11 just as the crisis began to worsen. During the last two weeks of October, communications between London and Washington almost completely broke down.

This was doubly tragic, for as the Middle Eastern situation deteriorated, rebellion erupted in Eastern Europe. The two events became closely related. Having unleashed unknown forces with his denunciation of Stalin, Khrushchev lost control of Poland's rapid de-Stalinization program headed by Wladyslaw Gomulka. Khrushchev flew to Warsaw, moved Soviet military forces into striking position, and delivered a blistering speech against the Polish changes. Gomulka responded by threatening to call out the Polish people. Khrushchev backed down. The news of Gomulka's success spread to Hungary. On October 23 students moved into the streets to demand that longtime Stalinist Ernö Gerö be replaced with Imre Nagy. When the secret police attempted to put down the protests, workers joined the students. One huge demonstration destroyed a gigantic statue of Stalin in central Budapest. The Soviets agreed to replace Gerö with Nagy, but that was no longer enough. The crowds demanded removal of Russian troops stationed in Hungary and the creation of a political party in opposition to the communists. On October 28 the Soviets began withdrawing the tanks that had moved to the outskirts of Budapest.

The next day Israeli troops made a lightning attack that in hours nearly destroyed the Egyptian Army and conquered much of the Sinai peninsula. In close cooperation with Israel, England and France delivered ultimatums to Israel and Egypt on October 30, warning both nations to keep their forces away from the canal. When Nasser rejected the note, British and French planes began bombing Egyptian military targets. The next day, October 31, the Presidium reversed its policy toward Hungary. Nagy had announced the withdrawal of Hungary from the Warsaw Pact. This was going too far, much further, for example, than Gomulka was going in Poland.

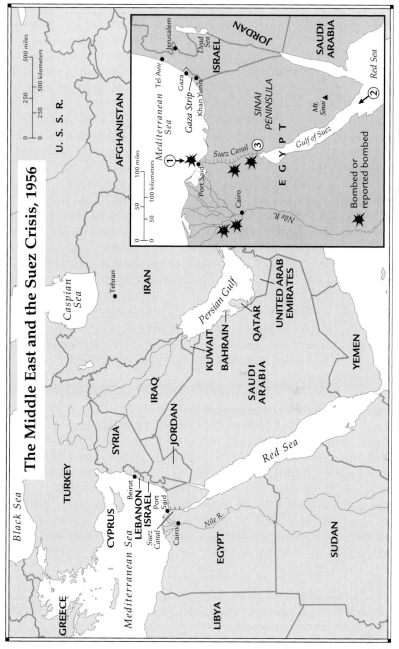

The Middle East and the Suez Crisis, 1956

The confrontation in the Middle East provided Khrushchev with the perfect opportunity. As Anglo-French columns moved into the canal area on November 4 and 5, Russian tanks crushed the Hungarian uprising. The Soviets captured Nagy under false pretenses, shipped him off to Russia, and executed him sometime in 1957. The State Department watched all this helplessly. As one high official later remarked, Dulles, "like everybody else in the Department was terribly distressed," but "none of us had whatever imagination it took to discover another solution. We just were boxed."[17] At the height of the crisis on November 3, Dulles underwent emergency surgery on the cancer which would later kill him.

Having smashed the Hungarian rebellion, Khrushchev paraded into the Middle Eastern scene. He suggested to the State Department that a Russo-American settlement be imposed upon the area and warned Anglo-French forces that, unless they quickly withdrew, the Soviets would use force, perhaps long-range rockets, to squash their armies. On November 6, as Americans went to the polls in a presidential election, Eisenhower responded to Khrushchev's demands by placing American military forces on an emergency alert. He was not, however, primarily afraid of Soviet military action in the Middle East. The greater danger was that Khrushchev might inveigle his way into negotiating a settlement and thereby interject Soviet power in an area which for centuries Western Europe had fought to keep free of Russian influence.

Attempting to short-circuit the Soviet move, the State Department put tremendous pressure on the British, French, and Israelis by passing a resolution through the General Assembly urging a truce. Then Eisenhower cut off oil supplies from Latin America that his close allies, England and France, needed to replace their oil, which could not get through the clogged canal. Hours before they would have seized the canal area, the British and French agreed to a cease-fire and pullback. Throughout November Washington carefully rationed the oil flow to Europe. Not until the UN resolution was obeyed and the troops withdrawn did the oil flow freely. American officials argued that they could not afford to turn on the oil too quickly,

---

[17]Interview with Robert Murphy, Dulles Oral History Project, Dulles Papers, Princeton. For a revealing discussion by Eisenhower and his top advisers of their many crises at this time, see chapter VIII documents at the www.mhhe.com/lafeber website.

for this would infuriate the Arab nations which held huge reservoirs of oil leased to Americans.[18]

By December 22 the armies had left, and a UN emergency force restored the canal area to Egyptian control. The Suez crisis was a graphic study of how the newly emerging peoples were reordering the power balance at the expense of the older and more powerful nations. These lessons had been learned the hard way in Washington and Moscow.

The events in Poland and Suez occurred at the climax of the presidential campaign in the United States. Beginning at a time of relative quiet in foreign affairs, the early weeks of the campaign were marked by a discussion of farm issues and the possible effects of the heart attack suffered by Eisenhower a year before. Democratic nominee Adlai Stevenson tried to overcome this apathy, but he did so in a curiously paradoxical manner. At times he argued that disarmament must be placed at the heart of American policy, urged a restudy and possible discontinuance of the military draft, suggested the suspension of nuclear weapons tests, and accurately pinpointed "events in Eastern Europe and the Middle East" as "symptoms of a vast new upheaval in the balance of world power." At other times, however, Stevenson reaffirmed the Cold War clichés: half of Indochina had "become a new Communist satellite and . . . America emerged from that debacle looking like a 'paper tiger'"; NATO's decline threatened the entire Western world; and in his last speech, Stevenson detailed how Harry Truman had stood up to the Russians while Eisenhower rejected the "great opportunities to exploit weaknesses in the Communist ranks and advance the cause of peace."[19]

In playing such a political game with Eisenhower, Stevenson was outmatched. Republican spokesmen could detail the times Dulles had gotten "tough" with the Russians (or had "gone to the brink" of war, to use Dulles's phrase), while Eisenhower could pose

---

[18]Douglas Little, *American Orientalism: The United States and the Middle East Since 1945* (Chapel Hill, 2002), pp. 90–93, especially for U.S.-Israel; Robert Engler, *The Politics of Oil* (New York, 1961), pp. 261–263; "Memorandum of Conference with the President," November 20, 1956, White House Memoranda Series, Box 4, Dulles Papers, Eisenhower Library, Abilene, Kan.

[19]Adlai E. Stevenson, *The New America* (New York, 1957), pp. 27–34, 40–41.

as the military man who made peace in Korea and knew just when to step back from the brink. When the United States and Russia again approached the brink in the last hours before the election, most Americans had no doubt whom they would entrust with their lives and their Middle Eastern interests.

Eisenhower overwhelmed Stevenson partly because of the President's personal popularity; he received 57 percent of the vote, but the Democrats captured both Houses of Congress, the first time that such a split had occurred since 1848. Yet in judging the rhetoric of the campaign and the postelection analyses, the results clearly demonstrated something more than personal popularity. They marked a consensus of ideology. Voting analyses later revealed that a small majority of Americans preferred Democratic domestic policy, but a larger majority supported Republican foreign policy.[20] Since 1952 Eisenhower had brought nearly all sectors of the Republican party into the internationalist camp. He added numerous Democrats and independents by combining appeals for peace with his history of brinksmanship.[21]

Eisenhower wove this consensus into policy—and an even stronger presidency—just a few months after his reelection.[22] The Suez crisis had seriously weakened the Baghdad Pact and had stimulated Nasser to attempt to increase his power in the Middle East. On January 5, 1957, Eisenhower tried to reverse those trends by replaying his performance of 1954–1955 in the Formosa Straits crisis. He asked Congress for authorization to extend economic and military cooperation and, if necessary, to employ American military forces in the Middle East if any nation in that area requested help against communist-instigated armed aggression. Dulles also secretly informed congressional leaders that the CIA was launching massive covert actions against pro-Soviet groups in the region. The Middle East Resolution, or the "Eisenhower Doctrine" as it came to be known, sailed through the House. The Senate, however, balked.

Senators attacked the resolution as being anti-Israeli, too vague, and injurious to the Western alliance. Dulles did not lessen this last criticism when he remarked that Anglo-French forces must stay out

---

[20]Angus Campbell, et al., *The American Voter* (New York, 1960), pp. 198–200, 526–528.
[21]*Life*, May 14, 1956, p. 184; *New Republic*, October 29, 1956, p. 11.
[22]Reinhold Niebuhr, "The Limits of Military Power." In *The World Crisis* (New York, 1958), pp. 114–121, outlines Niebuhr's role in this consensus.

of the Middle East, for "If I were an American boy . . . I'd rather not have a French and British soldier beside me, one on my right and one on my left." Such a remark was hardly tactful, but in a single sentence Dulles had given his view of how collective the security decision making should be in the Middle East.[23] With the help of Majority Leader Lyndon Johnson, the administration finally passed the resolution in March, 72 to 19. It did so despite little public support. Heavy congressional mail, in fact, ran 8 to 1 against the proposal in February. The passage of the Eisenhower Doctrine had interesting political overtones. A Democratic Congress formally surrendered some of its most important power, especially that of controlling the outbreak of war, to a Republican President. (The text of the Eisenhower Doctrine speech can be found in the chapter VIII documents at the www.mhhe.com/lafeber website.)

If anyone doubted that Eisenhower would use this gift of power, they learned otherwise within a month after the Senate completed action. In April 1957, young King Hussein of Jordan came under attack from pro-Nasser elements within his country. Hussein asked for help and was shrewd enough to announce that he was under attack from "international Communism and its followers." The Eisenhower Doctrine specifically and the general American ideological view of revolutions now faced a test: would the United States help Hussein defend the status quo against the Nasserite elements by brandishing the argument that Hussein was being saved from "international Communism"? Eisenhower responded by sending $10 million to Hussein and dispatching the Sixth Fleet to the Mediterranean area near Jordan. The CIA also apparently sprang into high gear. The official State Department announcement on the sending of this aid did not directly blame "international Communism"; instead it explained the action as safeguarding "the preservation of the independence and integrity of the nations of the Middle East."[24]

[23]U.S. Senate, Committee on Foreign Relations, 85th Cong., 1st Sess., *Hearings . . . to Authorize the President to Undertake Economic and Military Cooperation with Nations in the General Area of the Middle East* (Washington, 1957), Parts 1 and 2, especially pp. 4–41. This and the previous paragraph are also based on Douglas Little, "A Puppet in Search of a Puppeteer?" *International History Review*, XVII (August 1995): 516–525. An excellent detailed analysis is Salim Yaqub, *Containing Arab Nationalism* (Chapel Hill, 2004), especially chapters 2–4.

[24]Department of State, *American Foreign Policy: Current Documents, 1957* (Washington, 1961), p. 1024; Little, "A Puppet in Search of a Puppeteer?" pp. 524–526.

With such ease was a resolution giving the President military powers to fight international communism transformed into presidential power to intervene in any Middle Eastern situation which, by the President's definition, threatened the independence and integrity of any nation in the area. Anticommunism had become a rather strange phenomenon. It had also been integrated into a global Monroe Doctrine. The Eisenhower Doctrine was an extension of the dogmas of 1823 into the Middle East in the same sense that, as Dulles observed, SEATO extended the original doctrine into Southeast Asia.

Having scored triumphs over Congress, the British and French, Nasser, Khrushchev, and Stevenson—not a bad year's work for a sixty-six-year-old with a bad heart—Eisenhower also launched a cultural offensive. His main weapon was the U.S. Information Agency, which his administration set up in 1953. The glamorous, highly publicized offensive had two targets: to counter Khrushchev's attempts to use Soviet ballet, circuses, and science as bait to reel in support from third-world nations; and to demonstrate globally the vitality of American music, literature, film, and theatre. One project, only declassified a half-century later, was Project Pedro. This was a secretly funded effort, helped along by Coca-Cola advertising, to create newsreels for Mexico showing pro-U.S. propaganda and favoring Mexican politicians who favored the United States. Project Pedro, however, lasted only about a half-dozen years before its often boring films, failed attempts to change Mexicans' admiration of Cuba's Fidel Castro, and failure to balance budgets finished off Pedro. Hollywood-style news films, for all their slickness, sometimes could not overcome widely held images of American imperialism in Guatemala and Cuba.

The most popular American art form was jazz, but the USIA at first downplayed this music, perhaps because of its origins a half-century before in New Orleans brothels, perhaps because classical music supposedly had more prestige. In 1955, however, USIA began sending jazz musicians, led by Benny Goodman and the pioneer of jazz, Louis ("Satchmo") Armstrong. In a 1956 tour of Africa and Europe, Armstrong attracted huge crowds, including 100,000 for a concert in Ghana. CBS television filmed the trip, so "Ambassador Satch" triumphed in American homes as well as abroad. The most popular program on Voice of America (the U.S. government-supported radio beamed around the world) was Willis Conover playing jazz and rock-and-roll records. Conover's offerings so affected the young behind the Iron Curtain that, as one observer noted, if Communist officials had understood what was happening, "they would have jammed the music, not the news," to prevent their people from being touched by Armstrong and Elvis Presley.

Notably, the most effective American music came not from white mainstream artists, but from rock-and-rollers condemned by some religious leaders, and from black artists who suffered discrimination and segregation in their own society. The cultural offensive went well until Armstrong saw television pictures of African-American children being spat upon by whites and prevented from attending newly integrated schools in Little Rock, Arkansas. When Eisenhower did little to protect the children, Armstrong denounced the President as "two-faced" with "no guts," then cancelled his next USIA-sponsored trip to the USSR. Criticism rained down on Armstrong, but he stood his ground until pressures built and Eisenhower finally sent federal troops to protect Little Rock students and enforce integration. Cultural offensives overseas that trumpeted American freedoms were, in Armstrong's hands, fair game for being questioned, given the reality of rampant racism at home. Eisenhower and Dulles had never been big fans of the cultural tours. Now their enthusiasm disappeared. The USIA struggled until the Kennedy administration's passion for fighting the Cold War reinvigorated the agency after 1961.[25]

In the early spring of 1957, the Eisenhower administration could believe that it had emerged from the winter crises with increased powers and prestige. Such was not the case with Nikita Khrushchev.

---

[25]On Project Pedro, see the sweeping, pioneering analysis by Seth Fein, "New Empire into Old . . . ," *Diplomatic History*, 28 (November 2004), pp. 703–748. This and the previous paragraph on jazz draw from Penny M. Von Eschen, "'Satchmo Blows up the World': Jazz, Race, and Empire During the Cold War," in Reinhold Wagnleitner and Elaine Tyler May, eds., *"Here, There and Everywhere . . . ."* (Hanover and London, 2000), pp. 163–174; Reinhold Wagnleitner, "The Empire of Fun . . . ," *Diplomatic History*, 23 (Summer 1999); Richard Pells, *Not Like Us: How Europeans Have Loved, Hated, and Transformed American Culture Since World War II* (New York, 1997), pp. 84–86; Lawrence Bergreen, *Louis Armstrong, An Extravagant Life* (New York, 1997), pp. 471–478. On Kennedy, see Mark Haefele, "John F. Kennedy, USIA, and World Public Opinion," *Diplomatic History,* 25 (Winter 2001), pp. 63–84; on the Little Rock crisis and foreign policy, see Cary Fraser, "Crossing the Color Line in Little Rock," Ibid., 24 (Spring 2000), pp. 233–264.

Despite his triumphant proclamation that Dulles's failure to interfere in the Hungarian uprising had proved the hollowness of "liberation," the fiasco of Khrushchev's policies in Eastern Europe and his
inability to take advantage of the power vacuum in the Middle East
immersed him in deep political trouble in Moscow. He came under
vigorous attack for having invited Chinese officials to fly to Warsaw
at a critical moment to quiet the Poles. Having the Chinese play the
role of mediator in Eastern Europe because of Khrushchev's mistakes at the Twentieth Congress gave Molotov, Malenkov, and
Kaganovich their opening. Khrushchev soon counterattacked with
his tactics of 1953–1955. "We are all Stalinists," he loudly announced
at a New Year's Eve party, and then launched into a denunciation of
"capitalist countries" who wanted "a feverish arms race." His talk
became increasingly tough. For the first time since 1955 the Soviet
press accused the United States of following, in the words of a joint
Chinese-Soviet announcement, "a policy of aggression and preparation for war."[26]

During the summer of 1957 Khrushchev gained supreme power.
His first target was the military. Having helped make him, Marshal
Zhukov could perhaps help break him. Khrushchev's opportunity
arose when the marshal began to issue pronouncements on sensitive
political issues as well as on military strategy. Party leaders interpreted this as a direct and dangerous threat to the supremacy of the
party over the military. In late October Zhukov was stripped of his
post as defense minister. When he apparently tried to fight back, he
was also removed from the Presidium and the Central Committee.[27]
Khrushchev next attempted to educate the Soviet intellectuals who
had apparently misunderstood the de-Stalinization campaign to
mean that more candid criticisms of Soviet society would be tolerated. At a garden party, Khrushchev made such a verbal assault upon
the invited intellectuals that one woman fainted. That harangue climaxed with Khrushchev's shouting that Hungary would have
remained orderly if several writers had been shot at the proper time;
if such a threat ever faced the Soviet Union, he added, "My hand

---

[26]A superb account of the communist split is Chen Jian, *Mao's China and the Cold War*
(Chapel Hill, 2001), especially pp. 64–71; and see H.S. Dinerstein, *War and the Soviet
Union*, revised edition (New York, 1959, 1962), pp. 154–163.
[27]Raymond L. Garthoff, *Soviet Military Policy* (New York, 1966), pp. 52–54.

would not tremble."[28] The following year when the distinguished Russian author Boris Pasternak expressed some doubts about the results of the 1917 revolution in his novel *Dr. Zhivago,* the book was banned from mass circulation inside Russia, and Pasternak was prohibited from traveling to Stockholm to receive the Nobel Prize in literature. De-Stalinization had its limits, particularly if it threatened the power of the party and Khrushchev.

After a four-year struggle Khrushchev was supreme. In the United States Eisenhower began his second term in power. The world outside Moscow and Washington had greatly altered between 1953 and 1957. Having created an acceptable status quo in Europe, Washington shifted more and more of its energies to fighting the Cold War in the Third World. In the Soviet Union Khrushchev brought about changes that allowed his government to exploit opportunities within the newly emerging nations. Dwight Eisenhower provided the proper epitaph for the history of those years: "Somehow or other," he wrote Dulles in February 1955, "it seems not all extraordinary that you should celebrate your birthday in Bangkok."[29]

[28]Edward Crankshaw, *Khrushchev, A Career* (New York, 1966), pp. 253–255.
[29]The President to Secretary of State, February 15, 1955, Correspondence, Dulles Papers, Princeton.

Nikita Khrushchev and John F. Kennedy meet for the first time at their fateful conference in Vienna, June 1961.
(Courtesy of John F. Kennedy Library)

CHAPTER 9

New Frontiers and Old Dilemmas (1957–1962)

On the morning of October 4, 1957, the Soviet Union successfully launched the world's first artificial satellite. Named "Sputnik," Russian for "traveling companion," the 184-pound satellite swirled above the earth at 18,000 miles per hour. More significant than the satellite was the powerful booster rocket that thrust Sputnik into orbit, for it indicated Soviet capability of sending a nuclear weapon at very high speeds to targets within a 4000-mile radius. The launching also demonstrated the skill of Soviet missile science. Niebuhr's argument that scientists could be as efficiently exploited by a totalitarian as by a democratic society seemed true—and ominous.

Americans were extremely disturbed. Strategic air force units were dispersed and placed on alert, short-range Jupiter missiles were installed in Turkey and Italy to offset the long-range Soviet weapons, money was poured into missile and bomber programs, and "gaps" were suddenly discovered in everything from missile production to the teaching of arithmetic at the preschool level. Dulles attempted to play down the Soviet feat because he understood the impact it would have on world affairs. The newly emerging nations could view Russia as a people who in 1917 had been generations behind other industrialized nations but who, through harsh regimentation, had rocketed into first place in the race for control of outer space. They could also interpret the launching as a dramatic swing in the balance of military power toward Moscow. In August 1957 the Soviets had fired the world's first intercontinental ballistic missile (ICBM) and that same month had announced, "Co-existence is not only the absence of war between the two systems, but also peaceful economic competition between them, and concrete cooperation in economic, political, and cultural areas."[1] Khrushchev could welcome such competition with the knowledge that the Soviet gross national product (the total amount of goods and services in the economy) had increased on the average of 7.1 percent annually between 1950 and 1958, nearly 50 percent greater than the American rate.

This economic growth was real, but the Soviet lead in ICBMs was not. The Soviets secretly made a basic decision in 1957 not to build an elementary first-generation ICBM complex but to wait for the second- and third-generation models. This meant that for the next few years Russian foreign policy would attempt to exploit an imaginary lead. One interesting way Khrushchev did this was to have Russian radio and newspapers quote back to the West the West's own greatly exaggerated views of Soviet missile capacity, thereby reinforcing the exaggerations.[2]

U.S. arms experts and politicians meanwhile gravely warned that Americans faced the looming danger of being on the wrong side of a "missile gap." Such warnings from Senators John F. Kennedy and Lyndon Johnson grew more shrill as these Democrats opened early campaigns for the 1960 presidential election. In late 1957 their warnings received support from the Gaither Report. A top secret investigation of American military posture, it had been commissioned by Eisenhower's National Security Council. Named after its author, Rowland Gaither, the report updated NSC-68 of seven years before. The report ominously informed Eisenhower that unless U.S. military spending increased 50 percent in the near future, the "expansionist" Soviet threat "may become critical in early 1959 or early 1960." Along with a massive arms buildup, the paper urged a $25-billion ("simple, even spartan") program of fallout shelters which would not only supposedly protect Americans from Soviet attack but permit "our own air defense to use nuclear warheads with greater freedom." Such vast spending would have few bad effects on the U.S. economy and could even "help to sustain production and employment."

---

[1]"The Leninist Course of Peaceful Coexistence," *Kommunist*, No. 11, 1957, p. 5.
[2]Arnold Horelick and Myron Rush, *Strategic Power and Soviet Foreign Policy* (Chicago, 1966), pp. 36–38.

Eisenhower (correctly, as it turned out) dismissed the Gaither Report as badly misguided. He ordered it pigeonholed, and it did not become public until 1973. The President knew from his intelligence sources that Soviet missile forces posed little threat to the United States. He blamed much of the post-Sputnik panic (again correctly) on ambitious politicians such as Kennedy or Johnson, whose major priority was the 1960 election, or on longtime defense specialists—such as Paul Nitze, an author of both the Gaither Report and NSC-68, and later a top Reagan administration official—who could apparently not be satisfied no matter how large U.S. nuclear forces became. As one Republican senator recalled, "Ike took the heat, grinned, and kept his mouth shut."[3]

Eisenhower believed that current programs more than sufficed: between 1958 and 1960 the nation's nuclear stockpile stunningly tripled, from 6,000 to 18,000 weapons. These included fourteen virtually untouchable Polaris nuclear submarines (each with sixteen missiles), the first of which went into service in 1960. Allies and new domestic pressure groups—such as SANE, or the National Committee for a Sane Nuclear Policy—meanwhile pushed Eisenhower to stop nuclear testing and to negotiate arms reduction. Testing temporarily stopped in late 1958 after a series of huge Soviet and American explosions released dangerous amounts of radioactive materials into the atmosphere and, ultimately, into rain and even milk. But Eisenhower and Khrushchev never took the second step to arms control, particularly given the pressures of the Gaither Report and Democratic rhetoric on the President, and of Soviet military officials on the premier.[4]

Despite those pressures Eisenhower refused to panic. He also refused to further skew the economy by dramatically increasing military spending. His refusal required courage, because in 1957–1958 and again in 1959–1960 the economy suffered its second and third significant

---

[3]This and the previous paragraph are based on Robert A. Divine, *The Sputnik Challenge* (New York, 1993), pp. 35–41; and the text available in Joint Committee on Defense Production, 94th Cong., 2nd Sess., *Deterrence and Survival in the Nuclear Age (The "Gaither Report" of 1957)* (Washington, 1976), especially pp. 12, 22–23, 30–31. A good study of the overall response is Peter J. Roman, *Eisenhower and the Missile Gap* (Ithaca, N.Y., 1995).
[4]Robert A. Divine, *Blowing on the Wind: The Nuclear Test Ban Debate, 1954–1960* (New York, 1978), especially chapters 9–11; David Alan Rosenberg, "The Origins of Overkill," *International Security*, VII (Spring 1983), p. 66; David Holloway, *The Soviet Union and the Arms Race* (New Haven, Conn., 1983), pp. 38–40.

downturns of the decade. In retrospect the years between 1957 and 1960 marked a historic turn: in such key areas as Detroit's automobiles and Pittsburgh's steel, the U.S. manufacturing economy became less competitive in world markets than Japan's and West Germany's. Unable to maintain large, favorable trade balances and forced to continue paying the costs of acting as a global policeman, Americans had to begin shipping abroad large amounts of gold to pay their bills—$2 billion of gold in 1958 alone. The dollar, the foundation of the West's economic and military system, wobbled. A top government official finally declared in 1960, "This is the first time in my lifetime that the credit of the United States has been questioned. A serious shadow lies over the American business picture."[5]

Eisenhower privately blamed the problem on greed and a lack of discipline in the United States which he believed threatened to undermine the capitalist system. In a cabinet meeting he also singled out the huge sums spent on weapons that were "just negative stuff adding nothing to the earning capability of the country." In 1960 he blasted the "almost hysterical fear among some elements of the country" that prevented slashes in military budgets.[6] He obviously had Democratic party presidential candidates in mind.

This line of thinking climaxed in early 1961 with the President's famous farewell speech, which warned that a military-industrial complex threatened to distort the economy. At the same time, however, Eisenhower's own view of both the Soviet Union and revolutionary dangers in the Third World prevented him from trying to negotiate arms control agreements or even to educate his fellow Americans on the need to rethink foreign policy in the aftermath of the astonishing events of 1956–1959. Eisenhower understood the causes and costs of the Cold War better than most of the post-1945 Presidents. He also reigned when U.S. military superiority allowed him to negotiate on the causes and reduce the costs. Because of his anticommunism and caution, Eisenhower did neither. But he did manage to pigeonhole (at least until John F. Kennedy moved into the White House) the Gaither

[5]Godfrey Hodgson, *America in Our Time* (New York, 1978), p. 7; Walt Whitman Rostow, *Diffusion of Power, 1958–1972* (New York, 1973), pp. 60–61.
[6]"Minutes of Cabinet Meeting, June 3, 1960," Cabinet Meetings of President Eisenhower, pp. 1–3, Dwight D. Eisenhower Library, Abilene, Kans. On Eisenhower and capitalism, see Robert Griffith, "Dwight D. Eisenhower and the Corporate Commonwealth," *American Historical Review*, LXXXVII (February 1982): especially 117–122.

Report's recommendations for an even greater military buildup. (Eisenhower's "Farewell Address" can be read in the chapter IX documents at the www.mhhe.com/lafeber website.)

Eisenhower could thus afford to ignore Khrushchev's game of missile bluff, but for the rotund Russian leader the game turned out to be most costly. In months it contributed to a widening of the surprising split between the two communist giants. Khrushchev began by being properly cautious; he termed the ICBM the "ultimate weapon" and painted a picture of the horrible destruction that could result from a nuclear exchange. Mao Ze-dong, however, insisted in 1957 that "the international situation has now reached a new turning point. There are two winds in the world today; the East wind and the West wind. . . . I think the characteristic of the situation today is the East wind prevailing over the West wind."[7] Mao assumed, as a Chinese newspaper commented in February 1958, that the Soviet successes had created a "qualitative change in the distribution of world power [which] had . . . torn apart the paper tiger of American imperialism and shattered the tale of the 'position of strength.'"[8] The Chinese urged strong support for "wars of liberation" in the newly emerging nations, wars that could be safely fanned because the American strategic power had been neutralized. Khrushchev refused to cooperate in such recklessness. He knew that his ICBM program was considerably more of a "paper tiger" than the American long-range bombing force.

The break between China and Russia also became evident in other areas. The Soviets strongly disagreed with Mao's "Great Leap Forward" economic program in 1958, with its emphasis on forced collectivization. This disagreement pinpointed internal communist differences, for the Russians, as they had historically, insisted first upon industrial productivity and only secondarily upon infusing the masses with revolutionary ideology. Mao, however, was trying at best to balance the two and, in fact, actually to reverse the Soviet priorities in order to mobilize his tremendous manpower through mass revolutionary indoctrination. The Chinese became increasingly critical of Khrushchev's emphasis on consumer goods instead of military

[7]William Zimmerman, "Russia and the International Order," *Survey*, 58 (January 1966): 209–213.
[8]Donald Zagoria, *The Sino-Soviet Conflict, 1956–1961* (Princeton, 1962), pp. 160–162.

hardware and of the Soviet insistence on aiding "bourgeois" regimes in the underdeveloped world instead of fomenting revolution.

Dulles precisely and colorfully described the new Soviet attitude in May 1958. He no longer feared that the Soviets would pose a greater threat with their disavowal of force and "this policy of the smile." Dulles found hope in the belief "that a nation tends to become what it pretends to be. . . . I have seen lots of tough guys who have made their pile, who come to New York, wanted to get into society, and who have to behave differently."[9]

In these last months of his life, Dulles tried to influence the newly emerging areas by readjusting American policies. An increased emphasis upon Southeast Asia indicated the Eisenhower administration's growing concern over Mao's China. The President's policy became clear in late summer and autumn 1958, when the Chinese began to shell the offshore islands. Mao probably did not plan to invade the islands but hoped that, with the United States immersed in another Middle Eastern crisis, one of two results would occur: either the Quemoy garrison would surrender without being invaded, or the United States would strike back by bombing mainland China and thus bring the Soviets into the affair back of the Chinese. Neither occurred. The American Seventh Fleet escorted Nationalist troops and supplies into the islands. Dulles announced that Quemoy was "increasingly related" to Taiwan's safety, and American Marines moved into Quemoy eight-inch howitzers capable of firing atomic shells. Eisenhower's tough stand on the Chinese problem and his emphasis on tactical atomic weapons had merged into a concrete policy position. Khrushchev did little except assure Mao that Russia would help if China were actually attacked.

The Chinese calculations of the probable American response and the Soviet-American balance of power should have been more accurate, for Mao could have drawn the appropriate conclusions from the

---

[9]"Remarks to U.S. Ambassadors to Europe," Paris, May 9, 1958, NATO ministerial meeting, Conference Dossiers, Dulles Papers, Princeton. For the Chinese view of the Soviet changes and also of the Quemoy crisis discussed in the next paragraph, note especially Chen Jian, *Mao's China and the Cold War* (Chapel Hill, 2001), pp. 170–204. For Japan's increasingly important dissent from U.S. policies toward China, notably on economic issues, see Sayuri Shimizu, *Creating People of Plenty* (Kent, Ohio, 2001), especially pp. 122–147, 202–209.

Middle Eastern crisis of July 1958. In that episode the United States landed marines in Lebanon without any counterstroke from Moscow. Two months before the landings, Dulles had expressed the fear that the growing power of Nasser and the United Arab Republic (formed by Egypt, Syria, and Yemen in early 1958) would endanger Jordan, Iraq, and Lebanon. On July 14 the Iraqi military overthrew the Baghdad government and established a regime friendly to the UAR. The Baghdad Pact suddenly had a gaping hole. Repercussions were felt in Lebanon where pro-Nasser Moslems had been fighting Christians.

The news of the Iraqi coup and the turmoil in Lebanon arrived in Washington early on the morning of July 14. Lebanese President Camille Chamoun, a Maronite Christian, urgently requested help from the United States. At 9:45 A.M. Dulles began explaining to congressional leaders "recent Soviet political activities" in the area. He declared that "it was time to bring a halt to the deterioration in our position in the Middle East." The administration wanted to land troops in Lebanon. There would be no military problem. General Nathan Twining of the Joint Chiefs assured Dulles, as General Twining later recalled, that the "Russians aren't going to jump us," and "if they do jump us, if they do come in, they couldn't pick a better time, because we've got them over the whing whang and they know it."[10]

The only problem was again the proper interpretation of the Eisenhower Doctrine (see p. 194). Some congressmen argued that, because any communist threat was not evident, Dulles was asking them to condone intervention in a Lebanese civil war. Eisenhower shot back that "the crucial question is what the victims believe," and Chamoun believed "Soviet Communism" was the villain. Actually, Chamoun had no evidence the Soviets were involved, but he no doubt knew Americans would pay more attention if he said "Communism," even though the real danger was pro-Nasser Arab nationalism. At 2:30 P.M. the President issued the order. While British paratroopers landed in Jordan to help King Hussein once again stabilize his government, 14,000 American troops waded ashore around surprised public bathers on Lebanon's beaches to quiet the threat of civil war. The size of the force warned both the new Iraqi government

[10]Interview with General Nathan Twining, Dulles Oral History Project, Dulles Papers, Princeton. See also the detailed account in Salim Yaqub, *Containing Arab Nationalism* (Chapel Hill, 2004), pp. 220–236.

and Nasser that any threat to Western oil resources in the area would not be tolerated.

Kassim assured the West that its Iraqi interests were safe, and his government soon moved away from Nasser's influence. The Egyptian leader, so one top American official believed, received "one of the greatest lessons in world power politics that he ever had."[11] When Nasser flew to Moscow during the crisis to request Soviet help, Khrushchev refused to make any significant response. As for the United States, Dulles informed the cabinet that again the free world had ruined Stalin's and Lenin's prophecies that communism would march through the newly emerging nations to conquer the capitalist West. In 1959 Kassim destroyed the shell of the Baghdad Pact by formally withdrawing Iraq. The United States then immediately signed new bilateral military aid treaties with Pakistan, Turkey, and Iran, while the remaining members of the pact formed the Central Treaty Organization (CENTO). Dulles's "pactomania" continued.

By the autumn of 1958 Eisenhower had turned Khrushchev's game of missile bluff into a string of real American victories. The Soviet leader suddenly moved to play for much higher stakes: the control of West Germany. Some of the Cold War's most tense moments followed in 1958–1959. Eisenhower had to respond to Khrushchev's challenge, moreover, amidst a bitter debate that threatened to divide the Western alliance.

The debate had been triggered in 1956 when West Germany dragged its feet on building conventional forces. Chancellor Adenauer instead ominously began to request missiles, artillery capable of firing nuclear shells, and fighter bombers that could haul nuclear bombs. The West soon delivered the artillery and bombers. This turn in German affairs set off speeches by European leaders, who proposed the neutralization and reunification of Germany before Central Europe entered a full-fledged arms race. In the United States the debate climaxed in an angry exchange between two architects of postwar policy, George Kennan and Dean Acheson. In words strikingly similar to those of

---

[11]The context and the Eisenhower quote are in Douglas Little, *Americans Orientalism; The United States and the Middle East Since 1945* (Chapel Hill, 2002), pp. 131–137; Interview with Robert Murphy, Dulles Oral History Project, Dulles Papers, Princeton; Burton I. Kaufman, *The Arab Middle East and the United States* (New York, 1995), pp. 26–29.

Walter Lippmann's proposals of ten years earlier, Kennan proposed that before Germany received nuclear arms, the threat of such a possibility should be used to negotiate with the Soviets a neutralization of Central and Eastern Europe. Terms would include the withdrawal of both the Soviet and American armies.[12] This plan soon became known as "disengagement."

Acheson's response in January 1958 was acerbic. If the United States withdrew its troops from Germany and Western Europe, he declared, the Soviets would sooner or later exterminate "independent national life in Western Europe." Acheson particularly feared that Communist parties in Europe would gain the initiative. This indicated his belief that NATO shaped the internal political life of European countries, not just the overall military strategies. Withdrawal from and neutralization of Germany would be disastrous, Acheson warned, for, as he had once remarked, without American troops "to monitor the continued integration of Germany into the West, we should be continually haunted by the spectre of a sort of new [Nazi-Soviet] Agreement." As for Kennan, Acheson specifically recalled that Mr. "X" had tried but had failed to convince any "responsible leader" of these ideas as early as 1949. "Mr. Kennan has never, in my judgment," Acheson commented sarcastically, "grasped the realities of power relationships, but takes a rather mystical attitude toward them. To Mr. Kennan there is no Soviet military threat in Europe."[13]

Kennan, however, was not alone in saying that in a post-Stalin Cold War some fundamental rethinking was necessary. The European status quo was further shaken in June 1958 when Charles de Gaulle returned to power in France. Franco-American relations had not improved since the Suez debacle. Dulles watched de Gaulle with some concern, for he appreciated how the general hoped to regain the *grandeur* of France through the reorientation of French foreign policy.[14] The reorientation would require considerable freedom of action, and that, Dulles believed quite accurately, would result in "neutralist" policies advanced by de Gaulle within the NATO alliance. At the same time that the communist bloc was dividing into Russian, Chinese, and Yugoslav factions, the Western alliance was also splitting apart.

---

[12]George F. Kennan, *Russia, the Atom and the West* (New York, 1957).

[13]*U.S. News and World Report*, January 17, 1958, p. 63.

[14]Alfred Grosser, *La Politique extérieure de la République* (Paris, 1965), p. 44.

The postwar world, like most thirteen-year-olds, was entering a new and uncertain stage. The widening split within NATO became more evident in late 1958 when France, West Germany, Italy, and the Benelux prepared for the formal initiation of the European Economic Community, or Common Market, on January 1, 1959. Following an accord first reached in March 1957, these nations agreed that within fifteen years they would form an economic union by eliminating tariffs and equalizing taxes within the community while creating a common tariff for outside goods. The immediate impact was political as well as economic, for in a stroke "the six" had decreased their economic dependence upon the United States, tied West Germany firmly to the rest of Western Europe, taken their first step toward possible political federation, and were moving to create a middle bloc between the United States and the Soviet Union.

In the last months of 1958, Great Britain attempted to enter the Common Market, but it failed after refusing to cut its economic ties to its Commonwealth and to the United States. The British countered by forming, in November 1959, the Free Trade Association (or "Outer Seven") comprising themselves, Sweden, Switzerland, Portugal, Austria, Norway, and Denmark. The new grouping, however, failed to keep pace with the booming Common Market, and Washington watched as the British became increasingly isolated from Western Europe's economic upsurge.

Moscow feared these developments even more than Washington did. The success of the Common Market and, above all, West Germany's possession of artillery and aircraft that had nuclear capabilities, raised once again before the Soviets the specter of a militarized and economically aggressive Germany. After several days of publicizing his growing ICBM arsenal, Khrushchev began a series of moves on November 10, 1958. They climaxed in the demand that the United States, Great Britain, and France withdraw their 10,000 troops from West Berlin, make it a "free city," and negotiate with the East German government (which none of the Western powers recognized) for access into Berlin. With complete Western support, Dulles rejected Khrushchev's demands, refused to contemplate recognition of East Germany, and intimated that, if the East Germans did gain control of the access routes and refused to allow Western vehicles through, NATO would retaliate "if need be by military force." Khrushchev replied that this would mean World War III.

In focusing upon West Berlin, the Soviet leader had pinpointed the fulcrum that could change the balance of power within Europe. For American policymakers feared that, if the United States did evacuate West Berlin, the Adenauer government's confidence in NATO and the Common Market would be shaken and the basis laid for a West German–Russian deal. It soon became evident, nevertheless, that Khrushchev had concluded that the fulcrum was not worth a nuclear exchange. Denying that he had issued an ultimatum, he modified the six-month limit so that discussions could be held. Over strong Chinese protests the Soviet leader visited the United States in September 1959. Just before his arrival a Soviet "Lunik" (a rocket shot with a scientific payload) hit the moon. Khrushchev reminded the world of his nation's capabilities by presenting a replica of the Soviet pennant aboard the "Lunik" to the President. The visit produced few diplomatic results. Plans were made for a summit conference in Paris the following spring, after which Eisenhower was to visit Russia.

On May 5, 1960, the eve of the summit conference, Khrushchev suddenly announced that the Soviets had shot down a U-2 American reconnaissance plane which had been violating Russian territorial sovereignty. The United States first denied that the aircraft had been on a spying mission but then became trapped when Khrushchev produced the pilot who had parachuted to safety. After some hesitation Eisenhower accepted full responsibility for the incident. He also finally announced that there would be no future overflights. The damage, however, had been done. The Paris Summit quickly was aborted.

Khrushchev's major concern was not his relationship with Eisenhower; the President would shortly leave office anyway. More important was the embarrassing position in which the U-2 flights, which had been occurring over Russia for at least four years, placed the Soviet leader's entire foreign policy, not least his relations with Mao. Khrushchev now recalled Stalin's snickering that "soon after my death, the arrogant Americans would wring your necks, like chickens."[15] There could be little doubt that on previous U-2 flights the United States had discovered the truth about the weakness of Russian ICBM forces. This thought probably influenced Khrushchev to call off the Berlin crisis temporarily while intensifying his threats that Russia would destroy any American ally allowing U-2 planes to

---

[15]Anatoly Dobrynin, *In Confidence* (New York, 1995), p. 41.

leave from its territory. He particularly seized upon an issue in the summer of 1960 that somewhat appeased China and at the same time allowed him to wave his strategic power before the United States: Khrushchev welcomed Fidel Castro as a new force in Latin America and threatened to destroy the United States, "figuratively speaking," if it tried to attack Castro. The Monroe Doctrine, Khrushchev announced, was dead.

This incredible turn of events had begun on July 26, 1953, when the young middle-class lawyer, a species which the unbalanced Cuban society turned out in overabundance, led an armed assault on the regime of Fulgencio Batista. Castro was jailed, but he escaped to Mexico, organized a small revolutionary band, and landed in Cuba in 1956. Batista's police were waiting, and Castro struggled into the mountains with only ten other survivors. American officials paid little attention, believing Batista's word that Castro was dead. In 1957 *The New York Times* correspondent Herbert Matthews found the rebel's hideaway and revealed to the world Castro's program and his astonishing success among the Cuban peasants. Matthews's reports had little positive effect on Washington, however.

The American failure to worry about or understand Castro was not the major mistake, for this was symptomatic of a Cuban policy that had left much to be desired ever since the United States had first taken de facto control in the summer of 1898. By 1956 Americans owned 80 percent of Cuba's utilities, 40 percent of its sugar, 90 percent of its mining wealth, and the island's key strategic location of Guantánamo Bay. The Cuban economy could be manipulated simply by changing the amount of Cuban sugar allowed into the American market. The United States had also landed marines three times after 1902 in efforts to stabilize Cuban politics. Washington had not intervened when Batista overthrew a constitutionally elected government in 1952 and began consolidating his power by following such diverse policies as allowing American advisers to train his military forces while inviting Cuban Communist party members to assume governmental positions. The communists were so close to Batista that they almost missed joining Castro's movement before Batista was driven from power.

In Washington, officials did little until it was too late. They believed, as a U.S. intelligence officer phrased it, that "moderates" would replace Castro, or else "Cuba's economic dependence on the US" would force the revolutionaries to their senses. In 1960 the American ambassador to

Cuba during Batista's last years, Earl E. T. Smith, more accurately summarized past Cuban-American relations and implicitly explained how disastrous the American colonial policy had been in Cuba for sixty-two years: "Senator, let me explain to you that the United States, until the advent of Castro, was so overwhelmingly influential in Cuba that . . . the American Ambassador was the second most important man in Cuba; sometimes even more important than the President. . . . Now, today, his importance is not very great."[16]

His importance declined because, upon grasping power on New Year's Day 1959, Castro determined to balance the Cuban economy and rectify the social injustices within the society. To accomplish this, a thoroughgoing revolution would be required. In the new ruler's mind this meant ending Cuba's dependence on Washington. Castro's trip to the United States in April almost inevitably produced no positive results. The following month he announced an agrarian reform program which met American resistance. By the summer Castro's personal power was unquestioned, but in his need for organized political support to carry out the revolution, he moved closer to the communists within his 26th of July movement. By the end of the year, the anticommunists within the movement were isolated and leaving Cuba. Confiscations of American property intensified, signaling increased anti-Americanism, as well as Castro's need for resources to finance socioeconomic changes. That need, moreover, prohibited him from paying for the confiscated property. (Castro's 1960 speech at the UN outlining his anti-U.S. views can be read in the chapter IX documents at the www.mhhe.com/lafeber website.)

In February 1960 the Russians signed a trade agreement to exchange Cuban sugar for Soviet oil, machinery, and technicians. Ironically, as Cuban-Soviet bloc trade increased from 2 percent of the island's trade in 1960 to 80 percent by the end of 1961, Castro was forced to accept the position as a mere food and raw material producer which he had so strongly condemned in past Cuban-American relations. In July 1960 the United States cut the Cuban sugar quota from the American market. In August Washington began to mobilize hemispheric opposition to Cuba, and three months later American naval

---

[16]The best account is Thomas Paterson, *Contesting Castro* (New York, 1994), especially pp. 250–256; Robert F. Smith, *What Happened in Cuba? A Documentary History* (New York, 1963), p. 273.

forces moved to Central American waters to quell a rumored invasion from Cuba. At this time Eisenhower accepted a Central Intelligence Agency–State Department plan to train an anti-Castro army. Preparations began for an invasion in early 1961. In the first days of January 1961, U.S.-Cuban diplomatic relations were formally severed.

The attention of Americans now focused on this bearded jungle fighter who made four-hour-long speeches to entranced Cuban audiences and who had the gall to defy the world's greatest superpower just ninety miles away. But Castro was only an incredible symbol for a larger danger that confronted U.S. policy in its own hemisphere. In the late 1950s Latin America began passing through its most important change since it had obtained independence from Spain 140 years earlier.

Latin America was fundamentally different from most of the newly emerging areas in Asia or the Middle East. It was more highly developed and, in some areas, in an intermediate stage of economic growth that presented sophisticated economic and social problems. Large areas of Latin America were controlled by extremely conservative governments (the "oligarchs") that could not be removed from power as Africans and Asians removed European colonial rulers from their continents. In Vietnam, for example, the radical nationalists could fight an anticolonial war to send the "foreigners"—the French—back to Paris. But in El Salvador, Nicaragua, or Bolivia, the radical nationalists had to fight a revolution against oligarchs who were of their own nationality. The oligarchs, moreover, received strong support from the military elite and the United States, which had frowned on Latin American revolutions throughout the twentieth century.

The southern nations largely remained quiet between 1948 and 1958 as Latin America's economy grew at an impressive annual rate of 4.3 percent. But this growth occurred in a powder keg: the region's population grew 3 percent annually, an amount greater than that of any area of the world. By the year 2000, experts predicted, some 600 million people would live where 200 million lived in 1960. The economic growth also varied from country to country. Venezuela's oil and Mexico's viable political system gave those nations strong advantages. Elsewhere, poor resources and highly corrupt political systems contributed to internal pressures that threatened to explode in revolution. Outside democratic Costa Rica and Mexico, 2 percent of the population owned 75 percent of the agricultural land on a continent whose people had to live on their ability to scratch a living from the soil. Many of the poor moved out of the countryside to exist in some of the world's worst slums on the outskirts of major cities.

Then in 1957–1958 economic recession in the United States dragged down an already stumbling Latin American economy. Since 1945 Washington officials had made no major effort to correct inequities in the economies of the southern nations—many of which were dependent for survival on American producers and consumers. Between 1945 and 1960 Washington had given three times more aid to Belgium, Luxembourg, and the Netherlands than to all twenty Latin American nations. Private American capital, meanwhile, had invested $1 billion in oil, $500 million in mining, and $750 million in manufacturing, thus increasing the imbalance of the Latin American economies.

After signing their first trade agreement with Argentina in 1953, the Soviets tried to take advantage of these conditions. By 1957 Soviet trade with Latin America amounted to only $200 million annually. It increased to only $450 million by 1960. Nevertheless, it had doubled within three years (while the U.S. proportion of that trade had slipped), and it focused on a few select countries, such as Argentina, Brazil, and later Cuba.[17] During these same years anti-Yankeeism spread. Its intensity was not appreciated in Washington until April 1958 when Vice President Richard Nixon and his wife visited several Latin American nations. The North Americans were spat upon, had eggs and stones hurled at them, and in Caracas had their limousine attacked by mobs. Eisenhower rushed a thousand marines to U.S. bases in the Caribbean, but the Nixons escaped and flew home before further outbreaks occurred.

President Juscelino Kubitschek of Brazil seized this opportunity to push for Eisenhower's acceptance of a proposed "Operation Pan America," in which the United States and Latin America would cooperate to promote long-term development. A pivotal part of the plan was an Inter-American Development Bank that would channel low-interest U.S. loans into the southern nations. Eisenhower had been cool toward this proposal in 1957—he wanted only private

---

[17]Ronald James Clark, "Latin-American Economic Relations with the Soviet Bloc, 1954–1961," unpublished doctoral dissertation, Indiana University, 1963.

capitalists to handle development—but after Nixon's encounters and Castro's sudden appearance, Eisenhower's view changed. The bank was established in 1959 with $1 billion in capital. In 1960, with the Act of Bogotá, the hemispheric nations began working out details for a comprehensive program of economic development.

These events marked the real beginnings of what John F. Kennedy would later popularize as the Alliance for Progress. But they appeared too late to prevent the rise of Fidel Castro and the stirring of revolutionaries in Central and South America. Indeed, U.S. aid was given in such a way that it made the rich richer and the poor poorer in Latin America, and thus actually helped accelerate the revolutions against U.S.-supported regimes.

Castroism and the rumbling problems in other newly emerging nations dominated the foreign-policy debates in the 1960 presidential campaign. The Democratic nominee, John F. Kennedy, charged the Republican nominee, Richard Nixon, with allowing a "missile gap" in the Soviets' favor. But Kennedy started a more significant debate when he suggested American support of "non-Batista democratic anti-Castro forces." Nixon appeared appalled at even the suggestion of American support for such intervention. He later explained that, having access to the secret invasion plans already under way, he was forced to act surprised publicly at Kennedy's suggestion. Outside these exchanges the two nominees differed significantly on few other foreign-policy issues. The Eisenhower consensus, forged in 1956, was making its mark, and each candidate simply tried to exploit, not destroy, it. In one of the closest presidential elections, Kennedy won by a margin of 114,000 votes out of 68.3 million cast. The electoral college vote went to the Democrats 303 to 219.

John F. Kennedy was a most sensitive and astute politician, and the narrow victory margin affected the development of his foreign policy. Presidential assistant Theodore Sorensen defined the problem: "President Kennedy is acutely aware of Jefferson's dictum: 'Great innovations should not be forced on slender majorities.'"[18] Kennedy tended to defer to military and intelligence experts and to those in Congress who preferred to fight the Cold War rather than risk negotiating

---

[18]Theodore C. Sorensen, *Decision-Making in the White House: The Olive Branch or the Arrows* (New York, 1963), pp. 44–48.

Central and South America, 1954–1990

UNITED STATES

ATLANTIC OCEAN

CUBA
Batista overthrown 1959;
Attempted anti-Castro invasion 1961;
Soviet military aid, U.S. quarantine 1962

DOMINICAN REPUBLIC
U.S. broke diplomatic ties 1960;
Trujillo assassinated 1961;
Diplomatic ties restored 1962;
U.S. and O.A.S. intervention 1965

MEXICO
Threatened by $80 billion foreign debt 1980s

Miami

BAHAMAS (Br.)

HAITI

Mexico City

JAMAICA

BELIZE

HONDURAS
U.S. naval and air bases 1981–

Puerto Rico (U.S.)
Pérez Jiménez overthrown 1958;
Anti-Nixon riots 1958

GUATEMALA
Arbenz overthrown 1954;
Castillo Armas eassassinated 1957

NICARAGUA

BARBADOS

GRENADA *Invaded by U.S. 1983*

EL SALVADOR
Canal Zone

COSTA RICA
Arias peace plans, 1987–;
Sandinistas overthrow Somoza 1979;
U.S. supports anti-Sandinista "contras"
1981–1990

Caracas

VENEZUELA

TRINIDAD AND TOBAGO

GUYANA

Suriname (Neth.)

Fr. Guiana

Bogotá

COLOMBIA

PANAMA
Anti-U.S. riots 1959;
U.S. returns canal zone to Panama by treaty 1978;
Noriega seizes power 1983;
U.S. relations strained 1987;
U.S. invades and overthrows Noriega 1989

Quito

ECUADOR

U.S.-Colombian military attacks on drug cartels, 1988–1989

BRAZIL
Military seizes power 1964 and rules 1964;
Threatened by $90 billion foreign debt 1980s

PERU
Lima

Anti-Nixon riots 1958;
Military coup 1962;
Military coup 1968

BOLIVIA
La Paz

Brasília

**Average annual per capita income
1978–1981**

Argentina	$2,300
Barbados	3,000
Bolivia	510
Brazil	1,500
Chile	2,000
Colombia	1,100
Costa Rica	2,200
Cuba	840
Dominican Rep.	1,200
Ecuador	1,050
El Salvador	640
Grenada	500
Guatemala	1,080
Guyana	600
Haiti	260
Honduras	822
Jamaica	1,340
Mexico	1,800
Nicaragua	800
Panama	1,100
Paraguay	1,040
Peru	650
Trinidad & Tobago	4,800
Uruguay	2,800
Venezuela	3,600
United States	10,600

PARAGUAY
Asunción

Rio de Janeiro

CHILE
Salvador Allende elected 1970;
Overthrown by military and died 1973

Santiago

URUGUAY
Montevideo

Buenos Aires

ARGENTINA

Punta del Este Conferences 1961, 1962

Threatened by $50 billion foreign debt 1980s;
Returns to civilian government 1983

PACIFIC OCEAN

217

its problems. His experiences abroad while his father, Joseph P. Kennedy, was ambassador to Great Britain in the late 1930s convinced him that democracies moved too slowly in reacting to totalitarian aggression, a view that permeated his widely read book, written while he was a Harvard senior, *Why England Slept*. His sensitivity to the political climate was also demonstrated during 1950–1954, when he was extremely reluctant to oppose Senator McCarthy.

As a young senator from Massachusetts, Kennedy nevertheless realized that the growing importance of the newly emerging nations required changes in foreign policy. A 1957 speech was outspoken in support of Algeria's fight against France. In 1954 he warned against any American attempt to prop up the French regime in Indochina, but on this issue Kennedy changed, once the United States replaced the French. In June 1956 he lauded Diem as an "offspring" of the American effort to keep Southeast Asia free. Aware of the challenge of the newly emerging peoples and fearful that the United States would not respond quickly or properly, Kennedy emphasized in a special message to Congress on May 25, 1961, "The great battleground for the defense and expansion of freedom today is . . . Asia, Latin America, Africa and the Middle East, the lands of the rising peoples."[19]

In his first annual message on January 30, 1961, the President listed the priorities for waging the conflict between "Freedom and Communism," by noting "First, we must strengthen our military tools." Upon entering office, the administration had discovered that the "missile gap," which Kennedy had heavily emphasized in the campaign, was only fictional. The Soviets and the Chinese also knew this, and, consequently, Kennedy and his advisers feared that the communists would place more emphasis on conventional, local wars. In 1961 the administration increased the defense budget 15 percent by doubling the number of combat-ready divisions in the army's strategic reserve, expanding the marines, adding seventy vessels to the active fleet, and giving a dozen more wings to the tactical air forces. General Maxwell Taylor returned to act as the President's military adviser.

---

[19]U.S. Government Printing Office, *Public Papers of the Presidents, J. F. Kennedy, 1961* (Washington, 1962), p. 397. For the influence of his British experiences and books on Kennedy, note John D. Fair, "The Intellectual JFK: Lessons in Statesmanship from British History," *Diplomatic History*, 30 (January 2006): 119–142.

Varying little in objective from Eisenhower's approach, this policy was a different kind of attempt to contain communism and revolutionary instability. The policy had been thought through and widely publicized by the reports of the Rockefeller brothers in the late 1950s and was the result of a logical progression of thought on the part of intellectuals such as Henry Kissinger. In this sense particularly, the Kennedy administration seized upon American intellectuals in a manner unmatched since 1933. The scholars gladly responded.

Other parts of the society also responded. In his farewell address in January 1961, Eisenhower had warned the American people against the "conjunction of an immense military establishment and a large arms industry" which was "new in American experience," and whose "total influence . . . is felt in every city, every state house, every office in the federal government. . . . In the councils of government, we must guard against the acquisition of unwarranted influence, whether sought or unsought, by the military-industrial complex." The President declared, "The potential for the disastrous rise of misplaced power exists and will persist." For Eisenhower this was strong language.

The Kennedy administration, however, dismissed this speech. Determined to help noncommunist nations militarily, and worried over the outflow of American gold caused by an unfavorable balance in the nation's financial and trade exchanges with the rest of the world, the new President established in 1961 a special post in the Defense Department to sell American arms through private corporations to foreign nations. By 1965 American companies exported $1.9 billion worth of arms to Europe, Japan, Iran, Venezuela, and Saudi Arabia, among others. General Dynamics Corporation alone sold more than $1-billion worth of arms overseas between 1962 and 1965. Most of the goods were sophisticated and expensive electronic equipment. As one business periodical observed, in the 1930s such companies were known as "'Merchants of Death.' . . . Times have changed."[20]

The drive for a unified but multimilitary response to foreign-policy problems was typified by Secretary of Defense Robert McNamara's management of the Pentagon. No more would individual services have wholly independent programs. McNamara instead brought the

---

[20]*Forbes*, February 1, 1966, pp. 15–16.

various services together under "program elements" in which the military units were coordinated for efficient war making on various levels. The professional soldiers lost some of their political power, but they gained greatly in military efficiency. By mobilizing resources in this way, the administration could supposedly massively retaliate on many military levels. Particular emphasis was placed upon preparing the United States for guerrilla wars. The Jungle Warfare School in the Canal Zone and another at Fort Bragg, North Carolina, brought U.S. Army Special Forces troops together with Latin American units. More than 600 Latin American policemen sharpened their talents in counter-intelligence work and the handling of mobs by undergoing training in the Canal Zone school established by the Agency for International Development. At the end of 1966 anti-American guerrillas nevertheless operated in Venezuela, Bolivia, Colombia, Peru, Nicaragua, and Guatemala.

Kennedy picked Latin America for special attention. Besides the training of antiguerrilla forces and the establishment of the Peace Corps (young men and women trained to perform teaching and technical services in newly emerging nations), the President announced, on March 13, 1961, the Alliance for Progress.[21] To the Eisenhower policies of 1959–1960, Kennedy added a ten-year commitment of $20 billion of American money and an appropriate image. The plan was worked out at the Punta del Este, Uruguay, conference in August. The U.S. aid, including $300 million annually from private capital, would quadruple the annual economic assistance given the area between 1946 and 1960. In return Latin America pledged $80 billion of investment over the ten-year period and, most important, land, tax, and other socioeconomic reforms. Kennedy hoped these efforts would result in a 5.5 percent increase in Latin America's growth rate, or a modest net increase of 2.5 percent over the population increase.

These ambitious plans quickly encountered major difficulties. The programs were undercut by bureaucratic fighting in Washington; the marked reluctance of such major Latin American nations as Brazil, Argentina, and Mexico to submit their development programs to hemispheric scrutiny; and particularly the inability or unwillingness

---

[21]Elizabeth Cobbs Hoffman, *All You Need Is Love; The Peace Corps and the Spirit of the Peace Corps* (Cambridge, Mass., 1998), is an excellent, and partly autobiographical, account.

of many governments to undertake the promised reforms. In some nations the requisite political stability could not be established; between 1961 and 1966 military forces overthrew nine Latin American governments. The Kennedy administration, trapped between the alternatives of intervening in the affairs of sovereign nations or watching the Alliance grow increasingly weaker, could not work out an effective response. By 1963 Alliance officials claimed that 35 million Latin Americans had benefited from the program, but only at the end of the first five years would the 5.5 percent growth rate be in sight, and not even then would there be evidence of the reforms which could ensure fair distribution of the benefits.

The Alliance was designed to create a stable and orderly Latin America without having the hemisphere endure a series of Castro-like revolutions. The Cuban ruler had become a primary concern of American officials, and they moved to eradicate him on April 17, 1961, when Kennedy launched an invasion at the Bay of Pigs by a group of Cuban exiles. This force had been trained for months in Guatemala by the Central Intelligence Agency. Although it was supposedly a secret operation, news of the preparations was widespread in American newspapers by April. President Kennedy was assured by the CIA, State, and military officials that the invasion could succeed if, under American-provided air cover, the anti-Castro units could establish a beachhead and then link up with other guerrillas in the mountains. Taking the word of his experts, Kennedy acquiesced, demanding only that no American troops be committed. Fifteen hundred Cubans waded ashore on the morning of April 17, only to find that one key air strike had been canceled because of clouds, that other naval and air supporting units had been immobilized by Castro's small air force, that the beachhead was indefensible, and that they had no hope of reaching the mountains. In the aftermath American Ambassador to the United Nations Adlai Stevenson was caught lying about U.S. support of the operation. Kennedy ordered an investigation of the CIA and removed some top officials. In Cuba Castro was ensconced more securely in power than ever before.

"All my life I've known better than to depend on the experts," the President wondered aloud shortly afterward. "How could I have been so stupid, to let them go ahead?" Robert McNamara later gave one answer, "We were hysterical about Castro. . . ." No one was more hysterical than the President's brother, the attorney general. Moreover, the

Guatemala operation of 1954 colored the view of both the CIA and the White House when they analyzed the Cuban project. The political-military philosophy of the invasion, moreover, was quite compatible with the new emphasis placed by the administration upon guerrilla-like warfare. Nearly forty years later, it was discovered that not only did the Soviets and Cubans know about the plans for the attack, but the CIA knew they knew—and went ahead anyway.[22]

The more fundamental problems were revealed by a State Department White Paper, written by White House aide and Harvard historian Arthur Schlesinger, Jr., which attempted to rationalize the invasion just days before the tragedy occurred. The paper condemned the Castro movement as communist and attempted to place the United States on the side of social and economic reform within the hemisphere. It was, however, an unfortunate example of how history was misconstrued to serve political ends. From the first, when the paper claimed that "the hemisphere rejoiced at the overthrow of the Batista tyranny" (a fact not overly obvious in Washington in January 1959), until the conclusion that the "inter-American system was incompatible with any form of totalitarianism" (which failed to show how Trujillo, Duvalier, Somoza, and even Batista, among others, had prospered within that system, almost always with U.S. support), the State Department paper was more propaganda than a sober recital of facts.[23] But the paper revealed the dilemma of American policy toward Latin America. The Bay of Pigs was a public confession by the United States that it had failed to understand or deal with the most significant political change in the hemisphere in fifty years. This conclusion would have been tenable whether the invasion had succeeded or failed.

The President publicly accepted complete responsibility for the Bay of Pigs, and it was in the weeks immediately following this debacle that he traveled to Europe to visit West European leaders and Premier Nikita Khrushchev. The meeting in Vienna on June 3 and 4 with the Soviet leader resulted in an agreement to stop the growing

---

[22]Theordore C. Sorensen, *Kennedy* (New York, 1965), p. 309; Ronald Steel, *In Love with Night* (New York, 2000), p. 78, a superb analysis of Robert Kennedy. The CIA revelation is in *Washington Post*, April 29, 2000, p. A4.

[23]Smith, *What Happened in Cuba?* p. 211. Excerpts from this paper can be read in the chapter IX documents at the www.mhhe.com/lafeber website.

conflict in Laos. Otherwise it only increased Kennedy's apprehension that the Soviets were determined to create dangerous tensions by supporting what Khrushchev called "wars of liberation," that is, support of nationalist and pro-communist elements in the newly emerging countries which were fighting Western political and economic influence. Worst of all, Khrushchev was militant about the necessity of eliminating Western power in West Berlin. The six-month notice was reimposed by the Soviet ruler, who became deeply angry at Kennedy's repeated warning not to miscalculate American intentions. "I will tell you now," the President reported to the American people upon his return, "that it was a very sober two days."

Worried about the effects of the Bay of Pigs upon American credibility and disturbed at public reports that Khrushchev had brow-beaten him at Vienna, Kennedy accepted Dean Acheson's argument that the Berlin issue was a "simple conflict of wills" and that no negotiations could be considered until the Soviets lifted their threat of turning over the access routes to East Germany. This argument refused to touch the Soviet premier's real problems: the growing military power of West Germany, its strengthened ties with the West, its attractiveness to technicians and other experts living in East Germany, the very weak position of the East German communist regime, the position of West Berlin as an espionage and propaganda center within the communist bloc, the growing fear of the Soviet peoples over West Germany's power, and, finally, Khrushchev's realization that with his ICBM braggadocio punctured as only myth, he needed a major strategic victory.

Kennedy's reaction came in a national broadcast on July 25, 1961. He asked that National Reserve troops be placed on active duty and announced a dramatic increase of nearly 25 percent in American military strength. His premise was simple. The Berlin "outpost is not an isolated problem. The threat is worldwide," endangering Southeast Asia, "our own hemisphere," and "wherever else the freedom of human beings is at stake," as well as Berlin. That city and Saigon, the capital of South Vietnam, were, in this crucial sense, alike. Kennedy, like Eisenhower, defined the communist threat in global terms.

On August 13 the Soviets suddenly built a cement wall, complete with barbed wire and heavily armed guards, to separate East and West Berlin. The flow of young and skilled labor from East Germany to the West stopped, and Khrushchev partly sealed the bloc from

Western influences. The United States protested, but the wall stood, a final obstacle to hundreds of East Germans who were shot trying to escape to the West. It was mute and bloody testimony to the policy of both East and West which, since 1945, had preferred a divided rather than a neutralized and united Germany.

The wall had solved one of his problems, at least temporarily, but Khrushchev's supposed strategic power continued to come under attack in the West. In mid-1961 the Defense Department revealed that only a "handful" of Russian ICBMs were operational. Administration officials wondered aloud about Soviet credibility in the military realm. This no doubt made Khrushchev's political situation in Moscow uneasy, a situation already under attack because of the Sino-Soviet split. The division within the communist world had become irreparable by late 1960. Two weeks after the Berlin Wall appeared, Khrushchev broke the three-year Russian-American moratorium on the testing of nuclear bombs by beginning a series of tests which climaxed with the explosion in November of a 58-megaton weapon, 3000 times more powerful than the bomb that had obliterated Hiroshima.

Kennedy responded with underground testing in September 1961, but he remained fully confident that the United States held a wide lead in nuclear weapons capability. Indeed, his National Security Council decided that if it were necessary to break the Soviet "blockage to our access to Berlin," the United States would use "selective nuclear attacks" and, if necessary, escalate to "general nuclear war." (Khruschev had said to Secretary of State Rusk that since the Soviets were not foolish enough to start a nuclear war over Berlin, he thought Americans also were not. Rusk responded in what apparently was meant as a joke, "Mr. Chairman, you will just have to take into account the possibility that we Americans are goddamn fools.")

The Soviets again refused Western demands for inspection and international control. On April 25, 1962, Kennedy ordered the first of some thirty American tests that occurred during the following year. Amidst this too-easy talk about nuclear war, on the Fourth of July 1961, a Soviet nuclear submarine off Norway's coast suddenly had an accident with its reactor. The crew frantically fixed the problem before an explosion might have contaminated thousands of square miles, although eight of the sailors finally died of the radiation. A Soviet official later said that if an explosion had occurred, the United States and NATO might well have believed it was a nuclear strike, and World

War III would have begun with a thermonuclear exchange. Luckily, the West knew nothing until after the reactor was fixed.[24]

The President viewed his first eleven months in office as a period of continual international crisis, and it was in this context that he made two of his most fateful decisions. The first involved Laos. That former French colony was a key to Southeast Asia, for it rimmed China, both Vietnams, Cambodia, Thailand, and Burma. When Pathet Lao communist forces began major guerrilla action, the United States stepped up aid until, by April 1961, over 300 American military advisers were in Laos, and the country's right-wing government received $32 million in economic assistance, three times the annual rate of 1955–1959.

As China began building roads to the Laotian border for its own military power, the Soviets and Americans decided that the war must stop. With the support of Kennedy and Khrushchev, Great Britain and Russia reconvened the Geneva conference members of 1954. The sessions agreed on neutralizing Laos. This opened the way for a coalition government to be formed under neutralist Souvanna Phouma in June 1962. Nineteen nations, including China, promised to respect Laotian territorial integrity and sovereignty, and the SEATO powers explicitly excluded Laos from their area of control. It was a tenuous agreement, but a Soviet-American decision to enforce neutralization of a key area had moved Laos outside the torrid zones of the Cold War. "Thank God the Bay of Pigs happened when it did," Kennedy remarked privately. "Otherwise we'd be in Laos by now—and that would be a hundred times worse."[25]

The implications of that remark were not quite accurate, however, for meanwhile the President was making a pivotal commitment of American power to South Vietnam. The U.S.-sponsored regime of Ngo Dinh Diem had become very unpopular by 1958. It had stopped

---

[24]The Rusk remark is in Thomas W. Zeiler, *Dean Rusk* (Wilmington, 2000), pp. 48–49; National Security Action memorandum no. 109, October 23, 1961, in *Documents of the National Security Council*, 6th Supplement, reel 9 (University Microfilms of America, Bethesda, Md.); an excellent overview of the Berlin crisis and recent scholarship on it is Thomas A. Schwartz, "The Berlin Crisis and the Cold War," *Diplomatic History*, 21 (Winter 1997): 139–148. The 1961 submarine episode is recounted in "Gorbachev Proposes Soviet Sub Crew for Nobel Peace Prize," Moscow Interfax news service, February 1, 2006.
[25]Sorensen, *Kennedy*, p. 644.

agrarian reforms begun by Ho in the countryside, canceled elections, arrested political opponents, and concentrated power in the hands of Diem, his brother, and his brother's wife, Madame Ngo Dinh Nhu. Anti-Diem guerrilla attacks stepped up in 1958. Two years later Ho's government in Hanoi acknowledged and encouraged the southern pro-communists by establishing the National Liberation Front (NLF). The American-trained South Vietnamese Army could not handle the guerrillas, but it also disliked Diem and tried unsuccessfully in November 1960 to overthrow the president.

With this civil war intensifying, President Kennedy sent Vice President Johnson on a fact-finding mission in May 1961 and followed this with a mission in October headed by General Maxwell Taylor and State Department official Walt Whitman Rostow, a fervent disciple of thwarting communism with guerrilla warfare. The Taylor-Rostow team recommended increasing the number of American military advisers and pledging complete support to Diem. Kennedy faced a momentous decision. Restraining him were the inability and unwillingness of the SEATO allies as a whole to make any major commitment, his knowledge that the Vietnamese situation was extremely complex, and his own doubts that the "domino theory" had any validity. He apparently believed that whenever Red China exploded a nuclear bomb, its influence would be dominant in Asia, regardless of what the United States did in Vietnam.[26] Military members of the "Never-Again Club" and some State Department officials, particularly those who gave first priority to European affairs, also warned against any large commitment.

Opposing these views were some of the President's highest advisers, including Vice President Johnson, who, during his trip to Vietnam, had called Diem the "Winston Churchill of Asia" (which Diem unfortunately believed). Johnson warned the President that the United States must make a "fundamental decision . . . whether we are to attempt to meet the challenge of Communist expansion now in Southeast Asia . . . or throw in the towel."[27] Others argued that this was the opportunity to contain China, and that Vietnam's long coastline and apparently stable government provided optimum conditions for a get-tough-with-China policy. Most important, however,

[26]Arthur Krock, in *The New York Times,* February 14, 1965, p. E9.
[27]Philip Geyelin, *Lyndon B. Johnson and the World* (New York, 1966), pp. 34–40.

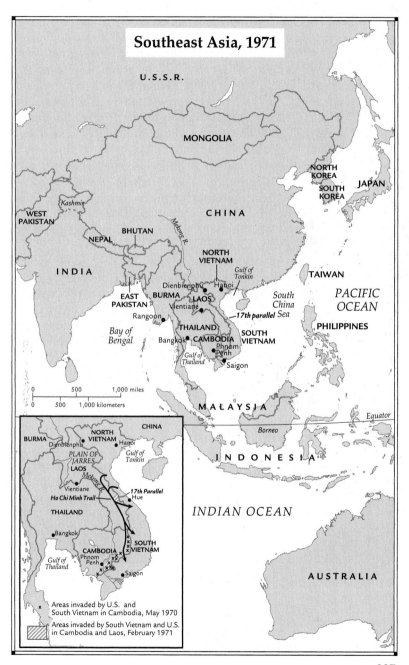

Southeast Asia, 1971

U.S.S.R.

MONGOLIA

NORTH KOREA
SOUTH KOREA
JAPAN

Kashmir

WEST PAKISTAN

NEPAL

BHUTAN

CHINA

Mekong R.

INDIA

TAIWAN

NORTH VIETNAM

Gulf of Tonkin

PACIFIC OCEAN

Dienbienphu Hanoi

EAST PAKISTAN BURMA LAOS

Vientiane

South China Sea

Rangoon

17th parallel

PHILIPPINES

Bay of Bengal

THAILAND

Bangkok CAMBODIA SOUTH VIETNAM

Phnom Penh

Gulf of Thailand

Saigon

| 0 | 500 | 1,000 miles |
| 0 | 500 | 1,000 kilometers |

MALAYSIA

Equator

Borneo

INDONESIA

INDIAN OCEAN

AUSTRALIA

Inset map

BURMA

CHINA

NORTH VIETNAM

Dienbienphu Hanoi

PLAIN OF JARRES

Gulf of Tonkin

LAOS

Mekong R.

Vientiane

Ho Chi Minh Trail

17th Parallel
Hue

THAILAND

Bangkok

CAMBODIA

SOUTH VIETNAM

Phnom Penh

Gulf of Thailand

Saigon

× Areas invaded by U.S. and South Vietnam in Cambodia, May 1970

Areas invaded by South Vietnam and U.S. in Cambodia and Laos, February 1971

the President began to see Vietnam as part of the global communist menace. If the Vietminh were not stopped, the whole world balance might be upset.[28] Kennedy soon found himself no longer questioning the Eisenhower-Dulles policies he had inherited, including the "domino theory," but adopting them. Kennedy also had more motivation, since abroad (and at home) he was determined to blot out the terrible image given his administration by the Bay of Pigs, the Vienna meetings, and the Berlin Wall. For an administration that prided itself on its "realism," its political pragmatism, and its determination to save the newly emerging nations, which were in Kennedy's own words, "the great battleground . . . of freedom," these arguments were irrefutable. The force was already present. The U.S. Pacific Command was a great military power with its 300,000 men, the largest mobile force on the globe (the Seventh Fleet), and logistics problems solved by bases in Okinawa, the Philippines, and Japan.

Within fifteen months following the Taylor-Rostow report, Kennedy expanded the American commitment from 500 to 10,000 men. He allowed these "advisers" to engage in combat, ordered U.S. Air Force units to strike Vietminh strongholds in South Vietnam, and promised full support to Diem. The Vietnamese president interpreted this promise to mean that he could intensify his authoritarian methods without worrying about any questions, or a possible pullout, from the American side.[29] The American-Diem forces attempted to secure the countryside with a strategic hamlet program which uprooted and then concentrated peasants in fortified villages.

These decisions were signal and symbolic, for they, like many other policies adopted in 1961 to mid-1962, indicated that the Kennedy administration could not lessen but only intensify Cold War tensions. When a reporter remarked in the autumn of 1961 that he wanted to write a book about the President's first year in office, Kennedy inquired, "Who would want to read a book about disasters?"[30]

---

[28]Arthur M. Schlesinger, Jr., *A Thousand Days: John F. Kennedy in the White House* (Boston, 1965), p. 548.

[29]David Halberstam, *The Making of a Quagmire* (New York, 1965), pp. 67–69.

[30]Told by Elie Abel, quoted by I. F. Stone in *The New York Review of Books*, April 14, 1966, p. 12.

In the first hours after John F. Kennedy's assassination, President Lyndon Johnson (at center in the photo) met with his top advisers to make far-reaching decisions about the Vietnam war. Here he confers with, from left, Ambassador Henry Cabot Lodge, Secretary of State Dean Rusk, Secretary of Defense Robert McNamara, and Undersecretary of State George Ball. (LBJ Library Photo by Cecil Stoughton)

CHAPTER 10

Southeast Asia—and Elsewhere (1962–1966)

What could have been the greatest of disasters nearly occurred one year later. The Cuban missile crisis, as President Kennedy remarked to Premier Khrushchev, at one moment approached the point "where events could have become unmanageable." This confrontation rechanneled the policies of the United States and the Soviet Union. It affected many areas of world affairs.

The roots of the crisis ran back to Khrushchev's ICBM-oriented foreign policies after 1957 and his intense concern with removing NATO power from West Berlin. By 1962 these policies were related, for the Soviets needed credible strategic force if they hoped to neutralize Western power in Germany. By the spring of 1962, however, high American officials had publicly expressed their skepticism of Soviet missile credibility. President Kennedy further observed in a widely publicized interview that under some circumstances the United States would strike first. In June, Defense Secretary McNamara indicated that American missiles were so potent and precise that in a nuclear war they could spare cities and hit only military installations.[1]

Khrushchev angrily responded that, contrary to McNamara's beliefs, cities would be the first victims in any nuclear war. The Soviet premier warned Kennedy against engaging "in sinister competition as to who will be the first to start a war." For the first time in five years, however,

---

[1]Stewart Alsop, "Kennedy's Grand Strategy," *Saturday Evening Post*, March 31, 1962, p. 14; Richard P. Stebbins, ed., *Documents on American Foreign Relations, 1962* (New York 1963), pp. 232–233.

Khrushchev emphasized Soviet bomber strength instead of missiles. As for West Berlin, the building of the wall and Kennedy's quick military buildup in 1961 had quieted Khrushchev's demands. During the summer of 1962 Khrushchev moved to regain the initiative in the strategic realm. In late August an American U-2 reconnaissance plane flying fourteen miles above Cuba reported the first Soviet surface-to-air missile site (see map, p. 217). Forty-two Russian medium bombers were next observed on Castro's airstrips. On September 19, 1962, U.S. intelligence, in an official estimate, assured the President that the Soviets had not tried, and would not try, to install nuclear-headed missiles ninety miles from the American coast. As late as October 14, 1962, U.S. officials expressed disbelief publicly that the two communist leaders would emplace offensive ground-to-ground missiles—especially after Kennedy had expressly warned Moscow about this the month before. The disbelief was also based on Khrushchev's assurances that he would not jiggle East-West relations during the volatile U.S. election campaign of 1962.

The Soviet leader, however, was secretly moving not one, but two types of nuclear weapons into Cuba. According to later Soviet testimony Khrushchev risked nuclear war for several reasons. First, as he told his ambassador to Cuba, Aleksandr Alekseyev, the United States was planning to invade Cuba again, this time not with mercenaries, as at the Bay of Pigs, but "with its own armed forces." Second, "Since the Americans have already surrounded the Soviet Union with a ring of their military bases and various types of missile launchers, we must pay them back in their own coin . . . so they will know what it feels like to live in the sights of nuclear weapons." No opposition to Khrushchev's gamble appeared among his top advisers. But Soviet records released in the 1990s also indicated that Khrushchev and those advisers had not thought through how—or even whether—they would use the weapons if Kennedy challenged them. In a sense, as his opponents later claimed, Khrushchev's Cuban Missile policy was half-baked. In June 1962 Raul Castro, Fidel's brother and head of Cuba's armed forces, flew to Moscow and worked out details. Four months later, on October 16, Kennedy received the first photographs, taken by a U-2 plane, showing a launchpad under construction that could fire nuclear missiles 1000 miles. Several days later a site for weapons with a 2200-mile capability was photographed.[2]

The President was in a delicate political situation. His hands were not exactly clean. Throughout 1962 he had authorized a top-secret campaign, Operation Mongoose, to overthrow Castro, possibly by U.S. military intervention. Publicly, for weeks some Republicans had warned of threatening Soviet moves in Cuba. These warnings, plus the frustrations which Castro was causing many Americans, created in the early autumn what one acute observer called "a war party" which demanded military action against Cuba.[3] The elections were less than three weeks away. In this pressure tank a special committee (the EXCOM) of top administration officials began virtual round-the-clock meetings to consider a response to the Soviets. The alternatives narrowed down to a blockade or an air strike against the missile sites. Dean Acheson (invited back out of retirement by Kennedy) and General Maxwell Taylor, along with the Joint Chiefs of Staff, argued vigorously for the air strike, even though they knew that such an attack would probably kill Soviet technicians working on the sites. Other officials changed their minds several times in the course of five days of secret discussions, but Undersecretary of State George Ball slowly won support for a blockade. (As Ball later phrased it, he opposed a "surgical air strike" that the military proposed because he had closely studied U.S. bombing in the Second World War and was amazed at its inaccuracy. He "concluded from the record of Allied bombing in Europe that if the medical profession should ever adopt the air force definition of 'surgical,' anyone undergoing an operation for appendicitis might lose his kidneys and lungs yet find the appendix intact.") McNamara supported Ball with the argument that, if the blockade failed, the air strike could then be ordered. Acheson so strongly opposed the final decision

---

[2]Foreign Broadcast Information Service (FBIS), Daily Report Annex: Soviet Union, January 17, 1989, pp. 6–11; Dino A. Brugioni, *Eyeball to Eyeball* (New York, 1992) on the U-2, especially pp. 181–220, 276–277; on Khrushchev's failure to think through his policy, see Raymond Garthoff, "New Evidence on the Cuban Missile Crisis," *Cold War International History Project Bulletin,* Issue 11 (Winter 1998): 251–262.

[3]Richard H. Rovere, "Letter From Washington," *New Yorker,* October 6, 1962, pp. 148–157.

merely to blockade that the crusty Cold Warrior resigned from EXCOM.[4]

At 7 P.M. on October 22, the President broke the well-kept secret to the American people. Because the Soviets were building bases in Cuba "to provide a nuclear strike capability against the Western Hemisphere," Kennedy announced, the United States was imposing "a strict quarantine on all offensive military equipment" being shipped into Cuba. American military forces, he added, were on full alert, and the United States would "regard any nuclear missile launched from Cuba against any nation in the Western Hemisphere as an attack by the Soviet Union on the United States, requiring a full retaliatory response upon the Soviet Union." He appealed to Khrushchev to remove the offensive weapons under UN supervision. (Kennedy's message can be read in the chapter X documents at this book's www.mhhe.com/lafeber website.)

A terrified world, as well as U.S. and Soviet nuclear forces, went on a full alert. Three days into the crisis, however, Russian ships headed for Cuba began to turn around. They were not going to challenge the blockade. Other Soviet vessels offered no opposition when U.S. warships stopped and searched them for missile parts. A break appeared on October 26 when Khrushchev, in a rambling letter, offered removal of the missiles in return for a U.S. pledge not to invade Cuba. The next day, however, the crisis again escalated when a Soviet officer in Cuba shot down a U-2 plane and killed its pilot.

That same day (October 27) Khrushchev seemed to raise the stakes: he demanded the dismantling of American short-range Jupiter missiles in Turkey. EXCOM was now worn down by ten days of the most intense pressures. "I saw first-hand," Theodore Sorensen recalled, "how brutally physical and mental fatigue can numb the good sense as well as the senses of normally articulate men." One U.S. official became so tired and frightened that he drove his car into a tree at 4:00 A.M.[5] That the world survived the missile crisis was in part plain dumb luck.

---

[4]James G. Hershberg, "Before the Missiles of October . . . ," in James A. Nathan, ed., *The Cuban Missile Crisis Revisited* (New York, 1992), especially pp. 237–238; George Ball, "JFK's Big Moment," *New York Review of Books*, February 13, 1992, p. 18; Elie Abel, *The Missile Crisis* (Philadelphia, 1966), pp. 63–64, 70, 81, 88, 118–119.

[5]Note especially Eric Alterman, *When Presidents Lie* (New York, 2004), pp. 108–116; Theodore Sorensen, *Decision-Making in the White House* (New York, 1963), p. 76.

The EXCOM began to plan for a military strike the following week to destroy the missile sites before they became operational. Invasion preparations were also accelerated. But the President, at the suggestion of his brother, Attorney General Robert Kennedy, made the crucial decision to bypass the second Khrushchev letter and accept the more moderate first note. He also secretly dispatched his brother to tell a Soviet official in Washington that the order had gone out months earlier (as it had) to remove the outdated and unneeded Jupiters from Turkey. Khrushchev was receptive, not least because he had information that U.S. bombing of Cuba could begin in three to four days. On October 28, as U.S. officials prepared to strike the island on October 30, Khrushchev accepted Kennedy's offer.[6] (The minutes of the climactic October 27th meeting can be read in the chapter X documents at the www.mhhe.com/lafeber website.)

The crisis, however, was not over. Khrushchev made the decision to withdraw the missiles without consulting Castro. He knew that if he did, the Cuban leader would not agree and could delay a deal until it was too late to stop a military exchange. A furious Castro therefore refused to allow UN inspectors into his country to observe the missiles' dismantling, as Kennedy had required, and then refused to return Soviet long-range bombers. U.S. forces remained on highest alert until November 20, 1962, when Castro finally returned the bombers. Meanwhile Kennedy toughened his position. Contrary to what was believed then and for the next quarter century, the President did not give ironclad assurance that the United States would not invade Cuba. Instead, in a letter to Khrushchev on December 14, 1962, Kennedy wrote that his no-invasion pledge depended on two conditions: the final removal of "all offensive weapons" from Cuba, and the assurance "that Cuba itself commits no aggressive acts against any of the nations of the Western Hemisphere." The second part was a major loophole. It was not known publicly until the letter was declassified in 1992. Had it been known in the 1970s and 1980s

---

[6]U.S. Department of State, *Foreign Relations of the United States, 1961–1963. Volume VI. Kennedy-Khrushchev Exchanges* (Washington, D.C., 1996), pp. 169–190; Ernest R. May and Philip Zelikow, eds., *The Kennedy Tapes* (Cambridge, Mass., 1997), pp. 431–432—an indispensable source on the crisis. FBIS, January 17, 1989, pp. 8–10; *Documents on American Foreign Relations, 1962*, pp. 392–404; good context is Bruce R. Kuniholm, "Turkey's Jupiter Missiles and the U.S.–Turkish Relationship," in Douglas Brinkley and Richard T. Griffiths, eds., *John F. Kennedy and Europe* (Baton Rouge, 1999), pp. 119–124.

when leftist revolutions erupted in Central America, there could have been loud demands heard in the United States to destroy Castro. Also kept secret until 1992 was Kennedy's willingness to trade the missiles in Turkey for those in Cuba if that were necessary to avoid nuclear war. Until 1992, it had been thought that Khrushchev had surrendered unconditionally.[7]

The Soviets made an even more stunning revelation when they released information in 1991–1992. Kennedy's EXCOM had thought no nuclear warheads had been placed on the missiles in Cuba. The Americans indeed had planned an air strike for October 30 before, they believed, such nuclear tips could be installed. Soviet officials later revealed, however, that forty-two intermediate-range missiles with warheads were in place during the crisis. Able to obliterate U.S. cities up to the Canadian border, they were guarded by 40,000 Soviet troops. Equally ominous, there were nine short-range nuclear missiles ready to be used against an American invasion. The EXCOM had known nothing about these warheads. A shaken Robert McNamara declared in 1992 after he learned this information, "This is horrifying. It meant that had a U.S. invasion been carried out . . . there was a 99 percent probability that nuclear war would have been initiated." McNamara added, "The actions of all three parties were shaped by misjudgment, miscalculations, and misinformation."[8]

The aftershocks of the near-tragedy rippled on. The possible horrors of nuclear war overhung the lifetime of the generation that lived through those days of October 1962. Immediately after the crisis, Khrushchev began to try to prevent another such confrontation. Now that the "burning flames of thermonuclear war" had been "felt more tangibly," he told Kennedy, it was time to sign a nonaggression pact and prepare to break up the U.S. and Soviet blocs. The President was not interested in moving that rapidly. But he responded more favorably in December when Khrushchev made the first offer in Russian history to have "2–3 inspections a year" of possible Soviet nuclear test sites.[9]

---

[7] Anatoly Dobrynin, *In Confidence* (New York, 1995), p. 73; *Washington Post,* January 7, 1992, p. A12; *New York Times,* January 7, 1992, p. A5; Ernest R. May and Philip D. Zelikow, eds., *The Kennedy Tapes,* pp. 518, 549, 692.

[8] *New York Times,* January 15, 1992, p. A11; *Washington Post,* January 14, 1992, p. A1.

[9] *Washington Post,* January 7, 1992, p. A12.

That offer opened the way to the historic nuclear test ban of 1963. In the summer of 1963 the United States and the Soviet Union negotiated and signed their first agreement to limit the arms race by prohibiting aboveground nuclear testing. These 1962–1963 events intensely angered the Chinese and widened the Sino-Russian split to the edge of a complete break. The Chinese called Khrushchev foolish for putting the missiles into Cuba and cowardly for removing them. They feared the growing cooperation between Moscow and Washington and ridiculed the less militant Soviet policy. The Chinese continued to believe that Americans were "paper tigers"; Khrushchev said such a characterization was "dung."

The crisis had not enhanced the Soviet leader's personal power within the communist bloc. His decline, combined with the Sino-Soviet breach and the warmer East-West relations, opened new opportunities for the satellites in Eastern Europe to regain more autonomy. The communist bloc was fragmenting. "If Stalin were alive," a high Soviet official complained, "he would do everything quietly, but this fool is blurting out his threats . . . and is forcing our enemies to increase their military strength."[10]

In contrast to Khrushchev's decline, President Kennedy emerged from the missile crisis with new support and political charisma. His own conception of this power was exemplified at American University in Washington, D.C., on June 10, 1963. There Kennedy spoke of peace "as the necessary rational end of rational men" and dramatically appealed to the Soviets to seek a relaxation of tensions. This speech sped the negotiations of the nuclear test ban treaty, a pact which Kennedy then drove through the Senate over the strong opposition of American military officials and a few scientists led by Edward Teller of the University of California. Private transnational peace groups, led by concerned nuclear scientists, played a crucial role in convincing Khrushchev and the Kennedy administration to sign the treaty.[11]

---

[10]Vladislav Zubok and Constantine Pleshakov, *Inside the Kremlin's Cold War* (Cambridge, Mass., 1996), pp. 261–263 relates Khrushchev's fall to his failed Cuban missile and other foreign policies; *New York Times*, January 22, 1992, p. A3.

[11]U.S. Senate, Committee on Foreign Relations, 88th Cong. 1st Sess., *Nuclear Test Ban Treaty* (Washington, 1963), pp. 422–423, 427. The critical role of the transnational groups from the 1950s to 1980s is explored for the first time in Matthew Evangelista's splendid *Unarmed Forces* (Ithaca, N.Y., 1999), especially chapter 2 on the test ban.

The new warmth toward Russia did not improve the NATO alliance. De Gaulle and Adenauer had been angered when Kennedy offered to negotiate bilaterally with the Soviets over Berlin in August 1961, and when the United States twice rejected (in August 1961 and January 1962) de Gaulle's pleas for establishing a joint directorate for military strategy. These rejections reaffirmed the French determination to build an independent nuclear force. De Gaulle viewed the British application for admission to the Common Market in 1961–1962 as the stalking horse of American economic and political power. The French pondered Kennedy's July 4, 1962, speech, which urged Europe to join in a "declaration of interdependence," but which pointedly omitted any mention of possible nuclear sharing. This speech, together with American trade legislation that allowed large reciprocal cuts in tariffs, indicated that the United States sought increased economic leverage in Europe. De Gaulle's mistrust intensified during the missile crisis, when Acheson flew to Paris to "inform" not "consult" (the words were de Gaulle's) the French on the confrontation. The French president fully supported Kennedy, but the episode convinced Paris officials that the United States would involve them in a nuclear war without consulting them beforehand.

De Gaulle's views were confirmed at the conference between Kennedy and British Prime Minister Harold Macmillan at Nassau in December 1962. The United States unilaterally canceled its development of the Skybolt missile on which the British had hoped to base their nuclear striking force. Instead Kennedy offered nuclear submarine and warhead information to Macmillan. The President pointedly did not make a similar offer to France. In January de Gaulle dramatically announced that he would veto the British entry into the Common Market. He explained that Great Britain had nitpicked for sixteen months of negotiations in an effort to bend the Common Market to British interests but had surrendered control of its own defense to the United States in a mere forty-eight hours at Nassau. De Gaulle, however, had made this decision for a more fundamental reason. He feared that if Great Britain entered the European Economic Community, "the end would be a colossal Atlantic Community dependent on America and directed by America, which would not take long to absorb this European Community." Shortly afterward a Franco-German friendship treaty was signed, which de Gaulle hoped would be the axis for an independent European diplomacy.

De Gaulle correctly believed that in the wake of the missile crisis East-West tensions would ease. In the long run a united Europe led by France might be able to influence international diplomacy if that Europe was free of both Russian and American control and if France had its own nuclear force. He also feared unchecked American military and economic power. De Gaulle was convinced that, because the United States would use the power unilaterally and irresponsibly, the French could suffer annihilation without representation.

The missile crisis did not advance Kennedy's "Grand Design" for Europe, but it tragically accelerated the American rush into Vietnam. Key Washington policymakers assumed that the one result of the October confrontation was a nuclear standoff between the two superpowers. Both had clearly indicated their reluctance to use nuclear force. The United States had won primarily because Khrushchev unwisely challenged Kennedy in the Caribbean, where American conventional naval power was decisive.

Within months both sides were discussing the easing of Cold War tensions. If the assumption was correct that the two great powers mutually feared each other's nuclear arms, then, the Kennedy administration concluded, the leaders of the emerging nations might feel that they had considerable opportunity to play West versus East, or, as in Southeast Asia and Africa, to undertake revolutionary changes without fear that either the United States or Russia would be able to shape these changes. If nationalist leaders acted on these beliefs, the newly emerging world could become increasingly unmanageable, perhaps dangerously radical from Washington's point of view. Kennedy especially feared that black–white racial wars, threatening to erupt in southern and Portuguese-controlled parts of Africa, would offer golden opportunities to communists. U.S. officials devised new policies to contain racial conflicts.[12] Such a view meshed perfectly with the other American fear that the communist policy line of support for (but not direct involvement in) "wars of liberation" had been established

---

[12]Thomas Borstelmann, "Hedging Our Bets . . . John Kennedy and Racial Revolutions in the American South and Southern Africa," *Diplomatic History,* 24 (Summer 2000): 451–452; Walt Whitman Rostow, "Domestic Determinants of U.S. Foreign Policy; The Tocqueville Oscillation," *Armed Forces Journal,* June 27, 1970, pp. 16D–16E; see also Rostow's *From the Seventh Floor* (New York, 1964).

in 1960–1961 precisely to exploit the emerging nationalisms. The New Frontiersmen dedicated themselves to rolling back such "wars of liberation." Vietnam would be used as the example.

The President also focused on Southeast Asia because he hoped to puncture what he believed to be the expansiveness of Communist China. In 1949–1950 Kennedy, then a member of the House of Representatives, had joined Republicans in denouncing the Truman administration for supposedly "losing" China. He softened these views during the 1950s, but in preparing to run for the presidency in 1960 he was reluctant to consider disavowing the use of nuclear weapons: "I wonder if we could expect to check the sweep south of the Chinese with their endless armies with conventional forces?"[13] After the missile crisis, Kennedy summarized his position in a conversation with André Malraux, French cultural affairs minister. Assistant Secretary of State for European Affairs William R. Tyler described the talk:

> [Kennedy] wanted to get a message to de Gaulle through Malraux . . . that really there was no reason why there should be differences between us and France in Europe, or between us and our European Allies, because there was no longer a likely Soviet military threat against Europe [since the Cuban missile crisis]. . . . But the area where we would have problems in the future . . . was China. He said it was so important that he and de Gaulle and other European leaders should think together about what they will do, what the situation will be when China becomes a nuclear power, what will happen then. . . . This was the great menace in the future to humanity, the free world, and freedom on earth. Relations with the Soviet Union could be contained within the framework of mutual awareness of the impossibility of achieving any gains through war. But in the case of China, this restraint would not be effective because the Chinese would be perfectly prepared, because of the lower value they attach to human life, to sacrifice hundreds of millions of their own lives, if this were necessary in order to carry out their militant and aggressive policies.[14]

---

[13]Kennedy to George Kennan, January 21, 1960, Oral History Interview with Mr. Kennan, March 23, 1964, Kennedy Library. Used by permission. For a succinct context on JFK and China, see Warren Cohen's review of Noam Kochavi, *A Conflict Perpetuated*, in *Diplomatic History*, 28 (January 2004): pp. 155–158.

[14]Oral History Interview with William R. Tyler, March 7, 1964, Kennedy Library; and Mr. Tyler to author, December 10, 1971.

The missile crisis and the Berlin confrontation in 1961 also rein-forced the administration's belief that it knew how to threaten to apply or, if necessary, actually apply conventional military power to obtain maximum results. White House officials joked that poor John Foster Dulles had never been able to find a suitable war for his "massive retaliation"; these pragmatic Kennedyites, however, had apparently solved the great riddle by perfectly matching power to crisis. One false premise ultimately wrecked this self-satisfaction: in Berlin and Cuba the Russians had backed down (Castro, noticeably, had been willing to fight to keep the missiles); in Vietnam the United States dealt with nationalist Vietnamese who, like Castro, had much to win by continuing to fight against apparently overwhelming American firepower.[15]

This fatal flaw did not clearly appear in 1962–1966. On the con-trary, during the autumn of 1962 the President's policies seemed to be proved correct during the brief war between India and China. India provoked the war during a border dispute over territory more important to the Chinese than to the Indians. The Chinese attacked with devastating force, destroying both the myth of Indian power and the American hope that India could serve as a cornerstone in the containment of China. The Chinese carefully occupied only some of the disputed territory, then voluntarily withdrew from other con-quered areas. On November 20 Prime Minister Nehru urgently asked Kennedy for aid. An American aircraft carrier moved across the southern Pacific toward India, but before it could become a factor, the crisis ended.[16] Some Washington policymakers nevertheless drew the mis-taken conclusion that the Chinese had backed down only after receiving warnings from the United States and, independently of the American move, from Russia.

Kennedy's advisers displayed similarly unwarranted confidence in their ability to control power in late 1962 when they decided to turn Laos into a pro-American bastion. They thereby helped destroy the Geneva Agreements which the United States had solemnly signed in midsummer 1962. Under the agreements, all foreign troops were to withdraw from Laos. The communist Pathet Lao were to join

[15]David Halberstam, "The Programming of Robert McNamara," *Harper's*, February 1971, p. 68.
[16]Allen Whiting's review of Neville Maxwell's *India's China War* in *Washington Post*, May 25, 1971, p. B6.

neutralist Souvanna Phouma's coalition government. American military advisers, indeed, began to leave, but the Central Intelligence Agency stepped up the supplying of the Meo tribesmen, an effective guerrilla army operating behind Pathet Lao lines.

In April 1964, however, a right-wing coup in Vientiane made Souvanna only a figurehead leader. The Pathet Lao retaliated with an offensive that threatened to conquer the entire Plain of Jarres. The United States then began initially small but systematic bombing raids on Laos, which Washington carefully tried to keep secret. To save a supposedly pivotal domino, the Kennedy-Johnson advisers confidently escalated their application of power.[17] The result, however, was that at the very time the United States escalated its commitment to South Vietnam, the key area of Laos became uncontrollable and formed an open channel for communist aid to the National Liberation Front in South Vietnam.

In 1962–1963 the assumptions that governed American policies in Vietnam fell into place. First, Vietnam was vital to American interests because, in John F. Kennedy's wildly overstated words of 1956, "Vietnam represents the cornerstone of the Free World in Southeast Asia, the keystone to the arch, the finger in the dike. . . . Her economy is essential to the economy of all of Southeast Asia; and her political liberty is an inspiration to those seeking to obtain or maintain their liberty in all parts of Asia—and indeed the world."[18] As Kennedy emphasized in his May 25, 1961, address to Congress, the battle of "freedom versus tyranny" was being waged in newly emerging areas such as Vietnam. While belittling the foreign policies of the previous administration, the Kennedy advisers gulped down whole the Eisenhower "domino theory." More precisely, the Dulles and Eisenhower formulation of the 1950s remained valid because, without an open Southeast Asia for its raw materials and markets, Japan, essential to the entire American strategic policy in the western Pacific, would have to turn toward its traditional market of China.

Second, the Kennedy administration assumed that China was to be not only isolated but, as some thought it had been in India, militarily disciplined. Both the Chinese and the Russians were to be taught that "wars of liberation" were not possible in areas the United States considered vital to its interests. Third, the missile crisis, the India-China

---

[17]D. Gareth Porter, "After Geneva: Subverting Laotian Neutrality." In Nina S. Adams and Alfred W. McCoy, eds., *Laos: War and Revolution* (New York, 1970), pp. 179–212.
[18]Quoted in Chester Cooper, *Lost Crusade* (New York, 1970), p. 168.

conflict, and the emerging Laotian situation gave the administration confidence in its ability to escalate military power while keeping it under control. Because of McNamara's work, moreover, the military power was available. For the first time in their history, Americans entered war with a great army at the ready, a force created by self-styled "realists" who, in the tradition of Forrestal and Acheson, believed that they could ultimately shape world affairs with American firepower.

These assumptions—the validity of the "domino theory" (particularly its economic implications for Japan), the century-old American fear of the "Yellow Peril," and the belief held by American liberal spokesmen that, as children of Niebuhr, they knew the secrets of using military force effectively—governed the Kennedy administration as it moved deeper into Vietnam.

Not, unfortunately, for the last time, U.S. officials sent their soldiers into a newly emerging nation convinced that no one could stand up to American firepower and good intentions. In 1962 Secretary of Defense McNamara had observed, "Every quantitative measurement we have shows we're winning this war."[19] Some factors in Southeast Asia, however, could not be computed. Twelve thousand American military personnel were involved in the conflict, yet the Vietminh continued to gain ground. The strategic hamlet program, geared to secure the countryside, was failing despite, or perhaps because of, the determination of the Diem regime. The peasants disliked being forced to leave their homes and to resettle elsewhere, particularly by a government that had condemned any meaningful land reform program. "No wonder the [Vietminh] looked like Robin Hoods when they began to hit the hamlets," one civilian American official remarked.[20] Vietminh successes mounted despite their kidnapping and brutal murdering of village and hamlet officials.

Kennedy's hope of reversing the situation rested on the ability of Diem's government to wage a successful military campaign while stabilizing South Vietnam's political problems. Saigon's military capability was dramatically called into question on January 2, 1963, in the village of Ap Bac, approximately fifty miles from Saigon. A small

---

[19] Arthur M. Schlesinger, Jr., *A Thousand Days* (Boston, 1965), p. 549. For an important analysis of how U.S. military superiority blinded Washington officials, see Gareth Porter, *Perils of Dominance* (Berkeley, 2005), chapters 4–5 on Kennedy's policies.
[20] David Halberstam, *The Making of a Quagmire* (New York, 1965), pp. 186–187.

Vietminh force was surrounded by a Vietnamese unit that was ten times larger, but despite the demands of American advisers to attack, the South Vietnamese refused. The Vietminh then methodically shot down five American helicopters, damaged nine more, killed three Americans, and disappeared. Apparently only U.S. soldiers had the will to fight in Vietnam, but Kennedy carefully pointed out after one firefight between Vietminh and American personnel that the U.S. forces in Vietnam were not "combat troops," and that if the situation changed, "I, of course, would go to Congress."[21] He was not prepared to do this in 1963. Nor was the White House even prepared to inform adequately the Congress and the public.

With an American presidential election little more than a year away, and his own belief that in 1964 his main challenge would come from the right wing of American politics, Kennedy carefully threw the best possible, even if misleading, light on Vietnamese affairs. American newspaper correspondents who candidly reported Diem's failures were rewarded either with Kennedy's unsuccessful attempt to give one critical correspondent a "vacation" from Vietnam, or with rejoinders to their questions like the one given by Admiral Harry Felt, commander of American forces in the Pacific: "Why don't you get on the team?"[22] In 1963 there was a widening abyss between the actual situation in Vietnam and the self-assurance of the Kennedy administration that it could manipulate military power to control nationalist revolutions.[23]

By late summer 1963 the abyss was so wide that it could no longer be ignored. Throughout the early part of the year, Diem, with the assistance of his brother Nhu Dinh Diem and Madame Nhu, ruthlessly suppressed domestic opposition. When Washington protested the Nhus' activities, Diem and his brother openly objected to this pressure. The beginning of the end for Diem and Nhu occurred on

---

[21]Cooper, *Lost Crusade,* pp. 193–194; also in U.S. Government, *Public Papers of the Presidents . . . Kennedy, 1962* (Washington, 1963), p. 228.

[22]Halberstam, *Making of a Quagmire,* p. 72. For this legacy that a contradictory Kennedy policy left to Lyndon Johnson, note especially Fredrik Logevall, *Choosing War* (Berkeley, 1999).

[23]For a succinct analysis of Kennedy's confused policies in his last months, see Robert David Johnson, "The Kennedy Myth," *Diplomatic History,* 28 (June 2004): pp. 467–471. James Aronson, *The Press and the Cold War* (New York, 1970), pp. 182–183. For Kennedy's public statement of his commitment to Vietnam in September 1963, see his television interview in the chapter X documents at the www.mhhe.com/lafeber website.

May 8, when Diem's troops shot into a crowd of Buddhists who were celebrating Buddha's birthday by waving religious flags, thereby violating the regime's rule that forbade the exhibit of any banner but the government's. The firing climaxed years of bitterness between the Roman Catholic regime of Diem and the Buddhists, who comprised more than 80 percent of the country's population. Many Buddhist leaders wanted no part of the war, no part of any foreign intervention in their nation, and no part of the Diem regime. They represented a new, potentially radical nationalism that neither the Diem regime nor the American officials in Vietnam could understand, let alone cope with. In June Buddhist-led antigovernment riots spread through Saigon. Diem retaliated by raiding Buddhist pagodas. Several Buddhists burned themselves to death in public protest, an act that Madame Nhu sarcastically welcomed as a "barbecue show." Students in normally quiet schools and universities joined the Buddhists. Diem confronted a full-scale rebellion.

The Kennedy administration's confusion in dealing with the revolutionary situation became glaringly evident during the crisis.[24] While continuing to announce that the military program was going well, the White House attempted to push Diem into making necessary domestic reforms by cutting off relatively small amounts of military and economic aid. That move, however, was sufficient to encourage anti-Diem elements in the army. On November 1 and 2, with, at least, the knowledge and approval of the White House and the American ambassador in Saigon, Henry Cabot Lodge, a military junta captured Diem and his brother.[25] Within hours the two men were shot and the junta assumed power. Three weeks later President Kennedy was assassinated in Dallas, Texas.

[24]*The Pentagon Papers,* as published by *The New York Times* (New York, 1971), pp. 163–177, 191–196. *The Pentagon Papers* is a condensed version of a massive study of Defense Department documents on the involvement in Vietnam. Commissioned by Secretary McNamara as a secret analysis, the larger study was written and compiled by three dozen experts and finally covered 3000 pages of analyses and 4000 pages of supporting documents. The shorter *Pentagon Papers* is crucial and revealing, but it should be used carefully because it contains little from either State Department or presidential files. See especially, George Kahin, "*The Pentagon Papers:* A Critical Evaluation," *American Political Science Review,* LXIX (June 1975): 675–684.

[25]*The Pentagon Papers,* pp. 158–159, 215–232, especially Lodge to Bundy, October 30, 1963, No. 57, pp. 226–229. This interpretation is supported with evidence found later and collected in Anne E. Blair's analysis, *Lodge in Vietnam* (New Haven, Conn., 1995), pp. 63–75.

President Lyndon B. Johnson inherited a set of badly decomposed foreign policies. In the last weeks of his life, Kennedy had said that the war was for the Vietnamese to win or lose. But the American consent given for Diem's overthrow, and the administration's full commitment to fighting what were intended to be limited wars with the conventional forces that Kennedy had so painstakingly developed, indicated that the United States would, if necessary, become further involved in Southeast Asia. Certainly Kennedy would have done nothing to change radically the American involvement until after the 1964 elections. By then he might have been unable to throw four years of policy suddenly into reverse. In Europe the administration's "Grand Design" was coming apart piece by piece, allowing de Gaulle to assume the leadership in the Western European community. The Alliance for Progress was crumbling, the victim of the false assumption that enough money and bureaucratic technicians could tinker with and adjust the dynamic nationalisms of an economically unbalanced Latin America to the policy objectives of a prosperous, satisfied, and expanding United States.

As these policies encountered the inevitable obstacles, bitter infighting appeared among Washington officials. The White House staff blamed the State Department for not having sufficient imagination and initiative to solve important diplomatic problems. Two talented biographers of Kennedy who were on the White House staff, Theodore Sorensen and Arthur Schlesinger, Jr., wrote their histories from this point of view. Their interpretation was questionable, for it glossed over several points. For example, there was no indication that President Kennedy and Secretary of State Dean Rusk differed on fundamental points of policy. This is important, for Kennedy must have appointed, and kept, this key official in the full knowledge that Rusk, having served under Dean Acheson and Robert Lovett, accepted the military-oriented policies that those two officials had followed. Rusk had also been assistant secretary of state for Far Eastern affairs during the Korean conflict. It did not require Kennedy's acute perception to conclude that Rusk, like the President himself, might have an uncommon commitment to building positions of military strength around the periphery of China. Consequently, the Kennedy administration bequeathed to Lyndon Johnson not only deteriorating foreign policies along with the test ban but also, much to Johnson's discomfort, the overpowering, handsome image and somber rhetoric of the fallen President.

The new Chief Executive's first important diplomatic pronouncement explained that he would continue his predecessor's Vietnam policies. The policies that followed, as well as the style with which they were carried out, could be understood in terms of the President's own history and resulting world view. A sharp British official caught several of Johnson's important traits:

> In view of the proximity of the Presidential election, and the urgency of the outstanding problems of Civil Rights and taxation, he will have to devote most of his time and energy to domestic affairs. In foreign affairs he is relatively inexperienced. . . . He speaks a language that Mr. Khrushchev understands, and his ability to hammer out a compromise may in time stand the West in good stead. Despite his desire for social reform, he has firm ideas about the pre-excellence of the American Way of Life, and tends to regard it as the only possible form of democracy.[26]

Lyndon Johnson's administration marked the point at which the historical legacies of Woodrow Wilson, Franklin D. Roosevelt, and the American frontier merged in the 1960s. Wilson believed that the American mission was to extend individual liberties throughout the world, but not out of altruism; it grew out of the belief that American liberties could not long exist at home unless the world was made safe for democracy. The basis of liberty at home was found in the economic system, for, as Wilson once observed, without "freedom of enterprise there can be no freedom whatsoever." Lyndon Johnson's own version was that "the very basis of a great nation is an educated mind, a healthy body, and a free enterprise system." With this established, the President could repeat time after time during the 1964 campaign, "Our cause has been the cause of all mankind." Whether the American system could work as well in the boiler houses of newly emerging nations as it had during its 300-year growth, and several mutations, in the United States was not discussed by the President. He simply moved to the conclusion: "Woodrow Wilson once said: 'I hope we shall never forget that we created this nation, not to serve ourselves, but to serve mankind.'"[27]

---

[26]F. O. Minute by J. L. N. O'Laughlin, December 2, 1963, FO371AU1012/5, Public Record Office; *The Pentagon Papers,* pp. 232–233.
[27]The Johnson quotes are cited from *The New York Times,* June 28, 1967, p. 24; and *Public Papers of the Presidents, 1964,* pp. 1242, 1103.

Emerging as a national political figure during the 1930s, and further developing the New Deal's domestic programs in the 1950s as the most powerful Senate leader in history, Johnson understood that even a well-functioning free enterprise system needed frequent governmental injections to provide balance and some economic justice. The New Deal, for example, had developed a previously poverty-stricken region of the United States through the Tennessee Valley Authority's electrical-power system in the 1930s. "The overriding rule which I want to affirm," the President remarked in Denver in 1966, "is that our foreign policy must always be an extension of our domestic policy. Our safest guide to what we do abroad is always what we do at home." This concern was easily translated to Vietnam: "I want to leave the footprints of America there. I want them to say, 'This is what the Americans left—schools and hospitals and dams. . . . ' We can turn the Mekong [River area] into a Tennessee Valley." The role of the government, therefore, both in the United States and Vietnam, was first to clear away the obstacles (the unenlightened American businessman in the 1930s, the Vietnamese communist in the 1960s), build the infrastructure (the Tennessee Valley and the Great Society at home, the Mekong Valley projects in Vietnam), and then let free enterprise develop the resources, and therefore the freedoms, of the areas. As one historian notes, Air Force generals wanted to bomb the Vietnamese back to "the Stone Age," but Johnson and such theorists as Walt Whitman Rostow and Samuel Huntington, who believed the newly emerging peoples could be taught to "modernize" along U.S. lines, somehow concluded they "could bomb the Vietnamese into the future."[28]

Johnson had an equally simple view of how this was to be accomplished, a view formed when he grew up in the frontierlike region of central Texas. His incredible ambition and energy exploited the opportunities of Texas and Washington, D.C., until he was privately wealthy and politically supreme. He had risen by making sharp distinctions between friends and enemies. "We are not a formal people," he observed

---

[28]The key work is Michael E. Latham, *Modernization as Ideology* (Chapel Hill, 2000), especially p. 151 which has the quote. This theme and its tragic implications are spelled out in the important study by Lloyd C. Gardner, *Pay Any Price: Lyndon Johnson and the Wars for Vietnam* (Chicago, 1995), especially chapters 1–3 and 9–11. *The New York Times,* August 27, 1966, p. 10; Interview with Henry Graff in *The New York Times Magazine,* March 20, 1966, p. 133.

in 1965, "We are not a people so much concerned with the way things are done as by the results that we achieve. Since the frontier really opened we have been this way." This remark, perilously close to an end-justifies-the-means point of view, could serve as a rationalization for both the Kennedy and Johnson conduct of the Vietnamese conflict. After all, as the President declared in 1965, "America wins the wars that she undertakes. Make no mistake about it." If the struggle became difficult, Johnson could again use the development of the American frontier as an example to reassure Americans that not they but a more supernatural power put them into Vietnam: "We had the good fortune to grow from a handful of isolated colonies to a position of great responsibility in the world. We did not deliberately seek this position; in a real sense the force of history shaped it for us."[29] History during the 1960s became a political tool to wield rather than a burden requiring understanding and humility.

Given this vision of American history, the President determined he must do nothing less than create a Great Society at home and wage the Cold War abroad. He demanded consensus for these objectives: "We cannot keep what we have and we cannot preserve the brightening flame of hope for others unless we are all—repeat *all* committed; all—repeat *all* willing to sacrifice and to serve wherever we can, whether it be in Vietnam, whether it be at home." Johnson justified using the widest possible presidential powers in foreign policy to shape this consensus. For there was the other side of the coin if Americans did not "sacrifice": "There are 3 billion people in the world and we have only 200 million of them. We are outnumbered 15 to 1. If might did make right they would sweep over the United States and take what we have. We have what they want."[30] Given such a world view, if discontent appeared at home the anti-war dissenters could be labeled "appeasers" of the "Munich variety"; national press and television could justifiably be manipulated; and policies could be acquitted by the latest poll, pulled from Johnson's coat pocket, which demonstrated through apparently incontrovertible quantitative data that "body count" indicated the war was being won in Vietnam and consensus reigned at home.

---

[29]*Public Papers of the Presidents, 1965,* pp. 770, 821; *Public Papers of the Presidents, 1966,* p. 984.
[30]*Public Papers of the Presidents, 1964,* p. 1640; *Public Papers of the Presidents, 1966,* p. 1287.

Johnson's policies in Vietnam were not aberrations but the culmination of nearly three-quarters of a century of American foreign policy. He only presented those policies—and their consequences—more starkly than had his predecessors. In this sense his continuation of Kennedy's approach to Vietnam was natural, but like the New Frontier, the Great Society's hope for military-imposed stability in Southeast Asia soon vanished. Saigon politics were in chaos. Seven different governments rose to power in South Vietnam during 1964, three during the weeks of August 16 to September 3 alone. This was the struggle within the civil war.

Nor was the civil war itself abating. State Department Director of Intelligence Thomas Hughes remarked on June 8, 1964, that "by far the greater part of the Vietcong forces in South Vietnam are South Vietnamese, the preponderance of Vietcong weapons come not from Communist countries but from capture, purchase, and local manufacture."[31] In such a civil war the United States could not find sufficient leverage to roll back the National Liberation Front. When Hanoi offered to negotiate in August 1964, the United States consequently rejected the proposal. U.S. officials argued fifteen months later, when the offer was finally revealed, that Ho Chi Minh was not serious about making an equitable settlement and that the military situation at the time gravely weakened the American negotiating position. The presidential campaign in the United States may also have been a factor. Johnson did not want to be open to the charge of appeasement, particularly when his overmatched Republican opponent, former Senator Barry Goldwater of Arizona, urged a "Let's win" policy of total military victory. (A 1964 example of Goldwater's tough language can be found in the chapter X documents at the www.mhhe.com/lafeber website.)

The war entered a new phase on August 2, 1964, when North Vietnamese torpedo boats attacked the American destroyer *Maddox* in the Gulf of Tonkin. Bounded by North Vietnam and China, the gulf was a sensitive strategic area. Despite American warnings and the reinforcement of the fleet, the attack was apparently repeated on August 4. Hanoi claimed that the American ships had been participating in South Vietnamese raids on two North Vietnamese shore areas. *The New York Times* also reported that the destroyers had collaborated

---

[31]Quoted in Philip L. Geyelin, *Lyndon B. Johnson and the World* (New York, 1966), p. 193.

with South Vietnamese commando raids.[32] President Johnson, however, interpreted the attack as "open aggression on the high seas." He added in an ironic historical prophecy, "We Americans know, although others appear to forget, the risk of spreading conflict." He insisted that "the attacks were unprovoked."[33] Without consulting NATO or SEATO allies or the U.S. Congress, the President ordered the first American air attack on North Vietnamese ports in retaliation.

Four years later in congressional hearings, Secretary McNamara admitted that the American warships attacked in the gulf had been cooperating with South Vietnamese forays against North Vietnam. Since February 1964 the United States had developed a program of clandestine attacks on North Vietnam. Termed 34A, these operations included parachuting sabotage teams, commando raids, and the bombardment of coastal installations. As the Saigon political situation deteriorated, the raids were stepped up, although the administration concealed them from Congress. This evidence contradicted McNamara's statement of August 6, 1964: "Our Navy played absolutely no part in, was not associated with, was not aware of, any South Vietnamese actions, if there were any."[34]

The truth, however, appeared much too late to prevent Congress from making one of its worst foreign-policy errors. The President requested a resolution supporting "all necessary measures" that the President may take to "repel any armed attack" against American forces. He demanded and received more, for Congress also gave advance consent that the President could "prevent further aggression" and take "all necessary steps" to protect any nation covered by SEATO

---

[32]*The New York Times,* August 5, 1964, p. 4; and August 4, 1964, p. 2. See especially the well-researched overview, Eric Alterman, *When Presidents Lie* (New York, 2004), pp. 190–222.

[33]*Public Papers of the Presidents, 1964,* p. 928; for the actual U.S. and North Vietnamese views on this turning point, see Robert McNamara, et al., *Argument Without End* (New York, 1999), pp. 167–170, 202–204.

[34]U.S. Senate, Committee on Foreign Relations, 90th Cong., 2nd Sess., *The Gulf of Tonkin, The 1964 Incidents* (Washington, 1968). *The Pentagon Papers,* pp. 234–242, 258–279, also analyzes the 34A operations and Gulf of Tonkin attack. Johnson's message, the Tonkin Gulf resolution, and part of the Senate debate, including Morse's sharp criticism, can be read in chapter X documents at the www.mhhe.com/lafeber website. In 2005, a secret National Security Agency study was made public that concluded U.S. intelligent analysts "deliberately skewed" information to suggest, falsely, that North Vietnam attacked the U.S. ships in the supposed second raid. (*New York Times,* December 2, 2005, p. A11.)

which might request aid "in defense of its freedom." In August 1964, this Gulf of Tonkin Resolution sailed through the House of Representatives after forty minutes of debate by a vote of 416 to 0. In the Senate, however, Senator Gaylord Nelson, Democrat of Wisconsin, attempted to amend the resolution so that it would not justify a widening of the conflict. He was stopped by J. William Fulbright, Democrat of Arkansas and chairman of the Foreign Relations Committee, who argued that the President should be trusted and that an amendment would require further consideration by the House at a time when speed and the appearance of national unity were essential. The Senate then voted 88 to 2 (Democratic Senators Wayne Morse of Oregon and Ernest Gruening of Alaska dissenting) to give the President virtually unlimited powers in the Vietnamese conflict.

During the next four years Johnson waged war without an explicit declaration of war from congress. He argued that the Gulf of Tonkin Resolution and the President's powers as commander in chief of the military gave him sufficient authority to send one-half million Americans into combat in Vietnam. The Senate finally repealed the resolution in 1970.

To examine the Vietnam War in isolation would be a grave historical error. The conflict was not an exception to the world view of American foreign policymakers during the 1960s. Vietnam was only one of a number of revolutions in the newly emerging world with which Johnson had to deal during his first eighteen months in office. Since 1960 Africa had been the most chaotic area. In all of Africa in 1945, only Egypt, Ethiopia, Liberia, and South Africa could lay claim to independence. Otherwise the continent was under Belgian, British, French, Spanish, or Portuguese control. World War II destroyed the power of European colonialism; the Suez crisis of 1956 (see p. 189) and then the termination of British control of Ghana in 1957 (giving the first black African state its independence in the postwar era) set off a chain reaction. In 1960 sixteen new African states joined the United Nations. By 1970 fifty African nations were independent. Many of these states were national entities only in the sense that colonial authorities had formerly imposed central governments over the areas. Tribal ties often remained stronger, factionalizing the new nations, creating insoluble problems for nationalistic leaders, and thereby allowing army generals to use military force to consolidate their own as well as their nations' power. Nearly all new African nations, moreover, had been poorly prepared by the colonialists for independence. Necessary capital, technical skills, stable governmental institutions, and educated elites were in short supply.

The United States held a precarious position among black Africans because it refused to use sanctions to penalize the Republic of South Africa for its policy of apartheid, under which a small white minority of less than 20 percent of the population isolated and ruthlessly suppressed the black majority. That dilemma intensified in November 1965, when Southern Rhodesia, with a white population of 200,000 and a black population of nearly 4 million, broke away from the British Empire to establish another apartheid system. The United States publicized its dislike for these apartheid policies but refused to go further. Vast economic investments, strategic naval ports in South Africa, a reluctance to oppose military allies (such as Portugal) that still controlled colonial African territories, and a fear that such action would be a precedent for other nations to condemn the violent American domestic racial situation—all these prevented the United States from effectively opposing the brutalities of apartheid.

Washington officials, however, did not hesitate to intervene in the Belgian Congo during the 1960s. This area, tragically unprepared by Belgium for independence, became a sovereign nation on June 30, 1960. Katanga Province, led by Moise Tshombe and bolstered by European and American copper and cobalt interests, attempted to secede from the Congo and become an independent state. In the ensuing two-year struggle the most popular nationalistic—and, to Eisenhower, radical and dangerous—Congolese leader, Patrice Lumumba, was murdered by Katanga authorities who were at least encouraged by the CIA. Order was restored only after the United Nations, with vast American support, helped the Congolese government capture Tshombe and reunite the country in January 1963. The United States had decided that removing Tshombe was less distasteful than allowing the continuation of a civil war that could become an open invitation to Soviet or Chinese intervention. The Soviets actually supported UN intervention, but not when the intervention was under U.S. control.

Congolese stability proved short-lived. In the spring of 1964 left-wing nationalists attempted to overthrow the government. By this time the United States had replaced Belgium as the most powerful foreign element and had spent more than $6 million attempting to bolster the central government. As rebellion spread, the Central Intelligence Agency formed a mercenary army and air force, many of whose planes were piloted by exiled Cubans. The multilived Tshombe returned to head this central government. He recruited white mercenaries from southern Africa, Europe, and the United States. The rebels opened contact with Communist China, although communist influence in the movement was extremely small. The antigovernment forces tortured and executed perhaps 20,000 opponents. When they gathered 280 Belgians and 16 Americans as hostages, the United States organized a quick Belgian paratroop strike.[35] On November 24, 1964, the hostages were freed, and the rebels were dispersed.

Shortly thereafter Tshombe was driven from power by a military regime led by General Joseph D. Mobutu. The political structure remained unstable, and Tshombe's use of white mercenaries had enraged African nationalists. American influence continued to grow until by 1967 Belgians had to make appointments through the U.S. embassy to talk with Congolese governmental officials.[36] When rebellion again erupted in the summer of 1967, however, powerful senators, led by Richard Russell, Democrat of Georgia, so strenuously objected to further aid for Mobutu that the State Department acquiesced. Racial tensions at home as well as the rising combat fatalities in Vietnam were beginning to limit American initiatives in other newly emerging nations.

Africa ranked much lower on Washington's priority list than either Vietnam or Latin America. In the latter area, Johnson continued the downgrading of the Alliance for Progress. He placed control of policy under a new assistant secretary of state, Thomas C. Mann. A no-nonsense fellow Texan, Mann's top priorities were the stabilization of Latin American politics, protection of American private investments in the area, and a vigorous struggle against radicalism. He willingly accepted military governments in Latin America, particularly if these regimes replaced liberal reform governments that

---

[35]Richard J. Barnet, *Intervention and Revolution: The United States in the Third World* (New York, 1968), pp. 248–251. On the U.S. and Lumumba's murder, note George Lardner, Jr., "Did Ike Authorize a Murder?" *Washington Post*, August 8, 2000, p. A23.
[36]*The New York Times*, August 3, 1967, p. 2.

threatened to pass economic measures aimed at making private investors more accountable and responsible. U.S. encouragement and acceptance of such a military coup d'état occurred first in Brazil in 1964. The new Brazilian military regime became one of the most stable—and repressive—governments in the hemisphere.

When President Johnson did attempt to increase investment in Latin American social enterprises such as education or health, his policies were questioned by the Treasury Department and its new secretary, Henry Fowler. The secretary's uppermost concern was not Latin American development but the correction of the worsening dollar deficit being incurred by the United States in international trade. Since the late 1950s (and for the first time since the 1870s), Americans had spent more overseas than they had sold. The deficit was made up by shipping gold abroad. By the mid-1960s the U.S. gold supply had shrunk 40 percent since 1945, and the situation threatened to get out of hand as Vietnam costs spiraled upward in 1965–1966. One of the first victims of America's inability to balance its international budget was the Alliance for Progress.

Fowler and the Treasury insisted that support for American exports (the most important suction for drawing money back into the United States) receive preference over all overseas social investments. The department inserted an "additionality" clause in aid grants. Under this clause Latin American recipients of American aid promised to spend all of that money on American goods, even though those goods were more expensive than, say, similar British or French goods. "Additionality" drastically drove up the cost of development for the Latin Americans. The president of Colombia observed sardonically in 1968, "Colombia has received two program loans under the Alliance. I don't know if we can survive a third."[37]

By 1966 the Alliance had miserably failed to achieve its objectives. It had created rising expectations in Latin America, expectations that demanded more than American support for military regimes or the use of Latin America as a mere export market for U.S. goods. But worse was to come.

In the Dominican Republic on April 24, 1965, a civilian government headed by Donald Reid Cabral was attacked by liberal and

[37]Jerome Levinson and Juan de Onís, *The Alliance That Lost Its Way: A Critical Report on the Alliance for Progress* (Chicago, 1970), is the best analysis; see especially, pp. 120–123.

radical followers of Juan Bosch (see map, p. 217). The nation's 3.3 million people were among the poorest in Latin America. Between 1916 and 1940 the government had been controlled by American Marines and customs officers, but the United States had withdrawn by 1940 in favor of Rafael Trujillo. The dictator, whom Franklin D. Roosevelt accurately characterized as "an s.o.b." but "our s.o.b.," brutally ruled and ruthlessly exploited his countrymen until he was gunned down by assassins in May 1961. When the dictator's relatives attempted to claim his power, President Kennedy deployed American naval units to safeguard the provisional government. In December 1962 the reform party led by Juan Bosch obtained 60 percent of the votes in a national election. Ten months later, Bosch fell to an army coup d'état that was supported by conservative businessmen, landholders, and church leaders. Neither the White House, whose staff had become dissatisfied with Bosch and viewed him as a mere "literary figure," nor the State Department protected Bosch's popularly elected government. The Reid Cabral junta which assumed power was soon deserted by both conservative and radical forces; it was deserted by everyone, apparently, except the United States. When Reid Cabral insisted on running for president in the June 1965 elections, and when Washington then extended a $5-million loan to his regime, pro-Bosch forces overthrew what was only the shell of a government.

Two days of fighting between the rebels and army forces followed. On Monday, April 26, the rebels began arming thousands of civilians. By April 28 the military seemed to have the upper hand, but Washington officials, acting on conclusions too hastily formed by the American embassy in Santo Domingo, concluded that marines would have to land to prevent a Castro-like revolution. Johnson and Mann had taken a tough line on Castro. Despite approaches from the Cuban government in the autumn of 1963 which hinted at its desire to have normal relations with the United States, Washington had replied very cautiously. When Castro then suggested an agenda for the talks, Johnson was President. Although he saw the Cuban memorandum, Johnson had refused to make any conciliatory move.[38] By late 1964 the United States, working through the Organization of

[38]Oral History Statement by William Attwood, November 8, 1965, Kennedy Library, Boston. Used by permission.

American States (OAS), had successfully pressured every Latin American nation except Mexico to break off diplomatic relations with Cuba. Faced with the Dominican revolt, the administration adopted a view that American policymakers had amplified from the Truman Doctrine to the Kennedy-Johnson interpretation of Vietnam: the revolt was part of a larger challenge in the newly emerging world, and a challenge in any area was thus a challenge to American security everywhere.

The initial public pretext for landing nearly 23,000 troops was the protection of Americans in strife-torn Santo Domingo. (This rationale was probably publicized in part because the U.S. action violated Articles 15 and 17 of the OAS Charter, which prohibited intervention "directly or indirectly, for any reason whatever, in the internal or external affairs of any other State.") On April 30, however, Johnson gave a different reason: "People trained outside the Dominican Republic are seeking to gain control." Unfortunately for the President, the CIA told him that no communists were involved. Furious, Johnson ordered the FBI to "Find me some Communists in the Dominican Republic." As a result the American embassy issued a poorly documented list of fifty-eight (or fifty-three) "identified and prominent Communist and Castroite leaders" in the rebel forces. American newspapermen on the scene considered the list propaganda, not fact, and agreed with Bosch's assessment that "this was a democratic revolution smashed by the leading democracy of the world."[39] In intervening unilaterally, the United States maneuvered a very reluctant vote of consent from the OAS, but Johnson's disdain for the organization's failure to be enthusiastic about the American Marines was great. "The OAS," the President remarked privately, "couldn't pour———out of a boot if the instructions were written on the heel."[40]

The President went further. On May 2, 1965, he announced that the "American nations cannot, must not, and will not permit the establishment of another Communist government in the Western Hemisphere." He warned that change "should come through peaceful process" and pledged that the United States would defend "every free country of this hemisphere." The importance of this "Johnson

[39]*Newsweek,* May 17, 1965, p. 52; Randall B. Woods, *Fulbright* (New York, 1995), p. 382.
[40]Geyelin, *Lyndon B. Johnson and the World,* p. 254.

Doctrine," like both the Truman and Eisenhower doctrines, depended on how broadly the United States would define "communism" and how easily an unrestrained President, could, without obtaining Congress's consent, order troops to defend "every free country." The contradictions inherent in the administration's policies (in both Southeast Asia and Latin America) appeared on May 9 in an interview with Mann. Having just intervened with a large military force, the assistant secretary of state declared that the United States only wanted every nation to choose its "own government free of outside interference."[41]

In the spring of 1966 a conservative government led by Joaquin Balaguer assumed power through nationwide elections. Four years later Balaguer was reelected amidst increasing violence. Although the opposition refused to participate in what it considered to be a fixed election, more than 200 political murders occurred. During the first six months of 1971, political killings occurred at the rate of one every forty-eight hours. Balaguer's police evidently committed most of the crimes. "Even under Trujillo we had nothing like this," observed a veteran Dominican reporter.

The effect of Johnson's intervention was incalculable among the Latin Americans themselves. But it also turned out to be incalculable at home. Johnson's good friend, J. William Fulbright, Democrat of Arkansas and powerful chair of the Senate Foreign Relations Committee, gave a speech in September 1965 carefully specifying how the administration had misled the American people about the danger of communism in the Dominican Republic. Fulbright never mentioned Johnson directly, but any attack on the Texan's policies, as the senator put it, meant "that's the end of you from his point of view." The President paid dearly for the break. For the next three years Fulbright used the Foreign Relations Committee as a launchpad for devastating attacks—largely from a conservative viewpoint—on Johnson's policies, above all those in the killing fields of Vietnam.[42]

The administration's policy thus came under severe attack at home. Most critics were concerned with the evolving pattern of

---

[41]*The New York Times,* May 9, 1965, p. E3. Johnson's May 2nd speech may be read in the chapter X documents at the www.mhhe.com/lafeber website.
[42]*Washington Post,* July 15, 1971, p. F7; Woods, *Fulbright,* pp. 390–484. Fulbright's attack can be read in the chapter X documents at the www.mhhe.com/lafeber website.

American intervention around the globe and the resulting justifications issued by official sources. As was, and is, too often the case, a bad—or duplicitous—secret foreign policy was covered up by misleading public statements.

During the 1964 presidential campaign Johnson had answered Goldwater's demands for bombing North Vietnam with the remark on September 25, "We're not going north and drop bombs at this stage of the game" because "I want to think about the consequences of getting American boys into a war with 700 million Chinese." The same day, however, William P. Bundy, assistant secretary of state for Far Eastern affairs, commented, "Expansion of the war outside South Vietnam . . . could be forced upon us by the increased pressures of the Communists." Bundy proved the more accurate prophet. At the time Johnson was campaigning, his closest advisers had decided that North Vietnam would have to be bombed. Target lists were drawn up, bombings were expected to begin at the outset of 1965, and only the President's permission, which his advisers now thought to be "inevitable," remained to be obtained. These counselors further understood that the bombing, once undertaken, would be only a stopgap measure to shore up the revolving South Vietnam regimes until American ground troops could be rushed into action. U.S. officials believed no one could long stand up to the American military, the most powerful on earth.[43]

On February 8, 1965, the American bombing raids on North Vietnam began. The ostensible reason was a Vietminh attack on the American camp at Pleiku, killing seven Americans; this was one of a series of attacks against U.S. bases that had taken place since the autumn. In March the President began "Rolling Thunder," a systematic long-term bombing program against the North. Curtis LeMay, air force chief of staff, thought it time: "We are swatting flies when we should be going after the manure pile." By April, however, the bombing had only stiffened Hanoi's resistance. Johnson ordered more than 20,000 American troops into Vietnam, and now they were openly instructed to enter into combat. The inescapable logic of the commitment began to become apparent.

---

[43]*Pentagon Papers,* pp. 307–342; McNamara, et al., *Argument Without End,* pp. 205–217 on the confusion in both Washington and Hanoi. For the supposed superiority of the U.S. military's position, see Porter's important interpretation, *Perils of Dominance,* especially chapters 6–8.

Over 100,000 U.S. troops went to Vietnam in approximately four months. The escalation saved the tottering South Vietnamese government, but at an unimagined price.

"Rolling Thunder" aimed to cut off supplies being infiltrated from North Vietnam and to help stabilize South Vietnam politically. It accomplished neither objective. Hanoi, with aid from Russia and China, matched the American escalation step by step by sending 60,000 men into South Vietnam in 1966 (three times the number of 1965) and increasing daily tonnage of supplies by 150 percent. Bombing had little effect on the primitive supply route, which needed to provide only six tons of goods a day (an amount that could be carried by several hundred people) to keep the Vietminh refueled. Bombings north and south, moreover, probably killed a ratio of two civilians to one Vietminh, according to one estimate; American-Vietnamese search-and-destroy operations on the ground perhaps killed as many as six civilians for each Vietminh. Ground fighting increased, with Americans assuming the burden. In April 1966, for the first time, more Americans than South Vietnamese were killed in action. A year earlier, in March 1965, Johnson realized he was horribly trapped. "I can't get out and I can't finish it with what I've got," he told his wife. "And I don't know what the hell to do."[44]

On the political side prospects only slightly improved. In June 1965 strongman Air Vice Marshal Nguyen Cao Ky came to power as premier. A North Vietnamese who had fought with the French against Vietnamese independence forces and later made a widely publicized remark praising Adolf Hitler, Ky was nevertheless welcomed by American officials because he promised to provide the necessary political stability. But desertions continued to rise dramatically in the South Vietnam Army. Inflation and corruption, appearing almost in proportion to the intensified American effort, decimated the Vietnamese economy. By February 1966 McNamara admitted that even if bombing destroyed all of North Vietnam's power systems, oil, harbors, and dams, "they could still carry on the infiltration of the men and equipment necessary to support some level of operations in the South."[45]

---

[44]Roger Hilsman, *To Move a Nation* (New York, 1965), p. 530; Alterman, *When Presidents Lie,* p. 220.
[45]*The New York Times,* February 16, 1966, p. 1.

These disasters were visible in 1966 for any American who cared to see them. Too often the scene was blurred by statistics that poured out of Washington, most of them misleading. "Ah, *les statistiques!*" a Vietnamese general explained to an American, "Your Secretary of Defense loves statistics. We Vietnamese can give him all he wants. If you want them to go up, they will go up. If you want them to go down, they will go down."[46] The view was also distorted by various peace initiatives. In an April 7, 1965, speech at Johns Hopkins University, President Johnson offered what he termed "unconditional discussions" and proposed an internationally financed Asian Development Bank for peacetime reconstruction. Actually, peace discussions were impossible from the American view because of the deteriorating military situation. During his first months in office, moreover, President Johnson had ruled out any neutralization of South Vietnam. This undercut totally his call for "unconditional discussions."[47]

For their part the North Vietnamese would settle for nothing less than a complete withdrawal of American power and the reunification of the country on their terms. They were not about to be betrayed as they felt they had been in the 1954 Geneva Conference. By 1965 the Vietnamese civil war could no more be compromised than the American Civil War could have been a century earlier.

In this larger sense, the enemy of the 1960s was China. On the one hand, the Johnson administration believed that because of internal difficulties the Chinese would not intervene in Vietnam as long as the fighting remained away from their borders. On the other hand, "Over this war—and all Asia—is another reality: the deepening shadow of Communist China," as the President told the nation in his Johns Hopkins speech. "The contest in Vietnam is part of a wider pattern of aggressive purposes." During the same month McNamara explained most fully in a private conversation why the United States was in Vietnam.

The alternative to fighting, he observed, was not to negotiate a neutral noncommunist South Vietnam, for this was impossible. The

---

[46]Hilsman, *To Move a Nation,* p. 523.

[47]*Pentagon Papers,* pp. 285–286, especially cable from President to Lodge, March 20, 1964, Document No. 65. Johnson's Johns Hopkins speech may be read in the chapter X documents at the www.mhhe.com/lafeber website. Senator Fulbright's powerful 1967 attack on U.S. policies in Vietnam can be found at this website as well.

real alternative was a Chinese-dominated Southeast Asia, which would mean a "Red Asia." If the United States withdrew, a complete shift would occur in the world balance of power. Asia would go Red, American allies would be shaken, and at home there would be a "bad effect on [the] economy and a disastrous political fight that could further freeze American political debate and even affect political freedom." Chinese attitudes might soften over the decades, but this would take longer than had the Russian change, for China "started from farther back than [the] Soviet Union in [the] industrializing process. The Soviet Union was contained by a military alliance in an expansionist period. So [it is] possible to contain China in her expansionist phase by similar alliances." To stop China, the United States would not recognize "any sanctuary or any weapons restriction. But we would use nuclear weapons only after fully applying non-nuclear arsenal." In 2001, newly opened records revealed that after China exploded its first atomic device in 1964, U.S. officials indeed debated whether to bomb the Chinese facilities and help India develop its own nuclear weapon to contain China. They finally decided to try other tactics first.[48]

These U.S. debates occurred at a time when the Chinese were suffering a series of devastating foreign-policy setbacks that helped trigger a severe internal upheaval within China between 1966 and 1968. A domestically generated coup in Indonesia led by nationalist army elements, and having little to do with the American presence in Vietnam, destroyed pro-Beijing communists in a bloodbath. Castro's Cuba, revolutionary Algeria, Egypt's Nasser, and a number of African nations publicly attacked Chinese policies, restricting or severing diplomatic ties. Despite China's explosion of a thermonuclear device in May 1966, that nation's diplomatic leverage declined.

These failures influenced Mao to launch a "cultural revolution" within China that transformed foreign policy and enabled him to eliminate personal enemies within Beijing. The turning point came in September 1965, when General Lin Piao, second in command to Mao, announced that China would encourage wars of liberation throughout the newly emerging nations. But Lin Piao gave no hint that China

---

[48]"Memorandum" of Background Session with Robert McNamara, April 22, 1965, Arthur Krock Papers, Princeton University Library; *New York Times*, January 13, 2001—I am indebted to Milton Leitenberg for this source.

would become directly involved in any of the revolutions. He warned other revolutionaries to help themselves as the Chinese had done.

In Washington, however, policymakers led by Secretary of State Dean Rusk immediately compared Lin Piao's statement to Hitler's *Mein Kampf*, in which the German revealed how he planned to conquer much of the world. The President announced that Lin Piao had confirmed that, if the domino of Vietnam fell, others would follow.[49] Nearly 200 scholars of Asian affairs urged a reevaluation of the policy toward China, but without success. They observed that, regardless of how the rhetoric was interpreted, Chinese capabilities and power could not and might never be able to achieve Lin Piao's objectives. Developments in Indonesia, Cuba, and Africa confirmed this view.

As usual, the greatest irony could be found in Vietnam. Following the Lin Piao statement, China pleaded with Hanoi to fight a protracted struggle that would tie down and bleed American power. Ho Chi Minh disliked such advice. He wanted to defeat the United States rapidly. A long war would leave a weakened North Vietnam more open to Chinese pressure.[50] Meanwhile, much to the consternation of the Chinese, the Soviet Union replaced China as the most important source of aid and support for Ho's regime. Worse, in early 1966, clashes between Chinese and Russian troops occurred along their long common border. At this point in 1965–1966, the Johnson administration decided to send 400,000 American soldiers to save Vietnam from China.

The Soviet Union was the primary, perhaps the only, nation that benefited from American intervention. Documents opened in the 1990s show that Soviet officers secretly operated missile sites in Vietnam that shot down U.S. planes. Thus the Soviets at once gained military experience, countered Chinese influence, took American lives, and won favor with the North Vietnamese. With U.S. attention and resources tied down in Southeast Asia, Russia made a dramatic recovery in world affairs between 1965 and 1971. After 1958 the Russian economy had grown at a considerably slower rate than previously, thus discouraging Khrushchev's hopes of challenging American economic

[49]*Public Papers of the Presidents, 1966*, p. 936; for the next sentence see also *The New York Times*, August 31, 1966, p. 9.

[50]David Mozingo, "China's Foreign Policy and the Cultural Revolution," Interim Report: Number 1, International Relations of East Asia Project, Cornell University, Ithaca, N.Y., 1970.

supremacy. The decline also weakened his power within the Kremlin. Dissenting party leaders and some military officials combined to oust Khrushchev in October 1964. The victors divided his posts between two former protégés of Stalin, Aleksey Kosygin, who became premier, and Leonid Brezhnev, the new first party secretary. This change occurred as the United States stepped up its effort in Vietnam. Kosygin was actually visiting Hanoi at that moment in February 1965 when the United States chose to begin the bombing. As Soviet influence grew in Hanoi, Moscow did nothing to mediate the war, partly because the two sides seemed irreconcilable but also because the conflict—as long as it remained limited—drained the United States and benefited the Soviet Union. The Soviets, moreover, had their own fear of China. Johnson continually hoped that Moscow would help him mediate a face-saving U.S. retreat from Vietnam, but as a top Soviet diplomat later noted, "Moscow had no intention of applying strong diplomatic pressure on Ho Chi Minh lest it drive him into the arms of the Chinese."[51]

The Russians further gained as the war helped divide the Western Alliance. France, the former colonial power in Southeast Asia, now condemned the "foreign intervention" of the United States. (In the spring of 1966 American policies received a further blow when de Gaulle pulled France out of the NATO military organization.) The Western Europeans refused outright to send troops for the American buildup in South Vietnam. Of the forty nations linked to the United States through treaties, only four (Australia, New Zealand, South Korea, and Thailand) committed combat troops. Korea and Thailand did so only after the United States promised to pay handsomely for their troops. Japan also grew critical of the escalation in the war. Meanwhile the Japanese made at least $1 billion per year 1966–1975 by selling war supplies to both Americans and their North Vietnamese enemy. U.S. soldiers used Japanese watches, cameras, beer, and toilet paper, while their dead returned home in Japanese-made polyethylene body bags. For some, Vietnam became a profitable war, even as they condemned it.[52]

---

[51]Anatoly Dobrynin, *In Confidence* (New York, 1995), p. 115; I. V. Gaiduk, *The Soviet Union and the Vietnam War* (Chicago, 1996), traces Soviet involvement.
[52]Thomas R. H. Havens, *Fire Across the Sea; The Vietnam War and Japan* (Princeton, N.J., 1987), pp. 87, 94–97, 103–104.

No matter where he looked, Johnson had difficulty finding support for his policies. The trouble with foreigners, the President lamented, "is that they're not like folks you were reared with." By mid-1966, however, the problems with the allies were rapidly becoming less important than the eruptions of the "folks" back home.

President Richard Nixon and Soviet leader Leonid Brezhnev looked forward to better relations aboard the President's yacht. As shown in this photo they looked in quite different directions.
(National Archives and Records Administration)

CHAPTER 11

A New Containment: The Rise and Fall of Détente (1966–1976)

Ironically, as the United States escalated the war in Vietnam to contain communism, the Johnson administration deescalated conflict with the Soviets. The seeds of détente, or lessening of international tension, were sown in 1967–1968, at the moment U.S. forces suffered setbacks in Vietnam, and blossomed in 1971–1972 as American bombers obliterated people and villages in large areas of Southeast Asia. Thus détente did not signal an American retreat from world affairs but was a new—and necessary—tactic for carrying on traditional containment policy. Overall the power of the U.S. economy and military (not to mention American culture, especially music, art, and McDonald's) remained dominant on the globe.

Johnson initially pursued détente in the hope that the Soviets, who were the largest suppliers of military goods to North Vietnam, might be able to pressure Ho Chi Minh to make peace. The Americans' hope was badly misplaced. The Russians would do nothing to take this pressure off the United States. On the battlefields the war dragged on, while at home the inflation rate doubled to 5 percent and antiwar protests intensified. Johnson's beloved Great Society program, created to erase domestic poverty and injustice, became a victim of a war 11,000 miles away. A top White House official revealed the President's dilemma with the remark, "What the hell do you say? How do you half-lead a country into war?"[1]

---

[1]Harry McPherson Oral History Interview, Tape #4, p. 20, Lyndon B. Johnson Library, Austin, Tex. (Hereafter cited as LBJ Library.)

Intensifying problems thus forced Johnson to approach the Soviets. Brezhnev and Kosygin were willing to talk, but not necessarily about Vietnam. Their influence in Southeast Asia increased each day the war dragged on. Unlike their late mentor, Stalin—whom Khrushchev once sarcastically described as thinking that "foreign policy meant keeping the antiaircraft units around Moscow on a twenty-four-hour alert"[2] —the new Russian leaders pushed their influence into such areas as the Middle East and South and Southeast Asia. Their military power was burgeoning. After the 1956 Suez crisis the Russians began a rapid buildup of conventional land and sea forces until by the late 1960s their fleet, once a subject of ridicule, began to appear regularly in the Mediterranean, Indian Ocean, and even Caribbean areas.[3] As for their nuclear forces, after the 1962 missile crisis a Soviet official warned an American that "you'll never be able to do that to us again," and by 1968 the Russians approached strategic parity with the once-supreme American arsenal.

The Vietnam morass and the new balance of power therefore also required that Johnson deal with the Soviets. Brezhnev and Kosygin were receptive, for although the Russians' military power had sharply increased, their economic growth rate had dropped drastically in the 1960s. They needed economic relief. The Russians, moreover, have always delighted in bargaining as an equal with the United States, a nation they simultaneously fear, dislike, and try desperately to copy. The time was ripe for a deal.

But the first deal on Vietnam was never struck. Rusk urged the Soviets to call off their North Vietnam ally because, he warned, if Russia was "backing the north to seize the south, then we [the United States and U.S.S.R.] were in trouble," for the United States would never allow it. The Soviets responded by threatening to give Ho new surface-to-surface missiles and flatly announcing that "since North Vietnam is a part of the Communist community, the Soviet Union must support and will assist it increasingly as the U.S.

---

[2]Nikita Khrushchev, *Khrushchev Remembers,* translated and edited by Strobe Talbott (Boston, 1970), pp. 392–393.

[3]J.M. McConnell and Bradford Dismukes, "Soviet Diplomacy of Force in the Third World," *Problems of Communism,* XXVIII (January–February 1979): 15–20.

escalates its efforts."[4] Americans acted, moreover, as if the Soviets could actually force Ho to give up his struggle; that was a highly doubtful assumption.

Johnson was luckier in his attempts to slow the nuclear race. At a summit meeting with Kosygin at Glassboro, New Jersey, an impassioned warning by Defense Secretary McNamara about the suicidal arms race both nations were running helped lead to an announcement that a nonproliferation agreement had been reached. Each power pledged to halt the distribution of nuclear weapons. Ominously, China, France, and India, among others, refused to sign the pact.

Détente seemed to be moving ahead. And then it suffered two stunning setbacks. The first began in February 1968, when the North Vietnamese launched a surprise Tet (New Year) offensive that was not beaten back until they threatened even the grounds of the U.S. embassy in Saigon. Until that occurred, Johnson could claim that the war was going better and Americans could see "light at the end of the tunnel." Now the light seemed to be an onrushing freight train engineered by Ho. The North Vietnamese suffered heavy casualties during Tet, but they broke the illusion held by many Americans that the war could soon be won.[5]

Johnson consulted a group of elder statesmen, and the most famous "wise man," Dean Acheson, bluntly told the President that his advisers had led him "down the garden path." A month later Senator Eugene McCarthy, Democrat of Minnesota, ran on an antiwar platform and nearly defeated Johnson in the New Hampshire presidential primary. On March 31, 1968, the President dramatically announced on national television that he was pulling out of the presidential race so that he could devote all his energies to making peace with Ho. Johnson turned down a military request for 206,000 more men to be added to the nearly 500,000 already in Vietnam, but he secretly allowed the numbers to rise to 549,000. He planned to

[4]Memorandum of conversation between Rusk and Ambassador Anatoly F. Dobrynin, May 26, 1966, White House Confidential File (Asia), Box 7, LBJ Library; Thomas L. Hughes to Rusk, May 4, 1967, National Security Files, Country File, U.S.S.R., LBJ Library; Memorandum of Conversation between Zbigniew Brzezinski and Yuri Zhukov, April 13, 1967, National Security File, Country File, U.S.S.R., LBJ Library.
[5]McPherson Oral History, Tape #9, p. 10, LBJ Library.

turn up the military pressure as he moved toward negotiations; if Ho refused to talk, then, as the State Department secretly informed U.S. ambassadors in Asia, it would "give us a clear field for whatever actions" were "required."[6]

At home the United States seemed to be approaching a crisis. Between 1964 and 1968 ghetto riots claimed dozens of lives in Los Angeles, Detroit, and Newark. After Martin Luther King, Jr., was murdered in April 1968, even Washington erupted in flames, as army troops moved into the city and used the Capitol Hill lawn as a bivouac area. Three major political assassinations (John Kennedy in 1963, King and Robert Kennedy in 1968) shocked the world. After Senator Robert Kennedy's murder, the American Advertising Council ran a campaign for gun control that told viewers to "Write your senator—while you still have a senator."[7] When the Democratic National Convention met in Chicago during the summer of 1968, massive antiwar riots broke out. Six thousand troops were flown into the city, and Johnson could not attend his own party's meeting because of the danger. Amidst the chaos, Vice President Hubert Humphrey became the party's nominee. Maine's Senator Edmund Muskie (who fought against a proposed peace resolution at the convention) accepted the vice presidential nomination.

When Republicans met in Miami, three blacks died in a ghetto riot, but the media paid scant attention. Instead the nation watched Richard Nixon arise from the political grave. His 1962 defeat in the California gubernatorial race, one liberal columnist wrote at the time, had supposedly sent Nixon "to that small place in history which belongs to national disasters which did not happen." But Nixon refused to go. By 1968 he had become the most important Republican spokesman on foreign policy. With surprising ease he beat back the challenge of New York Governor Nelson Rockefeller (whose foreign-policy speeches were largely drafted by Harvard Professor Henry Kissinger) and won the Republican nomination. Maryland's governor, Spiro Agnew, who admitted his name was not "a household word," became Nixon's running mate. While Nixon

---

[6]*The Pentagon Papers,* as published by *The New York Times* (New York, 1971), pp. 622–623.
[7]Charles Kaiser, *1968 in America* (New York, 1988), p. xi.

pictured himself as a statesman during the campaign, Agnew took a lower road and accused Humphrey of being soft on communism. These rapid political changes slowed the détente process, but it was knocked off its tracks in August 1968 by a second event: the Soviet invasion of Czechoslovakia. Since the mid-1960s the Soviets and their satellites had moved in different directions. Some Eastern Europeans experimented with more liberal economic policies. The Czechs, during their so-called Prague Spring, even discussed a loosening of their one-party political system. The United States encouraged the process by opening trade channels.

The Brezhnev-Kosygin regime, meanwhile, stolidly and unimaginatively tightened its control within Russia. Stalin's image was refurbished, and a centralized planning system (tagged "Stalinism with computers") emphasized military and heavy industry investment. Intellectuals—especially Jews—were arrested, deported, or declared "insane" when they questioned governmental policies. Brezhnev, who survived an assassination attempt and became the most powerful figure in the politburo, warned that dissent could not be tolerated because "we are living in conditions of an unabating ideological war."[8] Détente meant a lessening of military and political tensions with the West, but ideological coexistence could not be allowed.

The Prague Spring strained this rigid ideological line to the limit. Soviet officials were divided over how to respond. Some Foreign Ministry officials, who did not want to endanger détente, were among those opposing intervention. But they were overbalanced not only by party leaders who feared ideological and economic contamination from Czech liberalism but also by some military and secret police officials who believed the Czech policies might infect the entire bloc. Brezhnev at first equivocated. As the prointervention faction gained strength and threatened his own power, however, he joined it and ordered Soviet troops to smash the Czech regime.[9]

He did so at the moment Johnson prepared to meet the Soviet leaders at a summit conference. The President quickly canceled the meetings. Brezhnev's willingness to sacrifice détente indicated the

[8]Wolfgang Leonhard, "The Domestic Politics of the New Soviet Foreign Policy," *Foreign Affairs*, LII (October 1973): 59–74; John Dornberg, *Brezhnev, The Masks of Power* (New York, 1974), chapters XV, XVI.
[9]Jiri Valenta, "The Bureaucratic Politics Paradigm and the Soviet Invasion of Czechoslovakia," *Political Science Quarterly*, XCIV (Spring 1979): 55–76.

extent of his fear of disorder and liberalization in the bloc, as well as his keen sense of how to survive cutthroat Moscow politics. He capped the performance by issuing a "Brezhnev Doctrine" that justified Soviet intervention on the ground that a socialist nation had the right to save another from "world imperialism" and thus preserve the "indivisible" socialist system. Johnson did little in response, not only because of the military realities but perhaps also because the Brezhnev Doctrine for Eastern Europe was not unlike the Johnson Doctrine of 1965 for Latin America. Neither superpower would tolerate new ideological challenges in its own sphere.

As détente stalled, Nixon stumbled toward the White House. His 15-percentage-point lead in the polls during September dwindled to less than 1 percent in the November election. Nixon was the first newly elected President in the century who failed to give his party control over either house of Congress. Throughout the campaign he refused to take a clear stand on the war and said only that he had a mysterious "plan" to end it honorably. Privately he told aides, "I've come to the conclusion that there's no way to win the war. But we can't say that, of course." He preferred not to discuss concrete issues at all. ("You still have to put out a folder saying what you're for and against . . . ," he complained privately. "Women particularly like it. They don't have the slightest idea what it means."[10])

As usual, the election results were not a mandate on foreign policy. Despite the antiwar protests on the campuses, the prowar, racist, third-party ticket of Alabama Governor George Wallace received more support from voters under the age of thirty than it did from the population as a whole. (Throughout 1965–1973, the war was most firmly opposed by older, not younger, Americans; by blacks who were doing a disproportionate share of the fighting and dying, rather than whites; by females rather than males; and by lower-class rather than middle-class Americans.[11] As for the winner, Americans

---

[10]Richard J. Whalen, *Catch the Falling Flag* (Boston, 1972), pp. 137, 154.
[11]William L. Lunch and Peter W. Sperlich, "American Public Opinion and the War in Vietnam," *Western Political Quarterly*, XXXII (March 1979): 21–44; Richard M. Scammon and Ben J. Wattenberg, *The Real Majority* (New York, 1970), pp. 38–49, 92–93. Walter LaFeber, *The Deadly Bet; LBJ, Vietnam, and the 1968 Election* (Lanham, Md., 2005), especially chapters 6 (on Nixon) and 9 and "Conclusion," has further sources on foreign policy issues in this pivotal election.

knew he stood for "law and order in the streets," but few knew his plans for Vietnam or détente.

Nixon, however, understood what had to be done, and he thought he knew how to do it. His plans became clearer when, surprisingly, he picked Henry Kissinger as national security adviser. Both men believed that unless policy changes were made, the 1970s would be shaped by developments that were sapping U.S. dominance in world affairs: the Soviet military buildup; the rising economic and political power of Western Europe and Japan, which threatened American markets and worked against Washington's policies in such areas as Vietnam and the Middle East; and the apparently bottomless pit of the Vietnam War.

Above all, as Kissinger liked to say, the greatest problem was how to "manage" the Soviets as they emerged as a global, instead of merely a regional, superpower. Containment was as important in the 1970s as in the late 1940s, but because of the new Russian strength, and the relative decline of American power, containment now had to be constructed differently than when Acheson or John Kennedy made policy. Nixon and Kissinger believed that the Soviets could be contained not by a massive arms race or increased U.S. global commitments (which neither the American public nor the economy could tolerate) but by making a deal: the Soviets could have sorely needed economic help if they cooperated in Vietnam and agreed to arms limitation.

In the new containment, Nixon also planned to open talks with China. For twenty years Mao had been the Asian villain to Americans, but since the late 1950s he had also become Russia's main concern. The realization that one communist power could be played against the other allowed Nixon to believe that an "era of confrontation" was ending and an era of negotiations beginning.[12] Once the relationship between the Americans and the Soviets was properly adjusted, Nixon and Kissinger concluded, the other problems—Vietnam and the Allies—could be resolved.

All this required time, order, and support at home. With various devices, both legal and criminal, Nixon gained time over the next

---

[12]For the new containment policies see especially Stanley Hoffman, "The Case of Dr. Kissinger," *The New York Review of Books,* December 6, 1979, p. 24; and I. F. Stone, "The Flowering of Henry Kissinger," *The New York Review of Books,* November 2, 1972, p. 26.

five years. He also created—temporarily—order and support at home. For above all else, he and Kissinger sought order and control, both at home and abroad, with an awesome single-mindedness. When once asked whether he favored a revolution with justice or an orderly state that was unjust, Kissinger quoted Goethe: "If I had to choose between justice and disorder, on the one hand, and injustice and order on the other, I would always choose the latter."[13] At home this passion for order led Nixon to use criminal means in attempts to squelch antiwar protesters. Kissinger could not understand why college students refused to fight in Vietnam: "Conscientious objection is destructive of a society. The imperatives of the individual are always in conflict with the organization of society. Conscientious objection must be reserved for only the greatest moral issues, and Vietnam is not of this magnitude."[14] At that point more than a million people had been killed or wounded in Vietnam.

This determination to have order also led Nixon and Kissinger to control policymaking with an iron grip. Perhaps the President could have both directed policy and restored the public's shattered faith in government by structuring political coalitions in which his policies were debated and obtained support. In 1969 political analyst Richard Scammon thought such an opportunity existed. As ethnic and trade union voters became middle class and moved away from their loyalty to the Democrats, Scammon remarked, "There is a possibility that by following a centrist line—. . . moderately conservative—[Nixon] could build up a great new party of the center."[15] Other observers proclaimed the advent of an "emerging Republican majority." Nixon might well have been able to resolve one of the great problems in U.S. foreign policy: how to use American political institutions to gain support from Congress and the public, instead of resorting to an imperial Presidency that acted without public debate and too often created support through lying.

Nixon never tried to create such political institutions. Instead, he planned all of his policies, including foreign relations, around one supreme objective: his reelection in 1972. As early as mid-1970 one top aide said that Nixon was preparing to "gear everything to '72." He did

---

[13]John G. Stoessinger, *Henry Kissinger: The Anguish of Power* (New York, 1976), pp. 12–14.
[14]Quoted by Clayton Fritchey in *The New York Review of Books,* September 25, 1969, p. 26.
[15]William Whitworth, "Profiles," *The New Yorker,* September 20, 1969, p. 52.

so while believing mighty forces were intent on destroying him. Highly insecure personally, the President was "the most complete loner I've ever known," said Senator Barry Goldwater. "The man operates all by himself." Carrying the scars of too many political wars, the President preferred to circumvent a Democratic Congress. Nixon did not even trust the CIA: "It was staffed by Ivy League liberals" who had always opposed him politically. As for the State Department, he believed that "no Secretary of State is really important. The President makes foreign policy."[16]

Nixon consequently named William Rogers, a New York lawyer and an old political ally in the Eisenhower years, as secretary of state to keep the department quiet while the White House made foreign policy. Kissinger ensured State's impotence by keeping information from Rogers (and other cabinet members), encouraging Nixon to believe that Rogers was not a loyal team player, courting reporters and congressmen who heard only Kissinger's side of a story, and conducting critical negotiations without informing the State Department. Nixon understood all this. He remarked privately, "Henry thinks Bill [Rogers] isn't very deep and Bill thinks that Henry is power crazy. In a sense they are both right."[17] But then Kissinger often did not consult even his own staff. "Henry's chief lieutenants are like mushrooms," went the joke. "They're kept in the dark, get a lot of manure piled on them, and then get canned."[18]

Without assured congressional support, the trust of the State Department, or sometimes the confidence of Kissinger's staff, the President and his closest adviser had only each other. They considered this to be enough. When Kissinger was the ghost writer for Nixon's "State of the World" report in 1970, an observer thought it resembled a message from the Vatican, except that "the Pope quotes Scripture" while "Mr. Nixon quotes himself 31 times directly."[19] Kissinger meanwhile controlled the foreign policymaking process

---

[16]Jussi Hanhimäki, *The Flawed Architect; Henry Kissinger and American Foreign Policy* (New York, 2004), pp. 23–28; *Washington Post,* May 18, 1994, p. A6; Ibid., October 17, 1976, p. C4; Henry Kissinger, *White House Years* (Boston, 1979), p. 11; Whalen, *Catch the Falling Flag,* pp. 253–256.

[17]Leslie Gelb, "The Kissinger Legacy," *The New York Times Magazine,* October 31, 1976, pp. 78–79; William Shawcross, *Sideshow* (New York, 1979), p. 103.

[18]Bruce Mazlish, *Kissinger* (New York, 1976), p. 231.

[19]Hans Morgenthau, "Mr. Nixon's Foreign Policy," *New Republic,* March 21, 1970, p. 23.

from the White House and, as the President's personal assistant, did not have to be accountable to Congress. Rogers, although knowing little about any policies, had to testify before committees in what one senator frostily called "a rather empty exercise." Instead of building political institutions, Nixon was systematically undermining them.

Despite his firm control over policy, Nixon enjoyed few early successes. He was reluctant to deal with the Soviets in the aftermath of the Czech invasion. The President knew, moreover, that he could not negotiate with Brezhnev from a position of strength until the Vietnam War and the uproar at home were brought under control. He announced in 1969 that U.S. troops would leave Vietnam in a phased withdrawal. This policy promised to wind down the war and end the antiwar protests. Nixon, however, had no intention of following what he bitterly called "isolationism." The United States must retain its global obligations, but it had to uphold them with different policies than it had during the post-1945 years when it enjoyed overwhelming power.

In Vietnam Nixon pursued a policy of "Vietnamization," that is, building the South Vietnam Army so that it could replace the departing Americans. This approach actually resembled the failed policies of 1954–1965. As one U.S. official said, it simply meant "changing the color of the corpses." Elsewhere the President followed a "Nixon Doctrine." It provided that as the United States pulled back from some of its military commitments, Americans would help certain friends take up the burden of containment. In Asia the friend was to be Japan; in the Middle East, the shah of Iran; and in Africa, Zaire (the former Belgian Congo) and the white-dominated, but black majority, countries of Angola (a Portuguese colony) and South Africa.

Nixon and Kissinger sought containment-on-the-cheap. They even planned to make a profit. Overseas sales of American military arms amounted to $1 to $2 billion in the mid-1960s, but they surged toward $10 billion by the time Nixon left office. Iran alone bought $2.5 billion of arms in 1972–1973. Nixon ordered that the shah could have the newest equipment, and all that His Majesty desired. The shah responded by ordering planes and other equipment "as if he was going through the Sears, Roebuck catalog," in the words of one official. In all, the Nixon Doctrine encouraged a dangerous military buildup in the Middle East and southern Africa; nearly bankrupted some nations and encouraged others, such as Iran, to raise oil prices rapidly to pay for the inflation-priced U.S. equipment; made these nations more likely to use force rather than negotiations to settle disputes; helped create dangerously strained relations with Japan when it refused to become an Asian policeman; and caused Nixon to become a political bedfellow of the shah and white supremacist regimes in Africa. The doctrine's redeeming virtue was that it gave the President a rationale for pulling back from Vietnam.

But even that virtue was not immediately apparent. As Nixon pulled out troops, he secretly escalated the bombing, particularly in Cambodia, which—although a neutral state—was used by the communists to funnel troops into South Vietnam. The bombings turned out to be a catastrophe. *The New York Times* published a story on the "secret" bombing in March 1969. Nixon secretly set up a "Plumbers" unit to stop such leaks "whatever the cost." This decision led to a series of criminal acts by the Plumbers that climaxed in their attempt to break into Democratic party headquarters at Washington's Watergate Hotel in 1972.

The bombings meanwhile only drove the communist forces deeper into Cambodia and destabilized the country. In early 1970 the government of Prince Norodom Sihanouk, who miraculously had kept Cambodia out of the path of the war's destruction, was overthrown by a right-wing military officer, Lon Nol. The United States apparently was not directly involved in the overthrow, although the CIA certainly knew of Lon Nol's plans. But Nixon rushed to take advantage of the coup. On April 30, 1970, he announced in an emotional speech that the United States must not act as a "pitiful, helpless giant." American troops were therefore invading Cambodia to clean out the communist camps. In the name of winding down the war, Nixon expanded it.[20]

Both Cambodia and American campuses were soon devastated. Lon Nol proved to be an incompetent partner who watched helplessly as his own ally's planes, as well as communist armies, savaged his nation. By 1971 the communists controlled half the country. (By 1975 they had all of it. More than 250,000 persons had been killed, massive starvation began, and one of the world's most beautiful countries lay

---

[20]The standard account is Shawcross, *Sideshow,* especially pp. 102–121; Kissinger and Nixon quotes to be found in *The New York Times,* December 9, 1973, p. 76; *Washington Post,* February 19, 1974, pp. 1, 12–14.

in ruins.) In the United States students at nearly 500 colleges went on strike to protest Nixon's invasion. At Kent State in Ohio and Jackson State in Mississippi, protesters were shot and killed. Thousands of antiwar Americans descended on Washington. Troops were stationed in the White House basement to repel a possible assault.

Nixon, Kissinger feared, was on the edge of a nervous breakdown. The President would shout, "Let's go blow the hell out of them," as embarrassed aides looked on in stunned silence. But public opinion polls showed that 50 percent of the Americans surveyed supported Nixon's invasion, although 52 percent did not believe his claim that the action would shorten the war. Congress loyally acted as a lightning rod, absorbing the antiwar protesters' fury but doing nothing until they left Washington and Nixon pulled the troops out of Cambodia. Congress followed the President, not the people in the street.[21]

The Cambodian tragedy was one in a series of disasters that marked 1970–1971 as a nadir in recent U.S. history. In 1971 Nixon authorized South Vietnamese troops to clean out communist sanctuaries in Laos. "Vietnamization" turned out to be a failure as American television showed South Vietnamese troops clinging desperately to departing American helicopters in order to escape communist gunfire. Nixon responded by stepping up the bombing of Laotian supply trails until Laos became the most heavily bombed country in history. By mid-1971 the communists were in a stronger position in Laos than at any time since 1962.

Vietnamization failed despite an enlarged war and the dropping of bombs at the rate of one ton for every minute Nixon was in office. Between 1969 and 1972, 20,000 Americans died in Vietnam, and over 300,000 Asians were killed while the war was supposedly winding down. In frustration one popular Saigon newspaper ran a daily contest in which readers submitted stories of such atrocities as rape or homicide committed by Americans. North Vietnam, that "raggedy-ass little fourth rate country," as Lyndon Johnson once called it, was tormenting the United States. Americans tired of supporting a South Vietnamese regime that was corrupt and incapable. Many were also sickened by the slaughter dramatized during early 1971 when a military court-martial

---

[21]Shawcross, *Sideshow*, pp. 152–153; Marie Gottschalk, "Bring Us Together: Congressional Reaction to the Invasion of Cambodia, 1970," unpublished paper, 1980, pp. 54, 72–74 (in author's possession).

convicted Lieutenant William Calley, Jr., of killing at least twenty-one South Vietnamese civilians in 1968 at the village of Mylai. It was a war in which the enemy and the civilians were indistinguishable. Meanwhile, American soldiers, unwilling to be, perhaps, the last to die in such a war, used drugs in increasing amounts to avoid combat. Over 9000 were arrested for drug use in Vietnam during 1970, and their superior officers estimated that 65,000 U.S. troops had used drugs.[22]

And as Vietnamization failed, so too did the American economy. The gross national product (the sum of all services and goods produced) rose over the $1-trillion mark, but an apparently uncontrollable inflation accounted for half the increase in 1971. The nation's industries, moreover, were becoming so uncompetitive that, for the first time since 1894, Americans imported more merchandise than they sold abroad. As the economy weakened, so did the dollar—the foundation that had undergirded the remarkable post-1945 global trading system. In 1971 nearly $50 billion was held abroad, and more and more dollars were being printed in Washington, then pumped overseas, to pay for the nation's military expenditures and private investments. Overseas, dollars increased in number as they decreased in value. Europeans, watching helplessly as these dollars bought up their industries, grew angry and began to raise walls against the dollars and U.S. trade. "The rest of the world," French President Georges Pompidou announced, "cannot be expected to regulate its life by a clock [the dollar] that is always slow." The efficient Japanese economy sent streams of cars, steel, and electronic goods into American ports, and in 1969 had replaced the United States as Asia's leading trade partner. Nixon became furious when Japan refused to stop certain exports voluntarily until the United States regained its economic health. The Nixon Doctrine, indeed the entire alliance system, was in deep trouble.[23]

In 1970 Nixon promised he would never impose wage and price controls to stop the inflation that was making American goods more expensive than Japanese or West European products. But in mid-summer

---

[22]Robert Shaplen, "Letter from Indo-China," *The New Yorker,* May 16, 1970, p. 125. On drug use, see *The New York Times,* January 11, 1971, p. 13.

[23]Lewis Beman, "How to Tell Where the U.S. Is Competitive," *Fortune,* LXXXVI (July 1972): 54–55; Seymour Melman, *The Permanent War Economy* (New York, 1974), pp. 112–114; *Washington Post,* May 27, 1971, p. A27.

1971 the balance of payments suddenly showed the possibility of an unbelievable $48-billion annual deficit. The dollar, and hence the Western trading structure, threatened to collapse. In a Kansas City speech, the President discussed the "five great economic superpowers" (the United States, Russia, Japan, Western Europe, China), four of whom "challenge us on every front." "Because economic power will be the key to other kinds of power . . . in the last third of this century," he continued, and since domestic and foreign policies were so interlinked, Americans had to discipline themselves and their economy before they groveled in the "decadence" that had toppled Ancient Greece and Rome.[24]

In August 1971 the President suddenly imposed a wage-price freeze to curb inflation. He also placed a surtax on foreign imports to stop the inflow of goods from Europe and Japan, a nation that—as a State Department briefing paper reportedly warned Nixon—must be viewed as a potential enemy. He and his secretary of the treasury, tough-talking Texan John Connally, put tremendous pressure on the Allies to revalue their currency while the United States devalued the dollar, thus making the dollar cheaper and more competitive in world markets. Finally, Nixon announced that the dollar would no longer be redeemable in gold. The French bitterly called this program "a Marshall Plan in reverse." Unfortunately it was not enough. In 1973 the economy and the dollar again began slipping after Nixon removed the wage-price freeze. The dollar again had to be devalued. As in 1807, 1893, and 1914, a failing economy forced the United States to change its foreign policies. The era of the all-powerful dollar temporarily ended, and with it went much of Washington's political power (and the good times abroad once cheaply enjoyed by American tourists).

A year before the 1972 presidential campaign began, Nixon was plagued with troubles. Then occurred a remarkable turnabout. The wage-price controls temporarily halted inflation. The economic picture brightened. The military draft was cut back and student anti-war protests disappeared as if by magic. But most dramatically, in

---

[24]*Public Papers of the Presidents . . . Richard Nixon . . . 1971* (Washington, 1972), pp. 806–812. This remarkable 1971 speech can be read in the chapter XI documents at the www.mhhe.com/lafeber website for this book.

July 1971 Nixon seized the diplomatic initiative with the startling announcement that he would be the first President to visit China.

Since 1969 the two nations had sent subtle signals encouraging a new relationship. Nixon and Mao hoped to use the other to check Soviet power. China's fear of the Russians jumped in 1969–1970, when nearly 1 million Soviet soldiers encamped in a broad area along the Sino-Soviet border. Clashes occurred with Chinese troops. Nixon also hoped to develop a China market so that American businessmen could find economic relief—and enter China before the Japanese locked up the most promising trading ventures. Mao was receptive.

The President's major problem might have occurred at home, where for thirty years an anticommunist China Lobby had worked, often with Nixon's help, to make Americans believe that Chiang Kai-shek's government on Taiwan, not Mao's, was the real China. Opposition did develop, particularly from the American Federation of Labor (which feared both China's communism and cheap labor), but the President enjoyed wide maneuvering room. A mid-1960s poll showed that about 25 percent of Americans were unaware that China even had a communist government.[25] Nixon, moreover, could not be charged with being soft on communism. He had made his political reputation with such remarks as calling the 1952 Democratic presidential nominee, Adlai Stevenson, "the appeaser . . . who got a Ph.D. from Dean Acheson's College of Cowardly Communist Containment." In 1971 Nixon was not threatened by politicians resembling the earlier Nixon.

His 1972 journey to China was a huge success. A friendship treaty was signed, trade opened up, the Soviets were made fearful of a possible Sino-American alliance, and within months the Chinese entered the United Nations while Chiang's delegation was expelled. (Chiang died in 1975, the last survivor of World War II's Big Four. U.S. officials increasingly considered Taiwan as an internal Chinese problem, and by 1980 China and Taiwan were cooperating on some economic policies.)

The China trip and the slowing of the Vietnam War placed Nixon in a position to travel to Moscow. He became the first President

[25]Barry B. Hughes, *The Domestic Context of American Foreign Policy* (San Francisco, 1978), p. 57. For the Chinese views of Nixon and U.S. policies, see Chen Jian, *Mao's China and the Cold War* (Chapel Hill, 2001), pp. 245–276.

to visit the Soviet capital. Before his scheduled trip was due to begin in mid-1972, however, the North Vietnamese launched surprise attacks that threatened to overturn the South Vietnam government. Nixon, already called the "biggest bomber in world history," responded with intensified air attacks. In a dramatic departure called "Operation Linebacker" (the President was a devoted football fan), American planes bombed and sowed mines in the vital North Vietnam ports. Lyndon Johnson had refused to mine the ports; he feared that Russian and Chinese ships would be hit and the war escalated to a big-power crisis.

Nixon, however, believed he had to show American toughness as American troops left Vietnam and the presidential campaign approached. "Look," Kissinger later explained, "it wasn't just a matter of this summit—his political ass was on the line." Kissinger talked tough with the Soviets. Although the war had destroyed Johnson, he informed them, "Nixon will not permit three Presidents in a row to leave office under abnormal circumstances."[26] Then he tossed in the bait. Politics and economics had always been closely related in Russian-American relations, Kissinger noted. If the Soviets wanted economic help, they must cooperate politically. This "linkage" was a key to the summit's success.

Nixon calculated correctly. Regardless of events in Vietnam, the Soviets wanted to negotiate. Their readiness had been announced at the Twenty-fourth Party Congress in 1971 when Brezhnev presented a "peace program" that shaped Soviet views, especially détente policy, through the 1970s. Brezhnev's 1971 program rested on four legs, but only one of these was strong.

The strong leg was the military. In his era Khrushchev had tried to expand Soviet influence primarily through Russian economic successes and taking advantage of revolutionary situations in newly emerging areas. The plodding Brezhnev held no such illusions; the economy was in trouble and most revolutionaries mistrusted heavy-handed Russians. Brezhnev, a civilian who loved to parade around in a military uniform, placed his faith in a large buildup of military power. He increased defense budgets at a steady 3 percent annually

---

[26]William Safire, *Before the Fall* (Garden City, N.Y., 1975), pp. 434–436, 452. For this crisis and Nixon-Kissinger disagreements over handling the Soviets, note Hanhimäki, *The Flawed Architect*, pp. 202–218.

(while the United States cut its post-Vietnam conventional military) and drafted every able male at the age of seventeen for two-year active service and reserve service until the age of fifty. A force of 5 million stood at the ready. Brezhnev planned to wield it as a diplomatic weapon to obtain political dividends, especially in negotiations with the United States. Americans now had to deal with him as an equal superpower. For his part, he badly needed their help to prop up the other three, weaker, legs on which the success of Soviet policies depended.

One was Eastern Europe. Despite the tragedy of the Czech "spring" in 1968, the satellite states, particularly Rumania and Poland, slowly evolved national policies that did not fit the Russian model. The area was in a greater state of flux, and being more drawn to the booming Western economies, than Moscow desired. In a crisis the bloc could be controlled by force; that was one reason for the Russian military buildup. But the army could not resolve the deeper problems. In 1971 Brezhnev therefore made a deal in which the West Germans finally recognized the Eastern European boundaries imposed by the Red Army in 1945; in return, he settled the long-festering Berlin question by guaranteeing Western access to the city. He now wanted Nixon to agree to that arrangement and thereby further stabilize this weak leg.

The second wobbly leg was Sino-Soviet relations. This problem was indeed so dangerous that it provided a central reason for the military's expansion. The fear of "encirclement" that had haunted earlier Soviet leaders now reappeared, especially after the Chinese opened talks with Japan and the United States. Brezhnev designed his détente policy in part to ensure that it would remain in Nixon's interest to deal with him instead of moving closer to Mao.

The leg that needed the most support was the Soviet economy. The five-year plan of 1966–1970 had failed to reach its objectives. Despite, or because of, decades of coercion, Russian farm workers were only one-sixth as productive as the Americans. This economic decline, moreover, was part of a larger breakdown that was producing not only famous dissenters such as physicist Andrei Sakharov, and author Aleksandr Solzhenitsyn, but also a growing underground anti-Soviet literature among educated classes. Brezhnev wanted U.S. technology and agricultural products. A mammoth wheat deal, part of a trade agreement worked out at the summit, nearly doubled Soviet-American trade. Unfortunately, the Russian negotiators outfoxed their capitalist counterparts, bought the wheat at bargain-basement prices, and helped create a grain shortage in the United States that worsened inflation. To Nixon and Kissinger, however, the "Great Grain Robbery" was a cheap price to pay. They opened new markets for American farmers while reaping diplomatic benefits.

Given, therefore, the economic problems of both nations, and their need to bring spreading military commitments under some control, Brezhnev as well as Nixon designed a détente policy. The two leaders signed a Strategic Arms Limitation Treaty (SALT I). The pact was supposed to end the race to develop a defensive antiballistic missile system (ABMs) that promised to be enormously expensive and highly ineffective. SALT I also froze the number of nuclear missiles so that the Soviets had no more than 1600 and the United States 1054. Those numbers, however, deceived. For the United States had developed a new monster weapon, the MIRV (multiple independently targeted reentry vehicle) that contained—on one missile—multiple warheads capable of hitting widely separated areas. With the MIRV, Americans enjoyed a 2 to 1 lead in deliverable warheads—another good reason why Brezhnev wanted an agreement that limited the number of missiles. One American submarine possessing MIRVs was capable of inflicting 160 Hiroshima blasts. The United States had over thirty such subs. "What are 3,000 MIRVs among friends?" Kissinger later joked to the Russians. But he soon admitted that not controlling MIRVs was one of his greatest errors—especially when the Soviets moved rapidly to deploy their first MIRV in the mid-1970s. SALT I therefore only placed a few limits on, but did not stop, the arms race.[27]

The summit was a triumph for both Brezhnev and Nixon. The Russian leader successfully carried out his détente program announced at the Party Congress. In Vietnam the communist offensive ground to a halt; the Chinese and Russians did little publicly to retaliate for the U.S. bombing and mining. Nixon's policy had worked.

During the 1972 campaign the Democratic nominee, Senator George McGovern of South Dakota, had little chance. His left-of-center politics alienated many Americans and left him open to the unfair Republican charge that McGovern was the champion of "amnesty [for men who had illegally avoided the draft], acid, and abortion." He presented

---

[27]William Burr, ed., *The Kissinger Transcripts; The Top Secret Talks with Beijing and Moscow* (New York, 1998), p. 217; chapter 5 and the Introduction are superb in giving the context of these talks.

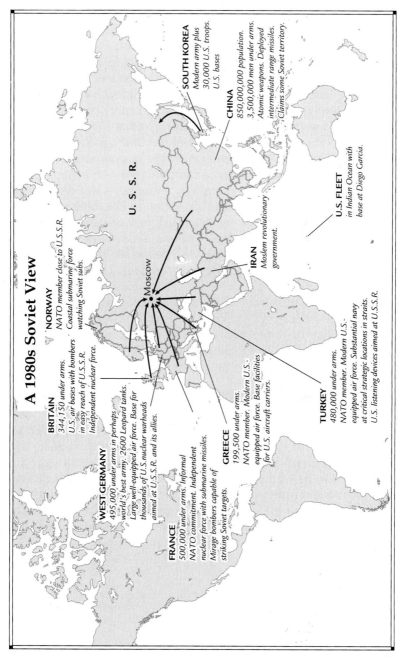

A 1980s Soviet View

NORWAY
NATO member close to U.S.S.R. Coastal submarine force watching Soviet subs.

SOUTH KOREA
Modern army plus 30,000 U.S. troops. U.S. bases

CHINA
850,000,000 population. 3,500,000 men under arms. Atomic weapons. Deployed intermediate range missiles. Claims some Soviet territory.

BRITAIN
344,150 under arms. U.S. air bases with bombers in easy reach of U.S.S.R. Independent nuclear force.

WEST GERMANY
495,000 under arms in perhaps world's best army. 2600 Leopard tanks. Large well-equipped air force. Base for thousands of U.S. nuclear warheads aimed at U.S.S.R. and its allies.

FRANCE
500,000 under arms. Informal NATO commitment. Independent nuclear force with submarine missiles. Mirage bombers capable of striking Soviet targets.

GREECE
199,500 under arms. NATO member. Modern U.S.-equipped air force. Base facilities for U.S. aircraft carriers.

IRAN
Moslem revolutionary government.

TURKEY
480,000 under arms. NATO member. Modern U.S.-equipped air force. Substantial navy at critical strategic locations in straits. U.S. listening devices aimed at U.S.S.R.

U.S. FLEET
in Indian Ocean with base at Diego Garcia.

U. S. S. R.

Moscow

285

a carefully prepared foreign-policy program that urged an immediate withdrawal from Vietnam and a sharply reduced defense budget. But McGovern could not stir up a debate. As Nixon isolated himself in the White House, Republicans accused McGovern of following an "isolationist" foreign policy. When the Democratic nominee pointed to the Watergate break-in and claimed that the Nixon administration was the most politically corrupt regime in American history, the voters were unmoved. Playwright Arthur Miller observed that Americans tend to respond to calls for righteousness when they think it is also a call for lunch. The President won reelection by the second largest electoral vote margin in twentieth-century American history.

Kissinger enhanced the margin by announcing just days before the voting that "peace is at hand" in Vietnam. The timing had been carefully calculated. Nearly two years before, Kissinger had wanted the war to drag on, and then have "a pullout right at the fall of '72 so that if any bad results follow, they will be too late to affect the election" (as he was quoted by a top Nixon aide). The celebration in October 1972, however, proved premature. Kissinger had reached agreement with the communists, but he could not convince South Vietnam's President Nguyen Van Thieu to accept terms that allowed large numbers of communist troops to remain in South Vietnam. The deal collapsed. (The Kissinger pre-election announcement can be read in the chapter XI documents at the www.mhhe.com/lafeber website.)

After the election Nixon began the most devastating bombing attack yet launched on North Vietnam. Parts of the country were carpet bombed. Congress merely watched, nearly 60 percent of Americans polled supported the "Christmas bombing," and no one stopped the President. As one journalist recorded Nixon's private conversation, he "did not care if the whole world thought he was crazy for resuming the bombing," because "the Russians and Chinese might think they were dealing with a madman and so better force North Vietnam into a settlement before the world was consumed in a larger war."[28]

---

[28]*Washington Post,* May 18, 1994, p. A6; Thomas L. Hughes, "Foreign Policy: Men or Measures?" *Atlantic Monthly,* CCXXXIV (October 1974): 56; Seymour Hersh, *The Price of Power* (New York, 1983), chapter 39.

Tragically, however, it was South Vietnam that held up a peace treaty. Nixon finally won Thieu's agreement with huge amounts of supplies and a secret letter assuring Thieu that if he would "go with us, you have my assurance of continued assistance in the post-settlement period and that we will respond with full force should the settlement be violated by North Vietnam."[29] So assured, Thieu agreed. The treaty was signed in February 1973. American prisoners of war returned home. The United States had retreated from its longest conflict.

Nixon stood unchallenged at the peak of his power. Free of the Vietnam quicksands, and with the Russians apparently better "managed" by détente and linkage, the President turned to other foreign-policy problems. Kissinger grandly announced that 1973 was to be the "year of Europe"—that is, the United States would now deal with the increasingly bitter Western European allies to whom it had paid little attention while making momentous deals with China and Russia. Critics, who believed the Western alliance was beyond repair, remarked that Kissinger's phrase resembled the words of a long unfaithful husband who grandly announced this was to be the "year of the wife."

In the Western Hemisphere, Nixon dealt with the Chilean government of Salvador Allende, a devoted nationalist and sometime Marxist who, since his election to the presidency in 1970, had moved to break Chile free from its dependence on large landowners and American multinational corporations (see map, p. 216). Allende nationalized nearly $1 billion of American investment. At least one multinational, International Telephone and Telegraph (ITT), urged Nixon to get tough. The President did so, but not primarily because of ITT. He and Kissinger viewed Allende's Chile as a potential Soviet satellite, a second Cuba, whose infection could spread through the hemisphere and demonstrate that Nixon was too weak to secure his own backyard. With the help of the CIA and close ties between the U.S. and Chilean military, Kissinger systematically undermined the Chilean government. Allende lost control of his nation's economy. "We set the limits of diversity," Kissinger bragged, and in September 1973 Allende died as Chile's army seized power. The military established a brutally repressive regime. When the U.S. ambassador protested

[29]*The New York Times,* May 1, 1975, p. 16.

the torture methods, Kissinger ordered him "to cut out the political science lectures."[30]

Nixon also moved to control, or intimidate, key parts of the federal government. He gained some of this power through illegal wiretapping, breaking and entering, and misusing campaign funds. Kissinger passed all this off with the joking comment, "The illegal we do immediately; the unconstitutional takes a little longer." But a fundamental question remained: could American foreign policy be drastically changed, and a public consensus built to support new policies, without an imperial Presidency that distorted the truth and manipulated the people? The Nixon presidency did not provide a happy answer to that fundamental question. Even Kissinger was apparently not safe. The daring diplomat, winner of a Nobel Peace Prize for his role in ending the Vietnam War, the man with the German accent and gravylike voice—"Superkraut" as he was happy to be called—was popular and powerful. Rumors spread in Washington that a jealous President was prepared to fire Kissinger. Then in mid-1973 Congress began hearings on the Watergate break-in of 1972. Nixon's political career and American foreign policy suddenly changed. A new era was about to begin.

The most dramatic event in this new era occurred when Richard Nixon became the first American President to resign from office. That historic turn had begun when he tried to cover up the break-in by his Plumbers unit at the Watergate hotel complex in 1972. But his foreign policy also hastened his exit. In 1973 Congress and public opinion so turned against his brutal bombing of Southeast Asia that the House and Senate finally ordered an end to the attacks. Resembling other Presidents, before and after, who found themselves becoming mired in political trouble at home, Nixon tried to save himself with foreign-policy spectaculars. Instead of firing the popular Kissinger as he had planned, the President named him secretary of state in the autumn of 1973. The two men then flew to Moscow for another highly publicized summit meeting. But it was too late; the House prepared impeachment articles. Nixon grew increasingly

---

[30]Roger Morris, *Uncertain Greatness* (New York, 1977), p. 241; Hanhimäki, *The Flawed Architect*, pp. 100–105; *The New York Times,* March 6, 1975, p. C37. Nearly thirty years later, the CIA still would not be honest with the American people and release its documents on Chile, even after President Clinton asked it to be more forthcoming. See *Washington Post,* August 11, 2000, p. A23.

unstable and, since his finger remained on the nuclear button, increasingly dangerous. In August 1974 his aides and several Republican leaders convinced him to resign.

The imperial Presidency had collapsed. In its place arose what some worried observers called an imperial Congress. The legislature had repealed the Gulf of Tonkin Resolution by 1971, and by 1974 it had passed measures preventing American troops from reentering Vietnam. The House and Senate similarly outlawed military involvement in parts of Africa without their explicit consent. In 1974–1975 the Senate struck at the heart of Kissinger's détente policy by attaching conditions to the Soviet-American trade treaty that made the pact unacceptable to the Soviets. (These conditions included the widely discussed Jackson-Vanik amendment demanding that Moscow allow more Jewish dissidents to leave Russia if they wished, and—more important from the Soviet view—a Stevenson amendment sharply limiting the amount of money the stumbling Russian economy could borrow from the United States.) "The same sons of bitches who drove us out of Vietnam," Kissinger raged privately, were now trying "to destroy détente and assert that it is our moral obligation to change internal Soviet policies."[31]

Apart from these riflelike limitations, Congress used a political shotgun in its attack on presidential powers. The War Powers Act of 1973 required that "in every possible instance" the President must consult with Congress before sending troops into hostilities; when the President commits the forces, he must send a full explanation to Congress within two days and he must withdraw the forces within sixty days unless Congress expressly gives him permission to keep them in battle. The act, in reality, gives the President the power to wage war for sixty days without congressional approval, a power that the founders wisely did not give the chief executive in 1787. Congress hoped, however, that the law could prevent future Vietnams.

Kissinger was furious. He warned that perhaps Congress could deal with domestic issues but, because of its supersensitivity to public opinion and interest groups, it was not designed to carry out long-term foreign policies. When his plans for Vietnam and Africa failed during 1975–1976, the secretary of state blamed Congress and the

[31]Burr, ed., *The Kissinger Transcripts,* p. 221; Hanhimäki, *The Flawed Architect,* pp. 340–344, 378–385.

effects of Watergate. He apparently did not understand that his and Nixon's foreign policies in Southeast Asia between 1969 and 1973 had caused congressional anger and the Watergate scandal. He also failed to understand that by the mid-1970s congressional authority grew precisely because of legislative power in domestic affairs, for domestic and foreign policies were becoming one.

That intimate relationship became dramatically clear in 1973–1974 when Americans found themselves short of gasoline at home because of a war in the Middle East. An Arab-Israeli clash was, as usual, the eye of the conflict. After the Suez crisis of 1956, the Soviets had rebuilt the Egyptian Army while the United States helped make Israel the most powerful military force in the area. In 1967 the Egyptians threatened the Gulf of Aqaba, the entranceway to Israel's key southern port of Elat. On June 5 Israel suddenly struck. In a six-day war the Israelis drove the Egyptians back across the Suez, the Jordanian Army across the Jordan River, and the Syrians away from the strategic Golan Heights. Israel seized the old city of Jerusalem.

The United States and Russia did not intervene, but within months each helped refill its ally's arsenal. To block the Soviets and leftist Arab nationalists, Lyndon Johnson placed U.S. policy on the so-called Three Pillars: Israeli power (including nuclear weapons), Iran's oil and military, and Saudi Arabia's massive oil reserves and strategic bases.[32] As the Soviets established port bases in Egypt, a confrontation loomed between the two superpowers. The new Egyptian president, Anwar el-Sadat, proposed negotiations, but only after Israel withdrew from lands taken in 1967. The Israelis, having paid a heavy toll for their withdrawal from the Sinai peninsula following the 1956 war, refused Sadat's conditions and rejected U.S. pressure to withdraw from all occupied territories. In October 1973, on Yom Kippur, the holiest day in the Jewish calendar, the Egyptians and Syrians launched a sudden attack that drove the Israeli Army back in a surprising show of strength. The shocked Israelis counterattacked, surrounded the Egyptian Army in the Sinai, and threatened to open all of Egypt to invasion. Sadat appealed to Brezhnev. The Soviet leader declared he would act alone to enforce a cease-fire if the Americans would not cooperate with his policy.

---

[32]Douglas Little, "Choosing Sides." In Robert A. Divine, ed., *The Johnson Years, Volume 3* (Lawrence, Kan., 1994), pp. 151, 169, 183; and Little's important overview, *American Orientalism: The United States and the Middle East Since 1945* (Chapel Hill, 2002), especially pp. 98–103, 106–108, 240–245.

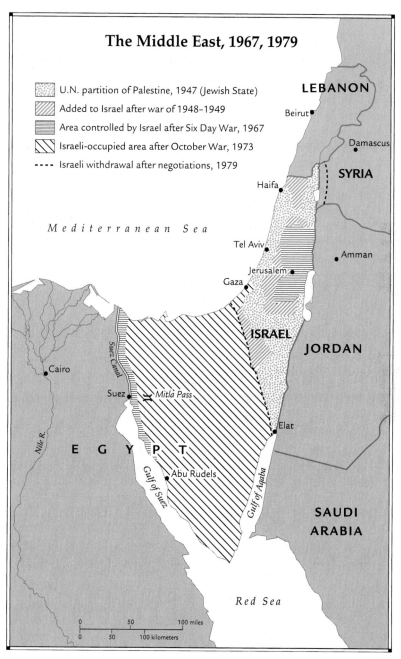

The Middle East, 1967, 1979

U.N. partition of Palestine, 1947 (Jewish State)
Added to Israel after war of 1948–1949
Area controlled by Israel after Six Day War, 1967
Israeli-occupied area after October War, 1973
---- Israeli withdrawal after negotiations, 1979

LEBANON

Beirut

Damascus

SYRIA

Haifa

Mediterranean Sea

Tel Aviv

Amman

Jerusalem

Gaza

ISRAEL

JORDAN

Suez Canal

Cairo

Suez

Mitla Pass

Elat

Nile R.

E G Y P T

Gulf of Suez

Abu Rudels

Gulf of Aqaba

SAUDI ARABIA

Red Sea

0   50   100 miles
0   50   100 kilometers

Kissinger and Nixon warned Brezhnev to stay out of the area. They emphasized their warning by putting the nation's nuclear strike forces on alert. But the Americans also offered the olive branch. They demanded an Israeli cease-fire and the supplying of the surrounded Egyptian forces. Kissinger held back military supplies needed by Israel until it agreed with his demands. With fresh support from Sadat, who had expelled all Soviet military advisers from Egypt when they seemed to threaten his own power, Kissinger began a series of trips among Middle East capitals to work out a settlement. Despite two years of exhaustive efforts (his plane was tabbed the "Yo-Yo express" because it went up and down so often), the secretary of state worked out a cease-fire but could not find the key to a full settlement.

His diplomacy focused on two objectives. He wanted peace, but without Soviet participation. Resembling the nineteenth-century British statesmen he had studied as a historian, and also resembling Acheson and Dulles, Kissinger determined not to allow Russian strength to shape affairs in the Middle East. To block the Soviets, he and Nixon willingly took the chance of destroying détente. They also sought to end the danger that the Arabs might try to blackmail the West. This nearly occurred in 1973. When the United States supplied weapons to Israel, using NATO bases in Western Europe as transport points, the Arab-dominated Organization of Petroleum Exporting countries (OPEC) imposed an oil embargo that threatened to strangle the Western and Japanese economies.

OPEC consisted of thirteen nations, including seven Arab countries, Iran, and Venezuela. It had been formed in 1960 to protest attempts of major oil companies (mostly owned by Americans, British, and Dutch) to reduce oil prices and payments to the producers. By the early 1970s the great international companies suddenly faced a unified bloc of producers. OPEC forced the companies to increase payments drastically, quadrupled the price of oil by 1974 to nearly $12 for a forty-two-gallon barrel, threatened nationalization of the companies' properties, and firmly believed that "we are the Masters."[33] Amidst a sudden energy crisis New York Stock Exchange shares lost $97 billion in value in six weeks.

---

[33]Gurney Breckenfeld, "How the Arabs Changed the Oil Business," *Fortune*, LXXXV (August 1971): 113–117. A superb analysis on the important books that have analyzed the background is Douglas Little, "America and the Middle East Since 1945," *Diplomatic History*, XVIII (Fall 1994): 513–540.

Japan and Western Europe began switching from pro-Israeli to pro-Arab policies. This change further strained the alliance system, for the United States, which imported only 12 percent of its oil from the Middle East (compared with 80 percent for the Europeans and over 90 percent for Japan), remained staunchly committed to Israel. As the allies changed, Kissinger bitterly commented that they were "craven" and "contemptible."[34] Not only had hopes for the "year of Europe" turned to ashes, but he believed that Western Europe had become his "deepest problem."

The energy crisis would have occurred in the not distant future regardless of the Arab-Israeli conflict. Between 1945 and the late 1970s, the West and Japan consumed more oil and minerals than had been used in all previous recorded history. With 6 percent of the world's population, the United States used nearly 40 percent of that wealth.[35] The West could not continue to increase its energy use 5 percent annually, pay low oil prices, yet sell inflation-priced goods to the petroleum producers. This was emphasized by the shah of Iran, whose nation was the world's second-largest oil exporter, and who was Washington's most trusted Middle East friend, according to the Nixon Doctrine. "Of course [the price of oil] is going to rise," the shah declared. "Certainly! and how! . . . You [Westerners] increased the price of wheat you sell us by 300%, and the same for sugar and cement. . . . You buy our crude oil and sell it back to us, refined as petrochemicals, at a hundred times the price you've paid to us. . . . It's only fair that, from now on, you should pay more for oil. Let's say . . . 10 times more."[36]

The Nixon-Kissinger policies were falling apart. They had focused on Russia and China, but the challenge now came from the Third World. American power was under attack even in Latin America, an area Kissinger had supposedly once dismissed as "a dagger pointed at the heart of—Antarctica." The Republicans devised no alternative to the moribund Alliance for Progress. As terrorism and guerrilla activities increased, Nixon's only major response was to propose doubling

---

[34]*Washington Post,* March 17, 1974, p. A12.

[35]Richard Barnet, "The World's Resources," *The New Yorker,* April 23, 1980, pp. 45, 47; *Washington Post,* February 24, 1975, p. 1.

[36]*The New York Times,* December 12, 1973, p. 64; for the background, see James E. Akins, "The Oil Crisis: This Time the Wolf Is Here," *Foreign Affairs,* LI (April 1973): 470–472.

the amount of military arms sold by the United States and, in Chile, helping a military regime overthrow Allende. But Allende's death did not remove a more fundamental danger. In 1975 the secretary of state worried that Latin Americans and other newly emerging nations were "tending to form a rigid bloc of their own," a development "particularly inappropriate for the Western Hemisphere."[37] Again his big-power diplomacy was being undercut by the Third World. Again the energy crisis made the challenge possible, for the Latin American bloc was organized and financed in large part by Venezuela and its oil revenues, which quintupled between 1970 and 1975.

A similar danger appeared to the north. Canada's television, periodicals, banks, and half its industry were dominated by the United States. Canadians began playing their own balance-of-power game. Trade was opened with China. Pierre Trudeau became the first Canadian prime minister to travel in the Soviet Union, signing consultation and trade pacts with the Russians. In 1973 strict controls were placed on foreign investments for the first time. During the 1970s, exports of Canadian oil and natural gas, upon which large sectors of the United States depended, rose dramatically in price, and then exports were cut back so that Canadians themselves could be assured of long-term cheap energy. While Kissinger searched for new relations with the four major blocs, hemispheric unity, which Americans tended to take for granted, fragmented.

U.S. officials could at least be relieved that the Soviets were not directly involved in the new developments in the Western Hemisphere and Middle East. In Africa, however, the superpowers nearly confronted each other in a crisis that typified the new Cold War that was developing in the 1970s. Their confrontation in little-known Angola became a major reason for the death of détente.[38]

Since 1970 Kissinger had assumed that the Portuguese, through their colony in Angola, would help maintain stability in Africa. In 1974, however, the forty-year dictatorship in Portugal fell. Angola became independent and black revolutionaries vied for power. The Americans and Chinese supplied one faction, while the Soviets backed the group

---

[37]*Department of State Bulletin*, March 24, 1975, pp. 365–366.
[38]Anatoly Dobrynin, *In Confidence* (New York, 1995), pp. 360–361. The best background and the key document are in Mohamed A. El-Khawas and Barry Cohen, eds., *NSSM 39: The Kissinger Study of Southern Africa* (Westport, Conn., 1976).

that ultimately won, the Popular Movement for the Liberation of Angola (MPLA). Most startling of all, the Russians flew thousands of Cuban troops into Angola in a move that Kissinger condemned as a dangerous escalation of the Cold War. He asked Congress for massive aid to stop the Soviet aggression "by proxy," but the legislators flatly refused to become immersed in a possible Vietnam-like conflict in Africa. The MPLA triumphed and then, in a wondrous turn of events, used the Cuban troops to protect the American-owned Gulf Oil refinery (one of the nation's most important facilities) and turned increasingly to Washington for technological help. Both superpowers were learning how little Africans cared about a Cold War that obsessed some Americans and Russians.

But Kissinger did not draw that lesson. He believed that Americans, especially the young who "have been traumatized by Vietnam as we were in Munich," lacked the will to stand up to the Soviets.[39] His concern increased in 1974–1975, when the United States sank into its worst economic recession since the 1930s. He had hoped to use the nation's economic power to "manage" the Russians. Congress, however, had already undercut the 1972 trade treaty, and in 1975, when Kissinger tried to use an embargo on wheat exports as a weapon to make the Soviets behave in Africa, a tremendous uproar of protest from American farm communities forced him to back down. He reflected on how difficult it was for policymakers to protect what they considered to be the national interest when that job had to be done in an individualistic, private enterprise economy.[40]

American foreign policy improved little after Gerald Ford replaced Nixon in August 1974. Appointed by Nixon to be Vice President when Spiro Agnew had to resign for taking illegal payments, Ford had been a leader in the House of Representatives. But he had little personal prestige and no background in foreign policy. When he made a serious error while discussing the Middle East, one journalist passed it off: "What the hell, it was just Jerry talking about things he doesn't understand."[41]

---

[39]Speech of April 17, 1975, *Department of State Bulletin,* May 5, 1975, p. 560.
[40]Remarks in Los Angeles, February 2, 1976, *Department of State Bulletin,* March 1, 1976, p. 272.
[41]Richard Reeves, *A Ford, Not a Lincoln* (New York, 1975), pp. 174, 181, 200.

Ford became President as Vietnam was finally falling to the communists. The agreement that Kissinger negotiated in 1973 with North and South Vietnam had never worked. President Thieu attacked the communists emplaced in South Vietnam, and in late 1973 they began retaliating. Thieu's forces lost more soldiers in 1974 than during the height of the fighting in 1967. At the same time a recession-ridden United States cut its aid from $1 billion to $700 million. In early 1975 the South Vietnamese Army began to disintegrate. Thieu called for President Ford to provide the American "full force" promised by Nixon in 1973. But Nixon's 1973 promise was of no effect. He and Kissinger had not made the letter public (indeed, Kissinger publicly denied in 1973 that any secret understandings existed), and Congress had prohibited the reintroduction of American forces in Vietnam. In April 1975 South Vietnam fell into communist hands. The thirty-year war was over.[42]

Kissinger asked Americans to put Vietnam behind them—a strange request coming from a former history professor, for the lessons to be learned were many and critical. The war demonstrated that militarily the United States could not single-handedly defeat nationalist movements in Asia. Nor did it have the economic and social resources to fight such a long, inconclusive war. The United States bore great responsibility for the downfall of South Vietnam. The involvement was not comparable to American responsibility for China in the 1940s. The governments of both South Vietnam and Cambodia were Washington's creations. Both depended upon the United States for their existence. Both collapsed after the American forces withdrew. In this sense the "domino theory" actually worked. (Dominoes is a game in which the pieces are laid flat. It requires special effort outside the rules to set them upright so that they can collapse.) American Presidents, supported in the early years by Congress and public opinion, made a mighty effort to prop up the dominoes in Southeast Asia, and the collapse duly occurred. (To read a revealing Kissinger speech about these crises in April 1975, see the chapter XI documents at the www.mhhe.com/lafeber website.)

---

[42]The best brief account is T. Christopher Jesperson, "The Bitter End and the Lost Chance in Congress," *Diplomatic History*, 24 (Spring 2000): 265–293.

Ford and Kissinger tried to reinvigorate foreign policy (and Ford's hopes for the 1976 presidential race) with two dramatic acts. They traveled to Russia in late 1974 and agreed with Brezhnev on the outline for a SALT II agreement that set new limits on nuclear arms. (Unknown to the Americans, Brezhnev suffered several seizures during and after the meeting. He began a rapid physical and mental decline but remained in power until his death in 1982.) The other drama occurred in May 1975, when Cambodian naval units seized an American cargo ship, the *Mayaguez*. The seizure occurred just after Vietnam fell, OPEC had quadrupled oil prices without an American response, and Kissinger had been unable to stop the MPLA in Angola. In this political climate Ford, with Kissinger's strong encouragement, did what Presidents have often done in similar situations: he used military force to show that he was decisive and not afraid to get tough with communists. Unknown to Ford, however, the Cambodian government had released the thirty-eight crew members. Forty American troops were killed in a needless raid on Cambodian territory. Public opinion polls nevertheless showed strong support for the President's use of military force.

The *Mayaguez* "rescue" and the arms agreement were not enough to save Ford's campaign in 1976. Indeed, Kissinger's foreign policy became an issue. Right-wing Republicans attacked détente until Ford outlawed using the word in his speeches. Kissinger remarked that détente "is a word I would like to forget." Soviet activities in Angola and Cuba, and continued repression of dissidents within Russia, had soured many Americans on the idea that détente could work. Meanwhile, the Democratic nominee, Jimmy Carter, hit Kissinger from the liberal side for being too secretive, supporting dictatorial regimes, and arguing for higher defense budgets. In a style that was typical of Carter, he then blasted the administration from the other direction for giving away too much in the arms talks, and especially for Kissinger's work in the 1975 Helsinki agreements.

At Helsinki, Finland, thirty-five countries, including the Western nations, accepted the East European boundaries as permanent; in return, the Soviets pledged to follow a more liberal human rights policy. Moscow leaders tried to modify their pledge ("We are masters in our own house," they declared), but, as a top Russian diplomat later noted, the Helsinki accords "gradually became a manifesto of the dissident and liberal movement, a development totally beyond the imagination of the Soviet leadership." The stage was being set for the U.S.S.R.'s later collapse. Carter, however, condemned the deal for not doing enough to protect individual liberties inside Russia.[43]

The Democratic candidate took different sides on so many issues that unfriendly critics charged that Carter's image could never be carved in stone on Mount Rushmore because there was room on the monument for only one more face. But his tactics worked. He lost most of his 30 percent lead over Ford in polls taken during late summer but held on to win by a slim popular vote.

Carter's triumph brought a remarkable decade to an end. Between 1966 and 1976 Americans had roller-coasted from heights to depths: from near victory in Vietnam to embarrassing defeat; from a powerhouse economy to a thieflike inflation; from an imperial Presidency to the presidential humiliation of Watergate and the War Powers Act; from cheap gasoline to bending before demands of OPEC oil producers; from condemning Chinese communism to cooperation with it; and, most important, from détente to increasing confrontation with the Soviet Union.

For at the heart of détente lay a fatal contradiction. On the one hand, the Soviet leaders saw détente as a form of class struggle in which they would employ the newly emerging nations to triumph over capitalism, while, of course, carefully avoiding a direct military confrontation with the United States. On the other hand, U.S. leaders viewed détente as a way to contain and manage Soviet power. "All in all," observed Soviet ambassador to the United States Anatoly Dobrynin, "one could say that détente was to a certain extent buried in the fields of Soviet-American rivalry in the Third World."[44]

The U.S. ability to contain and manage that Soviet power in the post-1960s world had dwindled. Frustrated Americans concluded that trying to manage Moscow through détente had been a great failure. The question now became whether a better approach could be devised. Jimmy Carter, Ronald Reagan, and—above all—Mikhail Gorbachev were to give quite different answers to that fundamental question.

---

[43]Henry A. Plotkin, "Issues in the 1976 Campaign." In Gerald Pomper, ed., *The Election of 1976* (New York, 1977), pp. 50–52; Dobrynin, *In Confidence,* p. 346.
[44]Dobrynin, *In Confidence,* pp. 468, 473.

A scene that generations of Americans and Russians thought they would never see: The U.S. President (Ronald Reagan) and the Soviet leader (Mikhail Gorbachev) laugh in front of a hospitable fire as they move toward ending the Cold War.
(Courtesy Ronald Reagan Library)

CHAPTER 12

From Cold War to Old War: Reagan and Gorbachev (1977–1989)

In the late 1970s Americans finally emerged from the crises of Vietnam and Watergate only to confront a new Cold War. It was a conflict more ominous and unmanageable than anything they had faced before. In the old Cold War Americans had enjoyed superior nuclear force, an unchallenged economy, strong alliances, and a trusted imperial President to direct this incredible power against the Soviets. In the new Cold War, however, Russian forces achieved nuclear equality. Each side could only plan to destroy the other many times; the plan involved a military doctrine known as Mutual Assured Destruction, or MAD. The U.S. economy reigned supreme, but in such key areas as steel, automobiles, and textiles it no longer could compete in world markets. It certainly could no longer bear the crushing burden of satisfying Americans' demands to be both the globe's greatest consumers and its unquestioned policeman. Meanwhile the alliance system further cracked and the imperial Presidency was overthrown. In the early 1980s Ronald Reagan moved to solve these challenges by trying to roll back time and recapture the happier days of the earlier Cold War. But first, Jimmy Carter, after much indecision and confusion, launched policies that prepared the way for Reagan.

As a little-known Georgia governor in 1973, Carter appeared on the television show "What's My Line?" and none of the panelists could guess who he was or what he did. Three years later Carter turned this anonymity into a political weapon. He ran against the Washington scandals by emphasizing that he had never been associated with the capital's politics. Carter instead stressed his decency and religious beliefs, and promised, "I'll never tell you a lie." He was also a tough politician. The two sides of his character, the realistic politico and the caring Christian, combined in his appraisal of Nixon: "I despise the bastard but I pray that he will find peace."[1]

The 1976 election produced no obvious foreign-policy mandate. Carter often refused to take clear positions. Working both sides of the political street, he evoked the name of a famous Southern conservative when he described himself as "a Populist in the tradition of Richard Russell." (One observer commented that that made as much sense as saying he was "a socialist in the tradition of Herbert Hoover."[2]) With such wordplay, Carter received strong support from independents as well as regular Democrats, who applauded his fight against the Washington "establishment." Independents could recall the words of Carter's top aide, Hamilton Jordan: "If, after the inauguration, you find a Cy Vance as Secretary of State and Zbigniew Brzezinski as head of National Security [Council], then I would say we failed. And I'd quit. . . . You're going to see new faces, new ideas." Vance and Brzezinski, deeply rooted in the "establishment," became secretary of state and national security adviser, respectively. Jordan did not resign.

Carter's foreign policy quickly became confused as Brzezinski and Vance clashed. Brzezinski saw the world more in bipolar terms and believed that the Soviets posed immediate global dangers. An immigrant and the son of a Polish diplomat, Brzezinski had taught at Columbia University, where he wrote many books on communist systems. A fellow White House official only half-joked that Brzezinski enjoyed being "the first Pole in 300 years in a position to really stick it to the Russians." He had condemned the détente policies of Kissinger, a person with whom he had competed professionally since the early 1950s. Brzezinski both urged the "independence" of such bloc states as Rumania and criticized the SALT deals, especially if the Russians did not then behave in Africa or the Middle East. He refused, moreover, to believe "that the use of nuclear weapons would be the end of the human race. . . . That's egocentric."[3] (His view had its counterpart in official Soviet military doctrine that Russia could survive a nuclear

---

[1]James Wooten, *Dasher* (New York, 1978), pp. 33–37.
[2]C. Vann Woodward, "The Best?" *The New York Review of Books,* April 3, 1980, pp. 10–11.
[3]Elizabeth Drew, "Brzezinski," *The New Yorker,* May 1, 1978, p. 126; *Washington Post,* February 18, 1979, p. C4; Ibid., February 5, 1977, p. A10.

exchange and, therefore, that blueprints for such an exchange be part of overall military planning.[4]) A close friend since 1972, Carter called Brzezinski "my teacher" in foreign policy. Brzezinski explained the closeness by referring to a passage in the novel *Sophie's Choice*, in which the author, William Styron, "describes a surprising affinity between Poland and the South, two peoples bred on a history that overcame defeat, on a code of chivalry and honor that proudly compensated for backwardness."[5]

Vance, on the other hand, agreed with the views of Marshall Shulman, his chief adviser on Soviet affairs and a former Columbia University professor who had been debating Brzezinski for a quarter century. Vance and Shulman believed that peace rested on negotiations and economic ties between the superpowers—not, as Brzezinski argued, by viewing any crisis anywhere in the world as a Soviet challenge. Unlike Brzezinski, Vance and Shulman saw SALT II as the central diplomatic issue and believed that no problem, even Russian aggressiveness in the Middle East, should be allowed to endanger arms talks. Shulman hoped to influence Soviet behavior through "soft linkage," that is, by saying quietly to Moscow officials that they had a greater chance of receiving badly needed American economic help if they respected human rights within their country and sought peace elsewhere. Shulman's hope rested on those Russians he called "within-the-system modernizers," that is, young and middle-aged technicians and professionals who would work with the West to improve Soviet society. He saw the modernizers as a check on the older, neo-Stalinist factions, but Shulman understood that time and not a few funerals were required first. Vance and Shulman would never be given that time. They did, however, predict rather accurately what indeed occurred a decade later in the Soviet Union.

If trouble developed in the newly emerging nations, Vance and Shulman, unlike Brzezinski, believed it could usually be handled as a problem of new nationalisms, not a superpower confrontation. Their view received strong support from Andrew Young, the U.S. ambassador to the United Nations. Young believed profitable political and

[4]Harriet Fast Scott and William F. Scott, *The Armed Forces of the U.S.S.R.* (Boulder, Colo., 1979), pp. 44–45, 52–62.
[5]Zbigniew Brzezinski, *Power and Principle: Memoirs of the National Security Adviser, 1977–1981* (New York, 1983), pp. 20–21.

economic cooperation would develop between the United States and the newly emerging peoples, if they could be kept clear of great power conflicts. He later proved his point with major diplomatic successes in Zimbabwe and Nigeria. Finally, Vance and Shulman differed from Brzezinski in believing that Eastern European changes had to occur slowly. They believed that any rapid development of independent policies could produce a rerun of the 1968 Czech tragedy.

Between these two views stood the final decision maker. President Carter clearly wanted to hear conflicting advice, but he had to choose between these complex alternatives without having any significant personal foreign-policy background. Between 1973 and 1976 he had been the token Southern politician on the Trilateral Commission, a private group of Americans, Western Europeans, and Japanese that Brzezinski and banker David Rockefeller organized to discuss the mushrooming problems of industrial nations. A number of Trilateralists (including Vance and Young) joined the Carter team, but the commission seldom agreed on common policy. One member dismissed his colleagues as mere "boosters," "a bunch of very sophisticated Rotarians."[6] Even Brzezinski, a founder, grew disillusioned. By 1975 he had concluded that resolving the industrial world's problems was less important (and obviously more difficult) than facing up to the Soviets.

Carter learned no useful framework for a consistent foreign policy from the Trilateralists, and he was unable to devise such a framework himself. A trained engineer, he studied problems case by case, "like an engineering student thinking you can cram for the exam and get an A," as one official remarked. He had little historical knowledge and hence little sense of how to construct a comprehensive strategy. Carter admitted in 1979 that he had read more history since entering the White House than in all the rest of his life.[7] Sometimes he simply split the difference. When Vance and Brzezinski sent him quite different policy memoranda for an address on Soviet policy, Carter solved the problem by stapling the two memos together as the basis for his speech.[8]

Such an approach had worked with American voters, but it quickly failed in the world of U.S. foreign policy. Carter, for example, declared that his commitment to human rights was "absolute."

[6]*Washington Post,* January 16, 1977, p. A4.
[7]Interview by Don Oberdorfer, *Washington Post,* February 18, 1979, p. C4.
[8]James Fallows, "Zbig Without Cy," *New Republic,* May 10, 1980, p. 19.

In 1977 he openly encouraged Russian dissidents, who demanded more political freedoms. The gesture infuriated Brezhnev. The dissidents suffered under new crackdowns. Because Carter was simultaneously trying to negotiate arms reductions with them, the Russians speculated that his human rights policy was a mere "bargaining chip" to trade. In reality, as Andrew Young admitted, the policy was never "thought out and planned," so it remained ineffective.[9]

Carter's tough line, which included sharply reducing aid, did cause military regimes such as those in Brazil, Chile, and Argentina to act more decently. The oppressive South Korean government was more important to U.S. security, however, so it received fewer public lectures and more arms. When Carter urged China to ease its dictatorial immigration rules in the interest of human rights, Vice Premier Teng Hsiao-p'ing (Deng Xiaoping) smilingly responded that he would be glad to do so and "send you 10 million immigrants right away." Carter dropped the issue.[10] Soviets soon noted that he said little about the thousands of political prisoners in China, even as he condemned holding such prisoners in Russia. The most glaring and costly inconsistency occurred in Iran. SAVAK, the shah's secret police, tortured and imprisoned upward of 50,000 Iranians. But on New Year's Eve 1977 Carter visited Iran, a vital link in U.S. defense plans. He toasted the shah for making Iran "an island of stability" and for deserving "the respect and the admiration and love which your people give you."[11] A year later a revolution drove the shah from power.

Not all the confusion was Carter's fault. At home he inherited a political structure that had historically depended on a strong party system. He had not helped by running against party leaders and the "establishment," but in any case the system was in an advanced stage of disintegration before he appeared on the national scene. Into the vacuum rushed hundreds of private groups, many representing a single interest (for example, doctors, used-car dealers, educators, pro- or antiabortion advocates), whose members lobbied hard in Washington. No national consensus could be shaped out of

[9]See especially Stephen F. Cohen's comments in Fred Warner Neal, ed., *Détente or Debacle* (New York, 1979); and Stephen F. Cohen, "Why Détente Can Work," *Inquiry,* December 19, 1977, p. 16; author's interview in Moscow, November 14, 1980.

[10]*Washington Post,* February 4, 1979, p. A10.

[11]*Public Papers of the Presidents . . . Jimmy Carter, 1977* (Washington, 1978), p. 2221.

these narrowly focused groups.[12] Special economic interests became ever more active as inflation skyrocketed to an annual rate of 13 percent in 1979–1980. In addition OPEC nations tripled oil prices to nearly $35 a barrel, draining the United States of $100 billion each year without any effective response by the President or a fragmented Congress. Severe economic recession set in. Allied leaders grew disenchanted with such disarray in the nation that supposedly led the noncommunist world.

Despite these problems and a lack of conceptual planning, Carter did score diplomatic victories. He did so most notably when he followed the Vance-Shulman-Young approach. In 1978 the Senate ratified the President's treaty that returned the Canal Zone to Panama over the next twenty-two years while protecting the American right to use and defend the waterway (see map, p. 217). Since 1947 the Panamanians had frequently rioted against the American zone that since 1903 had divided their country. When both sides lost lives in a 1964 outbreak, Lyndon Johnson began a new relationship that would recognize Panama's sovereignty in the Canal Zone. It took fourteen years to complete the arduous process. The decisive Senate figures were the leaders, Democrat Robert Byrd of West Virginia and Republican Howard Baker of Tennessee, who amended the two treaties submitted by Carter to make them acceptable to Republicans. Byrd and Baker took high political risks in fighting such opponents as Republican Senator S.I. Hayakawa of California, who proudly noted how the United States had seized the canal regions in 1903 and then claimed, "It's ours. We stole it fair and square." Carter and the Senate scored the most important advance in U.S.–Latin American relations since the 1930s.

The President also followed Vance's suggestions about Africa, despite Soviet intervention and Brzezinski's opposition. When warfare erupted on a border between Zaire (a U.S. associate) and Angola (where Soviet advisers and 19,000 Cuban troops remained), Brzezinski urged direct involvement to teach the communists a lesson. Andrew Young argued instead that the United States help find "African solutions for African problems." Carter accepted Young's advice and the warfare subsided. The Soviets, however, did not show similar restraint. They intervened in the strategic Horn of Africa to aid Somalia, Sudan, and

---

[12]Theodore Lowi, *The End of Liberalism* (New York, 1979), pp. 50–61; Joel Sibley, "The End of American Politics, 1980–1984?" unpublished paper, 1980, pp. 8–10.

Ethiopia. But Somalia and Sudan soon threw out the Russians. Brezhnev and 15,000 Cuban troops then found themselves immersed in a costly, uncontrolled military campaign on behalf of Ethiopia. Until Young finally resigned as UN ambassador in 1979, his "cool" approach was effective in navigating the whirlpools of African nationalism.

A final Carter triumph occurred in the Middle East during September 1978. A year earlier Egyptian President Sadat had taken the historic step of personally flying to Israel to begin a peace process with Prime Minister Menachem Begin. Carter then invited the two leaders to his private retreat at Camp David, Maryland, where for thirteen nerve-racking days he helped them hammer out an agreement that ended the thirty-year war between Israel and Egypt. The pact provided for Israeli withdrawal from the strategic Sinai peninsula, which had been Egypt's until the 1967 war. Carter helped ease Begin's acceptance with $3 billion of military aid. It was the Georgian's proudest moment as President.

From that point in September 1978, the Carter presidency began a long decline, pulled downward by internal divisions and uncontrollable external events. Soviet-American relations became the most important victim of the confusion. Even the Camp David agreement worsened relations, for in 1977 Carter and Brezhnev had issued a joint statement on the Middle East. The Russians made significant concessions in return for the President's assurance that they could help construct a Middle East peace. The Egyptians, Israelis, and powerful pro-Israeli lobbying groups in Washington loudly protested reintroducing Brezhnev's heavy hand in the region. Awestruck by the reaction, Carter simply "walked away from the statement," to use Brzezinski's words.[13] Infuriated Soviet leaders rushed more arms to friends in the region, including Syria, Israel's archenemy.

Perhaps the crucial turn in the superpowers' relationship, however, occurred in May 1978, when Brzezinski, over Vance's objections, flew to Beijing and began the process that climaxed in the opening of formal diplomatic relations with China on New Year's Day in 1979. Brzezinski hoped to play this "China card" to trump Soviet policies in Africa and the Middle East, and on arms control. In Beijing he enthusiastically engaged in a game with Chinese leaders to see who was the most anti-Soviet. Brzezinski was "so overwhelmed with the Chinese,"

---

[13]Brzezinski, *Power and Principle*, p. 175.

Carter recorded later, that "I told him he had been seduced." It is not seduction, however, when one travels halfway around the world to propose. Brzezinski's courtship produced immediate results. U.S. exports to China nearly doubled in 1979; thus Americans scored against their Japanese rivals in the game to see which would develop the long-fabled China market. Coca-Cola (a Georgia-based firm close to Carter) later opened its first plant in China, with guests drinking "Ke Kou Ke Le" (translated as "Tasty Happiness") as Beethoven's "Ode to Joy" played in the background.[14] (Pepsi-Cola, whose officials were close to Nixon, had earlier obtained a monopoly on the Soviet soft-drink market.)

Nowhere was the Carter-Brzezinski pro-China policy more evident—and Carter's willingness to sacrifice his supposed commitment to human rights more obvious—than in the bombed-out, war-devastated country of Cambodia. There, in the horrible aftermath of the Vietnam war, the Chinese-backed Pol Pot regime brutally gained power. Pol Pot became one of the worst murderers in human history, and given the recent examples of Hitler and Stalin that is a remarkable condemnation. Pol Pot killed millions in this small country, especially professionals and the educated in cities which he believed threatened his barbaric rule. But Carter, led by Brzezinski, supported Pol Pot, opposed a Soviet-backed invasion by Vietnam to overthrow the murderer, and then supported a Chinese attack on Vietnam that actually aimed to bring Pol Pot's Khmer Rouge party back to power in early 1979. Carter and Brzezinski put their support of China, and their growing opposition to the Soviets, ahead of Carter's much trumpeted human rights policy that would have opposed Pol Pot's genocide.[15]

Meanwhile, China played an "American card" effectively against the Russians. Chinese leaders shrewdly timed the announcement of formal diplomatic ties with the United States so that it poisoned a meeting between Vance and the Soviets to discuss SALT II. The SALT process consequently was fatally delayed. Then China's powerful leader, Vice Premier Teng Hsiao-p'ing, visited the United States in early 1979. After his return home he launched the invasion of Vietnam, Russia's ally in Southeast Asia. By his timing, Teng made it appear as if the United

---

[14]Jimmy Carter, *Keeping Faith: Memoirs of a President* (New York, 1982), p. 196; *The New York Times*, April 16, 1981, p. A3; U.S. Department of State, *Gist*, November 1979, p. 1.

[15]Kenton Clymer, "Jimmy Carter, Human Rights, and Cambodia," *Diplomatic History*, 27 (April 2003), pp. 245–278.

States had been a silent partner in the invasion. Moscow, at least, must have thought of it as collusion by Russia's two leading enemies. In retrospect mid-1978 marked a turn in Soviet-American relations. Brzezinski's influence rose as Vance's fell, especially on Chinese affairs.[16] The Soviets were locked out of the Camp David arrangements. Months later a high Chinese official captured the moment when, in splendid White House ceremonies, he praised Carter and Brzezinski, then turned to his translator and said publicly in Chinese, "I suppose I should also mention the Secretary of State; what's his name?"[17]

Brzezinski was amused by the incident; Brezhnev, no doubt, less so. Soviet leaders were still stunned by Nixon's resignation and the Senate's emasculation of the 1972 trade treaty that had undergirded détente. Carter was becoming a political bedfellow of the hated Chinese. Evictions from Egypt, Somalia, and Sudan were sharp setbacks for the Russians. Brezhnev nevertheless moved cautiously.[18] Scuttling détente could involve paying a high price, especially in the economic and military realms.

The Soviet economic system became less efficient as official communist ideology (that "fig-leaf" of the system, as Kennan had called it in 1947) withered. Few people still shared the old hope that other revolutions would follow the Soviet model. Nor did anyone believe that a utopian communist community was just over the horizon—unless, as a Russian joke put it, "you understand that an horizon is an imaginary line that recedes as you approach it." But the ideology could not be disavowed because, bankrupt or not, it legitimized the Communist party's monopoly on power. After 1971 Brezhnev had attempted to solve these complex problems with a dual approach: increasing trade with the West to invigorate the Soviet economy, but treating dissidents brutally (while allowing more Jews to emigrate to Israel) to ensure the party's control. By the late 1970s this policy had failed. The expected economic payoffs from détente never appeared.

---

[16]For differing views on the debate over this turn and Carter's human rights policies, note Burton I. Kaufman, *The Presidency of James Earl Carter, Jr.* (Lawrence, Kan., 1993); and David F. Schmitz and Vanessa Walker, "Jimmy Carter and the Foreign Policy of Human Rights," *Diplomatic History*, 28 (January 2004), pp. 113–143.

[17]Brzezinski, *Power and Principle*, p. 418.

[18]Paul Marantz, "Foreign Policy." In Alexander Dallin, ed., *The Twenty-Fifth Congress of the CPSU* (Stanford, Calif., 1977), pp. 89–90.

The Soviet Union actually outpaced the United States in coal, steel, and cement production, and was the world's largest oil producer, but a disproportionate share of the wealth went to nonproductive military budgets or disappeared in the floundering Cuban economy or devastated Vietnam system. With the world's largest area of tillable land, Russia could not feed its own population. Equally embarrassing to the communists, under 3 percent of the farm area was privately owned, but it contributed as much as 40 percent of the meat, dairy goods, and vegetables. As computers, electronic items, and other high-technology goods became crucial for highly industrialized societies, a system run by narrow party officials and fearful bureaucrats gave little encouragement to innovation. Projections indicated that Russia might even have to import oil by the mid-1980s unless it could buy massive American or Japanese technology to exploit new fields.

The outlook was bleak. Since 1945 the Soviets had tended to increase their gross national product not through innovation but simply by employing more laborers. In the 1970s, however, Soviet growth rates declined from 5 percent annually during Brezhnev's first years in power to 0.8 percent in 1979. A sharp drop in the birthrate during the 1950s and 1960s meant fewer laborers after 1975. Astonishingly, death rates and infant mortality rose rapidly in the 1970s, the first time such increases had been noted in such a developed nation. Poor medical care, alcoholism, bad safety facilities, and the tendency of Soviet women to have several abortions before finally bearing children relatively late in life contributed to these embarrassing figures. Population increases occurred almost wholly in Central Asia among Moslem groups. But historic hatreds divided these peoples from the Great Russians who ruled the land. Soviet leaders feared giving the ethnic peoples extensive economic power.[19] Brezhnev and his closest associates meanwhile grew older, slower, and more enfeebled. Brzezinski remarked to Carter that "under Lenin the Soviet Union was like a religious revival, under

---

[19]Michael Binyon, *Life in Russia* (New York, 1983), pp. 39–40, 58–65; John P. Hardt, "Highlight: Problems and Prospects," in U.S. Congress, Joint Economic Committee, 97th Cong., 2nd Sess., *Soviet Economy in the 1980s: Selected Papers* (Washington, 1983), pp. vii–xiii; Marshall I. Goldman, *U.S.S.R. in Crisis: The Failure of an Economic System* (New York, 1983), especially pp. 100–102.

Stalin like a prison, under Khrushchev like a circus, and under Brezhnev like the U.S. Post Office."[20]

In foreign affairs the Russians began to shiver from their old Stalinist fear of "capitalist encirclement"—only now it was communist as well as capitalist. Parts of the long Chinese-Russian border continued to be armed camps. A possible American-Chinese-Japanese partnership loomed on the Soviets' eastern flank. In Eastern Europe, economic crises and the energy crunch made the satellite states restless. Yugoslavia became unpredictable as Tito (who had cooperated with, as well as fought, the Soviets) became less active and then died in 1980.[21]

The most startling crisis loomed on Russia's own southern border. The shah of Iran's dynasty suddenly collapsed. Iran had been enduring terrible strains: half the population was younger than sixteen; the urban population was expected to quadruple to 20 million in just twenty-five years; an oil-dependent economy produced few jobs for an expanding population; 70,000 Iranians educated each year abroad (35,000 alone in the United States) returned with liberal, often anti-shah ideas; and—of special importance—modernization threatened the country's ancient religious ties, especially the Moslem leaders (the mullahs), who were becoming implacable foes of the shah. The shah meanwhile squandered the nation's wealth by importing more arms from the United States in the 1974–1978 era than Iran had bought in its entire history. He used SAVAK, his secret police that had close ties to the CIA, to silence enemies. By 1978 he was nevertheless losing control to the religious leaders and political fanatics (moderate leaders were dead or in prison), and suffering from cancer.[22]

American, and probably Soviet, officials understood few of these developments. At the "King of Kings" demand, U.S. intelligence had virtually no contacts with opposition parties. As the revolution gathered force, Brzezinski and Vance split over a response. Brzezinski urged

---

[20]Carter, *Keeping Faith,* p. 223.

[21]Paul Marantz, "Probing Moscow's Outlook," *Problems of Communism,* XXVIII (March–April 1979): 49–50; Ernest Kux, "Growing Tensions in Eastern Europe," *Problems of Communism,* XXIX (March–April 1980): 21–37.

[22]Abul Kasim Mansur [a pen name for a former U.S. Department of State official], "Why the U.S. Ignored a Quarter-Century of Warning," *Armed Forces Journal International,* January 1979, pp. 27–33. This document can be read in the chapter XII documents at the www.mhhe.com/lafeber website.

helping the shah establish a military regime to drown the revolt in bloodshed or, if that failed, mobilizing U.S. parachute troops for actual intervention. Vance urged Carter to contact the revolutionary leaders, distance himself from the shah, and assume that any military move could lead to the disintegration of the weakened Iranian Army. Carter again could not make a clear choice. On February 20, 1979, the leading religious figure, Ayatollah Ruholla Khomeini, led forces that drove the shah from power.[23]

U.S. foreign policy had suffered a major defeat. The Soviets publicly applauded this setback, but they could not take too much pleasure because Khomeini led a violently anticommunist Moslem group whose fanaticism could easily spread to the large and expanding Moslem population in Russia. As these revolutionary fires burned in the autumn of 1979, David Rockefeller, Henry Kissinger, and Brzezinski, all with close ties to the shah, convinced Carter to allow the fatally ill monarch into an American hospital.[24] Enraged mobs invaded the U.S. embassy in Tehran and seized sixty-nine hostages. Khomeini released sixteen women and African-Americans but would not free the remaining fifty-three, who, with their defiant captors, began to dominate television screens as the American presidential campaign got under way.

Carter's foreign policies began to unravel ever more rapidly. At a summit conference in Vienna during mid-1979, Carter and Brezhnev finally agreed on a SALT II pact that limited the number of nuclear arms launchers on each side to 2400 (with no more than 1320 to have MIRVs, the multiple warhead rockets). Each side retained its high card. For the United States the card was its small cruise missile, which could fly too low for Soviet detection; for the Russians it was their 300 huge land-based missiles. As Carter sent the treaty to the Senate, however, a group called the Committee on the Present Danger attacked the treaty. Established in 1976, the committee was headed by Paul Nitze and Eugene Rostow, both with long Washington experience, and both driven by the fear that Americans were losing their will to oppose communism. The seventy-two-year-old Nitze resurrected his old rhetoric from NSC-68 of thirty years before and lobbied the Senate incessantly until he and other opponents finally stalled the treaty.

[23]Brzezinski, *Power and Principle*, pp. 355, 388–393.
[24]Carter, *Keeping Faith*, pp. 452–453.

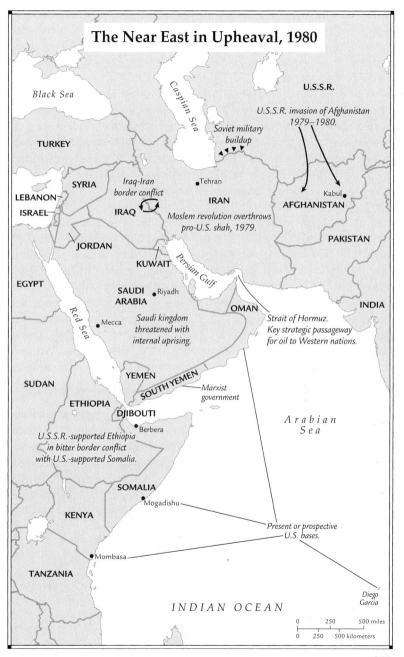

The Near East in Upheaval, 1980

Black Sea

Caspian Sea

U.S.S.R.

U.S.S.R. invasion of Afghanistan 1979–1980.

TURKEY

Soviet military buildup

SYRIA

Iraq-Iran border conflict

•Tehran

LEBANON

ISRAEL

IRAQ

IRAN

Kabul•

AFGHANISTAN

Moslem revolution overthrows pro-U.S. shah, 1979.

JORDAN

KUWAIT

Persian Gulf

PAKISTAN

EGYPT

SAUDI ARABIA

•Riyadh

OMAN

INDIA

Red Sea

•Mecca

Saudi kingdom threatened with internal uprising.

Strait of Hormuz. Key strategic passageway for oil to Western nations.

YEMEN

SOUTH YEMEN

Marxist government

SUDAN

ETHIOPIA

DJIBOUTI

•Berbera

Arabian Sea

U.S.S.R.-supported Ethiopia in bitter border conflict with U.S.-supported Somalia.

SOMALIA

•Mogadishu

KENYA

Present or prospective U.S. bases.

•Mombasa

TANZANIA

INDIAN OCEAN

Diego Garcia

| 0 | 250 | 500 miles |
| 0 | 250 | 500 kilometers |

Nitze and others against détente gained the upper hand. They did so even after Brezhnev suddenly allowed more than 50,000 Jews—the highest number in history—to emigrate from Russia in 1979. He thus met a key demand of the antidétente forces, but neither they nor Carter now reciprocated.[25]

The President was under attack from all sides. The Iranian debacle triggered a jump in oil prices. Western European allies blamed the United States for the jump, and they criticized Carter's indecisiveness in planning a weapons program to defend Western Europe. After a summit meeting with West European leaders in 1979, Carter recorded in his diary, "We then had a luncheon that was very bitter and unpleasant. [West German Chancellor Helmut] Schmidt got personally abusive toward me."[26] The President and his advisers also grew angry over attempts by Schmidt and other West Europeans to profit from moving closer to Moscow. Secretary of Defense Harold Brown remarked caustically that the allies seemed to say, "Yes, there should be a division of task—we'll sell stuff to the Russians and you defend us." Brown added, "That's not what I mean by a division of task." Brzezinski glibly rationalized these failures by writing that the "world had entered a new post-Eurocentric era."[27] To paraphrase, this meant that his Trilateral approach of closely working with Europe and Japan was dead. The United States had few, if any, friends in the industrialized Western world who would fully cooperate in containing Soviet power or disciplining Third World revolutionaries.

Even the "American backyard" seemed unsafe. In July 1979 the revolutionary Sandinista forces overthrew the dictatorial Somoza dynasty that, with strong U.S. support, had been ruling Nicaragua since the mid-1930s. Named after the peasant fighter Augusto Sandino, who had successfully fought U.S. Marines in his country between 1927 and 1933, the Sandinistas had been battling Somoza's brutal national guard for nearly twenty years. By the late 1970s the dictator's greed (he personally owned 25 percent of Nicaraguan land) and the

---

[25]Fred Kaplan, *The Wizards of Armageddon* (New York, 1983), pp. 378–384; Adam Ulam, *Dangerous Relations: The Soviet Union in World Politics, 1970–1982* (New York, 1983), p. 250.

[26]Carter, *Keeping Faith*, p. 112.

[27]Brzezinski, *Power and Principle*, p. 515; the Brown quote is from *The New York Times*, December 7, 1980, p. 44.

guard's terrorism had turned most Nicaraguans, including leading business figures, to the Sandinistas' side. As Anastasio Somoza was about to fall, however, Jimmy Carter tried to mobilize the Organization of American States to intervene so that the revolutionaries could not gain power. The President could not find a single significant Latin American supporter. He then tried to make the best of a bad situation by asking Congress for $75 million in aid to draw the Sandinista government closer to Washington. The new regime, however, did not want to move closer to the nation that had helped kill its supporters for two decades. The Sandinistas determined to follow a nonaligned foreign policy, but then turned to Cuba, which had supported them in the final months of the war and now sent thousands of teachers, health experts, and military advisers.

Relations with Nicaragua approached the breaking point in 1980 as the Sandinistas supplied revolutionaries fighting to overthrow the military government in El Salvador. With one of the most inequitable societies and brutal militaries in the hemisphere, El Salvador was ripe for revolution. Carter actually cut off aid to the government after four American Roman Catholic churchwomen were murdered (three had also been sexually assaulted) in late 1980 and Salvadoran officials did nothing. Their military forces, after all, had committed the crime. But revolutionaries launched a major offensive in January 1981, and Carter quickly reopened aid channels to the government. His Latin American policy, resembling his policies with the allies and the Soviets, lay in fragments.

Unable to devise coherent policies, in mid-1979 Carter seized the only alternative. He embarked on a major military buildup that, in retrospect, was the first chapter of the massive military spending program undertaken by the Reagan administration in the 1980s. The Defense Department budget began to grow as Carter built bases in the Persian Gulf region and authorized a so-called Rapid Deployment Force that (at least on paper) could strike quickly into Third World regions, especially in the oil-rich Middle East. Brzezinski later admitted that by this time, "There was neither dialogue nor deterrence in our relationship" with Moscow.[28] The relationship had been

---

[28]Two fine analyses are Melvyn P. Leffler, "From the Truman Doctrine to the Carter Doctrine," *Diplomatic History,* VII (Fall 1983): 245–266; and Stanley Hoffmann, "In Search of a Foreign Policy," *The New York Review of Books,* September 29, 1983, p. 54.

reduced to SALT II, and the pact was nearly dead because arms control proved too fragile, too politically exposed, to carry the entire burden of Soviet-American relations. It needed the kind of supporting political and economic structure that Nixon and Brezhnev had tried to create and that had now been dismantled.

As Carter turned to the military, so did Brezhnev. On Russia's border the Islamic state of Afghanistan began to move away from the control that the Soviets had wielded through puppet governments. In the nineteenth century British colonialists had talked about "the great game of empire" in the Near East, a game between the British and the Russians in which Afghanistan, because of its pivotal location, was a critical pawn. Now, to Soviet eyes, a hostile China and an Iran run by Moslem fanatics threatened the country. In 1979 the Soviets decided the stakes were worth reopening the game. An ill Brezhnev was convinced by a few civilian advisers that strategic and ideological reasons demanded a war—which, they assured him, would be brief. He was also persuaded by badly informed intelligence which mistakenly told him that Carter intended to move into both Iran and Afghanistan. Brezhnev then overruled his uniformed military, who feared and strongly objected to the operation. On December 27 the Red Army invaded Afghanistan, executed the ineffective Marxist leader, and soon committed nearly 100,000 troops to a long, costly struggle with Moslem guerrillas. American experts speculated it would be the Soviets' Vietnam. To avoid such a disaster, the Russians used brutal force, including the killing of college students who demonstrated against the occupation. Brezhnev also ordered new arrests of Russian dissidents, one of whom was Nobel Prize winning physicist Andrei Sakharov, the leader of the Soviet human rights movement. A high State Department official believed that the invasion and arrests resulted in part from a "domestic crisis within the Soviet system. . . . It may be that the thermodynamic law of entropy has finally and fully caught up with the Soviet system, which now seems to expend more energy on simply maintaining its equilibrium than on improving itself. We could," he concluded, "be seeing a period of foreign movement at a time of internal decay."[29]

---

[29]Christian Friedrich Ostermann, "New Evidence on the War in Afghanistan. Introduction," *Cold War International History Project Bulletin*, 14/15 (Winter 2003–Spring 2004), pp. 139–140; Anatoly Dobrynin, *In Confidence* (New York, 1995), pp. 438–439; Charles W. Maynes, "The World in 1980," U.S. Department of State, *Current Policy*, April 1980, pp. 1–2.

A beleaguered Carter, naively complaining that the Soviets had "lied" to him about their peaceful intentions, accelerated his military buildup, which had begun before the Afghanistan invasion. He withdrew SALT II from the Senate (where it was nearly dead anyway), began registering young men for the draft, embargoed U.S. wheat and technology exports to Russia, and ordered American athletes to withdraw from the 1980 Olympic Games in Moscow. He promised to increase defense spending by 5 percent in real terms. Finally, the President dramatically announced a "Carter Doctrine" that pledged American intervention—unilaterally if necessary—if the Soviets threatened Western interests in the Persian Gulf region. Brzezinski persuaded Carter to announce the doctrine by directly comparing the crisis to Truman's in 1947. The Georgian, who revered the earlier President, now saw himself once again propping up the dominoes of Western civilization.[30]

Cyrus Vance refused to join the crusade. He believed that the Soviets had invaded Afghanistan because they had a "dangerous problem" on their border and, moreover, had little more "to lose in [their] relationship with the United States."[31] In April 1980 Vance finally resigned when, over his protests, Carter ordered a secret military mission to rescue the fifty-three American hostages in Iran. The complex mission failed as a collision between two of the helicopters and a transport plane killed eight American soldiers.

The President entered the 1980 presidential campaign with one of the lowest approval ratings in recent history (77 percent negative, with 82 percent negative for his handling of foreign policy). Spirits sank so low that when Carter stood up to Senator Edward Kennedy's challenge for the Democratic party nomination by replying "I'll whip his ass," Carter's staff told the President that it had done more for their morale than anything "since the Willie Nelson concert" of months before.[32] Carter tried to regain the initiative with his arms buildup. He signed Presidential Directive 59 (PD-59), which ordered massive new forces built to fight a prolonged, limited

---

[30]Brzezinski, *Power and Principle*, pp. 30–31, 444–445. The Carter Doctrine speech can be read in the chapter XII documents at the www.mhhe.com/lafeber website. A good, succinct context for the CIA's activity in Afghanistan at this time is Douglas Little, "Mission Impossible . . . ," *Diplomatic History*, 28 (November 2004), especially pp. 688–691.

[31]Cyrus Vance, *Hard Choices* (New York, 1983), pp. 388–389.

[32]Carter, *Keeping Faith*, p. 464; polls in *Washington Post*, July 30, 1980, p. A12.

nuclear war. Critics quickly compared PD-59 with NSC-68 of three decades earlier when Soviet military power had been exaggerated.[33]

The nation's policy was taking a turn back to 1950. Unfortunately for Carter his political fortunes turned not at all. In his foreign policy he tried to outflank the Republican nominee, Ronald Reagan, from the right—a mission impossible.

Reagan received 51 percent of the popular vote but won overwhelmingly in the electoral college. Exit polls showed that most voters simply thought "it was time for a change"—that is, they wanted new leadership. They were especially disturbed by such domestic problems as inflation, but Americans were also angry over an apparent "loss of control" in foreign affairs. Of those polled, 84 percent believed the nation had sunk into "deep and serious trouble." They favored more money for defense and the use of force in crises.[34] Reagan rode these frustrations into power.

A former New Dealer, Reagan changed after dealing with communists in Hollywood, tiring of paying high personal income taxes, divorcing actress Jane Wyman, and marrying actress Nancy Davis, whose family was severely conservative. As television pitchman for General Electric in the 1950s and governor of California in the late 1960s, he blasted federal governmental powers. Governor Reagan also gained national attention for getting tough with antiwar and civil rights protesters on California campuses. In the 1970s he became the best-known spokesman for a neoconservative movement that demanded social order and reduced government spending at home but costly anticommunist military policies abroad. One neoconservative said that "the campus revolts of the 1960s, the rise of the counterculture, [LBJ's] Great Society," and the "takeover" of the Democrats by the liberal "McGovernite wing" had created the movement. But neoconservatism had also been spawned by millions of dollars given by business groups to establish such right-wing think tanks as the Heritage Foundation and the

---

[33]Fred M. Kaplan, "Our Cold-War Policy, Circa '50," *The New York Times Magazine*, May 18, 1980, p. 94; and Milton Leitenberg, "Presidential Directive (P.D.) 59," *Journal of Peace Research*, XVIII (1981): 309–317. Carter's foreign policy problems, amid the election campaign, come alive in his television interview in the chapter XII documents at the www.mhhe.com/lafeber website.

[34]Terry Deibel, *Presidents, Public Opinion and Power. The Nixon, Carter and Reagan Years* (New York, 1987), pp. 14–15; *The New York Times*, November 9, 1980, p. 28.

American Enterprise Institute. The neoconservatives took ideas seriously. Believing that liberalism had seen its day, they worked to come up with new programs. Reagan rode an intellectual as well as a populist wave into power.[35]

The new President's foreign policy was simple and direct: it rested entirely on opposing the Soviet Union. Gone were Nixon's sophisticated détente and Carter's earlier emphasis on North-South issues. Reagan instead took Carter's 1979–1980 anticommunist policies to an extreme. "Let's not delude ourselves," he declared during the 1980 campaign. "The Soviet Union underlies all the unrest that is going on. If they weren't engaged in this game of dominoes, there wouldn't be any hot spots in the world." If asked to be more specific, however, Reagan could seem vague and confused. He toasted his hosts in "Bolivia" while visiting Brazil, and in a critical national security meeting he mistakenly assumed the Soviet SS-19 missile was larger than the SS-18 because nineteen is a larger number than eighteen. By late 1981 his National Security Council (NSC) adviser found him so ignorant of foreign-policy fundamentals that he began showing the President simple government-made instructional movies. In these sessions Reagan asked few questions except "What do I have to say?"[36]

But he devoted hours to preparing for public appearances in which he used his Hollywood training to sell his policies. "To grasp and hold a vision . . .—that is the very essence, I believe, of successful leadership—not only on the movie set where I learned it, but everywhere."[37] Reagan envisioned defeating the Soviet Union in the Cold War. He described the U.S.S.R. to fundamentalist religious leaders as "the evil empire," and he told the British Parliament in 1982 that "Marxism-Leninism" was doomed to "the ashheap of history." In 1981 Leonid Brezhnev, buffeted by war in Afghanistan, Chinese hostility, and a declining economy, sent a nine-page letter asking for talks on arms reductions. Reagan refused; he wanted instead to talk about Soviet "imperialism." His popularity remained firm. "He operates on

[35]Sidney Blumenthal, *The Rise of the Counter-Establishment* (New York, 1986), p. 250; *The New York Times*, December 28, 1980, p. E5; *Washington Post*, May 12, 1985, p. F4.
[36]*Time*, December 8, 1986, p. 34; Strobe Talbott, *Deadly Gambits* (New York, 1984), p. 274; *Washington Post*, March 27, 1988, p. C4; *Wall Street Journal*, June 3, 1980, p. 1.
[37]Terry Deibel, "Reagan's Mixed Legacy," *Foreign Policy*, No. 75 (Summer 1989): 50–51; Neil Postman, *Amusing Ourselves to Death. Public Discourse in the Age of Show Business* (New York, 1985), pp. 125–128.

a separate plane from the rest of us," a Senate leader noted. "We may find him flawed because he doesn't know the details. . . . But he can have a simple dialogue with the voters. . . . Jimmy Carter agreed with you and you didn't like it. This guy can disagree and you think he's great." The reasons for Reagan's effectiveness went beyond his personality and movie manners, however. His vision exploited Americans' anti-Soviet feelings, the roots of which went back to the 1940s, if not the 1890s. And he constantly assured them they were God's Chosen People who would wage the great struggle according to what Reagan had called a "divine plan."[38]

His foreign-policy tactics for throwing the Soviets on history's "ash heap" were not as grand as his vision. Indeed, during the first five years of his presidency his foreign policy largely turned out to be his military budget. Reaganites charged that the 1970s arms race had been run only by the Soviets. Others, however, pointed out that, during the 1970s Americans had modernized 500 Minuteman missiles; introduced the deadly MIRV missile, with its multiple nuclear warheads; launched Poseidon submarines, with their powerful and highly accurate Trident missiles; built 200 newly developed cruise missiles that could avoid Soviet radar tracking; and deployed a new strategic bomber more advanced than any the Soviets deployed. In reality, Reagan's military-force blueprint looked little different from Carter's. But there was to be much more of it: $1.6 trillion over five years instead of Carter's planned $1.2 trillion. In the 1990s, Pentagon investigators discovered that the U.S. military and civilian officials had grossly underestimated costs—and grossly overestimated Soviet capabilities—to wring billions of dollars from Congress. For example, B-2 aircraft, costing $2 billion each, were demanded to penetrate certain Soviet air defenses—which did not exist. The money nevertheless flowed out from Congress, many of whose constituents wanted waste and fraud cut from government, but not if it affected their own profitable war contracts.

Reagan's anti-Soviet military plans rested in part on a 1976 analysis known as "Team B." The CIA, then headed by George H. W. Bush, had

---

[38]Blumenthal, *Rise of the Counter-Establishment*, pp. 252–253; Steven R. Weisman, "Can the Magic Prevail?" *The New York Times Magazine*, April 29, 1984, p. 41; *Washington Post*, November 21, 1983, p. A13; Ibid., March 29, 1981, p. A6; Strobe Talbott, *The Russians and Reagan* (New York, 1982), pp. 70–71. A classic Reagan anti-Soviet speech, given before the British Parliament in 1982, can be read in the chapter XII documents at the www.mhhe.com/lafeber website.

concluded a secret study of Soviet military plans that some—especially the Pentagon—damned as too optimistic. In response, Bush named Team B, which included hard-liners Paul Nitze, author of NSC-68, Richard Pipes, and Paul Wolfowitz. This group measured not only Soviet capabilities but stated intentions, and consequently concluded Moscow was "preparing for a Third World War as if it were unavoidable." The danger was to crest within the next ten years. In reality, Team B moved from false assumptions to wrong conclusions. The sad state of the Soviet economy limited such a major buildup, and within the next ten years the U.S.S.R. began its collapse. But Team B influenced Reagan, especially when some members, including Pipes and Wolfowitz, joined the administration.[39]

Secretary of Defense Caspar A. Weinberger was nicknamed "Cap the Knife" because he had earlier fought for cutting government budgets. Now, however, he presided over plans to build vast forces that could fight three and one-half wars around the globe. (Nixon had thought the capability to fight one and one-half wars was enough.) The buildup also aimed to give Americans the means to "prevail" in a "protracted" nuclear war. Scientists and some military officers thought such planning absurd—the first nuclear exchanges could make much of the earth uninhabitable. Planning, nevertheless, went ahead until Weinberger's projected five-year budget seemed too small. The administration, moreover, repeatedly hinted it would disavow Carter's SALT II deal with Brezhnev in order to build beyond the pact's limits. But just as often, U.S. military leaders warned that if SALT II were junked, the Soviets could build up faster than Americans. Reagan, who had roundly condemned Carter for the treaty, consequently now decided to abide by it.[40]

The buildup, however, continued and caused increasing concern. T. K. Jones, a Pentagon official, played down the concern. If a nuclear

[39]The last two paragraphs are drawn from Don Oberdorfer's analysis in the *Washington Post*, October 12, 1992, p. A11; the Team B report declassified manuscript, *NIE 11-3/8-76*, especially pp. 3–15, 19–24; and for the U.S. buildup in the 1970s, Thomas J. Downey, "We Never Dropped Out of the Arms Race," *Washington Post*, November 29, 1983, p. A17; Hans A. Bethe, "The Inferiority Complex," *The New York Review of Books*, June 10, 1982, p. 3; *The New York Times*, July 13, 1980, p. 14; *Washington Post*, July 12, 1980, p. A8. The Pentagon investigations are noted in the *The New York Times*, June 28, 1993, p. A10.
[40]Robert Dallek, *Ronald Reagan, The Politics of Symbolism* (Cambridge, Mass., 1984), p. 157; Ulam, *Dangerous Relations*, p. 248; Jeffrey Record, "Jousting with Unreality; Reagan's Military Strategy," *International Security*, VIII (Winter 1983/1984): 3, 18; *Washington Post*, March 5, 1981, p. A1; Ibid, March 8, 1982, p. A1.

war began, he declared, "Dig a hole, cover it with a couple of doors and then throw three feet of dirt on top. It's the dirt that does it." One newspaper editor wondered if Jones was actually a character in the "Doonesbury" comic strip. Another Reagan official assured Congress that the U.S. mail would be delivered after a nuclear war "even if the survivors ran out of stamps." He further refused to change his mind after a congressman noted that delivering mail could be difficult when "there will be no addresses, no streets, no blocks, no houses." Others in the administration seemed similarly misinformed. In 1983 Reagan astounded aides by admitting he had just discovered that the Soviets had 70 percent of their strategic nuclear weapons on the land-based missiles, while Americans had only 20 percent of theirs land based. Now he realized, Reagan added, why for two years the Russians had opposed his proposal to cut land-based systems drastically. But no reevaluation occurred. His team stubbornly clung to the scenario of "winning " a nuclear war.[41]

In 1983, as he prepared to run for a second term, Reagan tried to counter the criticism by proposing a Strategic Defense Initiative (SDI): a space-based, computer-controlled defense that would shoot down nuclear missiles before they reached their targets. Pentagon advisers had long discounted the possibility of "Star Wars," as this proposal was labeled. Reagan ignored them and also most American scientists, who believed that such a defense was not only impossible to build but dangerous even to suggest, because it could destabilize both U.S. and Soviet faith in mutual deterrence. The Soviets, for example, might build many times more missiles so that they could simply overwhelm any Star Wars defense. Nor were critics reassured when it was suggested that Reagan might have stolen the idea from his 1940 movie, "Murder in the Air," in which an imaginary "inertia projector" knocked down enemy planes.[42]

During his first term in office, Reagan's defense plans had little visible effect on Soviet policies. Each side understood that Russian domination of Eastern Europe, or even Afghanistan, could not be dealt with by even the threat of nuclear war. More immediate, nonmilitary

[41]Robert Scheer, *With Enough Shovels* (New York, 1982) is the standard source; Kaplan, *The Wizards of Armageddon*, p. 388; Dallek, *Reagan*, pp. 146–157; Weisman, "Can the Magic Prevail?" p. 48; *The New York Times*, March 19, 1982, p. A30.
[42]Garry Wills, *Reagan's America* (New York, 1987), p. 361; *Washington Post*, June 16, 1985, p. A14.

tactics were needed to pressure the Soviets. Reagan, however, had surrendered to U.S. farmers' pressure and lifted the grain embargo Carter had imposed against the Russians. Conservative columnist George Will bitterly declared, "This administration evidently loves commerce more than it loathes communism."

But something more interesting, and historic, occurred in Poland. In 1978, Cardinal Wojtyla of Krakow became John Paul II, the first Polish Pope to head the Roman Catholic Church. A secret, 1978 CIA analysis was stunningly accurate. Noting that the Pope represented a religious-inspired Polish nationalism which had fought Russian influence for centuries, the CIA predicted the new Pope would force openings for religious and human rights demands in Poland. Since Poland already had "a higher degree of social tension" and anti-Soviet feeling than any other East European country, the situation could turn explosive—not only in Poland but in the other communist regimes where nationalist demands for openness, religious rights, and Western principles could spread.

Poland had saddled itself with a $20-billion debt from badly managed 1970s industrial modernization plans. In 1980–1981 debts and food shortages led to widespread unrest. Next came the stunning appearance of Solidarity (an independent, noncommunist labor union). Then came the predictable crackdown by Polish communist military leaders, who decided they would do it before the Red Army did it for them. Reagan imposed economic sanctions on the Polish communist regime, but meanwhile he sent more grain to the Soviets. He found himself starving the oppressed and feeding the oppressors. Poland entered into that empty gray twilight that many Russians had long wished upon their neighbors, but now with a Polish-born Pope stirring up centuries-old anti-Russian nationalism.[43]

As the West Europeans watched all this in wonder, they became Reagan's next target. West Germany (by far the largest Western trading partner with the U.S.S.R.) had worked out a multibillion-dollar

---

[43]For this and the previous paragraph, see Gerald K. Haines and Robert E. Leggett, eds., *CIA's Analysis of the Soviet Union, 1947–1991* (Washington, D.C., 2001), pp. 101–104. Goldman, *U.S.S.R. in Crisis*, pp. 158–161; *Newsweek*, January 18, 1982, p. 100; two excellent analyses of Washington's response and Soviet policy are Francis J. Meehan, "Reflections on the Polish Crisis," *Cold War International History Project Bulletin*, Issue 11, (Winter 1998): 43–47; and Vojtech Mastny, *The Soviet Non-Invasion of Poland in 1980/81*, Cold War International History Project, Working Paper #23. (Washington D.C., 1998), pp. 28–35, which note Soviet fears of resistance from Solidarity and the Polish army.

deal to help the Soviets build a 3600-mile pipeline that would carry natural gas from Siberia to six West European countries. U.S. officials condemned both European development of—and possible dependence on—Soviet resources. (West Germany planned to obtain 35 percent of its natural gas from Siberia.) The West Europeans replied that Soviet gas supplies were more dependable than the Middle East's. Moreover, they added, Reagan should believe his 1980 campaign oratory that government had to get "off the backs of the people" and not interfere in the marketplace. Nevertheless, Reagan declared "it's time we laid the wood to the Russians" and then announced that European corporations would not be allowed to use U.S.-licensed technology to help build the pipeline. Shocked European officials angrily responded that he had no business interfering with corporations in their countries. The President backed down in late 1982, and the pipeline was built. In 1962 President Kennedy had forced the West Germans and Italians to give up plans to build a Soviet oil pipeline. Twenty years later, in the changed conditions of the third Cold War, Reagan could no longer dictate policy to Western Europe.[44]

He enjoyed better results, however, in 1983, when he worked closely with the West German conservative government to carry through Carter's promise of 1979 to install new Pershing intermediate-range missiles on German soil. The missiles were to counter Soviet weapons installed after 1977. Massive antiwar protests erupted in Europe, where fear grew that these were first-strike weapons that could start nuclear war. But with the European governments' cooperation, the Pershing deployment began. The Soviets walked out of arms talks in Switzerland in protest.

The Reagan administration's problems stemmed in part from its policies' contradictions. For example, the President could not get the government "out of the marketplace" and at the same time fight the Cold War by imposing economic sanctions. Moreover, after he declared that the massive Latin American debt (which approached $500 billion) must be resolved by private banks, he quickly reversed himself during a single weekend in 1982: the President allowed the U.S. government to send Mexico $3 billion to prevent the southern

---

[44]Superb accounts of the 1962 and 1982 pipeline controversies are in Bruce Jentleson, *Pipeline Politics* (Ithaca, N.Y., 1986), especially chapters 4 and 6; and in the final chapter in Frank Costigliola, *France and the United States; the Cold Alliance Since World War II* (New York, 1992).

neighbor from defaulting on its $81-billion debt and possibly bank-rupting U.S. banks to whom it owed money.[45]

Such policy contradictions, moreover, seemed worsened by questionable leadership. The administration focused on domestic issues, especially a tax cut. Reagan knew and cared too little to master foreign policy. Between 1981 and 1987 he went through five White House NSC advisers before he found one, General Colin Powell, who both understood foreign affairs and could successfully coordinate policy. In 1981–1982 Secretary of State Alexander Haig alienated the top White House staff and more importantly the President's wife, Nancy Reagan, with his abrasive personality, his undisguised ambition to control foreign affairs, and his policies. The White House maneuvered Haig into resigning. In June 1982 George Shultz became secretary of state. Nixon's secretary of the treasury, a tough Washington infighter, conservative economist, and multinational corporation executive who passionately believed in freer marketplaces, Shultz soon talked Reagan into retreating on the pipeline issue.

Shultz became the dominant U.S. foreign policymaker. "He was a Buddha, hard to read—and he looked like one," a White House official observed. With great energy, even in his late sixties, he "was beyond fatigue." Shultz had once been a proud U.S. Marine. The secretary of state fervently believed that the threat of force had to be clearly seen behind his diplomacy. As a staunch conservative, however, Shultz hated the idea of others using force to overthrow governments—unless the force was used to overthrow Soviet-supported regimes. He had no doubt about whose side history was on: "The Soviet system is incompetent and cannot survive," he had declared in 1979. Using force could give history a useful push, especially in the newly emerging nations. Shultz and Reagan's ambassador to the United Nations, Jeane J. Kirkpatrick, disliked each other personally, but she provided an important argument for the Reagan-Shultz policies. In a widely noted article Kirkpatrick urged that Americans strongly support "authoritarian" governments, such as the shah's in Iran, because they followed capitalist economic principles, cooperated with the United States, and were open to change. She wanted all-out opposition, on the other hand, to "totalitarian" regimes, such as the communists', because they abhorred capitalism,

[45]*Washington Post,* January 30, 1983, p. A1.

were anti-American, and were not open to liberal change.[46] She believed that communist-totalitarian regimes would never move toward real democracy unless pressured to do so by military force—a belief that was disproved in Eastern Europe before the 1980s were over.

Kirkpatrick's and Shultz's views about using force against Third World troublemakers fit with Reagan's belief that Americans had a mission to spread democracy throughout the earth. A belief in such a mission dated back to the seventeenth century and had found a twentieth-century champion in Woodrow Wilson. Thus Reagan drew on a deep vein of American faith. He stated his policy clearly in his "Reagan Doctrine" of 1985 when he declared: "Our mission is to nourish and defend freedom and democracy." Americans had to support those "on every continent, from Afghanistan to Nicaragua—to defy Soviet-supported aggression and [to] secure rights which have been ours from birth. . . . Support for freedom fighters is self-defense."

This policy, however, faced a major problem: since at least the Vietnam conflict, Americans disliked spending their money, not to mention their lives, to fight faraway conflicts. Reagan tried to overcome this problem by calling Vietnam "a noble cause," but many Americans disagreed. A 1982 poll revealed that 72 percent of those surveyed believed "the Vietnam war was more than a mistake; it was fundamentally wrong and immoral." The Reaganites dealt with this problem by supporting the strategy of "low-intensity conflicts" (LICs). Instead of Vietnam-type wars, LICs used small, specially trained counterinsurgency forces (native or U.S.) who through political action and guerrilla-type warfare could, over a long period, wear down opponents. LICs, moreover, were relatively cheap and so low-key that most Americans would pay little attention to them. But both the Reagan Doctrine and the LIC strategy soon came under attack. Critics warned that LICs could easily escalate (as in Vietnam) and that it was absurd to expend resources in distant areas (such as Cambodia, now renamed Kampuchea) where U.S. interests were, at

---

[46]George P. Shultz, *Turmoil and Triumph* (New York, 1993), p. 6; Larry Speakes, *Speaking Out* (New York, 1988), p. 78; Jeane J. Kirkpatrick, *Dictatorships and Double Standards* (New York, 1982), especially pp. 23–52.

best, vague. Military officers questioned LIC tactics for being imprecise and too open-ended.[47]

This division over LICs revealed a deeper, more dangerous split among Reagan's advisers. Shultz believed that the threat of force had to be used in dealing with foreign affairs and that, at times, force itself had to be used in newly emerging nations to make the threat credible. But Secretary of Defense Weinberger usually opposed using force or the threat of force. Weinberger's views reflected studies by top military scholars who had concluded that U.S. forces must never again be dragged into another Vietnam or detoured from their main business of opposing Soviet (not Kampuchean or Nicaraguan) forces. In November 1984 Weinberger, in a remarkable speech, publicly announced that the United States should use military power only when certain conditions were met: an assurance of long-term public and congressional support, a guarantee that the commitment would be made "wholeheartedly" and with full intention of "winning," and a clear definition of the objectives that were to be sought.[48] (In the 1990s and after, these beliefs were to become famous, and highly influential, as the "Powell Doctrine" [see p. 385].) An angry Shultz publicly questioned Weinberger's list of conditions and privately wondered why the military needed a $300-billion budget if it apparently did not intend to fight.

These contradictions and divisions in Reagan's Third World policies caused major disasters. The first, and one of the worst, occurred in the Middle East during 1982–1983. Fixated on keeping the Soviets out of the region, U.S. officials were uncertain how to deal with the region's fundamental problem—the Israeli-Arab conflict. Reagan and Shultz

[47]Reagan's statement of the doctrine is in U.S. Government, *Weekly Compilation of Presidential Documents*, XXI (February 11, 1985): 145–146; Robert W. Tucker, "Reagan's Foreign Policy," *Foreign Affairs*, LXVIII, 1 (1989): 21; Richard E. Neustadt and Ernest R. May, *Thinking in Time* (New York, 1986), p. 305. Note especially on the "noble cause" quote, Robert J. McMahon, "Rationalizing Defeat. . . ." *Rhetoric and Public Affairs*, 2 (no. 4, 1999), pp. 539–540. On low-intensity warfare: Secretary George Shultz, "Low-Intensity Warfare," *Current Policy*, No. 783; D. Michael Shafer, "The Unlearned Lessons of Counterinsurgency," *Political Science Quarterly*, CIII (Spring 1988): 75, 77–78; Gabriel Kolko, "Foreign Policy After the Election," July 1988, manuscript in author's possession; Michael T. Klare, "The New U.S. Strategic Doctrine," *The Nation*, January 4, 1986, p. 697.
[48]"The Use of Military Power," News Release, Office of Assistant Secretary of Defense (Public Affairs), November 28, 1984. This highly important Weinberger statement can be read in the chapter XII documents at the www.mhhe.com/lafeber website for this book.

stood by in mid-1982 when Israel invaded Lebanon to destroy the missiles of archenemy (and Soviet friend) Syria. The Israelis then drove into Lebanon's capital, Beirut, to destroy the Palestinian Liberation Organization, which represented Palestinians who vowed to return certain areas occupied by Israel to their own control. The Israelis became bogged down amid cutthroat Lebanese politics, the lack of a political consensus in Israel, and Syrian arms supplied by Moscow. When Israelis and Lebanese Christians carried out bloody massacres against Palestinians who lived in Israeli-controlled camps, Israel suffered a political crisis and—pushed by the United States—withdrew its troops. In 1982 at Shultz's urging and over Weinberger's objection, U.S. forces moved into Beirut to try to protect Palestinians, encourage Israeli withdrawal, and keep peace between Christian and Moslem factions inside Lebanon. In April 1983 lives were lost when the U.S. embassy in Beirut was bombed. Meanwhile U.S. troops, hunkered down near the Beirut airport, not only were open to sniper fire but were never clear about their mission. On October 23, 1983, a terrorist bomb killed 239 U.S. soldiers in their barracks. Reagan declared that keeping troops in Lebanon was now "central to our credibility on a global scale." But the President—facing strong public and Defense Department opposition, having no workable Middle East policy, and preparing to run for reelection—soon reversed himself. He pulled out the remaining 1600 soldiers. Lebanon became a bloody war zone in which Soviet-supported Syria gained the upper hand. Reagan's Middle East policy never recovered from the disaster.[49]

On October 25, 1983, two days after the Beirut barracks' bombing, Reagan and Shultz again deployed their military forces. They ordered an invasion of the Caribbean island of Grenada to destroy a regime that had close Cuban ties. The President declared he had acted to save 500 U.S. medical students and to aid neighboring governments who had asked for U.S. troops. The President's press secretary, Larry Speakes, later claimed that the White House believed the students were not endangered and that the invasion played little part in the U.S. decision. The real reasons were Reagan's desires to attack a pro-Cuban regime and to get American minds off the Beirut disaster. The President's good friend, British Prime Minister

[49]Douglas Little, *American Orientalism; the United States and the Middle East Since 1945* (Chapel Hill, 2002), pp. 245–248; Talbott, *Russians and Reagan*, pp. 34–36; *Washington Post*, October 30, 1983, p. C1; *The New York Times*, January 22, 1984, p. A1.

Margaret Thatcher (the "Iron Lady" who usually liked to use force), strongly opposed the invasion as unjustified. But when she tried to call Reagan, a middle-level U.S. official refused to connect her call until the troops had landed. Again, the U.S. military had severe reservations about the operation. And indeed, it became a close-run thing. Some 1900 badly prepared U.S. troops landed and finally overcame a small Grenadan force and 784 Cubans (most of whom were working to enlarge the island's airport), but only after the arrival of 4000 more U.S. troops and six days of fighting. Nineteen American soldiers were killed and 116 wounded. The Cubans counted 71 dead and 59 wounded. The Grenadans suffered 110 killed and 337 wounded. Five years after the invasion and $110 million of U.S. aid, Grenada's politics were anticommunist, but the economy was mired in depression and high unemployment.[50]

For Reagan, however, it proved to be an important political success at home. So were his encounters with Libya. That North African nation's pro-American monarchy had been overthrown in 1969 by Moslem army officers led by Mu'ammar Qaddafi. His expansionist plans, hatred of Israel, growing military ties with Moscow, and—especially—links with terrorists put Qaddafi on a collision course with the United States. In 1981 U.S. jets shot down two Libyan warplanes over disputed territorial waters. In April 1986 Reagan blamed Qaddafi for a bloody terrorist raid in West Berlin, called him "the mad dog of the Middle East," and ordered a bombing raid that killed Qaddafi's adopted daughter and injured at least a dozen other people. Libya, it turned out, had little connection with the West Berlin episode, although Qaddafi was intimately involved with other acts of international terrorism.

The President's tough talk, his command of the media ("You'd be surprised how much being a good actor pays off," he observed), his limited but successful use of force in Grenada and Libya, and the booming (if debt-ridden) economic times enabled him to win forty-nine of fifty states in a landslide reelection victory over former Vice President Walter Mondale in 1984. His advisers later admitted they

[50]Speakes, *Speaking Out*, p. 161; *Washington Post*, October 25, 1988, p. A23; *The New York Times*, May 2, 1994, p. A6; Center for International and Security Studies at Maryland, *The National Security Council Project . . . The Bush Administration* (Washington, D.C., 1999), p. 47.

had urged him to avoid foreign-policy issues in the campaign because these were Reagan's main weaknesses. But he rode the crest of a "new patriotism" that reached its extreme with the popularity of "Rambo," a movie character who ignored the supposed appeasers in Washington and, in the best U.S. unilateral tradition, single-handedly returned to Vietnam, used new military technology, and taught the communists a lesson. The craze included a Houston nightclub, Rambose, where waitresses wore fatigues, issued .50-caliber machine guns, and served buffet from a military stretcher.[51]

But not even Rambo's and Reagan's rhetoric could mask the failure of the President's original policies. Taking Shultz's advice, Reagan finally broke down and met the Soviet ambassador to Washington, Anatoly Dobrynin. He told Dobrynin that "there are some problems that can and should be tackled now. Probably, people in the Soviet Union regard me as a crazy warmonger," Reagan continued, "But I don't want a war. . . . We should make a fresh start."[52] Kirkpatrick's advice to support "authoritarians" failed in both Haiti and the Philippines, where longtime dictators fell (despite Reagan's personal support of them until the last minute). In Haiti a bloody military group took over after the United States finally helped push the "Baby Doc" Duvalier dictatorship from power. In the Philippines U.S. officials finally helped replace the corrupt dictatorship of Ferdinand Marcos with Corazon Aquino's government in 1986. Even with U.S. aid, however, she was unable to stop the spread of both corruption and a communist-led insurgency.

In South Africa, where 5 million whites ruled 21 million blacks through the brutal apartheid (enforced segregation) policy, Reagan followed a policy of "constructive engagement"—that is, using talk and economic ties rather than tough sanctions to ease apartheid. By 1986 the approach had failed. Congress, over the President's objections, imposed economic sanctions that began to squeeze the South African economy and helped convince more than half the 300 U.S. firms in the country to leave. In 1990 the besieged white regime finally freed the top black leader, Nelson Mandela, after he had spent 27 years in jail. But apartheid mostly remained.

---

[51]Richard Barnet, *By the Rockets' Red Glare* (New York, 1990), Part IV; Elizabeth Drew, "A Political Journal," *The New Yorker,* December 3, 1984, especially p. 107.
[52]Dobrynin, *In Confidence,* pp. 517–518.

Nor could the Reagan Doctrine and Kirkpatrick's approach save the President's policies in Central America. The 1980 Republican platform promised to replace Nicaragua's Sandinistas with a "free and independent" government. Reagan publicly declared he intended to make the Sandinistas cry "uncle." In November 1981 he signed the secret National Security Decision Directive 17 (NSDD 17), which authorized the CIA to spend millions to train and to equip Nicaraguan exiles, or "contras," who would fight the Sandinistas. In clear violation of U.S. neutrality laws, the CIA trained contras in the southern United States, then shipped them through Honduras to fight in Nicaragua. The Sandinistas, however, responded by building a force of 65,000 troops, strengthening their political hold on the country, and obtaining help from Western Europeans as well as the Soviet bloc. By late 1983 the contras' failures led the CIA to take over operations that destroyed oil refineries, mined Nicaraguan harbors, and aimed at assassinating Sandinista officials. A stunned U.S. Congress discovered these secret CIA missions, cut off military aid to the contras, and—as opinion polls indicated—received support from a large majority of Americans. U.S. military leaders again wanted no policy that might force them to fight an unpopular war in Nicaragua. Reagan's economic sanctions proved more effective. They helped make Nicaragua an economic basket case that lacked many necessities and, by 1989, suffered an unbelievable 33,000 percent inflation rate. The Sandinistas, nevertheless, held to power, despite the 40,000 killed by the contra war.

In neighboring El Salvador Reagan suffered another defeat when he attempted to destroy the revolutionary Farabundo Martí National Liberation Front (FMLN) that tried to overthrow the U.S.-supported government (see p. 315). He refused to follow up the 1982 FMLN offer to negotiate and instead poured about $1 million into that small country each day over the next six years. Americans virtually took over the wrecked Salvadoran economy. When U.S. trained and equipped Salvadoran soldiers massacred 800 unarmed peasants in late 1981, both El Salvador and the Reagan administration lied: they denied it happened. They feared Congress would cut off U.S. aid to the Salvadoran military killers. The CIA tried to keep out of power both the left and the far-right groups that hired "death squads" to kill thousands of suspect civilians. In 1989, nevertheless, the far-right party, Alianza Republican Nacionalista (ARENA), won national elections. The country polarized. On the left, the FMLN's 7000 troops carried out bloody attacks even in the capital city. On the right, U.S.-trained and supplied Salvadoran military massacred six Jesuit priests (who had led the attempt to end the war and its brutalities against civilians) and two women. U.S. officials, either because of ignorance or an attempted cover-up, at first blamed the FMLN for the massacre. When it became clear that army officers had ordered it, Washington demanded an investigation and convictions. The ten-year war had claimed 70,000 lives; at least two-thirds were civilians slaughtered by right-wing military-related death squads, but not a single military official had been convicted by the terrorized Salvadoran governments. In early 1990 U.S. military officials admitted that the FMLN could not be defeated.[53]

Recognizing the failure of U.S. policy, Costa Rican President Oscar Arias Sanchez won the Nobel Peace Prize in 1987 for stitching together a plan that tried to end the fighting in Nicaragua and El Salvador and to begin a process for democratic elections. U.S. officials disliked Arias's plan because it allowed the Sandinistas to remain in power but demanded that the contras disband. Arias's plan enabled Central Americans, not North Americans, to shape Central American affairs for the first time in a century. The Reagan Doctrine was not working well in what the United States liked to call its "backyard." Actually, the backyard and the house seemed to be much the same thing: more than 500,000 Salvadorans (or about one in eight) lived, illegally for the most part, in the United States to escape the bloodshed. Elsewhere in the neighborhood, General Manuel Antonio Noriega seized power in Panama during 1983. A longtime informant for the CIA, Noriega had also grown rich from the international drug traffic that flooded U.S. streets. Washington officials, including Shultz and Vice President George Bush, ignored Noriega's drug-running and political corruption. They even sent him millions of dollars because he helped fight the Sandinistas. When they finally tried to overthrow Noriega in 1987–1988, he defied them. As Arias feared, U.S. policy was making the neighborhood more, not less, violent.[54] (See map, p. 217.)

[53]On Nicaragua see Mary B. Vanderlaan, *Revolution and Foreign Policy in Nicaragua* (Boulder, Colo. 1986), especially pp. 127–209; Barry Rubin, *Secrets of State* (New York, 1985), p. 219; *The New York Times,* December 24, 1981, p. A14. On El Salvador see especially *New York Times,* March 8, 2005, p. A5.

[54]*Christian Science Monitor,* April 25, 1988, p. 1, reprinted in *Central America NewsPak,* April 25–May 8, 1988, p. 1; *The New York Times,* January 28, 1982, p. A10; Ibid., July 30, 1982, p. A6; Ibid., January 21, 1990, p. 21; Nora Hamilton, et al., *Crisis in Central America* (Boulder, Colo., 1988), especially the Sharpe, Arnson, and Karl essays on El Salvador; *Washington Post,* April 5, 1988, p. A16; W. LaFeber, *The Panama Canal* (New York, 1989), pp. 193–215.

These Third World problems created Reagan's gravest crises. In 1984 Middle East terrorists, supported by Iran, seized U.S. citizens (including several CIA agents) as hostages. Reagan, who had condemned Carter in 1980 for negotiating the hostage issue, continually denied he would ever bargain with terrorists. In 1985, however, he secretly accepted an Israeli proposal to send antitank, and later antiaircraft, missiles to Iran. When the first U.S. weapons were sent, six hostages were being held; by mid-1987 nine Americans were held hostage. At the same time, Congress ordered that all military aid be cut off to the hapless contras in Nicaragua.

Lieutenant Colonel Oliver North, of Reagan's National Security Council, proposed secretly to bypass the congressional order by diverting funds from the Iranian arms sales to supply the contras. Reagan later denied he knew about this illegal act, even though it was probably devised by his close friend William Casey, the CIA director. In late 1986, however, a Lebanese journal revealed the arms deals. A disclosure of the illegal contra aid followed. One independent investigation (by a commission headed by former Republican Senator John Tower of Texas) concluded that Reagan had failed to supervise his NSC staff or to properly oversee U.S. policy. North was brought to trial in 1989 and received a suspended prison sentence for lying to Congress, destroying documents, and accepting illegal payments. Casey died of a brain tumor before the scandal broke. When the scandal did break and fester in 1986–1987, Reagan's presidency reached its nadir.[55] A *Washington Post* reporter, Joanne Omang, grew so tired of being constantly lied to about Central America by U.S. officials Elliott Abrams and Robert McFarlane that she chose to resign and become a novelist rather than to continually mislead her readers. Corrupted foreign policies led to corruption and lying to cover them up in the United States.

This political crisis coincided with economic dilemmas. The U.S. arms budget approached $300 billion by 1986. The Soviets were spending nearly $250 billion. (Altogether the world's nations spent about $980 billion, or more than the combined income of the poorest half of the world, on arms in 1986.) America produced five nuclear

---

[55]Eric Alterman, *When Presidents Lie* (New York, 2004), especially pp. 270–277; U.S. House and Senate, 100th cong., 1st Sess., *Report of the Congressional Committees Investigating the Iran-Contra Affair* (Washington, 1987), especially pp. 3–51 on Nicaragua, 157–209 on Iran, and 327–392 on North; I am indebted to Max Miller for a copy of this document.

warheads each day. The Soviets, according to CIA estimates, had actually leveled off their arms budgets to no more than a 2 percent annual growth rate after 1976. The CIA's news arrived just as analyses disclosed that the $1.1 trillion of U.S. military spending between 1981 and 1985 had bought remarkably few new weapons. But corruption seemed rampant as $600 toilet seats and $7000 coffeemakers were discovered on the military ledger books. Forty-five of the nation's largest military contractors came under criminal investigation for illegal kickbacks and overcharges. Northrop Corporation was charged with buying parts from a local Radio Shack store to meet a deadline for producing a missile's incredibly intricate guidance system. One congressman wondered whether those missiles would hit "Washington or Moscow if we get into a war."[56] Reagan had demanded a 7 to 10 percent increase each year in the military budget. He had received less than half that amount by 1984 and only enough to cover the inflation rate by 1988.

Because of this spending and an inability to reduce domestic programs, the U.S. budget overflowed in red ink until more than $1 trillion of debt piled up in the Reagan years. At the same time, the U.S. economic machine became less competitive. In 1987 the Japanese outpaced the Americans in the amount of goods and services produced per person. Trade deficits hit record highs as Americans bought $171 billion more from abroad than they sold. (In addition, experts estimated that a booming $100 billion drug trade in the United States resulted in $5 to $25 billion being illegally sent abroad each year to pay for the drugs.) The astronomical deficit was made up in part by foreign investors: by 1989 they held $300 billion of U.S. industry, $400 billion of the $3-trillion national debt, and 21 percent of the U.S. banking assets. Nearly all that money had arrived since 1974—that is, during the years of the third Cold War. By 1985 a historic watershed occurred. Just four years before, when Reagan had entered the White House, the United States had been the world's proud leading creditor nation, but now it had suddenly slid below Brazil and Mexico to become the world's largest debtor. One authority declared, "The United States has lost control of its financial markets to foreigners." In the 1980 race for the

---

[56]Raymond L. Garthoff, *Détente and Confrontation* (Washington, 1985), pp. 795–796; *The New York Times,* March 2, 1986, p. 8; Ibid., April 12, 1987, p. F3; Ibid., May 19, 1985, p. 28; the production figure is in *Washington Post,* April 23, 1987, p. A10; the Radio Shack quote and references are in Ibid., December 1, 1988, p. B22.

Republican nomination, George Bush had accused Reagan of following "voodoo economics." By 1985 a conservative columnist noted that "Reaganomics is giving voodoo a bad name."[57]

The two superpowers each had spent trillions of dollars on defense to checkmate the other, only to discover that they had gone far in undermining their own domestic societies. The Soviets found themselves much worse off than the Americans. In 1959 Khrushchev had promised that Soviet industry would surpass the American system in per capita production by the 1970s. By the mid-1980s the top Soviet leadership had to admit that this had been a pipe dream. Until the mid-1970s Brezhnev had built up his military by spending as much as 25 percent of the gross national product on it. (Americans spent about 6 percent of a much larger gross national product.) Brezhnev did so at the expense of the investment and civilian sectors. A corrupt, disheartening stagnation set in. The economy's growth rate flirted with zero percent increase. As the world's largest oil producer, and dependent on petroleum exports for 60 percent of its badly needed hard-currency earnings (dollars, yen, marks, etc.), the Soviets suffered severely as their production leveled off and world oil prices skidded downward in the 1980s. Consumer goods were shoddy; the U.S.S.R. was the world's largest producer of shoes, but the shoes fell apart in weeks or rotted in warehouses because so few wanted them. Producing twice as much steel as the United States, the Soviets were always short of steel because they wasted so much and produced so little of good quality. Male life expectancy continued to decline alarmingly (sixty-six years in 1964, sixty-two and one-half years by 1984), while female life expectancy remained about ten years longer. Infant mortality rates soared to levels unheard of in the industrialized world.[58]

---

[57]William Safire, "Reagan's Next Term," *The New York Times Magazine*, January 13, 1985, p. 22 has "voodoo" quote; *The New York Times*, March 26, 1988, p. 1; Ibid., September 11, 1988, p. F3; Ibid., August 22, 1989, p. D3; *Los Angeles Times*, December 6, 1987, p. 1; *Washington Post*, March 18, 1988, p. B1. Drug trade figures are drawn from Professor William Walker's work, and author's conversation with Professor Walker, September 19, 1989.

[58]Condoleezza Rice, "Gorbachev and the Military," *The Harriman Institute Forum*, II (April 1989): 1, 3; Goldman, *U.S.S.R. in Crisis*, p. 101; John P. Hardt, "Highlight: Problems and Prospects," in U.S. Congress, Joint Economic Committee, 97th Cong., 2nd Sess., *Soviet Economy in the 1980s . . . Selected Papers* (Washington, 1983), pp. vii–xiii; Seweryn Bialer, "Gorbachev's Program," *Political Science Quarterly*, CIII (Fall 1988): 412.

Alcoholism, horrid hospital facilities (especially for women giving birth), and food shortages abounded. The aged, ill Brezhnev could find no solutions. A bitter joke circulated among Russians. Stalin, Khrushchev, and Brezhnev were riding on a train when it broke down. To solve the problem, Stalin advised shooting the engineer, Khrushchev suggested pardoning the crew and giving them another chance—and Brezhnev thought it would be best to pull down the window shades and pretend they were moving.

Brezhnev's incapacity also further undermined Soviet bloc strength. The bloc was economically linked by U.S.S.R. shipments of raw materials (especially oil) to such satellites as Poland and Czechoslovakia, who sent Soviets increasingly inferior manufactured goods. As oil prices sank and the quality of the manufactured goods worsened, the trade links frayed. Even militarily, the Warsaw Pact relations soured because the Soviets could not modernize their allies' forces. Hungary responded economically by trying to inject some private-market reforms. Hard-line regimes in Rumania, East Germany, and Czechoslovakia responded by jailing dissenters. Poland moved close to collapse and was finally propped up with martial law in 1981.[59]

Brezhnev died in 1982; he was followed by Yuri Andropov, who died in 1984, and then by an aged, ill, and inexperienced Konstantin Chernenko, who died in 1985. Andropov, the longtime KGB (secret police) chief, knew the system's weaknesses and tried to remedy them with fresh policies and younger, better-trained leaders, such as Mikhail Gorbachev. But both Andropov and Chernenko used the Stalinist tactics of seizing dissenters, such as Nobel Prize winning scientist Andrei Sakharov, and either exiling them or committing them as "insane" to psychiatric hospitals. Police limited the use of the relatively few copying machines and personal computers, because these "forbidden fruit," as they were known, threatened the state's absolute control. Such police action meant, however, that the stagnating economy fell further behind roaring Western systems that were fueled by the new technology. Only 50,000 personal computers were in the U.S.S.R. (Americans had 30 million), and they were generations behind Western machines. To copy an article, a Soviet scientist needed two or three days, if a photocopier could be found. Even the Soviet Foreign Ministry held up talks with

[59]*The New York Times*, February 19, 1984, p. 2F; Gordon A. Craig and Alexander George, *Force and Statecraft* (New York, 1983), p. 149; *Washington Post*, February 14, 1985, p. A23.

U.S. diplomats for hours while typing out documents on carbon paper that could have been copied in seconds.[60]

By early 1985 the Russian system resembled a science-fiction movie's huge gray blob that looked threatening but moved ever more slowly. Soviet-American relations reached a dangerously low point. In March 1985 Chernenko died and was replaced as party leader (in a closely contested secret election) by Mikhail Gorbachev. Born in 1931, the new leader possessed remarkable political skills that had rapidly pushed him through the party ranks until in 1980 he became by far the youngest full member of the all-powerful politburo. But not only age made him unusual. Unlike the Brezhnev-Chernenko group, he had been well educated at Moscow State University, where he had read Western philosophy, as well as the Leninist tracts, and had studied at the elite school of law. His wife, Raisa, had received her doctorate in philosophy. In a regime that tried to destroy religious practices, Gorbachev's mother was a devout Christian who had baptized her son. (As Soviet leader in 1988, he removed many restraints on the Russian Orthodox Church as it celebrated its 1000-year anniversary.)

Gorbachev's personal translator, Pavel Palazchenko, revealed another influence on this Russian generation:

> I am sure that the impact of the Beatles on the generation of young Soviets in the 1960s will one day be the object of studies. We knew their songs by heart. . . .
> In the dusky years of the Brezhnev regime they were not only a source of musical relief. They helped us create a world of our own. . . . [The] Beatles were our quiet way of rejecting "the system" while conforming to most of its demands.[61]

---

[60]Seweryn Bialer, "Danger in Moscow," *The New York Review of Books,* February 16, 1984, p. 6; Alex Beam, "The USSR: Atari Bolsheviks," *The Atlantic,* March 1986, pp. 28–32; *Washington Post,* January 16, 1984, p. A11; Ibid., January 16, 1986, p. A16.

[61]Pavel Palazchenko, *My Years with Gorbachev and Shevardnadze* (University Park, 1997), p. 3. The CIA's problems, and the Reagan administration's use of intelligence to support its preconceived hard-line views is an instructive story told in Dan Arbel and Ran Edelist, *Western Intelligence and the Collapse of the Soviet Union* (London, 2003). The following paragraph is based on Bialer, "Gorbachev's Program," pp. 407–408; Shultz, *Turmoil and Triumph,* pp. 490–491; 892–893; Walter LaFeber, "Technology and U.S. Foreign Relations," *Diplomatic History,* 24 (Winter 2000): 12–18 gives further references for this point; Michael Cox, "The End of the Cold War and Why We Failed to Predict It," in Allen Hunter, ed., *Rethinking the Cold War* (Philadelphia, 1998), pp. 166–168. An important Schultz speech on these topics can be found in the chapter XII documents at the www.mhhe.com/lafeber website.

Gorbachev was not an isolated, weird phenomenon. He represented a new Soviet generation that had become adult after Stalin's death, was well educated in the professions, had been inspired by Khrushchev's attempted reforms, was repelled by what it termed Brezhnev's repressive "stagnation," knew something about the West, and understood how far the country was falling behind the West in technology. This new class's politics ranged from radical to reactionary, but numerically it was the largest professional class in the world. Gorbachev and this new class demanded what they soon called "new thinking"—not because they feared Reagan's military buildup but because they understood that the Soviet system they inherited could not keep up with, and adjust to, the technological changes (computers, satellites, instant international television coverage) that were revolutionizing Western societies. Secretary of State Shultz understood what was happening. When other U.S. officials (especially in the CIA and Pentagon) did not want to negotiate with the Soviets, Shultz urged Reagan to do so because he could deal from a growing position of strength created by the new technologies of the dawning information age. Americans were exploiting these inventions. The Soviet system, Shultz preached, was doomed because it could not adjust.

Gorbachev sounded the theme: "Only an intensive, highly developed economy can guarantee the consolidation of the country's positions in the international arena." To achieve this goal, he proposed "perestroika" (a restructuring of the economy) and "glasnost" (publicity and political openness to encourage individual initiative). At the pivotal Twenty-seventh Communist Party Congress in February 1986, Gorbachev called for "radical reform." The reform included more independence and even profit making for farm and industrial managers. It also included a slow revamping of the price and market systems so that they would more accurately reflect reality and force farm and industrial workers to meet marketplace demands. This new thinking even allowed previously impossible private "cooperatives"; between 1985 and 1988, 13,000 producing cooperatives and 300,000 family-owned businesses appeared. The initiative also allowed new partnerships with Western corporations. A Soviet economy closed to most capitalists suddenly had American Express building hotels, Baskin-Robbins selling its thirty-one flavors of ice cream along Red Square, Merck Pharmaceuticals working with Soviet research scientists, the world's largest McDonald's frying "bolshoi Macs," and Nabisco making Russian breakfast cereals.[62]

But Gorbachev's reforms ran into a stone wall of opposition made up of some politburo members (who feared such reforms in principle), the massive party and government bureaucracies (which feared loss of their own power and privileges), and many workers (it was estimated that 16 million could lose their jobs in perestroika). He fought back with a whirlwind of political changes. First he brought trusted advisers onto the politburo to replace many of his conservative opponents. In mid-1985 he appointed a longtime colleague, Eduard Shevardnadze, only fifty-seven, to replace the seventy-nine-year-old Andrei Gromyko as foreign minister. The new regime, moreover, publicly condemned key parts of Soviet history and opened that history to a reexamination that had (as does much historical analysis) enormous potential consequences. The regime declared that "The guilt of Stalin is enormous and unforgivable" because of his crimes against the people. Hundreds of political exiles, including scientist Andrei Sakharov and his wife, Yelena Bonner, won their release, although many more remained in prison.

By 1988 Gorbachev's economic reforms were not working. Productivity lagged. Food was scarcer than before 1985. He tried to raise productivity and stop rampant alcoholism by sharply limiting sales of wine and vodka. Gorbachev became known as "Lemonade Joe." His action led to loss of tax revenue and a severe sugar shortage as Russians began making home-brewed liquor (often with a poisonously high alcohol content). Sugar scarcity even led to a shortage of ice cream, one of the Russians' most loved foods.

Glasnost meanwhile resulted in sudden demands by ethnic minorities in provinces far from Moscow for more independence and freedom. Gorbachev had not anticipated these outbreaks, and the authorities put some of them down with force.[63] In mid-1989 more than 300,000 coal-mine workers went on strike. They were among the most favored of Soviet workers, but they lived in hovels

---

[62]Martin McCauley, ed., *The Soviet Union Under Gorbachev* (New York, 1987), especially pp. 1–9, 210–227; Serge Schmemann, "The Emergence of Gorbachev," *The New York Times Magazine,* March 3, 1985, especially pp. 44–46, 55–57; Hedrick Smith, "On the Road with Gorbachev's Guru," *The New York Times Magazine,* April 10, 1988, pp. 38, 42; *Washington Post,* February 27, 1986, p. A32.

[63]Useful on the nationalities issues: McCauley, ed., *Soviet Union Under Gorbachev,* pp. 4, 86–95; Basile Kerblay, *Gorbachev's Russia* (New York, 1989), pp. 62–66.

and lacked necessities (for example, many received only one cake of soap every two months). Unrest spread across the country.

Throughout these crises Gorbachev's response was consistent: he purged political opponents and bureaucrats who, he claimed, were trying to use the crises to destroy his reforms. The climax of this policy came in March 1989, when he conducted nationwide elections for a new 2250-member People's Congress. Many Communist party leaders suffered humiliating defeats in the election. Debates in this pioneering parliament were even carried on television to enthralled Soviets. Gorbachev thus tried to use glasnost, or openness, to kill opposition to perestroika. He played to intellectuals and encouraged openness in the arts. Orwell's *1984* and even some of Aleksandr Solzhenitsyn's bitterly critical novels of Soviet history were made available. Movies such as "Little Vera" and "Is It Easy to Be Young?" gave grim views of workers and alienated youths, as did stunningly popular rock music that emerged from underground.[64]

It was a remarkable performance—a performance topped in February 1990 by the previously unthinkable: Gorbachev and the Communist party leadership surrendered the party's seventy-three-year-old monopoly of power in the U.S.S.R. They had little alternative. Economic reform and decentralization required some political decentralization as well. The party was supposed to remain supreme, but it instead quickly divided between reformers and conservatives. To free himself further from party conservatives, Gorbachev moved toward a more Western-style presidency and cabinet system of government whose power was based on the popularly elected People's Congress. He was opening windows that had been sealed for seventy years.

Gorbachev's chances for success depended not only on his control of Soviet politics but also in cutting back wasteful, costly commitments abroad. Most immediately, his success depended on making arms deals with Americans so that he could reduce his runaway military budget. The prospects looked grim when he came to power in 1985. U.S.-Soviet relations were tense. Reagan, moreover, now repeated

---

[64]Richard Stites, "Soviet Popular Culture in the Gorbachev Era," *The Harriman Institute Forum*, II (March 1989); useful chronology of Gorbachev's reforms is in *Washington Post*, December 31, 1988, p. A14; *The New York Times*, July 24, 1989, p. A1. Gorbachev's March 1988 speech exemplifying this "new thinking" can be found in the chapter XII documents at the www.mhhe.com/lafeber website.

Richard Nixon's tactics in order to pressure Moscow. Having once declared that the Chinese regime was "based on a belief in destroying governments like ours," in 1984 the President suddenly reversed course. He visited China and returned to call it "this so-called Communist China." He even sent high-tech weapons to the Chinese as Sino-American trade boomed. The Soviets, obsessed with fear of a giant, well-armed Chinese neighbor, saw a Sino-American axis forming against them.

Just before Reagan had gone to China, moreover, the Soviets had shot down a civilian Korean airliner that, they claimed, had intentionally flown over their highly sensitive eastern military bases. A U.S. congressman had been among the 269 people killed. Moscow called the flight a "deliberate provocation." Washington denied that the plane had been on an intelligence mission and called the August 1983 shootdown an inhuman act. One Soviet leader declared, "Comrades, the international situation at present is white hot, thoroughly white hot." A U.S. Marine Corps general announced that a U.S.-Soviet limited war was "an almost inevitable probability" in this generation. Reagan himself admitted, "There have been times in the past when people thought the end of the world was coming . . . but never anything like this."[65]

Then a slow but certain change began. Preparing to run for reelection in 1984 and aware that, as one poll revealed, more than one-third of Americans feared he would take them into a war, Reagan cooled his rhetoric. Moreover, at no time had even the most hawkish U.S. officials believed they could push the Soviets into a quick collapse. The secret National Security Decision Directive 75 of late 1982 planned only for "long haul" containment and the pious hope that the U.S.S.R. would somehow become more pluralistic. Reagan's rhetoric was more aggressive than his long-term policies.

The turning point in the Cold War came when Gorbachev assumed power in March 1985. He had already publicly declared that a détente was possible. His economic plans now made détente necessary. Gorbachev simply reversed Soviet doctrine. Moscow had argued that only socialists would survive nuclear war; Gorbachev

[65]Dallek, *Ronald Reagan,* p. 174; *The New York Times,* May 2, 1984, p. A1; Joel B. Harris, Bruce H. Turnbull, and Jeffery P. Bialos, *Compliance with U.S. Export Control Laws and Regulations* (Washington, 1984), pp. 39–41; *Washington Post,* November 21, 1984, p. A1; Ibid., June 22, 1984, p. A15; *The New York Times,* October 21, 1984, p. 32 on "Armageddon."

said it would spare no one—not even socialists. "Security," he announced, could "only be resolved by political means," not military face-offs. He further argued that the world's pressing problems, such as the environment and resource scarcity, had to be solved by cooperation, not confrontation: global "interdependence . . . is such that all peoples are similar to climbers roped together on the mountainside. They either can climb together to the summit or fall together into the abyss."

As Matthew Evangelista has shown, Gorbachev came to this conclusion in part because U.S. private arms-control groups educated him about the need to end the 1980s system of arms buildup. Led by the Pugwash organization (Western nuclear scientists and arms experts who worked closely with their Soviet counterparts), these non-government organizations (or NGOs) convinced Gorbachev that an arms builddown, rather than buildup, provided the most security. (The Pugwash group won the Nobel Peace Prize for its forty-year effort to stop the arms race.) In other words, private peace groups were perhaps more important than Reagan's military buildup in convincing Gorbachev to wind down the arms race.[66]

Gorbachev pressed Reagan to meet him at the summit. The first summit meeting in six years occurred during November 1985 in Geneva. The two men agreed in principle on a 50 percent cut in strategic forces and to reopen cultural exchange programs. In a whirlwind fourteen-hour meeting at Reykjavík, Iceland, in October 1986, they shocked the world by agreeing to eliminate all intermediate missiles (such as the Pershings) in Europe. They nearly agreed on eliminating almost all other nuclear missiles. But this last stunning proposal collapsed when Gorbachev demanded that it be linked to the U.S. termination of its "Star Wars" program and Reagan refused.

---

[66]This and the previous paragraph are based on Matthew Evangelista, *Unarmed Forces; The Transnational Movement to End the Cold War* (Ithaca, N.Y., 1999), especially chapters 11–14; Raymond L. Garthoff, "Letters to the Editor," *Foreign Affairs*, LXXIV (May/June 1995): 198; Paul Marantz, *From Lenin to Gorbachev* (Ottawa, 1988); Marantz's "Gorbachev's New Thinking," *Current History*, October 1988, pp. 3–6; FBIS, *Daily Report: Soviet Union* (Washington, February 17, 1987), pp. AA15–AA16; *Washington Post*, December 26, 1983, p. A3. Well-researched essays stressing the internal, rather than external, reasons for the Soviet collapse in the 1980s is a series of essays in the *Journal of Cold War Studies*, edited by Mark Kramer. Note especially those in the Volume 5, Fall 2003 issue.

A year later Gorbachev paid his first visit to Washington. The two men signed a treaty eliminating medium- and short-range nuclear missiles (that is, all those with a range of up to 3000 miles). This historic pact marked the first time an entire class of U.S. and Soviet nuclear weapons was not merely limited, but eliminated. In mid-1988 Reagan made a successful goodwill trip to Moscow. He and Gorbachev strolled arm-in-arm through Red Square. In December 1988 the Soviet leader returned to the United States and let the other, conventional-force, shoe drop: he announced that his armed forces would be reduced unilaterally by 500,000 men and 10,000 tanks in two years. Six tank divisions were to be withdrawn from East Germany. He also declared that Soviet law would be rewritten to ensure that no one would be persecuted for political or religious beliefs. As for "Star Wars," the United States had continued funding research, but Gorbachev concluded that Reagan's original plan was nearly dead—the victim of scientific realities, huge U.S. budget deficits, and the Pentagon's refusal to trust such a questionable system with the nation's security.[67]

These arms deals were astonishing, but also important were Gorbachev's economic and human rights proposals. Reagan later joked, "When I told him we should put our cards on the table, he took out his Visa and his Mastercard." For his part, the President said in Moscow that he believed the Soviets were no longer "an evil empire." He added, "We can look with optimism on future negotiations." After their first meeting in 1985, Reagan whispered to Gorbachev, "I bet the hardliners in both our countries are squirming."[68]

One of those hard-liners, Zbigniew Brzezinski (top adviser to former President Jimmy Carter), blasted people for "going bananas over Gorbachev simply because he happens to wear a clean shirt . . . and his wife does not look like a beast." But the persistent Gorbachev helped undercut hard-liners in both countries by allowing increased numbers of Soviet Jews to leave the U.S.S.R. Since 1969 the numbers of dissidents allowed to emigrate had

[67]Strobe Talbott, *The Master of the Game: Paul Nitze and the Nuclear Age* (New York, 1988), pp. 362–368; 374–383; *Washington Post,* December 8, 1988, p. A1.

[68]*Washington Post,* February 1, 1988, p. B8; *The New York Times* text of press conference, June 2, 1988, p. A16.

fluctuated according to U.S.-Soviet relations and how badly Moscow wanted an arms deal and economic help:

1967: 4498	1980: 21,471
1971: 13,022	1984: 896
1972: 31,681 (Nixon-Brezhnev	1986: 914
SALT I agreement)	1987: 8155
1975: 13,221	1988: 19,286[69]
1978: 28,864	1989: 70,000 (estimated)
1979: 51,320 (Carter-Brezhnev	
SALT II arrangement)	

Gorbachev's decisions amazed Westerners. Some U.S. officials simply could not see what was happening. The CIA frequently underestimated Gorbachev and overestimated Soviet power, perhaps because it was trapped in a Cold War mentality, perhaps also because it had been penetrated by a Soviet agent, Aldrich Ames. The CIA's top Soviet expert, Robert Gates, told a highly doubtful Secretary of State Shultz in 1986 that Gorbachev was nothing new, and that "the Soviet Union is a despotism that works." Gorbachev soon proved Gates wrong. For example, since 1946 Americans and Russians had waged wars, both hot and cold, to control key newly emerging regions. When he assumed power, Gorbachev increased Soviet commitments to such divided, war-wracked nations as Afghanistan and Angola. By 1986, however, he reversed course. These nations, along with Cuba, annually absorbed tens of billions of Soviet rubles with too little return for Moscow. Gorbachev disavowed Soviet-sponsored "wars of liberation" by declaring, "It is inadmissible and futile to encourage revolution from abroad." He angered Castro by repeating that policy in Cuba, then warned Castro to get his house in order because the Soviets could no longer pump in more than $10 million each day to keep the Cuban economy afloat.[70]

Peace began to break out on several fronts. Gorbachev supported a deal, patiently brokered by U.S. Assistant Secretary of State Chester Crocker, to stop the fourteen-year-old U.S.- and South

---

[69]*Congressional Quarterly,* February 25, 1989, p. 401; the Brzezinski quote is in Costigliola, *France and the United States,* p. 264.

[70]Fred Kaplan, "Soviets Recasting Foreign Policy," *Boston Globe,* April 10, 1988; *Time,* July 27, 1987, p. 40; *The New York Times,* August 7, 1988, p. 11; Shultz, *Turmoil and Triumph,* p. 703.

African-supported revolt against the Marxist Angolan government. Some 215,000 had died in the conflict. In return, the 30,000 Cuban troops who had protected the Angolan regime were to return home. It was a defeat for the Reagan Doctrine but a victory for U.S. and Soviet diplomacy, and especially for the long-suffering Crocker. Gorbachev also visited China to strengthen ties.

Most important, he pulled all 115,000 Soviet troops out of Afghanistan by early 1989. This "bleeding wound," as he termed it, had infected Soviet soldiers with drug addiction and alcoholism while claiming 15,000 Soviet (and 85,000 Afghan) lives. In the great (if short-term) triumph of the Reagan Doctrine, Washington had pumped in over $2 billion since 1979 to help the fundamentalist Moslem guerrillas fight the Soviet Army. The turn came in 1986 when, with strong support from Congress, the CIA gave the guerrillas Stinger antiaircraft missiles that could shoot down Soviet helicopter gunships. The irony was (as perhaps Gorbachev had calculated) that once the Red Army withdrew, the Afghans fell to fighting viciously among themselves. Numbers of Islamic fighters, led by a young, wealthy Saudi Arabian, Osama Bin Laden, began to turn their battle-tested skills (including, experts feared, their control of many Stinger antiaircraft missiles) against the United States and its allies. (See below, ch.15.) Bin Laden took advantage of the chaos that threatened when the Soviets left Afghanistan, and Americans simply pulled up stakes and went home. "Everybody was against the Russians," a guerrilla leader observed, "but now people are confused."[71]

Gorbachev not only escaped from these costly traps but redirected Soviet energies to profitable areas. Downplaying Angola and Nicaragua, he strengthened relations with India, Argentina, and Mexico—larger nations that offered economic as well as political benefits to him. Most significant, he launched a huge campaign to sweeten ties with Western Europe. Trips to Bonn, Paris, and London created "Gorby fever," and he used his popularity to call

---

[71]Christian Friedrich Ostermann, "New Evidence on the War in Afghanistan. Introduction," *Cold War International History Project Bulletin,* 14/15 (Winter 2003–Spring 2004), pp. 140–141, 166–172; *Washington Post,* December 23, 1988, p. A14; Ibid., October 4, 1986, p. A14, lists the sanctions; Matthew Evangelista, "'New Thinking' in Foreign Policy," *The Nation,* June 13, 1987, pp. 795–799; *The New York Times,* June 6, 1989, p. A4; Ibid., December 15, 1988, p. 27. Essential reading is John F. Burns, "Afghans: Now They Blame America," *The New York Times Magazine,* February 4, 1990, pp. 24–37.

for "a common European home" that stretched from Great Britain through the Soviet Union.[72]

The world was changing at a dizzying pace. In the early 1900s the great historian Henry Adams played with laws of physics to prove (to his own satisfaction) that the very pace of history had accelerated during the 1870–1910 era of the industrial revolution and Western imperialism. If Adams had been alive in the late 1980s, amid the incredible Soviet transformation, the rising powers of Western Europe and Japan, and the revolution brought to daily lives by computers, satellites, and bioscience, even he would have been left in wonderment at the increased speed and depth of change. In one area, however, Adams would have felt at home. Between 1900 and 1914 he was one of the few prominent Americans who, terrified by the possible catastrophes that could result from a disintegration of Russia, wanted to cooperate with the Russians and help them adjust peacefully to a new world. Most officials in the new George Bush administration were in agreement with Adams.

[72]Neil MacFarlane, "The USSR and the Third World," *The Harriman Institute Forum*, I (March 1988): 4–5; Mikhail Gorbachev, *Perestroika* (New York, 1987), p. 190; Alexander Yakovlev, *On the Edge of an Abyss* (Moscow, 1985), pp. 12, 33, 39, 142–146.

President Bush and British Prime Minister Margaret Thatcher confer in Colorado during August 1990 to plan what became known as the Persian Gulf War of early 1991.
(George Bush Presidential Library)

CHAPTER 13

A New World Order—Or the Age of Fragmentation? (1989–1993)

On December 25, 1991, the seventy-four-year-old Soviet Union disappeared as if by the stroke of a magician's wand. No one had predicted the timing or the exact nature of the disappearance, but one person had prophesied the breakup:

> I cannot but think . . . that the future growth of Russia . . . [is] not a little overrated. Without a civiliz[ing] of the hordes nominally extending the Russian dominion over so many latitudes and longitudes, they will add little to her real force, if they do not detract from it; and in the event of their civiliz[ing], and consequent increase, the overgrown empire, as in so many preceding instances, must fall into separate and independent states.[1]

So wrote former U.S. President James Madison in 1821. But Madison's prophesy instructed post-1989 Americans in yet another way. As the most important author of the Constitution in 1787, Madison had insisted on creating a flexible (and, as it turned out, federal) political system that could expand across a vast "empire," as he and his generation termed it. In the 1990s the United States survived as incomparably the world's greatest power. Russia meanwhile began to emerge from a nightmare of economic breakdown, rampant crime, and even civil war, to pose new problems for the United States. The Cold War was over, but the roots of the century-long competition between Americans and Russians remained,

---

[1]Madison to Richard Rush, November 20, 1821, in James Madison, *Letters and Other Writings of James Madison* (Philadelphia, 1867): III, pp. 235–236.

not least because of the thousands of nuclear weapons whose triggers were fingered by Moscow and Washington officials.

These two characteristics of the 1990s—the exceptional power of the United States and an increasingly frustrated, explosive Russia—were framed by a third theme: the political, ethnic, religious, and economic fragmentation of the global system. The divisions within the two superpowers' camps had begun in the 1950s (see p. 177), but with the end of the Cold War, the fragmentation seemed close to being out of control. The Soviet Union's fifteen members became a commonwealth of separate nations. Czechoslovakia and Yugoslavia splintered, African and Southeast Asian nations sank into domestic warfare, and even industrialized nations such as Canada, Italy, and India were threatened by major splits. New York Democrat Senator Daniel Patrick Moynihan worried in 1993 that ethnic division "promises to get savage. Get ready for 50 new countries in the world in the next 50 years. Most of them will be born in bloodshed."[2]

In their moment of Cold War triumph, Americans loved to honor their principle of self-determination, but that principle threatened to become dangerously unpredictable. As Russian Vice President Aleksandr Rutskoi worried in 1992, "More than 130 . . . ethnic groups live on Russia's territory, so that if this right [of self-determination] is implemented in practice, we may end up with more than 100 'banana republics.' " Rutskoi became increasingly willing to use armed force to prevent the existence of such "banana republics."[3] One authority noted that although the United Nations recognized that some 185 countries existed, they contained about 250 ethnic-religious groups who could argue for statehood.[4]

Americans were not immune to the growing disorder. Once the domestic pressures of opposing communism lifted, the Democratic and especially the Republican political parties lacked cohesion. Third parties became more popular. As the economy lost some of its Cold War underpinning, the gap between rich and middle-class incomes widened, and frustration deepened. More bloodily, so-called militias,

---

[2]David C. Rapoport, "Interventions and Ethno-Religious Violence; Self-Determination and Space," Working Paper No. 8, The Center for International Relations, UCLA (Los Angeles, 1994), especially pp. 6–7.
[3]*Foreign Broadcast Information Service—Russia,* January 21, 1992, p. 52.
[4]The analysis by David Binder and Barbara Crosette in *The New York Times,* February 7, 1993, p. 14, is a useful overview of the developing ethnic wars.

which advocated using armed violence if necessary to oppose U.S. laws, grew to between 10,000 and 40,000 members. One such fanatic was allegedly responsible for the deadly explosion of the Oklahoma City federal building that killed 169 people in 1995. Evangelical Christians became politically powerful in many states as they waged "cultural warfare" (in the words of one of their leaders) on post-Cold War American society. The head of the Christian Coalition, Ralph Reed, explained the reason for this new, more fragmented America: "The truth is, the ends of wars bring the most divisive politics recorded in American history." Reed believed that "the old dichotomies of liberal-conservative, internationalist-isolationist, dove-hawk are breaking apart. There are some ideological categories being formed that don't have any history in the politics of the Cold War." He emphasized the pivotal point: "The end of wars don't [sic] bring stability. They [sic] bring chaos and recriminations. Postwar eras are periods of an enormous realigning of political lines."[5]

George Bush and Bill Clinton became the first U.S. Presidents who had to deal with this fragmenting world and a new, less predictable Russia, while facing a primary problem: quieting the anger and bridging growing divisions in American society so that the country could survive and prosper in an increasingly fragmented, but also interdependent, world.

Raised in wealth by an athletically talented mother and a father who had been an international banker and a U.S. Senator, George Herbert Walker Bush had been the Navy's youngest flier in World War II. He became a hero after being shot down and rescued, and then returned to fly 1200 more combat hours. Making his fortune in Texas oil, Bush used Houston as a base for helping to create the modern Texas Republican party. One of his closest friends, especially on the tennis court, was James Baker, a well-off scion of an old-money, politically powerful Houston family. Some work in African-American and Hispanic neighborhoods helped Bush broaden a virtually nonexistent party, and in 1966 he won election to Congress. A run for the Senate failed, but between 1971 and 1981 he gained wide experience as ambassador to the United Nations, U.S. representative in China, head of the CIA, then Vice President. He earned the reputation of being in the moderate, pragmatic wing of Republicanism. In foreign policy, however, he had at times been an arch-Cold Warrior, as in 1965 when he declared that "I will back the President no matter what weapons we use in Southeast Asia," or in 1980 when at times his anticommunist rhetoric was actually stronger than Reagan's.[6]

Bush named Baker as his secretary of state. Baker had managed several of Bush's campaigns, including the politically brutal dissection of Democratic nominee Michael Dukakis in 1988. Known as "a political genius" with "the perfect Washington résumé" (White House chief of staff, secretary of the treasury, proven political operator, masterful manipulator of the press), Baker knew little about foreign affairs. Admitting he was "more interested in the game than in philosophy," and neither profound nor deeply reflective about foreign affairs, Baker was as fine a politician as anyone who had sat in the secretary's chair since William Seward in Lincoln's administration. Bush's national security adviser, General Brent Scowcroft, was more reflective but highly cautious and a specialist in arms control—a subject of declining importance as Gorbachev disarmed. Baker had a tight group of four younger persons surrounding him whose political talents few disputed, but whose ability to shift forty-five years of U.S. foreign policy—and move a huge, stolid bureaucracy to shift with it—remained to be seen. A senior official warned, "Neither Bush nor Baker reads history." Much historical memory disappeared, moreover, when Baker rather savagely fired George Shultz's highly successful professional staff and replaced it with his own close associates, few of whom knew much about the U.S.S.R.[7]

Baker's political skills stunningly appeared when he dealt quickly with the Central American questions that had torn apart American politics, and, finally, the Reagan administration, in the 1980s. The secretary of state realized that the Nicaraguan contras, whom Reagan had created and lauded as "freedom fighters," were actually losers, and that they were not worth more struggles with Congress. Baker resolved to disband the contras in return for a Sandinista pledge to hold an open

---

[6]Randall Rothenberg, "In Search of George Bush," *The New York Times Magazine*, March 6, 1988, pp. 29–49; David Hoffman's analysis in *Washington Post*, December 7, 1988, p. A26; Ibid., May 3, 1979, p. A2.
[7]George Bush and Brent Scowcroft, *A World Transformed* (New York, 1998), p. 20; John Newhouse, "Profiles: The Tactician," *The New Yorker*, May 7, 1990, pp. 50–51; Jack F. Matlock, Jr., *Autopsy on an Empire* (New York, 1995), p. 185.

election in February 1990. It was a calculated gamble that the Sandinistas would lose the election, a gamble most observers thought Baker would lose. But he covered his bet by receiving Gorbachev's assurances that the Soviets would cut off arms aid to Nicaragua and pressure the Sandinistas to abide by the election results. Baker threw the dice—and won. The Sandinistas lost to a coalition led by Violeta Chamorro, a revered newspaper publisher, and surrendered power. In 1991 Baker scored a similar victory by pushing the bloodstained right-wing government in El Salvador to make peace with the leftist revolutionary FMLN. Again the Soviets cooperated. Another hero was the former Costa Rican President, Oscar Arias, whose 1987 peace plan Baker followed but seldom mentioned.[8]

Highly visible beneath this velvet-gloved diplomacy was an iron fist. On December 20, 1989, as Gorbachev was renouncing both the use of force and Soviet imperialism, Bush used massive force and raised memories of U.S. imperialism by invading Panama with 27,000 troops. It was the largest U.S. military operation since the Vietnam War. Bush said he invaded to shield the Panama Canal; protect U.S. citizens (a U.S. Marine had been killed on Panama's streets, and other Americans had been attacked); halt the vast drug traffic through Panama; and capture Manuel Noriega, the dictator who had defied Reagan and Bush. Critics doubted these reasons. No case was convincingly made that the Canal was threatened. U.S. citizens endangered in other countries were protected without overthrowing governments and losing between 250 and 1200 (mostly civilian) lives. Drug traffickers had other routes to out-of-control American drug users; indeed, drug traffic through Panama actually increased after the invasion. Other reasons seemed more important. Observers noted Bush's statement that Noriega was an "enormous" personal "frustration," recalled how the President had been termed a "wimp" for not removing Noriega when a chance arose several months earlier, and concluded that Bush's motives were personal and political.

Two results of the invasion were of special interest. First, the President had not consulted Congress before going to war with Panama, and neither the Senate nor the House ever cared enough to investigate

---

[8]U.S. Department of State, "Secretary Baker: Democracy and American Diplomacy," *Current Policy*, no. 1266; Don Oberdorfer, *The Turn: From the Cold War to a New Era. The U.S. and the Soviet Union 1983–1990* (New York, 1991), pp. 268–270, 338–342.

thoroughly the causes and bloody consequences of his decision. Bush's foreign-policy powers approached those of the 1960s imperial Presidency. Second, although the President and Congress promised much aid to the new Panamanian regime, little was forthcoming. The United States, as Bush admitted, had the "will" but not the "wallet." The nation's economic decline was affecting its ability to help its friends. The U.S.-installed Panamanian government meanwhile proved inept and depended on U.S. military help to put down its own army's revolts. Corruption, laundered drug money, and unemployment plagued Panamanians—so much so that they asked the U.S. military not to move its bases (and its dollars) out of the country on December 31, 1999, as the 1977–1978 treaties provided (see p. 306). With Cold War threats over, however, and the Canal losing its importance in a new age of supertankers and ship-railroad systems, Americans were also losing their interest in Panamanians.[9] On schedule, the United States turned the Canal over to Panama in late 1999, while retaining the right to protect the waterway in any crisis.

Unlike his handling of Panama, Bush approached Gorbachev and the rapidly evolving Soviet bloc with a caution that puzzled observers. His presidency seemed to become schizophrenic. One part was a "personal" presidency marked by a dizzying pace of meetings, globetrotting, golf, jogging, and fishing. The sixty-five-year-old Bush always seemed to be in motion. His hero was Theodore Roosevelt, whose picture now hung in the White House, and the new President clearly followed TR's booming call to "the strenuous life." But the other was a cautious, even passive presidency when it came to making complex policy decisions.[10] His attitude of "Let's wait and see whether it will work out on its own" became most noticeable on domestic issues. He took much the same approach as the most important event of the last half of the twentieth century, the disintegration of the Soviet Empire, unfolded.

[9]Richard E. Cohen, "Marching Through the War Powers Act," *National Journal,* December 30, 1989, p. 3120; *The New York Times,* January 21, 1990, p. E3, February 11, 1990, p. 20, and January 18, 1992, p. 5; *Washington Post,* February 4, 1995, p. A14; Eytan Gilboa, "The Panama Invasion Revisited," *Political Science Quarterly,* 110 (Winter 1995–96): 551–559.

[10]Charles O. Jones, "Meeting Low Expectations." In Colin Campbell and Bert A. Rockman, eds., *The Bush Presidency; First Appraisals* (Chatham, N.J., 1991), pp. 37–59.

In March 1989, two months after Bush took office, Gorbachev held the first free elections in the Soviet Union since 1917. They resulted in humiliating defeats for the Communist party candidates running for the new national legislature. Discontent spread as perestroika did nothing to stop the sliding economy. One official tagged it the "'Perestroikamobile': the key is in the ignition . . . but it has not moved." The danger grew that the Soviet Union itself would fall apart, creating chaos and the possibility that its 30,000 nuclear warheads would fall into the wrong hands. This danger had many sources, including the pluralistic, multiracial population that stretched across eleven time zones; the hatred of many of these people for the Great Russians, who had long dominated the central government; long-smouldering religious hatreds; and Gorbachev's reforms that decentralized power but produced economic disasters. Conservatives warned that only brutal Stalinist methods could force the Russian people to work harder. Others, including many in the West, argued that, to the contrary, the economy would improve only when Gorbachev turned completely to free markets and thus destroyed the Communist party—a move that the Soviet leader, a committed communist, refused to take.[11]

Bush's response to these dramatic events was to do little in early 1989. He declared that his advisers were carefully analyzing the situation. After five months the results were finally announced: U.S. policy would be "status-quo plus," an empty term, given the immense changes going on, that was quickly ridiculed. In a speech at Texas A&M University in May, Bush declared that the 1947 containment policy had worked, but before the U.S.S.R. could be allowed into the Western community, Gorbachev had to meet a series of conditions—including sharply reducing Soviet involvement in Eastern Europe and the Third World. He valued his personal friendship with Gorbachev. (Bush often seemed to want to deal with foreign leaders as if they were old school chums.) He certainly did not want to see Gorbachev's central government dissolve. On the other hand, U.S. officials could not figure out how to help Gorbachev, given the growing demands on a stumbling U.S. economy and his commitment to communism. Bush's confusion

---

[11]"The Nationalities Policy of the Party in Present-Day Conditions," *Reprints from the Soviet Press,* October 31, 1989, p. 22; Angela Stent, "Doctrinal Discord," *New Republic,* January 8 and 15, 1990, p. 17; *The New York Times,* January 1, 1990, p. 33.

grew for another reason: Gorbachev was ending the Cold War and, especially, the obvious need for the Americans' NATO military presence in Europe where "Gorbymania" was rampant. The United States had little other leverage over a booming Western Europe that was already moving away from Washington. As Secretary of Defense Richard Cheney admitted in 1989, the reduced Soviet threat "makes it more difficult for us to maintain the kind of cohesion and unity within the Alliance" that had existed.[12]

Gorbachev then stunned Bush in the autumn of 1989 by more than meeting the President's demands. In April the Solidarity movement became a legal noncommunist political party in Poland. Solidarity had clout; since 1981 it had been led by Lech Walesa, a shipyard welder who had won the Nobel Peace Prize for trying to reform Poland nonviolently. In July Gorbachev publicly destroyed the Brezhnev Doctrine, and protected Walesa, by declaring that it was "inadmissible" for one nation forcibly to "restrain the sovereignty" of another. He was admitting that the Soviets could no longer afford to fix the failures of the East European regimes. Their people lacked food while West Europeans enjoyed both food and VCRs—a gap in living standards glaringly shown in television and newspapers that filtered through the Iron Curtain. But Gorbachev also believed that left on their own, the East European reformers—good communists like himself—would triumph and keep the party in power in a better, happier Eastern Europe. The Brezhnev Doctrine, a Moscow official said, was to be replaced with the "Sinatra Doctrine"—that is, East Europeans could do things "their way."[13]

The results were electric. Solidarity put Gorbachev to the test by demanding a dominant voice in the Polish government. Flustered Polish communists called Gorbachev for help and advice. There was no help, only advice: the Poles were on their own. The dam had been broken. Or, more accurately, the communist dominoes began to topple. As Solidarity won stunning election victories in Poland, fresh winds of

[12]Michael Cox, "From Super Power Détente to Entente Cordiale?" in Bruce George, ed., *Jane's NATO Handbook*, 3rd ed. (Surrey, U.K., 1990), pp. 278–279; Oberdorfer, *The Turn*, p. 333. For the internal Bush administration debate, see Bush and Scowcroft, *World Transformed*, pp. 152–155.

[13]The background is in *The New York Times*, December 11, 1989, p. D10; Richard Barnet, "After the Cold War," *The New Yorker*, January 1, 1990, pp. 66–69; and Larry Martz, "Into a Brave New World," *Newsweek*, December 25, 1989, p. 40; the "Sinatra" reference is in Oberdorfer, *The Turn*, p. 355.

change also blew in Hungary, which already had the bloc's most liberal economic system. Reformers drove out communists and free elections were set for 1990. When the new Hungarian regime opened its doors to the West in September 1989, East Germans flooded through Hungary into West Germany. The East German communists could not control the chaos, and this time, unlike 1953, Gorbachev ensured that the Red Army would not do it for them. Old regimes also collapsed in Czechoslovakia (where hundreds of thousands of young people lay siege to Prague streets for weeks until a noncommunist government gained power) and Bulgaria. The changes occurred with surprisingly little violence except in Romania,[14] where longtime dictator Nicolae Ceauşescu defied reformers and, along with his wife, was quickly executed. Most dramatically, on November 9, 1989, Communist East Germany suddenly opened the Berlin Wall, perhaps the Cold War's best known and most hated symbol. The twelve-foot-high barrier was then destroyed by workers, and pieces were sold for high prices by the new capitalists, while Germans sang their version of "For He's a Jolly Good Fellow." Under the "Sinatra Doctrine," Gorbachev had refused to use the Red Army, so East European communism collapsed. A surprised CIA director in Washington admitted, "It is going much faster than anyone might have anticipated."[15]

By the end of these astonishing events in 1989, Bush had thrown his political support fully behind Gorbachev. But this misled. The President could not deliver the massive economic aid that the Soviet leader needed. Indeed, although Secretary of State Baker admitted that the Soviet leaders were panicked and "men in a hurry" to solve their problems before they were destroyed by the onrushing chaos, the United States even refused to grant the U.S.S.R. most-favored-nation (mfn) trade status, which would give preference to Soviet goods in the U.S. market. Bush, however, did grant mfn status to China, even after the aged Chinese communists brought in tanks and bloodily smashed student demonstrations for democratic changes in June 1989. U.S. officials demanded immediate economic and emigration reforms before they would give similar trade preferences to the Soviets. The Bush administration, moreover, had no idea

---

[14]Through much of the post-1945 years, Rumania was the common spelling; following Ceauşescu's execution, the people of that country preferred Romania.

[15]Janine R. Wedel, "Lech's Labors Lost?" *World Monitor,* II (November 1989): 44–45; *Washington Post,* November 4, 1989, p. A4; Ibid., January 15, 1990, p. A12. The useful background account is in *The Chicago Tribune*'s special publication, *Communism: A World of Change* (1989).

Turning Points in Eastern Europe, 1989

EAST GERMANY
Nov.

POLAND
Aug.

SOVIET UNION

WEST GERMANY

CZECHOSLOVAKIA
Nov.

AUSTRIA

HUNGARY
Oct.

ROMANIA
Dec.

YUGOSLAVIA

ITALY

BULGARIA
Nov.

Key dates in the transition from communist domination

how to devise a policy that could replace the forty-three-year-old containment policy. In 1947 Mr. "X" (George Kennan) had argued that containment would lead to "the breakup or mellowing" of the Soviet Union (see p. 71). Now confronted by the "breakup" and potential chaos, U.S. officials grew worried. Even the eighty-five-year-old Kennan warned that the dangerous "disintegration," especially in East Germany, had to be stopped "one way or other."[16]

[16]The late William Appleman Williams noted the links between containment and 1989–1990 affairs; and Paul Dukes's seminal *The Last Great Game: USA Versus USSR* (London, 1989), especially chapters 7 and 8, is most helpful. *The New York Times,* January 18, 1990, p. A8, has excerpts of Kennan's testimony. Oberdorfer, *The Turn,* pp. 369–370, has Baker's quote.

A broad debate erupted in the United States over how to respond to these shocks. One popular argument was Francis Fukuyama's "end-of-history" thesis. Fukuyama, who served in Bush's State Department, argued that the Cold War was over and "political liberalism" had totally whipped communism. The great historical struggles between competing ideologies had ended with capitalism's triumph. Critics, however, warned that far from meaning the "end of history," communism's fall could mean the return of the unpredictable, combustible history of pre-1914 that had produced two world wars. Other critics admonished that there was not a single capitalism, but many different kinds—and that in the past, as in the case of the United States and Japan, they had dangerously clashed. One U.S. official began to worry that the world was beginning to look more like "1939" than "1989."[17]

This vigorous debate did not seem to influence Bush. He and Gorbachev took major steps toward reducing the number of nuclear missiles and banning the production of chemical weapons. But they could not agree on how to deal with that historical dilemma sitting at the heart of Europe—Germany—which was rushing toward reunification now that the Berlin Wall was rubble. Gorbachev wanted no unified Germany and demanded that if it did unify, it must not be a NATO member. Bush's position was more complex. For decades Western leaders had said they supported German unification; they did so because they privately thought it would not occur. Now that it was about to happen, the leaders of France and Great Britain secretly begged Gorbachev not to allow it. Bush was also fearful. He finally supported unification, but he also sent Baker to ask East German officials to slow their merger with West Germany. Matters, however, were out of all these leaders' hands. Germany's unification movement, propelled by history and a rich West Germany that offered to rebuild a devastated East, developed a momentum of its own. In July 1990 Gorbachev and West German leader Helmut Kohl made their own deals—some of which (such as forbidding NATO maneuvers in the former East German area) Bush did not like. The President nevertheless wisely decided to support a Germany that was "whole and

---

[17]Francis Fukuyama, "The End of History?" *The National Interest*, no. 16 (Summer 1989): 3–18; *Washington Post*, December 23, 1989, p. A11; see also "Z," "To the Stalin Mausoleum," *Daedalus*, CIL (Winter 1990): 295–340; Martin Sherwin, "Gorby and Z," *The Nation*, February 12, 1990, p. 189. Fukuyama acknowledged the multiplicity of capitalisms in his later book, *The End of History and the Last Man* (New York, 1990), especially pp. 122–128.

free"—but to tie it to the West through NATO, as well as through the flourishing European Economic Community. Gorbachev had to agree; in return he demanded that the Germans limit their army to 370,000 troops, continue to swear off nuclear weapons, and give up former German lands once and for all by agreeing to the German-Polish border set in 1945. Gorbachev also now played down his "common European home" theme and literally begged Bush to retain U.S. power in Europe to keep a close eye on Germany.[18]

Bush and Baker, along with other observers, were again surprised in February 1990 when Gorbachev overrode bitter hard-line resistance and broke the Communist party's monopoly on power for the first time since 1917. In the spring, noncommunists won sweeping victories, including the election of Boris Yeltsin to the head of the Russian Federation, the largest by far of the fifteen Soviet republics. Gorbachev had purged Yeltsin from the Moscow party leadership in 1987 because the upstart demanded more rapid reforms. Yeltsin now had the beginning of his revenge: he had been legitimately elected by the people while Gorbachev, although the U.S.S.R.'s President, had not been. Gorbachev had been put in office by party functionaries. Hard-line communists now moved to stop the reforms. In January 1991 tough Interior Ministry troops killed fifteen people while using force to keep Lithuania in the U.S.S.R. Gorbachev tried to placate the hard-liners with appointments and his refusal to move even more rapidly toward free-market policies.

Clearly, Yeltsin was legitimate, wanted to undertake far-reaching democratic reforms and arms reductions, and was surrounded by young advisers who were also tough and prodemocratic. He was ready to assume power. But the White House instead demanded that no U.S. government official build up Yeltsin or undercut Gorbachev. "It has become a Gorbachev-centered foreign policy," a U.S. diplomat observed, but there was no conceptual thinking about "where his disintegrating country might be headed." Bush had grown dependent on his personal friendship with Gorbachev and had grown deeply suspicious of Yeltsin, who threatened to break up Gorbachev's

---

[18]Bush and Scowcroft, *World Transformed*, pp. 249–258, 279–292; Frank Costigliola, "An 'Arm Around the Shoulder': The United States, NATO and German Reunification, 1989–90," *Contemporary European History*, III, no. 1 (1994): 100–108; Oberdorfer, *The Turn*, p. 381; Cox, "From Super Power Détente," p. 281; Martz "Into a Brave New World," p. 42.

central control—and who also had appeared to be both an alcoholic and a boor during an unfortunate visit to Washington. U.S. ambassador to Moscow Jack Matlock watched Gorbachev sinking and Yeltsin rising, then urged Baker to deal with both men. But White House "apologists" for Gorbachev, as Matlock called them, refused his good advice. Critics instead snickered that Yeltsin's most important American friend was Jack Daniel.[19]

Bush's inability to take advantage of the Soviet opportunities was not because of America's public opinion. Perhaps the President's great caution was caused by the inability of himself and his top advisers, all of whom had grown up in the Cold War, to imagine a world without the Soviets or a Cold War. Perhaps it was because Bush, Cheney, Baker, and Scowcroft had all been involved with Gerald Ford in 1976 when détente turned sour and Ford went down to defeat in the presidential election. Perhaps it was due to the administration's fear that if Yeltsin won, the Soviet Union could become so chaotic as to present new dangers.[20]

A military crisis did arise, but it had little to do with the Soviet Union. On August 2, 1990, Saddam Hussein, the military ruler of Iraq, invaded the neighboring oil kingdom of Kuwait. Saddam was then poised, U.S. officials feared, for an invasion of Saudi Arabia, oil-rich and since the 1940s a close ally of Washington's. Saddam took Kuwait for many reasons. He hated the Kuwait-Iraq boundary line (actually imposed on Iraq by British imperial officials in 1922) because it largely cut him off from the sea. He hated the Kuwaitis for pumping large amounts of oil, and thus keeping prices low, when he needed to sell high-priced oil from his wells to pay off a huge debt he had incurred during an incredibly bloody eight-year war against Iran. He aimed ultimately at dominating the Arab world. And finally, he believed that the United States and its allies would not respond.

After Saddam came to power in a 1968 military coup, the United States had normal relations with his regime. When the 1978–1979 Iranian revolution destroyed U.S.-Iranian relations, the Reagan administration

[19]*Washington Post*, February 13, 1990, p. A1; privileged interview, February 11, 1992; John Morrison, *Boris Yeltsin* (New York, 1991), pp. 56–73; Stephen White, *Gorbachev and After* (New York, 1991), pp. 68–69, 167; Matlock, *Autopsy on an Empire*, pp. 508–509; Michael R. Beschloss and Strobe Talbott, *At the Highest Levels* (Boston, 1993), p. 105.
[20]*The New York Times*, December 2, 1989, p. 33; Ibid., February 3, 1992, p. A8; *Washington Post*, February 13, 1990, p. A1; Newhouse, "Profiles: The Tactician," p. 76.

moved much closer to Saddam. In 1981, a fearful Israel destroyed the dictator's plant for developing nuclear weapons. But Washington supported the UN condemnation of Israel. During 1983, Reagan sent Donald Rumsfeld (George W. Bush's Secretary of Defense after 2001) to assure Saddam that the United States would regard "any major reversal of Iraq's fortunes as a strategic defeat for the West." This was said even though U.S. officials knew Saddam was using outlawed chemical and biological weapons against Iran. Later in the 1980s, the Reagan administration provided top-secret intelligence to Saddam, despite knowing he was using chemical agents against not only Iranian forces, but some of his own people who were siding with Iran. This was part of his "scorched-earth" strategy to kill inhabitants of entire villages. The Pentagon "wasn't so horrified by Iraqi use of [outlawed] gas", said one American who was involved. "It was just another way of killing people . . . , it didn't make any difference." The United States helped Saddam develop his chemical and biological weapons for which, in part, Americans condemned and overthrew him in 2003. They also gave him $40-billion worth of arms in the 1980s to fight Iran, nearly all of it on credit.

And until hours before the invasion, U.S. officials said privately to him and publicly to Congress that while Bush and Baker did not want force used, they would not take any position on the Iraqi-Kuwaiti boundary dispute and did not want to become involved. Not that Americans had illusions; they knew that Saddam had personally executed political opponents, had hung their bodies on meat hooks for public display, had publicly threatened "to make fire eat half of Israel" (the closest U.S. ally in the region), and had ordered tens of thousands of his young people to die in suicidal attacks against Iran. It was just that to Washington Iran, not Iraq, seemed more of a danger. Reagan and Bush, moreover, sent billions of dollars of arms and food to the brutal dictator to keep him apart from the Russians. American farmers and arms dealers, who happily profited, raised no objections. "We looked like fools," a high U.S. State Department official admitted, for not anticipating the invasion.[21]

---

[21]The last two paragraphs are based on *The New York Times*, October 18, 2002, p. A1; Ibid., December 8, 2002, p. 2 wk; *Washington Post*, December 30, 2002, p. A1; the superb account by Bruce W. Jentleson, *With Friends Like These* (New York, 1994), pp. 14–16, 94–97, 132–171; Judith Miller and Laurie Mylorie, *Saddam Hussein and the Crisis in the Gulf* (New York, 1990), pp. 3–23; Daniel Yergin, *The Prize: The Epic Quest for Oil, Money, and Power* (New York, 1991), pp. 770–775; the U.S. official is quoted in *Washington Post*, October 28, 1991, p. A9.

Bush again responded cautiously for several days. Kuwait, after all, had been the most pro-Soviet and anti-Israel state in the entire region. But he was pushed especially by the tough British prime minister, Margaret Thatcher, who happened to be in Colorado meeting with Bush when the invasion occurred. Her country profited from billions of dollars of Kuwaiti investments and bank deposits. "George," Thatcher told Bush bluntly, "this is no time to go wobbly." Both U.S. and British policies were dictated by domestic needs and interests. Bush also believed that the world's price of oil, and therefore the control of the world economy, was at stake. He decided, moreover, that it was 1938 and Munich all over again: if this "Hitler," as Bush called Saddam, succeeded, the world would be pushed back to a 1930s state of affairs, when aggressors ran rampant. He spelled out the meaning: "What is at stake is more than one small country, it is a big idea—a new world order" where "peace and security, freedom and the rule of law" reign. (Bush's outline of this new world order can be read in his 1991 State of the Union address in the chapter XIII documents at the www.mhhe.com/lafeber website.)

With help from Gorbachev and, especially, the British, Bush mobilized the United Nations to resist, although he was actually in full command of the UN effort. Japan and Germany, which had cut their own deals with Middle East oil producers, were reluctant to help, but Bush extracted $13 billion from Tokyo and $11 billion from Bonn. He even went to Congress (unlike all other post-1945 U.S. Presidents) and after a hard-fought battle obtained a constitutional authorization for war. (Bush later spoiled this victory by declaring, incorrectly, that he had the "inherent right" to take the country to war without congressional authorization.) The President carefully reassured his able chairman of the Joint Chiefs of Staff, General Colin Powell, that this time—unlike in Vietnam—the military would be allowed to fight its war and fight to victory. Powell used U.S. airpower and technology spectacularly. After a month of bombing, 550,000 U.S.-UN forces unleashed "Operation Desert Storm" on February 27, 1991. In 100 hours they liberated Kuwait and occupied southern Iraq. Saddam had threatened to wage "the Mother of all battles," but instead faced massive defeat.[22]

---

[22]Theodore Draper, "Presidential Wars," *New York Review of Books*, September 26, 1991, pp. 64–74; Yergin, *The Prize*, pp. 775–779; Bush and Scowcroft, *World Transformed*, pp. 319–321.

Of the Americans 146 were killed; the estimated Iraqi death toll ran as high as 100,000, many of them civilian. Bush waited for Saddam to leave or for the Iraqis to overthrow him. Neither occurred. A blunder in U.S. military planning allowed most of Saddam's elite troops to escape. The dictator's chemical- and nuclear-weapons projects were not destroyed. A year later Saddam held a survival celebration in Baghdad. Bush had also held back in fear that if he obliterated Iraq, Iran's Islamic regime would emerge as the unchecked regional power—especially if, as many (including America's Arab allies) feared, the removal of Saddam's iron fist would allow Iraq to collapse into civil war among its Islamic factions.

Bush and Powell had liberated Kuwait, but U.S. diplomacy had failed to anticipate or stop the invasion, and U.S. strategy had failed to remove the cause: Saddam. Secretary of State Baker did use the military success to forge a historic Middle East peace conference in which, for the first time, Israeli and Arab officials talked to each other about a lasting settlement in the war-torn region. Baker threw himself into his Middle East travels. (Bush joked, "Baker has a sign on his door. It reads '10 to 3.' They're not his hours, but his odds of not being there."[23])

During the Iraqi war Gorbachev had cooperated with Bush, but Soviet Army officers, who had helped equip and train the Iraqis, supported Saddam to the bitter end. One Soviet general even predicted that "The war in the Gulf will end in a major U.S. defeat." Embarrassed by the Iraqis' collapse, and humiliated both by Gorbachev's withdrawal from Eastern Europe and by German reunification (which seemed to throw into question even the great Russian victory in 1945), Soviet military officers moved closer to frustrated civilian conservatives who wanted to get rid of Gorbachev. Several opponents even charged that he was secretly dealing with Bush to make the U.S.S.R. totally dependent on the United States. Gorbachev, however, was also feeling pressure from his left, especially from Yeltsin and other leaders of the fifteen republics which were moving toward independence. In July 1991 Gorbachev agreed with nine of these republics on a treaty for a historic new, looser union in which the

---

[23]William Schneider, "Vietnam Syndrome Is Alive and Well," *National Journal*, April 13, 1991, p. 902; *Washington Post*, January 12, 1992, p. C1. The much-argued reasons why Saddam survived are discussed in a useful essay on important books about the war: Robert Divine, "The Persian Gulf War Revisited," *Diplomatic History*, 24 (Winter 2000): 129–138.

'HOW COZY IT IS ON THESE COLD WINTER EVENINGS, TO SNUGGLE DOWN IN FRONT OF
TV AND WATCH THE WAR.'

republics would be termed "sovereign," instead of "socialist," states
as in the past. The treaty was to be signed on August 20, 1991.[24]

Hours before that ceremony, the hard-liners struck. They placed
Gorbachev under house arrest and tried to clamp Stalinist restrictions
on the press and people. Yeltsin and his Russian government held out
in a Moscow building not far from the Kremlin. They defied the
takeover. When the army was ordered to take control of the building
and other outlying areas where opposition was rising, the military
split. The army refused to fire on Yeltsin and several hundred thousand supporters (who were mostly older people—younger students
did not appear in number to face down communist repression as they
had in Czechoslovakia or China). Meanwhile the coup-plot leaders
were disorganized, and, it turned out, some were quite drunk. Nor
could they lie about their failures: the new technology of CNN television news, fax machines, and satellite pictures kept the world's eyes

---

[24]*Wall Street Journal,* March 20, 1991, p. 8; *The New York Times,* December 26, 1991, p.
A13; Ibid., October 7, 1991, p. A7; Cox, "From Super Power Détente to Entente Cor-
diale?" pp. 282–283; *Foreign Broadcast Information Service,—Soviet Union—Economic,*
April 24, 1991, p. 37.

riveted on Moscow's streets. But Bush and his NSC adviser, General Scowcroft, were confused. The State Department, whose professionals Baker had largely shunted aside, was unable to help. The White House even came close to recognizing the desperate right-wing coup when Scowcroft declared "we should not 'burn our bridges' with them." Bush was luckily saved from such foolishness when Gorbachev refused to join the plotters. The entire plan began to collapse. Some plotters tried to flee and were captured. Others committed suicide. Gorbachev reappeared in triumph, but Yeltsin emerged with the new, decisive power. Gorbachev was blamed for having placed the coup-plotters in their government positions. As Yeltsin began systematically to uproot Communist party strength, Gorbachev finally resigned from the party and moved to disband the powerful Central Committee.[25]

The hard-liners' perfect failure, and Gorbachev's beheading of the party, meant that communism had ended in the Soviet Union with a whimper, more in farce than tragedy. The larger question became whether Gorbachev himself could survive at the top. Bush seemed to be doing all he could to save his friend. While the White House issued stories about Yeltsin's boorishness and "ego," Bush, on August 1, 1991, stunned the Ukrainian legislature, which was set to quit the Soviet Union, by telling it that the 52 million Ukrainians (a population twice the size of Canada's) should remain under Gorbachev. (That comment, and the President's appeasement of China's brutal leaders, led conservative columnist George Will to charge that Bush preferred "order before freedom.") The U.S. leader tried to help his Soviet counterpart by slashing nuclear weapons costs; he pulled out nuclear artillery shells from Europe, tactical nuclear weapons from warships, and the nuclear-armed B-52 bombers from their round-the-clock airborne alert (where they had been since Eisenhower's presidency). Both sides further cut the number of nuclear missiles and warheads, and also conventional forces, in Europe in 1991.[26]

Neither Gorbachev nor Bush, however, could revive the disastrous Soviet economy. A Russian's per capita annual income had

[25]Matlock, *Autopsy on an Empire*, pp. 585–595; *The New York Times*, August 25, 1991, pp. 1, 16; *Washington Post*, August 30, 1991, p. A29; Ibid., August 23, 1991, p. A27; Richard Barnet, "Reflections; The Disorders of Peace," *The New Yorker*, January 20, 1992, p. 69; Bush and Scowcroft, *World Transformed*, pp. 515–517.

[26]Will's quote is in *Washington Post*, January 12, 1992, p. C7; Ibid., June 21, 1991, p. A20; *The New York Times*, October 7, 1991, editorial. Bush's Kiev speeches can be read in the chapter XIII documents at this book's www.mhhe.com/lafeber website.

dropped to one-tenth that of an American's $19,780, and was falling. In 1990 the U.S.S.R. had one of its greatest grain harvests, but starvation threatened because handling and transportation were so bad that 40 percent of the crop rotted or was eaten by worms and rats. As production fell, the state paid bills by printing more money, which in turn triggered runaway inflation. As the ruble became worthless, Russians turned to a primitive barter economy. Vodka became a kind of exchange currency. Lacking money to purchase medicines, and as antiquated pharmaceutical plants were closed because they endangered the environment, even the most basic drugs such as aspirin often could not be found. The world's largest oil producer (11.5 million barrels daily in 1990) was about to become an importer of oil because of broken-down wells. Bush tried to help, especially at West European urging, but the United States could not afford to send much aid, and even the $4 billion of credit he offered for the purchase of U.S. food was dribbled out too little, too late. U.S. private investment did increase after the coup's failure. Pepsico (Pepsi-Cola, Frito, Pizza Hut) had more than $3 billion invested, General Motors had $1 billion, and Chevron continued its hunt for oil, while Colgate planned a toothpaste factory after noting that 280 million Russians are "a lot of teeth." But most U.S. ventures were dormant or losing money.[27]

Gorbachev had made several critical mistakes. He assumed the fifteen republics and 120-plus ethnic groups would remain loyal to the central government. He fatally underestimated the power of nationalism and ethnicity. Gorbachev also assumed that given some liberty and democracy, the Soviet people would work harder for the communist system—as he had. But they had been more terrorized or bought off by the system than loyal to it.

Yeltsin quickly took power from the politically wounded Gorbachev. In December the Russian Federation, Ukraine, and Belarus declared their independence and formed a Commonwealth of Independent States (CIS). By the end of 1991 eleven of the fifteen former Soviet republics had joined the CIS. Only the Baltic States and Georgia's reactionary regime remained apart. When Yeltsin's Russia refused to pay Gorbachev's bills, the president found himself without a government. On December 25, 1991, he announced his resignation over national television. He had

---

[27]*The New York Times,* February 4, 1991, p. A1; Ibid., January 14, 1992, p. D2; Ibid., September 1, 1991, p. 6F; *Washington Post,* January 30, 1991, p. F3; Ibid., August 15, 1991, p. A41.

Trying to Control Nuclear Weapons, 1963–1993

Date	Treaty	
August 1963	Limited Test Ban Treaty	Prohibits nuclear testing or any other nuclear explosions in the atmosphere, in outer space, and under water.
January 1967	Outer Space Treaty	Prohibits sending nuclear weapons into Earth's orbit or stationing them in outer space.
July 1968	Nuclear Nonproliferation Treaty	Prohibits the transfer of nuclear weapons to other countries and prohibits helping countries without nuclear weapons to make or acquire them.
May 1972	Antiballistic Missile Treaty	Bans space-based defensive missile systems and limits the United States and the Soviet Union to one ground-based defensive missile site each.
June 1979	Strategic Arms Limitation Treaty	The first formal strategic arms treaty sets an initial overall limit of 2400 intercontinental ballistic missile launchers, submarine-launched missiles, heavy bombers, and air-to-surface missiles.
December 1987	Intermediate-Range Nuclear Forces Treaty	Provides for the dismantling of all Soviet and American medium- and shorter-range land-based missiles and establishes a system of weapons inspection to guard against violations.
July 1991	Strategic Arms Reduction Treaty—START I	Brings the number of Soviet long-range nuclear warheads down from 11,012 to 6163, and the number of U.S. warheads down from 12,646 to 8556.
January 1993	Strategic Arms Reduction Treaty—START II	Reduces the superpowers' arsenals to one-third of their current size, limiting them to 3000–3500 warheads and bombs.

accomplished the historic task of opening his country to the democracy and openness of perestroika and glasnost. In the end, he was overwhelmed by the very forces he had let loose. As one Russian official remarked, Gorbachev "tried to reform the unreformable." Some thirty-three minutes after his speech, the Soviet Red Flag flying above the Kremlin was pulled down, and the traditional white-blue-red Russian flag was raised. The chimes on the Spassky Tower clock, which ring only on historic occasions, were heard. "Never before," observed the philosopher Sir Isaiah Berlin, "has there been a case of an empire that caved in without a war, revolution, or an invasion."[28]

In February 1992 Bush welcomed Yeltsin to Washington as the leader of the new Russia. Yeltsin's background differed from Bush's. Baptized (and nearly drowned during the ceremony) by a drunken Orthodox priest in a tiny Ural Mountain village, Yeltsin lived with five family members in a single-room hut where they slept huddled against the family's goat to keep warm. They had a cow and a horse, but both died. Yeltsin's father was arrested by Stalin's police. The son, however, rose through Communist party ranks after obtaining fine grades as an engineering student. He quickly gained power within the party, but he never forgot his roots and was (to Gorbachev's frustration) always pushing for more reform. Now, in early 1992, Bush and Yeltsin declared the Cold War over and planned further arms cuts. The Russian, however, wanted more. He presented a well-prepared, detailed list of proposals. But Bush either was not prepared to respond or felt the U.S. economic recession and his own upcoming reelection campaign gave him no room for a positive response. Yeltsin, as had Gorbachev, needed help quickly.[29]

Yeltsin pushed the economy toward free markets and privatization, but the gross national product continued to fall. One-third of Russia's people lived below the poverty line. Many of the old communist "apparatchiks" remained in place to slow reform and save their own jobs. During the winter of 1991–1992, a massive U.S.–West European airlift of food and medicines helped the people of Moscow, St. Petersburg (formerly Leningrad), and other cities avoid starvation. U.S. and European investors continued to show interest, not

---

[28]*Foreign Broadcast Information Service—Soviet,* December 10, 1991, p. 56; *The New York Times,* December 26, 1991, p. 12; Ibid., December 15, 1996, p. 22; *Economist,* December 26, 1992–January 8, 1993, p. 67.

[29]Morrison, *Boris Yeltsin,* pp. 33–35; *The New York Times,* July 28, 1991, p. 10.

least McDonald's, which during the attempted coup had sent truck-loads of hamburgers and coffee past Soviet tanks to the besieged Yeltsin and his allies. But the dangers that finally toppled Gorbachev also threatened Yeltsin. One was nationalism and ethnicism. Ukraine, for example, issued its own currency and created an army of 300,000. A right-wing reactionary movement, with deep roots in Russian history and vicious antiforeign feelings, also appeared.[30]

Bismarck once declared that Russia is never as strong or as weak as it appears. The Cold War's end proved that Bismarck was right about the "strong" part; Bush and other Western leaders hoped the nineteenth-century German was equally right about the "weak." Otherwise the growing chaos in Russia could, as it had in the past, spread to other regions. Announcing that "By the grace of God, America won the Cold War," Bush declared the United States "the undisputed leader of the age."[31] The "leader," however, had neither saved its closest Russian friend, Gorbachev, nor destroyed its sworn enemy, Saddam Hussein, in the 1991 war.

Bush paid for those failures in the 1992 presidential election. Seldom had a President fallen so far, so fast. Bush called Democratic presidential nominee Bill Clinton (the Governor of Arkansas) and his running mate Albert Gore (Senator from Tennessee) "two bozos" who knew less about foreign policy than did Millie, the Bushes' dog. But as an economic slump plagued the country, a Democratic bumper sticker appeared that read: "Saddam Hussein Still Has His Job. What About You?"[32] Bush flew to Japan in early 1992 to force that nation to buy more U.S. cars, only to get sick, vomit on the Japanese prime minister, and have the American automobile executives who were along condemn the trip as a failure. Clinton attacked Bush for refusing to cooperate with the world community at the historic Rio de Janeiro conference on the environment in 1992, for not stopping the killings in the civil war that erupted in the former Yugoslavia, and for stopping and returning refugees trying to flee military dictatorship in Haiti. Meanwhile the

---

[30]*Foreign Broadcast Information Service—Soviet,* January 21, 1992, p. 52; Ibid., February 5, 1992, p. 50; *Washington Post,* February 2, 1992, p. A19; Dimitri K. Simes article in *Washington Post,* January 19, 1992, p. C4.

[31]The text is in *The New York Times,* January 29, 1992, p. A16.

[32]Fouad Ajami, "Lucky Jim," *New Republic,* January 1, 1996, p. 35; Thomas Omestad, "Why Bush Lost," *Foreign Policy* LXXXIX (Winter 1992–1993): 70–81.

Areas of Discontent, 1988–1994

ESTONIA
LATVIA
LITHUANIA
POLAND
Volga R.
Moscow
SOVIET UNION
UKRAINE
ROMANIA
BULGARIA
Black Sea
Chechnya
GEORGIA
Caspian Sea
ARMENIA
Nagorno-Karabakh Region
TURKEY
AZERBAIJAN
IRAQ

Republican party split. Since the 1950s it had united against the Soviets. With the U.S.S.R. no longer a threat, Republicans disagreed over foreign commitments and costs; some simply wanted to forget about foreign policy altogether. Foreign affairs played an important role in the election, as Bush, the supposed "foreign-policy President," went down to defeat. The post–Cold War era had begun.

The Clinton Doctrine in action as dollars again replace bullets. Before a huge bust of Ho Chi Minh, who led the Vietnamese against U.S. forces for over twenty years, President Bill Clinton visited Vietnam in 2000 to recognize American-Vietnamese diplomatic relations and also champion U.S. investments in the former enemy's country.

(© Reuters/Corbis)

CHAPTER 14

The Post–Cold War Era of Fragmentation: Clinton, Yeltsin, and Back to a Bush (1993–9/11, 2001)

William Jefferson Clinton, the first President from the baby boom generation (that is, those born in the 1946–1964 years), moved into the White House as the world endured its most wrenching change in at least a half-century. The end of the Soviet Union certainly did not mean the end of crises with Russia. It did mean, however, the end of a kind of predictability that had become a most important part of the Cold War. Before 1991, it had usually been good guys versus bad guys, and in most instances the bad guys could quickly be identified. Each side had also learned to know the other quite well, and each had a stake, especially with thousands of nuclear weapons in position, to keep the world as stable as possible. By 1994, however, one respected observer declared that "chaos . . . is the real threat to international stability now."[1] The Soviet Union, Yugoslavia, and Czechoslovakia split apart. Portions of Africa collapsed into bloody civil wars. Unknown terrorists rather than familiar Soviet officials haunted American minds. Somehow, with the end of the Cold War, foreign policy was becoming more complex—and dangerous.

Such dangers grew as the globe shrank. By the mid-1990s, thirty-five major conflicts (those with more than 1000 deaths each year) tore apart regions of the world even as that world was supposedly becoming a "global village" (as new technology guru Marshall McLuhan had famously called it in the 1960s). Two people might live on opposite

[1]Joe Klein, "'Hard' vs. 'Soft' vs. 'Viral' Power," *Newsweek,* June 6, 1994, p. 39.

sides of the globe, but computers and earth satellites made them neighbors. The information revolution allowed many to see news instantaneously. Many, but not all. Half the world's population could not make a phone call in the 1990s, whereas the other half seemed to be constantly on their phone or computer. A most fearful result of the information revolution was that it widened the gap between the world's rich and poor. New technologies have never automatically meant a new and better world.

By the 1990s, Ted Turner's CNN, Rupert Murdoch's News Group (best known in the United States for the Fox television network), and ESPN (the sports network) used new cable technology and earth satellites to flood television sets around the world—often with American cultural values. In many countries, Nike became the shoes and other apparel of choice for youngsters; McDonald's replaced the locally owned corner restaurant; posters of Chicago Bulls basketball star Michael Jordan hung on walls that once held pictures of Mao Ze-dong or Cuban revolutionary Che Guevara; and English became the international language because Americans controlled so much of the computer technology (and, above all, controlled the money that produced the technology and culture).

Even for Americans, however, there was another side. Terrorists used the new technology to coordinate such plans as setting off fatal explosions at New York City's mammoth World Trade Center in 1993, or killing seventeen U.S. sailors in an attack on a destroyer in 2000. Enemies, including Iraq's Saddam Hussein, might more easily acquire information needed to build biological, chemical, and nuclear weapons of mass destruction. In southern France, a farmer who despised American fast-food culture used his tractor to destroy a McDonald's that was being built. The French government, along with many people across the globe, applauded the farmer and made him a national hero.

Bill Clinton thus came to power with a long domestic agenda, but little idea of how to deal with this new world. An initial idea came from Anthony Lake, director of Clinton's National Security Council. In a September 1993 speech, Lake argued that Americans had emerged from the Cold War into "a moment of immense democratic and entrepreneurial opportunity." He urged that post-1947 "containment" (see p. 71) be replaced by "enlargement"—that is, "enlargement of the world's free community of market democracies."[2] (Lake's speech can be read in the chapter XIV documents at the www.mhhe.com/lafeber website.)

Clinton's first attempt to apply "enlargement" was a catastrophe. It also vividly demonstrated how the wonderful information revolution could help produce bloody tragedy. Somalia is an east African nation that Americans and Soviets had fought over because of its strategic location. This competition stopped in the 1990s, but the two superpowers left so many weapons behind that, as one observer noted, Somalis had enough arms to shoot one another for a hundred years. War did erupt between rival clans. Americans paid little attention until December 1992 when their televisions showed grisly pictures of the starving and wounded. President Bush and President-Elect Clinton agreed to send a U.S.-led force, under UN authority, to distribute food and medicine. Television spectacularly covered the U.S. troop landing that occurred at night, but was well lit for a global audience. The intervention marked the first time a UN force had interfered in any nation's internal affairs without the agreement of local authorities. In mid-1993, however, Clinton changed the mission. He decided that any enlargement of peace could not occur until one militant clan leader was arrested. That leader's forces struck back by killing eighteen U.S. soldiers. Stunned Americans watched on television as earth satellites instantly showed their soldiers' bodies being dragged through the mud of the nation they thought they were trying to save. The demand rose to evacuate the troops. Clinton did so in late 1993.[3]

The Somalia debacle deeply affected the new President. During the 1992 campaign, he had demanded that the United Nations take more responsibility for policing the world. But after the Somalia tragedy, the UN, through some fault of its own, had a bad name. Clinton played to some Americans' mistrust of the world organization by saying that the United States just had to learn to say "no" to UN requests. Television, especially CNN, had actually been more important than the UN in leading

---

[2]Anthony Lake, *From Containment to Enlargement* (Washington, D.C., 1993), pp. 3–5; Larry Berman and Emily O. Goldman, "Clinton's Foreign Policy at Midterm," in Colin Campbell and Bert A. Rockman, eds., *The Clinton Presidency, First Appraisals* (Chatham, N.J., 1996), especially pp. 296–299.

[3]*Washington Post,* November 19, 1993, p. A52 for the overview; Michael Mandelbaum, "Foreign Policy as Social Work," *Foreign Affairs,* 75 (January–February 1996): especially pp. 16–19. An excellent account of this episode is Mark Bowden, *Black Hawk Down* (New York, 1999), especially pp. 304–311.

Americans into Somalia, then forcing them out. Clinton seemed to be at the mercy of the media, so like most politicians, he played to it. "Mr. and Mrs. Couch Potato want us to stop civil wars and save the hungry," one senior U.S. official groused. "They see the military as the best way to do that, but when people get killed they won't stand for it."[4]

The Pentagon's fear of becoming trapped in another Vietnam resurfaced. Clinton, who had gone to some lengths to avoid being drafted during the Vietnam conflict, shared that fear. Thus when Liberia (founded by freed American slaves in 1837) suffered a civil war bloodier than Somalia's, Clinton would not intervene. Nor would he and the UN use force to stop even more disastrous tribal wars in Rwanda (where estimates of the dead ran to 800,000), or Burundi. As one observer concluded, the end of the Cold War "set America free to pursue its own interests in Africa—and found that it did not have any." But that remark misled. Because of Africa's great oil and mineral wealth, the civil and tribal wars that wracked the continent, and a rising U.S. fear of terrorism, American special forces trained thirty-one of the fifty-four African militaries in tactics and, supposedly, the values of human rights. Forces such as Rwanda's learned the tactics and discarded the values.[5]

Lake's plans for "enlargement" did not disappear. The targets only changed. After all, the Clinton administration's ardent quest for the enlargement of foreign markets for American business had deep historical roots. They ran back at least to the 1890s when President William McKinley and later Woodrow Wilson energetically tried to find new customers for the goods produced by the American-led industrial revolution. Their (and Clinton's) approach assumed that the battering down of trade and political barriers around the globe would spread wealth and happiness. Most notably, this world view also fervently believed that accelerating commerce and investment would also accelerate the need for more open and democratic political systems. The slogan of the 1960s was "Make love, not war." The slogan for the 1990s was becoming "Make profits, not war."[6]

---

[4]*Newsweek*, December 27, 1993, p. 13.
[5]*New York Times*, March 7, 1993, p. E3; Ibid., July 31, 1995, for op-ed, "Anatomy of a Massacre," by Milton Leitenberg. Also *Washington Post*, July 14, 1998, p. A1.
[6]Martin Sklar has written several influential books and essays on this theme, but a good summary is "The Open Door, Imperialism, and Post-Imperialism: Origins of U.S. Twentieth Century Foreign Relations, circa 1900," in David G. Becker, et al., eds., *Postimperialism and World Politics* (Westport, Conn., 1999), pp. 317–336. For a good summary of the debate in the 1990s, note *The New York Times*, December 28, 2000, especially pp. A16–A17.

But resembling the 1960s, not everyone in the 1990s agreed with the conventional slogans. College students worked with labor unions to protest U.S. corporations' abuse of women and child laborers in Latin America, Asia, and even the United States. Protests against this brutal globalization climaxed with massive riots in Seattle, Washington, in late 1999, and disrupted international economic meetings in Switzerland and Toronto. Clinton nevertheless continued to give his overseas trade and investment policies top priority, even after they suffered setbacks in Congress in 1997–1998.

The President's foreign policies had been driven by two motors, both domestic: a determination to help the U.S. business community reach new (and stable) markets, and, not surprisingly, to win reelection in 1996. The two were closely related. They also pushed out of the way other priorities, including Clinton's promise in the 1992 campaign to give very high priority to human rights.

A "Clinton Doctrine" emerged. It threw all the power the President could muster back of the quest for foreign trade and investment markets. His first major domestic success was the passage of a 1993 measure that raised taxes in order to begin wiping out a $5 trillion national debt. His closest economic adviser, former Wall Street investor Robert Rubin, and Alan Greenspan, chair of the Federal Reserve system, convinced Clinton that by lowering the debt, money —that would otherwise be used to pay off the nation's debt—would be freed up to move into the stock market to finance corporate expansion, including new technology businesses. Clinton pushed the tax bill through Congress, although not a single Republican voted for it. The results were as Rubin predicted. Lower interest rates and the availability of money combined with an explosion of new information businesses to create the greatest wealth over six years that any nation ever enjoyed. As was usually the case, domestic successes led to foreign-policy successes[7]—at least in the economic realm.

The Clinton Doctrine's first foreign-policy triumph occurred in 1994 when Congress completed the historic North American Free Trade Association (NAFTA). U.S. dreams of a North American common

---

[7]Bob Woodward, *The Maestro* (New York, 2000), a biography of Alan Greenspan, tells the story of the 1993 debates and also the Mexican bailout; a good overview of this Clinton-Rubin policy is in *The New York Times*, December 28, 2000, p. A16. Clinton's statement of his "Doctrine" can be read in his November 1998 speech in the chapter XIV documents at the www.mhhe.com/lafeber website.

market without barriers ran back as far as the 1850s. But Ronald Reagan took the first important step in 1988 when he signed a treaty with Canada that brought down trade barriers over ten years. Americans and Canadians already conducted the greatest two-way trade in the world—greater than U.S. trade with Japan and Mexico combined. Six years later Clinton moved to bring Mexico into NAFTA. He met angry opposition from his own Democratic Party and, especially, union members who feared losing jobs to low-paid Mexican labor. The President had earlier promised that his NAFTA agreements would include real protection for U. S. labor and the environment. But the final treaty had few effective safeguards. Mexico, as well as most U.S. businesses, did not want to be dictated to by environmentalists and labor leaders.

NAFTA opponents warned that Mexico's one-party system was corrupt and its economy highly suspect. Soon after Congress ratified the treaty, Mexico's former President was indeed sought for various crimes. In 1994–1995 the country's inability to pay its debts and keep its currency propped up resulted in a near-collapse. Mexico's problems threatened to spread to other nations heavily involved in the Mexican economy, including the United States. Clinton and Rubin (now the U.S. secretary of the treasury) again took a giant risk. They believed Mexico could only be saved with a quick infusion of billions of U.S. dollars. The two men discovered that Congress would never appropriate such money for Mexico; it might appear to folks back home that their hard-earned tax dollars were being given away. Clinton and Rubin consequently found a fund that could be tapped without Congress's approval. They rapidly sent in $12.5 billion. The economy stabilized, conditions improved, and the Mexican government repaid the loan, with interest, ahead of schedule.

Meanwhile, between 1990 and 1998, Mexico's exports to the United States and Canada accelerated at a remarkable average rate of 16 percent a year. In 2000, Mexican voters threw out the highly corrupt PRI (Institutional Revolutionary Party) that had controlled Mexico for seventy years. They elected the flamboyant Vicente Fox, once an executive of a U.S. corporation. Fox fully agreed with the Clinton Doctrine. He even urged that the border between the two countries be thrown completely open so Americans and Mexicans could move back and forth at will. (Given that at least 300,000 Mexicans braved armed guards and barbed wire to work illegally each year in the United

States, not even the Clinton Doctrine, nor most Americans, seemed ready to accept Fox's idea.) Elsewhere in Latin America, as even Clinton officials admitted, free-market economics were not working. The rate of poverty remained the same as in 1979. Some 150 million, or more than one-third of Latin Americans, lived on less than $2 a day.[8]

The effects of NAFTA on Canada were dramatic. A leader of a Canadian nationalist group admitted that "we are, for all intents and purposes, becoming part of the United States." Canada's military was shaped to work with U.S. forces. Canadians sold more goods to Americans ($1 billion each day in cross-border trade) than they sold to other Canadians outside their own provinces. U.S. investment grew until Canada controlled only 70 percent of its productive capacity, that is, less than any other industrial nation owned of its own production. The 80 percent of Canadians whose first language was English read U.S. magazines and watched Hollywood films and television shows (many of them starring Canadian-born actors who had moved south). The other 20 percent, who spoke French in Quebec Province, grew frustrated and sought to establish a separate nation, an attempt that apparently peaked in the mid-1990s and then declined, in part because of U.S. economic opposition. After a decade of NAFTA, a remarkably high one-third of Canadians polled said it was likely that Canada and the United States would become one nation within twenty-five years. But there was considerable anger about this. As noted by the Canadian official who negotiated the 1988 agreement: "Americans are proud of what they are—which is Americans. Canadians are proud of what they are not—which is Americans."[9]

With his NAFTA success, Clinton next marched into battle for the world's most populous market, China. In 1992 Clinton declared that President George Bush had "coddled" the "butchers of Beijing," and had put trading privileges above human rights in China. By 1994, however, Clinton was downplaying human rights (which were worsening

[8]Nicholas Guyatt, *Another American Century?* (New York, 2000), pp. 14–21 on the Mexican bailout and the repercussions; *Economist,* August 26, 2000, p. 25, on Fox; Melvin Small, *Democracy and Diplomacy* (Baltimore, Md., 1996), with the useful final chapter on Clinton; Jim Hoagland, "Heeding the Voice of Silent Cal," *Washington Post,* February 9, 1995, p. A29; *Washington Post,* May 14.

[9]Steven Pearlstein, "The Americanization of Canada," *Washington Post,* September 5, 2000, p. A1; a widely noted analysis in Canada is Richard Gwyn, *Nationalism Without Walls: The Incredible Lightness of Being Canadian* (Toronto, 1995).

in China) to keep the Chinese as growing trade partners. In 1995 another problem appeared. The World Trade Organization (WTO) was created by 135 nations to replace the forty-seven-year-old General Agreements on Tariffs and Trade. The WTO enjoyed new—and great—power as it set about creating rules for global trade. China badly wanted to have a role in making these rules. It could not join the WTO, however, until it worked out a long-term agreement with WTO's most powerful member, the United States.

Clinton again pushed for the agreement even though, to the dismay of his Democratic party members in Congress, it had no significant provisions for protecting labor rights or the environment in China. He did receive strong support from a new China Lobby. The old lobby of the 1950s had protected Taiwan's interests in Washington against Communist China. In an interesting turnabout, however, the new lobby protected Communist China's interests in Washington against Taiwan's, and the Democratic party's, criticism of Chinese human-rights abuses. The lobby included the most powerful U.S. corporations (AT&T, Microsoft, General Motors, Motorola, Boeing—which shut down a large Kansas plant and shifted its operations to China—along with farm export groups) who believed their future depended on the China market. As Jack Welch, head of General Electric, declared, if GE's investment in China turned out to be wrong, it is only "a couple of billion dollars. If it is right it is the future of this company for the next century." China fully cooperated with the lobby according to the traditional Chinese belief: "Use barbarians to control barbarians." By 2000, one set of the "barbarians" (the Americans) had $24 billion invested in China.[10]

As U.S. trade negotiator Charlene Barshefsky moved to negotiate the deal, the Clinton Doctrine hit four major obstacles. First, some Chinese officials feared that opening up their long-protected markets, and allowing in freewheeling American businesses, would fatally weaken Communist party control (much as the Clinton Doctrine hoped and predicted). The Chinese military, which had billions of dollars invested in industries and resorts, could suddenly be faced with competition, as

---

[10]*The New York Times*, September 21, 2000, p. A12; *Washington Post*, March 24, 1994, p. A29; Ken Silverstein, "The New China Hands," *The Nation*, February 17, 1997, pp. 11–16; *Washington Post*, March 18, 1997, p. D1. The best overall account of Clinton's China policy is in chapters 16–18 of James Mann, *About Face* (New York, 1999). On Clinton's 1992 accusation of Bush, see John F. Harris, *The Survivor* (New York, 2005), p. 43, the best account of Clinton's presidency.

would 900 million peasants who sold and bought goods in controlled markets. In the end, Beijing officials agreed with Barshefsky's demands—in part because they wanted to get into WTO, in part because they knew that without U.S. help they could fall behind in the information revolution, and in part (as Washington suspected) because they intended to drag their feet in carrying out their promises anyway. The second obstacle was Taiwan, which China considered its own, and Taiwan's powerful U.S. friends in Congress. When Chinese leaders tried to influence Taiwan's politics in 1996 by holding military exercises close to the island and firing missiles around Taiwan's shores, Clinton ordered U.S. aircraft carriers into the area. A military confrontation loomed, then the Chinese backed off. But tensions over Taiwan remained high.

The third obstacle distracted Clinton more generally throughout 1997–1999. Accused of having sexual relations with a White House intern, Monica Lewinsky, the President lied by saying, "I did not have sex with that woman." When evidence proved otherwise, the Republican-controlled House of Representatives impeached him on charges of perjury and obstruction of justice. Clinton became only the second U.S. President to be impeached. The Senate finally acquitted him in February 1999. But two years of sensationalism had drained, and nearly ruined, his presidency. The fourth obstacle was his own Democratic party and the labor unions that provided millions of Democratic votes. They wanted protection against cheaper Chinese labor, and also demanded environmental and human rights provisions that had teeth. These opponents noted that Americans already suffered an annual $70 billion trade deficit with China, and the treaty could make it worse.

Clinton, Republican leaders, and the new China Lobby of U.S. corporations replied that without the treaty (in which the Chinese promised to open key sectors of their economy to U.S. investors and traders), Americans would never be able to close the trade deficit. U.S. businesses would, moreover, lose the potentially largest market in the world to Japanese and Europeans. Clinton added a national-security argument: rejecting the treaty would help anti-American hard-liners in Beijing who wanted confrontation, not trade, with the United States. As for human rights, the Clinton Doctrine bet that as China allowed in Internet and computer software companies, political discussions would multiply and weaken the Communist system (much as technology's challenge forced Mikhail Gorbachev and the

Soviet Union to change and open until the U.S.S.R. disappeared). On September 19, 2000, the Senate voted 83–15 to ratify Barshefsky's work and extend permanent normal trade relations to China.[11]

Within weeks after the vote, Chinese police rounded up and imprisoned hundreds of people they considered dangerous dissidents, including members of the growing Falun Gong group. Falun Gong started in the early 1990s as a quasi-religious, self-improvement movement. It quickly grew to an estimated several million members and began to stage peaceful demonstrations in Beijing. Falun Gong used computers to publicize itself internationally, communicate internally, and stay in touch with its founder who lived in exile in the United States. China claimed that Americans thus not only prevented unification with Taiwan, but now helped dissidents such as the Falun Gong who threatened the Beijing government. In late 2000, Chinese defense documents and other government releases picked out the United States as enemy number one. These documents also revealed that China's small land-based missile force could strike the United States, while submarine-launched missile technology was developing rapidly.

Increasingly tense relations nearly reached the breaking point in the May 1999 U.S. air war against Serbia (see p. 386). One bomb destroyed China's Embassy in Belgrade and killed three Chinese journalists. Clinton apologized and insisted it was accidental. (Skeptics noted that the highly precise weapon hit the floor housing Chinese intelligence operations.) Beijing refused to accept his explanation. In the long run, whatever that happened to be, the Clinton Doctrine might have helped U.S.-Chinese relations. In the short run, it did not seem to produce the hoped-for political results.[12]

In November 2000, the Clinton Doctrine dramatically reappeared. Clinton became the first U.S. President to visit Vietnam. In a politically courageous move, he had lifted the twenty-year economic embargo in 1994, then opened diplomatic relations with the former

---

[11]*The New York Times*, September 20, 2000, pp. A1, A16 has a useful and full overview.
[12]This and the previous paragraph are based on *Washington Post*, November 15, 2000, p. A1; Owen Harries, "A Year of Debating China," *The National Interest* (Winter 1991–2000), p. 144, analyzes the bombing; Thomas D. Weiss, et. al., *The United Nations and Changing World Politics*, 2nd ed. (Boulder, Colo., 1997), p. 22; James Lilley and Carl Ford, "China's Military: A Second Option," *National Interest* (Fall 1999), p. 75; a helpful analysis with excellent context on U.S.-China is David Mosler and Bob Catley, *Global America; Imposing Liberalism on a Reluctant World* (Westport, Conn., 2000), pp. 147–150.

enemy in 1995. Some Vietnam veterans objected. Others, however, wanted to turn a new page on Vietnam. U.S. businesses (including Coca-Cola which had a huge sign welcoming people to the capital, Ho Chi Minh City) demanded government help before other Asians and Europeans dominated Vietnam's market. Executives from fifty U.S. corporations accompanied Clinton on his trip. Vietnam needed economic aid. It also needed Washington's understanding of Vietnam's thousand-year on-and-off conflict with neighboring China. As the Clinton Doctrine prescribed, the President believed trade would gradually transform Vietnam's tightly controlled Communist state into "Asia's newest capitalist recruit," as one observer (perhaps with his fingers crossed) phrased it.[13]

Back of the trade offensive stood the world's number-one military power. (Of course, it should have been number one: U.S. military budgets in the 1990s exceeded those of the next ten military powers combined, and half of those were American allies.) Long-time allies in Western Europe, led—as usual—by French dislike of U.S. policies, did begin in the late 1990s to create an independent, multinational military force of 60,000 that could be deployed quickly to hot spots. Some Europeans demanded the force be independent of the United States—indeed, even act as a check on Washington policies. Americans saw this new unit as a direct threat to NATO, which continued to be the backbone of the entire U.S. alliance system. NATO remained the single most important American presence throughout Europe and gave Americans considerable power to shape European affairs, especially military policies.

In 1994 Clinton pledged to take the historic step of enlarging NATO. It was to move eastward (that is, toward Russia) by bringing in Poland, the Czech Republic, and Hungary as members. Intense debate erupted. Russian officials saw the expansion of NATO toward their borders as a direct military threat (and a step they believed President Bush and Prime Minister Thatcher had promised in 1990 not to take if

---

[13]*The New York Times,* July 14, 2000, p. A3 has the quote and excellent analysis by Joseph Kahn; *Washington Post,* November 18, 2000, p. A18 has texts of Clinton's remarks in Vietnam and good background; James C. Moore's "Twenty Years after the Fall," manuscript in author's possession, by a thoughtful Vietnam veteran who served as President of the New York State Bar Association.

the Russians, as they did, accepted the reunification of Germany and its membership in NATO).

Three reasons finally drove NATO expansion. First, it integrated Europe militarily under U.S. direction. Second, the need to rebuild the Polish, Czech, and Hungarian militaries meant profitable contracts for U.S. arms producers (including Boeing, Lockheed Martin, and Raytheon). In 1997–1998 alone, American arms manufacturers spent over $50 million to lobby Congress to pass NATO expansion. The massive 1999 celebration in Washington to celebrate NATO's fiftieth birthday (and when the three new nations became official members) was underwritten in large part by arms dealers. Third, many U.S. officials continued to value NATO in the twenty-first century, as officials had in the late 1940s, for its ability to carry out a double containment—that is, contain both German power (by integrating it into the organization) and Russian power (by setting up military barriers along its western borders). Germany would thus have to continue to be a "good citizen," as one observer put it. And, as Henry Kissinger remarked about Russia, "Of course history does not always repeat itself. But expansion extending over four centuries does reflect a certain proclivity." The new NATO was to be a cold shower on such a "proclivity."[14]

NATO, fortunately, had never gone into battle during the Cold War. After the Soviet Union disappeared, however, it went to war for the first time. This tragedy began in 1991. Until then, Yugoslavia's three major peoples—the dominant Orthodox Christian Serbs, the Roman Catholic Croats, and the Bosnians (who included some Serbs but especially many Moslems)—had remained uneasily together through the Cold War. Then Croatia and Bosnia, with encouragement from their longtime friends in Germany, moved to realize their ancient dream of independence. The Serb-dominated central Yugoslav government dispatched military forces to maintain its control and protect Serbs in the two breakaway areas.

---

[14]The Kissinger quote is in *Washington Post,* August 13, 1991, p. A17; an authoritative participant's view is Strobe Talbott, *The Russia Hand* (New York, 2002), especially pp. 93–115, 377–382; the debate is spelled out in Coit Blacker, Daniel Fried, and Alexander Vershbow, "U.S. Offers Moscow an Alliance," *Christian Science Monitor,* October 14, 1995, p. 15; for the other side, Owen Harries, "The Collapse of the West," *Foreign Affairs,* 72 (September–October 1993): 28–53; Michael E. Brown, "The United States, Western Europe and NATO Enlargement," in Frances G. Burwell and Ivo H. Daalder, eds., *The United States and Europe in the Global Arena* (New York, 1999), pp. 20–22; on the arms dealers see *The New York Times,* March 30, 1998, p. A1.

As the Bush administration showed little interest, conflict escalated. Serbs began "ethnic cleansing," that is, mass slaughter of those from a different religious or ethnic group. UN forces tried to help, but for two years Americans wanted nothing to do with this killing ground. Television pictures of civilians being blown up in market squares helped change that feeling. After Serbs massacred Moslems in 1995, Clinton acted. Serb defeats on the ground, helped along by U.S.-led NATO bombing, resulted in an American-brokered peace agreement in Dayton, Ohio. Sixty thousand NATO troops, including 20,000 U.S. personnel, moved in to enforce the peace. The President unfortunately declared the troops would remain only a year. A decade later they were still there to maintain peace. But Clinton had again taken a gamble. If Americans were killed, it could become another Somalia and undermine his 1996 reelection chances. But the success of the peace-keeping operation helped raise Clinton's foreign-policy poll ratings a surprising 15 percent. Vigorous diplomacy, rather remarkable personal political charisma, and especially a prosperous economy gave Clinton a near landslide reelection victory over Republican Senator Robert Dole in 1996.

The Yugoslav peace held off and on until 1998 when the brutal Serbian President, Slobodan Milosevic, began slaughtering opposition in Kosovo province and burning villages before international television audiences. A new U.S. secretary of state moved front and center. In 1997 Madeleine Albright had become the first woman, and the first native of Eastern Europe (Czechoslovakia), to serve as U.S. secretary of state. Because of her background and an academic career at Georgetown University, she intimately knew the considerable complexities of the Balkans. As U.S. Ambassador to the UN between 1993 and 1997, she talked and acted tough. When the top U.S. military officer, General Colin Powell, once expressed reluctance to commit U.S. troops to a risky situation, Albright angered him by asking what he was keeping all that high-priced military for, if he didn't want to use it. As a young woman, she had to flee Europe twice, once from Nazis in 1938, then from communists in 1948. "She watched her world fall apart," one friend noted, "and she was not going to let that world do so again.[15]

---

[15]For the last two paragraphs, note Harris, *The Survivor*, especially pp. 216–219; and *Washington Post*, December 16, 1996, p. A25.

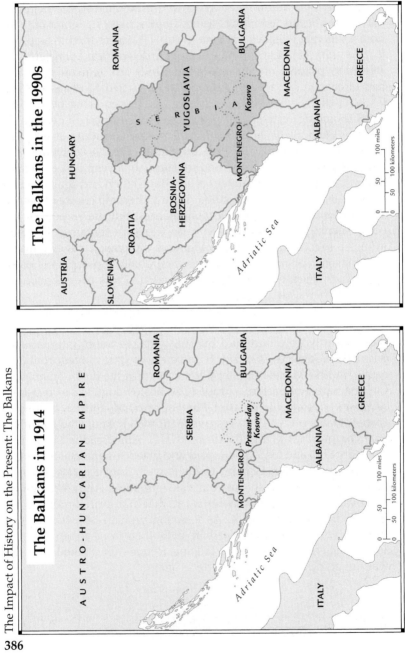

The Balkans in 1914

The Balkans in the 1990s

As Europeans hesitated, Albright pushed Clinton into launching a NATO bombing campaign in early 1999 to stop Milosevic. It was the first major war for NATO in its half-century of history. At the urging of his NSC adviser, Samuel Berger, Clinton declared no U.S. ground troops would be sent. As the air war wore on, the President came under sharp attack from critics for having crossed off the possibility of using the infantry. Stories circulated that Clinton, who had an explosive temper, privately berated Berger for his advice. The President should have thanked him. If troops had entered, and the body bags of the dead began to return home, support for such a mission would have disappeared as it did in Somalia, and Clinton would again have been embarrassed. Instead, the bombing began to take its toll as NATO planes escalated their attacks to obliterate power plants, communications, factories, and bridges. The Russians, Milosevic's staunchest supporter, pressured him to back off. After seventy-eight days of bombing, Serb forces withdrew from Kosovo. NATO forces, including American troops, moved in to rebuild and keep peace. A year later, the Yugoslav people removed Milosevic from office through elections. Clinton succeeded in revitalizing NATO and stabilizing a highly unstable part of Europe.[16]

The military was, despite Powell's reluctance, there to be used. Even without a Cold War, Clinton raised his military budgets from $260 billion to over $300 billion. Meanwhile, he and Bush sent U.S. troops into more conflicts during the 1990–2000 era than had been sent during any other post-1950 decade. One of those conflicts occurred in Haiti, the poorest country in the Western Hemisphere, which since 1915 had experienced U.S. invasions for, supposedly, the sake of restoring order.

In 1991 the elected President, Jean-Bertrand Aristide, was overthrown by the Haitian military which acted for the small elite that had long ruthlessly exploited their own people. As Aristide moved to Washington, Haitians in large numbers began to flee to Florida. To prevent a political uproar in that state, Clinton captured and detained the refugees—the exact act for which he had condemned Bush in the 1992 campaign. In 1994 Clinton decided to end the

---

[16]A good brief overview of the context and Clinton's Balkan policy is in Harris, *The Survivor*, pp. 361–367; *The New York Times*, December 28, 2000, p. A17; for a critical view, Ibid, December 25, 2000, p. A16; the effect of the economic sanctions imposed on Yugoslavia is discussed in Ibid., October 15, 2000, p. 4bu.

problem by landing troops. Haiti's military rulers left, taking large amounts of money with them. Aristide regained the presidency. But by 2001, when he again won office, he had accomplished little, Haitians suffered even worse poverty, and frustrated U.S. officials (and the public) threw up their hands and turned to problems that could be more easily solved.[17]

Clinton believed that one of the solvable problems might finally be the Middle East. Forty-five years of wars between Israel and its Arab neighbors suddenly turned into a promising peace process in 1992–1994. Clinton tried to broker a final peace, but the parties could never solve the toughest problems, including an agreement on which people, Arabs or Jews, would control Jerusalem's holy sites that were central to each side's religion. Nor could Clinton find a solution in Colombia, where drug lords and armed rebels threatened to take over large areas of this once democratic, prosperous nation. Colombia had become the source for most of the cocaine and heroin that enslaved too many Americans. To destroy the drugs and help the besieged Colombian government, Clinton devised a $7.5-billion "Plan Colombia" that would send U.S. military advisers and arms to rebuild the ineffective military, promote crops other than those used for drugs, and expand human rights. Critics feared the United States was being sucked down into another Vietnam. The often undependable Colombian military had been brutal to its own citizens. Key members of Congress began to pull back their support with the warning that the United States was on the brink of a "major mistake."[18] Clearly, the end of the Cold War did not mean the end of dangerous, complex foreign-policy problems.

Russia became one of the most important of those problems in the 1990s. With the end of the Cold War, the competition between Soviet communism and American capitalism disappeared. But problems that dated back into the nineteenth century returned to haunt both nations. For example, over many generations the Orthodox Christian Russians had tried to protect their cobelievers in Serbia. President

---

[17]The context and importance of the Haiti decisions are noted in *Washington Post,* January 15, 2001, p. A4.

[18]*The New York Times,* November 17, 2000, p. A10; Kenneth E. Sharpe, "Addicted to the Drug War," *Chronicle of Higher Education,* October 6, 2000, p. B14; Rafael Pardo, "Colombia's Two-Front War," *Foreign Affairs,* 79 (July/August, 2000): especially pp. 64–71.

Boris Yeltsin consequently disliked, and only reluctantly (or not at all) cooperated with, Clinton's policies during the Yugoslav crises.

To take another example (which will have much greater impact on Americans who live through most of the twenty-first century), the United States and Russia bitterly competed over who would develop the vast oil and gas reserves in the Caspian Sea area. With a potential worth of more than $6 trillion, these resources were perhaps second only to the Middle East's rich pools of petroleum. Until 1991, the Soviet Union and Iran controlled the region. Then five states broke away from Russia to become independent, and also quite corrupt, sometimes unstable, and possibly very rich. Several of the new states signed profitable contracts with such U.S. oil companies as Chevron (which negotiated a potential $20-billion deal with one of the breakaway states, Kazakhstan) and Exxon to develop their oil fields.

Of equal importance was a growing fight over the possible routes of the pipelines that would take the oil and gas to world markets. U.S. officials pushed hard for the pipelines to be built westward through Turkey and the Black Sea, not northward through an unpredictable Russia or southward through a hostile Iran. The Russians put great pressure on the new states, including the use of military threats, to bring them around to accepting northern pipelines. Again, history helped explain what was occurring. As noted earlier (see p. 316), the British and Russians had a century before ruthlessly played what was called "the great game of empire" to see who would control this region that was even then highly important strategically and economically. Because of its importance, Hitler had sent his invading army straight into this region in 1941, but was finally stopped by the Soviets with incredible cost in lives. Now the "great game" restarted, only this time not only between Americans and Russians, but Chinese, Iraqis, Iranians, and Europeans who played for the immense prizes.[19]

[19]An expert overview by a former U.S. government official is Sheila N. Heslin, "Key Constraints to Caspian Pipeline Development," April 1998, The James A. Baker Institute for Public Policy, Rice University, Houston, Texas; Stanley Kober, "The Great Game, Round Two," Cato Institute of Foreign Policy Briefing, no. 63, October 31, 2000, Washington, D.C., a critical account of U.S. policy; Geoffrey Kemp, *Energy Superbowl* (Washington, D.C., 1999), especially pp. 24–29, 49–62, a comparative study of the Middle East's resources.

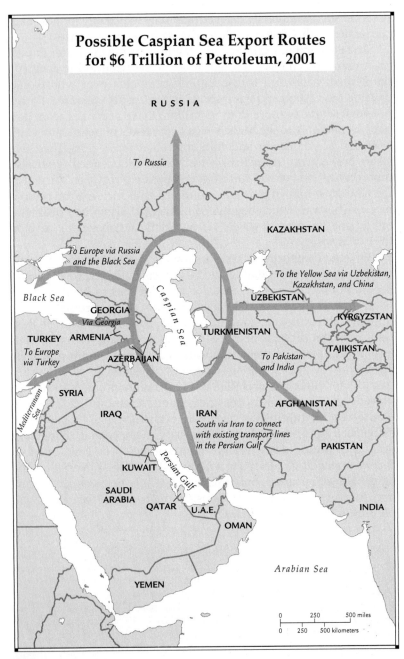

Possible Caspian Sea Export Routes for $6 Trillion of Petroleum, 2001

RUSSIA

To Russia

To Europe via Russia and the Black Sea

KAZAKHSTAN

To the Yellow Sea via Uzbekistan, Kazakhstan, and China

Black Sea

Caspian Sea

UZBEKISTAN

KYRGYZSTAN

GEORGIA

Via Georgia

TURKMENISTAN

TURKEY ARMENIA

TAJIKISTAN

To Europe via Turkey

AZERBAIJAN

To Pakistan and India

Mediterranean Sea

SYRIA

AFGHANISTAN

IRAQ

IRAN

South via Iran to connect with existing transport lines in the Persian Gulf

PAKISTAN

KUWAIT

Persian Gulf

SAUDI ARABIA

QATAR

U.A.E.

INDIA

OMAN

Arabian Sea

YEMEN

| 0 | 250 | 500 miles |
| 0 | 250 | 500 kilometers |

Clinton committed so much U.S. power to this region—running from the Balkans through the Middle East (including Iraq, where Saddam Hussein survived despite U.S. bombing raids and economic sanctions), and into the Caspian Sea region—that critics termed it "The Third American Empire." The first empire had been the possessions taken in the Pacific and Caribbean during the War of 1898. The second empire was the post-1945 expansion of U.S. power into the western European and Asian continents.[20] Boris Yeltsin liked this third empire no better than his communist predecessors in the Kremlin had liked the second. But he was not in a strong position to stop the growth of American influence. Yeltsin's ground forces declined rapidly in numbers, morale, and combat-readiness because he could not juice up either the Russian economy or the military's morale. He did, however, control thousands of nuclear weapons. As one authority observed, "They can do nothing much in Moscow, but they can wipe out New York."[21]

Russia still extended over ten time zones. The empire's vastness nevertheless threatened to pull the country apart, much as James Madison had prophesied 170 years earlier. The country had eighty-eight constituent regions, each led by local governments, as well as over a hundred ethnic groups. Local officials defied Yeltsin's attempts to expand the control of his central government.[22] His economic headaches were even worse. The Soviet military-industrial complex had once swallowed one-third of everything the nation produced, as well as employing at least one of every five adults.[23] (The comparable U.S. figures were approximately one-sixteenth of gross national product and about one of every sixteen in the workforce.) To turn the Soviet military complex into a market-based civilian economy without wrenching problems was beyond the ability of any mortal.

In 1991 President Bush helped open the channels for aid by bringing Russia and twelve of the other former Soviet republics into the International Monetary Fund and the World Bank. In 1995 Russia also became a charter member of the new World Trade Organization.

---

[20]Jacob Heilbrunn and Michael Lind, "The Third American Empire," *The New York Times,* February 2, 1996, p. A15.

[21]*Washington Post,* March 24, 1993, p. A24.

[22]*The New York Times,* October 10, 1993, p. 12. For the broader view, note Talbott, *The Russia Hand,* pp. 73–74.

[23]Leon Aron, "Russia's Recent Political Developments. . . ." in The Aspen Institute, ed., *Russia, Ukraine, the Caucasus, and the U.S. Response* (Queenstown, Md., 1994), p. 38.

Massive aid, however, did not appear, least of all from the U.S. government. Lenders mistrusted Russian bureaucrats who tried to solve problems by printing more money and thus generating inflation, as too much money chased too few products. In 1986, under Soviet rules, you needed two-thirds of one ruble to buy a dollar; ten years later you needed 4600 rubles.

Yeltsin appointed young market-oriented advisers, but they soon quit or were forced out. Their replacements were persons such as Viktor Gerashchenko, head of the powerful Central Bank that supposedly controlled the nation's money supply. "I understand the meaning of a bank," he told a group of Americans. "I like the words 'micro' and 'macro,' but not in economics. I don't understand all this stuff about micro and macro."[24] Not surprisingly, the Central bank bent easily to political pressures that urged solving problems simply by printing rubles. As prices inflated, the elderly, disabled, military, and others on fixed incomes grew angry as their money became worthless.

Westerners nevertheless continued to invest in Russia until the late 1990s. Led by such giants as Procter & Gamble, Chevron, and McDonald's, as well as Ben & Jerry's ice cream, Americans became the top foreign investors in the country. U.S. television shows including soap operas and a Russian version of *Wheel of Fortune* (called *Field of Wonders*) invaded television sets. But investment was too small to help the mass of people. Tremendous gaps arose between the rich, who bought off politicians to obtain access to Russian resources, and the poor. Perhaps as much as $100 billion of Russian money was moved out of the country, often by mobsters, to safer banks.[25]

Mob crime seemed to be one of the fastest-growing businesses. Police identified some 3000 gangs operating in Russia; nine or ten large mobs competed in Moscow alone. FBI experts tried to help Russian authorities make the country safer for living and investing. An American who owned several restaurants in Moscow believed that "this country is going from Communism to recklessness overnight." The effects went far beyond individual crime. For example, mob leaders paraded their fancy cars, bodyguards, and women

[24]*The New York Times,* January 23, 1994, p. F1; the fate of the reformers is analyzed in *Washington Post,* September 9, 1997, p. A14.
[25]*The New York Times,* January 2, 1996, p. A3; Ibid., January 30, 1994, p. H31; Jack F. Matlock, "Russia: The Power of the Mob," *The New York Review of Books,* July 13, 1995, p. 14; Talbott, *The Russia Hand,* pp. 275–292.

in short Lycra suits—exhibitionism that made some ordinary citizens believe they could improve their own fortunes only through crime. Others concluded that a strong Stalin-type government was preferable to this kind of democracy. Crime in the streets, moreover, quickly translated into crime in disposing of dismantled nuclear weapons. Arrests occurred throughout Europe as groups tried to smuggle nuclear materials from Russia into such anti-American nations as Iran and Iraq. "The chaos scares me," said one official from the Reagan-Bush years. "Here we have a 1930s situation in Chicago, except that Al Capone has access to nuclear weapons."[26]

Meanwhile life expectancy, already lower than that of any other developed country, dropped for men from sixty-four years in 1990 to fifty-seven years by 1994, while women's dropped from seventy-four to about seventy-one. (U.S. life expectancy was seventy-two for men and seventy-nine for women and had been steadily rising since 1900.) Death from alcohol-related causes skyrocketed 60 percent in the 1990s. Death from infectious and parasitic diseases shot upward 100 percent, especially because medicines were often unavailable to the poor. In 1993, 14,000 women were estimated to have been murdered by husbands, lovers, or former partners—twenty times the equivalent number for American women. Feminist groups formed to protest both such murder and the blatant economic discrimination women experienced. The first major feminist political party, Women of Russia, won a surprising eleven percent of the vote in 1991. Unfortunately, it was able to do little more.[27]

By 1992 Vice President Rutskoi, a powerful conservative voice, expressed disgust with the Western presence, especially the giant McDonald's in midtown Moscow where, he charged, "'Big Macs' with ketchup" overwhelmed the glory of "plain Russian meat pies," and where long lines of Russians seemed to be not merely "waiting for food" but "waiting for holy communion." Rutskoi condemned "the spiritual decline which has paralyzed our society." In 1993 Yeltsin tried to neutralize Rutskoi and his conservative colleagues in parliament. They responded in October by joining some communists,

---

[26]*The New York Times,* August 16, 1993, p. A6; Seymour Hersh, "The Wild East," *Atlantic Monthly,* June 1994, pp. 61, 79.
[27]*The New York Times,* August 1, 1995, p. 1; *Economist,* August 12, 1995, pp. 44–45; *The New York Times,* December 3, 2000, p. A1.

neo-Nazis, and extreme nationalists in an attempt to overthrow Yeltsin. The coup lasted only hours before being smashed, but it was a near miss, and Yeltsin's use of military units to blast the building in which the plotters holed up was seen globally on CNN. Reaction, however, had only begun.[28]

As unrest and anti-Westernism grew, Yeltsin shifted his ground. He tried to appease nationalists with a move that turned out to be perhaps the worst mistake he made. In 1994 Yeltsin ordered 40,000 troops to prevent the Chechnya region's separation from Russia. Living 1000 miles south of Moscow, the Chechens for centuries had gloried in defying the Great Russians. Yeltsin quickly found himself immersed in a Vietnam-like struggle. Chechens seized thousands of Russian hostages, while inflicting humiliating losses on Yeltsin's dispirited and badly equipped troops. One observer remarked that Russia apparently could not even invade itself.[29] Yeltsin bounced back from an unbelievably low 3 percent approval rating in 1996 to win reelection to the presidency—thanks to a weak opposition, much help from the newly rich "oligarchs" who owned television and newspapers (and wanted continued access to the Russian treasury), and support from the West which preferred Yeltsin to a possible communist or radical nationalist government. Bedeviled by alcoholism, a weak heart, and an ungovernable country, Yeltsin accomplished little. Then things turned worse.

Many Russians thought the rule of law useless. As an old Russian proverb put it, the law is like a wagon axle: it goes in any direction you want to pull it. Unable to collect taxes, stop the large illegal black market, or halt the outflow of money to safe Swiss banks, Yeltsin devalued the ruble in 1998. He also announced the government could not make payments on loans recently given by the West. Foreign investment rushed out of the country. Nearly $3 billion each month left over the next year. Investment dried up. Money disappeared. One observer believed that the difference with the Soviet era was that then there was money but no goods; now there were goods but no money. Clinton's Secretary of the

---

[28]*Foreign Broadcast Information Service—Russia*, February 5, 1991, p. 50; Aron, "Russia's Recent Political Developments," pp. 37–38; Leon Aron, *Yeltsin* (New York, 2000), pp. 516–550.
[29]Michael Mandelbaum, quoted and with a succinct analysis of Yeltsin's policies, in Paul Marantz, "Russian Foreign Policy during Yeltsin's Second Term," *Communist and Post-Communist Studies*, 30 (no. 4, 1997): 345–351. An excellent critical account, placed in context, is Matthew Evangelista, *Chechen Wars* (Washington, D.C., 2002).

Treasury Robert Rubin saw that a Russian collapse could create panic on world money markets (and indeed did help bring down one major U.S. fund). The President and Rubin pushed the International Monetary Fund to pump money into Russia in return for promises of reform. The money went in, the reforms never appeared, and much of the money then resurfaced in Swiss bank accounts of corrupt Russian businessmen and politicians. The crisis finally subsided as the world price of oil, Russia's largest export, rapidly rose during 1999–2000.[30]

Yeltsin was at the end of his political road. Just hours before the calendar turned from 1999 to 2000, he dramatically announced he was resigning and leaving the government in the hands of the little known Prime Minister, Vladimir V. Putin. The new President had been a KGB official who conducted Cold War spy ventures against the West while stationed in East Germany. He had shown a flair for bare-knuckle politics as a key cog in the political machine that controlled St. Petersburg after 1991. Putin gained attention when, after Yeltsin named him Prime Minister, he urged that as many Chechens as necessary be killed so the war could end on Russia's terms. He had also become famous for being superb at judo and a form of wrestling that involved strangling neck grips—talents for which he was called "Russia's Bruce Willis."

Putin easily won election on his own in 2000. He quickly centralized power. A leading liberal judge in Moscow who tried to build a rule of law was removed from power. Owners of media who disagreed with Putin were faced with arrest or exile. When investigating journalist Oleg Lurye appeared on NTV (Russia's only nongovernmental television channel) to reveal massive corruption among officials around Putin, four men attacked Lurye and his wife the next day. They slashed his face with a razor, then beat him unconscious.[31]

Yeltsin's disasters and Putin's crackdown embarrassed President Clinton, while giving Republicans a club to use against Vice President

---

[30]*Washington Post,* November 24, 1999, p. A17; *The New York Times,* October 18, 1998, p. 18 superbly analyzes the role of U.S. investment in the 1998 crash; Michael Waldman, *POTUS Speaks* (New York, 2000), pp. 228–242, the President's speechwriter's account of the 1998 economic crisis; Boris Yeltsin, *Midnight Diaries* (New York, 2000), chapter 10, gives Yeltsin's rather detached view of the crisis; Aron, *Yeltsin,* pp. 669–685 analyzes the Russian context and decision to devalue.

[31]This and the previous paragraph are based on *Washington Post,* January 22, 2001, p. A18; Ibid., October 17, 2000, p. A18 on the judge; *Wall Street Journal,* January 3, 2000, p. A8 on Bruce Willis.

Albert Gore (who had tried to work closely with his Russian counterparts) when he ran for President in 2000. The West had poured at least $100 billion into Russia since 1991, most of it in U.S. dollars. As one congressional observer noted, it was "worse than wasted." An analysis concluded that the Russian economy produced one-third less in 1999 than it had in 1989. A good result for the West was immense economic pressure on Russian military forces. Putin believed he would have to cut one-third of the 1.2-million-member army (it had been 2 million in 1991). The bad results for the West included a deteriorating, increasingly unpredictable nuclear force; a restless military badly divided between those wanting larger armies and those demanding more nuclear weapons; and significant (including secret) sales for profit of nuclear technology and conventional weapons to some of the leading enemies of the United States, especially Iraq and Iran. A new Russian military strategy issued in 2000 attacked U.S. policies expanding NATO and bombing Yugoslavia. Given the weakness of Russia's conventional forces, the strategy report ominously increased the possible use of nuclear weapons if crises occurred. The end of the Cold War was not ending the danger of nuclear attacks.[32]

Clinton was the first U.S. President in more than a half-century to serve his entire tenure in a world without the Cold War. He and his advisers were unable to come up with a comprehensive policy for the new world (a policy, for example, such as Truman's containment theory that was understandable to Americans and seemed to fit the world of the Cold War). But then, the globe was no longer simply divided between the free and the enslaved, as Truman had defined it. The complexities of technology, nationalisms, uneven economic development, and religious fundamentalism had taken over an international arena once seen as dominated by only communists and capitalists. Clinton tried to escape the problem by using his considerable intelligence and personality that had often allowed him to succeed in politics at the last moment. One observer believed that Clinton was convinced "he's so damn good he can come in in the fourth quarter and rescue the team." In Kosovo, where U.S. airpower was decisive, this approach worked. In Somalia, Haiti, and the Middle East, it did not. But his foreign policy will be most remembered for the Clinton Doctrine that tried

---

[32]This and the previous paragraph are based on Dimitri K. Simes, *After the Collapse; Russia Seeks Its Place* . . . (New York, 1999), pp. 208–209; *The New York Times*, October 10, 2000, p. 16; Joseph M. Siracusa and David G. Coleman, "Scaling the Nuclear Ladder; Deterrence from Truman to Clinton," *Australian Journal of International Affairs*, 54 (no. 3, 2000): 278, 292–293; Janne E. Nolan, *An Elusive Consensus: Nuclear Weapons and American Security After the Cold War* (Washington, D.C., 1999).

to use the American domination of world trade and revolutionary information technologies to create a new era in global economic affairs.[33]

In the 2000 presidential campaign between Democratic candidate Al Gore and Republican nominee George W. Bush, foreign-policy differences were usually blurred. They campaigned mainly on domestic issues. Gore won the popular vote, but Bush, the governor of Texas, won the electoral college and thus the election. As the son of former President George H. W. Bush, one of the most internationalist (and internationally experienced) of American Presidents, the Texas governor should have learned about foreign policy since his first breath. But he had shown little interest in the subject (or in much else involving politics) through the initial forty years of his life. He traveled abroad little (Bush had never, for example, visited London, Paris, or Berlin, the capitals of America's three closest allies), and led a largely provincial life of searching for oil or running the Texas Rangers baseball team. He made money in both businesses (in oil, it should be added, mainly because of his father's contacts in Texas and the Middle East). His political skills developed late, but powerfully. He also seemed intensely determined to use those skills (and his parents' contacts) to revenge his father's loss to Bill Clinton in 1992. Once a playboy in college (and after), he was on a mission in the 2000 campaign.[34]

The President-Elect understood he knew little about foreign policy, so he named Richard Cheney (secretary of defense during the Persian Gulf War, and a quarter-century-long Washington insider) to be his Vice President. Donald Rumsfeld, another insider who had been secretary of defense in the mid-1970s, returned to head the Pentagon. Condoleezza Rice, an expert on the Soviets who was influential in the National Security Council under Bush I, now led the NSC. Bush named one of the most popular and experienced of all American public figures, Retired General Colin Powell, to be secretary of state. Bush received less than 10

---

[33]*Washington Post,* January 15, 2001, p. A4 is a good overview, as is Samuel R. Berger, "A Foreign Policy for the Global Age," *Foreign Affairs,* 79 (November/December 2000), especially pp. 22–30.

[34]James Traub, "W's World," *New York Times Magazine,* January 14, 2001, pp. 28–34 is a critical overview of the careers and beliefs of Bush and his closest foreign policy advisers; Molly Ivins, *Shrub; The Short But Happy Political Life of George W. Bush* (New York, 2000) nicely analyzes the oil and baseball careers; Bill Minutaglio, *First Son* (New York, 1999) is a more conventional biography; *New York Times,* May 7, 2001, p. A9 on lack of travel to Europe.

percent of the African-American vote in the election, but Powell became the first African-American to be the premier of the Cabinet, while Rice was the first woman and only the second African-American (Powell was the first, under Reagan) to head the NSC.

Bush and his advisers seemed to share one central principle that indeed had deep roots in American history: unilateralism. This term did not mean isolationism, one of the most misunderstood words in the U.S. vocabulary. Bush (and few Americans since 1620) ever wanted to isolate the country—which in any event became impossible after the seventeenth century, given the nation's economic dependence on world markets. As a unilateralist, however, Bush questioned the continuing U.S. involvement with Europeans in Yugoslavia, and Rice even announced that the 6000 remaining American troops in Kosovo should be pulled out. Or, as she phrased it, "We don't need to have the 82nd Airborne [Division] escorting kids to kindergarten" in Bosnia and Kosovo. Regional powers, that is, Europeans, were to do this, while the U.S. military would be used only to fight major conflicts—of which, admittedly, there had been very few since 1975. Europeans and others immediately worried whether this meant a U.S. withdrawal from its longtime commitments which had won the Cold War and shaped the 1990s. In most parts of the world, moreover, there were no regional powers that could keep the peace, at least not on behalf of American interests and values.[35]

The Bush officials took the same unilateral approach to parts of the Clinton Doctrine. They accepted NAFTA and freer trade. Bush even committed himself to create a Western-Hemisphere-wide free-trade area, an idea Republicans had nurtured since James G. Blaine dreamed up the Pan-American movement in the 1880s. But the new President attacked the International Monetary Fund for often worsening economic problems. His new secretary of the treasury, Paul O'Neill (formerly head of the multinational giant Alcoa), called the 1998 financial help to Russia "crazy." Bush and his advisers showed little interest in adding provisions that would protect labor rights or the environment in new trade treaties. Globalization (for both investors and laborers) was apparently to be left to the discipline of the marketplace, with the government providing only a safety net with very large holes.[36]

---

[35]*The New York Times,* October 21, 2000, p. A10.
[36]Ibid., October 30, 2000, p. A16; Ibid., December 18, 2000, p. C23 on plans for Latin America.

Bush also sharply criticized Clinton's willingness to work with China, and termed the Chinese a "strategic competitor," a major threat to U.S. interests. The new President as well condemned his predecessor's attempts to work with the corrupt Soviet elite, although he had no alternative but to deal with Putin in trying to stop the proliferation of nuclear weapons. Most of all, Bush determined to build a National Missile Defense (NMD) that would be targeted, he argued, on rogue states (such as Iraq or North Korea) which might have only several nuclear weapons. The Russians, Chinese, and Europeans did not buy that argument. They believed Bush aimed to neutralize their nuclear forces with NMD. These nations, especially the first two, bitterly condemned his plan. The Russians refused to renegotiate the 1972 treaty, signed by Richard Nixon, that outlawed NMD. In the best tradition of unilateralism, Bush was apparently ready to disavow the treaty if Putin could not be brought around (or bought off) to accept its modification. Europeans and others feared that Bush's plan would trigger an arms race since, they argued, the Russians and Chinese would try to overwhelm NMD with new generations of missiles, and many of them.[37]

The NMD, the Powell Doctrine, and the Bush-Rice criticisms of financial bailouts and interventions for humanitarian reasons nicely exemplified American unilateralism in the early twenty-first century. Whether these policies would survive in the "global village" of twenty-first century globalization and information technology became a central question. It was, for example, one thing to say that U.S. officials should not work with a person like Putin to liberalize Russia, but one Moscow editor warned that if they did not work with him, "They will end up dealing . . . with a nuclear barbarian." Meanwhile, after Bush's first months in office, America's closest European friends condemned his administration's unilateral policies toward the environment, China, Communist North Korea, and international organizations—policies that were shaped with apparently little regard for the views of U.S. allies. The influential German magazine *Der Spiegel* termed the Bush administration "the snarling, ugly Americans."[38]

And then, on September 11, 2001, Americans suddenly came face-to-face with a tragically new world.

---

[37]An overview is in *Washington Post,* October 27, 2000, p. A14; Ibid, January 15, 2001, p. A15 on Bush and Russia; *The New York Times,* October 30, 2000, p. A16; Ibid., December 17, 2000, p. 5 on Powell.

[38]*Washington Post,* January 15, 2001, p. A15; *New York Times,* May 7, 2001, p. A9.

New York City, September 11, 2001.
(© Richard Orpw / AP Wide World Photos)

CHAPTER 15

The World Turned Upside Down (2001–2006)

On September 11, 2001, terrorist attacks dramatically changed the United States and, consequently, its foreign policies. Americans had spent the 1990s riding a wave of post-Cold-War triumphalism, proclaimed by politicians and scholars alike, that made them feel invulnerable. They watched *Forrest-Gump*-type movies, the Monica Lewinski scandal, a post-1995 booming stock market, and network nightly news programs whose coverage of overseas events declined by at least one-third between 1989 and 1999. Americans thus happily neglected complex, costly, and often-bloody foreign policy problems that festered around the world. These festered, after all, mostly far from U.S. shores. If Americans glanced overseas, it was to demand markets for their exports and investments, or to celebrate the seemingly endless expansion abroad of their McDonald's, Nike clothing, Pizza Huts, Disneylands, and military bases, all apparent indications of the global popularity and superiority of their culture.[1]

Then on September 11, two passenger jets, each hijacked by five men and revved up to 500 mph, hit and brought down the 110-story Twin World Trade Towers in New York City in a horrifying cloud of smoke and fire. A third plane controlled by five hijackers flew at 300 mph into the Pentagon, just south of Washington, D.C. The Pentagon was the seat of the globe's most powerful military whose duty was, in part, to protect the financial network reaching around the world

---

[1]A valuable, detailed, critical overview of this U.S.-led globalization movement is Jan Aart Scholte, *Globalization; A Critical Introduction* (New York, 2000), especially chapter 3.

from New York's Twin Towers. A fourth passenger jet, seized by four hijackers, was apparently to hit another Washington target but crashed in southern Pennsylvania after heroic passengers tried to retake the controls. Some 3000 people instantly died in the attacks. These included not only Americans, but men and women from more than fifty other nations, including 200 British citizens who perished in the Twin Towers collapse. A number of victims tried to escape the conflagration by jumping from 90- or 100-story windows.

The horrors clearly flashed worldwide on television, in part because it was a sunny, cloudless day on the East Coast. In another sense, however, the terror did not come out of the blue. Smaller-scale terrorism had become commonplace thirty-five years earlier in the 1960s when radicals captured business leaders for ransom, robbed banks, or killed police and innocent bystanders. Terrorism claimed seventeen victims including eleven Israeli athletes at the 1972 Olympic Games in Munich; 241 U.S. marines in Lebanon on October 23, 1983; at least six fatal crashes of large passenger planes between 1983 and 1990; and 161 lives in the 1995 bombing of the Oklahoma City Federal Building by a former U.S. soldier, Timothy McVeigh. Americans were growing up in an age of terrorism that targeted civilians.[2]

Beginning in 1993 a new pattern of terror appeared. That year, a car bombing of New York City's World Trade Center basement resulted in casualties, but little structural damage. The terrorists, linked to Osama bin Laden, were captured. Americans continued to believe they were invulnerable, at least at home if not overseas. As the world's self-proclaimed sole superpower, they had diplomats in 162 countries and 260,000 military personnel stationed abroad in more than an astounding 700 U.S. bases. In 1995, five U.S. advisers died in the bombing of a training school in Saudi Arabia. The next year a truck bomb killed nineteen Americans and injured 240 at a U.S. Air Force base in Saudi Arabia. In 1998 more than 224 people died, and 5,500 were injured, when terrorists bombed U.S. embassies

---

[2]Some noted that "one person's terrorist is another's freedom fighter," especially in parts of the world where groups used terrorism to gain independence or human rights. Terrorism has been defined by the U.S. government agency that keeps lists of such international acts: "premeditated, politically motivated violence perpetrated against noncombatant targets by subnational groups or clandestine agents, usually intended to influence an audience." Quoted and discussed in Paul R. Pillar (a CIA counterterrorist expert), *Terrorism and U.S. Foreign Policy* (Washington, D.C., 2001), pp. 13–18.

in Kenya and Tanzania. Two years later, seventeen American sailors died when their destroyer, the USS Cole, was attacked in Yemen.[3]

Three characteristics separated these post-1993 events from those before. First, the earlier attacks were usually nation-based (for example, terrorists were based in Libya or Syria), while the later strikes came from small, informal organizations that had many temporary homes and, for the most part, were inspired by an individual, Osama bin Laden, and his close associates. Second, earlier terrorism was often a specific response (Libya killed Americans, the U.S. bombed Libya, Libyans then destroyed a U.S. airliner) in a tit-for-tat exchange. But after 1993, "We began to have indiscriminate mass killings designed to shake the system to its core," in the words of one terrorist expert.[4] Third, the pre-1993 attacks were notably driven by forms of nationalism (for example, Palestinians who demanded from Israel their own country). But post-1993 terrorism was motivated primarily by religious belief, such as bin Laden's particular form of Islam.[5]

To say, however, that religious belief alone caused the September 11 terror is misleading. Bin Laden was a Muslim, a member of the world's second largest religion. (Christianity had 2 billion members, Islam 1.3 billion, Hinduism 900 million.) Many Muslims, including 3 to 5 million living in the United States, condemned the attacks and claimed that such terror against civilians had no place in their religion.

Nevertheless, some American Muslims tragically became targets. Mosques in Texas were fire-bombed and vandalized. A Muslim businessman was killed in Arizona. Fortunately, such tragedies remained few in number. American Muslims overall had done well in their adopted nation. An analysis of the 600,000 foreign-born New York City Islamic community showed that nearly three-fifths had already become U.S. citizens, and that they were better educated and earned more than the average American worker. Their most frequent occupations were "executive" or "manager of a business."[6]

---

[3]*The New York Times,* September 12, 2001, p. A18 has a good summary of post-1993. For an overview of the four planes and those who seized them on September 11, see Ibid., September 15, 2001, p. A22.

[4]Pillar, *Terrorism and U.S. Foreign Policy,* pp. 58–59.

[5]Ibid., pp. 129–196 has a detailed discussion separating "groups" from state-sponsored terrorism.

[6]Chart in *The New York Times,* November 14, 2001, p. G1.

More relevant to the terrorism was the importance of two Islamic nations, Saudi Arabia and Egypt. In other words, U.S. foreign relations were central to the September 11 tragedies. Both Saudi Arabia and Egypt were longtime allies valued by U.S. officials. The Saudis, controlling 25 percent of the world's petroleum resources, had used these riches to help keep oil prices relatively low and stable in the West. Egypt received the second-highest amount of U.S. foreign aid (second only to Israel), for opposing Islamic radicalism and sometimes working to dampen the fifty-year-long Palestinian-Israeli struggle.

Bin Laden came from Saudi Arabia. His family had grown rich in construction and other businesses. Some of his brothers had extensive holdings in the United States, and he was personally worth as much as $300 million, although this figure has been disputed. Fifteen of the nineteen hijackers on September 11 were also Saudis. Bin Laden's second-in-command, and other high officials of his al Qaeda terrorist organization, came from Egypt. Saudi Arabia remained a tightly controlled monarchy run by families grown incredibly rich by oil revenues. Egypt was a military-dominated authoritarian state. Repressive governments in both nations were necessary because the two economies enriched relatively few citizens while not helping the larger population. In Egypt, one-third of all workers were employed by the government and paid so little (about $71 a month), that they worked other jobs or turned to corruption. Saudi Arabia's economy was even more unbalanced, and both nations overflowed with young people (more than a majority in each nation were under age twenty-five), who grew more restless and radical as the economies stagnated. McDonald's golden arches rose throughout Egypt, but Egyptians and Saudis were barely touched by globalization. Most people in both countries had no access to the Internet, partly because of low income and partly due to the governments' desire that their people not have information "contrary to Islamic values."[7]

---

[7]Pippa Norris, *Digital Divide: Civic Engagement, Information Poverty, and the Internet Worldwide* (New York, 2001), pp. 55–56, 61; inequality and the failure of globalization in Egypt is discussed in *The New York Times,* October 14, 2001, p. B5. A good overview of the Egyptian problem in the 1990s and choices faced by U.S. officials is Fawaz A. Gerges, *America and Political Islam* (New York, 1999), pp. 108–114, 171–191.

The Saudis also bought some peace by allowing their Wahabbi religious leaders to verbally attack the West and modernization—as long as the Wahabbi clerics did not criticize the Saudi government or royal family. Wahabbism, founded 250 years ago, is a version of Islam that urges a return to the purity of the religion's origin in the seventh century when it was founded by the Prophet Muhammad.[8] The Saudi royal family gave as much as $10 billion a year to allow Wahabbi clerics to spread their form of Islam, preach hatred of Western modernization (including rights for women), and supposedly provide some legitimacy for the royal family itself. Bin Laden and his associates were Wahabbi. They also received good chunks of the $10 billion that the Saudi monarchy laundered each year through so-called "private charities." Americans paid little attention. They had, after all, won the Cold War and set about profiting from that triumph.

The September 11 attacks were, however, the children of that Cold War. A straight line runs from the U.S.-Soviet struggle in the 1980s over Afghanistan (see pp. 316, 345), to the tragedies in New York City and Washington. This line can be traced by following Osama bin Laden's path.

Born in 1957, he was the seventeenth of fifty-seven children produced by his father, from Yemen. His mother, a Saudi, was one of many wives. Deeply religious, he left Saudi Arabia to help his fellow Muslims in Afghanistan fight the Soviet invaders. He soon worked with Pakistani and, more indirectly, U.S. intelligence agents who supplied his and similar groups with arms—especially 900 to 1000 Stinger missiles. A single soldier could carry and fire a stinger to bring down helicopters or low-flying airplanes. When the Soviets finally left in 1989, bin Laden turned his sights on the remaining superpower. As he later said, "The collapse of the Soviet Union made the U.S. more haughty and arrogant and it has started to look at itself as a master of this world and established what it called the New World order."[9]

---

[8]Karen Armstrong, *Islam, A Short History* (New York, 2000), pp. 135, 161–162 offers a good introduction to Islam and its Wahhabi followers.
[9]Quoted, with good context, in Peter L. Bergen, *Holy War Inc.; Inside the Secret World of Osama bin Laden* (New York, 2001), pp. 19–20. This is a useful biography of bin Laden. For a critical analysis of U.S. views and policies, 1989–1991, against which bin Laden said he was reacting, note Christian Alfonsi, *Circle in the Sand; Why We Went Back to Iraq* (New York, 2006), especially chapters 5–6.

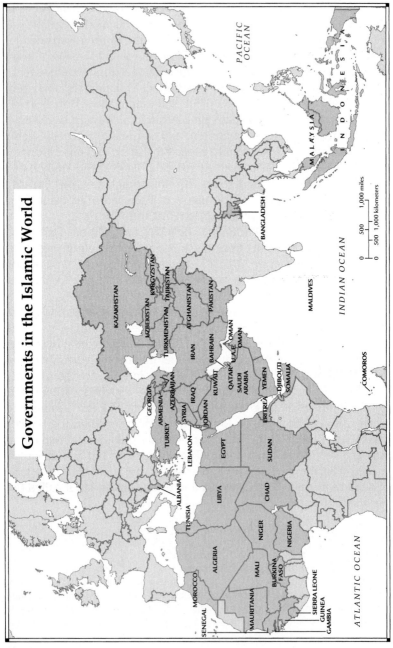

Governments in the Islamic World

His anti-American feelings were inflamed after the Gulf War of 1991 when U.S. military bases, with 20,000 personnel, remained in Saudi Arabia. In his eyes, the U.S. presence profaned the center of Islamic religion. He was now a hero to many Muslims around the world, for he had given up a plush lifestyle to fight for Islamic principles. His popularity and anti-Western ideas grew to the point that nervous Saudi leaders threw him out of the country in 1991. Bin Laden shrewdly looked for war-wrecked, politically divided nations where he could hide in the chaos. Americans, thinking the Cold War was over, were celebrating while cutting back aid and attention to areas devastated directly and indirectly by that Cold War. Two nations largely ignored by Americans were Sudan and, especially, Afghanistan, where the war with Russia had left 1.5 million dead and vast devastation. Bin Laden first went to Sudan, then in 1996 traveled in a chartered jet with his three wives back to Afghanistan.

That year a radical religious group, the Taliban, climaxed seven years of civil war by taking over most of Afghanistan. Their opponents, a loose coalition of warlords called the Northern Alliance, were largely contained in the country's north. As Wahabbis, the Taliban sought to return, literally, to Prophet Muhammad's world of 1400 years earlier. The Taliban forced women out of schools and work and into the home—and into clothing that covered head-to-toe so men would not be distracted from thinking religious thoughts. The Internet, televisions, telephones, music cassettes, and lipstick were banned. A number of foreigners and Afghans faced the death penalty for preaching Christianity. The new regime happily accepted as much as $100 million of protection money from bin Laden. The Taliban received further help from neighboring Pakistan.[10]

The Clinton administration showed little concern about the Taliban until 1996 when oil became an issue. The United States wanted to take the black gold out of the rich Caspian Sea area by running a pipeline through Afghanistan, thus avoiding both Russia and Iran (see map, p. 390). U.S. officials even offered to work with the Taliban. (For some Americans, oil profits were much more important than cultural differences.) But relations cooled when the country's religious leaders appeared to be beyond American influence.[11]

---

[10]Bernard Lewis, *Islam and the West* (New York, 1993), pp. 156–165 notes Islamic divisions.
[11]Ahmed Rashid, *Taliban; Militant Islam, Oil, and Fundamentalism in Central Asia* (New Haven, 2000), a superb analysis—see especially pp. xii–xiv, 29–33, 43–46; *Washington Post*, October 15, 2001, p. A1.

In 1998, bin Laden's terrorists attacked the two U.S. embassies in Africa. During February of that year, he announced a jihad (a religious striving) against "Jews and Crusaders [western Christians]." He blasted the United States for "occupying . . . the holiest of places, the Arabian Peninsula," and for bombing Iraq (which U.S. officials believed was, under Saddam Hussein's dictatorship, developing nuclear and other weapons of mass destruction). He issued a fatwa (a theological order) "to all Muslims." The order stated: "to kill the Americans and their allies—civilians and military—is an individual duty for every Muslim who can do it in any country in which it is possible to do it." The fatwa demanded Muslims "liberate" Saudi Arabia from the U.S. "grip."[12]

Americans asked, especially after September 11, "Who are these people who hate us so much?"[13] That question could begin to be answered by noting that bin Laden ordered not only a jihad against "infidels," but a class war against the world's richest nations. He appealed to Muslims, many of whom lived in some of the world's poorest states, to kill Americans. The overwhelming number of those who responded were not born and raised in North America or Western Europe, but in the Middle East and African nations such as Egypt and Saudi Arabia where few people were rich and many poor. Deeply studying their history, Muslims knew that centuries earlier Islam was more advanced in science and many other fields than was Christian Europe. Since the nineteenth century, the West had not only overtaken them but had conquered many of their lands. Muslims experienced firsthand the devastating development that in 1830 the globe's richest country had only three times the income as the poorest, but after 170 years of Western-led globalization, the richest enjoyed thirty times the income of the poorest, and too often Islamic, states.[14] It was a highly revealing statistic.

When al Qaeda terrorists attacked the two U.S. embassies in 1998, the Clinton administration responded with missile attacks on Afghanistan to kill bin Laden, and on Sudan to destroy one of his suspected chemical weapons plants. At least thirty people died but bin Laden escaped, apparently by only a few hours. The Sudan plant turned out to have no

---

[12]Statement issued by the World Islamic Front, February 23, 1998. The text can be found in the chapter 15 documents at this book's www.mhhe.com/lafeber website.
[13]*The New York Times,* October 15, 2001, p. A19; Tony Judt, "America and the War," *The New York Review of Books,* November 15, 2001, especially p. 4.
[14]Jeff Madrick, "Economic Scene," *The New York Times,* November 1, 2001, p. C2.

relationship to him. Because "the attack was so limited and incompetent," one U.S. expert believed, "we turned this guy into a folk hero."[15] By using missiles, moreover, Clinton showed terrorists he did not intend to put U.S. troops on the ground and in danger. The most he wanted was to land a small team of elite Special Operations troops in Afghanistan to track down bin Laden. But for the U.S. military chiefs, the Powell Doctrine (see p. 327) ruled out such a venture. Privately, these uniformed officials accused Clinton of "going Hollywood," that is, wanting a showy operation that would probably amount to nothing. When the military chiefs advised that only a major military commitment using tens of thousands of troops would work, Clinton pulled back. The President wanted no part of an attack on an entire country (Afghanistan) that protected terrorists, especially if such a war on Muslims could arouse the Islamic world.[16]

Clinton announced that antiterrorism was a top priority, then tripled the small amount of funds that had been available for fighting terrorism. He and his aides warned that a major terrorist act was imminent, but admitted they did not know where or when. CIA and FBI antiterrorist resources rapidly increased. The two agencies, however, mistrusted each other to the point that one sometimes refused to share information with the other. Both, moreover, lacked specialists who could speak the Arabic languages. A rapid fall-off of student interest in, and government support for, foreign-language training in U.S. universities had been another result of post-Cold-War American triumphalism. As a former FBI official groused, "If you don't have an Arab-American agent on your staff, how the hell do you recruit Arabs? You don't even understand the culture." Clinton meanwhile set out to work secretly with Pakistani agents to kill bin Laden, but Taliban spies infiltrated and spoiled the operation.[17]

In the thirty years before 9/11, Arab and Islamic terrorists had killed nearly 1000 Americans. The terrorism included the blasting of the American warship in Yemen even as the 2000 presidential campaign accelerated. Republican presidential nominee George W. Bush and his top foreign-policy adviser Condoleezza Rice, seemed relatively unconcerned about the rising terrorism. During the 2000 campaign, they

[15]*Washington Post,* September 24, 2001, p. A8; also Ibid., October 3, 2001, p. A18.
[16]Ibid., December 19, 2001, p. A1, an important analysis by Barton Gellman; Ibid., October 3, 2001, p. A18.
[17]Ibid., December 19, 2001, pp. A1 and especially A26; Ibid., October 3, 2001, p. A18.

stressed, in Bush's words, the "priorities" of "Russia and a strong NATO
...; China ...; our own hemisphere; as well as the Middle East."[18]

Once in control of policy during early 2001, the Bush administration
became known for the powerful, so-called neoconservatives who held
considerable power, especially in the Defense Department. Led by
Deputy Secretary of Defense Paul Wolfowitz, the group included Undersecretary of Defense Douglas Feith, personnel in the White House, and,
publicly, *The Weekly Standard*, edited by William Kristol, which along with
Fox Network became a media favorite of the administration. Neoconservatives believed in deploying the unmatched U.S. military power, unilaterally if necessary, to beat back any rising challenge from (they
emphasized in 2000–early 2001) China, and also to extend U.S. democratic principles across the globe. Many of the neoconservatives were
deeply concerned about Israel, the most important and powerful U.S.
ally in the Middle East, and consequently had long been committed to
destroying Saddam Hussein's dictatorship in Iraq. (Saddam had provided $25,000 to families of suicide bombers who had blown up Israelis
along with themselves.) They were committed to turning authoritarian
Islamic regimes in the Middle East into peaceful democracies. Other
powerful Bush officials—including Vice President Richard Cheney, Secretary of Defense Donald Rumsfeld, National Security Council adviser
Rice, and Attorney General John Ashcroft—also were determined to wield
American power to beat down global challenges and to work closely
with Israel in the Middle East. Taking a more traditional American conservative line, however, this group doubted the rougher parts of the
world (especially in the Middle East) were ready to be democratized, so
they diverged on this point from the neoconservatives. Secretary of State
Colin Powell stood apart from both the neoconservatives (he wanted no
part of a crusade to spread democracy, not after his experiences in the last
crusade, Vietnam), and the traditional conservatives (who, for his taste,
were too willing to put U.S. military lives at stake).[19]

[18]Ivo H. Daalder and James M. Lindsay, *America Unbound* (Washington, D.C., 2004),
p. 83; Jim Mann, *Rise of the Vulcans* (New York, 2004), p. 258.
[19]Daalder and Lindsay, *America Unbound*, p. 15; Stefan Halper and Jonathan Clarke,
America Alone: The Neo-Conservatives and the Global Order (New York, 2004), useful for
distinguishing these younger from an older generation of neoconservatives of the
1950s–1960s; Robert W. Merry, *Sands of Empire* (New York, 2005), pp. 153–173; John
Micklethwait and Adrian Wooldridge, *The Right Nation; Conservative Power in America*
(New York, 2004), especially chapters 7–8, a valuable account; James Risen, *State of
War* (New York, 2006), pp. 71–76.

But between January and early September 2001, all the new officials seemed to agree that terrorism posed no immediate danger to Americans. This quiet agreement arose in part because the outgoing Clinton administration warned them about terrorists, and the Bush team automatically discounted advice from the former President, especially if the advice implied cooperating with European (or many other) allies who might question U.S. intentions. When the top U.S. antiterrorism official, Richard Clarke, gave Rice a memo in January 2001 that argued a meeting on al Qaeda was "urgently needed," she never scheduled the meeting and effectively demoted Clarke. In May, 2001, Vice President Cheney became the head of a task force assigned to examine the threat of terrorism inside the United States. By early September, it had done little. When several lower officials wanted to change U.S. laws to fight terrorism and especially move against the financing of terrorists, they got nowhere.[20]

On August 6, 2001, U.S. intelligence warned President Bush in his morning briefing that it was possible "a group" of "bin Laden supporters was in the U.S. planning attacks with explosives." Bush and his top advisers seemed to have no response. While thinking about possible state rivals (China, Russia), they appeared to have trouble focusing on non-state entities, such as al Qaeda, whose cells easily moved around among many nations. Not until September 4, 2001 did the Cabinet discuss al Qaeda. On September 11 itself, Condoleezza Rice planned to give a speech on "The Threats and Problems of Today and the Day After." Her address implicitly attacked the Clinton administration for not dealing with the real problem: missile defense. When Rice's speech draft did mention terrorism, she linked it to rogue nations, such as Iraq.[21]

Along with most other administration officials, Rice instead spent part of September 11 in an underground bunker. Americans soon learned that the terrorists had prepared their mission in several areas, especially Florida, Minnesota, and New England, and al Qaeda

---

[20]Mann, *Rise of the Vulcans*, p. 292; Clarke, *Against All Enemies*, p. 196; Daalder and Lindsey, *America Unbound*, pp. 73–76.

[21]Clarke, *Against All Enemies*, p. 24; *Washington Post*, April 1, 2004, p. A1 for the Rice speech draft; *The 9/11 Report: The National Commission on Terrorist Attacks upon the United States* (New York, 2004), pp. xcvi–xcvii; *The New York Times*, April 4, 2004, p. 30; the August 6, 2001 memo can be found, courtesy of CNN.com, in this book's chapter 15 documents at www.mhhe.com/lafeber website.

members were rounded up in the Midwest. The total costs of the attacks were about $400,000 to $500,000 for al Qaeda, approximately a trillion dollars for Americans. Already weak because of overexpansion followed by rapid decline in high-tech businesses, the shocked economy staggered into its worst tailspin in a decade. Hundreds of thousands of people lost their jobs. There was no place to hide from the September 11 horrors.[22]

On September 12, President Bush called the attack an "act of war." But it seemed an odd war. As he observed, fighting terrorists was weird and complex, a conflict "without battlefields or beachheads." It seemed to be a war against not a nation, but an individual, Osama bin Laden, and his al Qaeda group that had cells in some sixty countries, including the United States. It seemed even more odd when Bush went on television and did not demand American sacrifice, as U.S. Presidents had in 1917, 1941, and 1950, but told the country instead to spend money "at the malls," and to "go down to Disney World."

The President's call to enjoy Mickey and Minnie Mouse was welcomed by nervous Americans, but also seemed quite misleading. For while he told those Americans to have a good time spending money, Bush immediately began to structure strong presidential powers based on the assumption that the nation was at "war," and that he was a wartime President—even though Congress never declared war, as the Constitution required. The nature of the conflict (that is, fighting scattered terrorists, while Americans spent as much money as possible) seemed to make the usual war declaration inadvisable. On September 14, Congress passed an authorization bill granting the President the right to use "all necessary and appropriate force" against terrorists associated with the attacks of three days before. The White House had wanted the wording to be broader and more permissive for the President's use, and not limited to those terrorists.

Over the next four years, Bush nevertheless took his power far beyond Congress's measure of September 14, until he became one of the most powerful presidents in American history. The Bush White House believed in a "unitary presidency," in which, its supporters claimed, the presidency was not merely equal to the other two branches of government (as the Constitution states), but superior to

---

[22]*The 9/11 Report*, p. xcviii.

Congress and the courts. Bush signed legislative measures (as one outlawing torture), then quietly recorded that he need not abide by the legislation. No president had ever done this so many times or over so many years. Congress—and the American people—did little in response. Those most worried seemed to be a few conservatives who feared what might happen if a liberal, say Senator Hillary Clinton of New York, would later take over these new powers.[23]

Bush was constantly pushed to extend his powers by Vice President Cheney, who believed that the public and congressional reaction against President Nixon's coverup of the Watergate break-in of 1972, and also the nation's reaction at the same time against the presidentially directed Vietnam War, had led Congress to limit unwisely the Executive's authority. Cheney was half-correct: the crimes of the Watergate break-in, and the lies and misleading information that took Americans into Vietnam had—correctly—led Congress to cut back the imperial presidency. The Vice President was mistaken in believing that Bush should try to regain, indeed go beyond, the powers Kennedy, Johnson, and Nixon had claimed—a claim that had destroyed the Johnson and Nixon presidencies.[24] Bush's powers grew until the "accidental president" of the hotly contested 2000 election exercised authority approaching that of Franklin D. Roosevelt's in World War II. As early as November 15, 2001, conservative columnist William Safire's analysis in *The New York Times* was headlined, "Seizing Dictatorial Powers."

Within forty-eight hours of the September 11 attacks, Rumsfeld and Wolfowitz, the two top Defense Department officials, began to argue that Iraq should have to pay, and heavily. No credible evidence emerged that al Qaeda was linked to Iraq's Saddam Hussein. Al Qaeda was devoutly religious, while Saddam's regime was secular, even as it ruled an Islamic country. In the 1980s and 1990s, Saddam had deeply mistrusted and even fought such religious groups. Wolfowitz apparently refused to believe that only al Qaeda had attacked the United States; Saddam, he argued, had to be involved—even though U.S. intelligence reports clearly told Bush that Saddam was not connected

---

[23]*Washington Post,* September 15, 2001, pp. 1–4; Bob Woodward, *Bush at War* (New York, 2002), pp. 44–46; David Bromwich, "A Republic Divided," *Daedalus* (Spring, 2006); Elizabeth Drew, "Bush's Power Grab," *New York Review of Books,* June 22, 2006, especially p. 15, for this and the previous paragraph.

[24]*Washington Post,* December 21, 2005, pp. A1 and especially A6.

to 9/11. The President overruled the two Defense officials, at least for a time. Bin Laden and al Qaeda were headquartered in Afghanistan, and that had to be the first target.[25]

Bush told the Taliban government controlling Afghanistan to deliver bin Laden "dead or alive" or face U.S. military strikes. The Taliban refused, partly on the ground that Muslims do not surrender other Muslims to infidels. With the approval of the nearby Russians and Chinese, the President moved small military forces into position. To find needed close-by bases, he reversed years of U.S. policy by making an informal—and by early 2002, formal—military relationship with Pakistan's military regime headed by General Pervez Musharraf. (Only months earlier, Washington had imposed economic sanctions on Musharraf because in 1999 he had overthrown an elected civilian government.) Bush also made base agreements with Uzbekistan, until 1991 a part of the Soviet Union, and since then a dictatorship with a horrible human rights record. But the Uzbek regime, with good access to neighboring Afghanistan, was commited to fighting its own Islamic terrorists.

Then, as war approached, came the crackdown within the United States itself. Bush tightened immigration policies, without asking for congressional action, by reorganizing the Immigration and Naturalization Service. Again without consulting Congress, he ordered that captured terrorists who were not U.S. citizens could be tried in military (not civilian) courts. Such an order had been rarely issued in American history, was highly controversial (especially since appeals could be made only to higher military authority or to Bush himself), and became an immediate target of those concerned about individual liberties.

Attorney General John Ashcroft, meanwhile, claimed the right to detain suspects secretly and to listen in on conversations between lawyers and their clients, even if the clients had not been charged with a crime. He issued a new, more flexible policy for tapping cell phones. Bush also announced that a sitting President could block the release of an earlier President's records. This order undermined congressional laws and policies dating back to the 1970s. The President

---

[25]Clarke, *Against All Enemies*, pp. 30–31; *The New York Times*, November 27, 2005, p. 11wk; Ron Suskind, *The Price of Loyalty; George W. Bush, the White House, and the Education of Paul O'Neill* (New York, 2004), pp. 72–76, 186–190.

could now, for example, make impossible the release of information about why his father had ordered Americans to fight and die in Panama and the Gulf War between 1989 and 1991. The Bush administration suddenly embarked on reclassifying records that had long been declassified and even published. Government agents began locking up documents from, say, the 1940s which had been public for years and seemed to pose no harm.[26]

A leading U.S. newspaper feared just three months after the September 11 attacks that Americans were being led "down a path that will surely wind up embarrassing the country and undermining our own standing as a defender of international human rights and global justice." The newspaper observed that the United States, after all, had condemned others—notably the Soviet Union—"for holding secret trials."[27]

Anti-war movements appeared on some college campuses, but polls reported that 80 percent of American college students supported the air strikes on Afghanistan, more than two-thirds approved using ground troops, and 60 percent trusted the federal government to do the right thing (only 36 percent had such trust a year earlier). Bush also rode a wave of patriotism that had begun to rise before the September terrorism. Films such as *Saving Private Ryan* and books (Tom Brokaw's *The Greatest Generation*) enjoyed huge audiences by extolling Americans who fought World War II. Purchases of gas masks, weapons (notably shotguns), and bottled water spiraled upward, but the biggest seller was the American flag.[28]

Meanwhile, as Bush prepared to strike Afghanistan, Secretary of State Colin Powell pieced together a coalition of allies, some quite surprising. Russia's Vladimir Putin was the first foreign leader to call Bush and offer help after September 11. The usual friends also rushed to support the United States, including Great Britain's Prime Minister, Tony Blair. The British leader also first made public some evidence linking bin Laden directly to the September 11 horrors.

---

[26]*Washington Post,* November 20, 2001, pp. A1, A14, for an overview; *The New York Times,* December 2, 2001, p. 14wk; Richard Reeves, "Writing History to Executive Order," Ibid., November 16, 2001, p. A25.

[27]*The New York Times* editorial, December 2, 2001, p. 14wk.

[28]*Washington Post,* November 1, 2001, p. A36 has the college student poll; *The New York Times,* September 14, 2001, p. A23 on the sales.

Blair thus quieted at least some in the Islamic world and elsewhere who argued that bin Laden had not been involved.[29]

On October 7, 2001, U.S. and British air forces began striking Afghanistan. A defiant bin Laden suddenly appeared in a videotape on television to exalt that "America is struck by God Almighty in one of its vital organs, so that its greatest buildings are destroyed. Grace and gratitude to God." He directly called up history as justification: "for more than 80 years,"—that is, since the breakup of the Ottoman empire led to the British and French colonial takeover in the 1920s of some Islamic areas—there had been "humiliation and disgrace." But now "God has blessed a group of vanguard Muslims . . . to destroy America." Then came eerie echoes of the early Cold War: bin Laden declared the world stood "divided into two camps, the camp of the faithful and the camp of the infidels." Bush picked up the same two-camp theme in his September 20 speech: "Every nation in every region now has a decision to make: either you are with us or you are with the terrorists."[30]

Bin Laden appeared on the al-Jazeera television network which was based in the small Gulf kingdom of Qatar. Al-Jazeera soon became one of the best known and influential of media; within five years it was so well known that it launched its own English-language programs available in Europe and the United States. It had a regular audience in the Middle East of at least 35 million. While al-Jazeera interviewed U.S. and European officials, its programs were often seen as anti-Western, especially anti-Israeli. When U.S. officials complained about this bias to Qatar's authoritarian ruler, the emir solemnly replied that, after all, democracies require a free media. Bin Laden and al-Jazeera threw back the new high-tech globalization against Americans who had originated so much of the technology.[31]

Although U.S. Special Operations troops launched ground attacks against the Taliban government in Afghanistan, the brunt of the fighting was done by the Americans' Afghan ally, the Northern Alliance. This collection of tribes and warlords supported itself largely by growing poppies for opium and heroin use in the United States and elsewhere. Washington officials, however, were in no

---

[29]*The New York Times,* October 5, 2001, p. A1 for the Blair statement and an analysis.
[30]*The New York Times,* October 1, 2001, p. B7. For the two-camp theme of the early Cold War, see above, ch.3
[31]Judt, "America and the War," p. 5.

position to examine badly needed allies too closely. By the end of 2001, the Taliban had been driven from the major cities, but bin Laden escaped. It was later revealed that Bush and Rumsfeld refused to commit more than one U.S. division to the fighting—that is, fewer troops were devoted to the supposed task of capturing bin Laden and his top advisers than the number of New York City police assigned to Manhattan. U.S. Special Forces and their Islamic experts were pulled out for reassignment to areas around Iraq.[32]

But even as President Bush shifted his attention to Iraq, the war in Afghanistan did not end over the next five years. About the size of Texas, with 26 million people, Afghanistan's eastern mountains provided mazes of protection for anti-U.S. groups, especially after bin Laden's construction crews created multilevel living spaces deep within. Taliban leaders joined him. Both received help from sympathizers from nearby Pakistan, which shared the eastern mountain boundary. Throughout the nineteenth century, British and Russian imperialists had fought each other in "The Great Game" to see which could control this "cockpit of Asia," as a London official tagged Afghanistan.[33]

This time, however, the Westerners were not taking on nineteenth-century natives on horseback. Bin Laden used U.S.-produced, computer-sized satellite phones costing $7,500. His anti-Western declarations were printed on Apple computers with the most advanced encryption software, sent electronically to al Qaeda cells, then beamed through satellites to printers in New York. A top U.S. intelligence official believed that bin Laden used better communication technology than did the United States. Such sophisticated technology allowed al Qaeda to decentralize its operations and to continue them even if, for example, bin Laden and, perhaps, cells in forty countries were destroyed.[34]

It turned out bin Laden resembled Americans in having a vision of globalization. The American version used new technology to create open markets, expand democracy, and spread U.S. popular culture.

[32]*The New York Times,* October 5, 2001, pp. A1, B5; Clarke, *Against All Enemies,* p. 245; on U.S. Special Forces note Tom Clancy with General Carl Stiner (ret.), *Shadow Warriors* (New York, 2002) for their history and makeup.

[33]Rashid, *Taliban,* p. 7; also *Boston Globe,* October 23, 2001, p. A12.

[34]Bergen, *Holy War, Inc.,* pp. 20–27, 197; *Washington Post,* December 13, 2001, p. A22, for U.S. high-tech weapons.

Bin Laden used the new technology to hasten globally the return of the Caliphate (the religious and civil head of a puritanical Islamic state that would rule believers while punishing infidels everywhere). U.S. troops discovered in Afghanistan that al Qaeda had attempted to draw up plans for weapons of mass destruction, including biological and chemical agents. Vice President Richard Cheney predicted that "for the first time in our history, we will probably suffer more casualties here at home in America [in this war] than will our troops overseas."[35]

By 2002, the all-important question for Bush seemed to be: if Cheney's prophesy about U.S. casualties caused by terrorism was to be avoided, where should American forces next move? One of the globe's distinguished scholars, Michael Howard of Oxford University, gave one answer at the moment Bush pondered the question.

Howard warned that the worst policy would be to invade sovereign Islamic nations, then call it a "war" against terrorism. Terrorists, he believed, should not be "dignified with the states of [country-based] belligerents: they were criminals" and should not be given "a status and dignity that they seek and that they do not deserve." He urged Bush to avoid a "catharsis"; that is, he should not try to avenge the 9/11 attacks with spectacular military actions. Such wars against Islamic nations would alienate even those Muslims who now despised al Qaeda. And to attack Iraq would resemble "the drunk who lost his watch in a dark alley but looked for it under a lamppost because there was more light there." Al Qaeda, Howard wrote, was not in Iraq, but did exist in many other countries. Bush should cooperate with other intelligence agencies, seize and break up the terrorist networks, then either kill the terrorists or bring them before courts. To invade Islamic nations could turn those nations into breeding grounds for terrorists, while "eroding the moral authority" of the United States as it killed innocent civilians in the attack. Such an invasion would resemble "trying to eradicate cancer cells with a blowtorch." Vital areas (Turkey, Egypt, Pakistan) could be consumed in the flames, while the cancer's cause, Osama bin Laden, could escape and "cannot lose."[36]

---

[35]Bergen, *Holy War, Inc.*, pp. 20–26; Scholte, *Globalization*, pp. 187–189, offers a brief overview of "religious globalization"; *The New York Times*, November 4, 2001, p. B7; Ibid., November 11, 2001, p. B1 for al Qaeda's attempts to build chemical weapons.
[36]Michael Howard, "What's in a Name? How to Fight Terrorism," *Foreign Affairs*, 81 (January–February 2002): 8–13.

Howard's argument appeared as a speech in London and as a paper published in the most prestigious U.S. foreign-policy journal. But Americans, and especially Washington officials, paid it little attention. They were too busy dismissing Islam for not fully supporting U.S. policies, or—as did neoconservatives Kenneth Adelman and Eliot Cohen—condemning Islam for being a "militaristic religion." They said this after Bush declared that "the face of terror is not the true face of Islam," which "is a faith that has made brothers and sisters of every race. It's a faith based upon love, not hate." Al Qaeda was not to be confused with a billion other Muslims, but Americans who wanted war with Iraq blurred the vast distinction and ignored Howard's ominous warning.[37]

By early 2002, Bush was quickly moving toward war with Saddam Hussein. His own approval rating ran steadily in the 80 to 90 percent range, an incredibly high number. George H. W. Bush's son now seemed determined to finish a job his father had not (for good reasons) finished in 1991 (see pp. 363–364). When later asked whether he had consulted his father, the younger Bush replied he mainly had talked with him about "tactics." "You know," the President added, "he is the wrong father to appeal to in terms of strength. There is a higher father that I appeal to." Until nearly the age of forty, Bush had suffered from alcoholism and little business success of his own. He then became a devout, born-again Christian and rid himself of his alcoholism (and saved his marriage).

Bush had come to define the world in simple terms. He believed "Moral truth is the same in every culture, in every time, and in every place," as he told West Point cadets in mid-2002. "We are in a conflict between good and evil, and America will call evil by its name."[38] But moral truths (for example, whether it is moral to execute a convicted killer) are far from being the same "in every culture." Bush was soon to discover, as Reinhold Niebuhr's writings could have informed him,

---

[37]*Washington Post*, November 30, 2002, p. A4; *9/11 Report*, p. 81.

[38]The important West Point speech can be read at the chapter 15 documents of this book's website: www.mhhe.com/lafeber; Woodward, *Plan of Attack*, p. 421 for Bush's "higher father" quote; Mel Gurtov and Peter Van Ness, eds., *Confronting the Bush Doctrine* (London, 2005), p. 6 for quotes and analysis; for insight into the religious beliefs of both Bush and his chief speech writer, see Jeffrey Goldberg, "The Believer," *The New Yorker*, February 13 and 20, 2006, pp. 56–69; an important discussion is in Morris Berman, *Dark Ages America* (New York, 2006), pp. 104, 151–152, 199–203.

that good and evil are considerably more complex and blurred in the harsh realities of international relations. Franklin D. Roosevelt and Winston Churchill, for instance, had not thought of Stalin as "good," certainly not after the Soviet dictator had slaughtered millions of his own countrymen, but they allied with him because Hitler was worse.

One senior White House official explained to journalist Ron Suskind (a former senior correspondent at the *The Wall Street Journal*) why the President could view the world as he did. Journalists and others, the official instructed Suskind, were "in what we call the reality-based community" and "study . . . discernible reality. . . . [But] that's not the way the world really works anymore. . . . We're an empire now," this top White House figure continued, "and when we act, we create our own reality. And while you're studying that reality . . . we'll act again, creating other new realities, which you can study too, and that's how things will sort out." To separate oneself (as this official was separating the President) from "the reality-based community" seemed a most unusual and worrisome thing to do for anyone exercising vast power (including over the nuclear button). To think that "discernible reality" could be replaced by the Bush administration creating "our own reality" was extraordinary. To some, it seemed to resemble an irrational person ignoring "discernible reality" in order to "create [his] own reality." For the President, his "own reality" became a view of the world which justified seeing it in black/white, good/evil, terms, and a view of Iraq which justified war—and which allowed him to disregard opposing intelligence information, say, from dissenting State Department officials or the United Nations.[39]

In early 2002, Bush announced that an "axis of evil"—Iraq, Iran, North Korea—existed, and implied he would deal with such "evil."[40] The President's call-to-action especially targeted Iraq, although available evidence strongly indicated that Saddam had nothing to do with the 9/11 attacks. By July 2002, eight months before the invasion and while the President publicly denied that he had invasion plans on his desk, British officials secretly learned firsthand that Bush had decided to "remove Saddam, through military action," and that the war was "inevitable." Top U.S. leaders, British Foreign Secretary Jack Straw secretly reported, were only looking for a proper

---

[39]Ron Suskind, "Without a Doubt," *The New York Times Magazine*, October 17, 2004.
[40]Woodward, *Plan of Attack*, pp. 86–89, 91–96.

justification for launching the war, but the case was thin. Saddam was not threatening his neighbors, and his WMD (Weapons of Mass Destruction) capability was less than that of Libya, North Korea, or Iran—none of which was threatened by a U.S. attack for having such weapons. The British believed two excuses for overthrowing Saddam, self-defense and humanitarian intervention, were much too weak. A third reason, however—Saddam's refusal to allow UN inspectors to go anywhere they pleased to ensure he had no WMD capability—might work.[41]

Having famously defined the world as simply "good" and "evil," Bush was having problems making a persuasive case, especially to potential allies, that Saddam was so evil that he was worth the possible sacrifice of thousands of lives and chaos in the explosive Middle East. The President was, however, helped in his hour of need by U.S. and British authors who took it upon themselves to convince Americans that as the world's greatest power, they had to follow the nineteenth-century British imperial example and bring balance and civilization to those parts of the world (especially the Middle East) which such widely published scholars as Bernard Lewis of Princeton were labeling anti-modern and, thus, anti-United States.

For example, British-born Sebastian Mallaby, a *Washington Post* columnist, argued that the destruction of British and lesser empires after 1945 had left a power vacuum in parts of the world. Nothing less than "chaos" was threatening, Mallaby warned, and he believed it was the United States' job to make the world right. Niall Ferguson, another author from England, wrote several popular books arguing that the British Empire (which at least one close relative had helped run) had made the world more civilized, and that Americans had to replace the British as, supposedly, helpful imperialists. For example, Ferguson wondered why graduates from the good U.S. colleges did not head out to help civilize dangerous parts of the Middle East or Africa instead of—as they seemed to prefer—make money at home. Best-selling books on that most admired of American imperialists, Theodore Roosevelt, appeared. The volumes seldom got around to explaining how, as president, TR had deliberately turned away from

---

[41]The British document can be found in the June 9, 2005 issue of *The New York Review of Books*, and it is quoted and analyzed at length by Mark Danner on Tomeditor@aol.com, May 15, 2005.

a U.S. empire in Asia after 1906 because he knew the policy could become, and indeed was already in 1907 becoming, a disaster. During 2002–2003, anti-imperialism, and more accurate history which did not fit in with their desire for some kind of military action, seemed not to be popular with Americans. Widely respected columnists and television news analysts accepted these pro-imperial arguments and joined the growing consensus for war.[42]

Deeply enraged by the 9/11 attack, while too often ignoring their own limitations and history (which included the first successful modern revolution against that supposedly beneficent British Empire), Americans willingly suspended their disbelief. When officials such as Wolfowitz suggested that rebuilding Iraq would resemble how Americans and their allies successfully rebuilt Germany and Japan between 1945 and 1951, informed scholars responded by pointing out that Iraq was in no important way comparable to Germany and Japan. Americans nevertheless seemed to accept, or at least act on, Wolfowitz's version of their history. For their part, Democratic party leaders were caught up in the surge toward war and, fearful of being branded as weak on defense, joined Republicans in pushing through a measure in the fall of 2002 giving Bush their permission to attack Iraq virtually on his terms. One critic noted, "Instead of . . . preserving the republican form of government, they gave the president unchecked power." Bush shrewdly timed the vote just before the November 2002 congressional elections. Few candidates wished to commit political suicide by questioning a series of administration claims about the great dangers coming from Iraq, claims which proved to be untrue.[43]

Secretary of State Powell had urged the President and NSC director Condoleezza Rice to be patient and ensure any attack on Iraq was supported by hard evidence and important allies. Powell warned Bush about "the Pottery Barn rule: You break it, you own it."

---

[42]Mallaby is discussed in *The New York Times,* January 12, 2002, p. B7; Niall Ferguson, *Empire* (New York, 2003), and *Colossus: the Price of America's Empire* (New York, 2004); Edmund Morris, *Theodore Rex* (New York, 2001); on commentators and columnists, note Norman Solomon, *War Made Easy* (Hoboken, NJ, 2005), especially chapters 9 to 15; excellent historical and contemporary background can be found in Eric Alterman, *When Presidents Lie* (New York, 2004).

[43]The critic was the distinguished presidential scholar of the Congressional Research Service at the Library of Congress, Louis Fisher, "Deciding on War Against Iraq: Institutional Failures," *Political Science Quarterly,* 118 (Number 3, 2003): especially pp. 403, 407.

Bush dismissed this warning. British documents indicated that by the time the Secretary of State talked with Bush in the summer of 2002, the President had decided to invade Iran, but he encouraged Powell by agreeing to wait for more United Nations support. Meanwhile, however, Vice President Cheney alleged "a pattern of relationships" had been discovered between al Qaeda and Iraq "going back many years." In August 2002 he mistakenly stated that Saddam "continues to pursue a nuclear weapon." Bush claimed, wrongly, in early 2003 that Iraq furnished al Qaeda with "bomb-making" experts and "chemical and biological weapons training." In this atmosphere, when the U.S. Senator from Georgia, Senator Max Cleland (Dem.)—who had lost three limbs fighting in Vietnam—raised questions about Bush-Cheney policies, well-financed Republicans attacked him as un-American and defeated his 2002 reelection bid. Republicans easily maintained their control of Congress in the elections.[44]

The false information which trapped Bush, Cheney, and other officials emerged from several sources. One was Ahmad Chalabi, the Iraqi expatriate leader in London and long a leader of the anti-Saddam group, the Iraqi National Congress. The United States had supported him with millions of dollars. But Chalabi, significantly, was also very close to the Iranians, who were members of Bush's "axis of evil." He, like nearly all Iraqi exiles, was a Shiia Muslim, as were the large majority of Iranians. (Saddam Hussein and his ruling party in Iraq were largely Sunni Muslim.)[45] Chalabi and Iran fully agreed on the central point: they wanted Saddam Hussein to be destroyed by Americans—preferably, to spare themselves the expense and loss of lives. Chalabi relayed highly dubious information to Washington officials about Saddam's plans for developing weapons of mass destruction. Some U.S. intelligence voices, including experts in the Defense Department itself, believed the exile's

---

[44]Woodward, *Plan of Attack*, pp. 149–152, for the Powell discussion; *The New York Times*, June 20, 2004, p. 4wk; *The New Yorker*, October 27, 2003, p. 81; for a retrospective on the Democrats, note *Washington Post*, August 22, 2005, pp. A1 and especially A4; for the evidence that Saddam's Iraq had "no link to al Qaeda," see Ibid., June 17, 2004, pp. A1 and A15.

[45]Soon after the death of Prophet Mohammed (the founder of Islam religion) in 632 A.D., his followers split over who should be the new *caliph*, or leader. Those who became Shiia believed the leader must be a direct descendant of the Prophet. Those who became Sunni believed the leader did not have to be a direct descendant if he held to other beliefs and high standards of the religion. The struggle soon became bloody and continued to be bloody in the twentieth and twenty-first centuries.

claims "of little or no value." When dubious State Department officials wanted to cut off Chalabi, he was defended by Cheney, Rumsfeld, and Wolfowitz "for providing unique intelligence on Iraqi WMDs." It turned out to be unique to the point of being untrue. Chalabi remained on the U.S. payroll and continued to pass on false information about Saddam's WMDs.

Some CIA assessments were on target, many others were not. During a tense moment during late 2002 when Bush asked for some evidence to support his claims that Iraq was developing WMDs, CIA director George Tenet assured him, with little evidence, that it was a "slam-dunk." One former CIA official later claimed that analysts who differed "were beaten down. . . . I've never seen a government like this." One other senior official believed that Cheney and his chief of staff, Lewis "Scooter" Libby, "sent signals, intended or otherwise, that a certain output was desired" from the CIA. *Time* magazine revealed in May, 2002, that Rumsfeld so badly wanted war he had asked the CIA on ten different occasions to link Iraq and Saddam Hussein to 9/11. No real evidence appeared, but the move to war neverthess accelerated. When CIA information was not sufficient to go to war, the administration could turn to Undersecretary of Defense Douglas Feith's quickly assembled, and heavily biased, intelligence-gathering group. Powell privately dismissed it as the "Gestapo office," and General Tommy Franks, who later led the invasion of Iraq, dismissed Feith as "the — stupidest guy on the face of the earth." But the Undersecretary, a leading neoconservative voice, helped give pro-war officials what they needed.[46]

By early 2003, Bush was ready to move. In September 2002, his new *National Security Strategy* had publicly argued for the U.S. right of preemptive attack, acting alone if necessary, for self-defense against terrorism. Such preemption, of course, assumed the President had solid evidence that the United States was about to be attacked. Bush, however, still lacked the evidence to support the invasion. He one time wildly imagined publicly that Saddam was creating a fleet of unmanned aircraft for "targeting the United States." In reality, Saddam had hardly

[46]The previous two paragraphs are based on Lloyd C. Gardner, "Mr. Rumsfeld's War?" in Marilyn Young and Lloyd C. Gardner, *Iraq and the Vietnam, Syndrome* (New York, 2007), the best analysis of Rumsfeld; Evgenia Peretz, et al., "The Path to War," *Vanity Fair,* May 2004, pp. 230, 234, 240, 283; Seymour M. Hersh, "The Stovepipe," *The New Yorker,* October 27, 2003, pp. 77–81; Woodward, *Plan of Attack,* pp. 281, 292, *Washington Post,* June 5, 2003, p. A1, for the comments on the CIA.

any functioning air force or navy at all that could even begin to contest areas around Iraq.[47]

The United Nations had gone along with the President's request to inspect Iraq for WMD and was finding no credible evidence. Rumsfeld continued to insist not only that Iraq had WMD, but also that he knew where they were—a claim that had absolutely no basis in fact, as many authorities inside and outside the UN were realizing. By early 2003, there seemed no possibility the United States could obtain the eight votes necessary in the fifteen-member UN Security Council to give Americans the authority to attack Iraq. Even if votes somehow appeared, the French and/or Russians would veto a war measure. Americans made fun of the French (as Freedom Toast replaced French Toast in restaurants, liquor salesmen publicly dumped fine French wine, and Rumsfeld dismissed Europeans who disagreed with him as "old Europe"). But French President Jacques Chirac was correct when he insisted that UN inspection teams had actually disarmed Iraq of all WMD in the 1990s.

In February 2003, a month before the actual invasion, Powell dramatically appeared at the UN to charge that Saddam was hiding WMD materials. (Three years later, he declared he had known his argument had no basis in fact and that "I never believed it.") The UN still refused to support the President's drive toward war. The Bush administration intensified its claims that it could take care of Saddam itself, and that the conflict would be inexpensive. Iraq's oil reserves, the world's second largest, would pay for the war—and keep American SUVs fueled with cheaper gas. One top U.S. official, Andrew Natsios, even insisted on television in April 2003 that Iraq would cost Americans about $1.7 billion. (Three years later the cost raced toward the $400 billion level.) On the eve of the invasion, Cheney echoed Wolfowitz's thinking by telling Congress that "We'll be greeted as liberators."[48]

---

[47]Mann, *Rise of the Vulcans,* pp. 328–329, succinctly discusses the *Strategy* document; *Washington Post,* October 22, 2002, p. A1, has Bush's quote about the unmanned aircraft and notes why at the time it was "dubious, if not wrong."

[48]This and the previous paragraph are based on Gardner, "Mr. Rumsfeld's War?" and *Washington Post,* April 22, 2006, p. A21 for the Powell quote; Daalder and Lindsay, *America Unbound,* p. 144, and Brian Urquhart, "Hidden Truths," *The New York Review of Books,* March 25, 2004, on the UN; Woodward, *Plan of Attack,* p. 470, for Cheney's quote; *The New York Times,* March 27, 2006, p. A1 on Bush's plans; *Washington Post,* March 19, 2004, p. 14, for the Natsios quote and the context. For the perspective of defenders of Bush's actions in undertaking the war, see *Iraq: Setting the Record Straight. A Report of the Project for the New American Century* (Washington, D. C., April 2005).

On March 19–20, 2003, the U.S.-British led force—the "coalition of the willing" as Rumsfeld and others called it to hide the lack of support from other former allies—struck. Within two weeks the small Iraqi military disintegrated. As one surprised American commentator remarked, "We were at war with the Flintstones." On May 1, Bush, costumed in a flight jacket for the television cameras, flew in a jet fighter onto an aircraft carrier off San Diego to announce "Mission accomplished." Saddam's Iraq, "an ally of al Qaeda," as he mistakenly called it, was no more. He and Cheney continued to emphasize the nonexistent Saddam-al Qaeda relationship, although by September 2003, the President finally had to admit, "We've no evidence that Saddam Hussein was involved with September 11."[49]

In May 2003, about a month after the conflict ended, the top U.S. official running Iraq, L. Paul Bremer, disbanded Saddam's Baathist forces. Without pay but with weapons and anger, many turned into guerrilla fighters to target Americans. Bush responded by proclaiming "Bring them on." As increasing numbers of Americans were killed or badly wounded, Rumsfeld refused to call the growing insurgency "anything like a guerilla war or an organized resistance." His refusal allowed the Secretary of Defense to cancel sending 16,000 more soldiers who were desperately needed to stop the looting, lawlessness, and growing insurgency. Then Rumsfeld refused requests from the U.S. military and Bremer for more troops before the resistance got further out of hand.[50]

By mid-summer 2003, it was too late. Iraq was under the Pentagon's (not the State Department's) responsibility as the country drifted first toward chaos and then spreading anti-U.S. insurgency. Powell was stunned that the State Department, which had done massive studies on how to deal with post-war Iraq, had been blocked out. When he appealed to Rice for help, she replied she could not do anything. For nearly three weeks after Saddam fell (and disappeared literally underground before he was found in December 2003), central parts of the nation became lawless. U.S.

---

[49]*The New York Times,* June 7, 2004, p. A15 for quotes and context; Daalder and Lindsay, *America Unbound,* p. 147 for the commentator.

[50]Michael R. Gordon and General Bernard E. Trainor, *Cobra II: The Inside Story of the Invasion and Occupation of Iraq* (New York, 2006), pp. 475–477, 484; Thomas Powers, "Bringing 'Em On," *The New York Times Book Review,* December 25, 2005, p. 13; *Washington Post,* July 1, 2003, p. A9 for Rumsfeld quote.

forces did protect Baghdad's oil offices. The country's petroleum reserves were a leading, some claimed the leading, reason for the invasion. But no one protected world-class museums holding thousands of years of priceless displays which had long revealed not only the evolution of Iraq and some of Islam's holiest sites, but the rise of civilization itself. At Babylon, preserved for centuries as one of the Seven Wonders of the Ancient World, 2000 U.S. Marines built a helicopter pad on the ancient ruins, caused a building roof to collapse with vibrations, and filled sandbags with invaluable archeological artifacts. Priceless items going back thousands of years were destroyed or looted in a matter of days. The resulting anger helped fuel Iraqi hatred for the invaders, even as many also celebrated the overthrow of the Saddam dictatorship.[51]

Over the next three years, the Iraqi resistance claimed 2500 American lives and uncounted tens-of-thousands of Iraqis. The insurgents were "very good at information operations," one U.S. artillery commander noted. "People are reluctant to help us." Meanwhile, U.S. troops ran low on bullets and had to buy ammunition from the British and Israelis. American soldiers also were short of bullet-proof vests for several years and could not obtain new armored trucks to protect them against the insurgents' explosive devices. The troops even had to move their crotch protectors to under their arms so bullets and bomb fragments would not slice through their sides where, because of Pentagon failures, they had no protection. The three-star general heading the U.S. Army Reserve (which had to provide increasing numbers of troops in Iraq) said in early 2004 that the Reserve "is rapidly degenerating into a 'broken' force."[52]

In late 2003, Libya, ruled by Mu'ammar Qaddafi, announced it would give up its nuclear and chemical weapons programs. After Qaddafi's orders had killed Americans in the 1980s, the United States bombed Libya, then imposed trade and other economic sanctions on the North African nation. Now Qaddafi exchanged his

[51]BBC news on http://news.bbc.cc.uk of April 14, 2006, "US Marines Offer Babylon Apology"; Chalmers Johnson, "The Smash of Civilizations," Tomeditor@aol.com.

[52]Rod Nordland, "Web Exclusive," *Newsweek,* April 17, 2004, http://www.msnbc.msn.com and also on Amy Davis's UNCLOUDED website, for casualty estimates; *The New York Times,* June 28, 2004, p. A9 for commander's quote on information; *Washington Post,* October 16, 2005, p. A1, and Ibid., July 22, 2004, p. E1 for stories on U.S. soldiers lacking protection; Ibid., January 6, 2004, p. A1 for Army Reserve commander's quote.

nuclear ambitions for capital to develop Libya's large oil reserves. Chinese, Japanese, and U.S. companies moved in. The Bush administration took credit for transforming Qaddfi into a cooperative (rather than murderous) person, and hoped that North Korea, Iran, and similar enemies would follow the Libyan example. It did not happen. The Iraqi invasion was followed by North Korea and Iran stepping up their nuclear program to help ensure that what happened to Iraq would not happen to them.

More immediately, terrorist attacks escalated around the globe after early 2003. The overwhelming number (90 to 95 percent, ran various estimates) of insurgents in Iraq were Iraqis, but the country turned into a training ground for foreigners associated with al Qaeda and other terrorist groups. The new CIA director, Porter Goss, said in early 2005 that Iraq was producing "a potential pool of contacts to build transnational terrorist cells, groups and networks in Saudi Arabia, Jordan, and other countries." (Just before Goss's comments, Vice President Cheney had remarked that the insurgency was in its "last throes." When asked to comment, the CIA director thought "not quite," but "very close to it." The war instead worsened in 2005–2006.) Al Jazeera television showed a videotape in mid-2004 displaying al Qaeda recruits also being trained in Afghanistan. U.S. government figures concluded that "significant" terrorist attacks around the world reached a record 175 in 2003, but leaped to 655 in 2004. When in 2005 Condoleezza Rice, the newly appointed Secretary of State, was asked by members of Congress to provide statistics on terrorist activities, she refused on the recommendation of her counselor, Philip D. Zelikow.[53]

"We've become the worst of all things," Bremer told Rice a year after the invasion, "an ineffective occupier." The supposed Iraqi weapons of mass destruction, used by the administration as the reason for the invasion, were never found—much as United Nations and some State Department intelligence sources had concluded, before the war, they would not be found because Saddam had destroyed them in the 1990s. Wolfowitz switched to emphasize not the WMD threat, but Saddam's evil regime and the opportunity to

[53]*Washington Post*, November 17, 2005, p. A1; Douglas Jehl column in *The New York Times*, June 22, 2005, p. A1; Ibid., June 17, 2004, p. A19 for terrorist training in 2004 Afghanistan; *Washington Post*, April 27, 2005, p. A1.

extend democracy through the region. (In 2004, he left to head the World Bank in an eerie resemblance to Defense Secretary Robert McNamara leaving his failed Vietnam policies in 1967–1968 to head the same bank.)[54]

Bush followed Wolfowitz and other neoconservatives in emphasizing the need, as the President proclaimed in his Second Inaugural Address, "to seek and support the growth of democratic movements and institutions in every nation and culture, with the ultimate goal of ending tyranny in our world." This pronounced commitment to spreading democracy had notably begun with Woodrow Wilson's presidency between 1913 and 1921. But Wilson had failed to "make the world safe for democracy" (as he famously phrased it), had died broken and embittered, and consequently was not emulated by Franklin D. Roosevelt, Harry Truman, and other presidents—until Ronald Reagan resurrected Wilsonianism to try to undermine the Soviet Union in the 1980s. Determined, as Bush's White House official had told journalist Ron Suskind, to "create our own reality," the President after 2003 seemed to deemphasize military power, especially as the U.S. military became trapped in the terrible aftermath of the Iraqi war. He instead emphasized an American mission to create new democracies. He appeared to be a reincarnation of the Woodrow Wilson from nearly a century earlier.

Bush's support of new, budding democratic governments in the former Soviet states of Ukraine and Georgia seemed successful in 2004–2006. Support for democratic movements elsewhere was less so. Scholars had long pointed out that to be successful, democracies first needed not elections, but an independent judiciary, a legitimate and accepted legal code, a functioning economy perceived as fair, and a broad consensus on the need for a democracy. For its part, the United States had taken some 150 years to develop these requirements before full-fledged democratic elections evolved between the 1830s and 1920 (when American women finally received the vote).

In the early twenty-first century, most nations did not have 150 years of democratic development. Instead, many went directly to holding elections. Egypt, along with Israel a major U.S. ally in the

---

[54]L. Paul Bremer III, with Malcolm McConnell, *My Year in Iraq* (New York, 2006), p. 358; *Washington Post*, September 12, 2003, p. A23 for Wolfowitz's change in emphasis; *The New York Times*, October 7, 2004, p. A1 and especially p. A28 for Saddam's destruction of WMD years earlier.

Middle East, conducted more-open elections and, as Islamic parties gained support, began to be destabilized. In Uzbekistan, which provided a major base for the U.S. invasion of Afghanistan, the government ordered the Americans to leave after Washington officials criticized the regime for anti-democratic, indeed murderous, practices. In Afghanistan, 2005 elections brought to power a government that could not control large parts of the country (where Taliban fought and al Qaeda hid). The Afghan government, according to one of its own newly elected legislators, faced a fundamental problem: "The foreigners have rules; Afghans don't have any rules." Hamas, an Islamic movement which since the 1980s had pledged to destroy Israel, came to power in Palestine through open elections, much to Bush's displeasure. He and Israel turned off hundreds of millions of dollars in aid which they had been sending the previous Palestinian government. And in Iraq itself, when 2005 elections produced a government highly open to Iran's influence, Bush moved to get rid of some of the elected leaders whom he did not trust. "We've sacrificed for democracy and now you want us to jump over the results of the elections," protested one such Iraqi leader. "What are you trying to tell us? That peace and wisdom are useless? That we believed a lie?" Creating the "reality" of democracy was proving to be even more difficult and dangerous for Bush than it had been for Woodrow Wilson.[55]

Besides the terrible traps he was encountering in trying to spread democracy, other major problems arose for Bush from his foreign policies. In early 2003, on the eve of the invasion, the President had used highly doubtful British intelligence to claim that Saddam had tried to buy "yellowcake" (a form of processed uranium for possible use in nuclear weapons) from Niger. At the U.S. government's request, Ambassador Joseph C. Wilson had earlier traveled to Niger and quickly discovered the story was untrue. After Bush nevertheless repeated the claim as truth, Wilson publicly disputed the President, and pointedly noted how Vice President Cheney had falsely claimed in the days before the war that Iraq was "trying once again to produce nuclear weapons." Scurrying to attack Wilson, especially as the 2004 presidential election loomed, the President secretly declassified

[55]Bush's Second Inaugural is from *Washington Post*, January 21, 2005, p. A24 and can be read at the website for this book, www.mhhe.com/lafeber under chapter 15 documents; the Afghan situation and quote are noted in *The New York Times*, December 19, 2005, p. A11; the Iraqi leader is quoted in Ibid., March 12, 2006, p. 1wk.

information (which he could do legally), and it was then passed to chosen reporters so they could discredit Wilson. The reporters wrote that Wilson's wife, Valerie Plame, was a well-hidden (until then) member of the Central Intelligence Agency. Revealing the identity of such a CIA agent was a crime. Cheney's Chief-of-Staff, Lewis "Scooter" Libby, was indicted in 2005 for lying to a grand jury about the case. Bush, it might be noted, had earlier declared publicly that he would fire anyone who leaked classified information.[56]

The White House worked successfully to keep this scandal from developing too dangerously for the 2004 election. Americans followed the Republican emphasis on such cultural issues as abortion, school prayer, and other religious questions, while Bush posed as being tough against terrorist attacks. Cultural values seemed to be even more important to American voters than an economy which between late 2000 into 2005 was nearly doubling corporate profits, and expanding the gross domestic product by 8.4 percent, but sinking the average weekly wage for Americans by .3 percent. Bush had won only a minority of the popular votes in 2000, but now became a majority president as he defeated the Democratic candidate, Senator John Kerry of Massachusetts. Kerry's own conflicted record in both supporting and opposing the Iraqi war was turned against him by the Republicans.[57]

By 2006, U.S. and British troops continued to fight in Iraq as many of the thirty-five other allies pulled out their small numbers of troops. After Saddam was overthrown, Wolfowitz had argued, echoing other officials, "France would have a strong interest in assisting Iraq's reconstruction." Rich oil and rebuilding contracts could—supposedly—buy the help of those, like France, who had refused to help before the war. But those who refused, including the French, before the war, also refused to help afterward, especially given the killing-zones now infesting important parts of the country. American-trained Iraqi forces and police grew in number, but much less in efficiency.

[56]Josh Gerstein, "Bush Authorized Leak to Times, Libby Told Grand Jury," *New York Sun* Web Exclusive, April 6, 2006, http://nysun.com; Joseph C. Wilson 4th, "What I Didn't Find in Africa," *The New York Times,* July 6, 2003, p. 9wk on op-ed page; on the administration's control of information, note especially, "Prewar Intelligence: Insulating Bush," *National Journal,* March 30, 2006.

[57]An excellent study of the cultural values in the election is Thomas Frank, *What's the Matter with Kansas? How Conservatives Won the Heart of America* (New York, 2004). The author is indebted to Hirschel and Adam Abelson for the economic information.

U.S. officials did not trust them to handle the insurgency. That insurgency not only continued, but also transformed. Iraq had long been divided between Shiia Moslems, who accounted for about 60 to 65 percent of the population, and Sunni Moslems, who were about 30 percent. (The remainder were mostly Kurds, who had long sought unsuccessfully to ally with their brethren in Turkey, and possibly Iran, to form their own nation.) Saddam, a member of the minority Sunni, had brutally kept the Shiia and Kurds in check. By mid-2006, these groups were at virtual civil war with each other, as tens and sometimes hundreds of Iraqis, including many women and children, were killed or wounded each day by bombs set in markets or after being pulled from their automobiles and slaughtered. U.S. troops could do little. They were too few in number and too distrusted by Iraqis. When this murderous civilian bloodshed began shortly after the 2003 invasion, Secretary of Defense Rumsfeld tried simply to brush it off by saying, "Stuff happens"—a phrase that haunted him thereafter. Over the next three years the "stuff" created one of the worst eras in nearly 250 years of American history.[58]

Bush now tried to bridge these considerable gaps between Iraqis, and to undercut the growing insurgency, by holding U.S.-sponsored elections. Between late 2003 and 2006, a series of such elections produced an interim Iraqi government controlled by the Shiia. Since the Shiia represented the majority of the population, their victories were not surprising, but the victories became ominous when the winners moved closer to Iran (a Shiia state). A number of the new Iraqi political leaders had sought refuge in Iran from Saddam during the 1980s–1990s. As a prominent Iraqi political analyst declared in early 2006, "America occupies Iraq, but Iran influences us." The Iranians were a charter member of Bush's famous "axis of evil," because of their sharp differences with the United States since 1979. By 2005 they also were developing a nuclear program which they claimed was for peaceful purposes, but which U.S. officials believed aimed at creating weapons. When Bush tried to rein in the Iranian nuclear plans, he was blocked by, among others, Russia and China, whose vetoes could stop any meaningful UN action against Iran.[59]

---

[58]The best analysis of this phrase and of Rumsfeld generally is Gardner, "Mr. Rumsfeld's War?" Also note Daalder and Lindsay, *America Unbound*, pp. 150–151.

[59]Jay Solomon, et al., "Rough Neighborhood," *The Wall Street Journal*, February 14, 2006, p. A1.

Several tentative conclusions could be reached about the historic turn in U.S. foreign policy after the 9/11 attacks. First, the Bush Doctrine of 2001 had declared that the United States possessed the right to attack other nations preemptively in order to stop an imminent enemy attack. The President assumed he could launch a preemptive war without either the permission or support of other powers. The great supremacy of U.S. military power, the reasoning went, allowed Washington officials to act unilaterally, if necessary. In Afghanistan, NATO and other U.S. allies supported the invasion of October 7, 2001, to overthrow the Taliban and perhaps capture Osama bin Laden (although his capture seemed to be of less importance to the Bush administration). In Iraq, however, helpful allies were in much shorter supply. Many longtime friends of the United States did not believe Saddam Hussein had the weapons to pose a significant threat, and they feared the explosive instability that could result in both Iraq and the wider Middle East if he were overthrown. President Bush nevertheless went ahead. Successful preemption, however, required that he act on the basis of sound intelligence that accurately analyzed the immediate danger. U.S. intelligence was confused, divided, and then cherry-picked by leaders such as Bush, Cheney, Rice, Wolfowitz, and Feith so they could use what they needed to support a drive toward war. When conditions quickly worsened after the invasion, Bush asked the United Nations and Europeans for help, but he received little. The alliance system that had supported U.S. policies throughout the Cold War seemed no longer to work. False claims for preemption had produced the realities of failure.[60]

A second conclusion emerged from the President's identification in early 2002 of Iraq, North Korea, and Iran as the "axis of evil." After these remarks, North Korea, a communist, totalitarian state, continued to develop its capacity for making nuclear weapons. The United States, preoccupied in the Middle East, stepped aside while

---

[60]For an account in 2006 of the dangerous and horrible conditions under which even Iraqis who work for the United States have to live three years after the invasion, see the U.S. Embassy's secret report to the secretary of state on this book's website at chapter 15 (www.mhhe.com/lafeber). Also note David E. Sanger, "Bush's Pre-emptive Strategy Meets Some Untidy Reality," *The New York Times,* July 12, 2004, p. A10; Robin Wright, "Iraq Occupation Erodes Bush Doctrine," *Washington Post,* June 28, 2004, p. A1; Congressional Research Service, "U.S. Military Operations in the Global War on Terrorism," August 26, 2005, especially pp. 1–11 on Afghanistan. On the European reaction, note T. R. Reid, *The United States and Europe* (New York, 2005), especially pp. 180–192.

China and South Korea led negotiations to try to rein in the North Koreans. Little was achieved. China and South Korea were especially reluctant to pressure North Korea out of fear that the North's impoverished system could break down and millions of desperate Koreans would suddenly move across Chinese and South Korean borders. But if North Korea merely managed to remain a nuclear threat, the other "evil," Iran, prospered. Bush treated this part of the "axis of evil" quite oddly. The United States destroyed Iran's arch-enemy to the west, Saddam Hussein. The U.S. invasion of Afghanistan removed another danger to Iran, the Taliban (who were Sunnis), on the other side. Working with Shiia Iraqis who had earlier sought refuge in Iran, Teheran's leaders exerted immense influence in southern Iraq, where huge oil reserves existed. As Iran developed its nuclear capacity, the United States seemed to have little leverage—especially when two of the world's leading powers, Russia and China, declared they would not allow Washington officials or the United Nations to impose sanctions on the Iranians. Two members of Bush's "axis of evil" were building, not yielding, power, and he seemed to be making one of them—Iran—more secure.[61]

A third conclusion arose out of Bush and his supporters' determination to go-it-alone (in the long tradition of American isolationism, only this time with the world's greatest military), and their belief they quite literally could create their own "reality" through Bush's use of unchecked presidential powers. In 2002–2003, the United States captured hundreds of suspected terrorists, and Bush invented the term "unlawful enemy combatants" for them. By using this term, he hoped to deny them the protections of the Geneva Conventions (international law which the United States had supported) or U.S. law.

Accommodating lawyers in the administration, including the future Attorney General of the United States, Alberto Gonzalez, developed legal rationales for ignoring international law and handling the prisoners in such secrecy. They were initially opposed by lawyers in the State Department. Secretary of State Powell secretly warned that reversing a century of U.S. support for the Geneva Conventions would

---

[61]*Washington Post*, March 14, 2006, p. A16 for Iran, China, and Russia; George Friedman, "Overdoing Chalabi," *The Stratfor Weekly*, May 28, 2004, at alert@stratfor.com—a useful intelligence/news site.

undermine the protection of American troops, who had been protected by those international laws, and lead to international condemnation of Washington's policy. Bush and Rumsfeld overrode Powell. Then came revelations that the prisoners in the Abu Ghraib prison in Iraq, as well as the Guantanamo prison in the U.S.-controlled sliver of Cuba, had been treated inhumanely, including being threatened by dogs, and even tortured. Others had been secretly spirited off, sometimes from European streets, to secret interrogation centers where U.S. laws could not protect them.

The U.S. Supreme Court threatened Bush's prisoner policy by declaring in 2004 that the Court's jurisdiction reached to Guantanamo and implied that prisoners could appeal to the Court for treatment in line with U.S. statutes and international law. Congress then passed a law, at Bush's request, which the Executive interpreted, with little justification, as taking away the Supreme Court's right to interfere. Justice Sandra Day O'Connor, a moderate swing vote on the Supreme Court, had acted with the majority on the 2004 case. Retired in 2006, O'Connor attacked Bush's legal reasoning for hiding prisoners by declaring, "It takes a lot of degeneration before a country falls into dictatorship, but we should avoid these ends by avoiding these beginnings." Torture was also producing questionable, if not dangerous, information. The story surfaced in 2005 that three years earlier a prisoner taken to Egypt tried to escape torture by giving information linking Saddam's Iraq to al Qaeda. It was later found to be totally false.

More ominously for Americans themselves, Bush developed new powers to spy within the United States. Under the 1978 Foreign Intelligence Surveillance Act (FISA), Presidents were required to go to a secret FISA court for permission to wiretap phones and other communications. The act had been passed when congressional investigations revealed that the FBI and other executive agencies had secretly wiretapped and spied on Americans who opposed the Vietnam War. After 1978, the court granted more than 99 percent of these secret presidential requests. Bush declared in the 2004 presidential campaign that Americans were protected because Chief Executives had to get court permission before they could tap, say, cell phones. In reality, he had ignored the FISA court, wiretapped masses of communications inside the United States, and when caught tried to justify it on grounds of his presidential authority and a highly strained interpretation of the 2001 and 2002 congressional measures giving him permission to attack Afghanistan and Iraq. Lawyers and others outside the administration disputed and condemned such justification. Congress did virtually nothing in response. The "war" against terror launched in 2001 was having vast consequences for U.S. presidential power, and for Americans directly.[62]

A fourth conclusion for the post-9/11 era involved the U.S. relationships with other major powers, especially Russia and China. The relationships deteriorated as the three nations competed for oil and other strategic resources in the Middle East, Africa, and Central Asia, and as Bush's mission to expand democracy encountered strong opposition, especially from Russia's leader, Vladimir Putin.

A famous story in American history recounts that when British troops surrendered to George Washington's bedraggled army at Yorktown in 1781 to end the Revolutionary War, their surprised commander ordered the military band to play a tune called "The World Turned Upside Down." The song could have been the background music for U.S. diplomacy after September 11. It seemed every important relationship was undergoing a transformation or reversal, and none more so than with that century-long enemy, Russia. So it seemed.

Shortly after becoming President, Bush had met Russian leader Vladimir Putin. Both were charmed, and Bush rhapsodized that he had looked into Putin's soul and saw an "honest, straightforward man . . . who loves his family." That the former KGB intelligence agent and tough political boss had such a transparent soul became a source of jokes on late night American television. Within hours after the September attacks, however, Putin was the first foreign leader to call Bush. The President had put U.S. forces on high alert, a move that usually automatically threw the Russian military into high gear

---

[62]*Washington Post,* June 24, 2004, pp. A1, A6 for background and quotes from both sides; Seymour M. Hersh, "The Gray Zone; How a Secret Pentagon Program Came to Abu Ghraib," *The New Yorker,* May 24, 2004, pp. 38–44; *The New York Times,* March 20, 2006, p. A24; Ibid., December 23, 2005, p. A12 for Adam Liptak's story on lawyers' views of the wiretapping; the context and analysis of the wiretapping can be found in Risen, *State of War,* especially pp. 43–46. For Secretary of State Condoleezza Rice's defense of Bush's new surveillance policy, note *The New York Times,* December 19, 2005, p. A28.

as well. But Putin now told Bush not only that his sympathies were with the victims of the terrorist attacks, but also that Russian forces would avoid a dangerous escalation by actually scaling back their alert status. The President declared that "he [Putin] understands the Cold War is over."[63] In a conversation later in September the Russian leader said he had no objections to U.S. bases being installed in Central Asia (once a part of the Soviet Union). He also promised valuable intelligence and logistical help. One U.S. government expert on Russia later said he never had expected in his lifetime to hear such words of cooperation pass between the top American and Russian leaders. Hard interests, however, not Putin's soul, had shaped his offer. In return, Putin had three issues on which he asked for Bush's understanding.

The first was Chechnya, the breakaway Islamic province. Chechnya had become a bleeding wound for seven years, and Americans had rubbed salt into it by condemning Russia for treating the Chechens brutally. The crisis was more troublesome because Chechen independence leaders were moderate, but terrorist groups once again had appeared to take advantage of the chaos. After intense debate among his advisers, Bush issued a statement that in reality supported Putin's actions in Chechnya. The Russians, after all, were dealing here with their own Islamic problem. U.S. officials understood, moreover, that Putin had gone out on a long limb to support Bush so publicly. The Russian political elite and especially its military deeply mistrusted the United States. They believed Bush would ultimately double-cross them, just as they believed earlier U.S. presidents had. The U.S. media then began to attack Bush for supporting a Russian policy that had killed more than 11,000 Chechens in just several years. By early 2002, as the Afghan war wound down, Bush was again criticizing Russian policy in Chechnya.[64] Post-September 11 diplomacy was forcing Americans to make some bitter choices.

---

[63]*Washington Post,* October 4, 2001, p. A14.

[64]*Washington Post,* October 4, 2001, p. A1, and *The New York Times,* October 9, 2001, p. B8 have useful overviews and material on Putin's domestic problems; *Washington Post,* January 9, 2002, p. A18 editorial criticizes Bush's pro-Putin policy on Chechnya. Two accounts that superbly provide different views of the Russian background for Putin's actions are Stephen Kotkin, *Armageddon Averted: The Soviet Collapse, 1970–2000* (New York, 2001); and Michael McFaul, *Russia's Unfinished Revolution; Political Change from Gorbachev to Putin* (Ithaca, NY, 2001).

The Middle East, 2001–2006

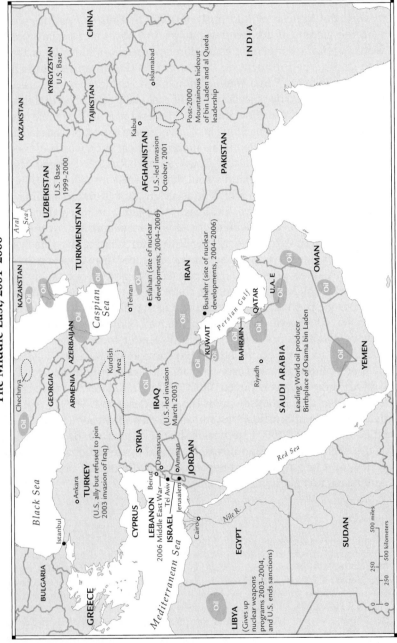

BULGARIA

GREECE

Black Sea

Istanbul

CHECHNYA
Oil

GEORGIA

ARMENIA

AZERBAIJAN
Oil

KAZAKSTAN

Aral Sea

KAZAKSTAN
Oil
Oil

UZBEKISTAN
U.S. Base
1999-2000

TURKMENISTAN

Caspian Sea

Oil

KYRGYZSTAN
U.S. Base

TAJIKSTAN

CHINA

INDIA

PAKISTAN

Islamabad

Post-2000
Mountainous hideout
of bin Laden and al Queda
leadership

Kabul

AFGHANISTAN
U.S.-led invasion
October, 2001

TURKEY
(U.S. ally but refused to join
2003 invasion of Iraq)

Ankara

Kurdish
Area

Oil

IRAN

Tehran

Esfahan (site of nuclear
developments, 2004–2006)

Oil

Bushehr (site of nuclear
developments, 2004–2006)

OMAN
Oil

Persian Gulf

U.A.E
Oil

QATAR
Oil

BAHRAIN
Oil

KUWAIT
Oil

Oil

IRAQ
(U.S.-led invasion
March 2003)

SYRIA

Damascus

CYPRUS

LEBANON
2006 Middle East War

Beirut

ISRAEL
Tel Aviv

Jerusalem

Amman

JORDAN

SAUDI ARABIA
Leading World oil producer
Birthplace of Osama bin Laden

Riyadh

YEMEN
Oil

Red Sea

Cairo

Nile R.

EGYPT

LIBYA
Oil
(Gives up
nuclear weapons
programs 2003-2004,
and U.S. ends sanctions)

SUDAN

Mediterranean Sea

0   250   500 miles

0   250   500 kilometers

After the terrorist attacks an influential Russian observer noted, "This is the first time since 1945 that the United States and Russia have a common enemy."[65] Putin at first hoped to play on that common fear of Islamic terrorism to deal with a second problem: Bush's determination to ditch the U.S.-U.S.S.R. 1972 antiballistic missile treaty (see chart, p. 368) so he could begin building a high-tech, antiballistic missile shield around the United States. Russia, and especially China, saw Bush's plans as a direct threat to their own nuclear strategies which rested on mutual deterrence—that is, the belief that neither side would use nuclear weapons because it could be destroyed by the other side's nuclear missiles.

The third issue Putin had in mind was the U.S. determination once again to expand NATO toward Soviet borders. In November 2001, Putin flew to the United States for talks with Bush. Publicly the two got along superbly. When he was treated to barbeque, catfish, and cornbread at Bush's Texas ranch, Putin even proclaimed, "A masterpiece of cooking!" In late 2001 a historic deal was worked out on NATO. Expansion would go forward, but for the first time since the organization's founding in 1949, Russia would participate more formally in discussions on such political items as terrorism, although not on military policies (most of which, of course, had been directed against Russia). The deal triggered intense debate. Henry Kissinger and Zbigniew Brzezinski, who never lost their mistrust of Russians, attacked it for watering down the most important U.S. military relationship and also for giving Putin more than they thought he deserved.[66]

On the ABM treaty, Bush stuck to his position. In December 2001, he announced the United States would withdraw from the 1972 treaty so it could test antimissile systems. Putin's response was moderate: "we consider it a mistake," especially since there should not be "a legal vacuum [that is, the lack of international treaty agreements] in the issue of strategic stability." But as the *The New York Times* editorialized, Bush was "rolling the dice." Critics feared other nations, including China, might set out to build many more nuclear missiles to overwhelm such a U.S. system. September 11 demonstrated to these critics, moreover, that Americans were most vulnerable not to missile attacks, but to terrorists who might slip a primitive nuclear

---

[65]*The Wall Street Journal*, September 24, 2001, p. A19.
[66]*The New York Times*, November 23, 2001, p. A1 analyzes the new arrangements; for an example of the criticism: Zbigniew Brzezinski, "NATO Should Remain Wary of Russia," *The Wall Street Journal*, November 28, 2001, p. A18.

device into any U.S. port and make the adjoining city unlivable for decades.[67]

Business deals nevertheless quickly followed, especially for the rich Russian mineral reserves that, even with poor technology, produced one-tenth of the world's oil and a stunning one-third of its natural gas. "This is the green light," a top U.S. official of ExxonMobil said of the Putin-Bush talks. ExxonMobil went through the green light to sign a $4 billion deal to develop Russian oil. OPEC (the Arab-dominated oil producing group) tried to raise gasoline prices by cutting back production. Putin undercut OPEC by expanding Russian oil output. The move further cemented his good relations with the West, but the gushing oil revenue also gave the blush of some prosperity, at last, to the Russian economy. Other U.S. firms such as ChevronTexaco planned new Russian ventures. "It's the same reason Bonnie and Clyde robbed banks," one tough-minded (if insensitive) U.S. petroleum executive declared. "This is where the oil is."[68]

Skeptics wondered whether the long U.S.-Russian relationship was actually turning as rosy as it seemed. Among the skeptics were the conflicted Russian people. In a late 2001 opinion poll, 42 percent said Americans were their best ally, but 43 percent of Russians believed Americans were their worst enemy. As Bush quit the ABM treaty and set up military bases along the Russian border, a Moscow political scientist called the President's policies "multilateral unilateralism." That is, the President talked cooperation but acted as he wished.[69] It turned out Putin did also. Despite U.S. protests, he signed a $300 million arms deal with Iran (a nation Bush defined as an enemy), then agreed to help Tehran build nuclear power stations. Russia also remained economically and militarily close to Saddam Hussein's Iraq, Washington's primary state enemy and a possible U.S. target once Afghanistan was settled.

---

[67]Good background is in Congressional Research Service, *Nonproliferation and Threat Reduction Assistance: U.S. Programs in the Former Soviet Union, Updated June 26, 2006* (Washington, D.C., 2006). The Putin, Chinese, and French concerns about Bush's ABM plans can be found in the December 13, 2001, document in chapter 15 of this book's www.mhhe.com/lafeber website; *The New York Times* editorial, December 13, 2001, p. A38.

[68]*The New York Times*, December 5, 2001, p. C1; Ibid., October 30, 2001, p. W1 for "green light" remark.

[69]The quote and polls are in Jim Hoagland, "Split Vision of America," *Washington Post*, December 14, 2001, p. A45.

More immediately, however, the United States needed both Russian and Chinese cooperation, or at least neutrality, in fighting terrorism. Chinese leaders were considerably less enthusiastic than Putin about Bush's responses to the September 11 attacks. They were more concerned about the new U.S. bases in Central Asia (their so-called backyard), which when combined with the American fleet guarding Taiwan and Washington's military cooperation with Japan, nearly surrounded China with U.S. military hardware. As a Chinese expert on the United States phrased it, the Americans could now exert "pressure on both fronts," east and west.[70] Chinese leaders did announce some support for Bush's antiterrorism efforts; this probably related to their own Islamic threat, the rebellious Uigher people in their western regions close to Afghanistan. However, Washington officials angered China at first by considering the Uighers freedom-fighters, not terrorists. Washington thus seemed to distinguish freedom-fighters from terrorists on the basis of whether the target of the attack was less cooperative with the United States (such as China), or more cooperative (such as Russia).

Leaders in Beijing found themselves facing several dilemmas. For a century China had feared Japanese militarism. The United States and Japan's own "nuclear allergy" (the result of being hit by two atomic weapons in 1945) had kept that militarism in check. After September 11, however, the United States asked Japan to help fight terrorism and to use its fleet—like its air force, one of the world's best—to protect Pacific sea lanes. The Japanese quietly responded. China now had something else to worry about. Chinese President Jiang Zemin had little room to maneuver. Many of his best educated people were anti-American, as was his military.[71]

Chinese leadership faced other serious problems. New, younger leaders replaced Jiang and his generation in 2002–2003. The heir apparent to the top post was Vice President Hu Jintao. A political star at home, until 2002 Hu had never visited Russia, Western Europe, or the United States. Jiang and Hu took the growing Chinese economy into world markets under the rules of the World Trade Organization (WTO), which China finally joined in 2001. The WTO's rules requiring openness and minimal government intervention directly threatened

---

[70]*Washington Post,* October 18, 2001, p. A26.
[71]Ibid., September 14, 2001, p. A26.

China's communist way of doing business as well as its military's profitable monopolies.[72] The sudden U.S. appearance in Central Asia and Japan's military movement after September 11 combined with these unpredictable political and economic transitions to make China a potentially dangerous problem for a United States already preoccupied with terrorism.

After September 11, China, Russia, and the United States focused their attention on, of all places, Central Asia. By 1900, Russia had conquered much of the area, despite British opposition and warnings that whoever dominated the region controlled the "geographical pivot of history": the nation that could develop it would dominate the vast Eurasian continents.[73] The Soviet Union, however, never succeeded in such development, in part because the Soviets' banning of religion ran against the region's historic allegiance to Islam. When the U.S.S.R. disbanded in 1991, five new nations suddenly appeared. Islam's long-dormant power surged.

Most Americans had never heard much about the five nations—Turkmenistan, Tajikistan, Uzbekistan, Kazakhstan, and Kyrgyzstan—unless they were in the oil business or loved Oriental rugs. After September 11, however, thousands of U.S. military personnel found themselves on new bases in Uzbekistan. They and folks back home suddenly discovered the United States had become perhaps a leading Central Asian power, the twenty-first-century counterpart to the nineteenth-century British and Russian empires. The surroundings did not resemble Thomas Jefferson's ideal. Four countries were run by dictators and their cliques, many of whom were former communists. Tajikistan at times seemed to be run by no one.

[72]The New York Times, June 3, 2001, p. 14 gives an overview; Gordon G. Chang, The Coming Collapse of China (New York, 2001) is by a U.S. lawyer who worked for two decades in China and sees the nation's WTO entry as the final straw for a regime that cannot maintain both communist control and integration with the modernizing world. A distinguished scholar provides a larger historical context for understanding recent U.S.–China relations in Warren I. Cohen, East Asia at the Center; Four Thousand Years of Engagement with the World (New York, 2000), especially pp. 474–484. Hu is analyzed in The New York Times, October 29, 2001, p. A3.

[73]Perhaps the most famous, and anti-Russian, statement, which remains instructive nearly a century later is H. J. Mackinder, "The Geographical Pivot of History," The Geographical Journal, XXIII (April 1904): 421–437.

For the United States, the most important states (as the p. 390 map indicates) were Kazakhstan (large, mineral rich, especially in oil), Turkmenistan (bordering the vast oil deposits of the Caspian Sea region), and Uzbekistan (a route for oil pipelines and with the best all-weather road access to Afghanistan). Uzbekistan became a vital U.S. ally in the fight against al Qaeda, but that greatly distressed human rights advocates. The Uzbek dictator, Islam Karimov, welcomed the Americans. Indeed he had welcomed teams of U.S. Green Beret Special Forces in 1999, two years before the September 11 attacks, when the Clinton administration quietly began a major program of military cooperation with the dictator. In the early 1990s, Karimov's brutal suppression (including sexual violence and fatal beatings by police) of Muslims who wanted an Islamic state had created a dangerous terrorist organization, the Islamic Movement of Uzbekistan (IMU) which roamed throughout the region. "Such people should be shot in the head," the newest U.S. ally had told his parliament. "If necessary, I'll shoot them myself." The U.S. Special Forces thus had three objectives even before 2001: help put down the IMU, set up bases to protect the potential oil pipeline route, and ensure that Karimov and other Central Asian leaders would turn increasingly to Washington, not Moscow or Beijing.[74] These policies became crucial to the United States after September 11.

Russian concern grew when it became clear in 2002–2004 that Americans were establishing permanent power bases in the region. U.S. investors had once been reluctant to shake Karimov's bloody hands (relations were so bad that "meetings with investors were like visits to a cancer clinic," one diplomat in the region recalled). But these investors worked with him after September 11. Some firms took heart from Chevron Texaco's $9 million oil-refining venture. As one expert on the region said, however, "Unless there's a major reform here, you're always going to be throwing good money into a bad hole." Pentagon, oil, and oil-pipeline officials all seemed ready to take that chance.[75]

---

[74]Superb, succinct historical background and analysis of the early 2002 situation are in Ahmed Rashid, "They're Only Sleeping," *The New Yorker*, January 14, 2002, pp. 23–41; the Green Berets' 1999 appearance is analyzed in *The New York Times*, October 25, 2001, p. A1; *Washington Post*, October 9, 2001, p. A16; the human rights problems are discussed in Raffi Khatchadourian, "Letter from Uzbekistan," *The Nation*, January 21, 2002, pp. 18–22.

[75]*The Wall Street Journal*, November 6, 2001, p. A20; *The New York Times*, December 15, 2001, p. C1.

As U.S. foreign policy evolved with the invasion of Iraq and its long, tragic aftermath, fewer officials in both Washington and Moscow were willing to take such chances. Indeed, deteriorating relations between Russia and the United States even reminded some analysts of the dangerous competition that surged during certain eras of the Cold War. In 2004–2006, Ukraine and Georgia, once parts of the Soviet Union, began to remove governments friendly to Moscow and, through elections, brought in new administrations which moved in a pronounced Western, rather than Russian, direction. The Bush administration provided considerable help to the new governments, and—notably—worked with Poland (bitterly anti-Russian since the early nineteenth century and especially 1945), which gladly did all it could to loosen the Russian grip. Putin was not pleased, especially since the loss of Ukraine and Georgia severely hurt his country both economically and strategically. When Belarus, an authoritarian, pro-Russian nation, also began to waver, Putin provided crucial support to keep the country with him. Bush viewed these openings as democracy-in-action. Putin saw them as U.S. expansionism-in-action.

By 2004, the much-noted American-Russian friendship after the 9/11 attacks had transformed into rising competition. Putin quickly consolidated his own power by jailing, or threatening to jail, Russians who had become rich obtaining bargain-basement-priced oil, manufacturing, and utility companies once owned by the Soviet government. Many of these entrepreneurs moved into the political realm to challenge Putin. He changed laws so that the leaders of far-flung Russian provinces were responsible to him, not primarily to their own people. The Russian leader cracked down on independent television and radio until the media essentially came under government direction. Questions began to be raised how he might change the electoral rules which prevented him from running in 2008 for another term as the nation's president. As Putin effectively consolidated his power, he also significantly turned against the United States and President Bush, who during happier times in 2001 had supposedly looked into Putin's "soul" and liked what he saw. In 2002–2003, the Russian leader refused to go along with U.S. attempts to get rid of Iraq's Saddam Hussein. One reason, other than the long military ties between Moscow and Baghdad, was that Saddam had secretly made at least fifty oil deals with Russians. Putin continued

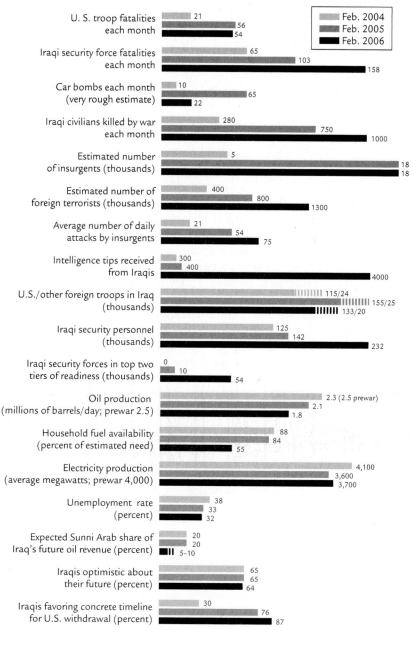

	Feb. 2004	Feb. 2005	Feb. 2006
U. S. troop fatalities each month	21	56	54
Iraqi security force fatalities each month	65	103	158
Car bombs each month (very rough estimate)	10	65	22
Iraqi civilians killed by war each month	280	750	1000
Estimated number of insurgents (thousands)	5	18	18
Estimated number of foreign terrorists (thousands)	400	800	1300
Average number of daily attacks by insurgents	21	54	75
Intelligence tips received from Iraqis	300	400	4000
U.S./other foreign troops in Iraq (thousands)	115/24	155/25	133/20
Iraqi security personnel (thousands)	125	142	232
Iraqi security forces in top two tiers of readiness (thousands)	0	10	54
Oil production (millions of barrels/day; prewar 2.5)	2.3 (2.5 prewar)	2.1	1.8
Household fuel availability (percent of estimated need)	88	84	55
Electricity production (average megawatts; prewar 4,000)	4,100	3,600	3,700
Unemployment rate (percent)	38	33	32
Expected Sunni Arab share of Iraq's future oil revenue (percent)	20	20	5–10
Iraqis optimistic about their future (percent)	65	65	64
Iraqis favoring concrete timeline for U.S. withdrawal (percent)	30	76	87

to sell his country's oil to the United States (Russian-controlled service stations even began to set up shop in and around U.S. cities). But he did not hide his anger when it came to dealing with neighboring western nations, such as Ukraine, which threatened to move toward the Americans and its NATO allies, not the Russian republics.[76]

Nor did he do so when he looked south to deal with the ever more important Central Asian nations. For decades, they had been part of the Soviet Union. After 9/11, however (indeed, by the late 1990s [see p. 443]), the United States was moving rapidly to stake out claims for oil, oil pipelines, and military bases. The Russians and Chinese initially responded in 2001 by forming the Shanghai Cooperation Organization (SCO). Its other members were all Central Asian (and Islamic): Kazakhstan, Kyrgystan, Tajikistan, and Uzbekistan. By 2006, the SCO was uniting to fight Islamic terrorism, chart cooperative ventures for oil and gas to form a common "energy strategy," develop Russian-Chinese cooperation—and quietly work to reduce the American political and military presence.

As noted previously, outbreaks in Uzbekistan, and the critical U.S. response, had led to the Uzbeks asking the Americans in 2005 to pick up their base and leave. The United States had other bases in the region, but the growing SCO efforts threatened to make highly difficult the U.S. efforts to clean up growing Taliban/al Qaeda opposition in Afghanistan, and, indeed, threatened Washington's hopes that Central Asia, with all its oil and gas reserves (and its strategic proximity to Russia and China), would move ever closer to U.S. interests. In 2006, moreover, SCO, which had said it would not expand, decided to allow in as full members Mongolia, India, Pakistan, and—perhaps most notably—Iran (as it moved toward having nuclear power).[77]

China's primary problems were largely internal, not external. The dynamic transformation of the economy produced dangerous inequality between classes and regions, increasingly threatening

---

[76]For fears of another Cold War, note *Washington Post*, April 3, 2006, p. A14; Stephen Cohen, "Did the Cold War Really End?" H-DIPLO @ H-NET.MSU.EDU, given in Moscow, March 1, 2006. Peter Baker and Susan Glasser, *Kremlin Rising; Vladimir Putin's Russia and the End of Revolution* (New York, 2005), especially pp. 217–230, and chapter 14, "Twilight of the Oligarchs"; Thomas E. Graham, Jr., *Russia's Decline and Uncertain Recovery* (Washington, D.C., 2002), especially chapters 4 and 6.

[77]M. K. Bhadrakuman, "China, Russia Welcome Iran Into the Fold," April 18, 2006, *Asia Times Online*.

environmental dangers, corruption (which Beijing repeatedly tried to limit by executing some of those charged with the crime), and rising unemployment as hundreds of millions of peasants moved into the cities. The communist government's failures, notably its brutal human rights abuse of dissidents or those suspected of dissenting, were challenged by those abroad (especially by the United States), and at home by rapidly growing numbers of protests which reached well into the tens-of-thousands annually by 2006. Despite such massive problems, the Chinese government could not stand by and allow the United States to move easily into Central Asia, attempt to take more desperately needed oil resources, or obstruct Beijing's determination to retake Taiwan. China thus needed Russian cooperation, even if the mistrust between the two sides was glaring and, much to Putin's disgust, large numbers of Chinese were surging across the boundary to populate parts of Russian Siberia.[78]

Russia and China have opposed each other, often violently, for centuries. The Soviet-Communist Chinese cooperation after 1950 (see p. 126) began to break apart within a decade, and the two became virtual enemies by the late 1960s. After the collapse of the Soviet Union in 1991, however, relations began to improve. By 2001–2006, the two powers had many differences (including along their long, shared border), but were also working out new means of cooperation, in part to counter the growing U.S. presence in Asia and the Middle East. Moscow and Beijing began to discuss how to transfer Russia's oil to petroleum needy Chinese factories and autos. (although Putin also shrewdly constructed a major pipeline toward Japan, in part so China, whose growing power he hardly welcomed, would not take him for granted). By the midpoint of the twenty-first century's first decade, Russian-Chinese relations were better than they had been for decades. The new relationship aimed at containing, indeed driving back, U.S. power which was attempting nothing less than to expand around the boundaries of the other two nations.

One of the Chinese targets became, surprisingly, Latin America. As the Chinese economy grew at unheard of rates of 8 to 10 percent annually, and began to dominate world commerce (and especially dominate the trade of the United States, which suffered an imbalance of several

---

[78]*The New York Times*, April 17, 2006, p. A1 story by Joseph Kahn has excellent background; Baker and Glasser, *Kremlin Rising*, pp. 193–195.

hundred billion dollars a year with China), Beijing searched around the world for badly needed oil. The Chinese had a rich supply of coal, but not of petroleum, and so discussed deals to obtain oil from African nations, Central Asia, Russia—and, rather shockingly to Washington, Venezuela, whose petroleum exports North Americans had developed and dominated in the 1930s and had absorbed ever since.

A populist, anti-U.S. regime headed by former general Hugo Chevez headed the Caracas government, and even survived a 2002 *coup* attempt (during which the pleased Bush administration congratulated the group that it thought had overthrown Chavez, but did so too early. Chavez survived.). The Venezuelan leader developed close ties with Fidel Castro in Cuba, and in 2004–2005 discussed with the Chinese how to switch his petroleum exports (nearly all of which went to the United States) to China. The switch was impossible at the time because the refineries and pipelines required for heavy Venezuelan oil were all linked to the United States. But Chinese trade with Venezuela and other Latin American nations began to expand rapidly. Chavez (and the Chinese) continued to discuss how to switch Venezuela's oil flow from the United States to Asia. The Bush administration responded by criticizing Chavez's increasingly authoritarian regime, even as Americans continued to depend heavily on Venezuelan oil.

The problems with Venezuela were only part of the growing difficulties the United States was having with Latin Americans. During the 1990s, democratic elections gave many (especially in Washington) hope that the Southern Hemisphere was moving fully toward both democracy and cooperation with the United States. By the late 1990s, however, Latin American economies were suffering, and so—as far as Washington was concerned—were the election results. In a number of nations, particularly Bolivia, Brazil, Ecuador, and even Chile, voters returned populist candidates who avowed left-wing positions and were critical of U.S. economic and political policies. A stunning event occurred in early 2006 when, for the first time, Latin American issues had to be discussed between officials from Washington and from—of all places—China. Theodore Roosevelt, who in 1904–1905 put the teeth of the American military into the Monroe Doctrine, would not have been pleased with Latin America's turn against U.S. influence in the twenty-first century. And TR, who thought the Chinese inefficient and well-down on his list of "civilized" people, would have been stunned to see Monroe's Doctrine threatened by a quite different Chinese government.

In early 2006, President Bush moved to counter China's surging power by signing a new agreement with India, the major Asian competitor of the Chinese since the 1950s. In the deal, Bush committed the United States to recognize and help develop India's nuclear program. American-Indian relations thus, in part, improved to challenge increased Russian-Chinese cooperation.[79] It resembled a similar alignment in the early 1950s.

Little more than a generation ago, Reinhold Niebuhr, then near the end of his life, worried that both Americans and Russians had too easily tried to escape political and economic dilemmas by placing their faith in military power:

> It is one of the mysteries of human nature that while most of us are unconscious of an inevitable mixture in our motives, we try to atone for this error by too constant emphasis on "the law in our members which wars against the law that is in our minds."[80]

As world affairs became less predictable after 1989–1991, and Americans continued to rely on their military superiority to deal with much of the unpredictability, Niebuhr's point remained crucial. It did not necessarily follow that with the end of the Cold War the earth was a safer place. The events of 9/11 made that clear to Americans. The spread of nuclear capability (in India, Pakistan, North Korea, and Iran, to name four of the countries which preoccupied U.S. officials) had helped transform the pre-1991 Cold War—when the two super nuclear powers offset one another—into a post-1991 world of increasing danger due to growing instability caused by terrorism, fragmentation, and aroused concern about the growth of nuclear weaponry.

---

[79]Congressional Research Service, "India-U.S. Relations," updated February 9, 2006; Henry A. Kissinger, "Working with India," *Washington Post,* March 20, 2006, p. A15; superb and necessary background can be found in Andrew J. Rotter, *Comrades at Odds; The United States and India, 1947–1964* (Ithaca, N.Y., 2000), which ranges far beyond 1964.

[80]Reinhold Niebuhr, "Toward New Intra-Christian Endeavors," *Christian Century,* December 31, 1969, pp. 1662–1667.

The dramatic turn in world affairs marked by the ending of the Cold War was symbolized by Mikhail Gorbachev's visit to Fulton, Missouri, on May 6, 1992. The former Soviet leader spoke at Westminster College, where in March, 1946, Winston Churchill had sounded a rallying cry for Cold War against the Soviet Union by warning that "an iron curtain" had fallen across Europe (see ch. 2). Gorbachev gently disagreed with Churchill's assessment by observing that in the late 1940s the Soviet Union "was exhausted and destroyed." But he admitted the Russians made a "major error" in misunderstanding and frightening the West while, he claimed, the West gravely erred by launching a nuclear arms race. He pleaded that such mistakes not be repeated: "It would be a supreme tragedy if the world, having overcome the 1946 model [by having ended the Cold War], were to find itself once again in a 1914 model," when much of the world surprisingly exploded.

As Gorbachev pleaded for a stronger United Nations, and as he warned Americans not to take a "monocentric" view that they had won the Cold War so could dominate world affairs as they pleased, he sounded much like Niebuhr. And above them loomed the spirit of James Madison warning about the dangers of fragmenting empires. The Russian and the American, once locked in Cold War, now agreed that if the world's people did not use "their minds" to solve the growing disorder and fragmentation caused by burgeoning economic, political, environmental, nuclear, and terrorist problems, then—as not only the Cold War's history, but post-9/11 conflicts, demonstrated—they could too easily resort to what Niebuhr called "the law in our members."[81]

[81]*The New York Times*, May 7, 1992, p. A1, analyzes and quotes from the Gorbachev speech. An important analysis of how "nationalism," as Gorbachev called it, and the post-1946 world can be understood through an approach combining cultural with political-economic analysis is Matthew Connelly, "Taking Off the Cold War Lens: Visions of North-South Conflict during the Algerian War for Independence," *American Historical Review,* 105 (June 2000): 739–769.

Bibliographical Note

In 2003 the Society for Historians of American Foreign Relations (SHAFR) published, under Professor Robert L. Beisner's general editorship, a two-volume set, *American Foreign Relations Since 1600; A Guide to the Literature, Second edition* (Santa Barbara, California, 2003). It is an enlargement and update of the pioneering 1981 *Guide* edited by Richard Burns. The 2003 *Guide* is available in nearly all college libraries. Arranged chronologically and with helpful annotations for thousands of entries, these volumes are indispensable for students wishing to pursue particular topics in the field. Chapter 18 of Volume I lists bibliography for 1941–1945. Volume II contains the references for 1945 to "the End of the Cold War, and After." (The references are also available online and frequently updated.) Each chapter contains both the important secondary books and articles and, also, lists of published primary documents. For example, students wishing to consult books, scholarly articles, and/or primary (documentary) materials on "The United States, North Africa, and the Middle East since 1961" can find in Chapter 19 the important sources with commentary on each source by the contributing editor for this section, Professor Douglas Little, a distinguished scholar on U.S. relations with the Middle East.

No single book's bibliography can match the scope and variety of the references found in this Guide, and consequently this 10th edition of *America, Russia, and the Cold War* suggests that students and other scholars rely generally on the 2003 *Guide* for sources. This edition of *America, Russia, and the Cold War* supplements the Guide by (1) expanding references in the footnotes of this tenth edition so some post-2003 materials, and many important newspaper and periodical articles and analyses, are noted, and (2) creating a general bibliography which students can use on the book's Internet's Web site for this tenth edition.

Index

452